Praise for *A Companion to American Cultural History*

"The thirty bibliographies of the most influential work in American cultural history would by themselves make the book very helpful to a wide audience. But the essays' historiographical and thematic overviews provide the most valuable contribution, for each essay is aimed squarely at the ways that the best works in the field have been in conversation with each other." *A Journal of Southern History*

"A monumental achievement. The breadth of coverage is staggering, and the depth of insight a credit to its multifarious authors. Rarely can one book offer so much." *Reviews in History*

"This excellent reader in US cultural history for undergraduates may also be useful to specialists as a general overview of the field as it has evolved, especially over the past four decades. Summing Up: Highly recommended. All levels/libraries." *CHOICE*

"A guide for scholars and students who are interested in developments over the past quarter-century ... No reader should come away from it without a good springboard to further study. It is an appetite-whetter, a conspectus and a guide." *Reference Reviews*

"The contributors to this indispensable volume have applied to scholarship in American cultural history the same keen imagination and appreciation for complexity that has made the field so exciting in recent years." *Joan Shelley Rubin, University of Rochester*

"This important collection of original essays provides a most useful and accessible survey of a new approach to United States history. It is not just a companion but a text in its own right, a new survey of the American past from many cultural perspectives." *Alan Trachtenberg, Yale University*

"This volume marks a major contribution to the field of American cultural history. Illuminating, accessible, and authoritative, it will indeed prove a trusty companion for students and scholars alike." *John Kasson, The University of North Carolina at Chapel Hill*

"This well-wrought collection is a must-read. Its essays do more than any other book to clarify the multiple meanings of cultural history and to document the thorough penetration of cultural approaches to all the sub-fields of American historical scholarship." *Richard W. Fox, University of Southern California*

"A comprehensive and timely overview of American cultural history, from its first pioneering examples to its most recent linguistic, visual, transnational, and performative turns. Students looking for a lucid and lively introduction to the themes, methods, and impact of the culturalist perspective on US history will find this volume indispensable." *Jean-Christophe Agnew, Yale University*

"This collection is a marvel of intelligent synthesis and concise interpretation. Karen Halttunen has assembled some of the best cultural historians in the United States and they have cast unprecedented light on their contentious field from a rich variety of chronological and conceptual perspectives. The resu'   :e." *Jackson Lears, Rutgers University*

EY BLACKWELL COMPANIONS TO AMERICAN HISTORY

This series provides essential and authoritative overviews of the scholarship that has shaped our present understanding of the American past. Edited by eminent historians, each volume tackles one of the major periods or themes of American history, with individual topics authored by key scholars who have spent considerable time in research on the questions and controversies that have sparked debate in their field of interest. The volumes are accessible for the non-specialist, while also engaging scholars seeking a reference to the historiography or future concerns.

Published:

A Companion to the American Revolution
Edited by Jack P. Greene and J. R. Pole

A Companion to 19th-Century America
Edited by William L. Barney

A Companion to the American South
Edited by John B. Boles

A Companion to American Women's History
Edited by Nancy Hewitt

A Companion to American Indian History
Edited by Philip J. Deloria and Neal Salisbury

A Companion to Post-1945 America
Edited by Jean-Christophe Agnew and Roy Rosenzweig

A Companion to the Vietnam War
Edited by Marilyn Young and Robert Buzzanco

A Companion to Colonial America
Edited by Daniel Vickers

A Companion to American Foreign Relations
Edited by Robert Schulzinger

A Companion to 20th-Century America
Edited by Stephen J. Whitfield

A Companion to the American West
Edited by William Deverell

A Companion to the Civil War and Reconstruction
Edited by Lacy K. Ford

A Companion to American Technology
Edited by Carroll Pursell

A Companion to African-American History
Edited by Alton Hornsby

A Companion to American Immigration
Edited by Reed Ueda

A Companion to American Cultural History
Edited by Karen Halttunen

A Companion to California History
Edited by William Deverell and David Igler

A Companion to American Military History
Edited by James Bradford

A Companion to Los Angeles
Edited by William Deverell and Greg Hise

A Companion to American Environmental History
Edited by Douglas Cazaux Sackman

A Companion to Benjamin Franklin
Edited by David Waldstreicher

A Companion to World War Two (2 volumes)
Edited by Thomas W. Zeiler with Daniel M. DuBois

A Companion to American Legal History
Edited by Sally E. Hadden and Alfred L. Brophy

A Companion to John Adams and John Quincy Adams
Edited by David Waldstreicher

In preparation:

A Companion to American Urban History
Edited by David Quigley

A Companion to the History of American Science
Edited by Mark Largent

A Companion to Supreme Court History (2 volumes)
Edited by John Vile

A Companion to American Sports History
Edited by Steven Riess

A Companion to Custer and the Little Big Horn Campaign
Edited by Brad D. Lookingbill

A Companion to the U.S. Civil War
Edited by Aaron Sheehan-Dean

A Companion to the Meuse-Argonne Campaign, 1918
Edited by Edward G. Lengel

PRESIDENTIAL COMPANIONS

Published:

A Companion to Franklin D. Roosevelt
Edited by William Pederson

A Companion to Richard M. Nixon
Edited by Melvin Small

A Companion to Theodore Roosevelt
Edited by Serge Ricard

A Companion to Thomas Jefferson
Edited by Francis D. Cogliano

A Companion to Lyndon B. Johnson
Edited by Mitchell Lerner

A Companion to George Washington
Edited by Edward G. Lengel

A Companion to Andrew Jackson
Edited by Sean Patrick Adams

A Companion to Woodrow Wilson
Edited by Ross A. Kennedy

In preparation:

A Companion to James Madison and James Monroe
Edited by Stuart Leibiger

A Companion to Harry S. Truman
Edited by Daniel S. Margolies

A Companion to Abraham Lincoln
Edited by Michael Green

A Companion to Dwight D. Eisenhower
Edited by Chester J. Pach

A Companion to Ronald Reagan
Edited by Andrew L. Johns

A Companion to the Antebellum Presidents, 1837–61
Edited by Joel Silbey

A Companion to the Reconstruction Presidents, 1865–81
Edited by Edward Frantz

A Companion to Gerald R. Ford & Jimmy Carter
Edited by V. Scott Kaufman

A Companion to Warren G. Harding, Calvin Coolidge, and Herbert Hoover
Edited by Katherine A. S. Sibley

A Companion to John F. Kennedy
Edited by Marc Selverstone

A COMPANION TO AMERICAN CULTURAL HISTORY

Edited by

Karen Halttunen

WILEY Blackwell

This paperback edition first published 2014
© 2014 John Wiley & Sons Ltd

Edition history: Blackwell Publishing Ltd (hardback, 2008)

Registered Office
John Wiley & Sons Ltd, The Atrium, Southern Gate, Chichester, West Sussex, PO19 8SQ, UK

Editorial Offices
350 Main Street, Malden, MA 02148-5020, USA
9600 Garsington Road, Oxford, OX4 2DQ, UK
The Atrium, Southern Gate, Chichester, West Sussex, PO19 8SQ, UK

For details of our global editorial offices, for customer services, and for information about how to apply for permission to reuse the copyright material in this book please see our website at www.wiley.com/wiley-blackwell.

Library of Congress Cataloging-in-Publication Data

A companion to American Cultural history / edited by Karen Halttunen.
    p. cm. – (Blackwell companions to American history)
    Includes bibliographical references and index.
    ISBN 978-0-631-2   -5 (pbk. : alk. paper) 1. United Stat   States–Civilization–Historiography.   3. Unit   tates–Historiography.   I. Halttunen, Karen, 19
    E169.1.C684 2008
    973–dc22

                                                            2007028573

A catalogue record for this book is available from the British Library.

Cover image: Poster for Ringling Bros circus, 1899. Library of Congress
Cover design by Richard Boxhall Design Associates

Set in 10 on 12 pt Galliard by Toppan Best-set Premedia Limited
Printed in Malaysia by Ho Printing (M) Sdn Bhd

1   2014

Contents

Notes on Contributors

Eric Avila is Associate Professor of Chicano Studies and History at the University of California at Los Angeles. He is author of *Popular Culture in the Age of White Flight: Fear and Fantasy in Suburban Los Angeles* (2004), and the co-editor of *The Chicano Studies Reader: An Anthology of Aztlan* (2001).

Daniel Belgrad is Associate Professor of Humanities and American Studies at the University of South Florida. He is the author of *The Culture of Spontaneity: Improvisation and the Arts in Postwar America* (1998).

Casey Nelson Blake is Professor of History and American Studies at Columbia University, New York. He is author of *Beloved Community: The Cultural Criticism of Randolph Bourne, Van Wyck Brooks, Waldo Frank, and Lewis Mumford* (1990) and editor of *The Arts of Democracy: Art, Public Culture, and the State* (2007).

James W. Cook is Associate Professor of History and American Studies at the University of Michigan. His publications include *The Arts of Deception: Playing with Fraud in the Age of Barnum* (2001), *The Colossal P. T. Barnum Reader* (2005), and (with Lawrence Glickman and Michael O'Malley) a forthcoming edited collection, *The Cultural Turn in US History*.

Janet M. Davis is Associate Professor of American Studies and History at the University of Texas, Austin. She is the author of *The Circus Age: Culture and Society under the*

American Big Top (2002), and the editor of *Burlesque Dancer, Circus Queen and Tinker Bell: The Memoir of Tiny Kline* (forthcoming).

Hasia R. Diner is Paul and Sylvia Steinberg Professor of American Jewish History at New York University. Among her many books are *Erin's Daughters in America: Irish Immigrant Women in the Nineteenth Century* (1984), *Hungering for America: Italian, Irish and Jewish Foodways in the Age of Migration* (2002), and *The Jews of the United States, 1645–2000* (2004).

Joel Dinerstein is Assistant Professor of English at Tulane University. He is the author of *Swinging the Machine: Modernity, Technology, and African-American Culture between the World Wars* (2003).

Nan Enstad is Associate Professor of History at the University of Wisconsin. She is the author of *Ladies of Labor, Girls of Adventure: Working Women, Popular Culture, and Labor Politics* (1999).

Demetrius L. Eudell is Associate Professor of History at Wesleyan University, Connecticut. He is the author of *The Political Languages of Emancipation in the British Caribbean and the US South* (2002).

Ann Fabian is Professor of American Studies and History at Rutgers University. She is the author of *Card Sharps, Dream Books, and Bucket Shops: Gambling in Nineteenth-Century*

America (1990) and *The Unvarnished Truth: Personal Narratives in Nineteenth-Century America* (2000).

Alice Fahs is Associate Professor of History at the University of California, Irvine. She is the author of *The Imagined Civil War: Popular Literature of the North and South, 1861–1865* (2000) and co-editor of *The Memory of the Civil War in American Culture* (2004).

Julia L. Foulkes is Associate Professor of History at the New School, New York. She is the author of *Modern Bodies: Dance and American Modernism from Martha Graham to Alvin Ailey* (2002) and the forthcoming *Culture Cities: Urbanization and the Arts after World War II.*

Joanne B. Freeman is Professor of History at Yale University. Her publications include *Affairs of Honor: National Politics in the New Republic* (2001) and *Alexander Hamilton, Writings* (2001).

J. Ritchie Garrison is Director of the Winterthur Program in American Material Culture, and Professor of History, University of Delaware. He is author of *Landscape and Material Life in Franklin County, Massachusetts, 1771–1860* (1991) and *Two Carpenters: Architecture and Building in Early New England* (2006), and co-editor (with Ann Smart Martin) of *American Material Culture: The Shape of the Field* (1997).

David Glassberg is Professor of History at the University of Massachusetts, Amherst. He is the author of *American Historical Pageantry: The Uses of Tradition in the Early Twentieth Century* (1990) and *Sense of History: The Place of the Past in American Life* (2001).

Lawrence B. Glickman is Professor of History at the University of South Carolina. He is the author of *A Living Wage: American Workers and the Making of Consumer Society* (1997), editor of *Consumer Society in American History: A Reader* (1999), and co-editor (with James W. Cook and Michael O'Malley) of a forthcoming collection, *The Cultural Turn in US History.*

Petra Goedde is Associate Professor of History at Temple University, Philadelphia. She is the author of *GIs and Germans: Culture, Gender, and Foreign Relations, 1945–1949* (2003).

Jane H. Hunter is Professor of History at Lewis & Clark College, Oregon. Her publications include *The Gospel of Gentility: American Women Missionaries in Turn of the Century China* (1984) and *How Young Ladies Became Girls: The Victorian Origins of American Girlhood* (2002).

Catherine E. Kelly is Associate Professor of History at the University of Oklahoma. She is the author of *In the New England Fashion: Reshaping Women's Lives in the Nineteenth Century* (1999) and the *Things Useful and Ornamental: The Aesthetics of Everyday Life in the Early Republic* (forthcoming), and co-editor of *Reading Women: Literacy, Authorship, and Culture in the Atlantic World, 1500–1800* (2007).

M. Alison Kibler is Assistant Professor of Women's and American Studies at Franklin & Marshall College, Pennsylvania. She is the author of *Rank Ladies: Gender and Cultural Hierarchy in American Vaudeville* (1999) and "The Stage Irishwoman" in the *Journal of American Ethnic History* (Spring 2005).

George Lipsitz is Professor of Sociology and Black Studies at the University of California, Santa Barbara. His many books include *Dangerous Crossroads: Popular Music, Postmodernism, and the Poetics of Place* (1994) and *The Possessive Investment in Whiteness: How White People Profit from Identity Politics* (1998).

Charles F. McGovern is Associate Professor of History and American Studies at the College of William and Mary, Virginia. He is the author of *Sold American: Consumption and Citizenship, 1890–1945* (2006), and co-editor (with Susan Strasser and Matthias Judt) of *Getting and Spending: European and American Consumer Societies in the Twentieth Century* (1998).

Peter C. Mancall is Professor of History and Anthropology at the University of Southern California. His many books include *Deadly Medicine: Indians and Alcohol in Early*

America (1995), and *Hakluyt's Promise: An Elizabethan's Obsession for an English America* (2007); he is also editor of *Travel Narratives from the Age of Discovery* (2006) and *Virginia and the Atlantic World, 1550–1625* (2007).

Lewis Perry is John Francis Bannon, SJ Chair and Professor of History at St. Louis University. He is the author of *Radical Abolitionism: Anarchy and the Government of God in Antislavery Thought* (1973), *Childhood, Marriage, and Reform: Henry Clarke Wright, 1797–1870* (1980), *Intellectual Life in America: A History* (1984), and *Boats Against the Current: American Culture Between Revolution and Modernity* (1993).

Carla Gardina Pestana is W. E. Smith Professor of History at Miami University. She is the author of *Quakers and Baptists in Colonial Massachusetts* (1991) and *The English Atlantic in an Age of Revolution, 1640–1661* (2004).

Sally M. Promey is Professor of Religion and Visual Culture in the Yale Institute of Sacred Music and Yale Divinity School, and Professor of American Studies in the Faculty of Arts and Sciences, Yale University. She is the author of *Spiritual Spectacles: Vision and Image in Mid-Nineteenth-Century Shakerism* (1993) and *Painting Religion in Public: John Singer Sargent's Triumph of Religion at the Boston Public Library* (2001), and co-editor of *The Visual Culture of American Religions* (2001).

Andrew J. Rotter is Charles A. Dana Professor of History at Colgate University, New York. He is author of *Comrades at Odds: The United States and India, 1947–1964* (2000) and *Hiroshima: The World's Bomb* (forthcoming).

Scott A. Sandage is Associate Professor of History at Carnegie Mellon University. He is the author of *Born Losers: A History of Failure in America* (2005) and an annotated abridgement of Alexis de Tocqueville's *Democracy in America* (2007).

Leigh E. Schmidt is Agate Brown and George L. Collord Professor of Religion, Princeton University, New Jersey. He is the author of *Holy Fairs: Scottish Communions and American Revivals in the Early Modern Period* (1989), *Consumer Rites: The Buying and Selling of American Holidays* (1995), *Hearing Things: Religion, Illusion, and the American Enlightenment* (2000), and *Restless Souls: The Making of American Spirituality* (2005).

Karin Wulf is Associate Professor of History and American Studies at the College of William and Mary, Virginia. She is the author of *Not All Wives: Women of Colonial Philadelphia* (2000), and the co-editor of *Milcah Martha Moore's Book: A Commonplace Book from Revolutionary America* (1997).

INTRODUCTION

Karen Halttunen

Among the many innovative approaches that have reshaped the discipline of history over the past twenty-five years, perhaps the most broadly influential has been the field of cultural history. Before the 1970s, American cultural history was a relatively small and insignificant field, situated on the margins of intellectual or social history, whose hybrid nature was routinely acknowledged in the course title, "American intellectual and social history," offered in many undergraduate curricula. As a form of intellectual history, cultural history focused on High Culture – what Victorian critic Matthew Arnold famously defined as "the best that has been thought and said" – in the fine arts and canonical works of literature. As a form of social history, cultural history concerned itself with the trivial ephemera of everyday life – sometimes called "pots-and-pans history" – with particular attention to matters of leisure and entertainment. Studies in the field were as likely to emerge from departments of literature as from history; in the 1950s and 1960s, literary scholars in the American Studies "myth-and-symbol" school produced some of the most important works in American cultural history, focusing on such popular literary forms as sentimental fiction, dime novels, and other bestsellers.

Since the 1970s, cultural history has emerged as a central area of interest for American historians, now armed with a more holistic concept of "culture" as the entire range of practices, representations, languages, and beliefs that make up a particular social group's way of life. The new cultural history owes a great debt to "the new social history" of the 1960s and 1970s (as Lawrence Glickman argues in Chapter 27 of this volume). As the new social historians uncovered mountains of information about the social and material lives of ordinary people in the past, they and others grew increasingly committed to uncovering the *meanings* of those experiences. Since the 1980s, cultural history has focused on decoding the meanings of the signs, gestures, artifacts, performances, and other expressive forms by which people communicate their values and their truths in a given society. Drawing insights from the symbolic anthropology of Clifford Geertz, Antonio Gramsci's concept of "hegemony," Pierre Bourdieu's work on cultural production, British cultural studies, and Continental postmodernism, American cultural history evolved into a dominant mode of practice – with its own distinct course title in college curricula – by the end of the twentieth century.

The new cultural history involves less an object of study – such as ballet or the Horatio Alger novel – than a distinctive set of approaches to all areas of historical study. The field of cultural history can, of course, still designate the study of High Culture, such as fine architecture or art museums; and it can still focus on popular literature and amusements – though in both pursuits, the new cultural history is more likely to address matters of production and reception than the old "intellectual and social history." Alternatively, cultural history can work on an ethnographic model, examining the behavior and values of such social subgroups as slaves or Shakers, gold miners or working-class suburbanites, zoot-suiters or Boston Brahmins. Some cultural histories focus on a specific medium of cultural expression, producing studies of visual or material culture, or performance studies. Among the most widely influential works in the field are those that identify and characterize some larger pattern of meanings and values that pervaded American society in a given time period – such as the "culture of refinement," the "culture of consumption," "Victory Culture" – and examine its expression and impact on a wide range of beliefs and practices. The mainstreaming of cultural history, finally, has generated many cultural histories of such conventional topics as the Columbian encounter, the American Revolution, imperialism, and the Cold War.

The aim of the Blackwell *Companion to American Cultural History* is to provide an introduction to the growing body of scholarship reflecting this rich range of approaches to the American past. Each chapter offers an historiographic overview of the scholarship, written by an expert in that field, with special attention to the major studies and debates that have shaped that area of interest, followed by a short, selective bibliography. This volume is designed to serve as a reference work for students, scholars, and others interested in the significant impact of cultural history on American historical practice over the past quarter-century. Though it does address high-level conceptual issues and historiographic debates, it has been written for an audience that includes undergraduates as well as senior scholars in the field.

In an effort to do justice to the complexities of this field of inquiry, and to ensure the widest possible usefulness of this volume, the essays have been organized along three different lines of approach. The first approach is chronological: the first three sections of this *Companion* concern three major periods of American cultural history. Part I covers the early American period, and offers chapters on cultures of encounter and of settlement, British provincialism in the eighteenth century, and the cultural history of the American Revolution and its aftermath. Part II moves to the nineteenth century, and includes chapters on various sub-periods and topics, including antebellum cultural history, religion and reform, African American cultures, the Civil War, the West, the Gilded Age, immigration and ethnic culture, and cultural watersheds at the turn of the century. Part III addresses the twentieth century, and offers chapters on consumer culture and mass culture, modernism, politics and culture in the 1930s and 1940s, American culture in the 1950s and 1960s, and the globalization of American culture. Parts I through III of this *Companion* are thus designed for ready accessibility by readers interested in specific time periods of the American past.

The second approach of this *Companion* volume is thematic and methodological. Part IV offers a series of chapters on some of the most vital and important subfields of American cultural history, defined conceptually and thematically more than topically. Chapters in this section cover such areas as the role of cultural theory in shaping the field, visual and material cultures, popular culture and performance studies, gender and sexuality, race and ethnicity, and studies in history and memory. Many of these chapters illuminate the importance of culture in "constructing" Americans' changing understandings of reality across time: the changing cultural constructions, for example, of gender systems, ethnicity and whiteness, and the American past itself. The chapters in Part IV are intended to engage readers whose primary interests lie in specific conceptual and thematic approaches across time periods.

The third and final approach, taken in Part V of this volume, involves the critical assessment of the impact of cultural history on older, more established fields of history. The "cultural turn" has strongly influenced the two fields from which it initially borrowed – intellectual history and social history – as well as religious history, political history, and the history of foreign relations. In Part V, leading practitioners in these five areas of specialization evaluate the ways in which cultural history has presented new problems, prompted new questions, and suggested new approaches in their fields of study. These five chapters invite readers to form their own critical assessments of the impact of the culture concept across the full spectrum of American historical practices.

The 30 essays in this volume do not adhere to a single, "cookie-cutter" approach to American cultural history. Rather, they illuminate the full range of possibilities presented by the concept of culture for American historical scholarship. Popular culture and High Culture, ethnographies and critical cultural studies, images and artifacts, religious belief and social rituals: all these and more feature in the essays that follow. This eclectic range of not only topics, but questions, methodologies, and conceptual frameworks, has characterized the development of the new cultural history over the past quarter-century and more. From the anthropological turn of the 1970s and 1980s, through the linguistic turn of the 1980s and 1990s, to the spatial-geographic turn of the 1990s and the early years of the twenty-first century, American cultural history has proved to be thoughtfully responsive to new intellectual opportunities offered by developments in other disciplines. This creative flexibility and persistent openness to new ideas and approaches promise to serve the field well for many years to come.

Part I

EARLY AMERICA

Chapter One

CULTURAL ENCOUNTERS: AMERICANS AND EUROPEANS

Peter C. Mancall

In 1576 Martin Frobisher made his first journey into the North Atlantic. He had gone in search of the Northwest Passage, the fabled water route that Europeans believed bisected the North American continent and connected the Atlantic Ocean with the Pacific. Frobisher sailed into waters surrounding territory still unknown to the English. Upon landing, the sailors encountered local Inuit. When the summer was drawing to a close and the English left for home, Frobisher left behind five men. A year later, when he returned to look again for the Northwest Passage, he also tried to find the five missing men. Once again he met Inuit. Though relations between them had grown tense (and would get worse), Frobisher believed that the natives knew where the five men might be. As his ships returned again for England, he left behind ink and paper. He hoped that the Inuit would either write a note telling where the men could be found, or that they would take the paper and ink to the men (Churchyard 1578: sig. Bvii^r–Bvii^v). He did not grasp that the Inuit had no understanding of the act of writing.

The encounter on those cold shores typified the kinds of cultural misunderstandings that would take place when Europeans met Americans during the sixteenth and seventeenth centuries. It was a classic example of what one historian in another context called a "dialogue of the deaf" (MacGaffey 1994). Over time, of course, Europeans and Americans would learn much about each other's cultures. The newcomers frequently hoped to change Americans' cultures; the natives, for their part, had fewer plans for their uninvited visitors, but often became effective proselytizers in their own right (Axtell 1975).

From the first efforts to write "American" history in the sixteenth century until the mid- to late twentieth century, European and Euro-American scholars who described cultural encounters in the Americas often emphasized the positive contributions that Europeans made to the cultures of the Western Hemisphere. Often these historians uncritically stressed the efforts to convert Native Americans to Christianity and ridiculed (and occasionally demonized) indigenous populations. By the 1970s that cultural consensus had begun to fracture, and by the 1990s apologias for European colonization were in full retreat. When the five-hundredth anniversary of Christopher Columbus's first voyage arrived in 1992, historical treatments of the earliest cultural encounters in the Americas bore little resemblance to earlier views.

Drawing on methods and insights from a variety of disciplines – notably anthropology, archaeology, and art history – historians reassessed the encounter between the so-called "old" and "new" worlds. Historians of the Anglo-American experience also came to realize that encounters in territories that became New Spain and New France had direct bearing on the ways that natives and newcomers understood each other. They began to pay more serious attention to oral history maintained within indigenous communities. Finally, historians became sensitive to the process of cultural encounters, especially the different forms of communication that allowed for the transmission of ideas over time and from one group to another – including the exchange of ideas across the cultural divides that often separated Europeans from Americans.

Cultural misunderstandings and hostility characterized the encounters between Americans and Europeans since the earliest known contact between the two continents. When Norse sailors decided to travel west from their settlement in Iceland – the first offshore colony of any European society – they ventured to territories they called Greenland, Helluland, Markland, and Vinland. Iceland had had no human residents before these northern Europeans arrived, but the other territories were inhabited by Inuit. The earliest surviving sagas, told orally from one generation to another in the North Atlantic region until finally recorded on vellum in the fourteenth century, spoke of tensions between the travelers and the peoples they met. The Norse referred to the Inuit as "Skraelings," a term whose exact meaning is lost but approximates "wretches." The Northmen made little effort to learn the culture of the Inuit. Their inability to understand each other led to such mistrust that the Norse once killed five Inuit they found asleep (Magnusson & Pálsson 1965; Crosby 1986).

The Norse cultural encounter with the Western Hemisphere stretched from the twelfth to the fifteenth century, but left little permanent mark on either the travelers or those they encountered. But the cultural encounter that began when Columbus arrived in the Bahamas in 1492 took a different course, in large part because the Spanish, unlike the Norse, immediately decided to establish significant settlements in the Western Hemisphere. Cultural encounters between Europeans and Americans, which had been sporadic and small scale in the North Atlantic, now became more extensive and, as it happened, permanent.

Christopher Columbus, as is universally known, was not quite sure where he was when he arrived in the Western Hemisphere in October, 1492, and hence labeled the people he met "Indians" in the mistaken belief that he reached the East Indies. He soon decided to kidnap several of the locals, he wrote, "so that they might learn our language and give me news of what existed in those parts." The plan worked, "for later they understood us and we them, either by speech or by signs: and they have been very useful to us" (Obregón 1991: 66). This action revealed Columbus's belief that the Spanish would have ongoing contact with Americans in the islands, and that only by learning each other's language could the Europeans control the situation.

In the decades following Columbus's voyages, Europeans continued to travel to the Americas and, on many occasions, Americans journeyed to Europe. One scholar has estimated that perhaps 1,600 Americans visited Europe by the early seventeenth century (Prins 1993). Every place they went they became objects of fascination, mobile and living spectacles of a world unknown to Europeans before 1492. Among the most dramatic of these occasions was the arrival in Rouen of perhaps 50

Tupinambas from Brazil in 1550. Their visit had been arranged by locals to honor the visit of King Henri II. The Tupinambas lived in a fabricated jungle, purportedly pursuing their normal daily tasks. The highlight of the visit was a staged battle between the Tupinambas and a group labeled as "Tagaberes" and advertised as the Tupinambas' mortal enemies. In actuality no Tagaberes showed up, in all likelihood because they probably did not exist. Still, the show went forward, with French soldiers attired in what they believed were native Brazilian costumes. A surviving image of the Tupinambas' temporary home reveals a miniature world of Brazilian-inspired lodges, game hunts, and domesticity (*C'est La Deduction* 1551; Wintroub 1998). Americans also became fixtures in European cultures, their images circulating in printed books for a variety of political and ideological purposes (Kupperman 1995; Schmidt 2001).

Most encounters between Europeans and Americans took place in the Western Hemisphere. During the sixteenth century, miscommunication was a common problem. Europeans usually believed that they held the upper hand in these encounters, but on the ground the situation was often less clear. When Francisco Pizarro marched his troops into the heart of the Incan homeland to confront (and eventually capture) the emperor Atahualpa, neither one of them knew how to read (Ortega 2003: 25). While some literate Europeans felt themselves superior to indigenes, the Incans preserved vast stores of information in a series of knotted strings known as *khipu* (or *quipu*). The great Venetian chronicler of overseas travelers Giovanni Batista Ramusio noted that the Peruvians possessed "public houses full of those ropes, through which the person who is in charge of them can tell the past events, although they are far in the past, in the same way as we do with our letters" (Ramusio 1556: sig. 4^r). The precise meaning of *khipu* has eluded Western scholars since the sixteenth century, though recent breakthroughs involving computer analysis of the patterns of knots on the strings has hinted that the vast storehouse of knowledge included ways of transferring information from one place to another – a process analogous on some level to the function of writing as Europeans understood it (Urton & Brezine 2005).

By the time the English arrived in North America, at least some of them were aware of the cultural conflicts that had arisen when other Europeans met Americans. What they knew best were the few texts that had been translated into English, beginning in 1555 with Richard Eden's edition of parts of the work of the humanist the English called Peter Martyr (known on the continent as Pietro Martire D'Anghiera). In 1583 English readers gained access to the writings of the Dominican friar Bartolomé de Las Casas, whose *Brevissima relacion de la destruycion de las Indias* (published first in Seville in 1552) appeared in English as *The Spanish colonie, or Briefe chronicle of the acts and gestes of the Spaniardes in the West Indies, called the newe world*. That book chronicled what Las Casas described as the atrocities perpetrated by Spanish conquistadores on the indigenous peoples of the Caribbean basin and the mainland. Though the book paid little attention to issues of culture, it had a permanent effect on English colonial plans. Las Casas's book became the central text in what became known as the "black legend" of the Spanish Conquest. Having read about what the Spanish did in the Western Hemisphere, the English resolved that they would educate rather than exterminate the Americans they met. In the past generation new editions of indigenous chronicles have provided additional insights into the brutality of the conquest as well as details about pre-contact life (e.g., Sahagún 1950–82).

In the 1580s the English launched their colonization of North America. The venture did not get off to a smooth start. Despite four journeys to modern-day North Carolina, the English were unable to establish a permanent settlement at the place known as Roanoke. Instead, the last group of settlers the English deposited there could not be found when the English returned to the site. They became the famous "lost colonists" who would feature prominently in the mythology of the United States.

If the fate of those settlers remains unknown, the English effort to settle Roanoke produced a text that had wide-ranging significance for European understandings of the culture of North Americans. The book was written by a young scholar named Thomas Harriot, who would later become famous because of the crucial role he played in the development of algebra. Entitled *The Briefe and True Report of the New Found Land of Virginia*, the book appeared as a small pamphlet in London in 1588. A year later the text appeared again, this time in the younger Richard Hakluyt's *Principall Navigations, Voiages and Discoveries of the English Nation*, a collection of travel accounts modeled on Ramusio's *Navigationi e Viaggi*. In 1590 Harriot's book appeared again, but this time it was printed in four languages (English, Latin, German, and French) and contained illustrations done by the Flemish engraver Theodor de Bry based on the paintings of an artist named John White who had accompanied Harriot to Roanoke in 1585 (Harriot 1590).

The text and images in the *Briefe and True Report* established a permanent idea of what Americans were like, at least in the minds of the English. Harriot detailed what he thought were the most significant aspects of the culture of the Carolina Algonquians, including the ways that they tended their children, dressed themselves, and maintained an economy based on fishing, hunting, and farming. He was careful to delineate their religious beliefs, including their notions about the afterlife and the rituals that they practiced. The engravings in the illustrated volume gave life to the texts. They continue to be the most widely circulated images of any pre-1800 American population.

Harriot's illustrated account offered European readers an image of Americans that challenged prevailing views. Ever since the circulation of the report announcing Columbus's discovery, known as the "Barcelona Letter" and first published in 1493, many Europeans had believed that Americans were primitives locked into lives of permanent savagery. The earliest visual evidence confirmed that view. A 1494 edition of the Barcelona Letter published in Basel depicted Columbus and his shipmates arriving in the islands on a sophisticated European sailing vessel capable of making a transatlantic crossing. Naked Tainos stand cowering on the shore. Subsequent images, notably a famous 1505 German broadside depicting the arrival of Europeans in Brazil, offered an even blunter contrast: European ships gracefully sailing toward the shore, where they were destined to meet local Tupinambas bedecked in feathers around their loins and little else. The Americans are gathered together in front of a rudimentary shack, and one of them is chewing on a human arm; a head and other limbs hang suspended from a rafter (Honour 1975). Though Columbus himself had not encountered any man-eaters, he did report that they existed on other islands. But other Europeans were more forthcoming. A half-century after the 1505 broadside appeared, a German named Hans Stade (or Staden) was taken captive in Brazil. When he was released he wrote an account of his travails, emphasizing widespread cannibalism in the Americas (Stade 1557). Though the French essayist Michel de Montaigne questioned whether American cannibalism was more brutal than the way that Europeans treated unfortunates in their own society (Montaigne 1580), the image of flesh-eating Americans became fixed for a time in European conceptions of Americans and figured prominently in the engraver de Bry's *America* series published in German in the 1590s.

Harriot's careful presentation of natives altered that dominant mode of interpretation. While he depicted the Carolina Algonquians as primitives in many ways, especially in their manner of dress, architecture, and bodily scarification, he also recognized their intellectual abilities. Like other European observers in the Americas, he described their polytheism and the presence of local idols. Since the Algonquians already possessed a distinct understanding of the divine, Harriot believed they could be readily converted to Christianity. The illustrated edition also presented a series of images of the Picts, the famed aboriginal inhabitants of northern Britain who terrorized the Romans. These images were more threatening than those of the Algonquians. Lest a reader not understand why the Picts were included, Harriot inserted a brief note that these early Britons had been more "savage" than the Americans found in Roanoke and that they had become civilized over time. In other words, if earlier European depictions had suggested that Americans were locked into a permanent state of savagery, Harriot's illustrated report suggested that they were instead merely at an earlier stage of cultural evolution. Read together, the illustrations in Harriot's book suggested that, with the proper tutelage, the Carolina Algonquians could become Christian and English. Culture was in this vision not dependent on race or ethnicity. It was instead transferable and learnable, a subject of endless fascination to European theorists (Hodgen 1964).

Harriot's text helped establish the context for the English colonization efforts of the early seventeenth century. But he did not act alone. Richard Hakluyt, who had ushered the illustrated edition of the *Briefe and True Report* towards its multilanguage publication, also prodded the English to embrace the colonizing venture. He did so by publishing travel accounts. In the two editions of the *Principal Navigations*, he instructed the subjects of the Queen (and anyone else who could read English) that the English had been engaged in long-distance travels since ancient times. He told them about the Empress Helena (mother of Constantine the Great), King Arthur, and the Welshman Madoc who in the twelfth century sailed deep into the Atlantic and came to lands that the English in the sixteenth century believed was America. Most of the accounts described more recent efforts of the English in Russia, Africa, East Asia, and the Americas. Though Hakluyt's goals were explicitly religious and economic – he wanted to spread Protestant Christianity and to establish long-distance commercial ties – these journeys had cultural consequences as well. By printing accounts of travelers who had met Americans, Hakluyt let his readers know about the natural resources to be found in the Western Hemisphere and those who controlled them. He also participated in a phenomenon that crossed borders within Europe: a publishing frenzy that led to the production of hundreds of books describing the Western Hemisphere and its peoples. Books about America came from presses in every major European city, and smaller towns too; wherever printers had presses, they churned out volumes telling of the wonders and dangers to be found across the Atlantic Ocean. The publication of the multi-volume *European Americana* has now made it possible to understand the vast extent of this enterprise (Alden 1980–97; Mancall 1998).

Printed books helped to establish the cultural context for the Virginia Company's efforts. These texts provided specific details about the Americans to be found along the Atlantic coast and allowed the English, like other Europeans, to speculate about the nature of Americans and their cultures (Chaplin 2001). Hakluyt's collections, among other sources, had frequently compared American and European resources, a process of analogous reading of the landscape that enabled the newcomers to arrive with firm ideas already in mind about how they could utilize the region (Pagden 1993). They brought cultural baggage with them, including views of how to treat colonized peoples shaped by the Elizabethan conquest of Ireland (Canny 2003; Hinderaker & Mancall 2003). But despite their preparation, the English did not recognize the difficulties they would face in the Chesapeake from local diseases (Earle 1979). Fortunately for the newcomers, the Powhatans at first tolerated their presence, probably because they saw the English as a potentially subsidiary tribe (Gleach 1997).

During their first decade along the James, the colonist John Rolfe planted some West Indian tobacco seeds; within a generation, the plant would shape the colony's culture as well as its economy. Historians of early Virginia have recognized this as a turning point in the colony's history. The profits produced by tobacco provided ongoing justifications for the migration of young English men and women to the Chesapeake, many of whom suffered from the diseases that had afflicted the first settlers. Only a profitable crop could justify the occupation of a place where, on average, over one-quarter of the foreign-born population succumbed each year. But tobacco's economic success was not obvious in the middle of the 1610s, when English polemicists waged a cultural battle over the fate of tobacco itself. Its proponents celebrated the plant for its health-giving properties and the pleasant sensations it produced. Its opponents, including King James (who in 1604 had published a tract warning of tobacco's dangers), argued that since tobacco played a crucial role in American rituals, it was better suited for the savage than the civilized. While those who loathed the plant accepted its medicinal benefits, they feared the cultural consequences of its adoption. By the late 1610s the opponents of tobacco had lost the battle. Tobacconists spread across London and the plant became a fixture in England, as it had elsewhere in Europe, with results that ensured the survival of Virginia (Mancall 2004).

But the long-term economic success came at a high price. Though Rolfe had married Powhatan's daughter Pocahontas, and she herself had gone to England and become the object of intense public interest when she dressed and lived like an Englishwoman (Townsend 2004), relations between the Powhatans and the English deteriorated. By 1622 both Powhatan and Pocahontas had died, and the Powhatans launched an attack on the English, killing 347. The English responded in 1623 and 1624, killing hundreds of Powhatans.

Yet despite the unfolding tragedy on the Chesapeake, Americans and Europeans also continued to meet peacefully. Tensions in Virginia subsided by 1625. By then the English had established themselves at Plymouth; by the end of the 1620s the

Massachusetts Bay Company organized its migration, which was far more substantial than the Pilgrim movement to Plymouth, and a new arena for intercultural exchange opened in southeastern New England. By 1642 approximately 21,000 Puritans had migrated to Massachusetts, a movement termed by later scholars the "great migration," though recent work has demonstrated that this movement was far less substantial than English and British migration elsewhere in the Atlantic basin (Bailyn 1986; Canny 1994; Games 1999). When the population of newcomers increased, so did tensions with locals, and relations between them eventually took a deadly turn: in 1637 the English, along with their Narragansett allies, attacked the Pequots. The most horrific moment came along the Mystic River, when the English and Narragansetts surrounded a village and set it on fire, shooting at those who escaped. The atrocity became a defining moment in New England culture. William Bradford, the first historian of Plymouth, claimed that the bloodshed signified divine support for colonization. The English "victory seemed a sweet sacrifice," Bradford wrote, quoting Leviticus 2:1–2, "and they gave the praise thereof to God, who had wrought so wonderfully for them, thus to enclose their enemies in their hands and give them so speedy a victory over so proud and insulting an enemy" (Bradford 1952: 296).

The violence that engulfed native and newcomer communities in the 1620s and 1630s did not lead to permanent cultural alienation in eastern North America, though neither community was able to forget what had happened. By the middle of the century the English relaunched their cultural initiative to convert Americans to English ways, specifically to Protestant religion, the market economy, and sedentary settlements. They did so by trying to establish schools in Virginia and in Massachusetts. The two schools, Henrico College in Virginia and Harvard's Indian College, had virtually no students and only a negligible effect on relations between the peoples of the still new colonies (Szasz 1988). But educational efforts continued nonetheless. The most successful (from an English perspective) was led by the missionary John Eliot, whose efforts resulted in the conversion of 1,100 natives in Massachusetts. The English called them "praying Indians," thereby ignoring the fact that the vast majority of Americans who did not embrace Christianity were nonetheless also religious. Eliot for his part translated the Bible into Massachusett and published it in 1663; it remains perhaps the least-read book produced in the Anglo-American colonies in the seventeenth century (Eliot 1663).

The cultures of Europeans and Americans remained distinct, though each proved willing and able to adopt elements of the other's lifestyle. Perhaps the most notable borrowing involved imported livestock. Before Europeans arrived the inhabitants of eastern North America had no domesticated animals other than dogs. Europeans brought cattle, horses, sheep, and swine with them, knowing that the creation of European-style communities required the continued keeping of these Old World animals (some later also imported honeybees). At first these creatures, and their close relations with colonists, mystified Americans. But the indigenes soon learned of the utility of these beasts, and many began to adopt them into their own economies. By the middle of the seventeenth century, according to one recent account, cattle and pigs had become widespread in indigenous communities. The inclusion of these animals did not always go smoothly; free-ranging English livestock routinely consumed natives' crops. Despite such problems, Americans nonetheless raised domesticated livestock. They even took to branding them as private property, although the concept made no sense in the pre-contact world where fish and game could be harvested but not owned – at least not until they were captured or killed (Cronon 1983; Anderson 2004). Cultural borrowing went in both directions: colonists adopted American ideas and practices too (Axtell 1981).

Despite such adaptations, tensions between the peoples of the mainland Anglo-American colonies remained. In the 1670s, warfare erupted in the most populous English colonies. In both the Chesapeake, where the conflict came to be known as Bacon's Rebellion, and in New England, where the violence gained the name King Philip's or Metacom's War (the terms are still used interchangeably by scholars), the deadliest warfare yet seen in the east spread across the landscape. Scholars who study this era have identified the economic and political roots of these wars, but in the end it is difficult to escape the notion that these were cultural battles. Many colonists came to believe that they could no longer co-habit with Americans and wanted them removed or exterminated, as the Governor of Maryland indicated when he paid a bounty for the scalps of 10 natives; natives captured in Metacom's War, including many of the "praying Indians," were sold into slavery. The Puritan cleric Cotton Mather, in one famous sermon, declared the violence to be worthy "the name of warr," as if previous conflicts were unworthy the appellation. The indigenous peoples of the region also recognized the gravity of the conflict and the lingering tensions it produced. When colonists threatened them again two decades later, these Americans recalled the brutality of the 1670s, drawing on their oral histories to fuel renewed battles with the English (Mather 1697; Gyles 1981; Lepore 1998).

The cultural conflicts that erupted in the 1670s cannot be understood in isolation. The value of a work such as Edmund Morgan's *American Slavery, American Freedom* (1975) lies in its ability to tie together the stories of indigenous peoples in the Chesapeake region with the growing perception among the English that they could not sate their economic desires if they relied exclusively on voluntary labor from abroad. The English turned toward bound African labor in the latter decades of the seventeenth century, at least in part because they had become convinced – correctly, it should be added – that it would also have been too difficult to hire or enslave Americans. The arrival of Africans and Afro-Caribbeans on the mainland complicated the cultural encounters in the colonial period. But the relatively small numbers of African migrants made such clashes less visible than they would become in the eighteenth century (Morgan 1975; Parent 2003).

By the latter decades of the seventeenth century many Americans inhabited what the historian James Merrell brilliantly perceived was a "new world" marred by the ongoing loss of population and land, among other tragedies (Merrell 1989). Though Americans and Europeans often encountered each other in towns and cities (Merrell 1991), hostilities lingered. Still, despite periodic violence, efforts to understand each other across the cultural divide continued. The colonial traveler John Lawson, for example, praised one American for being able to imitate his own writing "with more Exactness, than any European could have done, that was illiterate." Such talents were emblematic of a people who "are no Inventers of any Arts or Trades worthy mention" yet who could "learn any thing very soon." Many of Carolina's native peoples "wear the *English* Dress," Lawson wrote. He hoped they would adopt cattle too (if they had not already done so) since "such Inclinations in the Savages should meet with Encouragement." Like other colonists who preceded him (and many who arrived on the scene later), Lawson wanted to change native culture, but he recognized that such transformations might come at a price. "They are really better to us, than we are to them," he wrote in a passage praising native hospitality practices. "If we admit Reason to be our Guide, she will inform us, that these Indians are the freest People in the World," he added, "and so far from being Intruders upon us, that we have abandon'd our own Native Soil, to drive them out, and possess theirs."

Lawson believed that colonists were so offended by indigenous "strange Customs (uncouth to us)" that they could not take a proper measure of American cultures. Rather than living up to a sense of "Christian Duty," Lawson argued that colonists instead treated natives callously, introduced alcohol – and thus drunkenness – to them, and failed to show the compassion needed to convert them to English religion and mores. Lawson contended it would be better if the English intermarried with natives, a suggestion that many of his readers would have found shocking. Yet such intimate relations might "be a more reasonable Method of converting the Indians, than to set up our Christian Banner in a Field of Blood, as the Spaniards have done in New Spain, and baptize one hundred with the Sword for one at the Font." By invoking the legacy of the Black Legend, Lawson made a point about the ongoing clash of cultures in the Anglo-American colonies: recognition of the valuable parts of indigenous customs and practices would enable these Europeans to advance the original goals of the Elizabethan promoters (Lawson 1967: 57, 175, 200, 243–6).

Lawson's recommendations went nowhere. No English official embraced his call for intermarriage, and by the early decades of the eighteenth century the gap between Europeans and Americans remained firm. Though much had changed in the region between the Atlantic and the Appalachian Mountains, which served as the de facto western boundary for the Anglo-American colonies until the Seven Years' War, oral histories and colonial observations each testified to the persistence of cultural differences. In the famous "secret" account of searching for the boundary line between Virginia and North Carolina, for example, the colonial planter William Byrd frequently derided the opinions of his native traveling companions. At one point in October 1728 he wrote about one companion who had killed a deer while others had successfully hunted turkeys. As the bounty of the hunt was about to be prepared, "the Indian begg'd very hard that our Cook might not boil Venison & Turkey together, because it wou'd certainly spoil his luck in Hunting, & we shou'd repent it with fasting & Prayer." Byrd subsequently believed that such views were a "ridiculous Superstition," which it was better to mock and ignore than to take seriously (Byrd 1967: 193–5). But what he had observed was a widespread indigenous belief that success in the woods would only come when hunters paid proper obeisance to the divine forces that controlled the movement of animals on the earth (Martin 1978).

Byrd was not always hostile to indigenous belief systems. In his account he included the testimony of one native observer who told him about an afterlife that bore occasional similarity to Christian eschatology, including two distinct destinations – one for the good, the other for the bad. "At the Entrance into this blessed Land sits a venerable Old Man who examines every One before he is admitted," Byrd reported, "& if he has behav'd well the Guards are order'd to open the Chrystal Gates & let him into this Terrestrial Paradise." The other option was bleak indeed, inhabited by the hungry and the desperate; it was guarded by "a hideous Old Woman whose Head is cover'd with Rattle-Snakes instead of Tresses, with glaring white Eyes, sunk very deep in her Head." She determined who would be forced to remain in "this Region of Misery." Byrd did not dismiss this account; he in fact praised the openness of the man who told him about it (Byrd 1967: 199–203).

For all of their cultural biases, Lawson and Byrd were both able to overcome their society's lingering hostility toward American culture. Both left posterity with histories showing how they had personally wrestled with the differences between natives and newcomers. In the past generation a number of scholars have used such accounts, along with more prosaic documents such as account books, to tell how the peoples of eastern North America looked at and adapted to each other (see, e.g., Calloway and Salisbury 2004). The so-called "new imperial history" has invigorated a tired field of inquiry, formerly devoted to military strategy and high colonial policy, by taking seriously aspects of indigenous culture in the Americas and elsewhere (White 1991; Hinderaker 1997; Canny 1998). One imaginative historian has blended the insights of ethnohistorians and scholars of the New England town to create the first sustained analysis of a particular indigenous community, a place where the desire to preserve at least some elements of local culture provided stability for individuals who had to cope with the constant pressures brought on them by nearby colonists (Piker 2004). Scholars of material culture have studied specific examples of cultural adaptation, notably the transferal across the cultural divide of European clothing and technology (Shannon 1996) and the persistence of such vital practices as basketry and weaving (Wolverton 2003). In the past 15 years scholars of early American culture have also begun to take more seriously the nature of the sources used to explore and explicate early American culture. All have benefited from two seemingly unrelated developments: a discussion among scholars of literature and historians of the book who have made clear the instability of texts (McKitterick 2003); and a growing recognition, evident to early American historians since at least the late 1970s, of the crucial contributions that can come only from oral historians. For example, the Cheyenne scholar Henrietta Whiteman wrote an account of what she learned from her great-grandmother White Buffalo Woman, which includes a powerful assault on scholars who rely exclusively on the written word (Martin 1987). A recent partnership between a Narragansett tribal historian and an academic historian resulted in a path-breaking analysis of Rhode Island during the American Revolution. This study peeled back generations of cultural misunderstanding to get at the underlying persistence of a native population and its culture (Herndon and Sekatau 1997).

There was no way for either natives or newcomers to predict the outcome of the cultural clash that took place in the Americas in the early modern era. The arrival of Europeans along with their animals, diseases, and ideas about religion and landholding had far-reaching effects that have rippled across Indian Country for centuries (Crosby 1972, 1986; Kupperman 2000). Specific commodities altered individual lives and had cultural consequences. Alcohol, to take the most notable example, was unknown in eastern North America before Europeans arrived, and was available only in small quantities before the middle of the seventeenth century. But once the liquor trade developed as an integral part of the plantation economy of the West Indian sugar islands, the spread of rum into the English hinterland (and brandy in New France) had cultural as well as psychological and economic consequences. Europeans believed that Americans were morally deficient because their cultures were unable to put an effective check on the ways that drinkers, notably young men, behaved when inebriated. Americans, for their part, criticized Europeans for their decision to change a basic foodstuff into a deadly one. "You Rot Your grains in Tubs," the Catawba headman Hagler railed against colonial officials in 1754. In his mind the liquor trade represented nothing less than depravity on a massive scale, a telling sign that Europeans cared so much about making a profit that they were willing to transform food into poison (Mancall 1995).

By the middle decades of the eighteenth century, eastern North America belonged to a transplanted population. The landscape bore the mark of European agricultural and urban practices and a parent culture that had developed without any notion of the existence of the Western Hemisphere. The original inhabitants of eastern North America, like all indigenous peoples across the Americas, had suffered from the assault of pathogens, land-hungry interlopers, and soul-craving missionaries. If we follow the historian Daniel Richter's recent idea of looking at colonization not from the perspective of Europeans but instead eastward from Indian Country, the classic tale of "manifest destiny" takes on an inverted cultural meaning (Richter 2001). All Americans faced cultural challenges that came directly from Europe. By the middle of the eighteenth century the descendants of European invaders appropriated the term "American" for themselves. They defined the indigenous peoples as "merciless Indian savages," to use the words of the Declaration of Independence, or dealt with them along with "other foreign nations," as the United States Constitution put it. Native American cultures survived, but they became subversive instead of dominant. They persist today and should not be set aside in assessments of the nation's cultural legacy.

REFERENCES

Alden, John, et al., eds.: *European Americana: A Chronological Guide to Works Printed in Europe Relating to the Americas, 1493–1776*, 6 vols. (New York: Readex Books, 1980–97).

Anderson, Virginia DeJohn: *Creatures of Empire: How Domestic Animals Transformed Early America* (New York: Oxford University Press, 2004).

Axtell, James: "The Indian Impact on English Colonial Culture," *The European and the Indian: Essays in the Ethnohistory of Colonial North America* (Oxford: Oxford University Press, 1981), pp. 272–315.

Axtell, James: "The White Indians of Colonial America," *William and Mary Quarterly*, 3rd Ser., 32 (1975), 55–88.

Bailyn, Bernard: *The Peopling of British North America: An Introduction* (New York: Alfred A. Knopf, 1986).

Bradford, William: *Of Plymouth Plantation*, ed. Samuel Eliot Morison (New York: Alfred A. Knopf, 1952).

Byrd, William: *Histories of the Dividing Line betwixt Virginia and North Carolina*, ed. William K. Boyd (New York: Dover, 1967).

Calloway, Colin G. & Salisbury, Neal, eds.: *Reinterpreting New England Indians and the Colonial Experience* (Boston: Colonial Society of Massachusetts, 2004).

Canny, Nicholas: "English Migration into and across the Atlantic during the Seventeenth and Eighteenth Centuries," in Nicholas Canny, ed., *Europeans on the Move: Studies on European Migration, 1500–1800* (Oxford: Oxford University Press, 1994), pp. 39–75.

Canny, Nicholas, ed.: *The Origins of Empire*, vol. 1 of *The Oxford History of the British Empire*, gen. ed. William Roger Louis, 5 vols. (Oxford: Oxford University Press, 1998).

Canny, Nicholas: *Making Ireland British, 1580–1650* (Oxford: Oxford University Press, 2003).

C'est la Deduction du sumpeux ordre plaisantz spectacles et magnifiques theatres dresses, et exhibes par les citoiens de Rouen. Orig. published 1551; facsimile titled *L'Entrée de Henri II à Rouen 1550* (Amsterdam: Theatrum Orbis Terrarum, 1970).

Chaplin, Joyce: *Subject Matter: Technology, the Body, and Science on the Anglo-American Frontier, 1500–1676* (Cambridge, MA: Harvard University Press, 2001).

Churchyard, Thomas: *A Prayse, and Reporte of Maister Martyne Frobishers Voyage to META INCOGNITA* (London, 1578).

Cronon, William: *Changes in the Land: Indians, Colonists, and the Ecology of New England* (New York: Hill and Wang, 1983).

Crosby, Alfred: *The Columbian Exchange: Biological and Cultural Consequences of 1492* (Westport, CT: Greenwood Press, 1972).

Crosby, Alfred: *Ecological Imperialism: The Biological Expansion of Europe, 900–1900* (Cambridge: Cambridge University Press, 1986).

Earle, Carville V.: "Environment, Disease, and Mortality in Early Virginia," in Thad Tate & David Ammerman, eds., *The Chesapeake in the Seventeenth Century: Essays on Anglo-American Society* (New York: W. W. Norton for the Institute of Early American History and Culture, 1979), pp. 96–125.

Eliot, John: *Mamusse wunneetupanatamwe Up-Biblium God naneeswe Nukkone Testament kah wonk VVusku Testament* (Cambridge, MA, 1663).

Games, Alison: *Migration and the Origins of the English Atlantic World* (Cambridge, MA: Harvard University Press, 1999).

Gleach, Frederic W.: *Powhatan's World and Colonial Virginia: A Conflict of Cultures* (Lincoln: University of Nebraska Press, 1997).

Gyles, John: "Memoirs of Odd Adventures, Strange Deliverances, Etc.," in Alden Vaughan & Edward Clark, eds.: *Puritans Among the Indians: Accounts of Captivity and Redemption, 1676–1724* (Cambridge, MA: Harvard University Press, 1981), pp. 93–131.

Harriot, Thomas: *A Briefe and True Report of the New Found Land of Virginia* Orig. pub. Frankfurt, 1590; facsimile ed. (New York: Dover, 1992).

Herndon, Ruth Wallis & Sekatau, Ella: "The Right to a Name: The Narragansett People and Rhode Island Officials in the Revolutionary Era," *Ethnohistory* 44 (1997), 433–62.

Hinderaker, Eric: *Elusive Empires: Constructing Colonialism in the Ohio Valley, 1673–1800* (New York: Cambridge University Press, 1997).

Hinderaker, Eric & Mancall, Peter C.: *At the Edge of Empire: The Backcountry in British North America* (Baltimore: Johns Hopkins University Press, 2003).

Hodgen, Margaret T.: *Early Anthropology in the Sixteenth and Seventeenth Centuries* (Philadelphia: University of Pennsylvania Press, 1964).

Honour, Hugh: *The New Golden Land: European Images of America from the Discoveries to the Present Time* (New York: Pantheon, 1975).

Kupperman, Karen Ordahl, ed.: *America in European Consciousness, 1493–1750* (Chapel Hill: University of North Carolina Press for the Institute for Early American History and Culture, 1995).

Kupperman, Karen Ordahl: *Indians & English: Facing Off in Early America* (Ithaca: Cornell University Press, 2000).

Lawson, John: *A New Voyage to Carolina*, ed. Hugh Talmage Lefler (Chapel Hill: University of North Carolina Press, 1967).

Lepore, Jill: *The Name of War: King Philip's War and the Origins of American Identity* (New York: Alfred A. Knopf, 1998).

MacGaffey, Wyatt: "Dialogues of the Deaf: Europeans on the Atlantic Coast of Africa," in Stuart Schwartz, ed. *Implicit Understandings* (Cambridge: Cambridge University Press, 1994), pp. 249–67.

Magnusson, Magnus & Pálsson, Herman, trans.: *The Vinland Sagas: The Norse Discovery of America* (Harmondsworth: Penguin, 1965).

Mancall, Peter C.: *Deadly Medicine: Indians and Alcohol in Early America* (Ithaca: Cornell University Press, 1995).

Mancall, Peter C.: "The Age of Discovery," *Reviews in American History* 26 (1998), 26–53.

Mancall, Peter C.: "Tales Tobacco Told in Sixteenth-Century Europe," *Environmental History* 9 (2004), 648–78.

Martin, Calvin L.: *Keepers of the Game: Indians, Animals, and the Fur Trade* (Berkeley: University of California Press, 1978).

Martin, Calvin L., ed.: *The American Indian and the Problem of History* (New York: Oxford University Press, 1987).

Mather, Cotton: "A Narrative of Hannah Dustan's Notable Delivery from Captivity" (1697), in Alden Vaughan & Edward Clark, eds., *Puritans Among the Indians: Accounts of Captivity and Redemption, 1676–1724* (Cambridge, MA: Harvard University Press, 1981), pp. 161–4.

McKitterick, David: *Print, Manuscript, and the Search for Order, 1450–1830* (Cambridge: Cambridge University Press, 2003).

Merrell, James H.: *The Indians' New World: Catawbas and Their Neighbors from European Contact through the Era of Removal* (Chapel Hill: University of North Carolina Press for the Institute of Early American History and Culture, 1989).

Merrell, James H.: " 'The Customes of Our Countrey': Indians and Colonists in Early America," in Bernard Bailyn & Philip D. Morgan, eds., *Strangers within the Realm: Cultural Margins of the First British Empire* (Chapel Hill: University of North Carolina Press for the Institute of Early American History and Culture, 1991), pp. 117–56.

Montaigne, Michel de: *Essais*. Orig. pub. Bourdeaux, 1580; in Montaigne, *Complete Works*, trans. Donald M. Frame (New York: Alfred A. Knopf, 2003).

Morgan, Edmund: *American Slavery, American Freedom: The Ordeal of Colonial Virginia* (New York: W. W. Norton, 1975).

Obregón, Mauricio: *The Columbus Papers: The Barcelona Letter of 1493, the Landfall Controversy, and the Indian Guides* (New York: Macmillan, 1991).

Ortega, Julio: "Transatlantic Translations," *PMLA* 118 (2003), 25–40.

Pagden, Anthony: *European Encounters with the New World: from Renaissance to Romanticism* (New Haven: Yale University Press, 1993).

Parent, Anthony S., Jr.: *Foul Means: The Formation of a Slave Society in Virginia, 1660–1740* (Chapel Hill: University of North Carolina Press, 2003).

Piker, Joshua: *Okfuskee: A Creek Indian Town in Colonial America* (Cambridge, MA: Harvard University Press, 2004).

Prins, Harald E. L.: "To the Land of the Mistigoches: American Indians Traveling to Europe in the Age of Exploration," *American Indian Culture and Research Journal* 17: 1(1993), 175–95.

Ramusio, Giovannia Batista: *Terze Volume Delle Navigationi et Viaggi* (Venice, 1556).

Richter, Daniel: *Facing East from Indian Country: A Native History of Early America* (Cambridge, MA: Harvard University Press, 2001).

Sahagún, Bernardino: *General History of the Things of New Spain: The Florentine Codex*, trans. J. O. Anderson and Charles E. Dibble. 13 vols. (Santa Fe: 1950–82).

Schmidt, Benjamin: *Innocence Abroad: The Dutch Imagination and the New World, 1570–1670* (Cambridge: Cambridge University Press, 2001).

Schwartz, Stuart: *Implicit Understandings: Observing, Reporting, and Reflecting on the Encounters between Europeans and Other Peoples in the Early Modern Era* (Cambridge: Cambridge University Press, 1994).

Shannon, Timothy J.: "Dressing for Success on the Mohawk Frontier: Hendrick, William Johnson, and the Indian Fashion," *William and Mary Quarterly*, 3rd Ser. 53 (1996), 13–42.

Stade(n), Hans. *Warhafftige historia vnnd beschreibung einer landtschafft der wilden nacketen grimmigen menschfresser leuthen in der newen welt America.* Orig. pub. Frankfurt, 1557?), trans. Albert Tootal as *The Captivity of Hans Stade of Hesse: in AD 1547–1555, among the Wild Tribes of Eastern Brazil* (London: Hakluyt Society, 1874).

Szasz, Margaret Connell: *Indian Education in the American Colonies, 1607–1783* (Albuquerque: University of New Mexico Press, 1988).

Townsend, Camilla: *Pocahontas and the Powhatan Dilemma* (New York: Hill and Wang, 2004).

Urton, Gary & Brezine, Carrie: "Khipu Accounting in Ancient Peru," *Science* 309 (2005), 1065–7.

Vaughan, Alden & Clark, Edward, eds.: *Puritans among the Indians: Accounts of Captivity and Redemption, 1676–1724* (Cambridge, MA: Harvard University Press, 1981).

White, Richard. *The Middle Ground: Indians, Empires, and Republics in the Great Lakes Region, 1650–1815* (New York: Cambridge University Press, 1991).

Wintroub, Michael: "Civilizing the Savage and Making a King: the Royal Entry Festival of Henri II (Rouen, 1555)," *Sixteenth-Century Journal* 29 (1998), 465–94.

Wolverton, Nan: "'A Precarious Living': Basket Making and Related Crafts Among New England Indians," in Colin Calloway & Neal Salisbury, eds., *Reinterpreting New England Indians and the Colonial Experience* (Boston: Colonial Society of Massachusetts, 2003), pp. 341–68.

Chapter Two

CULTURES OF COLONIAL SETTLEMENT

Carla Gardina Pestana

The linguistic or "cultural" turn that began to reshape American historical study in the 1980s has had less influence on historians of early America than on those working in the nineteenth and twentieth centuries. Whereas scholars focusing on later periods have drawn significantly on intellectual developments in philosophy and literary criticism, colonial historians have continued to draw primarily on anthropological and sociological approaches to culture. Most obviously the clash of cultures – especially the meeting of Native American and European – has been a recurrent theme since the mid-1970s. A related endeavor, more narrowly focused on European settlers, is the study of cultural continuity and change. Historians have also explored the interplay of religion and culture in society, especially with regard to the New England region. Finally, efforts to understand the roots of a uniquely American character have focused on the early colonial period, in particular on its literature. These four areas of scholarship – the clash of cultures, cultural transplantation, religious culture, and cultural identity – all pre-date the linguistic turn in American historical study, and have been pursued to varying extents without regard for the theoretical innovations associated with recent cultural studies. Relying on these older models of culture has been both a strength and a weakness in the historiography of early settlement.

The mid-1970s marked a watershed for scholarly appreciation of the importance of cultural encounter in shaping early America – most notably in Gary Nash's *Red, White, and Black: The Peoples of Early America* (1974). Presenting an overview of early American history from the perspective of diverse peoples meeting in eastern North America, Nash showed how cultural interactions profoundly affected their histories. It is unusual for a book that changes the way scholars think about a field to present its new interpretation in the context of a historical overview, as *Red, White, and Black* did. Its impact on scholars was so dramatic that speakers at a 1997 conference celebrating Nash's career almost invariably mentioned the major impact of this work on their understanding of the history of early America. Because the work is synthetic in nature, it was quickly adopted in history classes, which brought its viewpoint to generations of college students. Shortly after the publication of Nash's text, Francis Jennings produced *The Invasion of America: Indians, Colonialism, and the Cant of Conquest* (1975), which argued that English settlement of North America constituted an invasion. This altered perspective explained Native American violence as a defensive posture adopted in response to aggression, and it required a rethinking of the rhetoric of the encounter. According to Jennings, colonists (and the historians who had subsequently read them) presented the Indians as uncivilized savages prone to unprovoked violence. He described this interpretation as "the cant of conquest," because it masked the colonizers' true role and the justified nature of the native response. Between Jennings's impassioned case for abandoning assumptions based unreflectively on self-serving sources and Nash's demonstration of the centrality of cultural interchange to the settlement experience, the way was prepared for a new paradigm of cultural interaction.

Since these path-breaking works by Nash and Jennings, early Americanists have devoted much attention to cultural encounter. Almost all such studies focus on the seventeenth century in North America, and treat Native Americans and Europeans but not Africans. The number of Africans in the mainland colonies remained low through most of the seventeenth century, and the best evidence of the cultural impact of Africans in North America dates from later centuries. For the early settlement period, one line of inquiry has explored the ways that encounter altered European participants. Karen Ordahl Kupperman (1980) analyzed English writings about Indians in order to understand how the newcomers perceived this new culture. Going beyond the "cant" that justified land expropriation, Kupperman was interested in efforts to grapple with the existence of a new world and new peoples. In a study of Mary Rowlandson's captivity narrative, Mitchell Breitwieser (1990) asserted that Rowlandson struggled but ultimately failed to understand her experience as a captive within the proscribed "Puritan" framework. Her reaction to the Native Americans she encountered undercut the values of her community. Kathleen Brown (1996) showed how English gender norms for work roles and sexuality affected the early encounter in Virginia. In Brown's telling the first meeting of Indians and English set the stage for later relations between European slaveholders and their African and African American slaves, and among members of the European settlement community itself. Elaine Breslaw (1996) offered the highly speculative but intriguing thesis that a central figure in the Salem witchcraft trials, the Indian slave Tituba, introduced strange attitudes toward witchcraft and the devil into the proceedings, ideas that were based on her exposure to Arawak and African beliefs in her native South America and on a plantation in Barbados. According to Breslaw these unfamiliar ideas increased the fears of the dominant community, which in turn further spread the scare. Understanding how the encounter with Native America transformed colonial society is one well-developed area in the scholarship.

Another approach has been to see the encounter as a two-way street. Neal Salisbury (1982) contrasted the cultural, especially religious, systems of Native Americans and New England settlers, finding them to be on a collision course as a result of their profound differences. Richard White's *Middle Ground* (1991), one of the most often cited books about the colonial period, found that for a century and a half after 1650 various cultures and peoples met on fairly equal terms in part of the Great Lakes region; there, while no one group dominated, an ongoing process of negotiation created a sort of cultural "middle ground." Recently, Faren Siminoff's study of Long Island focused on small-group interactions within a local framework, plotting interpersonal contacts and small-scale networks as the basis of cross-cultural encounters, and cautioning against seeing Native Americans and settlers as monolithic and homogenous groups (Siminoff 2004).

Other scholars have also explored aspects of encounter from both sides of the cultural divide. With a project that began as a simple revision of her *Settling with the Indians*, Karen Kupperman won the Atlantic History Prize for a new volume, *Indians and English* (2000). Studying English and Indian perceptions, she depicted the two groups as sharing mutual fear and wonder, as well as a hope to control the developing relationship. In the same year another book focused on the colonial drive to alter Native American marriage practices in early New England. Ann Marie Plane argued that European efforts to reshape native marital practices were fundamental to the wish to dominate the Indian peoples. The English viewed Indian customs as inferior, an analysis that would eventually lead to the construction of modern notions of culture. For their part Indians both resisted and adapted to the changing context brought by settler colonialism (Plane 2000). To explore the encounter from both sides has required an attention to non-literary sources such as oral traditions and archaeological sites as well as a careful reading of European-produced written sources and sensitivity to the nature of the different cultures on either side of the divide.

A third line of inquiry has involved comparing the experiences of different cultural groups present in the early North American colonies. James Axtell (1985) contrasted French and English approaches to the conversion of Indians. The greater French success was based on a host of factors, including different requirements for converts, the presence of missionary priests who were able to live among the native peoples, and a degree of cultural flexibility. In a more broad-ranging comparison, E. Brooks Holifield (1989) examined Europeans of various origins as well as Native Americans, arguing that all employed similar tools of persuasion that he found to be central to early colonial history in North America. Comparative colonialism is an area of research that is likely to grow, with the current scholarly interest in placing the North American settlements in Continental and Atlantic frameworks.

While most work on the clash of cultures in the seventeenth century has attended to the Indian–settler encounter, a few works have looked at Europeans. The Dutch in New Netherland, which became the colony of New York with the 1664 English conquest, have been the focus of a number of such studies. Donna Merwick published two books on the challenges that the conquest presented to the Dutch. In *Possessing Albany* (1990), she argued for dramatically different cultures among the Dutch and the English colonies. The Dutch, more interested in trade than in settlement, mapped the waterways and thought in terms of alliances with Indian peoples who served as trading partners. The English had less use for Native Americans but far greater interest in their land, since they sought settlement and individual ownership of farmland. These cultural differences influenced everything from map-making to legal systems, and the disjunction resulted in massive culture shock with the imposition of English rule on conquered Dutch people. Merwick's analysis of Dutch and English differences was consistent with the observations subsequently developed by Patricia Seed (1995), contrasting the different ways that various European colonizers laid claim to the land. Merwick later reexamined the conquest crisis on the micro-historical scale, with the tale of a Dutch notary who eventually committed suicide in despair over his inability to navigate the cultural and legal transformation (1999). Her vision of conquest as a wrenching experience fits well with a study of religion by Randall Balmer (1989), who charted post-conquest attrition and out-migration among the Dutch Reformed Church members. Joyce Goodfriend (1992), alternatively, saw the Dutch as relatively able to weather the English takeover. Cultural resilience was the order of the day, in Goodfriend's view, at least during the first decades after 1664. Cultural encounter, whether between rival Europeans or between Europeans and Indians, has been a major arena of cultural historical studies of the early settlements.

If cultural clash represented a new perspective dating from the 1970s, the study of the transfer of culture to America offered an older interpretive framework that received a boost around the same time. When the books by Nash and Jennings appeared, the prevailing paradigm was the town study, especially that of the New England town. Influenced by the French *Annales* School and by Peter Laslett's seminal *The World We Have Lost* (1965), a cohort of historians labored to uncover the lost world of the colonial village. These scholars were at the forefront of an avalanche of social history scholarship that overtook American history generally in the 1970s and 1980s. Joyce Appleby (1998) has vividly described these young scholars armed with computer punch cards, ready to utilize the latest technological breakthroughs in their efforts to recreate past social life. In the context of New England historiography, they sought to challenge Perry Miller's magisterial *New England Mind*, objecting to the idea that one overarching mind (discernible in the writings of the ministerial elite) represented colonial New England. Instead they sought to recreate the lives and worldview of ordinary colonists. These works, notably those by Kenneth Lockridge and Philip Greven (both published in 1970), understood culture in terms of premodern, communal values. Paradoxically, despite their intention of challenging Miller, most town studies (including Darrett Rutman's Boston study of 1965) adopted the declension paradigm – the idea that New England initially achieved a high level of social stability and community cohesion which eroded with time – that was associated with Miller's opus. According to this view, most baldly stated by Lockridge, early New Englanders were peasant villagers who set up highly traditional communities.

The idea that New Englanders were initially peasants dedicated to a traditional lifestyle formed the presuppositions that undergirded perhaps the single most popular book on the seventeenth-century colonies. Paul Boyer and Stephen Nissenbaum (1974) explained the witchcraft outbreak of 1692 as a reaction of traditional villagers against the encroachments of an innovative commercial segment within their society. *Salem Possessed* argues that witchcraft accusations were related to long-standing social and political tensions within Salem Village. In keeping with the prevailing view of New England culture, the authors link these tensions to the idea that New Englanders were agrarian traditionalists wedded to precapitalist economic and social relations. Like the town studies that influenced them, Boyer & Nissenbaum's interpretation ignored a vast European scholarly tradition linking the "Puritan" religious reform impulse with economic modernization and the birth of capitalism. Neither Boyer & Nissenbaum nor Lockridge nor Greven considered how traditional peasants managed to participate in transatlantic migration or how the region they settled moved so rapidly to the forefront of the commercialization of the Atlantic world. In the intervening years scholarship on England itself has undermined the idea of an isolated and traditional peasant culture flourishing anywhere in the seventeenth-century Anglophone world. In addition, the assumption that New England's religious orientation made it inherently hostile to commerce has been thoroughly discounted (Newell 1998). Despite the clearly flawed underpinnings to *Salem Possessed*, it continues to be frequently assigned to students of Salem witchcraft. The reason is perhaps that both students and their teachers feel more comfortable with economic interpretations than with serious analyses of unfamiliar beliefs about the supernatural.

Despite the continued popularity of *Salem Possessed*, numerous scholars have challenged the idea that New England's culture was highly traditional or that religion and commerce were antithetical. Richard Gildrie's study of Salem (1975) charted the history of a town that was contentious throughout the century, experiencing "crisis" in its first decade; the author posited that Salem offered a town type midway between the stable, traditional inland village and the bustling seaport of Boston. Like Gildrie, Byers (1987) studied a New England region that defied the paradigm. Nantucket developed as a tolerant community that did not sanction interference in personal affairs, breaking with the "Puritan" practice of community watchfulness and censure. In 1984 Christine Heyrman brilliantly inverted the prevailing view, and she did so working within the town-study genre. In Heyrman's telling, the seaport towns of Gloucester and Marblehead became more stable and harmonious as they became more highly commercial and prosperous. Commerce did not undermine religion but rather bolstered it. Although it is still possible to find the occasional scholar opposing Puritan traditionalism to non-Puritan commercialism (such as Breen 2001), Heyrman's insights have helped to reorient the field away from this older view.

Other works outside the town-study tradition have also contributed to challenging the view that to be Puritan was to oppose commercial development. Mark Peterson (1997) argued that economic success was fundamental to the creation and maintenance of congregationalist churches in New England. The church order most New Englanders embraced proved costly, and vigorous economic activity was necessary to the health of the churches and their efforts to extend their reach through missionary work. David Konig (1979) tackled the problem from another angle, noting the existence of other avenues for the creation of community harmony outside the local church. His legal history revealed that seventeenth-century New Englanders relied heavily on litigation to settle disputes, making law and legal institutions neither a sign of declension nor of increased concern for material acquisitiveness but rather basic to the creation of a stable society. After numerous scholars challenged the assumptions behind the declension model of New England's history, it has been largely undermined. Now, religion and economic growth are more typically seen as complementary, as in Gloria Main's *Peoples of a Spacious Land: Families and Culture in Colonial New England* (2001), which explores a "family gospel" of "personal piety, family labor, and congregational independence" (p. 237).

When New England town studies were at the height of their influence, scholars used their social science methods to conduct research on other colonial regions, initially contrasting them to the New England town. Because the town was not an important institution in other colonies, these studies were organized around such social units as the neighborhood, the county, or the colony as a whole. Concurrent with the arrival of the town studies upon the historical scene, Richard S. Dunn and the Bridenbaughs issued books on the seventeenth-century Caribbean (both in 1972). In contrast to the idyllic communalism of seventeenth-century New England, these scholars documented an atomized and exploitative society, entirely dedicated to the acquisition of material wealth. In a cleverly wrought contrast, Karen Kupperman's prize-winning *Providence Island* (1993) posited that Puritans in the tropics were as likely as any other English peoples to become exploitative and even piratical. More recent studies, especially Larry Gragg on Barbados (2003), have moderated the view that the Caribbean stood in complete opposition to a more stable New England model; just as later research on the colonies to the north found them to be less harmonious than once assumed, Gragg has found more evidence of ameliorating social institutions and community values. The Rutmans (1984) pushed against the prevailing view of an entirely atomized south with their study of the social networks that bound early Virginians together. A vast social history literature on early America was summarized by Jack Greene in his *Pursuits of Happiness* in 1988. He argued that the relative stability of New England made it anomalous, but that all the colonial regions converged over time, with New England becoming less stable and other areas more so. By the time Greene published, the image of stable town life in New England had already been seriously undermined, although most scholars would agree that the northern colonies had been relatively more stable than those further south. Although the image of the atomized Chesapeake and harmonious but repressive New England still pervades textbooks and lectures delivered in American history survey courses, it is not consistent with the latest literature on the subject.

Much of what has been written on the transfer of culture to the colonies has focused on this question of the prevalence of traditionalism, but some scholars have looked at the issue of cultural transfer in more general terms. The major book asserting that transplanted cultural forms shaped early America was David Hackett Fischer's *Albion's Seed* (1989). Initially intended as the first volume in a multi-volume cultural history of the United States, *Albion's Seed* posited the existence of distinctive folkways from Britain that were transferred to the colonies, decisively shaping regional variations. Fischer used a classic definition of culture, drawn from anthropology and focused on folkways, but was widely criticized for his reductive use of evidence. Other studies of the transfer of culture have been less ambitious and more successful than Fischer's. David Grayson Allen's study (1981) of a handful of towns in New England posited that the topography of England had affected agricultural forms and social organization, creating variations that emigrants sought to recapture. Allen found settlers migrating repeatedly from town to town within Massachusetts, in search of the specific agricultural practices and modes of life they had left behind. Michael Rozbicki (1988) explored the transfer of culture from England to Maryland, finding that the colonial setting brought out the acquisitive, individualistic, secular aspects of early modern English culture over the more communal and religious. Rozbicki's view relied on a more sophisticated understanding of the English cultural heritage than had the earlier town studies or Fischer's study of folkways. Even with this greater sophistication, Rozbicki adheres to the prevailing view in that his findings on Maryland offered an implicit contrast to the allegedly communal and religious northern town. Rozbicki also argued that the introduction of heavy reliance on slave labor reoriented the Marylanders toward English values of paternalism and the aristocratic ethos. As Maryland became more exploitative it also shifted its cultural values in a more communal direction, adopting another of the ideologies currently available in England. James Horn's study of the Chesapeake (1994) documented the mixed cultural heritage coming from England; he too argued that Chesapeake settlers tried to recreate what they had known. He found that the colonial environment hampered their efforts but that upholding conservative cultural values was as much a goal of many Chesapeake settlers as of their New England counterparts. Facile generalizations about the contrast between colonial regions have been significantly eroded by the literature of the last 30 years, although it remains to be seen how much impact this scholarship will have on the popular understanding of the early colonial period.

The religious culture of the seventeenth-century settlements has also been explored extensively. In one respect this area of research is intimately related to the vision of a stable New England, for the importance of religion in the major colonies of that region was pivotal to its representation as traditional and stable. While most scholars would still feel comfortable asserting that religion played a more important role in New England than elsewhere, there is no denying that we know more about religion (as about many other things) for that region due to the vagaries of record survival. Unsurprisingly, the one town study to minimize the role of religion (Innes 1983) dealt with Springfield, an unusual New England locale for which no church records are extant. In general, New England looms large in our understanding of the seventeenth century because it is by far the most heavily documented colonial region for that century. A welcome trend away from this dominance of New England can be seen in some recent works. For instance, Horn's book on the early Chesapeake includes an excellent chapter on religion, emphasizing how it shaped the worldview of early settlers. More recently, Edward L. Bond (2000) has further explored religion in early Virginia, focusing on the established church and how it was shaped by questions of empire and identity.

Given the predominance of New England, it is unsurprising that many of the books on early colonial religious culture treat the movement known as "Puritanism." The term "Puritan" was used to ridicule those within the Church of England who sought its reform prior to its collapse during the revolution of the 1640s. A loose coalition of godly Protestants that would fragment within England after 1643, the Puritans have a much longer history within New England than in the land of their origins. The moniker is applied by American historians to the mainstream (or orthodox) religious community within most of New England into the early eighteenth century, with minister Increase Mather (1639–1723) sometimes dubbed "the Last Puritan." In recent decades scholars have attempted to place early New England religion in this transatlantic context, uncovering the roots of the region's dominant religious culture and the ongoing dialogue between godly Protestants in England and America. Stephen Foster's *The Long Argument* (1991), although more concerned with the intellectual than the cultural history of the movement, is a prominent example. Theodore Dwight Bozeman (2004) looked at tensions over discipline and control, understanding the antinomian controversy of the 1630s as one result. Michael Kaufmann (1998) instead explored the tension within New England culture arising between individualism and such institutions as patriarchy. A brilliant but difficult book by Ann Kibbey (1986) wrestled with the role of violence in the Puritan tradition. *The Interpretation of Material Shapes in Puritanism* saw prejudice as intertwined with religious beliefs from the outset of the Puritan movement. Emphasizing the role of iconoclasm in the Protestant Reformation, Kibbey posits that the violence against objects of veneration developed into "sacrosanct violence against human beings," especially those who looked different from the Puritans (1986: 2). Thus violence against Native Americans had divine sanction, in the Puritan view. After the Hutchinson affair (1636) and the Pequot War (1636–7), both of which reveal the prejudicial aspect of religiously sanctioned violence, leading clerical figure John Cotton began advocating a holy war on Catholics. Despite their differences, these studies share an interest in placing Puritanism in its transatlantic context.

The popular religious culture of early America has also been explored extensively. The piety of the laity was the focal point of a study by Charles Hambrick-Stowe (1982), who saw Puritan piety as central to the lay experience of religion and as closely related to practices among other Christians, including Anglicans and even Roman Catholics. Hambrick-Stowe sought to demonstrate that ministers and the laity partook of a shared religious culture; in doing so he wanted to counter the criticism that studies of the ministers' concerns did not fully illuminate the content of the New England mind. Showing lay engagement in a shared religious culture was one way to counter that criticism. David Hall's important work *Worlds of Wonder, Days of Judgment: Popular Religious Belief in Early New England* (1989) shared the same goal. Hall explored providential thinking, popular religious literature, execution sermons, and a host of other evidence to argue in favor of a culture that united clergy and laity. Philip Gura's study of radicalism in early New England (1984) took a different tack, exploring heterodox beliefs in the period to 1660. Lumping together a range of unconventional views under the rubric of "Puritan radicalism," Gura sought to present early New England as seething with strange beliefs and practices. Despite his efforts to break down barriers between orthodox and other viewpoints, Gura's work focused largely on the margins of New England, especially Rhode Island. Other works on religious radicalism in this early period (such as Pestana 1991) have seen dissenters as embracing alternatives to the orthodox religious culture. If Hambrick-Stowe and Hall sought to present mainstream Puritanism as widely appealing and Gura tried to expand the boundaries of what was encompassed by the term, Richard Gildrie (1994) argued for fairly clear divisions within the religious culture of New England. Although happy to concede that Puritanism (as understood by Hall rather than by Gura) shaped the culture of the first decades, Gildrie asserted that by the later seventeenth century differences among "the profane, the civil, and the godly" were clearly evident. Interestingly, Gildrie's account returns to some of the evidence used to demonstrate declension but examines it in light of transatlantic cultural shifts that were not a result of simple decline.

Given the centrality of the 1692 witchcraft episode to our image of early America's engagement with the supernatural, it is unremarkable that beliefs about witchcraft and magic have occupied much scholarly (and popular) attention. Elaine Breslaw's argument that Tituba introduced exotic beliefs about the supernatural into the witchcraft controversy was unusual in looking beyond the European community for the source of disparate ideas. Other studies have been influenced by the idea, taken from European scholars, of a split between high and low culture over belief in magic and (to some extent) witchcraft. Sociologist Richard Weisman was the first to apply this view to the English colonies; his study of *Witchcraft, Magic, and Religion in 17th-Century Massachusetts* (1984) explored a break between elites, who worried over witchcraft because it represented interaction with the devil, and ordinary colonists, who focused on the material harm witches could do. Richard Godbeer (1992) further developed this line of reasoning in a study of early New England patterned on Keith Thomas's powerful *Religion and the Decline of Magic* (1971). Jon Butler went beyond either Weisman or Godbeer (or for that matter Thomas) in an influential article later revised for inclusion in his *Awash in a Sea of Faith* (1990), a general history of early American religion. Butler adopted the elite-versus-popular model in support of his view that most of the early settlers were largely irreligious. In his schema, evidence of magical beliefs demonstrated a rejection of organized Christianity. Hall responded to this assumption in *Worlds of Wonder* by demonstrating broad areas of overlap between elite and popular ideas about the supernatural. This debate revolves around questions of religious culture, including whether colonists shared a broadly similar understanding of the supernatural and whether orthodox theological positions might be held alongside magical beliefs or were mutually exclusive categories.

Witchcraft is one area in which religion and gender come together. Carol Karlsen's influential study (1987) explored the cultural assumptions that made women more likely to be accused as witches. Elizabeth Reis (1997) plumbed the intersection of theology and gender, showing how understanding of women's nature opened them to suspicions of witchcraft. Other works on gender and religion have ranged beyond witchcraft. Anne Hutchinson, as a woman who defied the authorities and was punished with excommunication and exile, has been analyzed in terms of the way her beliefs and her gender interacted to create a volatile confrontation that threatened to destroy the infant colony of Massachusetts. For Amy Schrager Lang (1987), Hutchinson offered an early example of the intertwining of female empowerment and antinomian ideas. More recently, Bozeman's study (2004) of the antinomian backlash against a harsh Puritan message argued that antinomians favored a more feminine and passive emphasis on grace. Leslie J. Lindenauer's *Piety and Power: Gender and Religious Culture in the American Colonies, 1630–1700* (2002) offers a wide-ranging, multiregional exploration of the ways in which gender shaped early American religious culture. This study of Congregationalist Massachusetts, Dutch Reformed New York, and Anglican Virginia develops the idea that Protestantism created new opportunities for female religious expression.

The origins of American identity is a final theme that has shaped the study of culture in the early colonies. This issue has been a central preoccupation of American studies scholarship for many decades. Like the scholarship on religion to which it is linked, work on this topic focuses largely on New England. A foundational text was Sacvan Bercovitch's *The Puritan Origins of the American Self* (1975). Bercovitch argued that American self-identification as an elect nation dated to New England's sense of its mission in the world. This argument expanded upon Perry Miller's idea, put forward in a 1956 essay entitled "Errand into the Wilderness," that the early New Englanders understood their presence in the New World in terms of a divinely ordained mission. Relying heavily on the writings of Cotton Mather, Bercovitch uncovered a later generation's reading of the meaning of the founders' history. His work is less about the way early settlers perceived their actions than about the meaning ascribed to them retrospectively by a man dedicated to creating a suitable past for his colonial region. Bercovitch subsequently explored, in *The American Jeremiad* (1978), the rhetoric of jeremiads as a major form of cultural expression. He viewed the jeremiad – the sermon style popular in the later seventeenth century that supplied key evidence for Miller's interpretation of declension – as having a signal impact on American culture, providing a rhetoric that could at once chastise and galvanize. Between them, Miller and Bercovitch directed studies of early American literature to the origins of the American character, a focus that has only recently begun to shift.

Whether Americans were on a mission, and what the nature of that mission was, has engaged a number of scholars since Miller and Bercovitch. Whereas Miller had posited that migrating New Englanders brought with them a sense of mission, Andrew Delbanco (1989) saw them as escaping from threatening circumstances in England. Rather than coming to America to create a new society or to serve as a model for England, they were simply fleeing, an act the implications of which they would later be forced to confront. Virginia Anderson (1991) analyzed the later settlers' desire to live up to the legacy of the first generation. She documented an emerging sense of mission, one that had to be understood in the context of the self-criticism that arose from contemplating the founders' heroic acts. Declension was part of the creation of a founding myth. The idea that the Puritans, as biblical primitivists, sought to return to an idealized past was developed by Theodore Dwight Bozeman (1988). Bozeman's argument put declension in a new light, since all churches were said to have declined not from those first founded in the colonies but from a millennia-old biblical ideal. More recently, Kristina Bross (2004) has seen the drive to convert the Indians as part of the revision of the New England mission. If the colonists dedicated themselves to Christianizing the Indians, they had a colonial project worthy of their aspirations, not to mention one that could impress an English audience.

Many subsequent works have taken up the question of the meanings ascribed to New England or, more broadly, to America. John Shields (2001) sought to decenter the literary foundations of early American culture, arguing that the classical tradition was equally significant to the emerging sense of identity. Experience offered an alternative source of authority for early settlers, one that shaped their literature as well as their sense of self, according to Jim Egan (1999). John Canup (1990) charted the colonists' struggle with the impact of the wilderness on their culture. Fearful that the wilderness would make them less English, colonists sought to convert Indians to both Christianity and civility as a way to allay those fears. Jill Lepore's study of the impact of King Philip's War (1998) was similarly interested in the links between Indians and the settlers' sense of identity, though she focused more narrowly on the role of the violence in a particularly devastating war. James F. Cooper, Jr. (1999) revived a tradition older than Perry Miller that portrayed New England as the seat of American democracy. De-emphasizing the role of the town meeting, Cooper instead looked to congregational polity, and especially its advocacy of communal checks on authority, as a source of American democratic values. Leo Lemay suggested that identifying America as a land of opportunity was the key element in the creation of an American character, and John Smith was the central figure. His *American Dream of Captain John Smith* (1991) attempted to displace New England and New Englanders from their presumed centrality. According to Jeffrey Richards (1991), America as a stage was a typical metaphor in colonial American literature. This conviction that the whole world was watching America was fundamental to a sense of mission and gave the colonists a way of presenting their own significance.

Recently, some literary scholars have broken with the idea that the early colonies laid the groundwork for a monolithic American identity. This shift in the literature is related to a new interest in the Atlantic context for colonization. Reintegrating the colonies into an early modern Atlantic world has undermined the faith in American exceptionalism, the idea that the United States and therefore the colonies out of which it arose were unique. Since the nation states throughout the Americas and the Caribbean were all born out of a colonial experience, privileging the United States' colonial origins makes little sense. Works such as Ralph Bauer's *The Cultural Geography of Colonial American Literatures: Empire, Travel, and Modernity* (2003) posited common themes between English North American and Spanish American colonial literature. Holifield's older comparative study of persuasive language within various colonial and native cultures in North America anticipated this turn. Other scholars have made more modest claims about the centrality of the English context to American literary developments. James D. Hartman (1999), for instance, placed witchcraft and captivity narratives into an English context, noting that the effort to combat atheism by presenting the supernatural world as real was a transatlantic agenda. In *By Nature and By Custom Cursed: Transatlantic Civil Discourse and New England Cultural Production, 1620–1660* (1999), Philip H. Round explicitly disclaimed the goal of uncovering the origins of American identity or analyzing the preoccupations of a monolithic New England. Thomas Scanlan (1999) had turned the argument about New England's concern with identity on its head, asserting that the central debate concerned the Protestant identity of England itself, and had nothing to do with a unique or even separate American self. The popularity of the project of locating American cultural roots in the colonial period probably means that books on the origins of the American self will continue to appear, yet many scholars now perceive that agenda as seriously limited. In American literary studies the early colonial period has routinely been neglected, so perhaps that field's focus on finding seventeenth-century origins for all of American cultural history amounted to special pleading.

Much of the literature on the cultural history of the seventeenth-century settlements has revolved around these four themes: the clash of peoples, the transfer of culture, religious culture, and the literary origins of American identity. These categories cannot be kept entirely separate, and indeed some of the more provocative work has combined them in interesting ways. For instance, Breslaw's biography of the slave woman Tituba brought together concerns about cultural differences that shaped European and native encounters, with ideas about witchcraft belief and lay attitudes that are basic to the study of popular religious culture. With the surviving evidence for the seventeenth century so heavily weighted toward New England, the history and culture of that region is likely to remain a central concern of the historical literature. Yet recent trends in the field, including the new emphasis on Atlantic history and the renewed attention to a transatlantic context, may help to decenter New England. Work that emphasizes similarities and connections between different colonial regions, such as Lindenauer's comparative history of gender and faith in three colonies and three faith traditions, offers another important corrective. Whether early American scholars will increasingly embrace the more theoretically informed approaches to culture is not at all clear – scholars of seventeenth-century English history may lead the way in this trend, but it is not certain that colonial historians (as opposed to literary critics) will follow. In other ways, however, the literature of the seventeenth century has been innovative, first in ushering in the social history of colonial towns, and later in inaugurating the shift toward cultural encounter. In general, the scholarship of this era is pulled between such innovative trends and such older concerns as the English cultural heritage and the origins of the United States' identity.

REFERENCES

Allen, David Grayson: *In English Ways: The Movement of Societies and the Transferal of English Local Law and Custom to Massachusetts Bay in the Seventeenth Century* (Chapel Hill: University of North Carolina Press, 1981).

Anderson, Virginia DeJohn: *New England's Generation: The Great Migration and the Formation of Society and Culture in the Seventeenth Century* (New York: Cambridge University Press, 1991).

Appleby, Joyce: "The Power of History," *American Historical Review* 103 (1998), 1–17.

Axtell, James: *The Invasion Within: The Contest of Cultures in Colonial North America* (New York: Oxford University Press, 1985).

Balmer, Randall: *A Perfect Babel of Confusion: Dutch Religion and English Culture in the Middle Colonies* (New York: Oxford University Press, 1989).

Bauer, Ralph: *The Cultural Geography of Colonial American Literatures: Empire, Travel, and Modernity* (New York: Cambridge University Press, 2003).

Bercovitch, Sacvan: *The Puritan Origins of the American Self* (New Haven: Yale University Press, 1975).

Bercovitch, Sacvan: *The American Jeremiad* (Madison: University of Wisconsin Press, 1978).

Bond, Edward L.: *Damned Souls in a Tobacco Colony: Religion in Seventeenth-Century Virginia* (Macon, GA: Mercer University Press, 2000).

Boyer, Paul & Nissenbaum, Stephen: *Salem Possessed: The Social Origins of Witchcraft* (Cambridge, MA: Harvard University Press, 1974).

Bozeman, Theodore Dwight: *To Live Ancient Lives: The Primitivist Dimension in Puritanism* (Chapel Hill: University of North Carolina Press, 1988).

Bozeman, Theodore Dwight: *The Precisionist Strain: Disciplinary Religion & Antinomian Backlash in Puritanism to 1638* (Chapel Hill: University of North Carolina Press, 2004).

Breen, Louise A.: *Transgressing the Bounds: Subversive Enterprises among the Puritan Elite in Massachusetts, 1630–1692* (New York: Oxford University Press, 2001).

Breitweiser, Mitchell R.: *American Puritanism and the Defense of Mourning: Religion, Grief, and Ethnology in Mary White Rowlandson's Captivity Narrative* (Madison: University of Wisconsin Press, 1990).

Breslaw, Elaine G.: *Tituba, Reluctant Witch of Salem: Devilish Indians and Puritan Fantasies* (New York: New York University Press, 1996).

Bridenbaugh, Carl & Bridenbaugh, Roberta: *No Peace beyond the Line: The English in the Caribbean, 1624–1690* (New York: Oxford University Press, 1972).

Bross, Kristina: *Dry Bones and Indian Sermons: Praying Indians in Colonial America* (Ithaca, NY: Cornell University Press, 2004).

Brown, Kathleen M.: *Good Wives, Nasty Wenches, and Anxious Patriarchs: Gender, Race and Power in Colonial Virginia* (Chapel Hill: University of North Carolina Press, 1996).

Butler, Jon: *Awash in a Sea of Faith: Christianizing the American People* (Cambridge, MA: Harvard University Press, 1990).

Byers, Edward: *The Nation of Nantucket: Society and Politics in an Early American Commercial Center, 1660–1820* (Boston, MA: Northeastern University Press, 1987).

Canup, John: *Out of the Wilderness: The Emergence of an American Identity in Colonial New England* (Middleton, CT: Wesleyan University Press, 1990).

Cooper, James F., Jr.: *Tenacious of Their Liberties: The Congregationalists in Colonial Massachusetts* (New York: Oxford University Press, 1999).

Delbanco, Andrew: *The Puritan Ordeal* (Cambridge, MA: Harvard University Press, 1989).

Dunn, Richard S.: *Sugar and Slaves: The Rise of the Planter Class in the English West Indies, 1624–1713* (Chapel Hill: University of North Carolina Press, 1972).

Egan, Jim: *Authorizing Experience: Refigurations of the Body Politic in Seventeenth-century New England Writing* (Princeton: Princeton University Press, 1999).

Fischer, David Hackett: *Albion's Seed: Four British Folkways in America* (New York: Oxford University Press, 1989).

Foster, Stephen: *The Long Argument: English Puritanism and the Shaping of New England Culture, 1570–1700* (Chapel Hill: University of North Carolina Press, 1991).

Gildrie, Richard P.: *Salem, Massachusetts, 1626–1683: A Covenant Community* (Charlottesville: University Press of Virginia, 1975).

Gildrie, Richard P.: *The Profane, the Civil, & the Godly: The Reformation of Manners in Orthodox New England, 1679–1749* (University Park: Pennsylvania State University Press, 1994).

Godbeer, Richard: *The Devil's Dominion: Magic and Religion in Early New England* (New York: Cambridge University Press, 1992).

Goodfriend, Joyce D.: *Before the Melting Pot: Society and Culture in Colonial New York City, 1664–1730* (Princeton: Princeton University Press, 1992).

Gragg, Larry: *Englishmen Transplanted: The English Colonization of Barbados, 1627–1660* (New York: Oxford University Press, 2003).

Greene, Jack P.: *Pursuits of Happiness: The Social Development of Early Modern British Colonies and the Formation of American Culture* (Chapel Hill: University of North Carolina Press, 1988).

Greven, Philip: *Four Generations: Population, Land, and Family in Colonial Andover, Massachusetts* (Ithaca, NY: Cornell University Press, 1970).

Gura, Philip F.: *A Glimpse of Sion's Glory: Puritan Radicalism in New England, 1620–1660* (Middletown, CT.: Wesleyan University Press, 1984).

Hall, David D.: *Worlds of Wonder, Days of Judgment: Popular Religious Belief in Early New England* (New York: Alfred A. Knopf, 1989).

Hall, Michael G.: *The Last American Puritan: The Life of Increase Mather, 1639–1723* (Middletown, CT: Wesleyan University Press, 1988).

Hambrick-Stowe, Charles E.: *The Practice of Piety: Puritan Devotional Disciplines in Seventeenth-Century New England* (Chapel Hill: University of North Carolina Press, 1982).

Hartman, James D.: *Providence Tales and the Birth of American Literature* (Baltimore: Johns Hopkins University Press, 1999).

Heyrman, Christine Leigh: *Commerce and Culture: The Maritime Communities of Colonial Massachusetts, 1690–1750* (New York: W. W. Norton, 1984).

Holifield, E. Brooks: *Era of Persuasion: American Thought and Culture, 1521–1680* (Boston: Twayne Publishers, 1989).

Horn, James: *Adapting to a New World: English Society in the Seventeenth-Century Chesapeake* (Chapel Hill: University of North Carolina Press, 1994).

Innes, Stephen: *Labor in a New Land: Economy and Society in Seventeenth-Century Springfield* (Princeton: Princeton University Press, 1983).

Jennings, Francis: *The Invasion of America: Indians, Colonialism, and the Cant of Conquest* (Chapel Hill: University of North Carolina Press, 1975).

Karlsen, Carol F.: *The Devil in the Shape of a Woman: Witchcraft in Colonial New England* (New York: Vintage, 1987).

Kaufmann, Michael W.: *Institutional Individualism: Conversion, Exile, and Nostalgia in Puritan New England* (Hanover, NH: University Press of New England, 1998).

Kibbey, Ann: *The Interpretation of Material Shapes in Puritanism: A Study of Rhetoric, Prejudice, and Violence* (New York: Cambridge University Press, 1986).

Konig, David Thomas: *Law and Society in Puritan Massachusetts, Essex County, 1629–1692* (Chapel Hill: University of North Carolina Press, 1979).

Kupperman, Karen Ordahl: *Settling with the Indians: The Meeting of English and Indian Cultures in America, 1580–1640* (Totowa, NJ: Rowman and Littlefield, 1980).

Kupperman, Karen Ordahl: *Providence Island, 1630–1641: The Other Puritan Colony* (New York: Cambridge University Press, 1993).

Kupperman, Karen Ordahl: *Indians and English: Facing Off in Early America* (Ithaca, NY: Cornell University Press, 2000).

Lang, Amy Schrager: *Prophetic Woman: Anne Hutchinson and the Problem of Dissent in the Literature of New England* (Berkeley: University of California Press, 1987).

Laslett, Peter: *The World We Have Lost* (London: Methuen, 1965).

Lemay, J. A. Leo: *The American Dream of Captain John Smith* (Charlottesville: University Press of Virginia, 1991).

Lepore, Jill: *The Name of the War: King Philip's War and the Origins of American Identity* (New York: Viking, 1998).

Lindenauer, Leslie J.: *Piety and Power: Gender and Religious Culture in the American Colonies, 1630–1700* (New York: Routledge, 2002).

Lockridge, Kenneth A.: *A New England Town: The First Hundred Years, Dedham, Massachusetts, 1636–1736* (New York: W. W. Norton, 1970).

Main, Gloria Lund: *Peoples of a Spacious Land: Families and Culture in Colonial New England* (Cambridge, MA: Harvard University Press, 2001).

Merwick, Donna: *Possessing Albany, 1630–1710: The Dutch and English Experiences* (New York: Cambridge University Press, 1990).

Merwick, Donna: *Death of a Notary: Conquest and Change in Colonial New York* (Ithaca, NY: Cornell University Press, 1999).

Miller, Perry: *The New England Mind*, vol. 2: *From Colony to Province* (Cambridge, MA: Harvard University Press, 1953).

Miller, Perry: *Errand Into the Wilderness* (Cambridge, MA: Belknap Press of Harvard University Press, 1956).

Nash, Gary B.: *Red, White, and Black: The Peoples of Early America* (Englewood Cliffs, NJ: Prentice-Hall, 1974).

Newell, Margaret Ellen: *From Dependency to Independence: Economic Revolution in Colonial New England* (Ithaca, NY: Cornell University Press, 1998).

Pestana, Carla Gardina: *Quakers and Baptists in Colonial Massachusetts* (New York: Cambridge University Press, 1991).

Peterson, Mark A.: *The Price of Redemption: The Spiritual Economy of Puritan New England* (Stanford, CA: Stanford University Press, 1997).

Plane, Ann Marie: *Colonial Intimacies: Indian Marriage in Early New England* (Ithaca, NY: Cornell University Press, 2000).

Reis, Elizabeth: *Damned Women: Sinners and Witches in Puritan New England* (Ithaca, NY: Cornell University Press, 1997).

Richards, Jeffrey H.: *Theater Enough: American Culture and the Metaphor of the World Stage, 1607–1789* (Durham, NC: Duke University Press, 1991).

Round, Philip H.: *By Nature and By Custom Cursed: Transatlantic Civil Discourse and New England Cultural Production, 1620–1660* (Hanover, NH: University Press of New England, 1999).

Rozbicki, Michael J.: *Transformation of the English Cultural Ethos in Colonial America: Maryland, 1634–1720* (Lanham, MD: University Press of America, 1988).

Rutman, Darrett B.: *Winthrop's Boston: Portrait of a Puritan Town, 1630–1649* (Chapel Hill: University of North Carolina Press, 1965).

Rutman, Darrett B. & Rutman, Anita H.: *A Place in Time: Middlesex County, Virginia, 1650–1750* (New York: W. W. Norton, 1984).

Salisbury, Neal: *Manitou and Providence: Indians, Europeans, and the Making of New England, 1500–1643* (New York: Oxford University Press, 1982).

Scanlan, Thomas: *Colonial Writing and the New World, 1583–1671: Allegories of Desire* (New York: Cambridge University Press, 1999).

Seed, Patricia: *Ceremonies of Possession in Europe's Conquest of the New World, 1492–1640* (New York: Cambridge University Press, 1995).

Shields, John C.: *The American Aeneas: Classical Origins of the American Self* (Knoxville: University of Tennessee Press, 2001).

Siminoff, Faren R.: *The Rise of Atlantic American Communities in Seventeenth-Century Eastern Long Island* (New York: New York University Press, 2004).

Thomas, Keith: *Religion and the Decline of Magic: Studies in Popular Beliefs in Sixteenth and Seventeenth Century England* (London: Weidenfeld & Nicolson, 1971).

Weisman, Richard: *Witchcraft, Magic, and Religion in 17th-Century Massachusetts* (Amherst: University of Massachusetts Press, 1984).

White, Richard: *The Middle Ground: Indians, Empires, and Republics in the Great Lakes Region, 1650–1815* (New York: Cambridge University Press, 1991).

Chapter Three

BRITISH AMERICA IN THE EIGHTEENTH CENTURY

Karin Wulf

Henry Hill of Philadelphia was a fashionable man. Whether he was too fashionable or hopelessly in need of fashion advice was the subject of some conversation among his kin. Starting out as a student of medicine, he was lured into the family business and rode both the rise in Madeira wine's fashionability, and the luck that had many decades earlier placed his near-broke father in the town of Funchal on Madeira in hopes of remaking himself as an island merchant in situ. The younger Hill then made an impressive fortune importing the Madeira that his family had been shipping around the Atlantic since the 1740s, and in 1786 he built an extraordinary home on Philadelphia's Fourth Street (to accompany his country seat south of the city).

A fabulous double fanlight, perhaps the largest such window of its kind in America at the time, crowned Hill's front doorway, ornamenting the exterior and allowing light to flood the front hall interior. With spokes (made of painted brass rather than the more typical lead) that radiated up and away from an anchoring glass crescent, Hill's fanlight included two separate tiers of "fanned" glass – the first with eight rounded, petal-shaped panes, and the second with sixteen slightly smaller, slightly blunted and tipped panes – but also an intermediate section of elaborate pattern. The effect was stunning. The critical central hall of the house, the place where guests would first be greeted and ushered toward the best parlor, was elegantly lit as well as decorated by the exquisite woodwork and glass. Those inside, including Hill himself, his wife, family, their guests and servants, would find their sensibilities stimulated by the light and the design, which enhanced an appreciation of the front hall's proportions, furnishings (including an entry stove to warm visitors in winter), and décor (including a blue-and-white checkerboard marble floor). From outside, the fanlight announced Hill's high social station and economic position, as well as his keen aesthetic sense.

American elites' taste for imported English glass was reflected in relatively lavish use of windows in their eighteenth-century homes. In the years before Henry Hill built and furnished his house dozens of advertisements in Philadelphia's *Pennsylvania Gazette* told of imported window glass that could be acquired in a wide range of sizes and from several English and European sources. Hill had a private source, however. One of his sisters, Mary Lamar, lived in London and was able to procure the fanlight and other essentials that would suit her brother's situation. But in aiding his quest for appointing his home appropriately, she had to put to rest some of his ideas: on the subject of mantles and other framework for a fireplace, he suggested something akin to one that was in the home of a Mr. White, whereas Mrs. Lamar insisted that "such, here, are only put in bed and back rooms; the best dining parlours of late have . . . entire marble pieces." She would see about getting something like that sent to Philadelphia, along with wallpaper: "Yellow is a colour quite the fashion at present, and from experience I know it wears and cleans the best of any." Other relations were less determined that Hill should display the finest and the latest of metropolitan fashions, whether on his walls or on his person. Among Hill's Quaker family were some relations with extraordinary wealth, but many of his kin nonetheless preferred simplicity. They circulated a teasing poem on the subject of the famous fanlight, noting that, "thou with Panes are truly blest" (Smith 1854: 197–8; Blecki & Wulf 1997: 190).

Henry Hill's fanlight, its style and fashionability, and the aesthetic commentary and experiences it provoked help illuminate the connection of material goods to eighteenth-century ideas about status and identity. Americans in the 1980s were assailed by fashion and home designer Ralph Lauren's advertising campaigns consciously connecting his wares to an imagined lifestyle; Lauren understood that he was selling neither sweaters nor bedsheets, but the life of leisure, health, and understated sexuality that was promised by his models and their interactions depicted in the photographs of his goods. From a longer historical perspective, Lauren was a bit of a Ralph-come-lately to this understanding of the attachment of material culture to identity, and identity to a performance on an appropriately decorated set (nominally, "lifestyle"): Henry Hill could well understand the connection between the life his fanlight advertised and the person he had come to be. Indeed we can find examples from most historical periods and situations of the ways that ownership, use, and display of particular material goods marked social position or ambitions. In the eighteenth century, however, British Americans came to this experience of the connection between the material around them and the performance of status, identity, and their selves in dramatically new ways, and with a dramatic intensity.

The desire for consumer goods and the cultural challenges and changes wrought by the consumer revolution were by no means the sole province of elites. In the middle decades of the eighteenth century consumer goods began to infiltrate the backcountry, and to appear in the homes and ultimately the estate inventories of rural farmers and middling yeoman. Many of those same goods, namely cloth and metals, became crucial components of Native American cultural practices. They made their way into native ritual and daily practice through diplomacy, namely as tribute, and as prized trade goods. Through the second-hand clothing market and vendue sales, as well as redistribution to servants, fine cloth goods became absorbed into working households. And the declining prices for goods such as tea and wool cloth made them more accessible as new purchases to a wider audience of consumers. People across a range of socioeconomic positions, free and unfree peoples, and people of varied ethnicities and cultural backgrounds absorbed, accommodated, and used consumer goods to display status, convey identity, or signify relationships between individuals or groups. Material items carry meaning. How did the meaning of consumer goods change in the eighteenth century, when so many more types and so much greater volume of stuff littered the landscape? One answer comes from T. H. Breen, who has written the most sweeping statement on the effect of the consumer revolution to date: "the colonists' shared experience as consumers provided them with the cultural resources needed to develop a bold new form of political protest" (Breen 2004: xv). Other scholars have asked how the consumer revolution may have changed cultural understandings and practices, and looked to the impact of an expanded world of consumer goods on expressions of status and identity.

There are many possible cultural histories of eighteenth-century British America. Two phenomena in particular have deeply engaged scholars of the period: the consumer revolution with its emphasis on an expanded, manufactured material culture, and the expressed necessity of articulating a sense of the "self." Goods always announced or affected status; more and new types of goods announced more elaborated and specified rank and status. As such, material things contributed to identity: they could be used both to assert a class, racial, and/or gender-based identity, and also to infer such identities. But the parallel emergence of an emphasis on comprehending human interiority and the sudden availability of vast quantities and varieties of commercial goods combined to promote a display that could challenge prevailing traditions about gendered, racial, and class hierarchies. A curious paradox developed: the interior self was best known by the exterior surrounding it, and the exterior was an increasingly problematic way of understanding the integrity of the interior it advertised. In the 1980s and 1990s, scholars across the disciplines of history, literature, and material culture in particular energetically explored this paradox and its component parts.

A New World of Material Goods

England's colonies in America experienced not one, but two eighteenth-century revolutions: the conjunction of social, economic, and political events that culminated in the war of the American Revolution, and a "consumer revolution" that transformed both the standard of living and the relationship between people and the material world in which they lived. The term "consumer revolution" encompasses two ideas. One is that the expansion of goods, in quantity and in variety, was truly revolutionary. The other is that it was consumers who drove this revolution. Their interests, their tastes, their desire for goods, and ultimately their purchasing power created and gave cultural meaning to this economic phenomenon. This transformation in the habits and expectations of consumption in British America was fueled by England's ability to produce and provide through trade more goods, and a wider variety of goods over the eighteenth century. The intensification of the trade relationship between England and the colonies made these goods newly available on the empire's periphery, and the nature of the economy and society within the colonies made at least some of these goods available across a wide swath of the socioeconomic spectrum. The emergent markets for goods aimed at elites, the striving middling sort, and laborers shared two premises: people would buy rather than make many goods, if they could, and most goods could connote identities of race, status, gender, and aspiration. The elaboration of the market for items that spilled into colonial ports, then, depended on a cultural as well as an economic understanding of their manufacture and sale.

Most recent scholarship concludes that the consumer revolution arrived in America in two stages. The first emerged in the late seventeenth century, and began to drive the economy after the 1720s. In this earlier period the revolutionary change in consumption was characterized by both new items and volume; new consumption patterns mimicked those in England, including an emphasis on caffeinated hot drinks – coffee, tea, and chocolate – sugar, and tobacco. After the 1760s and up to about 1820, patterns of acquisition and the profusion of consumer goods accelerated. As Paul Clemens has argued in a recent analysis of consumer culture in the Mid-Atlantic in this second period, "the great variety of goods, the global reach of the economy that supplied these goods, the regional variations in what was consumed, and the participation of ordinary householders (but usually not the poor) were each defining features of the evolution of America's first consumer economy" (Clemens 2005).

Over the full course of the eighteenth century the change in the volume and the diversity of material things, and their ubiquity in the daily lives of Americans, was stunning. These changes followed on the expansion of the colonial population, increases in per capita income, especially after 1720, and the consequent growth of the colonies as a significant market. Demand for European goods in particular increased as colonists moved to specialize as producers, increasing their ability and their desire to purchase goods they might have previously supplied themselves or could not have afforded at all, from other sources. As John J. McCusker and Russell R. Menard have noted, "Not all of these things happened everywhere, to everyone, or to the same degree, but their net impact caused a considerable expansion in colonial demand for goods and services over the period 1607–1775" (McCusker & Menard 1984: 278).

T. H. Breen, the historian arguably most responsible for highlighting the importance of the consumer revolution in early America, observes that, "for elite colonists, the flood of British imports quickly transformed an entire material culture. [But] for most Americans . . . the [British] empire first entered their lives as 'smole trifeles'" (Breen 2004: 247). Such a small trifle could be a single button, newly available in one of the shops lining Philadelphia's busy streets. While volume increase was important, the expansion of consumer choice in the second half of the eighteenth century across many types of goods may have been more profound in shaping the experience of acquiring and living with things. Breen offers the following example: New York advertisers before mid-century rarely mentioned gloves; in the 1750s they started to note the availability of men's and women's gloves in different types of cloth or pattern. In the 1760s buyers could choose from over 35 different types of gloves, including those made of worsted, chamois, lamb, and even dog skin, and colors from white and black to buff and purple (Breen 2004: 57). To read advertisements for accessories or adornments to clothing, such as gloves, is to realize both the current and contemporary expertise required to appreciate the distinctions among the wares offered by milliner Ann Pearson in late 1765. Ribbons, tapes, and laces, handkerchiefs, aprons, and mitts, hose, pumps, and clogs, and bonnets, caps, hats, and stays only skimmed the surface of the complex ground Pearson's wholesale and retail ("for cash only") customers would navigate in the quest of outfitting themselves (*Pennsylvania Gazette*, 1765). But discerning customers were expected to understand more than the distinctions among "German serges," "Devonshire kersey," "India satins," and "Genoa velvets." They would or should know that, at least in 1765, broadcloth could be had in many colors, "of the newest fashion, and . . . suitable for the summer season." They should care that a retailer had his goods "upon the best terms and from the best house in London," and that anyone was welcome to "see the sterling cost" to appreciate the fair price of these fine offerings (*Pennsylvania Gazette*, 1765). In other words, the consumer revolution produced both an expansion of goods and, ideally, an expanded population of new and educated customers.

By the 1770s probably 80 percent or more of the goods imported into America were processed, manufactured goods (as opposed to raw materials or food, or semi-processed foods such as wine); and an even higher proportion of imports from England, the colonies' most important trading partner, was in manufactured stuff (McCusker & Menard 1984: 285). Although goods flowed into America from other European countries and the Caribbean, trade regulation in conjunction with other factors bound England and her colonies in what Breen called a transatlantic "Empire of Goods" (Breen 1986).

That empire was dominated by its center (Gould 2000). Eighteenth-century fashions emanated from the metropole; fashions in clothing and home furnishings in particular signaled the wearer's or owner's participation in a transatlantic culture which privileged display. The same population that purchased and/or read cosmopolitan publications such as the *Gentleman's Magazine* or the *Spectator* would credit fashion as a force to be reckoned with, making the provenance of imports an important selling point. Newspaper advertisements shouted the arrival of imports from England. Magdalena Devine of Philadelphia advertised the cloth, clothing, household, and personal furnishings that she had "Imported in the Sally, Captain William Barber, from Glasgow, and sundry Vessels from London, Liverpool, and Bristol, and sold, wholesale and retail," at her establishment on Second Street. Devine's offerings included several colors of satins, damasks, and taffetas. Lawns, linens, cambricks, bombazine, gauzes, worsted, and broadcloth appeared in colors and patterns of gingham, stripe, check, as well as stampedor printed. Sheeting, blankets, even haircloth and rugs, as well as hose, breeches, and gloves, all promised valuable use, fashion, and comfort – itself a fashionable concept. Cloth goods comprised the bulk of her inventory, but Devine also noted that she had "green tea, mahogany tea chests . . . and sundry other goods, too tedious to insert, all of which she will sell at reasonable rates, for ready money or short credit" (Breen 2004: 69).

Consumers' choices and preferences interacted with metropolitan ideas of fashion to create pressure on producers. If producers were to succeed, they needed a stock that was "both marketable and therefore often [of] a fashionable design," but also conformed to the "strict visual specification embodying that marketability" (Styles 1993: 346). Retailers wanted to know that the glassware or items of clothing or plate they would receive comported with the patterns and samples they or their wholesalers saw, because they wanted to be confident that the items they ordered would appeal to their customers. Just as Henry Hill's London sister wanted her brother in Philadelphia to look and to *be* fashionable, she became an arbiter of fashion herself. By making selections for Hill's home furnishings based on the quality, design, material, and color, she interpreted fashion as well as responded to fashion (Haulman 2005: 626).

Many of the new goods that increased importation were accessories to other cultural and economic developments. The fashion for tea equipage, for example, obviously followed hard on the heels of the fashion for tea itself and for tea drinking as a social event and a social ritual. Although consumer goods classified as "durables" – cloth, plate, and the like – survive to tell us something of their acquisition and use, the consumer revolution was also marked by the increase and diversity of groceries, especially chocolate, coffee, and tea, and, later in the century, wines and other drink. These groceries offered new social possibilities, and new social realms were constructed around their consumption. Though not all households, obviously, could afford to indulge, a large part of the population could and did, and with ever more elaborate ritual associated with food and drink, and new specialized social spaces at home and elsewhere in the community, like the coffeehouses, that were furnished accordingly (Bushman 1992).

Coffeehouses sprang up in cities up and down the coast, and made their way into the American interior. In these spaces coffee *was* consumed, but it was the cultural contours of the space that made it distinctive. Coffeehouses became gathering places for men, particularly merchants, and important sites for the exchange of useful business and political news. Ship captains and merchants arranged shipping deals and letters were distributed at American coffeehouses, which emulated the mercantile character of London's great coffeehouses, as well as some of the masculine polite quality of those places. David Shields has elucidated, for example, the premium on wit, (mere) jest, and other forms of competitive politesse exhibited and appraised in these venues (Shields 1997: 55–98; Thompson 1998).

One could scarcely describe tea drinking in eighteenth-century America without reference to the role of tea in the resistance to British rule. Breen argues that tea's potency lay in its ubiquity. Although it entered the economy as a luxury, by the time of the Revolution plenty of ordinary, even poor, colonists were consuming tea daily – and many of them from porcelain teacups. "It had become the master symbol of the new consumer economy" (Breen 2004: 304). Not only its consumption, but also, importantly, the accessories to its consumption, were becoming ubiquitous. Tea drinking seemed to require, at a minimum, a teapot and teacups, but elaborate tea equipage could include sugar bowls and spoons or tongs, slop bowls, cream and tea containers, and of course tea tables on which to array them. Benjamin Franklin famously decried the rage among middling and working women for such display, in the guise of a letter from tradesman "Anthony Afterwit" to the *Pennsylvania Gazette* in 1732: "My Wife being entertain'd with *Tea* by the Good Women she visited, we could do no less than the like when they visited us; and so we got a *Tea Table* with all its Appurtenances of *China* and *Silver*" (quoted in Shields 1997: 115). (This instinct for mimesis continued with an acquisition of a maid, a clock, and a fine horse, all of which Afterwit sold, when his wife was out socializing, to avoid debt collectors.) Teapots could be enlisted in political sloganeering: during the Stamp Act protest teapots were marketed that famously sported the motto "No Stamp Act!" Gorgeously crafted silver teapots were among an elite household's most prized possessions, sometimes standing on curved feet, adorned with a coat of arms or perhaps the entwined initials of a marrying couple.

The ritual of tea drinking became highly elaborated and highly self-conscious among, at least, American middling and elites. Women's control over the tea table, the service of the tea, and the conduct of the conversation may be the closest American analogue to the social and political power of the European *salonières* of the same era. Men attended tea, but women held the reins of invitation and exclusion. In some American locales, earning a place at a particular tea table was not only a mark of distinction, but an essential social achievement (Shields 1997: 99–140). In urban circles sociability at tea also promoted the wearing and display of new fashions in clothing, and tea table conversations promoted gossip as well as a cultivation and evaluation of "sense," the combination of intellect and sensibility (ibid. 119).

While the preponderance of evidence for the availability and use of consumer goods comes from urban areas – primarily places like Philadelphia, New York, Boston, and Charleston where those goods entered through the ports and began the journey of distribution – it is also clear that rural folks – and less wealthy rural families – had access to these goods and stocked their homes and embellished their lives accordingly (Walsh 1983; Carr & Walsh 1994). Lorena Walsh and Lois Carr have been at the forefront of scholarship that demonstrates the transition of Chesapeake planters from forest to cleared land, and from rudimentary farms to more amply furnished (if still simple) dwellings that included more and more manufactured goods. Defining as "amenities" those items that were "nonessentials – things that made life more comfortable or inspired awe or envy in those who did not possess them" – Carr and Walsh found that amenities appeared in more households, and in greater number, as the eighteenth century progressed (Carr & Walsh 1994: 60). Even poorer planters in the Chesapeake region acquired items like bed and table linens, forks and knives, earthenware, spices, and tea and tea equipage. By the 1770s nearly a third of the poorest households could boast of knives and forks, tea and tea-ware (ibid. 78–80). Thus, what John Styles has called the "social shape" of the market included an interest and an ability on the part of poorer consumers to acquire goods that were useful, novel, and even fashionable (Styles 1993: 538).

By the end of the eighteenth century, "everyday life . . . was scarcely liveable without a cupboard or a chest of drawers full of things they used in their dealings with virtually everyone they encountered" (Carson 1994: 488). Advocating the repeal of the Stamp Act before Parliament in 1766, Benjamin Franklin warned that colonists could learn to make for themselves many of the necessities, such as cloth, that they imported from England and that the majority of English goods they could learn to do without; they were "mere conveniences, or superfluities" (quoted in McCusker & Menard 1984: 278). In other words, much of what was imported contributed not to a household or individual's subsistence but to a sense of comfort or a desire for adornment. The consumer revolution made amenities "essential to the conduct of social relations" (Carson 1994: 488).

Material things were always essential to the conduct of diplomatic relations; scholars of eighteenth-century Native Americans emphasize the importance of the "gift exchange" to creating and maintaining alliances among native groups or between natives and colonists. The gifts, meant to represent good will and to symbolize an ongoing relationship, were often the same items prized by natives and frontier traders; weapons and liquor, but also metal household items such as needles and kettles (the latter sometimes cut into pieces and worked into clothing or worn as jewelry), glass beads, and paint made their way into the colonial backcountry. Natives put these items, many of them explicitly requisitioned as trade goods, to both traditional and novel uses. British America experienced a consumer revolution, while Native

Americans experienced a revolution represented by the new goods in their midst (Merritt 2003; Richter 2003).

Expressions of the Self and about the Other

Cultural boundaries proved especially and maddeningly porous for men and women who moved between European and native societies and practices, confusing all sides even as they served all sides – and probably served primarily their own survival. Andrew Montour was born to an Oneida father and a Canadian Métis mother; he worked the Pennsylvania frontier as an interpreter, guide, soldier, and land speculator, among other jobs, from the early 1740s until his murder by a Seneca 30 years later. Montour's "countenance was decidedly European," declared the Moravian Count Zinzendorf. Montour spoke European languages, surprising Zinzendorf, who addressed him in French, by replying in English. But his clothing spoke of something different: he wore a coat, breeches, shirt, and waistcoat, but he also wore a "black Cordovan neckerchief, decked with silver bugles . . . [and] His ears were hung with pendants of brass and other wires plaited together like the handle of a basket." How Zinzendorf, and a succession of other European Pennsylvanians and Indians, interpreted Montour's "real" identity, his "self," is a fascinating question that can probably never be fully answered. How Montour understood his identity is also important, and probably similarly elusive, though clues such as his extensive combination of European and native customs and cultural practices suggest that he drew regularly if not equally from as many wells as possible. Is it possible, though, that Montour's approach to the colonizers can be read backwards through his self-conscious presentations of self? In other words, could we determine Montour's ideas about who and what "German Pennsylvanians" were, or even his distinction between Moravians and other Germans, by parsing his sense of audience (Merrell 1997; White 1997)?

Historians have paid close attention in the past decade to what Rhys Isaac, an early and energetic advocate of anthropologically inflected study of early America, has called "the Revolutionary power of the self." Over the eighteenth century, Isaac argues, an intensification of self-narratives in a variety of printed, manuscript, and performance forms "did not just contribute to the great spectacle that we call the American Revolution, but, in a profound sense, they were the Revolution" (Isaac 1997: 236–7). The evidence of emergent expressions of the self is plain to see in eighteenth-century literary and other sources: historians can locate articulations of self in text, image, and object. Though the timing of a preponderance of expressions around a "me-self" – defined autonomously – rather than a "we-self" – defined relationally, interdependently, communally – is difficult to ignore, the meaning of that timing is elusive (Sobel 1997). In a very general sense, the notion of the individual as being distinctive in capacity and understanding, and as having an awareness and appreciation of the interior realm of this distinctiveness, has long served the historical narrative which posits a transition from early modern to modern culture. The individual is one of the many features, but often the pre-eminent feature, signifying the arrival of modernity. The individual, for example, is the critical social unit for industrial capitalism, for the sentimental, nuclear family, and for other hallmarks of the modern mode. A consciousness of individuality proved as important in harnessing people to the modern world as their detachment from the firmly local contexts in which early modern culture had bound them culturally, socially, and economically (Sobel 1997: 200–5).

Capturing the emergence of a historically specific notion of self, or of the significance of that self in reflecting or producing historical change, is a bit like catching water with a butterfly net. One can observe its passage, but too little remains for sustained study. Introducing a volume of essays on histories of self in early America with a discussion of various disciplinary and philosophical approaches to the self, Greg Dening remarked that "History, arguably the most unblinkered of sciences, will try to represent the experiencing self rather than the model" (Dening 1997: 9). With a few notable exceptions, for historians of early America theorizing the nature of a historicized self has been secondary to analyzing the expressions and then sociocultural or political uses of self.

Early American elites were particularly attuned to displays of identity signaled by language, behaviors, and consumption. In turn, scholars have been particularly attuned to these elite displays, and what they suggest about the nature of colonial cultures of power. William Byrd (1674–1744), the quintessential anxious Virginia patriarch of Kathleen Brown's work (1996) and the quintessential raging patriarch of Kenneth Lockridge's (1992), built Westover in 1730, a house that is now described as perhaps the premier example of Georgian architecture in America. He courted beautiful and rich women, and married two of them – though to read Byrd is to suspect that neither wife was as rich or as beautiful as the women who rejected his advances. He amassed a library of some 3,000 volumes, extraordinary in any time but particularly in his own, and authored both published and unpublished work on subjects public (inoculation, and, famously, the boundary dispute between Virginia and North Carolina) and private (a "secret history" of the adventures of the dividing-line explorers, and his own secret diaries and commonplace book).

Byrd's misogyny and sexual frankness in his diaries and in a published essay (*The Female Creed*, 1725), as well as the sheer volume of his writings, have made him a worthy target of analytical attention. What scholars generally discover in Byrd may be in some measure applicable to a much larger group. Byrd's undoubted prominence in Virginia, not only as a white man in a society hierarchically structured to advantage just such a person, but as a very wealthy man of social and political position, seemingly gave him little security. Virginia's political elite struggled in the last years of the seventeenth century and into the first decades of the eighteenth to craft a legal regime that would concretize racial distinctions and ensure their dominance; they passed punitive legislation, for example, to make interracial unions increasingly onerous, especially for women. Ever more aggressively they equated slavery with blackness and freedom with whiteness, and sexual access to both white and black women a prerogative of white men. Teetering atop this hierarchy, Byrd's anxious, angry writings exposed not just the fragility of the authority which many like him longed to attach to the power they held so firmly, but also the fractured identity they attached to themselves. Men like Byrd could neither lay legitimate claim to the kinds of cultural and socioeconomic authority of elites in England, nor confidently command the obedience of their subordinates as fully as they would have liked. Racial slavery was the bedrock of the colonial hierarchy they had built. They feared its fault lines (Lockridge 1992; Brown 1996; Isaac 2004).

As in the case of colonial elites such as William Byrd, ideas about the self are essentially connected to ideas about "the other," and most histories of subjectivity have emphasized claims to identity in relation to assertions about others. Historically, otherness has been a mode of projecting and interpreting difference in the service of asserting hierarchy. For eighteenth-century British America, otherness was important in the colonial contexts of race relations, particularly vis-à-vis Native Americans and enslaved Africans, but notions of gender and sexuality intersected with – and were mutually constitutive of – ideas about race and status. Early explorers and then colonists accused Native Americans of being perversely backwards in their gendered behavior; women tilled fields, for example, which from a European perspective was clearly "man's work" (though plenty of European women, of course, had long been expected to do field work and in the colonial lands it was reasonable to expect more would). Indian men, meanwhile, hunted, which seemed a leisurely and lazy pursuit (it was neither, but rather a central means of providing protein for their diet). Enslaved African men were depicted as unnaturally beastly, and therefore fitted for unrelenting labor, while African women were characterized in both highly sexualized and dehumanizing ways.

As in the case of Virginia's codification of race through the laws of slavery, the principal objective in these narrative characterizations was to create and sustain a gendered and racial hierarchy (Brown 1996; Morgan 2004). Though we know that the generation of racial and gendered privilege did not guarantee that those privileges could always be sustained, and that the kinds of authority cultivated by those in positions of privilege was contingent, it is also plain that in colonial British America white men were in a far better position to determine the path of their lives than were other people. Writing so much about the ways that the politically and culturally powerful in colonial society described and proscribed "the other," however, Kirsten Fischer and Jennifer Morgan have cautioned that:

> historical investigations ostensibly organized around the sexual lives of African or Native American women are in danger of using the bodies of "other" women to outline once more only the figures of white men. The result is an increasingly complex rendition of the sexual/social order of things in the minds of white male colonists, together with greater insight into the way sexuality is intrinsic to the process of constructing new settlements and maintaining one's "progress of civility," but not a full understanding about the meaning of sex among the enslaved or the dispossessed either individually or as a group. Historians need to use whatever sources are available for their respective projects to try to include women's perceptions of "others" and of themselves. (Fischer & Morgan 2003: 198)

Fischer & Morgan's point is equally pertinent for other non-elites. How can we understand the subject position of the colonizers from the perspective of non-elites, and particularly of native people? One answer is to look for people who inhabited the liminal spaces between cultures. Andrew Montour may or may not have ever considered his interior "self," but through language, dress, and behavior he carefully articulated an identity as, in turn, European, Native, both, and something in between, that played on his audience's expectation that his performance reflected something inherent, real, and interior.

The Self in Goods

Our retrospective position makes it tempting to see the emergence of the modern within eighteenth-century society and culture as more clearly delineated than it actually was. And the relationship of the "self" as articulated in increasingly coherent terms over the eighteenth century to the modern, bourgeois individual is perhaps the murkiest aspect of this process. Bringing together a quantitatively and qualitatively new material culture in the eighteenth century, and the explicit expressions and display of identity that circulated around the "self," highlights the important interplay between material objects and the cultural meanings assigned to them. Perhaps this interaction enhanced the importance of both: more material goods allowed for more elaborate articulations of self.

The theatrical stage has proved a useful metaphor for understanding what the earliest scholarship on early modern selfhood called "self-fashioning" (Greenblatt 1980; Agnew 1986). Seeing contested colonial space as a stage for the performance of identities and ambitions has been useful in thinking about, for example, the interactions of Native Americans and Europeans – particularly because ritual enactment was so central to native cultures. Europeans understood the authority of the stage at a fundamental level: court culture and church ritual were played out on stages with full costuming. Material goods including clothing and furnishings provided ample costuming and props for the performance of self that became so consistent in the eighteenth century.

The idea that clothing can or should be a reflection of status is long-standing. Roman emperors confined the wearing of "imperial purple" to the use of their household; particular reds were long used in the Catholic Church to mark the status of cardinals. Sumptuary laws in England and the restrictions on the wearing of particular furs in the early years of the New England colonies drew on the same ideas about the importance of distinguishing status through outward appearance. But the relationship of such costuming to status shifted in the eighteenth century. No longer certain about the fixity of status, especially in a world where both social and economic mobility were more fluid, the power of clothing alone to mark identity declined. Certainly clothing could be read. The material, the cut of the clothing and its fashionability, the accessories worn with it, style of hat, men's choice of wig or their natural hair – all these could be read to indicate knowledge of and participation in a wider consumer culture. But indications of the self, of the internal, were less easy to read through these outward expressions. For one thing, as the volume of imported goods increased, access to goods among the poor also expanded. Vendue sales of second-hand or damaged goods, as well as the market for stolen property, made it possible for someone to pass for higher status in what seemed like high-quality clothing. Clothing was a more complicated marker of identity.

Leisure and manners were surer, though still uncertain, signs of identity, and surer signs of the interior self that was demonstrated through performances accessorized with material goods (Calvert 1994). Leisure and manners required both material apparatus and the knowledge of not only what was best to buy, but how and when and in what company to use it. The tea ritual's complexity as a dance of social positioning becomes more transparent when we factor in the angle of the table, the arrangement of the people around it, the setting of the silver or porcelain objects on it, and the way they were lifted and set down again.

The eighteenth-century "self" was, as Toby Ditz argues, "understood as complex but elusive and precariously integrated. It was, moreover, deeply intertwined with social imperatives: a socially conditioned self" (Ditz 2000: 242). This social conditioning relied in good measure on the new availability of material goods to represent the social. In eighteenth-century America, certainly in eighteenth-century British America, linking material goods to selves meant linking consumption and display to new ways of claiming and asserting identity, even as the acts of consumption and display were ambiguously related to an interior "self."

REFERENCES

Agnew, Jean Christophe: *Worlds Apart: The Market and the Theater in Anglo-American Thought, 1550–1750* (New York: University of Cambridge Press, 1986).

Blecki, Catherine & Wulf, Karin, eds.: *Milcah Martha Moore's Book: A Commonplace Book from Revolutionary America* (State College, PA: Pennsylvania State University Press, 1997).

Breen, T. H.: "An Empire of Goods: the Anglicization of Colonial America, 1690–1776," *Journal of British Studies* 25 (1986), 467–99.

Breen, T. H.: *The Marketplace of Revolution: How Consumer Politics Shaped American Independence* (New York: Oxford University Press, 2004).

Brewer, John & Porter, Roy, eds.: *Consumption and the World of Goods* (London: Routledge, 1993).

Brown, Kathleen M.: *Good Wives, Nasty Wenches, and Anxious Patriarchs: Gender, Race, and Power in Colonial Virginia* (Chapel Hill: University of North Carolina Press for the Omohundro Institute of Early American History and Culture, 1996).

Brown, Kathleen M.: "Beyond the Great Debates: Gender and Race in Early America," *Reviews in American History* 26, 1(1998), 96–123.

Bushman, Richard L.: *The Refinement of America: People, Houses, Cities* (New York: Alfred A. Knopf, 1992).

Calvert, Karin: "The Function of Fashion in Eighteenth-Century America," in Carson et al., *Of Consuming Interests: The Style of Life in the Eighteenth Century* (Chapel Hill: University of North Carolina Press, 1994), pp. 252–83.

Carr, Lois Green & Walsh, Lorena: "Changing Lifestyles and Consumer Behavior in the Colonial Chesapeake," in Carson et al., *Of Consuming Interests: The Style of Life in the Eighteenth Century* (Chapel Hill: University of North Carolina Press, 1994), pp. 59–166.

Carson, Cary: "The Consumer Revolution in Colonial America: Why Demand?" in Carson et al., *Of Consuming Interests: The Style of Life in the Eighteenth Century* (Chapel Hill: University of North Carolina Press, 1994), pp. 483–697.

Carson, Cary, Hoffman, Ronald, & Albert, Peter J., eds.: *Of Consuming Interests: The Style of Life in the Eighteenth Century* (Charlottesville: University Press of Virginia, 1994).

Clemens, Paul G. E.: "The Consumer Culture of the Middle Atlantic, 1760–1820," *William and Mary Quarterly* 62, 4 (2005), 577–624.

Crowley, John E.: *The Invention of Comfort: Sensibilities and Design in Early Modern Britain and Early America* (Baltimore: Johns Hopkins University Press, 2001).

Dening, Greg: "Histories of Self," in Ronald Hoffman, Mechal Sobel, & Fredrika J. Teute, eds., *Through a Glass Darkly: Reflections on Personal Identity in Early America* (Chapel Hill: University of North Carolina Press, 1997), pp. 9–12.

Ditz, Toby: "Shipwrecked; Or, Masculinity Imperiled: Mercantile Representations of Failure and the Gendered Self in Eighteenth-century Philadelphia," *Journal of American History* 81, 1 (1994), 51–80.

Ditz, Toby: "Secret Selves, Credible Personas: The Problematics of Trust and Public Display in the Writing of Eighteenth-Century Philadelphia Merchants," in Robert Blair St. George, ed., *Possible Pasts: Becoming Colonial in Early America* (Ithaca, NY: Cornell University Press, 2000), pp. 219–42.

Ellison, Julie: *Cato's Tears and the Making of Anglo-American Emotion* (Chicago: University of Chicago Press, 1999).

Fischer, Kirsten & Morgan, Jennifer: "Sex, Race, and the Colonial Project," *William and Mary Quarterly* 60 (January 2003), 197–8.

Gould, Eliga H.: "An Empire of Manners: The Refinement of British America in Atlantic Perspective," *Journal of British Studies* 39 (2000), 114–22.

Greenblatt, Stephen: *Renaissance Self-Fashioning* (Chicago: University of Chicago Press, 1980).

Hancock, David: *Citizens of the World: London Merchants and the Integration of the British Atlantic Community, 1735–1785* (New York: Cambridge University Press, 1995).

Haulman, Kate: "Fashion and the Culture Wars of Revolutionary Philadelphia," *William and Mary Quarterly* 62 (October 2005), 625–62.

Hoffman, Ronald, Sobel, Mechal, & Teute, Fredrika J., eds.: *Through a Glass Darkly: Reflections on Personal Identity in Early America* (Chapel Hill: University of North Carolina Press, 1997).

Isaac, Rhys: "Stories and Constructions of Identity: Folk Tellings and Diary Inscriptions in Revolutionary Virginia," in Ronald Hoffman, Mechal Sobel, & Fredrika J. Teute, eds., *Through a Glass Darkly: Reflections on Personal Identity in Early America* (Chapel Hill: University of North Carolina Press, 1997), pp. 236–7.

Isaac, Rhys: *Landon Carter's Uneasy Kingdom: Revolution and Rebellion on a Virginia Plantation* (New York: Oxford University Press, 2004).

Jaffee, David: "Peddlars of Progress and the Transformation of the Rural North, 1760–1860," *Journal of American History* 78, 2 (1991), 511–35.

Lockridge, Kenneth: *On the Sources of Patriarchal Rage: The Commonplace Books of William Byrd and Thomas Jefferson and the Gendering of Power in the Eighteenth Century* (New York: New York University Press, 1992).

Lockridge, Kenneth: "Colonial Self-Fashioning: Paradoxes and Pathologies in the Construction of Genteel Identity in Eighteenth-Century America," in Ronald Hoffman, Mechal Sobel, & Fredrika J. Teute, eds., *Through a Glass Darkly: Reflections on Personal Identity in Early America* (Chapel Hill: University of North Carolina Press, 1997), pp. 274–339.

McCusker, John & Menard, Russell G.: *The Economy of British America, 1607–1789* (Chapel Hill: University of North Carolina Press, 1984).

Merrell, James: "'The Cast of his Countenance': Reading Andrew Montour," in Ronald Hoffman, Mechal Sobel, & Fredrika J. Teute, eds., *Through a Glass Darkly: Reflections on Personal Identity in Early America* (Chapel Hill: University of North Carolina Press, 1997), pp. 13–39.

Merritt, Jane: *At the Crossroads: Indians and Empires on a Mid-Atlantic Frontier* (Chapel Hill: University of North Carolina Press, 2003).

Morgan, Jennifer: *Reproduction and Gender in New World Slavery* (Philadelphia: University of Pennsylvania Press, 2004).

Pennsylvania Gazette, December 5, 1765.

Perkins, Elizabeth: "The Consumer Frontier: Household Consumption in Early Kentucky," *Journal of American History* 78, 2 (September, 1991), 486–510.

Richter, Daniel: *Facing East from Indian Country: A Native History of Early America* (Cambridge, MA: Harvard University Press, 2003).

St. George, Robert Blair, ed.: *Possible Pasts: Becoming Colonial in Early America* (Ithaca, NY: Cornell University Press, 2000).

Shammas, Carole: *The Pre-industrial Consumer in England and America* (Oxford: Clarendon Press, 1990).

Shields, David: *Civil Tongues and Polite Letters in British America* (Chapel Hill: University of North Carolina Press for the Omohundro Institute of Early American History and Culture, 1997).

Smith, John Jay, ed.: *Letters of Doctor Richard Hill and His Children* (Philadelphia: privately printed for the descendants, 1854).

Sobel, Mechal: "The Revolution in Selves: Black and White Inner Aliens," in Ronald Hoffman, Mechal Sobel, & Fredrika J. Teute, eds., *Through a Glass Darkly: Reflections on Personal Identity in Early America* (Chapel Hill: University of North Carolina Press, 1997), pp. 163–205.

Sobel, Mechal: *Teach Me Dreams: The Search for Self in the Revolutionary Era* (Princeton: Princeton University Press, 2000).

Styles, John: "Manufacturing, Consumption, and Design in Eighteenth-Century England," in John Brewer & Roy Porter, eds., *Consumption and the World of Goods* (London: Routledge, 1993), pp. 527–54.

Thompson, Peter: *Rum Punch & Revolution: Taverngoing & Public Life in Eighteenth-Century Philadelphia* (Philadelphia: University of Pennsylvania Press, 1998).

Wahrman, Dror: *The Making of the Modern Self: Identity and Culture in Eighteenth-Century England* (New Haven, CT: Yale University Press, 2004).

Walsh, Lorena: "Urban Amenities and Rural Sufficiency: Living Standards and Consumer Behavior in the Colonial Chesapeake, 1643–1777," *Journal of Economic History* 43, 1 (1983), 109–17.

White, Richard: "'Although I am Dead, I am Not Entirely Dead, I have Left a Second of Myself': Constructing Self and Persons on the Middle Ground in Early America," in Ronald Hoffman, Mechal Sobel, & Fredrika J. Teute, eds., *Through a Glass Darkly: Reflections on Personal Identity in Early America* (Chapel Hill: University of North Carolina Press, 1997), pp. 404–18.

Chapter Four

THE REVOLUTION AND THE EARLY REPUBLIC

Catherine E. Kelly

In 1976, Kenneth Silverman published *A Cultural History of the American Revolution*. Like any number of other bicentennial authors, Silverman sought both to encourage and to capitalize on public interest in the nation's founding. Unlike his competitors, he directed readers' attention away from battles and statecraft to culture, which he defined as literature, painting, theater, and music. Organized into three sections, the book traces cultural development from the imperial crisis through the Revolution and the creation of the modern state. It moves back and forth between brief sketches of the arts at particular moments and longer narratives that frame political and military events through their effects on culture. In Silverman's hands, the Boston Tea Party figures not simply as ritualized resistance but also as the inspiration for songs and operas. The Declaration of Independence is not only a political manifesto but also a perfect match of syntax and content, whose rhythms are structured by traditions stretching back to *Paradise Lost* and *The Canterbury Tales*. If the Constitutional Convention marks a monumental political turning point, it also inspires Charles Willson Peale to dust off his display of moving pictures for the most cosmopolitan of the convention delegates. Cultural productions of all kinds were galvanized by war and nation-making. Unlike previous scholars, who were apt to cast eighteenth-century Anglo-American culture as a derivative wasteland, Silverman mapped it as a vibrant and dynamic landscape, one that had remained a scholarly *terra incognita* for far too long (Silverman 1976).

A Cultural History of the American Revolution drew praise for its magisterial sweep and painstaking attention to detail. But it was hardly a hit. Some reviewers took issue with Silverman's interest in the arts, faulting him for reducing all of culture to the cultural productions of the metropolitan few. Other reviewers remained altogether baffled by the broad significance that he ascribed to the early national arts. Certainly, the book seemed to diverge from contemporary scholarly preoccupations, which emphasized the intricacies of political ideologies, on the one hand, and the experiences of "common" Americans during the Revolution, on the other. Whether placed alongside other mass-market bicentennial books or assessed in terms of dominant academic paradigms, *A Cultural History of the American Revolution* seemed oddly out of place, even idiosyncratic.

Some 30 years later, in the wake of the "cultural turn," preoccupations that once seemed idiosyncratic have moved to the center of scholarly inquiry and debate. Literary culture, performances of all kinds, and the visual arts are no longer charming distractions from serious-minded investigations of politics and society. Instead, they have become far more significant to those investigations than Silverman could have imagined. After all, Silverman himself posited two revolutions, one giving rise to a new nation, the other to a metropolitan culture. Although the arts registered and commented upon political and social change, in his treatment they played little role in generating it. But over the past 20 years, literature, performance, and art have been recast as constituent elements of political and social transformation. At the same time, scholars investigating revolutionary and early national culture have benefited from shifts in the humanities more generally, especially the move toward interdisciplinarity and the growing attention to the reception of cultural productions. Taken together, the resulting scholarship offers remarkably rich and richly contextualized analyses of texts and artifacts. Even more importantly, it yields a far clearer understanding of the potential rewards of constructing a "cultural history of the revolution" as well as a more inclusive, expansive picture of culture itself.

Literary Culture

The close connections between the American Revolution and American culture, to say nothing of the scholarship that has illuminated those connections, are most obvious when we look at literature and reading. In the decades following the American Revolution, growing numbers of increasingly diverse readers gained access to a wide variety of printed texts, such as newspapers, books, almanacs, and novels. The early national literary marketplace was a decentralized, patchwork affair. It encompassed both the transatlantic book trade and the output of local publishers; it was plagued by rampant piracy, uneven distribution, and insecure profits. Despite the obstacles, booksellers found markets for their wares among readers who were both enabled and encouraged by the expansion of education in the years immediately preceding and following the war. Reliable figures on literacy are notoriously hard to come by. Yet all measures indicate that there were far more, and more sophisticated, readers in 1800 than in 1750. Male and female, elite and plebeian, these readers acquired books from hawkers and through subscriptions; they borrowed them from friends and commercial circulating libraries.

It would be a mistake to attribute the expansion of American print culture to any one cause. But surely much of the credit should go to the ways in which texts provided a vehicle for considering the problems of nationhood, and print encouraged Americans to construct and inscribe themselves in a national culture. Certainly this was the case with the novel. Increasingly popular among readers, novels remained deeply suspect into the first quarter of the nineteenth century. As ministers and haughty elites pointed out, fiction encouraged escapism, inviting readers to transgress convention and abandon their stations, if only in their imaginations. As literary historian Cathy N. Davidson has observed, the critics had a point; characters and plots resonated with the dilemmas and possibilities that characterized early national culture (Davidson 1986). Seduction novels, for example, privileged the *femme covert* by dramatizing the predicaments of growing numbers of female readers whose educations inculcated intellectual and social ambitions but whose futures led inexorably to the confinements of marriage. A young woman reading Hannah Webster Foster's bestseller *The Coquette* (1797) could simultaneously enjoy the heroine's romantic adventures and her attempts at self-determination; meditate on the injustices of patriarchal culture; and congratulate herself on her own conventional virtue. The rambling, structureless form of the picaresque – exemplified by Hugh Henry Brackenridge's *Modern Chivalry* (1792–1815) or Royall Tyler's *Algerine Captive* (1797) – allowed authors to experiment with multiple perspectives on matters as weighty as religious and political doctrine. The great variety of characters (Easterners, gentlemen, paupers) encountered by the traveling hero or heroine allowed writers to link particular points of view with the social "types" most likely to espouse them. The meandering plot structure made it difficult to declare any one perspective correct. The American picaresque thus indexed the multiplicity of interests – the emergent pluralism – which came to define political culture by the turn of the nineteenth century.

In fact, political culture was deeply embedded in print culture and vice versa. Numerous historians and literary critics have drawn on the theoretical insights of Jürgen Habermas, who sketched the emergence of the eighteenth-century public sphere, and Benedict Anderson, who pointed to print culture as a necessary component of the "imagined community" of the modern nation (Anderson 1983; Habermas 1989). Taken together, these scholars' work has illuminated the close connections between print culture, the public sphere, and nationalism. As Michael Warner suggested in his enormously influential *Letters of the Republic*, the rhetorical conventions of print and the aesthetics of typeface were well suited both to republicanism and to the tumultuous party politics that emerged after the ratification of the Constitution. Print conveyed an impersonal authority, one that was distinct from the personal modes of sociability that dominated colonial political discourse. It was precisely this suggestion of impersonality, Warner argues, that granted print its privileged status as the disembodied, discursive representation of "the people." Indeed, printedness was crucial to the authority of the federal Constitution. Unsigned and rendered in impersonal type, the Constitution seemed to "emanate from no one in particular and thus from the people" (Warner 1990: 108).

If print could project the fiction of a people speaking in a single voice, it could also exacerbate the partisan conflict that fueled American nationalism through the early nineteenth century. Newspapers, for example, played a key role in forging a national identity and a national political culture: reading about far-flung Americans helped men and women see themselves as part of a national whole. Moreover, as David Waldstreicher has observed, the proliferation of explicitly partisan newspapers after 1800 served to intensify and expand political debate (Waldstreicher 1997). Local politicians were forced to ratchet up their rhetoric in order to defend themselves against the (printed) insults of their political enemies. At the same time, these men refined their platforms, overhauled civic celebrations, and whipped up popular participation with an eye toward press coverage. Parades and toasts were real-time events that could take on an extended second life in print.

If print culture was deeply implicated in the construction of nationalism and politics, it was also implicated in the valorization of politicized emotion. Novels, poetry, sermons, and political tracts simultaneously disseminated a culture of sentiment and yoked it to political ideals. In the past two decades, the study of feeling has become a growth industry. Literary scholars and political historians have traced a transatlantic culture of sentiment over the long eighteenth century, enriching our understanding of literature and politics in the process. This burgeoning literature has generated serious and unresolved quarrels over whether sensibility was primarily masculine or feminine; over the similarities and differences between terms like "sensibility," "senti-ment," and "sympathy"; over whether emotions resonated strongest in republican or liberal political cultures. Nevertheless, taken together, it has confirmed the inter-penetration of literary and political cultures and alerted historians to a central com-ponent of Anglo-American culture (Barker-Benfield 1992; Van Sant 1993; Stern 1997; Burgett 1998; Ellison 1999; Burstein 2001).

Recent studies have demonstrated that the culture of sentiment was predicated on the assumption that virtue, both private and political, demanded feeling as well as reason. And the feeling that mattered most was sympathy, which allowed individuals to identify with the pain of others. Sympathy, like other feelings, was both physical and emotional. Information about the other entered the body through the eye (or the mind's eye), causing a nervous reaction and sparking emotion. The resulting feelings then manifested themselves in the body's appearance: flushed cheeks, spar-kling eyes, and pooling tears were all signs of emotion at work. Sentiment also demanded the exercise of reason, which prevented sympathetic men and women from straying into sentimental excess. Sentiment in general and sympathy in particular might be individual qualities, created internally and registered physically. But this capacity for emotional connection profoundly affected society. It was sympathy, without the distancing condescension of pity, which forged the "social affections" that bound citizens together. The culture of sentiment thus held far-reaching political implications. Feeling could transform persons into "the people" and then galvanize "the people" for virtuous political action (Fliegelman 1993; Waldstreicher 1997; Burstein 2001).

Although the culture of sentiment was a transatlantic phenomenon with roots stretching back at least to the early eighteenth century, Americans claimed it as their own during and after the Revolution. In 1776, British Americans declared indepen-dence from their "unfeeling" King and Parliament in a torrent of propaganda. Well into the nineteenth century, citizens of the United States affirmed their "mutual affections" in speeches, sermons, and toasts on July 4. Indeed, the culture of senti-ment played a significant role in the construction of George Washington's mythic reputation during his lifetime and after. During the horrific winter at Valley Forge, he violated the Congressional ban on theater so that he and his troops could benefit from a production of *Cato*, whose eponymous hero embodied courage and tender feelings in equal measure. En route to his New York inauguration in 1789, he passed beneath a triumphal floral arch erected by the "Ladies of Trenton," commemorating his decisive victory there some 13 years before. Moved by the memories of wartime valor and by the peacetime display of feminine patriotism, the president-elect wept. This sentimental tableau was reported throughout the United States in newspaper stories commending Washington's public display of republican feeling. And when Washington died, citizens throughout the nation commemorated him in elegiac poetry, celebrating his republican virtue while demonstrating their own capacity for politically correct sentiment. Americans embraced the culture of sentiment because it provided reassuring standards of character at a time of uncertainty and change. It also opened up expansive opportunities for participation in politics and society while delineating criteria for excluding those who lacked feeling, making it compatible with individual ambition and self-cultivation (Fuller 1999; Waldstreicher 1997; Cavitch 2003).

With so much riding on sentiment, small wonder that early national print culture spoke not only to readers' minds but to their hearts. Indeed, texts of all kinds were central to the elaboration of sentimental selfhood. Printed texts, ranging from novels and poetry to sermons and political and philosophical treatises, offered a primer on the physical and verbal conventions of sentiment. A rich manuscript culture (including letters, diaries, commonplace books, and privately circulated *belles lettres*) enabled women and men to fashion sentimental selves. Patriotic celebrations and sociable gatherings provided vehicles for the public displays of feeling, casting participants as simultaneous performers and spectators of virtuous emotion. The result was a remarkably reflexive relationship between literature, subjectivity, and society – one that promised individual gratification and virtuous social visibility (Fliegelman 1993; Waldstreicher 1997; Burstein 2001).

In practice, however, the culture of sentiment did not accord equal status to all. For example, elite women – often dressed in white – were conspicuous elements of early national political celebrations, where their bodies symbolized the nation and their feelings signaled patriotism untainted by political partisanship. But the meanings they conjured emphasized women's distance from the rough-and-tumble world of electoral politics and from the franchise itself. It was precisely their marginal relationship to national party structures and their disenfranchisement that made them such potent symbols of national unity and patriotic feeling. Women's capacity for experiencing and registering feeling thus guaranteed them a powerful symbolic role and excluded them from the exercise of political power (Waldstreicher 1997). Among African Americans, the culture of sentiment was similarly paradoxical. Both black and white abolitionists exploited the discourse of feeling. White abolitionists, in particular, lavished attention on tortured, bleeding, black bodies. While this literature challenged early national readers to acknowledge and sympathize with the plight of enslaved women and men, it could also provoke vicarious feelings of sadistic pleasure in a distinctly racialized pain. This emphasis on black pain and white empathy may have been an effective counter against those Americans who argued that blacks were characterized by a restricted emotional range. But, as John Wood Sweet has argued, the emphasis on sensibility resonated powerfully among white citizens precisely because it evaded and obscured the issue of equal rights across the color line (Sweet 2003).

Cultures of Performance

This expansive literary culture was situated in an equally rich, equally contradictory culture of oratory and performance. Recent scholarship has moved well beyond the simplistic and inaccurate assertion that "modern," "cosmopolitan" print culture supplanted "traditional" oral culture. Orality and oratory hardly disappeared as print culture expanded. Instead, orators enacted different sorts of authority depending on whether they appeared to speak spontaneously or read from prepared texts. And critics have long pointed to a distinct preoccupation with voice and verbal forms in American literature. By emphasizing how these two forms of communication intersected and conflicted, scholars have illuminated how different groups of Americans laid competing claims to power in the early republic.

Certainly, recent studies of oratory have challenged Michael Warner's contentions about the impersonality and abstraction of print culture. Taken together, the work of Jay Fliegelman (1993), Sandra Gustafson (2000), and Kenneth Cmiel (1990) has reminded us that eighteenth- and early nineteenth-century Americans were acutely sensitive to the ways in which the spoken, performed word could amplify and extend the meaning of the printed one. Thomas Jefferson, for example, intended the Declaration of Independence to be read aloud rather than silently. The manuscript original and a single surviving proof copy included marks signifying pauses of varying lengths and emphases, much as a piece of sheet music might convey instructions to singers or musicians. Regardless of whether revolutionary orators matched Jefferson's preferred cadences, many colonists encountered the Declaration primarily as an oratorical performance. The connections that Jefferson and his contemporaries drew between political texts and political performances were part of a transatlantic elocutionary revolution, which changed the goals and standards of oratory. No longer was a speaker merely to convey ideas or even feelings. Instead, his voice, face, and body had to manifest convincingly the seemingly spontaneous experience of those ideas and feelings. The goal was a natural theatricality, in Fliegelman's apt phrase. Eloquence demanded the expression of real feelings, but, paradoxically, those feelings could only be expressed through a precise repertoire of vocal tones and physical gestures. Mastering the codes that conveyed sincerity, would-be orators simultaneously honed their ability to deceive auditors. By performing their sincerity, skilled speakers thus exacerbated wide-ranging anxieties about authenticity and deception in the republic.

Debates over the conventions of oratorical performance came to resonate with tensions over the significance of social status and the stability of national identity. From the 1780s through the 1820s, arguments about the relative refinement of American English indexed the social and cultural dilemmas that grew out of the Revolution. In that context, overly refined language signaled more than ostentatious bad taste; it betrayed aristocratic pretension. No less an orator than George Washington was caught up in such conflicts. An ungainly speaker, Washington attempted to combine the rhetorical and elocutionary conventions of colonial gentility with those of republican simplicity. For ardently republican auditors, the president's awkwardness arose from his inexplicable and inappropriate penchant for aristocratic affectation. For his Federalist allies, Washington's poor delivery registered sincerity and the free play of virtuous feeling (Gustafson 2000). If the lingering forms of aristocratic oratory posed one set of problems, the rough speech of non-elites posed another. Americans were to speak simply but not too simply, for the republic demanded educated and articulate citizens. The pursuit of a democratic eloquence was most obvious in academies and common schools. Oratory had long occupied a privileged place in a gentleman's education. But following the Revolution, elite female academies offered rhetorical training modeled on that of young men. By the early nineteenth century, it was extended to young women and men throughout the northern hinterland. The spread of graceful speech was fostered by the press, which generated elocution manuals; monologues and dialogues written expressly for student recitation; and, especially, grammars, which provided thousands of men and women with a clear, affordable guide to spoken and written English. By refashioning speech, educators hoped to create a distinctly American English, one that would distance the United States from England while fostering republican social relations. From their perspective, a truly standardized American language held out the potential to create the disinterested harmony that stood near the center of the republican ideal. Noah Webster aspired to more than a national language; in the rancorous 1790s, he believed that a single standard of pronunciation would eradicate tensions between citizens of different regions *and* ranks (Cmiel 1990).

Webster's dreams notwithstanding, early national oratory never coalesced into a unifying republican dialect. By the early nineteenth century, politicians elaborated what Cmiel has called a "middling" speech, one that moved between grand rhetorical flourish and folksy colloquialism; this was the language of liberal pluralism rather than republican unity. And like political culture, oratorical culture placed clear limits on which vernacular forms were compatible with democratic eloquence and which categories of individuals could lay claim to the occasional rhetorical flourish. One speaker who fell outside those limits was Aupaumut, a Mahican Indian from Stockbridge, Massachusetts, who served as a captain in the Continental Army during the Revolution and as Washington's emissary to the western Indians in the 1790s. A consummate mediator, Aupaumut successfully staged dual identities in both oral and textual media: he mastered the oratorical conventions of both Native American and Anglo-American diplomacy. He understood why texts, like treaties, were the objects of Native American suspicion and also why they were central to the exercise of Anglo-American power; indeed, when his integrity as a diplomat came under attack, he defended himself in a written memoir. Despite this cultural and rhetorical fluency, Aupaumut nevertheless found himself marginalized within the United States. Excluded from the corridors of national power following his mission, he died on a Wisconsin reservation during Indian Removal (Gustafson 2000).

The sheer range and variety of early national oratory rendered it more cacophonous than harmonious. Its discordant accents derived from geography, race, and class. But they also derived from the unprecedented numbers and categories of people who claimed the right to speak authoritatively in ways that confounded the conventions governing republican letters and republican speech. For example, Deborah Sampson Gannett, who had served briefly in the Continental Army disguised as a man, recounted her experiences before a paying public during an 1803 lecture tour. At a time when women entered civic discourse as writers rather than as speakers, Gannett was an anomaly. Her performance both underscored and undermined women's ascribed roles in the republic: she closed her speech by instructing her audiences that men were destined for military and governmental service, while women belonged in kitchens and parlors. She followed this lesson with a complicated and strenuous series of rifle maneuvers and drills performed in military uniform. Gannett violated social norms even as she appeared to submit to them, thus highlighting the ambiguity of women's speech in the early republic (Gustafson 2000).

Other speakers intruding on an emergent public sphere were far more tenuously connected to the norms of civic discourse, either oral or textual. The Revolutionary and Federal eras witnessed a surge of millenarian prophecy, in which women and men alike exhorted Americans onto the path of spiritual righteousness. For example, the charismatic Rhode Island Quaker prophet Jemima Wilkinson, also known as the Publick Universal Friend, preached sermons of fire and brimstone during the Revolution. Likening herself to a king or a royal avenger, traveling with an entourage two-dozen strong, Wilkinson attracted equally fervent supporters and detractors before giving up her public ministry in 1790. On the eve of the War of 1812, former felon Nimrod Hughes created a national sensation by predicting that God was about to destroy one-third of humankind and visit unprecedented terrors on the rest of it. Hughes's bestselling pamphlet, *A Solemn Warning to All Dwellers upon Earth* (1811), extended his gloomy itinerant preaching to a wide audience. And his credibility was surely shored up by the calamities that filled the pages of American newspapers that year, which included not only British atrocities against American sailors, but also murders and suicides, fires and comets. Like Wilkinson, Hughes was a divisive figure, hailed as a prodigy and denounced as a confidence man. Doomsayers like Wilkinson and Hughes exposed and intensified conflicts pitting reason against mysticism and enlightenment against ignorance. Significantly, their detractors condemned them for manipulating the power of language in order to lead innocents astray. The persistence of prophets and the devotion of their followers reveal the operations of faith in a secular public sphere. But they also testify to the multiplicity of speakers who competed for listeners within that sphere (Juster 2003).

Scholarly interest in the performative dimensions of literature and language has also inspired a new interest in the revolutionary and early national theater. Anglo-American theater long seemed to pale in comparison to its English counterpart; it was regularly invoked to mark Anglo-America as a cultural backwater. Even critics who traced strong connections between other forms of literature and the creation of a national identity slighted drama in their assessments and analyses. But in the past five years, scholars have demonstrated that theatrical productions advanced competing visions of the nation before contentious communities who registered their response on the spot. From this perspective, theater did not register either American provincialism or a simplistic nationalism. Instead, it provided a forum for literally enacting contests over American politics and society.

Prior to the Revolution, dramas written in the colonies, such as *Androboros* (1714 or 1715) or *The Paxton Boys* (1764), stressed the need for loyalty to the Crown. But as relations between British authorities and colonists deteriorated in the decade preceding the Revolution, plays written in America reflected the divisive political culture. Loyalists and Patriots alike churned out pamphlet plays. Loyalist playwrights took special pleasure in lampooning the representative assemblies formed by Patriots throughout the colonies. Mercy Otis Warren, an ardent Patriot, wrote three plays on the eve of war (*The Adulateur* in 1772; *The Defeat* in 1773; *The Group* in 1775) that condemned British officials as corrupt and self-serving and vilified Massachusetts's wildly unpopular royal governor, Thomas Hutchinson. Loyalist or Patriot, these prewar pamphlet plays were rarely, if ever, read aloud; Warren's, in fact, were published serially. They are best understood as elements of an escalating propaganda war, offering their readers sharp commentary on unfolding events and fodder for their political commitments (Wilmer 2002; Nathans 2003).

The sternest Patriots were happy enough to exploit the conventions of written drama to further their cause, but theatrical productions proved another matter altogether. New England Puritans, Pennsylvania Quakers, and New York Presbyterians had long condemned the theater for religious reasons. For much of the eighteenth century, their complaints were more or less effectively countered by urban elites, who believed that the theater evidenced the Anglicization and concomitant civilization of the colonies. But in 1774, the Continental Congress banned theatrical productions for financial and political reasons: they were both too extravagant and too British. And given that the great majority of Americans had never attended the theater, prohibiting it afforded all the satisfactions of virtuous sacrifice and patriotic behavior with none of the discomfort or inconvenience. Moreover, it isn't clear that the Congressional ban did much to harden the hearts of theater devotees. As we have seen, George Washington staged a production of Joseph Addison's *Cato* at Valley Forge in the hopes that his troops would be heartened by that Augustan paean to self-sacrifice and republican virtue. Instead, the ban on theater, like the production of *Cato*, was a useful device for contrasting American virtue with British corruption. The contrast was made all the more potent by the British army's prominent use of the theater to entertain both its troops and the residents of occupied cities. Military productions of *The Fair Penitent* deployed the stock repertoire of the eighteenth-century theater to underscore the viability of English culture in America. *The Blockade of Boston*, written by British General Burgoyne, satirized Yankee customs. And the notorious *Meschianza*, staged by Major John Andre outside Philadelphia just days after Washington's *Cato*, dramatized the futility of the struggle for independence and the rewards awaiting Loyalists with a cavalcade of jousts, dances, fireworks, and ladies in "Turkish" costumes (Withington 1991; Fuller 1999; Wilmer 2002; Nathans 2003).

In any case, in the years immediately following the war, bans on the theater were overturned in city after city by organized elites like Philadelphia's Dramatic Association and Boston's Tontine Association. These men successfully argued that the theater could represent both cosmopolitan modernity and republican virtue. And by casting themselves as defenders of culture, such men also secured their positions among local cultural and political leaders. Advocates of the theater tirelessly championed its potential for inculcating a distinctly national character among audiences. But early national theaters were contradictory, hybrid creatures (Wilmer 2002; Nathans 2003). They owed as much to English as to American culture; they promoted partisan strife as well as patriotic nationalism. Consider the buildings themselves. American theaters constructed in the 1790s, for example, were explicitly modeled on European examples and incorporated scenery, curtains, and chandeliers imported directly from England. The imposing neoclassical exterior of Boston's Federal Street Theater bespoke a predictable republican aesthetic. Inside, above the proscenium, a medallion displaying the combined arms of the Union, the State of Massachusetts, and the masks of tragedy and comedy suggested the aestheticization of politics. And special rooms dedicated to dancing, card playing, and tea drinking suggested that the genteel sociability of political and cultural elites might play a crucial role in forging a national culture.

Moreover, in the decades following the Revolution, theaters did far more to further partisan politics than to shore up nationalism or inculcate republican virtue.

Not surprisingly, many plays reflected the rancorous political climate of the 1790s, when domestic and international politics split Americans into camps of Federalists, who viewed Britain as a model and a potential ally, and Democratic Republicans, who favored close ties with revolutionary France. For example, John Burk's *Bunker-Hill; or the Death of General Warren* (1797) depicted the Revolutionary general as a populist who eschewed the privileges of rank; lest the point be lost on audiences, Warren's coffin appeared surrounded by Democratic Republican slogans. This treatment was not well received in all quarters. Federalist President John Adams complained that the real Warren had been a "gentleman and a scholar" who had been reduced to a "bully and a blackguard" by a disrespectful playwright. But Federalist writers did not hesitate to stage equally partisan interpretations of the Revolution. William Dunlap's *Andre* (1798) caused a stir with its sympathetic portrayal of British Major John Andre, who had collaborated with Benedict Arnold in addition to staging the *Meschianza*. Dunlap, a Federalist, cast Andre as the victim of an unfeeling General Washington and urged American audiences to reconcile with England, leaving the contentious past behind them. Democratic Republican papers had a field day, castigating the long-dead Andre as a duplicitous spy and Dunlap as a disloyal dramatist. The political valences of plays placed theater owners in a difficult position, for, as Heather Nathans has observed, they needed patrons of all parties in order to stay afloat. Ironically, they attempted to avoid the appearance of partisanship by staging English plays, edited to appeal to American tastes. But even English dramas could not hold party strife at bay: audiences requested that orchestras play partisan songs before the entertainments. When the Federal Street Theater's orchestra refused to play a pro-French song, "Jacobins" in the audience pelted the musicians with debris, including broken glass. Indeed, the "Federal Overture," a medley of French and Federalist tunes, became popular in theaters precisely because it seemed to take both sides at once.

At least in northeastern cities, theater was a singularly visible and aesthetically adaptable vehicle for expressing national and partisan identities. These qualities made it especially attractive to newly, tenuously free blacks, who looked to the stage to articulate their own struggles and aspirations. Recent studies by Shane White and Marvin McAllister have not only mined fragmentary, ephemeral sources in order to recover the vibrant theater community centered on New York City impresario and playwright William Brown; they have also placed that theater at the center of blacks' efforts to confront racial oppression and to elaborate their own distinctive cultural forms (White 2002; McAllister 2003). In 1821, six years before the final abolition of slavery in New York, William Brown, a former ship steward and a free man of color, opened first a pleasure garden and then a theater company for Afro-New Yorkers. Blacks had been barred outright from the city's white-owned gardens, and although they were regular theater attendees, they were relegated to the rear galleries in the back of theaters. Brown's theater (variously called the African Grove Company, the African Company, and finally the American Company) staged entertainments for mixed audiences until 1823, when it closed in the face of financial problems and entrenched white harassment.

On the surface, productions staged by Brown's company were much like those staged in theaters throughout the North: his audiences would have seen a play, followed by a comic afterpiece; they would also have been entertained by interludes of music, song, and dance inserted into the program before, during, and after the play itself. But New York's tense race relations combined with Brown's own artistic and political agendas lent his company's performances a distinct edge. Brown acquired theater space only a block from the city's most prominent theater. His house admitted blacks and whites, although initially whites were confined to the rear galleries with the rationale that they did not "know how to behave at entertainments designed for ladies and gentlemen of colour" (McAllister 2003: 2). He regularly staged Shakespearean dramas (*Richard III* was the troupe's first performance) at a time when whites agreed that the bard's linguistic complexities placed him beyond the reach of blacks. But Brown's company did more than encroach on white turf, literally or rhetorically. His company's performances revealed a uniquely African American aesthetic emphasizing hybridity, parody, innovation, and improvisation (White 2002: 67). Reading white viewers' disparaging accounts of screeching music and "vigorous" dancing girls, White discerns the melodic forerunner of jazz and the kinetics of a rich, underground dance culture. And Marvin McAllister describes the prevalence of "stage Europeans" in the company as "whiteface minstrelsy," in which black actors not only performed white privilege but also publicly demonstrated the ways that a "black 'self' could identify and disidentify, subvert or celebrate" (McAllister 2003: 66).

Visual Culture

If nationalism and national identities, however contested, were articulated in print and performance, they also emerged as part of a complex visual field that included paintings, architecture and iconography, and a range of exhibitionary spaces. In the past 10 years, art historians and cultural historians have moved beyond formalism, on the one hand, or dismissals of American provincialism, on the other, in order to situate a variety of images and objects in increasingly sophisticated contexts. Most notably, scholars working in a variety of fields have brought insights drawn from studies of politics, literature, and culture on both sides of the Atlantic to bear on high-style and vernacular productions. They have also begun to consider objects and images as elements of a protean consumer market. It is still too early to know exactly how these studies will extend and challenge our understanding of the broad contours of the Revolutionary and early national period. But taken together, this interdisciplinary literature has already begun to generate arresting readings of particular artists, images, and objects. Just as important, it has heightened our awareness of the significance of visuality in the formation of national identities.

Art historians and cultural historians have long noted that unlike British patrons, who developed an interest in landscapes and history paintings early on, Americans purchased portraits. For better or worse, to be a working painter in British North America was to be a portraitist. Recent studies have done much to explain Americans' enchantment with portraiture during the long eighteenth century. As Margaretta M. Lovell has argued in a series of essays exploring the work of John Singleton Copley, portraits were bound up with family. These paintings were often commissioned in pairs, typically of husbands and wives, and generally marked a transition in the sitters' status, such as marriage. Hung in domestic spaces before an audience of kin and friends, they simultaneously instantiated lineage and provided clear messages about the values and characteristics that distinguished the best families, including ideals about childrearing and spousal relations. Portraits did more than simply depict affectional modes of childrearing or the rise of companionate marriage; they were constituent elements of shifts in family strategies and ideals precisely because of their didactic, normative functions (Lovell 2005).

During and after the Revolution, the prevailing popularity and modes of portraiture were harnessed to nationalist agendas, encouraging Americans to image the nation through likenesses of political elites. Paintings of the founders and various republican notables were commissioned by the sitters along with their family and friends to commemorate their contributions to the republic and to secure their places in a revolutionary legacy. Overtly politicized, these portraits also propelled the visages of important men beyond domestic settings. They adorned city halls, state houses, and universities. They served as ceremonial gifts to diplomats and foreign dignitaries. By the end of the 1790s, they circulated among a larger, more anonymous audience: copies of "official," commissioned portraits were often engraved as prints and sold either as single images or as components of matching sets. Not surprisingly, the founder who was depicted most frequently and on the greatest variety of media was George Washington. His likenesses ranged from Gilbert Stuart's famed *Lansdowne Portrait* (1796), a lavish oil portrait on an enormous canvas, to intimate miniature portraits watercolored on ivory and set into rings, brooches, and lockets. He appeared in framed prints and on crockery. Marble Washingtons graced stately public parks while life-size wax models were featured in traveling shows. A depiction of Washington on his deathbed was even printed on handkerchiefs, which were sold on both sides of the Atlantic. The proliferation of Washington's likenesses indexed more than veneration for the *patriae pater*, just as images of lesser statesmen resulted from and revealed far more than patriotic enthusiasm. Recent explorations of political and politicized portraits suggest both the intersection of artistic and market cultures and the multiple levels on which paintings signified (Kelly, forthcoming).

Painting Washington was a crucial career move for any artist lucky enough to secure a sitting. Charles Willson Peale, for example, began painting Washington on the eve of the Revolution and continued through his presidency, securing seven sittings in all. Gilbert Stuart returned to the United States from Ireland expressly to further his career by painting the first president. Painters pursued Washington not simply because a portrait taken from life guaranteed public exposure or provided an entrée into elite circles, but because the original portrait could be copied – and sold – over and over again. Consider Gilbert Stuart's famous "Athenaeum" head, which was commissioned along with a portrait of Martha Washington to hang at Mount Vernon. Stuart never finished the original, but he did complete and sell around 75 copies of it. Indeed, William Dunlap, who was trained as a painter before forging a career in the theater, likened his own steady stream of copied Washington heads to cash (Kelly, forthcoming).

Yet art historians have demonstrated that more was at stake than a painter's profits or the mechanistic expansion of market demand. Like novels and newspapers, a painted canvas provided artists and viewers alike with food for political thought. "Exact likenesses" of statesmen were in demand not simply as emblems of political affiliation but because they provided vital information about the statesmen themselves. As art historians and literary critics have pointed out, physiognomy – the belief that character was inscribed on the face – had wide currency in eighteenth- and nineteenth-century America. Although discussions of physiognomy became more common and more scientific following the publication of Johan Lavater's *Essays on Physiognomy* (1775–8), beliefs about the relationship between face and character were commonplace (Steinberg 1996). In the face of rising anxieties about sincerity and duplicity in the decades following the Revolution, portrait painters were charged with representing a sitter's innermost self and publicly confirming qualities that the sitter hoped would be obvious to mere acquaintances. Early national portraits, which were intended both to confirm and model character, emerged out of complex negotiations between sitter, painter, and patron. Charles Willson Peale, for example, depicted many of his sitters, including George Washington, with uniformly oval faces that signified the virtuous intelligence demanded by republican society. Peale's portraits were thus likenesses of particular individuals and allegories of desirable personal traits. Portraits could also serve as a defense of sitters' class interests. This was the case with Ralph Earl's depictions of Connecticut's Federalist elite (St. George 1998). Earl regularly posed his sitters in front of a window looking out onto the very house in which the sitter was depicted. The harmonious timelessness evoked by these double portraits of individuals and their homes served to naturalize the sitters' social, political, and economic dominance at the precise moment when it was being challenged by a capricious market, Democratic Republicans, and undeferential artisans.

Architecture and iconography provided Americans with even clearer political messages. Scholars have long noted that Federal-era public buildings owed much to the influences of classical architecture. The columns, porticos, and friezes that marked building exteriors, along with the round and octagonal rooms that distinguished interior spaces, were derived from the temples of both republican and imperial Rome. For example, the Virginia state capital, designed in 1785 by Thomas Jefferson with the assistance of a French architect, was modeled on a Roman temple at Nimes. As president, Jefferson influenced the design and construction of the United States Capitol, which he intended to serve as a "museum" of authoritative architectural forms that could educate public taste. But Federal-era architects and designers did more than copy idealized columns and friezes. In time-honored fashion, they embellished those forms to suit local purposes. Charged with transforming New York's city hall into the seat of the United States' government in 1788, French architect Pierre-Charles L'Enfant created a frieze with thirteen stars, window tablets with thirteen arrows, and a central pediment emblazoned with an enormous eagle. Similarly, Benjamin Henry Latrobe crowned the columns in the United States Capitol with magnolias, corncobs, and tobacco leaves. This penchant for the motifs and conventions of classical design was of a piece with educated citizens' fascination with the ancient world, which not only provided potent political antecedents but also validated Americans' own republican project (Stillman 1999).

Less obviously, these same buildings were also replete with motifs drawn from freemasonry, a transatlantic intellectual and cultural movement that was aimed at improving humankind through reason and that generated a rich symbolic vocabulary which referenced both the tools of the building trades and the ancient world. In the United States, freemasonry was closely associated with the creation and consolidation of the new government both because its core values (which included learning, morality, and non-sectarian Christianity) resonated with republicanism, and because so many of the new nation's military and political elites were themselves members of Masonic lodges. In fact, freemasonry was literally built into the new government; the cornerstone to the US Capitol was laid in 1793 by George Washington, decked out in his Masonic apron and accompanied by brothers from his Alexandria, Virginia lodge. More to the point, the Masonic preoccupation with the symbolic resonance of geometric shapes, columns, and domes meshed nicely with the conventions of neoclassical architecture. Indeed, architectural historian James Stevens Curl (1999) has suggested that the US Capitol is as Masonic as it is neoclassical. By the end of the eighteenth century, Masonic imagery, most notably the pyramid and the all-seeing eye, were prominently embedded in public buildings and national iconography. Whatever their decorative value, these images were primarily intended to serve didactic purposes. Influenced by Enlightenment ideas that tied education to sensory perception, Masons believed that visual symbols would serve as prompts, reminding viewers of the values graphically represented. They hoped that emblems characterized by simplicity, universality, and elevation, would create a visual language capable of instilling virtue in the observer (Bullock 1999).

Depictions of oval-headed statesmen or all-seeing eyes were potent signifiers not simply because of qualities inherent in the image but because of viewers' increasingly acute visual literacy. Their ability to read images and objects surely owed much to the consumer revolution of the long eighteenth century, which brought an increasing number and variety of goods within the reach of greater numbers of Americans. But it also resulted from the widespread conviction that visual perception was a crucial component of self-improvement and self-cultivation. Reading images, objects, and spectacles was akin to reading books and newspapers. Eager for information about the continent and even the world, early national Americans purchased scores of geography books, which included cartographic as well as textual representations. They purchased globes, like those made by James Wilson, a Vermont blacksmith who taught himself to make terrestrial globes in the 1780s. They were fascinated by optical devices like the camera obscura and the convex mirror, which played tricks on viewers' eyes, distorting perception and offering lessons on distinguishing between truth and illusion. They toured museums like Charles Willson Peale's famous Philadelphia Museum, which displayed natural and man-made artifacts with Linnaean order (Brigham 1995; Bellion 2002; Jaffee 2004). But they also flocked to Daniel Bowen's Columbian Museum, where arrangements of wax presidents, Chinese "mandarins," Barbary pirates, and eight-legged calves owed more to cultures of curiosity and spectacle than to the hierarchies of natural science. Scholars are only just beginning to recover the parameters of this visual culture, to say nothing of its full significance. And they have yet to consider the relationship between visual and print cultures. But if their research does not yet allow for broad generalizations, it clearly indicates the significance of the visual in the early republic.

Since the 1976 publication of Kenneth Silverman's *Cultural History of the American Revolution*, we have learned a great deal about revolutionary and early national culture and about the ways in which it shaped the emergence of nationalism and the creation of a republican state and society. Most obviously, explorations of various kinds of cultural productions have moved us beyond the canonical texts and images that once dominated early American cultural studies; there was more to the long eighteenth century than *The Federalist Papers* and the portraits of John Singleton Copley. Once-obscure individuals like Aupaumut, Deborah Sampson, and James Wilson are no longer curiosities or footnotes; instead, they have taken their places alongside Charles Willson Peale and Hugh Henry Brackenridge as creators of culture. Indeed, Silverman's catalogue of "culture" now seems a bit narrow. (But this insistence on the significance of early national cultural production, including the move toward more expansive, inclusive discussions of culture, has not extended to music. Despite growing interest in the history of the senses, historians of the Revolution and early republic have been markedly slow to consider music and sound more generally; Silverman's discussion of music remains cutting edge.) Yet the significance of this scholarship extends well beyond the recovery of obscure novels and forgotten plays. Literary culture, performances of all kinds, and visual culture now appear to be crucial constituent elements of a story that once centered on politics, very narrowly defined. Scholars working in multiple disciplines are well on their way not only to writing "cultural histories of the Revolution," but to writing histories of a revolution that was as grounded in culture as in politics.

REFERENCES

Anderson, Benedict R. O'G.: *Imagined Communities: Reflections on the Origins and Spread of Nationalism* (London: Verso, 1983).
Barker-Benfield, G. J.: *The Culture of Sensibility: Sex and Society in Eighteenth-Century Britain* (Chicago: University of Chicago Press, 1992).
Bellion, Wendy: "Pleasing Deceptions," *common-place* 3:1 (October 2002).
Brigham, David R.: *Public Culture in the Early Republic: Peale's Museum and Its Audience* (Washington, DC: Smithsonian Institution Press, 1995).
Bullock, Steven C.: "'Sensible Signs': The Emblematic Education of Post-Revolutionary Freemasonry," in Donald R. Kennon, ed., *A Republic for the Ages: The United States Capitol and the Political Culture of the Early Republic* (Charlottesville: University Press of Virginia for the United States Capitol Historical Society, 1999), pp. 177–213.
Burgett, Bruce: *Sentimental Bodies: Sex, Gender, and Citizenship in the Early Republic* (Princeton: Princeton University Press, 1998).
Burstein, Andrew: "The Political Character of Sympathy," *Journal of the Early Republic* 21 (2001), 601–32.
Cavitch, Max: "The Man That Was Used Up: Poetry, Particularity, and the Politics of Remembering George Washington," *American Literature* 75 (2003), 247–74.
Cmiel, Kenneth: *Democratic Eloquence: The Fight over Popular Speech in Nineteenth-Century America* (New York: William Morrow, 1990).
Curl, James Stevens: "The Capitol in Washington, DC, and Its Freemasonic Connections," in Donald R. Kennon, ed., *A Republic for the Ages: The United States Capitol and the Political Culture of the Early Republic* (Charlottesville: University Press of Virginia for the United States Capitol Historical Society, 1999), pp. 14–267.
Davidson, Cathy N.: *Revolution and the Word: The Rise of the Novel in America* (New York: Oxford University Press, 1986).
Ellison, Julie: *Cato's Tears and the Making of Anglo-American Emotion* (Chicago: University of Chicago Press, 1999).
Fliegelman, Jay: *Declaring Independence: Jefferson, Natural Language, and the Culture of Performance* (Stanford, CA: Stanford University Press, 1993).

Fuller, Randall: "Theaters of the American Revolution: the Valley Forge *Cato* and the Meschianza in their Transcultural Contexts," *Early American Literature* 34 (1999), 126–46.

Gustafson, Sandra M.: *Eloquence is Power: Oratory and Performance in Early America* (Chapel Hill: University of North Carolina Press, 2000).

Habermas, Jürgen: *The Transformation of the Public Sphere: An Inquiry into a Category of Bourgeois Society* (Cambridge, MA: MIT Press, 1989).

Jaffee, David: "Curiosities Encountered: James Wilson and Provincial Cartography in the United States, 1790–1840," *common-place* (4) 2004 <http://www.common-place.org/vol-04/no-02/jaffee/>

Juster, Susan: *Doomsayers: Anglo-American Prophecy in the Age of Revolution* (Philadelphia: University of Pennsylvania Press, 2003).

Kelly, Catherine E.: *Things Useful and Ornamental: The Aesthetics of Everyday Life in the Early Republic* (forthcoming).

Kennon, Donald R., ed.: *A Republic for the Ages: The United States Capitol and the Political Culture of the Early Republic* (Charlottesville: University Press of Virginia for the United States Capitol Historical Society, 1999).

Lovell, Margaretta M.: *Art in a Season of Revolution: Painters, Artisans, and Patrons in Early America* (Philadelphia: University of Pennsylvania Press, 2005).

McAllister, Marvin: *White People Do Not Know How to Behave at Entertainments Designed for Ladies and Gentlemen of Colour: William Brown's African and American Theater* (Chapel Hill: University of North Carolina Press, 2003).

Miller, Lillian B., ed.: *The Peale Family: Creation of a Legacy, 1770–1870* (New York: Abbeville Press in association with the Trust for Museum Exhibitions and the National Portrait Gallery, Smithsonian Institution, 1996).

Nathans, Heather S.: *Early American Theatre from the Revolution to Thomas Jefferson: Into the Hands of the People* (Cambridge: Cambridge University Press, 2003).

St. George, Robert Blair: *Conversing by Signs: Poetics of Implication in Colonial New England Culture* (Chapel Hill: University of North Carolina Press, 1998).

Silverman, Kenneth: *A Cultural History of the American Revolution: Painting, Music, Literature, and the Theatre in the Colonies and the United States from the Treaty of Paris to the Inauguration of George Washington, 1763–1789* (New York: Thomas Y. Crowell, 1976).

Steinberg, David: "Charles Willson Peale Portrays the Body Politic," in Lillian B. Miller, ed., *The Peale Family: Creation of a Legacy, 1770–1870* (New York: Abbeville Press in association with the Trust for Museum Exhibitions and the National Portrait Gallery, Smithsonian Institution, 1996), pp. 118–33.

Stern, Julia A.: *The Plight of Feeling: Sympathy and Dissent in the Early American Novel* (Chicago: University of Chicago Press, 1997).

Stillman, Damie: "From the Ancient Roman Republic to the New American One: Architecture for a New Nation," in Donald R. Kennon, ed., *A Republic for the Ages: The United States Capitol and the Political Culture of the Early Republic* (Charlottesville: University Press of Virginia for the United States Capitol Historical Society, 1999), pp. 271–315.

Sweet, John Wood: *Bodies Politic: Negotiating Race in the American North, 1730–1830* (Baltimore: Johns Hopkins University Press, 2003).

Van Sant, Ann Jessie: *Eighteenth-century Sensibility and the Novel: The Senses in Social Context* (Cambridge: Cambridge University Press, 1993).

Waldstreicher, David: *In the Midst of Perpetual Fetes: The Making of American Nationalism, 1776–1820* (Chapel Hill: University of North Carolina Press, 1997).

Warner, Michael: *The Letters of the Republic: Publication and the Public Sphere in Eighteenth-Century America* (Cambridge, MA: Harvard University Press, 1990).

White, Shane: *Stories of Freedom in Black New York* (Cambridge, MA: Harvard University Press, 2002).

Wilmer, S. E.: *Theatre, Society, and the Nation: Staging American Identities* (Cambridge: Cambridge University Press, 2002).

Withington, Ann Fairfax: *Toward a More Perfect Union: Virtue and the Formation of American Republics* (New York: Oxford University Press, 1991).

Part II

THE NINETEENTH CENTURY

Chapter Five

Antebellum Cultural History

James W. Cook

When I first thought about studying US cultural history, the antebellum period seemed a rather unlikely place to set up shop. In the broader sweep of American culture, these were the decades known as early or mid-"Victorian," a period typically defined by its rigid social strictures and cast as dour precursor to the more dynamic cultural experiments of *fin de siècle* "modernism." Adding to my doubts was a sense that much of the previous scholarship on antebellum culture seemed oddly out of sync with the era's great social, economic, and political upheavals. The decades before the Civil War were among the most volatile in the nation's history. Yet many key sources of that volatility – from northern emancipation to the anti-slavery crusade, the rise of the metropolis to the rapid expansion of market capitalism – appeared to fall within the methodological bailiwick of other historical subfields and modes of questioning.

Twenty years later, antebellum cultural history looks like another place entirely. The long-running caricatures of Victorian priggery have given way to a more nuanced understanding of middle-class cultural formation. The older emphasis on white social elites has been challenged by path-breaking studies of workers, women, immigrants, and African Americans. The antebellum period itself has been reconceptualized as a wellspring of the modern rather than its opposite or antipode. And the range of cultural forms generating scholarly attention has expanded to include a far more diverse mix of vernacular, commercial, and transnational sources.

Similarly dramatic has been the collective impact of all this methodological stretching. From the rise of "class cultures" and "racial formations" during the 1980s, to current debates about the "market revolution" and "empire," antebellum cultural historians have frequently set new research agendas for the discipline as a whole. And this is to say nothing of the many fruitful cross-pollinations across disciplines. Since the inauguration of the American Studies Association's John Hope Franklin book prize in 1987, roughly half of the winners have addressed antebellum topics, often venturing into historical terrain (such as the commerce of slavery) previously understood as well outside the boundaries of "cultural" analysis. During the same period, new cohorts of scholars conversant in transatlantic cultural studies have returned to many of the foundational forms of antebellum commercial entertainment (such as blackface minstrelsy), dramatically transforming our understanding of what a rigorous, interdisciplinary history of "the popular" might entail.

My larger purpose here, however, goes beyond subdisciplinary boosterism. More productively, I want to consider some of the reasons for the antebellum period's gravitational pull on US cultural historians over the past quarter-century. Why have so many recent culturalists (myself included) found themselves drawn to these well-traveled decades before the Civil War? How has the proliferation of new scholarship dislodged and complicated previous master narratives? Where might we look for the next waves of innovation?

Beyond Victorianism

One good place to begin addressing these questions is with the gradual erosion of "Victorian America" as a central organizing concept. As late as the mid-1980s, many leading scholars continued to invoke this concept (and its more explicitly ideological counterpart, American Victorianism) with all of the collective confidence and presumed legibility that well-established paradigms typically provide. Victorian, in this formulation, referred to a number of things. On a very basic level, it defined a particular nexus of social identities – white, Protestant, bourgeois, Anglo-American – although the most sophisticated studies were quick to point out important wrinkles within the larger patterns (such as the growing impact of German-American immigration after 1850). At the same time, "Victorian" offered a convenient shorthand for a complex series of historical processes understood as generative for the larger culture: the spread of Protestant evangelicalism following the Second Great Awakening; the emergence of separate spheres for bourgeois men and women; the promotion of an urban–industrial work ethic specifically tailored to the burgeoning market economy; and the rigorous cultivation of moral self-discipline (as, for example, in the various reform campaigns against prostitution, alcohol, and "low theatricals").

In all of these different respects, Victorian America served as a kind of master trope for mid-nineteenth-century cultural history, simultaneously signifying a period, a demographic amalgam, and a dominant set of values. For scholars working on later periods, moreover, Victorian culture provided a useful historical foil, conjuring with a single catchphrase the broader range of taboos, anxieties, and repressions against which subsequent modernist movements were said to have both defined themselves and decisively battled. How, then, are we to explain the striking absence of this trope/catchphrase in current US cultural history scholarship, the present volume being one obvious example?

Part of an answer can be found in the path-breaking work on women and gender that began to emerge in the late 1970s and early 1980s. Carroll Smith-Rosenberg's landmark essay collection, *Disorderly Conduct* (1985), is an important case in point. Written over the course of two decades, *Disorderly Conduct* straddles many of the methodological thresholds I have referenced thus far. In the opening chapter, "Hearing Women's Words," Smith-Rosenberg describes the volume as a work of "social history," but then goes on to champion many of the methodological touchstones of the "new cultural history" – from linguistic analysis and close readings of "mythic constructs," to the poststructuralism of Michel Foucault and the anthropological insights of Mary Douglas. In similar fashion, Smith-Rosenberg often notes inherited wisdom about Victorian "prudery" and "domesticity" only to complicate and challenge these assumptions through a series of revisionist readings. Moving through a wide range of volunteer networks, reform organizations, and evangelical meetings, the antebellum women who fill the pages of *Disorderly Conduct* are never simply confined to the domestic sphere and the activities of motherhood. Their campaigns against "moral licentiousness," we come to realize, were also forms of collective resistance against sexual "double standards"; their millenarian "anti-ritualism" in Protestant churches provided a strategy to "seize sacred space" from male authorities.

It was during the mid-1980s, too, that new waves of feminist historians began to expand and reconceptualize the role of antebellum women as cultural laborers. In *Private Woman, Public Stage* (1984), for example, Mary Kelley was among the first to challenge the prevailing notion that the era's most successful female authors were simply trapped in an ideological zero-sum game: either as victims of a pervasive "cult of domesticity" or as self-deluding peddlers of "feminine influence." Tracking the careers of prominent "literary domestics" such as Catherine Maria Sedgwick, Sara Parton (aka "Fanny Fern"), and Harriet Beecher Stowe, Kelley shows how these white middle-class women struggled to negotiate the competing demands of commercial celebrity and personal obligation, a deeply ambivalent process which often played out in the pages of some of the era's bestselling novels and newspaper serials.

More recently, Robert Allen's *Horrible Prettiness* (1991), Faye Dudden's *Women in the American Theater* (1994), and Renee Sentilles's *Performing Menken* (2003) have explored related questions about gender, representation, and power on the antebellum stage. While increasing numbers of women gained access to commercial theaters between the 1820s and 1870s, they did so within a male-dominated marketplace that often valued bodies over words and appearance over artistry. Yet this emerging hegemony of "sexual spectacle" was far from complete. Some antebellum performers, like the international opera star Jenny Lind, responded by turning dominant ideals of feminine virtue into mass-marketed forms of "family amusement." Others, like Charlotte Cushman, ventured abroad, using her novelty as an American actress to secure a broader range of roles, including a highly successful Romeo in "breeches." Still others, like the burlesque comedian Lydia Thompson and the poet/actress/provocateur Adah Isaacs Menken, explicitly flaunted their sexuality in an effort to cultivate public controversy around the very questions of what a woman can do and say in public.

The growing body of work on antebellum masculinity has demonstrated a number of important wrinkles, as well. One of the earliest and richest studies is Elliott Gorn's *The Manly Art* (1986), in which we discover large numbers of white-collar "sporting men" eagerly pursuing their passion for bare-knuckle boxing as part of conventionally mixed-class, mixed-race audiences. What Gorn helps us to see are the multiple social and cultural positions available within the larger rubrics of "bourgeois" and "working-class" masculinity, some of which gained their traction precisely by rejecting the bodily and behavioral proscriptions favored by Protestant evangelicals. In similar fashion, Ann Fabian's innovative history of gambling, *Card Sharps, Dream Books, and Bucket Shops* (1990), reveals a motley assortment of urban clerks and rural gentlemen who regularly balked at warnings to engage in slow and steady toil, careful savings, and rational profit seeking. Drawing on a variety of previously neglected sources,

Fabian skillfully explicates the "negative analogue" of antebellum market discipline – those badly behaved faro dealers and policy players who spent their money in all of the "wrong ways."

In *Honor and Slavery* (1996), Kenneth S. Greenberg extends this project of differentiating masculinities across the Mason–Dixon line. Particularly interesting is Greenberg's suggestion that southern slaveholders and northern merchants understood the meanings and functions of self-representation in very different ways. By the 1840s, he argues, northern merchants typically viewed words and gestures as the malleable instruments of market exchange, whereas southern landowners believed that words and gestures conveyed unequivocal meanings about the moral status of the speaker. In fact, it was the ongoing refusal of southern gentlemen to search beneath the surface meanings they manipulated (refusing, for example, to focus on the inner beings of their slaves, rather than on the social status ascribed to skin color) which helped to define and consolidate their power *as* southern gentlemen.

In many ways, though, the most fundamental challenges to the master narratives of American Victorianism can be found in Karen Halttunen's *Confidence Men and Painted Women* (1982) and John Kasson's *Rudeness and Civility* (1991), two widely influential histories of antebellum manners. In retrospect, one of the most striking features of both studies is their agile use of primary sources long understood as the cultural bedrock of bourgeois "respectability": etiquette books and conduct manuals, fashion advice and children's literature, city guides and parlor magazines. But whereas previous scholars had presented these didactic texts as transparent expressions of Victorian "hypocrisy" and "social control," Halttunen and Kasson read them in relation to a broader semiotic crisis, one in which the antebellum quest for fixed and legible forms of personal character grew out of the new perceptual challenges of anonymous urban crowds, rapid demographic mobility, and increasingly speculative forms of commerce.

On a very basic level, this line of argument offered a more dynamic set of explanations for the ideological origins of social and moral self-discipline. Suddenly, those pious souls of Sabbath school fame began to look like active improvisers in the swirl and flux of modernization (rather than a one-dimensional rearguard, anxiously holding back the floodgates). Also notable were Halttunen's and Kasson's rigorous efforts to connect the day-to-day rituals of social respectability to a more particular segment within the antebellum bourgeoisie: namely, the "new middle class," which began to take shape in northeastern cities during the 1820s and 1830s. In stark contrast to previous studies, which had mostly chortled over the behavioral ticks of an undifferentiated Victorian "social elite," Halttunen and Kasson helped us to see the deeper significance and functional value of these ritualized behaviors for the larger process of urban middle-class self-making.

From Class Cultures and Racial Formations
to Multiethnic Histories

Ultimately, this shift in conceptual emphasis from Victorian to new middle class was more than a simple matter of demographic fine-tuning. One might argue, in fact, that most of the books I have described thus far were part of a broader

ANTEBELLUM CULTURAL HISTORY

historiographical effort to supplant the conceptual monolith of American Victorianism with a more capacious series of "class cultures." It was during this very same period, moreover, that growing numbers of US historians began to explore the expressive forms, vernacular styles, and consumption habits of antebellum workers, particularly in the newly industrializing metropolises of the northeast. Initially, at least, the cultural components of these localized labor studies were relatively modest. Thus, we find a half-dozen pages on blackface minstrelsy, volunteer fire companies, and the Bowery Theater in Sean Wilentz's influential history of New York City artisans, *Chants Democratic* (1984); or a somewhat deeper exegesis of working women's uses of Five Points dance halls in Christine Stansell's *City of Women* (1986); or a final chapter on Bowery fashion, slang, and humor in Richard Stott's *Workers in the Metropolis* (1990).

More recent scholarship has complicated and enriched these early portraits in a number of different ways. Consider, for example, the methodological trajectory of Paul Johnson, whose most recent study, *Sam Patch, The Famous Jumper* (2003), explores the fascinating career of a Rhode Island mill worker-cum-waterfall daredevil. In Johnson's first book, *A Shopkeeper's Millennium* (1978), as in many of the best quantitative social and labor histories from the 1970s, someone with Patch's vocational profile would have barely registered as an individual subject. And more likely than not, he would have found himself operating within rigidly hegemonic "structures" of social, economic, and technological discipline.

In *Sam Patch*, by contrast, Johnson places his protagonist's daredevilry at the very center of analysis, reading each death-defying leap as a kind of oppositional performance art through which we can glimpse the struggles of thousands of anonymous mill workers who left behind no written records. This shift in analytical emphasis, it is important to note, should not be understood as a one-way movement away from the questions first posed by *A Shopkeeper's Millennium*. Again and again, Johnson skillfully juxtaposes Patch's drunken bravado with the disciplinary projects championed by bourgeois property owners and moral reformers; indeed, it is precisely in defiance of the latter's "rational amusements" and "languages of progress" that Patch's public acts accrue their deeper significance. More accurately, then, *Sam Patch* employs the conceptual tools of cultural history (thick description, discourse analysis, close attention to visual imagery, etc.) to expand what can be known about the localized impacts of the Industrial Revolution, as well as the day-to-day forms of resistance devised by antebellum workers caught in its vortex.

Other recent studies have focused on the construction of working-class racial identities. That antebellum workers frequently engaged in acts of racial discrimination had, of course, been acknowledged by previous social and labor historians. During the first half of the nineteenth century, white urban workers across the northeast increasingly excluded newly emancipated African Americans from entire professions and neighborhoods. And Irish-American workers, in particular, frequently vented their frustrations at the expense of black businesses, churches, and homes. Less clear was the specific relation between such forms of racial hostility and the manifold impacts of market capitalism. Nor had previous studies explained the specific ideological process by which large numbers of manual laborers came to define themselves as "white."

It was to these complex questions about working-class "racial formation" that Alexander Saxton's *Rise and Fall of the White Republic* (1990) and David Roediger's

Wages of Whiteness (1991) addressed themselves. Particularly influential was their use of linguistic analysis to track the shifting racial and economic identifications embedded in the era's dominant labor categories ("hirelings" and "slaves," or "masters" and "servants"). By reading such categories as both mutable and continuously interwoven with contemporary changes in industrial production, immigration, and party politics, Saxton and Roediger made it far easier to see that white workers actually had racial identities of a specific historical vintage. Their innovative modes of questioning, moreover, made it increasingly difficult to treat race and class as wholly separate issues. Today, in fact, most cultural historians would describe *all* identity categories (race, class, gender, sexuality) as chronologically contingent and mutually constituted.

This leads to what is arguably the single most important development in recent scholarship: namely, the ongoing effort to construct a more pluralistic and racially inclusive portrait of antebellum culture. Early signs of this effort can be found in a series of path-breaking histories of antebellum slavery, including Lawrence Levine's *Black Culture and Black Consciousness* (1977), Albert Raboteau's *Slave Religion* (1978), Charles Joyner's *Down by the Riverside* (1984), Deborah Gray White's *Ar'n't I a Woman?* (1985), and Sterling Stuckey's *Slave Culture* (1987). In many ways, *Black Culture and Black Consciousness* stands out in this stellar body of work, for it taught an entire generation of scholars how to read long-neglected vernacular forms such as spirituals, jokes, and animal tales as meaningful historical evidence. Initiated during the mid-1960s (as Levine was actively involved in the Civil Rights movement), *Black Culture and Black Consciousness* is a politically charged "history from below" which restlessly seeks out new ways of conceptualizing subaltern thought, identity, and resistance. "Black culture," in Levine's innovative formulation, is less a strict aesthetic category than a dialectical, multilayered "process." As the epic story unfolds, we come to see how the vernacular cultural expressions of African Americans were at once shaped by unique historical experiences and struggles, interwoven with the cultural life of other social groups; and continuously engaged in the broader battle to remake American society.

Over the past quarter-century, much of the best new scholarship has not only embraced this expansive, pluralistic vision of antebellum culture, but also worked to correct some of its lingering blind spots. Some, like Sterling Stuckey's *Going Through the Storm* (1994), Shane White and Graham White's *Stylin'* (1998), Shane White's *Stories of Freedom in Black New York* (2002), and Leslie Harris's *In the Shadow of Slavery* (2003), have explored the less familiar histories of post-emancipation community building and cultural politics initiated by African Americans in the antebellum North. Others, such as Frances Smith Foster's *Written by Herself* (1993), Carla Peterson's *"Doers of the Word"* (1995), and Nell Irvin Painter's *Sojourner Truth: A Life, A Symbol* (1996), have addressed the specific contributions of black women writers and lecturers in the struggles around suffrage and anti-slavery. Still others, such as Ramon Gutierrez's *When Jesus Came, the Corn Mothers Went Away* (1991), John Kuo-Wei Tchen's *New York before Chinatown* (1999), and Susan Johnson's *Roaring Camp* (2000), have pushed beyond the black/white binary to demonstrate the complex patterns of multiethnic cultural exchange and conflict that regularly emerged in southwestern colonial outposts, northeastern port cities, and California mining camps. In all of these different respects, the larger entity we now call antebellum culture looks far more syncretic, dynamic, and contested than it did when I first thought about becoming a professional historian. Indeed, one would be hard-pressed to find any chronological subfield that has been more productively stretched and complicated by the cultural turn in late twentieth-century historiography.

Theorizing the Popular

Thus far, much of my discussion has focused on problems of identity – those core questions of race, class, gender, and sexuality that have long shaped our prevailing portraits of antebellum culture. In actual fact, though, such identity questions are but one important piece of a much larger puzzle. Saxton and Roediger, for example, were key innovators in explicating the rise of working-class whiteness, but their studies also fueled important new debates about the origins of blackface minstrelsy, one of the era's most pervasive forms of popular culture. Similarly, studies such as Tchen's *New York before Chinatown* and White's *Stories of Freedom in Black New York* can be read on at least two different levels: both as powerful chronicles of subaltern struggle against the era's dominant racial ideologies, and as innovative histories of rapidly expanding entertainment industries which did much to produce and disseminate the ideologies. It is to these complex questions of popular cultural production and consumption that I now want to turn.

Antebellum historians, it seems to me, are particularly well positioned to trace changes in the meanings, production, and circulation of US popular culture, for it was during the decades before the Civil War that the very first commercial entertainment industries began to emerge. Key studies, in this regard, include Eric Lott's *Love and Theft* (1993), Ken Emerson's *DOO-DAH!* (1998), Dale Cockrell's *Demons of Disorder* (1997), and W. T. Lhamon, Jr.'s *Raising Cain* (1998) on blackface minstrelsy; David Grimsted's *Melodrama Unveiled* (1968), Lawrence Levine's *Highbrow/Lowbrow* (1988), Bruce McConachie's *Melodramatic Formations* (1992), and Don Wilmeth and Christopher Bigsby's *The Cambridge History of American Theatre, Volume One* (1998) on theater; Neil Harris's *Humbug* (1973), Bluford Adams's *E Pluribus Barnum* (1997), and James W. Cook's *Arts of Deception* (2001) on P. T. Barnum and the "show trade"; and Michael Denning's *Mechanic Accents* (1987), Ronald Zboray's *A Fictive People* (1993), Richard Brodhead's *Cultures of Letters* (1993), Scott Casper's *Constructing American Lives* (1999), Isabelle Lehuu's *Carnival on the Page* (2000), and Shelley Streeby's *American Sensations* (2002) on the explosion of antebellum print culture.

This rich body of scholarship has pointed to a number of broader conclusions. First and foremost, it has taught us that "the popular" was a thoroughly mutable category, never simply intrinsic to any particular cultural form. In some cases, this categorization grew out of carefully choreographed promotional campaigns designed to pitch elite artistry (such as Jenny Lind's opera singing) to a broader socioeconomic spectrum. In others, it reflected a specific performance location, ticket price, gender dynamic, or managerial policy (such as the decision to sell alcohol). In still others, it was a function of sales and distribution, which, in turn, became the very basis of a product's market identity (as, for example, when antebellum publishers advertised Sara Parton's *Fanny Fern* novels as "popular" on the basis of thousands of advance orders).

This leads to a second basic conclusion about the complex relationship between vernacular expression and capitalist expansion. The point here is not simply that vernacular forms such as songs, dances, fables, and jokes were becoming commercial products for non-localized markets – a process which had been underway for at least two centuries. Rather, what seem to have been new in the 1830s and 1840s were the increasingly self-conscious efforts of individual artists and managers to make vernacular authenticity a central feature of their cultural productions and marketing campaigns. P. T. Barnum, for example, spent much of the early 1840s promoting a young Irish-American street dancer named John Diamond as one of the Five Points' leading practitioners of "breakdowns" and "double shuffles." Similarly, F. S. Chanfrau, a New York actor, writer, and stage manager with working-class roots, scored one of the biggest theatrical sensations of the late 1840s by playing the character "Mose," a good-hearted but tough-as-nails "B'hoy," very much like the brash young men he had known growing up in the Bowery.

The historical rub here is that Diamond and Chanfrau really *were* from the old neighborhoods, a fact that makes it difficult to describe their performances as straightforward "appropriations" or "co-optations" of working-class vernaculars. Yet it would be equally misleading to ignore the ongoing impacts of their efforts to sell these vernaculars across ever-expanding market segments, a complex process which pushed the dance steps and theatrical gestures from street to stage and back again. Right from the start, Diamond and Chanfrau addressed themselves to urban publics far broader than their earlier working-class social milieux. And in ways both big and small, they adapted their performances to the shifting tastes, politics, and prejudices of each new public they encountered. What their careers help to illustrate, then, is not simply the movement of antebellum cultural products from vernacular seedbeds to larger regional and national markets, but also the production of "the popular" as an increasingly self-conscious and profitable promotional strategy.

A third key conclusion involves the transnational scope of antebellum popular culture. For many years, the broader circulatory patterns of the era's entertainment products were hard to see, a function both of US historians' long-running tendency to favor the nation state as their primary contextual rubric and an equally entrenched master narrative of US "dependency" on European art, literature, and music before the 1850s. Three recent document collections have offered a more complete picture. In Dale Cockrell's *Excelsior: Journals of the Hutchinson Family Singers* (1989) we discover that the antebellum era's most acclaimed evangelical singing group was also one of its most peripatetic cultural productions, covering hundreds of different venues on both sides of the Atlantic. Much like the recent groundswell of excellent work on religious publishing (such as Nathan O. Hatch's *The Democratization of American Christianity* [1989], R. Laurence Moore's *Selling God* [1994], David Morgan's *Protestants and Pictures* [1999], and David Paul Nord's *Faith in Reading* [2004]), Cockrell demonstrates that the moral proscriptions against antebellum "theatricals" were far from absolute. More accurately, Protestant reformers created their own forms of cultural commerce, both to compete with the secular mainstream and to provide an innovative vehicle for their numerous missionary projects.

W. T. Lhamon, Jr.'s rich collection of early blackface "plays, lyrics, and street prose," *Jump Jim Crow* (2003), paints a similarly transnational picture, showing for the first time that T. D. Rice (the key American innovator) was a major star in Britain by the mid-1830s – seven years *before* the first formalized "minstrel show" in New York City. In stark contrast to earlier studies of antebellum minstrelsy, which had generally confined their analyses to particular US cities or even neighborhoods, Lhamon points to a disturbing but crucial fact: namely, that blackface was the United States' first major cultural export. By the 1840s and 1850s, dozens of American minstrel troupes were "Jumping Jim Crow" in leading European theaters and music halls.

My own *Colossal P. T. Barnum Reader* (2005) documents the remarkable scope and complexity of the Great Yankee Showman's transnational projects. During the mid-1830s, Barnum had conducted his tours in a manner hardly distinguishable from his eighteenth-century forbears. Often traveling by horse-drawn wagon across the countryside – and living largely hand-to-mouth – Barnum's mode of production barely traversed the threshold of modern market relations. Less than a decade later, however, Barnum had amassed enough capital in lower Manhattan's burgeoning amusement markets to launch a series of foreign tours which extended across England, Scotland, Ireland, France, Spain, Belgium, Holland, and Cuba. Over the next four decades, Barnum imported and exported dozens of different acts, from the juvenile singing group known as the Bateman Children, to his massive three-ring circus venture with James A. Bailey, which traveled to Britain on a fleet of steamships. By the time of his death in 1891, Barnum's show business empire included a staff of thousands; separate publicity, advertising, and acquisitions departments; corporate mergers every few years; capital assets valued at over $10 million; and brand recognition across much of the globe.

A final point involves the complex power dynamics at work in such commercial enterprises. That popular culture itself has often functioned as an arena for social struggle is hardly news – indeed, it would be difficult to find any major study over the past quarter-century that has not explored this question in one way or another. What the best new work has offered, rather, are a series of fresh insights about patterns of domination and resistance in antebellum cultural forms specifically understood as national or transnational industries. In *American Sensations* (2002), for example, Shelley Streeby demonstrates that the newspaper serials and dime novels of early pulp luminaries such as George Lippard and E. Z. C. Judson (aka "Ned Buntline") were, in fact, highly politicized cultural productions which spoke to their increasingly national readerships through languages of "empire." By tracking these antebellum texts in relation to major political developments such as Indian Removal and the US–Mexican War, Streeby enables us to see the longer ideological trajectory of conquest and territorial expansion, a process which both preceded and helped to shape the rise of US imperialism in the Pacific.

Similarly, Tchen's *New York before Chinatown* demonstrates the rather surprising fact that widespread discourses of "commercial orientalism" actually preceded the arrival of significant numbers of Chinese immigrants in New York City, a pattern which forced antebellum performers such as Afong Moy (the "Chinese Lady") and Chang and Eng Bunker (the "Siamese Twins") to construct their self-representations in opposition to already pervasive public assumptions about Chinese difference. What Tchen helps to clarify, in this regard, is the emergence of a distinctly modern mode of minority cultural struggle, one in which the performers' efforts to achieve visibility, profits, and mobility were continuously interwoven with battles over representational

control. Cross-cultural struggles over the terms and meanings of racial/ethnic difference were well under way before the Civil War.

Speculating on the Future

Where might we look for the next waves of innovation? Even today, it seems relatively
clear that the transnational turn in antebellum cultural history has become something
more than a momentary correction of older patterns of American "exceptionalism,"
a conclusion only reinforced by recent publications such as Joseph Roach's *Cities of
the Dead* (1996), Peter Linebaugh and Marcus Rediker's *Many-Headed Hydra* (2001),
Sarah Meer's *Uncle Tom Mania* (2005), and Daphne Brooks's *Bodies in Dissent*
(2006). Less clear is the question of whether future transnational histories will continue to operate primarily within "circumatlantic" contexts and frameworks.

One broader lesson of the first wave of studies, it seems to me, is that antebellum
markets *mattered* – not simply as economic engines driving the movement of bodies,
goods, and aesthetic forms across borders, but also, simultaneously, as the very networks through which transnational counter-publics and oppositional ideas frequently
took shape. Once we focus our attention on the international flow of cultural capital,
however, even hemispheres begin to look rather small. Literary texts, songs, dance
moves, and performance companies circulating through the Atlantic world often
found their way to San Francisco, Honolulu, Hong Kong, Calcutta, Sydney, and
Auckland by the 1850s and 1860s. The number of "port cities" supporting US cultural exports quickly proliferated.

It also seems clear that antebellum cultural historians will continue to operate in
the vanguard of a much broader effort to stretch and enrich our understanding of
capitalist expansion. This effort, I would emphasize, is about as old as the cultural
turn itself. From sweeping, multigenerational studies of consumer culture and advertising, such as Richard Bushman's *Refinement of America* (1992) and Jackson Lears's
Fables of Abundance (1994), to more focused histories of particular consumer groups
and economic discourses, such as Michael Zakim's *Ready-Made Democracy* (2003)
and Scott Sandage's *Born Losers* (2005), antebellum cultural historians have long
explored the manifold ways in which antebellum market expansion played out at the
levels of identity, fashion, values, and even epistemology.

Yet we have engaged these fundamental questions with an equally diverse mix of
analytical strategies. Some have focused on market-driven changes in the production
and distribution of particular cultural forms (as in Denning's and Streeby's discussions
of early dime novels, or Nord's analysis of the American Bible Society). Others have
examined market expansion as a causal motor driving key shifts in antebellum race,
class, and gender relations (as in Halttunen's and Kasson's studies of middle-class
respectability, or Saxton's and Roediger's treatments of working-class whiteness). Still
others have sought to explain the ideological impacts of market exchange through
close readings of particular social types, moral thresholds, and cultural practices (as
in Fabian's examination of gambling, or my own explorations of Barnum's fakery).

Especially helpful in recent scholarship has been the growing effort to integrate
the larger process of capitalist development (what we now often characterize as the
"market revolution") with more subtle changes in language, perception, identity, and

social ritual (issues often bundled together as "market relations"). A powerful case in point is Walter Johnson's recent history of the "antebellum slave market," *Soul by Soul* (1999), which quite deliberately casts its subject in ambiguous terms: both as a localized New Orleans institution on which large numbers of slaves and slaveholders left their individual marks, and as an even larger system of commodity exchange, which impacted upon countless facets of identity, consciousness, and social experience. In all of these different respects, Johnson's study provides a useful model for historians seeking to reconnect "the social" and "the cultural," "macro-history" and "micro-history," "material conditions" and "patterns of discourse." What Johnson helps us to imagine is a more nearly complete history of antebellum slavery, a history neither disembodied by the numbing blur of statistical categories, nor set apart from the brutal commerce which inevitably constrained individual acts of will and agency.

Finally, I suspect that cultural historians will have much more to say in the future about the wide variety of antebellum individuals who explicitly chose to position themselves outside of, or in opposition to, the era's dominant moral, social, and political orders. The potential stakes (and dangers) of such willful iconoclasm can be glimpsed more clearly in a number of recent studies. In Martha Hodes's *White Women, Black Men* (1997) and Jonathan Ned Katz's *Love Stories* (2001), for example, we enter into the barely visible social worlds inhabited by so-called "amalgamationists" and "sodomites," whose most intimate choices about love, sex, and friendship were routinely condemned as moral "abominations." Similarly, in Patricia Cline Cohen's *The Murder of Helen Jewett* (1998), Helen Lefkowitz Horowitz's *Rereading Sex* (2002), and Jackson Lears's *Something for Nothing* (2003), we begin to appreciate why the "sporting men" who populated antebellum boxing arenas, race tracks, and gambling dens were often perceived as such a fundamental threat. At once within the white-collar professions and gleefully defiant of their ideological strictures, the antebellum sporting fraternity embodied a possibility almost unthinkable in national reform circles: namely, that large numbers of cash-carrying white men would demonstrate little interest in the normative doctrines of domestic virtue, moral self-discipline, and strict racial segregation.

Moving through a very different range of antebellum institutions, Paul Goodman's *Of One Blood* (1998) and John Stauffer's *Black Hearts of Men* (2002) illuminate long-neglected social relationships and political alliances that took shape across the color line. On a very basic level, these books help us to think beyond the conceptual monolith of antebellum "whiteness," demonstrating a multiplicity of racial identities and sympathies articulated by anti-slavery artisans, farmers, and philanthropists. At the same time, Goodman and Stauffer help us to imagine a more richly textured history of the origins of racial equality, a history that inevitably included political conventions, courtrooms, and abolitionist newspapers, but also fleeting acts of grassroots collaboration and localized sociability. It is to these more quotidian forms of interracial exchange that future studies promise to address themselves.

REFERENCES

Adams, B.: *E Pluribus Barnum: The Great Showman and the Making of US Popular Culture* (Minneapolis: University of Minnesota Press, 1997).

Allen, R.: *Horrible Prettiness: Burlesque and American Culture* (Chapel Hill: University of North Carolina Press, 1991).

Brodhead, R.: *Cultures of Letters: Scenes of Reading and Writing in Nineteenth-Century America* (Chicago: University of Chicago Press, 1993).

Brooks, D.: *Bodies in Dissent: Spectacular Performances of Race and Freedom, 1850–1910* (Durham, NC: Duke University Press, 2006).

Bushman, R.: *The Refinement of America: Persons, Houses, Cities* (New York: Vintage Books, 1992).

Casper, S.: *Constructing American Lives: Biography and Culture in Nineteenth-Century America* (Chapel Hill: University of North Carolina Press, 1999).

Cockrell, D.: *Demons of Disorder: Early Blackface Minstrels and Their World* (Cambridge: Cambridge University Press, 1997).

Cockrell, D., ed.: *Excelsior: Journals of the Hutchinson Family Singers* (Stuyvesant, NY: Pendragon Press, 1989).

Cohen, P.: *The Murder of Helen Jewett* (New York: Alfred A. Knopf, 1998).

Cook, J.: *The Arts of Deception: Playing with Fraud in the Age of Barnum* (Cambridge, MA: Harvard University Press, 2001).

Cook, J., ed.: *The Colossal P. T. Barnum Reader* (Urbana: University of Illinois Press, 2005).

Denning, M.: *Mechanic Accents: Dime Novels and Working-Class Culture in America* (London: Verso, 1987).

Dudden, F.: *Women in the American Theater: Actresses and Audiences, 1790–1870* (New Haven, CT: Yale University Press, 1994).

Emerson, K.: *DOO-DAH! Stephen Foster and the Rise of American Popular Culture* (New York: Da Capo Press, 1998).

Fabian, A.: *Card Sharps, Dream Books, and Bucket Shops: Gambling in Nineteenth-Century America* (Ithaca, NY: Cornell University Press, 1990).

Foster, F.: *Written by Herself: Literary Production by African American Women, 1746–1892* (Bloomington: Indiana University Press, 1993).

Goodman, P.: *Of One Blood: Abolitionism and the Origins of Racial Equality* (Berkeley: University of California Press, 1998).

Gorn, E.: *The Manly Art: Bare-Knuckle Prize Fighting in America* (Ithaca, NY: Cornell University Press, 1986).

Greenberg, K.: *Honor and Slavery* (Princeton: Princeton University Press, 1996).

Grimsted, D.: *Melodrama Unveiled: American Theater and Culture* (Chicago: University of Chicago Press, 1968).

Gutierrez, R.: *When Jesus Came, the Corn Mothers Went Away: Marriage, Sexuality, and Power in New Mexico, 1500–1846* (Palo Alto, CA: Stanford University Press, 1991).

Halttunen, K.: *Confidence Men and Painted Women: A Study of Middle-Class Culture in America* (New Haven, CT: Yale University Press, 1982).

Harris, L.: *In the Shadow of Slavery: African Americans in New York City, 1626–1863* (Chicago: University of Chicago Press, 2003).

Harris, N.: *Humbug: The Art of P. T. Barnum* (Boston: Little, Brown, 1973).

Hatch, N.: *The Democratization of American Christianity* (New Haven, CT: Yale University Press, 1989).

Hodes, M.: *White Women, Black Men: Illicit Sex in the 19th-Century South* (New Haven, CT: Yale University Press, 1997).

Horowitz, H. L.: *Rereading Sex: Battles over Sexual Knowledge and Suppression in Nineteenth-Century America* (New York: Alfred A. Knopf, 2002).

Johnson, P.: *A Shopkeeper's Millennium: Society and Revivals in Rochester, New York, 1815–1837* (New York: Hill & Wang, 1978).

Johnson, P.: *Sam Patch, The Famous Jumper* (New York: Hill & Wang, 2003).

Johnson, S.: *Roaring Camp: The Social World of the California Gold Rush* (New York: W. W. Norton, 2000).

Johnson, W.: *Soul by Soul: Life Inside the Antebellum Slave Market* (Cambridge, MA: Harvard University Press, 1999).

Joyner, C.: *Down by the Riverside: A South Carolina Slave Community* (Urbana: University of Illinois Press, 1984).

Kasson, J.: *Rudeness and Civility: Manners in Nineteenth-Century America* (New York: Hill & Wang, 1991).

Katz, J. N.: *Love Stories: Sex between Men before Homosexuality* (Chicago: University of Chicago Press, 2001).

Kelley, M.: *Private Woman, Public Stage: Literary Domesticity in Nineteenth-Century America* (New York: Oxford University Press, 1984).

Lears, J.: *Fables of Abundance: A Cultural History of Advertising in America* (New York: Basic Books, 1994).

Lears, J.: *Something for Nothing: Luck in America* (New York: Viking, 2003).

Lehuu, I.: *Carnival on the Page: Popular Print Media in Antebellum America* (Chapel Hill: University of North Carolina Press, 2000).

Levine, L.: *Black Culture and Black Consciousness: Afro-American Folk Thought from Slavery to Freedom* (New York: Oxford University Press, 1977).

Levine, L.: *Highbrow/Lowbrow: The Emergence of Cultural Hierarchy in America* (Cambridge, MA: Harvard University Press, 1988).

Lhamon, Jr., W. T.: *Raising Cain: Blackface Performance from Jim Crow to Hip Hop* (Cambridge, MA: Harvard University Press, 1998).

Lhamon, Jr., W. T., ed.: *Jump Jim Crow: Lost Plays, Lyrics, and Street Prose of the First Atlantic Popular Culture* (Cambridge, MA: Harvard University Press, 2003).

Linebaugh, P. & Rediker, M.: *The Many-Headed Hydra: Sailors, Slaves, Commoners, and the Hidden History of the Revolutionary Atlantic* (Boston, MA: Beacon Press, 2001).

Lott, E.: *Love and Theft: Blackface Minstrelsy and the American Working Class* (New York: Oxford University Press, 1993).

McConachie, B.: *Melodramatic Formations: American Theatre & Society, 1820–1870* (Iowa City: University of Iowa Press, 1992).

Meer, S.: *Uncle Tom Mania: Slavery, Minstrelsy and Transatlantic Culture in the 1850s* (Athens: University of Georgia Press, 2005).

Moore, R.: *Selling God: American Religion in the Marketplace of Culture* (New York: Oxford University Press, 1994).

Morgan, D.: *Protestants and Pictures: Religion, Visual Culture, and the Age of American Mass Production* (New York: Oxford University Press, 1999).

Nord, D.: *Faith in Reading: Religious Publishing and the Birth of Mass Media in America* (New York: Oxford University Press, 2004).

Painter, N.: *Sojourner Truth: A Life, a Symbol* (New York: W. W. Norton, 1996).

Peterson, C.: *"Doers of the Word": African-American Women Speakers and Writers in the North, 1830–1880* (New York: Oxford University Press, 1995).

Raboteau, A.: *Slave Religion: The "Invisible Institution" in the Antebellum South* (New York: Oxford University Press, 1978).

Roach, J.: *Cities of the Dead: Circum-Atlantic Performance* (New York: Columbia University Press, 1996).

Roediger, D.: *The Wages of Whiteness: Race and the Making of the American Working Class* (London: Verso, 1991).

Sandage, S.: *Born Losers: A History of Failure in America* (Cambridge, MA: Harvard University Press, 2005).

Saxton, A.: *The Rise and Fall of the White Republic: Class Politics and Mass Culture in Nineteenth-Century America* (London: Verso, 1990).

Sentilles, R.: *Performing Menken: Adah Isaacs Menken and the Birth of American Celebrity* (Cambridge: Cambridge University Press, 2003).

Smith-Rosenberg, C.: *Disorderly Conduct: Visions of Gender in Victorian America* (New York: Alfred A. Knopf, 1985).

Stansell, C.: *City of Women: Sex and Class in New York, 1789–1860* (New York: Alfred A. Knopf, 1986).

Stauffer, J.: *The Black Hearts of Men: Radical Abolitionists and the Transformation of Race* (Cambridge, MA: Harvard University Press, 2002).

Stott, R.: *Workers in the Metropolis: Class, Ethnicity, and Youth in Antebellum New York City* (Ithaca, NY: Cornell University Press, 1990).

Streeby, S.: *American Sensations: Class, Empire, and the Production of Popular Culture* (Berkeley: University of California Press, 2002).

Stuckey, S.: *Slave Culture: Nationalist Theory and the Foundations of Black America* (New York: Oxford University Press, 1987).

Stuckey, S.: *Going Through the Storm: The Influence of African American Art in History* (New York: Oxford University Press, 1994).

Tchen, J.: *New York before Chinatown: Orientalism and the Shaping of American Culture, 1776–1882* (Baltimore: Johns Hopkins University Press, 1999).

White, D.: *Ar'n't I a Woman? Female Slaves in the Plantation South* (New York: W. W. Norton, 1985).

White, G. & White, S.: *Stylin': African American Expressive Culture from Its Beginnings to the Zoot Suit* (Ithaca, NY: Cornell University Press, 1998).

White, S.: *Stories of Freedom in Black New York* (Cambridge, MA: Harvard University Press, 2002).

Wilentz, S.: *Chants Democratic: New York City and the Rise of the American Working Class, 1788–1850* (New York: Oxford University Press, 1984).

Wilmeth, D. & Bigsby, C., eds.: *Cambridge History of American Theatre*, Volume 1: *Beginnings to 1870* (New York: Cambridge University Press, 1998).

Zakim, M.: *Ready-Made Democracy: A History of Men's Dress in the American Republic, 1760–1860* (Chicago: University of Chicago Press, 2003).

Zboray, R.: *A Fictive People: Antebellum Economic Development and the American Reading Public* (New York: Oxford University Press, 1993).

Chapter Six

RELIGION AND REFORM

Lewis Perry

Participants in social movements sometimes feel that the significance of their actions will elude scholars and get lost from public memory. In his *History of American Socialisms* (1870), John Humphrey Noyes pointed to a connection between the rise of utopian communities, like the successful one he founded and led in Oneida, New York, and the spread of religious revivals in America. The revivalists' "great idea" was the regeneration of the soul, while communitarians advanced to the grand project of regenerating society. Looking back to the early 1830s, Noyes believed Americans had come "as near to a surrender of all to the Kingdom of Heaven" as they came, a decade later, to a new "Age of Harmony." Admittedly, neither the Millennium nor earthly harmony had been realized, but as a result of these two movements, "a yearning toward social reconstruction" was implanted in "the continuous, permanent, inner experience of the American people." Yet memories of the sources of that yearning grew dim. Noyes explained the fading of memory as a kind of repression:

> a man's deepest experiences are those of religion and love; and these are the experiences in respect to which he is most apt to be ashamed, and most inclined to be silent. So the nation says but little, and tries to think that it thinks but little, about its Revivals and its Socialisms; but they are nevertheless the deepest and most interesting passages of its history, and worth more study as determinatives of character and destiny, than all its politics and diplomacies, its money matters and its wars. (Noyes 1966 [1870]: 24–7)

To say that the American people forgot entirely about revivalism would surely be an exaggeration. After all, both Confederate and Union armies experienced revivals during the Civil War. Still, there is truth in Noyes's depiction of later generations' repression of once-cherished enthusiasm for the transforming power of religion. The Civil War isolated or cut short pacifist, feminist, communitarian, and other movements that a decade earlier had seized attention and gained adherents. After the war, urban growth and industrial change submerged the intense religious excitement that Noyes remembered with so much feeling. When postwar chronicles and memoirs took note of the religious fervor of an earlier time, they frequently spoke of fads and foibles, eccentricity, and charlatanism. In the historical profession that emerged in the late nineteenth and early twentieth century, influential professors revived charges

once voiced in pro-slavery defenses – that northern states with their excessive freedom
had been vulnerable to fanaticism, sometimes relatively harmless, but in its openness
to anti-slavery agitation dangerous to the nation. To the proponents of the major
historiographical movement of the first half of the twentieth century – the Progressives – religion and utopian socialism were, at best, distractions from more important
matters of sectionalism and economic cleavages. For the most part, progressive
America regarded revivalism as backward, rural, and anti-intellectual. It was a relic of
a passing era. In the 1930s and 1940s some writers began to praise reform movements, without much reference to their religious origins, as precursors of liberalism
and secular humanitarianism.

Amid prevailing traditions of US historical writing that neglected reform or linked
it to liberalism, some of the most influential works on the subject have taken a form
that Noyes might have predicted: they are recoveries and reassertions of the significance of religion. The outstanding early example was Gilbert Hobbs Barnes's 1933
reinterpretation of what he called "the antislavery impulse" (Barnes 1964 [1933]).
An economist who previously co-authored a textbook on social scientific ways of
thinking, Barnes was an unlikely scholar to criticize accounts of anti-slavery that
emphasized economic factors and to celebrate the workings of religious zeal as
"incomparably more significant." But he had found a trunk full of letters revealing
the story of a previously little-known figure, Theodore Dwight Weld, who, in Barnes's
treatment, deserved recognition as the most heroic and influential figure in the history
of the anti-slavery movement. Prior to his anti-slavery work as an organizer and
orator, Weld had been converted by the great revivalist Charles Grandison Finney
and served as Finney's assistant in one of America's grand eruptions of evangelical
fervor. Weld's *The Bible against Slavery* (1838) enunciated the message of slavery's
fundamental sinfulness that he instructed agents of the American Anti-Slavery Society
to spread across the North. After Barnes's resurrection of this forgotten hero, a link
between revivalism and anti-slavery reform was firmly established. It was significant,
however, that Barnes dedicated his book to one of his teachers, Ulrich B. Phillips,
the most prominent scholarly defender of southern race relations, and intensified
vilification of the radical abolitionist William Lloyd Garrison by elevating Weld against
his example. Though flawed and discredited as an account of factionalism in the
anti-slavery movement, Barnes's work remains a milestone in the study of religion
and reform. It was the first of many studies to reveal, often with notable excitement,
the importance of evangelical religious conviction in stirring Americans to social
compassion and fiery confrontations with sin. Especially influential have been biographies of Garrison, Lewis Tappan, and numerous other reformers (Mayer 1998;
Wyatt-Brown 1969; Walker 1978).

Barnes described his *Antislavery Impulse* to a skeptical friend as disproving the
view that "no revival of religion had or could produce a social movement of intrinsic
importance." In introducing a reissue of the book, William G. McLoughlin, a leading
religious historian of a later generation, convincingly placed Barnes among a cohort
of intellectuals who began in the 1930s to reject the genteel Protestant view that
regarded religious fervor with suspicion, social scientific orthodoxies that treated
religion solely as a product of social forces, and most of all, the derogatory attitudes
toward "puritanical" strains in American culture that had become fashionable in literary circles. Among theologians, this change was voiced clearly in H. Richard Niebuhr's

The Kingdom of God in America (1988 [1937]), which moved away from the socio-logical approach of his previous work and explored ideas of God's kingdom that had kept Christianity from becoming a mere function of culture, while renewing interest in the great doctrines and traditions of the Christian past and motivating successive generations of Christian believers to seek social reform in their times. In a chapter on abolitionism as exemplifying the millennial aspirations of pre-Civil War Americans, Niebuhr relied significantly on Barnes's portrait of Weld. The point in placing Barnes's work in the context of shifting intellectual attitudes toward religion is not that Barnes's personal religious views – about which we know little – distorted his presentation or argument. The point, rather, is that cultural changes under way at the time Barnes wrote facilitated more open-minded assessment of the religious experiences and quests of antebellum American reformers. This was part of a larger scholarly development sometimes called "the recovery" of American religious history (Loveland 1997).

But if historians' explorations of religion were freed from embarrassment or defen-siveness, they still took place in a professional milieu that was generally secular. In one sense, it had to be secular to include researchers who were by no means united in having a religious viewpoint, let alone a common faith, even as they participated in common inquiries in US history. In fact, readers of historical works generally know little of the religious faith, or unbelief, of their authors; and criticism of historical works in professional journals never engages in theological disputation. But the pro-fessional milieu was secular in a second sense. Regardless of the recovery of religion in history, academic communities retained many vestiges of earlier decades' suspicion of mixing religious fervor with public affairs. In his preface to a valuable anthology of scholarly writings on antebellum reform, David Brion Davis noted a continuing gulf between scholarly culture and religious motives. The subject was "uncongenial to twentieth-century scholars," he observed, because "most of the early reformers were devout Protestants whose public expressions of piety have appeared sanctimo-nious" to intellectuals who "equated social progress with secular, rational thought." To a society favoring permissiveness, tolerance, and pragmatic problem solving, "no traits appear more offensive and dangerous than sentimental piety and moral self-righteousness" (Davis 1967: 1–2).

About the personal faith of most scholars mentioned in this essay we know nothing, but one important exception is Timothy L. Smith, son of two "holiness preachers and friends of reform" (as he described them), who was himself a Nazarene pastor and revivalist, a Harvard PhD and leading figure in the recovery of religious history, and author in 1957 of *Revivalism and Social Reform*. This second milestone in the recovery of religion in the history of reform acknowledged Barnes's role in charting a course away from the prejudices of early twentieth-century intellectuals who took "great delight in pillorying religion." Too many historians had accepted uncritically the radical abolitionists' "strange libel" that the churches were the bul-warks of slavery; to the contrary, "the decisive body of Northern anti-slavery senti-ment lay in the hearts of moderate Christians." *Revivalism and Social Reform* was one of the last scholarly histories to view the Civil War as caused by avoidable blunders (Smith 1980 [1957]: 179–80). But the slavery controversy was not at the heart of this book, which proposed a new interpretation of American Protestantism in the 1840s and 1850s, one that looked at popular writings rather than intellectual treatises, focused on urban life rather than frontier challenges, took note of large numbers of Methodists, Baptists, Disciples of Christ, and other evangelicals in addition to the more-often-studied Congregationalists and Presbyterians, and called attention to incessant revivalism throughout the period, culminating in a great crest of revivals across the North in 1857–8 that some observers called an American Pentecost. For Smith, revivalism gave converts something more than an escape from eternal damnation; it raised expectations of living at a higher level of holiness, or perfection, almost always leading to a drive for righteousness – for aid to the poor, for women's rights (at least in religion), for peace, for temperance. Smith found fault with historians who attributed the social gospel movement, decades later, solely to responses to new social conditions and thereby overlooked important continuities with pre-Civil War holiness movements. For example, the Five Points Mission established in one of the poorest sections of New York City in 1850 by Phoebe Palmer, a beloved Methodist leader and author of widely read books on holiness, was a prototype of settlement houses in the Progressive era. And holiness leaders of the 1850s sounded a call for the Kingdom of God on earth as hopefully as did the Social Gospellers 50 years later.

In many ways Smith's emphasis on popular religion outside the supposed Puritan mainstream was ahead of its time. Certainly his view of revivalism anticipated the direction of later scholarship. At the time when he wrote, some scholars – Barnes's celebration of Weld's romantic heroism is a good example – referred to "the Revival" as unique and singular. But that was to ignore memories of "awakenings" and "outpourings" that had surged up and down North America for over a century. One common view of revivals held that they inevitably were ephemeral and left communities burned out after they subsided. But Smith found no evidence that spiritual excitements in the West or East before 1820 "ever burned out," and he added (by his own account, "with some sense of wonder") that "seasons of intense religious interest and measures to promote their frequent recurrence in local congregations became increasingly characteristic of the religious life of all the major American Protestant denominations from 1820 onward" (1980 [1957]: 254). This was to anticipate a view of evangelicalism, in all its varieties, as a major component of American democratic culture that now prevails in US scholarship (Hatch 1989; Dayton & Johnson 1991).

In a model study of repeated crests of religious enthusiasm and radical movements, Whitney Cross had already traced the transformation of regional culture in trans-Appalachian New York by round after round of religious excitement. He emphasized that religious ferment in New York had yielded "luxuriant new growths" including Mormonism, Adventism, spiritualism, and Noyes's Oneida as well as other utopias (Cross 1965 [1950]). In current literature on antebellum evangelicalism, the sources and outgrowths of revivalism include major movements in American religion, like the Baptists and Methodists, which had been previously neglected. Voluntary societies are likely to be presented, alongside revivals, as elements in "the evangelical arsenal" that mobilized Americans and reorganized their nation. Rather than attributing momentous consequences to specific revival campaigns, historians today are likely to speak more broadly of a sustained "evangelical surge" (Noll 2002: 161, 182). While the links to reform movements remain important, such consequences as doubling the active Protestant population and introducing religious themes into political life have demanded attention they never really received before (Carwardine 1997).

A perennial issue throughout the changes in scholarship concerns the charge that religious reform was a form of "social control." A half-century ago, this charge was stated powerfully in a prize-winning graduate-student essay by Clifford Griffin on the leaders of great national interdenominational societies founded in the decade after the War of 1812 (Griffin 1957). These "benevolent" organizations, dubbed by scholars "the evangelical united front," have long been regarded as a base point in the development of antebellum reform. They are the same organizations that more recent scholarship assigns to the evangelical arsenal. But Griffin identified their leaders with political Federalism and old-line denominations appalled by urban growth, westward migration, and democratic upheaval. Their campaigns to educate clergymen, distribute Bibles and moral tracts, and support home missions, in his view, reflected hopes to prevent crime and immorality in the tumultuous republic and to shore up a semblance of hierarchical authority, religious orthodoxy, and respect for law and order. Other movements joining the united front, notably those promoting temperance and supporting penitentiaries, enhanced the argument that the motives behind "reform" were repressive. Griffin's article was laced with the leaders' frank commentary about their fears and intentions, including the goal of keeping the poor and working classes "pacified." Later scholars highlighted distinctions reformers made between worthy, independent working families and dissolute, dangerous, poor people on whom charity would be wasted (though their children might deserve to be rescued from their control). Some have interpreted the revivals themselves as powerful mechanisms of social control over an emerging industrial workforce (Johnson 1978).

The view of religious benevolence as social control has been challenged repeatedly. In the case of antebellum reform movements, Griffin may have overemphasized the leaders' ties to the privileges of a fading social order; yet linking reform societies to an emerging evangelical order does not remove their goals of creating orderly, sober, moral citizens – in short, goals that could be called social control. Especially valuable is an essay by Conrad Edick Wright on "Charitable Motivations and Historical Writing" (it appears as an appendix in Wright 1992), which takes a calm, measured look at social control's many critics, some of whom reject any endeavor to understand religious and reform movements in sociological or psychological terms, especially if they wind up depicting philanthropists and reformers of an earlier day as cynical oppressors of the unfortunate. Wright challenges the accuracy of much that social-control scholars have said, but he does not dismiss out of hand the view that reforms aimed at shoring up social stability and inculcating habits and values that were civically useful. One might conclude that Griffin, especially in his youthful article, chose his quotations selectively, but he did show voluminous evidence of fear that social order in the new republic was unraveling. We may thank Wright for rejecting the false dichotomy that reforms must be motivated either by religious faith or by social and economic motives.

"Benevolence" was an historically important turning point in its own right. There is wide scholarly agreement that new conceptions of benevolence and sin made possible the proliferation of reform. Usually these new conceptions are traced to the eighteenth-century New England Calvinist theologian Samuel Hopkins, for whom true holiness meant complete selflessness, including a willingness to be damned, if need be, for God's glory. What linked Hopkins's "New Divinity," as it was called, to earthly reform was belief in the approaching millennium, which he portrayed as an age of peace and justice. Griffin's essay provoked so much discussion of social control that it is easy to forget his recognition that Hopkins and the New Divinity were fundamental to the evangelical united front. Reform leaders, he explained, believed that sanctified and benevolent persons experienced "an infinite concern for other people's souls" that motivated them to try to save and improve others (1957: 426). Timothy Smith pointed out a "kinship between 'Hopkinsianism' and the Methodist doctrine of perfect love" running through the nineteenth century (1980 [1957]: 160). Conrad Wright's essay on "Charitable Motivations" explains that disinterested benevolence became a cherished and practiced belief, not just of Hopkins and the New England Puritan tradition, but of Americans of many religious persuasions.

Hopkins's place in the history of Puritan theology is well understood, but it is not so easy to account for the influence of his "Consistent Calvinism" in nineteenth-century reform. His ideas originated in the religious life of congregations clinging to an old system in revolutionary times; were simplified through discussion from the pulpits of other ministers; and spread widely throughout the evangelical culture of antebellum America. In practical terms, the New Divinity discarded an overwhelming sense of original sin that could leave many Christians resigned to their sinfulness and discouraged from seeking holiness. As Richard W. Fox has recently explained, Hopkins (and his interpreters) redefined sin as "an array of discrete wrongful acts rather than a general condition against which natural resistance was futile." Thus a person could "chip away" at his or her own sinfulness in progressive steps. Besides the individual significance of the benevolent disposition to succor and improve others, there was a social dimension to the redefinition of sin. For society, too, sins could be combated one by one as institutions improved, evils were eliminated, and progress was made toward the kingdom of God on earth. In short, the New Divinity, in Fox's terms, "helped spark an era of broad social reform in America" (Fox 2004: 143). Such a redefinition underlay one important feature of American reform: its division into a multitude of separate reform societies, some of which might be called conservative or at least preoccupied with social order. But more radical reforms, including the elimination of slavery, and more exalted visions of a renovated world were also features of the millennial social order that Hopkins depicted.

The emergence of radicalism in the second quarter of the nineteenth century is another perennial issue in the study of antebellum reform. In an illuminating 1965 essay, John L. Thomas pointed out that radical reform "traced its origins to a religious impulse which was both politically and socially conservative." Like others discussed here, Thomas started with reformers' adoption of the idea of individual perfectibility in place of intractable human sinfulness. "Romantic" is his preferred term for humanitarian radicals who proceeded to view human nature as a "reservoir" of possibilities to be released rather than evil tendencies to be repressed. In its assault on oppressive social institutions, romanticism has been called "spilt religion" (Thomas took this definition of romanticism from the early twentieth-century English essayist T. E. Hulme). Conversion experiences much like those that occurred in revivals hit some individuals when they discovered suffering, injustice, and oppression that others dismissed as inevitable. "With the sudden transference of a vague perfectionist faith in self-improvement to urgent social problems there emerged a new type of social reformer whose whole life became identified with the reform process." In short, Thomas showed the usefulness of regarding reformers as a type extending and revising Christian beliefs in a time of rapid social change. Certainly some reformers assumed a role in society that gave them extraordinary freedom to redefine their lives while promoting bold changes in human society. Thomas quotes, for example, the experimental educator Bronson Alcott as a self-proclaimed "true reformer" who "studied man as he is from the hand of the Creator, and not as he is made by the errors of the world" (Thomas 1965: 656–7, 663–4).

Robert Abzug's *Cosmos Crumbling* – currently the single most important study of the reform impulse – analyzes the role of the reformer in greater depth. A sharp opponent of social science "reductionism" in the study of reform, Abzug foregrounds the individual reformer's quest for personal holiness and a sacred social order. He characterizes American reformers as "religious virtuosos" (a term adapted from Max Weber) – that is, as individuals with hearts and minds attuned to sacred rather than mundane considerations. Though overwhelmingly Protestant and notably individualistic, they were "voluntary orphans," similar to monks and mystics in other societies, in their alienation from the business of ordinary life and their dream of "sacralizing all the world's order in accordance with God's plan" (Abzug 1994: 4). Abzug highlights examples of exalted views of social transformation expressed by reformers who might be considered conservative, such as William Alcott, who commenced his career atop a Connecticut hill envisioning a "new world" and pledging "new dependence on God, and on his natural and moral elements." A prolific and influential writer, Alcott was one of several "moral physiologists" who sought to create a "neo-Mosaic law," a system of health and domestic principles obeyed in a spirit of everyday piety (1994: 169, 171). Frequently, as Abzug shows, campaigns for stricter adherence to principle led to divisions in the ranks of reformers over issues like Sabbath observance and total abstinence from alcoholic beverages well before such notoriously "ultra" reforms as absolute pacifism, immediate abolition, and women's rights made their appearance. Abzug's gallery of religious virtuosity also features memorable portraits of defiant individualism and radical social criticism. In 1836, Angelina Grimké took a stance of civil disobedience regarding society's laws that upheld slavery: "If a law commands me to *sin I will break it*; if it calls me to *suffer*, I will let it take its course *unresistingly*." The next year, distinguishing between woman's subjection to God and domination by men, Sarah Grimké wrote: "All I ask of our brethren is, that they will take their feet from off our necks, and permit us to stand upright on the ground which God designed us to occupy" (Abzug 1994: 211, 216).

Romantic reformers have for several decades been favorites of historians. Among those whom Thomas mentions, Dorothea Dix, Samuel Gridley Howe, and Horace Mann were notably successful in their advocacy of improved rights and conditions for the insane, for the deaf and dumb, and for schoolchildren, respectively (Gollaher 1995; Gitter 2001; Grasso 2002). Some of the best-known American writers, including Henry David Thoreau and Walt Whitman, have their place in romantic radicalism. Theodore Parker attracted many followers, and outraged evangelicals, with a radical theology and commitment to reform that did not rest on literal readings of the Bible (Grodzins 2002). New departures in anti-slavery, feminism, temperance agitation, and utopian communities are also part of the story.

Yet it would be misleading to describe reform movements as at their core made up of defiant individuals at odds with mainstream institutions. One point easily overlooked in histories of reform is the frequent failure of exceptional radicals to convert their associates. Abzug suggests, for example, that "business proved an important locus of creative religious virtuosity" and focuses attention on the merchant brothers Lewis and Arthur Tappan, who were "virtuosos bent on sacralizing all of their own business practices and the world in which they traded" (1994: 106–7). They dressed modestly, required clerks to reside in Christian boardinghouses, held morning prayer meetings in the workplace, and gave substantial funds to new churches, especially in New York City, where Finney came to lead a reformation of America's commercial capital. They were major benefactors of reform societies of the evangelical united front who moved on to take radical positions on total abstinence from alcohol and the immediate abolition of slavery (though they rejected the "ultra" stands on woman's rights and absolute pacifism that other abolitionists were promoting by the 1840s). The Tappans were absolutely central figures in the evolution of reform – ultras who resisted the further ultraism of others, "powerful actors" (as Abzug calls them) of considerable influence in American reform and religion. But to say that they were not representative of business is to state the obvious; more important, much of evangelical reform did not follow their lead on alcohol and slavery. In popular culture, they were despised and ridiculed for their insensitivity to the aspirations exhibited in the working classes' own temperance movement. In a second example of the resistance within reform's empire to new departures, Abzug observes that despite their "powerful arguments," the Grimkés at a key juncture in the late 1830s "could not even convince all their female comrades that woman's rights needed to be agitated as a separate issue" (1994: 224). The point is simply this: a fissure developed over radical perfectionism, and historians have paid more attention to those who embraced reform as revolutionary in principle than to those who existed comfortably in the evangelical empire created in the years after 1815. Scholars have favored the forces of change and neglected the existence of a reform universe that continued in its own way to be orthodox and businesslike.

Reform societies collected moneys, hired agents, issued publications, made investments, dispensed funds, elected officers, held meetings, sponsored social events, and engaged in other activities that left a public record, but historians have been far less interested in the business of reform than in public speeches by leading reformers. Anne M. Boylan's *The Origins of Women's Activism* is the outstanding exception. Through meticulous reconstruction and analysis of the records of dozens of women's benevolent organizations in New York and Boston, as well as further research to identify over a thousand officers and participants in these organizations, Boylan reveals overlooked dimensions of reform. When small groups of women first organized in the 1790s to raise money to help poor widows, to place children in orphanages, or to support missionary work or the education of ministers, they "forever altered the social field in which women could undertake collective religious, political, ideological, and economic activities" (Boylan 2002: 218). After 1812, women's organizations took on even more explicitly evangelical purposes: women played key roles in raising funds, selling Bibles, superintending Sunday Schools, visiting homes of the poor, and other activities essential to the benevolent empire that Griffin had reduced to social control. Boylan has assembled impressive accounts of the activities of women like Lydia Morris Shields Malcolm, who after her "new birth" in 1818 in Philadelphia served as a house visitor to the poor, manager of a society to distribute Bibles and a Baptist female education society, and superintendent of a Sunday school for black children; after her marriage to a Baptist minister in Boston she ran the girls' department of his new church's Sunday school, headed the maternal association, joined a Boston Bible society, and became directress of the Boston Infant School Society. Thus, she was able to express her religious conversion and conviction in a long series of organizational involvements. But careers like hers did not result in declarations of freedom from human conventions that might fit a pattern of romantic virtuosity. If sewing societies, tract societies, Sunday schools, or orphanage committees helped mark out a place for women in civil society, it was a circumscribed place that stressed subservience to God's authority and offered slight challenge to conventional understandings of "woman's sphere." Furthermore, though benevolent women made some claims for women's special sensitivity to issues vital to the common weal, their organizations generally excluded immigrant, African American, and Catholic women. Women from those groups set up their own organizations, but their efforts were never as well funded or influential, and one consequence was that in US cities the "chasms" separating women of different social backgrounds were deepened, rather than bridged, by benevolence (Boylan 2002: 218).

After years of assuming that early nineteenth-century women's organizations led directly, if not immediately, toward women's-rights activism, historians have come to see the picture as much more complex. Boylan's work adds instructively to the complexity. It is true that the first wave of women's organizations, starting in the 1790s, overcame objections that it was "unnatural" for "frail feeble women" in societies to do what wives individually could not do: for example, raise and invest funds, manage property, seek legal corporate status, bring suits, or employ workers. But they did not stretch this victory into a critique of gender or marital relations. They did not challenge the clergy's male preserve; they subordinated their voluntary careers to familial duties, raised funds to educate male clergymen, created male advisory boards, and in their internal governance preferred to elect married women – referred to as Mrs. – rather than single ones (except for the post of treasurer because of laws restricting married women's control of property). Yet they also moved their organizations outside the home and "opened up an arena of feminine action that was neither strictly familial nor wholly public" (Boylan 2002: 91). In a second wave of women's activism, 1812–20, marked by enhanced evangelicalism, there was if anything diminished emphasis on republican equality and a redefinition of women's collective action as an extension of domesticity.

Only in a third wave, 1823–40, did some women's evangelical organizations tackle controversial social issues – prostitution, liquor dealing, and slavery, with gender inequality soon to follow. Some women justified participation in these campaigns for "moral reform" by referring to the precedents of previous organizations. It was too late to claim that, "our sphere of action is limited to private life exclusively"; if that were true, one editor announced, "we have long since left our own province and entered that of the other sex" (Boylan 2002: 37). Yet the petition campaigns of women abolitionists and anti-prostitution reformers met sharp criticism from prominent clergymen, who deplored "unnatural" claims of independence from men's authority and protection. Prominent female writers such as Catharine Beecher, who were also close to the benevolent societies, joined in denouncing activities they deemed alien to woman's character (Sklar 1973). Few women with experience in the established benevolent organizations accepted the new assertiveness or joined the new reform endeavors. Those few who did join "invariably" dropped out of the old societies – or were expelled (Boylan 2002: 44). By the late 1830s, when Boylan's book ends, conflicts over perfectionist theology and sexual equality had begun to divide even the ranks of moral reformers, as many declined to take a next step into woman's rights activism. In subsequent decades, according to one probing analysis of the changing meanings of benevolence, "faith in the moral transformation of American society" declined and was replaced by a new emphasis on efficient restraint of "the sins they had been unable to eradicate" (Ginzberg 1990: 100–1). Are we back at social control?

The demise of slavery is a remarkable and still rather unfamiliar story – and one that transcends the bounds of American reform movements. In broad terms, modern scholarship has shown that slavery was, until the mid-eighteenth century, largely accepted in Europe and its colonies as divinely justified and part of the natural order of society. Enlightenment ideals of liberty and equality challenged traditional views of slavery, but by far the leading sources of anti-slavery feeling and action were found among dissenting Protestants, especially at first the Quakers. After providing a chronological table that begins with stands taken by Societies of Friends in England and North America in the 1770s and 1780s, and concludes with the abolition of slavery in Cuba and Brazil in the 1880s, Robert William Fogel identifies what he calls the century of emancipation: "within the span of little more than a century, a system that had stood above criticism for 3,000 years was outlawed everywhere in the Western world." The violence of emancipation in Haiti, where a black population won liberation through bloody revolution, and in the United States, where slave owners "resorted to full-scale warfare to halt the abolitionist trend," was exceptional. "Probably the majority" of slaves were freed under "more or less peaceful conditions" – that is, conditions in which religious and Enlightenment ideals could influence political change (Fogel 1989: 205–7). There has been criticism of the scholarly consensus that slavery was long accepted as natural and above criticism: the enslaved, it is said, always felt moral objections to slavery. The role of the slaves in effecting their own emancipation has become a leading topic of scholarly inquiry and surely will be so for years to come. There is no doubt, however, that the existence of an abolitionist critique of slavery was vital to the slaves. Despite efforts to cordon off the American South from outside information, slaves learned that the institution that controlled their lives was under international attack.

Scholars have not defined the periods of anti-slavery as well as they have woman's activism. There has been relatively little treatment of US anti-slavery movements in the 30 years or so after the Revolution, and the most recent work, while mentioning religion's primary importance in motivating abolitionists, explicitly de-emphasizes religious history. Richard S. Newman provides a close study of the Pennsylvania Abolition Society, its social composition (primarily elite white men), and its cautious but sustained commitment to the cause of gradual emancipation through legislative petitions and legal action in the courts. He examines the Massachusetts Anti-Slavery Society of the 1830s as a contrasting example of a "more democratic and emotional sensibility" prevailing in a second wave of abolitionism that was particularly open to "grassroots activism" and took advantage of the "rising prominence of African Americans and women in the public sphere" (Newman 2002: 8, 173, 175). The tactical and ideological escape of second-wave abolitionists from the elitist caution of their predecessors constitutes the "transformation" in his title. Newman's attention to local societies certainly points to an important direction for future research. There is still much to be learned about changes in religious and political thought in the postrevolutionary decades, about the American Colonization Society – the national movement for anti-slavery in the post-1818 evangelical empire – and the role of northern blacks in urging approaches to emancipation that would be less deferential to authority and to the interests of the slave owners.

The religious goals and behavior of post-1830 abolitionists have been studied extensively in the years since Barnes's *Antislavery Impulse* and especially since the 1960s. We can outline here some major themes, while noting that there are still issues to probe, and suggest that the conflicts within abolitionism over politics and religion after 1840 were important enough to be considered signs of further "transformations." Some of the main points about post-1830 abolitionism were especially well made by Ronald G. Walters. In keeping with the line of scholarship that began with Barnes, Walters acknowledged the importance of revivalism in the lives of some abolitionists, but he stressed difficulties in defining the connections. To start with, a good many abolitionists came from Quaker, Unitarian, Calvinist, or other non-evangelical backgrounds. Furthermore, most people converted in revivals never became abolitionists, and those who did seldom did so immediately and often agonized over choosing between commitments to revivalism and the cause of the slave. They found themselves in conflict with Finney, who sought to keep abolitionism subsidiary to revivalism, and with other evangelists, who took little interest in social problems. Some moved toward abolitionism out of disillusionment with the individual self-absorption that the revivals fostered. Further disappointment followed the high hopes of the early 1830s that the churches would take a leading role in condemning the immorality of slaveholding (Walters 1976: chap. 3). Before long, some abolitionists were ready to denounce the clergy and the churches, as well as the mainstream benevolent and missionary organizations, as bulwarks of slavery. Despite schisms in the abolitionist movement and in major national denominations, efforts to persuade northern churches to take at least a moderate anti-slavery stance did not cease. Even after southern churches split from their northern counterparts, and even in the midst of the Civil War, few northern denominations could be moved to condemn slavery or endorse emancipation, let alone racial equality (McKivigan 1984).

Nevertheless, many scholars (including Smith, as we have seen) have criticized Garrison and other radical abolitionists for denouncing the churches – how was this supposed to win public opinion to the anti-slavery cause? – and some have regarded the radicals' estrangement from youthful religious enthusiasm as evidence of ironic failure (Stewart 1982). The radicals had an answer. To the charge that an uncompromising stand hindered anti-slavery, James Russell Lowell replied in 1849: "The fanaticism of the Abolitionists has retarded emancipation, just in the same way that Luther retarded the Reformation." In other editorials in the *National Anti-Slavery Standard*, Lowell insisted that "*true* religious sentiment" remained the strongest weapon against slavery and all other social evils but was too seldom found in "the Church as it is," in which the clergy, who no longer held the privileged social status of colonial times, were too timid to take positions in defiance of current prejudices. "They are no longer the only priests, and there are other pulpits than those in churches . . ." (Lowance 2003: 189–92). Lowell, a popular satiric poet who would soon hold a chair in literature at Harvard, was keenly sensitive to changes in American public discourse. Walters is one of a few scholars who take abolitionist criticism of the churches as indicative of important new tendencies in American life. He perceptively delineates an "on-going spiritual quest" in the lives of a "surprising number" of abolitionist men and women, one that did not cease with loss of confidence in the churches. For them, the "logic of reform" led to a preference for practical piety and a "religion of humanity" over sterile formalism. Walters quotes a great popular evangelist of the next generation, Henry Ward Beecher, in describing the American Anti-Slavery Society as "an uncanonical Church . . . of the very best and most apostolic kind" (1976: 52). Since one group of abolitionists broke from the churches and a second group failed to reform them, we may well conclude that abolitionists were out of touch with popular religious belief. That conclusion might be strengthened by Mark Noll's comprehensive "social history" of theology, which identifies an important "American synthesis," a compound of evangelical religion, republican political beliefs, and a commonsense approach to morals. By the 1830s, all three parts of this synthesis rested on agreement that the Bible could be simply understood in a "literal hermeneutic" and that it was the source of basic, invariable truths (Noll 2002: 17, 367–70, 379–80). The abolitionists argued fervently that God created all races of one blood and that slavery violated both God's distinction between human beings and conveyable property and the golden rule taught by Christ. However, their contention that slavery was sinful was rejected even by northerners who disliked the institution and wished to see it gradually disappear. Noll comes close to saying that abolitionists had, in the context of their times, no convincing way – short of an "intellectual high-wire act" – to deny that the Bible sanctioned slavery. Whenever they seemed to circumvent the plain facts of the Old Testament or proposed interpretations based on the spirit or overall development of Christianity, they collided with the "overwhelming public attitude" of literalism and "reverential, implicit deference" to the Bible (2002: 392–3). It should be clear that Noll is not criticizing the abolitionists; he writes with regret of the inadequacy of mainstream American theology to come to terms with the slavery crisis or the war. Other studies have shown that there was little novelty in the interminable arguments over the Bible and slavery, which ended in stalemates already familiar in the eighteenth century. The continuation of these arguments may be as significant as their futility. Still, it does seem strange that a nation proud of its republican mission and with a population transformed by Christian revivals resisted the argument that the Old Testament's rules applied to a bygone era. Although E. Brooks Holifield, in another recent survey of American theology, also finds it to have been wanting in times of crisis, he is less dismissive of anti-slavery reasoning. He suggests that the controversy did acquaint an "educated public" with new approaches to interpreting the Bible and that arguments over whether American slavery differed substantially from ancient precedents resulted in "some modest abolitionist victories," including some calls for reform of laws respecting slavery (Holifield 2003: 501, 504).

African American religion, long neglected by historians who complained of insufficient sources, has been the subject of outstanding scholarship in recent decades. Albert Raboteau's *Slave Religion*, a beautifully written and carefully argued study based on abundant evidence "from the mouths of former slaves," provides an excellent overview (Raboteau 1978). Unlike social scientists, who interpreted persistent African beliefs and practices as "static 'Africanisms' or as archaic 'retentions,'" he views them as evidence of the adaptability of African traditions to living religions forged by generations of enslaved people in the various societies of the New World. In the United States, with a naturally increasing slave population and comparatively few direct importations from Africa, African theology did not survive to the extent it did in Cuba, Haiti, and Brazil, but African folk beliefs and styles of singing and dancing would still be evident in worship of the Christian God in a religion that American slaves had made their own.

The conversion of African Americans to Christianity, especially evangelical Protestantism, effectively began with the Great Awakening of the mid-eighteenth century and became more widespread with the work of Methodist and Baptist revivalists, including black lay preachers, in the 1790s and thereafter. Many factors – the transiency of revivalists, illiteracy of preachers, increasing separation of black and white congregations, and secrecy of some slave meetings – made precise tallies of Christian affiliation impossible. But it is clear that the Christian theology, built on depictions of human sinfulness and alienation from the divine, had little appeal to the slaves. Few if any scholars doubt the importance of the conversion of the slaves to a syncretic Christianity, in which they identified themselves as a people like the Hebrews once delivered from captivity in Egypt and in which they cherished hope for liberty, fulfillment, and reunification with loved ones in a place and time not too far off. Did this vision of a world "over Jordan" dampen the slaves' rebelliousness, as some masters believed and critics have charged? Raboteau assembles a wealth of evidence of slaves' rejection of the hypocritical Christianity promoted by white masters. Although the slaves' Christianity may only occasionally have motivated armed rebellions – never after 1831 – it provided an inner world in which to hold onto their own values and scorn those their masters sought to impose. In a recent and now-indispensable book on rural slave culture, Steven Hahn builds on the work of Raboteau and other scholars to describe a general pattern of religious life while explaining that what the slaves created was not exactly a unified religion. "Each slave community appears to have devised its own customs and rituals, some displaying the traditions of West Africa, some the forms of evangelical denominations, some the imprint of American republicanism, and some a complex combination of each." Instead of asking whether slaves were rebellious, Hahn examines a broader, uneven struggle in rural slave communities to "contest and transform the relations of domination under which they lived" (Hahn 2003: 51).

Historians have been frustrated in searching for links or similarities between rural slave culture and black Christianity in the North, where ministers often wrote in traditional denominational veins, including Calvinism, and black protest leaders, many of them clergy, promoted a reform ideology emphasizing morality, improvement, and respectability (Rael 2002; Holifield 2003). The problem surely deserves more exploration, but it should not be exaggerated. Fugitive slaves – about 1,000 per year in the 1850s – found support in black communities and from some white reformers in the free states. Some prominent black authors and orators, envisioning a shared destiny for America's slaves and free blacks, denounced the eloquent white divines who harnessed the Bible and theology to the defense of slavery. Some prophesied divine judgment on America if it failed to repent of the sin of slavery (Hinks 1997). When a black preacher in Cincinnati praised slaves and free blacks as "our nation, my brethren," and as God's chosen people, destined for great prosperity, his congregation stamped their feet and shouted "oh glory" (Perry 1993: 112). Hahn, though well aware that there are risks in "overemphasizing solidarities and cohesion among African Americans," let alone white reformers, notes the emergence in southern cities during the 1840s and 1850s of black churches, as well as schools and benevolent and mutual-assistance societies, that bore a resemblance to antebellum northern religious and reform culture. These institutions would provide crucial leadership in the years after emancipation (2003: 5, 120).

When the masters launched their rebellion and Union troops encamped in the South, slaves responded with "a form of rebellion that neither the Confederates nor the Yankees had quite imagined" – that is, by abandoning slavery in large numbers, sometimes with singing and preaching, sometimes by simply taking off for Union lines (Hahn 2003: 68). In the years that followed, northerners who came south as soldiers, officers, chaplains, missionaries, agricultural managers, relief workers, teachers, or journalists came into contact with the former slaves as a people they knew very little about, despite the decades of national political and theological controversy over slavery. These encounters have been the subject of a classic book by Willie Lee Rose on the South Carolina Sea Islands and, more recently, a major project documenting the experiences of the liberated across the South (Rose 1964, Berlin et al. 1992). Besides their significance to scholarship on slavery, war, and reconstruction, these encounters tested the limitations of antebellum understandings of benevolence and introduced themes of cultural diversity that would recur in subsequent intellectual and political life. Thus they mark a break in US cultural history and raise questions about the universality of the yearning for social reconstruction that, according to Noyes, lingered in the American character.

REFERENCES

Abzug, Robert H.: *Cosmos Crumbling: American Reform and the Religious Imagination* (New York: Oxford University Press, 1994).

Barnes, Gilbert Hobbs: *The Antislavery Impulse, 1833–1844* (New York: Harcourt Brace, 1964 [1933]). Recommended edition because of the introduction by William G. McLoughlin.

Berlin, Ira et al.: *Free at Last: A Documentary History of Slavery, Freedom, and the Civil War* (New York: New Press, 1992).

Boylan, Anne M.: *The Origins of Women's Activism: New York and Boston, 1797–1840* (Chapel Hill: University of North Carolina, 2002).

Carwardine, Richard: *Evangelicals and Politics in Antebellum America* (Knoxville: University of Tennessee, 1997).

Cross, Whitney R.: *The Burned-Over District: The Social and Intellectual History of Enthusiastic Religion in Western New York, 1800–1850* (New York: Harper Torchbook, 1965 [1950]).

Davis, David Brion, ed.: *Ante-Bellum Reform* (New York: Harper & Row, 1967).

Dayton, Donald, & Johnson, Robert K.: *The Variety of American Evangelicalism* (Knoxville: University of Tennessee, 1991).

Fogel, Robert William: *Without Consent or Contract: The Rise and Fall of American Slavery* (New York: W. W. Norton, 1989).

Fox, Richard Wightman: *Jesus in America: Personal Savior, Cultural Hero, National Obsession* (San Francisco, CA: HarperCollins, 2004).

Ginzberg, Lori D.: *Women and the Work of Benevolence: Morality, Politics, and Class in the Nineteenth-Century United States* (New Haven, CT: Yale University, 1990).

Gitter, Elisabeth: *The Imprisoned Guest: Samuel Howe and Laura Bridgeman, the Original Deaf-Blind Girl* (New York: Farrar, Straus & Giroux, 2001).

Gollaher, David L.: *Voice for the Mad: The Life of Dorothea Dix* (New York: Free Press, 1995).

Grasso, Christopher: "Skepticism and American Faith: Infidels, Converts, and Religious Doubt in the Early Nineteenth Century," *Journal of the Early Republic* 22 (2002), 465–508.

Griffin, Clifford S.: "Religious Benevolence as Social Control, 1815–1860," *Mississippi Valley Historical Review* 44 (1957), 423–44.

Grodzins, Dean: *American Heretic: Theodore Parker and Transcendentalism* (Chapel Hill: University of North Carolina, 2002).

Hahn, Steven: *A Nation under Our Feet: Black Political Struggles in the Rural South from Slavery to the Great Migration* (Cambridge, MA: Harvard University Press, 2003).

Hatch, Nathan O.: *The Democratization of American Christianity* (New Haven, CT: Yale University Press, 1989).

Hinks, Peter P.: *To Awaken My Afflicted Brethren: David Walker and the Problem of Antebellum Slave Resistance* (University Park, PA: Pennsylvania State University, 1997).

Holifield, E. Brooks: *Theology in America: Christian Thought from the Age of the Puritans to the Civil War* (New Haven, CT: Yale University, 2003).

Johnson, Paul E.: *A Shopkeeper's Millennium: Society and Revivals in Rochester, New York, 1815–1837* (New York: Hill & Wang, 1978).

Loveland, Anne C.: "Later Stages in the Recovery of American Religious History," in Harry S. Stout & D. G. Hart, eds., *New Directions in American Religious History* (New York and Oxford: Oxford University Press, 1997), pp. 487–502.

Lowance, Mason I., ed.: *A House Divided: The Antebellum Slavery Debates in America, 1776–1865* (Princeton, NJ: Princeton University Press, 2003).

McKivigan, John R.: *The War Against Proslavery Religion: Abolitionism and the Northern Churches, 1830–1865* (Ithaca, NY: Cornell University Press, 1984).

Mayer, Henry: *All on Fire: William Lloyd Garrison and the Abolition of Slavery* (New York: St. Martin's, 1998).

Newman, Richard S.: *The Transformation of American Abolitionism: Fighting Slavery in the Early Republic* (Chapel Hill: University of North Carolina, 2002).

Niebuhr, H. Richard: *The Kingdom of God in America* (Middletown, CT: Wesleyan University Press, 1988 [1937]).

Noll, Mark A.: *America's God: From Jonathan Edwards to Abraham Lincoln* (New York: Oxford University Press, 2002).

Noyes, John Humphrey: *History of American Socialisms* (New York: Dover, 1966 [1870]).

Perry, Lewis: *Boats Against the Current: American Culture between Revolution and Modernity* (New York: Oxford University Press, 1993).

Raboteau, Albert J.: *Slave Religion: The "Invisible Institution" in the Antebellum South* (New York: Oxford University Press, 1978).

Rael, Patrick: *Black Identity and Black Protest in the Antebellum North* (Chapel Hill: University of North Carolina, 2002).

Rose, Willie Lee: *Rehearsal for Reconstruction: The Port Royal Experiment* (Indianapolis: Bobbs-Merrill, 1964).

Sklar, Kathryn Kish: *Catharine Beecher: A Study in American Domesticity* (New Haven, CT: Yale University Press, 1973).

Stewart, James Brewer: "Abolitionists, the Bible, and the Challenge of Slavery," in Ernest R. Sandeen, ed., *The Bible and Social Reform* (Philadelphia, PA: Fortress Press, 1982), pp. 31–57.

Smith, Timothy L.: *Revivalism and Social Reform: American Protestantism on the Eve of the Civil War* (Baltimore, MD: Johns Hopkins University Press, 1980 [1957]).

Thomas, John L.: "Romantic Reform in America, 1815–1865," *American Quarterly* 17 (1965), 656–81.

Walker, Peter: *Moral Choices: Memory, Desire, and Imagination in Nineteenth-Century American Abolition* (Baton Rouge: Louisiana State University, 1978).

Walters, Ronald G.: *The Antislavery Appeal: American Abolitionism after 1830* (Baltimore, MD: Johns Hopkins University Press, 1976).

Wright, Conrad Edick: *The Transformation of Charity in Postrevolutionary New England* (Boston, MA: Northeastern University, 1992).

Wyatt-Brown, Bertram: *Lewis Tappan and the Evangelical War Against Slavery* (Cleveland, OH: Case Western Reserve University, 1969).

Chapter Seven

BLACK CULTURE IN THE EIGHTEENTH AND NINETEENTH CENTURIES

Demetrius L. Eudell

Those who came involuntarily, beginning in the sixteenth century, from Africa to the Americas during the Middle Passage embarked on a voyage that forever changed the world. They came from societies, cultures, civilizations, kingdoms, and villages that varied in language, cosmogonies, and social systems. Nevertheless, their forced deracination created something so extraordinary that its unintended consequences have yet to be fully comprehended. Although, before their tragic departures, they could not have identified themselves as "Africans" or "Negroes," through their recreations of their identities and social realities they became a people who, though lacking a common history, would over time come to share an increasingly common experience, playing a central role in the "New World" in which they found themselves.

Their journeys began in the wake of another set of paradigmatic voyages, those of the Portuguese, who in 1434, after a series of expeditions, rounded Cape Bojador off the west coast of Africa, and within a decade reached the shores of Sénégal. The Portuguese voyages had been enabled by the earlier colonization of, first, the eastern and, then, the western Mediterranean, as well as the "discoveries" of Madeira, the Azores, and the Canary Islands, together with the 1415 capture of Ceuta – which were a part of the Christian monarchs' pursuit of the "Reconquest" of infidel Islamic lands, and European attempts to enter the legendary Saharan gold trade (Fernández-Armesto 1987). In making such a trip, the Portuguese breached not only physical/geographical but also intellectual barriers: the conviction that no one could travel beyond the Pillars of Hercules without paying a price as dear as that paid by Odysseus, condemned to the Inferno of Dante's *Divine Comedy* for daring to venture beyond the *ne plus ultra* (Wynter 1995).

Consequently, these voyages shattered the feudal conception of the earth's geography, which was based on the idea of a fundamental divide between the inhabitable temperate realm of New Jerusalem (where West Europe was located) and the uninhabitable torrid zone (beyond the bulging Cape and western Atlantic), an understanding linked to the Scholastic representation of the physical universe, whereby the heavens were to have been constituted by a difference of substance from the terrestrial realm of the earth inhabited by fallen natural man. As was usually the case before the rise of the natural sciences, the representation of the cosmos would be employed to reaffirm the social hierarchies which, in the case of feudal Christian Europe, were supposed to have been as fixed by divine design as was the division between the heavens and the earth, between the temperate and torrid zones, and, most centrally, between the clergy and the laity. In addition to contributing to the dismantling of the feudal organization of the social reality (based on a metaphysics of supernatural causality), the voyages of the Portuguese also enabled the subsequent ones of Columbus beginning in 1492, a development directly leading to the formation of a "New World" from the Old Worlds of Europe, Africa, and the Americas.

The Middle Passage occurred in precisely this context of the "New World," and indeed, constituted an indispensable element in the unfolding of events that produced the post-1492 modern world system. For this reason, the often-acrimonious debate among historians concerning the actual numbers transported misses a more fundamental issue. Whether it was approximately 10 million, as Philip Curtin has argued, or substantially more, as other scholars have put forth, the issue of the legitimacy of the practice remains the central question (Curtin 1969; Thomas 1997: 861–2). Within what conceptual framework could such a practice be made to seem like the natural order of things? In the past, in an effort to answer this question, some scholars such as Basil Davidson, Daniel Mannix, and Malcolm Cowley have pointed to the active role of Africans in the slave trade – despite the fact that no such conception of an "African" existed before the encounter with Europe, and no slaves were marketed as personal and/or real property whose primary purpose was labor exploitation in agricultural or mining operations, as would occur later in the Americas (Foster 1976). The North African Islamic trade in sub-Saharan slaves, which began some seven centuries before the Western European/Christian transatlantic enterprise, did serve as a prelude, given that one could find slaves enduring harsh conditions in draining the salt flats of southern Iraq (which led to slave rebellions in the seventh and ninth centuries), or working the Saharan salt mines and the Nubian gold mines. Moreover, more than a hint of racial discourse gradually emerged in the Islamic narratives of justification for the enslavement of sub-Saharan peoples (Lewis 1990: 3–20).

But even when marginalized and treated cruelly, slavery in Africa did not structure the self-conception of their societies, as the institution would come to do in the Americas, where it became the basis of economic, social, legal, and political systems. In the Islamic and African examples (as in other societies such as Rome), it was not impossible for a slave to be incorporated into a specific family or culture-specific kinship network. Such was not the case in the Americas, where slaves were placed "outside the realm of moral obligation" (Fein 1979: 9), represented as not fully human, and prohibited from learning to read or making the formation of families and communities a priority. Only in this "Christian nation" of the United States would slaves be told that they were not part of the human family (Walker 1829).

The specific conception of the slave in the Americas therefore has to be understood within the terms of the historical and cultural context in which it emerged. The complex that gave rise to this particular mode of enslavement involved revolutionary changes underway in Europe at the time. In the wake of the social and intellectual movements of lay humanism, the Christian conception of being human was gradually secularized, causing a shift in power from the church doctrine of spiritual timelessness to the expansion of the temporal state and its related metaphysics of natural law. In this new field of meaning and political milieu, the peoples of African hereditary descent would come to embody the Conceptual Other (replacing the laity), as irrational beings (like Caliban in Shakespeare's *The Tempest*), in the terms established within the Renaissance/civic humanist discourse of the state (Pocock 1989 [1971]; Wynter 1995). This presumed irrationality provided the rationale for enslaving those of African descent, as well as appropriating the lands of the indigenous peoples of the Americas.

This dynamic tension, constituted by an Afro–Euro–Indio triad, profoundly shaped the societies that would come to define the Americas after 1492. The foodways of the indigenous peoples laid the basis for many of the dietary habits that have come to define the modern world. Whether it was potatoes from the Incas, maize corn from Mexico, chocolate from the Aztec civilization, tomatoes, peanuts, and sundry other food items, the contributions of the indigenous peoples to the agricultural practices and culinary traditions of the Americas and the world (for how else would the potato make it to Ireland and the tomato to Italy?) were epochal. Moreover, the role of forced labor of indigenous peoples on *encomiendas* (proto-plantations) or under the system of rotational labor drafts (*repartimiento* in New Spain, *mita* in Peru) would be indispensable for agricultural production as well as for the building of roads, churches, and public buildings (Weatherford 1988; Foster & Cordell 1992; Burkholder & Johnson 2001).

The role played by Western European cosmogonies in this triadic process has been amply detailed (and perhaps overemphasized) in official histories. From the influence of language to that of religion to culture-specific conceptions of law, property, and land, Western Europeans would leave an indelible mark on the hemisphere and, consequently, the world.

It was therefore in this context of the interactions with the two other founding civilizations to the cultural matrix defining the Americas that the forms of life produced by Negroes/blacks would arise. The specific manner in which these phenomena manifested themselves during the eighteenth and nineteenth centuries in British North America had already been prefigured by the earlier historical and political development in the Spanish and Portuguese colonies. Indeed, by the time that British North America was achieving its American foothold in the early seventeenth century, Africans had already been present in the Americas for over a century. Consequently, because of commerce, exchange, and relations between empires, there would be relations of both continuity and discontinuity, with respect to the development of slavery in the North American British colonies, with the earlier counterparts in Latin America and the Caribbean.

The slave trade that brought those of African hereditary descent to North America had begun a century earlier in the Caribbean, when the governor of Hispaniola requested, in 1501, that the Spanish Crown authorize the shipment of African slaves to the Americas. A year later the policy took effect, first with Africans (a term increasingly relevant) living in Spain and subsequently, in 1518, with slaves brought directly from Africa to the Americas (Palmer 2000). The Middle Passengers were uprooted and physically separated from worlds that had initially defined their self-understanding, worlds such as those of the Akan, the BaKongo, the Fon, the Igbo, the Wolof, and the Yoruba. But this social severance did not imply a complete break from African cultural forms during the transport and enslavement process (to invoke the infamous debate between Melville J. Herskovits and E. Franklin Frazier). The ongoing discussion of the nature of Negro/Afro-American culture has usually emphasized this question of African cultural "retentions," what some have identified as Africanisms (Frazier 1939; Herskovits 1958; Holloway 1990). But within these discussions, the meaning of "culture" has often been less than clear. Uses of the term often imply a mechanistic understanding of culture – in this case, Africanisms – as discrete elements that are created by pre-social beings who then create artifacts, values, beliefs, and norms. Against such an interpretation, Mikhail Epstein has argued that "culture" consists of both "what a human being creates and what creates a human being at the same time," and therefore humans "should be seen as being (simultaneously) creator and creation" (Epstein in Berry et al. 1993: 109–10). Frantz Fanon and Sylvia Wynter's formulations amplify Epstein's assertion. Both insist that to be human, to become human, one is always already socialized within the system of meaning of a specific culture. Being human is a dual nature/culture process – *bios/ logos*, gene/word – in which one has to be socialized to feel, desire, and attempt to realize a specific conception of what constitutes the ideal, the good, and all that is valuable (Fanon 1993 [1952]; Wynter 2001).

If it is true that one cannot be/become human except within the culture-specific terms of a model of being human, then both the assertion of lost culture and the defense of cultural survivals and retentions (Africanisms) become unnecessary. Both of these explanations implicitly depend on the presupposition that humans pre-exist the narratives that generate their being and their social frameworks. Such an assertion should not, however, be construed as an attempt to deny the centrality of African forms of life to the dynamic worlds invented by Blacks in the Americas. Rather it is to point out that the idea of Africanisms places the emphasis on origins and geneal-ogy, such as with Holloway's definition of them as "those elements of culture found in the New World that are traceable to an African origin" (Holloway 1990: ix). Alongside this approach, one could equally place the emphasis on these conceptual systems invented by the slaves as points of departure for the creation of totally original forms of life.

In other words, calling these inventions Africanisms could suggest that what became the Americas pre-existed what is now called Africa. Indeed, Africa, the Americas, and Western Europe (which before the fifteenth century could not have been conceptualized as a unified geopolitical entity) all came into being during the same historic moment in an interactive process of dynamic change. The problem has been that the centrality of the forms of life derived from the conceptual worlds of Africa (and indeed of indigenous America) to the formation of the general society has received inadequate recognition. Yet there were no Americas (in the present sense) before and without an Africa. The dual process referred to by John Blassingame as the "Americanization of the slave and the Africanization of the South" (Blassin-game 1972: 49–104) can therefore be extended to the breadth and length of the hemisphere. Moreover, the popular and scholarly understanding that societies in the Americas are generically white (with non-white add-ons) is a direct result of the belief system of race, the integrating principle itself of these societies.

What came to constitute slave culture would emerge in a dialectical relationship to the dominant society's official discourse in both a complementary and antagonistic manner. In the complementary aspect of the process in North America, slaves incorporated Christian beliefs and democratic ideals. Outside North America, slaves fused the multiple religious cosmogonies of Africa with hegemonic Judaeo-Christian beliefs (and sometimes with those of indigenous peoples as well) in such hybrid conceptual systems as Santería (in Cuba, Puerto Rico, and the Dominican Republic), Vodoun (in Haiti), Jonkunnu (in Jamaica), and Candomblé (in Brazil) (Raboteau 1978; Matory 2005). In the antagonistic aspect of the process, these new, specifically American, cultural forms would serve to contest the governing conceptions of the social reality, especially with respect to the understanding of what it meant to be fully human, in which the Black slave served as the ontological Lack. At the same time as the slaves were forced to challenge the putative universality of this order of domination, they engaged in a process of re-rooting neo-indigenization (as distinct from immigrants), in which these counter-cosmogonies would populate the hemisphere with gods, music, literary forms, and political philosophies specific to its cultural and intellectual context. They would therefore make possible subsequent challenges to the ruling groups as well as point toward comprehensive alternatives for ways in which the social order (including its core understanding of being human) could be conceptualized. While there would certainly be differences based upon geography and the specific regime under whose dominance the enslaved found themselves, at the same time, a pattern of institutions and ideas were put in place that emerged over space and time, to borrow a jazz phrase, as "variations on a theme."

One of the central issues at work in the question of Black/slave culture concerns language. Throughout the plantation Americas, the slaves retained much of the meanings, if not the structures, of their native tongues, generating vernaculars that differed from the dominant languages of the slaveholders. Thus, from the earliest moments of encounter and impact throughout the Americas, the languages of the dominant groups and those of the enslaved often diverged, whether it was the putative Queen's English versus English Creole, or French versus Haitian Creole/Kreyol, Dutch versus Papiamentu, peninsular Spanish versus that of the Americas (and within that further distinctions). While a substantial amount of debate has focused on the extent to which the speech of slaves constitutes a separate language, other research has emphasized the implications of the different speech patterns of the slaves. Lorenzo Dow Turner was one of the first to broach the topic with his groundbreaking study on the Gullah language in the Sea Islands. He noted the words taken directly from languages of African peoples, together with syntactical and morphological features, establishing that a specific logic did shape the linguistic patterns of Gullah speakers. Turner also noted the preponderance of slaves employing African naming practices, such as naming children based on the child's condition, appearance, temperament, or character, as well as by the day, week, year, or manner of birth (Turner 2002 [1949]). Building on Turner's original thesis, J. L. Dillard and Geneva Smitherman have further demonstrated the African influence in the formation/evolution of Black English with respect to the rules of grammar, structure, and sound; for example, the use of the non-differentiation of pronoun genders, the use of the past tense marker "did," and the pronunciation of the sounds "r" and "th." Moreover, the contribution of words to the English language such as yams, banana, cola, and chimpanzee

demonstrate the influence of African languages as well as the reciprocity of communication between slaves and non-slaves (Dillard 1972; Smitherman 1986).

Since Turner, much insightful scholarship has demonstrated that rather than constituting a "broken" or "corrupted" form of English in which the slaves attempted
to mimic the language of the slaveholders, Gullah and forms of Black Vernacular
English represent something far more significant. As Fanon argued, every dialect or
vernacular constitutes a way of thinking, because to speak does not only mean "to
be in a position to use a certain syntax" or "to grasp the morphology of this or that
language, but it means above all to assume a culture, to support the weight of a civilization" (Fanon 1952: 17–18). For this reason, the colonized, for Fanon (or in the
present example, the slave), "is elevated about his jungle status in proportion to his
adoption of the mother country's cultural standards," central to which has always
been the question of language (ibid. 18).

In other words, whether or not it is referred to as Pidgin (in the formal linguistic
sense of a language used by diverse speakers for a specific purpose, such as commerce),
or Plantation Creole (an ostensibly more formalized and standardized mode of communication), the central issue remains what the language was doing. Literally, it was
making meaning, a process in which all humans must engage in order to be and
become human. Because of the inability of the slaveholders to recognize that their
particular language was specific to their own system of meaning making, they represented the languages of slaves as derivative and deficient. Therefore, the extraordinary
feat that the language of slaves accomplished (at the various stages of evolution from
Pidgin to Creole to Black Vernacular English and/or Standard English) had to be
overlooked. For what it did was to take peoples from disparate backgrounds and
infuse their experiences with new meanings, able to create worlds in which they could
exist (however much subordinated) as fully human on their own terms. Such formulations would at times challenge the dominant understanding of why they found
themselves in such a predicament as slavery.

Moreover, as early as the colonial era in the United States, the acquisition of the
dominant language could have life-and-death consequences. For instance, advertisements for runaway slaves often used the linguistic status of the fugitives as a means
to facilitate identification. Always emphasized in capital letters, phrases such as "speaks
good English" (or French or Dutch) or "speaks proper English," or "remarkably
good English for a Negro," recurred throughout announcements in eighteenth-
century newspapers. Indeed, readers were often warned that runaways could be
"artful" (also placed in capital letters for emphasis) for having such ability, especially
when coupled with "can read and write," because these skills enabled runaways
to forge documents and attempt to pass as free people (anon. 1916: 164, 170,
176, 177).

The issue of religion is central to discussions of the culture of Blacks in the Americas. The conversion in the Anglo-Americas of Blacks to Protestant Christianity was
"a, perhaps *the*, defining moment" in the history of the population group (Frey &
Wood 1998: xi). This process would not occur immediately given that, during the
eighteenth century, formal exposure to the ideas of Christianity occurred intermit-
tently. Thus, as was the case with language, the original African intellectual and
cultural foundations remained evident in more explicit terms in the earlier phases of
adaptation to the situation in the New World. Moreover, using religion as the lens

through which to view the experiences of slaves can provide a useful alternative to viewing slave culture as a function merely of labor or class structure.

Historians often emphasize the importance of geographic and distinct plantation systems in shaping Black culture in North America. Ira Berlin, for instance, has distinguished four different slave societies in what eventually became the United States: the Chesapeake region, the coastal Low Country of the Carolinas and Georgia, the lower Mississippi Valley, and the non-plantation North (Berlin 1998). Such a model is unquestionably useful: it would be impossible to understand the development of the institution of slavery outside the production of tobacco in the Chesapeake, rice and indigo in the Low Country, cotton and sugar in Mississippi and Louisiana, and the slave trade in New England. However, despite the importance of regional variations in labor and commerce, reducing the understanding of slavery to such a framework may overstate the case. As John Blassingame has so insightfully asserted, "the social organization of the quarters was the slave's primary environment which gave him his ethical rules and fostered cooperation, mutual assistance, and Black solidarity. The work experience represented his secondary environment and was far less important in determining his personality than his primary environment" (Blassingame 1972: 105–6).

Although it is important to consider the diverse African backgrounds of American slaves, "similar modes of perception, shared basic principles, and common patterns of ritual were widespread among different West African religions" (Raboteau 1978: 7). Such a "fundamental similarity" in beliefs and values was rearticulated in the Americas to shape black/slave religion. For instance, many coming from African societies held beliefs in a Supreme Being/Creator, but these were accompanied by beliefs in lesser gods/deities/ancestors; an overarching monotheistic structure could include polytheistic beliefs (ibid. 8). Such fusion remained fundamentally at odds with the absolutism implicit in orthodox Judaeo-Christianity, whose foundational belief of a single pathway to salvation could not co-exist with competing conceptions of the human condition and destiny. As a result, the remarkable ingenuity of slave religion had to be maligned by many as a superstitious and primitive cult. And yet, this "primitive cult" would be responsible for much of the originality of what can be defined as prototypically American – that is, as an original cultural form that could only have been produced in the psycho-existential context of the plantation Americas.

Not until the First Great Awakening, which began in the 1730s and 1740s, were a significant number of slaves formally converted to Christianity. Before this time, in the United States, little attempt was made to convert slaves; many Euro-Americans were actually hostile toward such practices. However, toward the end of the eighteenth century, in the wake of a series of evangelical revivals, the number of enslaved and free Blacks who joined the Baptist and Methodist denominations (in particular) increased considerably. Yet, the religious consciousness of the slaves would continue to reflect the influence of African conceptual systems in terms of both belief and structure (Raboteau 1978: 128–9; Frey & Wood 1998: 80–117).

Since beliefs in general tend to be interwoven with ritual practices, the ways in which the slaves in the United States expressed their beliefs were linked to traditional West African religious expressions, although certainly transformed in the context of a new social reality. Music, for example, has played a central role in the structuring of slave religion and culture. Certain principles define the "musical and choreographic modalities" that connect Black peoples in the Western Hemisphere. Among other things, these include "the dominance of a percussive performance style, a propensity for multiple meter," and call and response in singing (Thompson 1983: xiii). As a result, dancing, singing, and drumming played an integral part in the invocation of the spirits. The "ring shout," first recognized by non-practitioners in the Sea Islands during the Civil War, was the most renowned of the slave dances. The counter-clockwise dance ceremony invoked its African ancestry with its call-and-response singing as well as with percussive clapping (Blassingame 1972: 134–5). The ritual is still practiced in coastal areas of Georgia.

The original creativity of slave music can also be seen from the invention of the spiritual. What W. E. B. Du Bois once referred to as the "sorrow songs" (Du Bois 1961 [1903]) were not only that, though they certainly spoke to the slaves' sense of exile and abjection. These were also songs of triumph, of overcoming, and, as one song goes, of "joy unspeakable." Nowhere are the agony and the ecstasy defining the human condition better expressed than in these songs. The brilliance behind their intellectual strategies also lay in the cutting across of the Judaeo-Christian belief system that created a chasm between the realms of the sacred and the profane.

For the African-descended slaves, such distinctions between the sacred and the profane were unnecessary; these songs were not performed solely in churches, but were also sung in work and social situations (Levine 1977). Moreover, the improvisational structure of the spirituals anticipated the "secular" variants of blues and jazz, though the boundaries between these genres could not always be clearly demarcated. This music, coming out of the slave experience, and then changing over time, can be identified as part of the classical musical tradition of the United States (and in the case of others such as salsa and rumba, of the Americas) because it belongs to this specific cultural field of meanings, and could not have been produced anywhere else. Not only music, but also musical instruments have been identified as having been created under slavery. The banjo and the xylophone originated in Africa: the former probably came from the Senegambia region; the latter, brought by African slaves during the sixteenth-century Spanish conquest, resembled the balafon of Ghana and the malimbe of the Kongo.

Slave songs also reflected a certain political acuity. Rather than adopting the submission to (civil) slavery urged, according to some interpreters, by the Pauline letters of the New Testament, slaves tended to identify with Old Testament figures in such songs as "Go, Down Moses," "Ezekiel Saw the Wheel," "Didn't My Lord Deliver Daniel?" and "Run Old Jeremiah," often performed with the ring shout. Although not every spiritual should be viewed as a coded protest song, an intellectual and political strategy can be identified in their central theme of the biblical liberation of a people from bondage. In this respect, the reinterpretation of the great story of Exodus, with the slaves as the chosen people, invoked the revolutionary origins of early Christianity in the Roman Empire. Here was another uprising against an empire, both intellectual and, less explicitly, political and economic as well. The slaves' enlistment of the analogy of the children of Israel under the tyranny of Pharaoh to understand their own situation represented an epistemological challenge to the dominant narrative of origin that underlay the plantation system. Rather than the origin of their enslavement lying in the "curse of Ham" or in the secular theory of polygenesis, this reinterpretation of the biblical story of Exodus (that contradicts certain streams of contemporary Afrocentric philosophical discourse in which Egypt represents a Black civilization and the fount of much of Western knowledge) implied that the origin of the group lay in the man-made political and social system of slavery.

In other words, both religious and secular justifications of the institution condemned slaves as the ontological negation of the conception of being fully human. In both schemas, there was no possibility for slaves to change their situation; in both narrative justifications, their condition had been extra-humanly determined. However, as David Walker proclaimed in his challenge to Thomas Jefferson's assertion that between Black and White "the difference is fixed in nature, and is as real as if its seat and cause were better known to us," it was not nature that produced these distinctions, but rather the Euro-American understanding of what it meant to be human that determined the treatment of Blacks. "Have they [Whites] not, after having reduced us to the deplorable conditions of slaves under their feet, held us up as descending originally from the tribes of *Monkeys* or *Orang-Outangs*?" (Walker 1965 [1829]: 10). In other words, on the basis of their own narrative of origin, the slaves refused to succumb to the most debilitating psychological aspects of their physical enslavement. In fact, this narrative fueled several slave insurrections in the eighteenth century – in New York (1712) and South Carolina (1739) – as well as the nineteenth century – Gabriel Prosser's Rebellion near Richmond, Virginia (1800), St. Charles and St. John the Baptist parishes in Louisiana (1811), (the now questioned) Denmark Vesey Revolt in Charleston, South Carolina (1822), and the most infamous rebellion of Nat Turner in Southampton, Virginia (1831). Gabriel Prosser was directly influenced by his having read and been moved by the story of the Israelites and their delivery from slavery.

Similarly, slaves theoretically redefined their social context by telling folktales and practicing conjuring, in which priests/medicine-men acquired power based on knowledge of roots and herbs to cure illness. Like Christianity, conjuring – also called hoodoo, voodoo, and rootwork – responded to questions that confront all human social systems. Thus, the distinction between religion and magic may not be the most efficacious way of understanding the phenomenon. For conjuring served as an explanatory model that placed slaves, both within the cosmos and in their social world, in terms that invoked African forms of life. For instance, the snake god that for Whydah, Fon, and Ewe embodied fertility, the dynamic quality of life, and both good and evil spirits, became Damballa in nineteenth-century Louisiana (Blassingame 1972).

Conjuring could work either with or against the beliefs and rituals of Christianity. Both of these not always distinct systems of thought posited a world populated with spirits (in the secular variant, nature eventually becomes the omnipotent unknowing force), and therefore both motivated behaviors specific to the way in which their respective field of meanings defined good and evil forces. In the world of conjuring, there existed a necessary unity in which all events and things were interlinked, and thus knowledge of this world could be essential for survival. It was for this reason that many in the slave community deferred to the expertise of those who could best understand these mystical forces. These divinatory practices determined causality by defining the nature of an illness and prescribing a cure. A slave could rely on certain charms to protect himself from the brutality of the slaveholder, as did Sandy in Frederick Douglass's narrative; or consult a conjurer to pursue personal health, romantic interests, or vengeance against an adversary. Although many slaves could be skeptical of the divination of conjurers, especially after consulting one without receiving the desired outcome, the truth of conjuring remained, in the extent to which the beliefs compelled the behaviors of its adherents.

Some medical practices of slaves were actually adopted by the slaveholding society. There is evidence not only of individual Whites' embracing aspects of conjuring, but also of official medicine taking up slave healing practices. In 1729, the governor of Virginia freed an elderly slave who had revealed his "many wonderful cures of diseases." In South Carolina, the cure for poison by a slave named Caesar was so effective that, in 1750, the legislature "ordered his prescription published for the benefit of the public" (Phillips 1966 [1918]: 323). Slave women often served as nurses or midwives on many plantations. According to one doctor in the state of Virginia, by the mid-nineteenth century, fewer than half of all births in the state were attended by doctors, and over 90 percent of all deliveries among Blacks were conducted by Black midwives. A significant number also attended deliveries by White women as well. Whether it was nursing, midwifery, pulling teeth, or administering medicine, Blacks played a central role in the Virginia health-care system (Savitt 1978).

Through such cultural practices as the invention of a vernacular, the reinterpretation of the biblical story of Exodus, the creation of new musical forms, and the use of African-based and transformed healing/conjuring metaphysics, the creative responses of the slaves constituted the basis for building what has been defined as the slave community. To this effect, the formation of institutions served an indispensable role in sustaining a society that was consistently under siege both politically and intellectually. From early in their New World experiences, enslaved and free Blacks throughout the Americas organized institutions that provided spiritual and financial support that enabled many to endure the harsh conditions to which they were subjected. As early as the mid-sixteenth century, Africans in Cuba established mutual aid societies, known as *cabildos de naciones de afrocubanos*, which maintained, while transforming, African customs. Initially started as unstructured recreational reunions, these voluntary associations gradually took on political functions, serving as intermediaries between the general Afro-Cuban community and the colonial government. By the middle of the nineteenth century, these societies would be modified as *sociedades de color*; unlike the earlier groups, these were not based on language and ethnic similarities, but rather extended their activities to the wider enslaved and free Black Cuban community. Although they carried over certain functions such as providing assistance for members, and through their long history maintained a reformist agenda, the goals of these organizations did become for a moment quite radical in the context of the first Cuban war of independence (1868–78) (Howard 1998).

This mode of institution building, which implied the redefinition of kinship (indeed, of belonging in a general human sense), would be paralleled in other parts of the Americas. In Brazil, "nations" also emerged in such modes as Catholic religious fraternities, mutual aid societies, and the army. These various associations were responsible for the preservation and adaptation of African ceremonies as well as planning armed rebellion against the ruling order. Indeed, the practice of candomblé in Brazil used the idiom of nations or "houses" that provided an alternative to the dominant sociopolitical system of racialized plantocracy. Like their Cuban counter-parts, these houses, besides providing methods for inviting the intervention of the living gods through spiritual possession and other ceremonies, gradually took on diverse social roles such as providing employment, temporary shelter for fugitives, and eventually an important constituency for politicians in electoral campaigns (Matory 2005).

In North America, the building of institutions by free Blacks in the North, and enslaved and free Blacks in the South, began in about 1775, with the founding of the Silver Bluff Baptist Church in South Carolina – often identified as the first separate Black church in North America. Founded by George Liele, David George, and several others, the church ushered in an era of Black evangelical leadership that created a network of churches linking Blacks throughout the diaspora. Liele, in the wake of the revolution of 1776, and the evacuation of British forces from Savannah, left for Jamaica, where in 1784 he established, with "four brethren from America," the first Baptist church in the colony. Differences in interpretation led to the splintering of the denomination, with one faction (led by another North American émigré, George Lewis), which emphasized speaking in tongues, having a substantial impact on Jamaican slaves. Although maligned by the more orthodox British Baptists (and Liele as well) for practicing "Christianized obeahs," the "Native Baptists" would not only serve the religious needs and desires of many slaves, but also have an important political role in the 1831 slave revolt, which many termed "the Baptist War." Liele's colleague David George also carried faith into international lands. After gaining his freedom and leaving for Nova Scotia in 1782, where he founded a Black church at Shelburne, George migrated a decade later to Sierra Leone, where he established another Baptist church (Raboteau 1978).

Many churches and non-church-related organizations were founded in the United States during the late eighteenth and early nineteenth century. The influence of the Methodists was significant. After forming the non-religious Free African Society in Philadelphia in 1787, designed to support widows, fatherless children, and those who had fallen ill, Richard Allen established in 1816 a new denomination, the African Methodist Episcopal Church. Rather than arising out of a specific theological doc-trine, the church emerged precisely to address the spiritual and social concerns of Blacks both slave and free (Porter 1936). Other associations were concerned not only with educating youth, but providing mutual aid and general moral reform. According to the Pittsburgh African Education Society, created in 1832, "ignorance is the sole cause of the present degradation and bondage of the people of color in these United States," and thus its objective was the "dispersion of the moral gloom that has so long hung around us" (Porter 1971: 120). These societies, while performing a neces-sary and useful service to the Black community, often reflected the larger society's understanding of being human. In their preamble to the charter of the Free African Society, Allen and Jones expressed a concern for "the people of their complexion whom they beheld with sorrow, because of their irreligious and uncivilized state" (Douglass 1862: 15). The constitution of the African Benevolent Society of Newport, Rhode Island, founded in 1808 to establish a free school, stipulated that a certain number of male members and White directors had to be present to transact any business (Porter 1971). These organizations demonstrated the difficulty of trying to transform ideas imposed by the dominant culture. Again, while humans produce culture, culture also produces specific modes of being human.

In addition to mutual aid, benevolence, and education organizations, Blacks, mostly in the North, also formed temperance and anti-slavery societies, the latter of which radicalized many White abolitionists and became central to the shift in the 1830s from advocating gradual emancipation to agitating for the immediate abolition of slavery. Literary societies also formed in the liberal, anti-slavery North, where "the presence of Negroes in white literary organizations was not wanted" (Porter 1936: 557); in fact, the Reverend Theodore S. Wright was thrown out of a literary meeting of the Alumni of Nassau Hall in New York City. Like the educational societies out of which many of the literary societies emerged, concern for the development of youth remained primary; the Philadelphia Library Company of Colored Persons was formed in 1833 on the model of Benjamin Franklin's 1731 Library Company, for the purpose of cultivating literary pursuits among youth as well as the "improvement of the faculties and powers of their minds" (ibid. 560).

Yet because these well-intentioned groups thought within the dominant terms (even as they challenged them), they did not see, as many have not since, that a new literature and poetics had already been born. The slave spirituals and folktales, together with the slave narratives, constituted what Arna Bontemps called "an American genre," produced as the result of the specific historical and cultural context of slavery in the Americas (Bontemps 1969). Slavery as a social phenomenon was not new. However, in the Americas, especially the United States, the literary production of slave narratives constituted a break with the history of this institution. Throughout the breadth and length of the slave societies of Greece and Rome, as well as other societies in Asia and Africa that tolerated slavery, no such literature had emerged to tell of the experiences under which the slaves suffered. Although often characterized as having low artistic value, the slave narratives should be understood on the basis of the conditions that made them possible, rather than for any presumed failure to transcend the specific culture context in which they were created.

The story of the rise of the (English) novel usually begins with the writings of Samuel Richardson and Henry Fielding, as well as the displacement of the romance and the rise of the middle class. Whichever perspective is adopted, it seems indisputable that, although adapted to American social realities, the novel's origins lay in Europe. In the nineteenth century in particular, literature (together with opera and museums) was used as a tool of cultural hierarchy to institute and reproduce the dominance not only of ruling groups, but of ruling ideas, which together informed the contemporary definition of "having culture" (Levine 1988). Yet, just as a useful history of the Western novel should convey something of the times that produced it, so too should the history of the American slave narrative. The slave narrative, which documented the existential reality of an enslaved population, made clear that the political claims of "the rights of man" foundational to the American republic could not incorporate "the rights of the Negro" (Lamming 1953: 334). Without the slave narratives, not only would there be no Black literature, but Mark Twain and William Faulkner could not have conceptualized many of their characters (Ellison 1986). Not unlike the *Aeneid*, in which the narrator self-consciously provided a history of how he became the ancestor of the Romans, slave narratives, born in part from the African oral tradition, were also self-conscious acts that told a different tale of the origin (and destiny) of the American republic.

Frederick Douglass always understood that rethinking origins was central to his political and intellectual project. In his 1854 speech, "The Claims of the Negro Ethnologically Considered," he pointed out that in order to justify holding Blacks in slavery, the slaveholding statesmen had to consult the reigning theorists of polygenesis (Josiah Nott, Samuel Morton, Louis Agassiz, George Gliddon), who sought to "read the Negro out of the human family" by casting "doubt over the Scriptural account of the origin of mankind" (Douglass 1950 [1854]: 295). Thus, the religion of slaves had to challenge the intellectual schemas upon which their subordination was legitimated. The ruling race, whether enlisting the Christian argument that Blacks were the children of Ham, or the scientific theories (such as polygenesis) that Blacks were inferior by nature, was committed a priori to the non-homogeneity of the human species. Thus, when the slaves reinterpreted the world by putting forth an alternative conception of social reality, they necessarily asserted another origin of the human species.

By the end of the nineteenth century, another form of a potentially transcendent discourse had emerged to re-enact the history of the nation. In Charleston, South Carolina, former slaves initiated a tradition whose origins have still not been fully acknowledged in popular memory. In the process of mourning the massive scale of death in the Civil War, Blacks in Charleston founded Decoration Day on May 1, 1865. An estimated 10,000 people, mostly former slaves, commemorated fallen Union soldiers with a parade followed by the decoration of graves. The event occurred at the planters' Race Course, a horseracing track that had been converted into a military prison, where more than 250 Union soldiers had died under appalling conditions and been unceremoniously buried in unmarked graves (Blight 2001).

It was thus in this moment of a profound symbolic rearticulation of meaning, a process that had always defined Black culture in the Americas, that the former slaves and their northern and free Black allies (including the 54th from Massachusetts as well as the 35th and 104th US Colored Troops), redefined the significance of their own deaths by identifying the "Martyrs of the Race Course" – generating meaning where there had been none. A few years later, this ritual of commemoration would appear in the North. But it was former slaves who, in their tradition of collapsing the sacred and the profane and redefining the meaning of sociality, would found Memorial Day "in a ritual of remembrance and consecration" (Blight 2001: 70). Their struggle was only just beginning with the end of slavery, for despite all their ecumenical and transformative intellectual strategies, the dominant society consistently refused to recognize the centrality of Black/African-derived forms of life to the formation of the new (as had also been the case with the old) nation. Both the creation of Memorial Day, and the subsequent forgetting of its origins, illustrated a central theme in the history of Blacks in the United States and throughout the Americas. That history was marked by a tension between triumph and tragedy, what Ralph Ellison defined as "that same pain and that same pleasure," whereby no matter how systematic the attempts to exclude Blacks from the mainstream, "Negro Americans are in fact one of its major tributaries" (Ellison 1964: 3–23; 1986: 108).

REFERENCES

Anon.: "Eighteenth Century Slaves as Advertised by Their Masters," *Journal of Negro History* 1 (April 1916), 163–216.

Berlin, Ira: *Many Thousands Gone: The First Two Centuries of Slavery in North America* (Cambridge, MA: Belknap/Harvard University Press, 1998).

Berry, Ellen E., Johnson, Kent & Miller-Pogacar, Anesa: "Postcommunist Postmodernism – An Interview with Mikhail Epstein," *Common Knowledge* 2, 3 (Winter 1993), 103–18.

Blassingame, John W.: *The Slave Community: Plantation Life in the Antebellum South* (New York: Oxford University Press, 1972).

Blight, David Blight: *Race and Reunion: The Civil War in American Memory* (Cambridge, MA: Belknap/Harvard University Press, 2001).

Bontemps, Arna: "The Slave Narrative: An American Genre," in *Great Slave Narratives, Selected and Introduced by Arna Bontemps* (Boston, MA: Beacon Press, 1969), pp. vii–xix.

Burkholder, Mark A. & Johnson, Lyman L.: *Colonial Latin America* (New York: Oxford University Press, 2001).

Curtin, Philip D.: *The Atlantic Slave Trade: A Census* (Madison: University of Wisconsin Press, 1969).

Dillard, J. L.: *Black English: Its History and Usage in the United States* (New York: Random House, 1972).

Douglass, Frederick: "The Claims of the Negro Ethnologically Considered, Address Delivered at Western Reserve College, July 12, 1854," in *The Life and Writings of Frederick Douglass, Volume II: Pre-Civil War Decade, 1850–1860*, ed. Philip S. Foner (New York: International Publishers, 1950), pp. 289–309.

Douglass, William: *Annals of the First African Church in the United States of America, Now Styled the African Episcopal Church of St. Thomas* (Philadelphia, PA: King & Baird, 1862).

Du Bois, W. E. B.: "Of the Sorrow Songs," in *The Souls of Black Folk* (Greenwich, CT: Fawcett Publications, 1961 [1903]), pp. 181–90.

Ellison, Ralph: "That Same Pain, That Same Pleasure: An Interview," in *Shadow and Act* (New York: Vintage, 1964).

Ellison, Ralph: "What America Would Be Like Without Blacks," in *Going to the Territory* (New York: Vintage, 1986), pp. 104–12.

Epstein, Mikhail: "An Interview with Mikhail Epstein," *Common Knowledge* 2, 3 (Winter 1993), 103–18.

Fanon, Frantz: *Black Skin, White Masks*, trans. Charles Lam Markman (London: Pluto Press, 1993 [1952]).

Fein, Helen: *Accounting for Genocide: National Responses and Jewish Victimization during the Holocaust* (New York: Free Press, 1979).

Fernández-Armesto, Felipe: *Before Columbus: Exploration and Colonization from the Mediterranean to the Atlantic, 1229–1492* (Philadelphia: University of Pennsylvania Press, 1987).

Foster, Herbert: "Partners or Captive in Commerce? The Role of Africans in the Slave Trade," *Journal of Black Studies* 6, 4 (June 1976), 421–34.

Foster, Nelson & Cordell, Linda S., eds.: *Chilies to Chocolate: Food the Americas Gave the World* (Tucson: University of Arizona Press, 1992).

Frazier, E. Franklin: *The Negro Family in the United States* (Chicago: University of Chicago Press, 1939).

Frazier, E. Franklin: *The Negro Church in America* (New York: Schocken Books, 1963).

Frey, Sylvia & Wood, Betty: *Come Shouting to Zion: African American Protestantism in the American South and British Caribbean to 1830* (Chapel Hill: University of North Carolina Press, 1998).

Herskovits, Melville J.: *The Myth of the Negro Past* (Boston, MA: Beacon Press, 1958 [1941]).

Holloway, Joseph E., ed.: *Africanisms in American Culture* (Bloomington: Indiana University Press, 1990).

Howard, Philip A.: *Changing History: Afro-Cuban Cabildos and Societies of Color in the Nineteenth Century* (Baton Rouge: Louisiana State University Press, 1998).

Huggins, Nathan: *Black Odyssey: The Afro-American Ordeal in Slavery* (New York: Pantheon Books, 1977).

Jones, LeRoi: *Blues People: Negro Music in White America* (New York: William & Morrow, 1963).

Lamming, George: *In the Castle of My Skin* (New York: Collier Books/Macmillan, 1953).

Levine, Lawrence: *Black Culture and Black Consciousness: Afro-American Folk Thought from Slavery to Freedom* (New York: Oxford University Press, 1977).

Levine, Lawrence: *Highbrow/Lowbrow: The Emergence of Cultural Hierarchy in America* (Cambridge, MA: Harvard University Press, 1988).

Lewis, Bernard: *Race and Slavery in the Middle East: An Historical Inquiry* (New York: Oxford University Press, 1990).

Matory, J. Lorand: *Black Atlantic Religion: Tradition, Transnationalism, and Matriarchy in the Afro-Brazilian Candumble* (Princeton, NJ: Princeton University Press, 2005).

Palmer, Colin: "The First Passage: 1502–1619," in Robin D. G. Kelley & Earl Lewis, eds., *To Make Our World Anew: A History of African Americans* (New York: Oxford University Press, 2000), pp. 3–52.

Phillips, Ulrich B.: *American Negro Slavery: A Survey of the Supply, Employment, and Control of Negro Labor as Determined by the Plantation Regime* (Baton Rouge: Louisiana State University Press, 1966 [1918]).

Pocock, J. G. A.: *Politics, Language, and Time: Essays on Political Thought and History* (Chicago: University of Chicago Press, 1989 [1971]).

Porter, Dorothy: "The Organized Educational Activities of Negro Literary Societies, 1828–1846," *The Journal of Negro Education* 5 (October 1936), 555–76.

Porter, Dorothy, ed.: *Early Negro Writing, 1760–1837* (Boston, MA: Beacon Press, 1971).

Raboteau, Albert J.: *Slave Religion: The "Invisible Institution" in the Antebellum South* (New York: Oxford University Press, 1978).

Savitt, Todd L.: *Medicine and Slavery: The Diseases and Health Care of Blacks in Antebellum Virginia* (Urbana: University of Illinois Press, 1978).

Smitherman, Geneva: *Talkin' and Testifyin': The Language of Black America* (Detroit: Wayne State University Press, 1986).

Thomas, Hugh: *The Slave Trade* (New York: Touchstone/Simon & Schuster, 1997).

Thompson, Robert Farris: *Flash of the Spirit: African and Afro-American Art and Philosophy* (New York: Vintage, 1983).

Turner, Lorenzo Dow: *Africanisms in the Gullah Dialect* (Columbia: University of South Carolina Press, 2002 [1949]).

Walker, David: *David Walker's Appeal, in Four Articles: Together with a Preamble to the Coloured Citizens of the* World (New York: Hill & Wang, 1965 [1829]).

Weatherford, Jack: *Indian Givers: How the Indians of the Americas Transformed the World* (New York: Crown Publishers, 1988).

Wynter, Sylvia: "1492: A New World View," in Vera Lawrence Hyatt & Rex Nettleford, eds., *Race, Discourse, and the Origins of the Americas: A New World View* (Washington, DC: Smithsonian Institution Press, 1995), pp. 5–57.

Wynter, Sylvia: "Toward the Sociogenic Principle: Fanon, Identity, the Puzzle of Conscious Experience, and What It is Like to Be Black," in Mercedes F. Duran & Antonio Gomez Moriana, eds., *National Identities and Sociopolitical Changes in Latin America* (New York: Routledge, 2001), pp. 30–66.

Chapter Eight

THE CIVIL WAR IN AMERICAN CULTURE

Alice Fahs

When Stephen Crane published his bestselling *The Red Badge of Courage* in 1895, numerous Civil War veterans commented that he was the first author who had captured their reality of war; many assumed that Crane must be a fellow veteran. But Crane, of course, was no Civil War soldier: born in 1871, six years after the conflict ended, he gleaned much of his detailed historical knowledge of the war from perusing old issues of the famous *Century Magazine* "Battles and Leaders" series.

Looking back, Crane reconstructed the war through memory and imagination; but for readers in the twentieth century his novel was itself a fresh experience of the war, one that would inform their own memories – not to mention continue today to influence our understandings of the Civil War. Like Crane's *Red Badge of Courage*, Margaret Mitchell's bestselling *Gone with the Wind* (1936) was not just a work of original imagination; among other influences on Mitchell's understanding of the war was D. W. Griffith's landmark film, *Birth of a Nation* (1915), which had been strongly influenced by Thomas Dixon's *The Clansman: An Historical Romance of the Ku Klux Klan* (1905). These works, which have had a powerful, continuing impact on American culture, are also a reminder of the densely accreted, geological nature of memory in general – and certainly of memories of the Civil War.

If one way to understand the impact of the Civil War in American culture is to drill downward through layers of memory, remaining sensitive to the complexities of proximity and influence along the way, another method is to stop at any one point in time and take stock of the surrounding landscape of Civil War remembrance. As Stuart McConnell usefully reminds us, the "geography of memory" is an "uneven physical, cultural, and political space" in which some forms of memory are "more available to some social groups than to others" (Fahs & Waugh 2004: 259). Questions of political and social power determine who gets to claim the memory of the Civil War at any given moment, especially as a means of affirming group identity or membership in the nation.

These questions of power are at the heart of the new Civil War cultural history. Examining both cultural artifacts (such as photographs, monuments, and literature) and the cultural processes by which these artifacts have been created and remembered, recent scholars have insisted that we can fully understand the Civil War only if we study its cultural history in addition to military, political, and social history. At issue, scholars from several disciplines have argued, is no less than understanding how freedom, citizenship, and nationhood have been and continue to be defined.

It should be noted at the outset that simply invoking the phrase "Civil War cultural history" with confidence marks a significant departure from the past. It was not so long ago, after all, that Civil War historiography was dominated by political and military history. Even today, the bookshelves of any large American bookstore reveal that among the estimated 60,000 books published on the war, political and especially military history remain the most popular forms of Civil War history for a wider reading public.

Yet among scholars a virtual revolution in Civil War studies has taken place over the last decade and a half. Studies of the memory of the war, Civil War literature, the home front, Civil War nationalism, local communities, and wartime gender dynamics are but a few of the most prominent new approaches that have widened and reshaped our ideas of the war itself. With a striking interest in narratives of war as a form of social and cultural power, Civil War scholars have decisively (if somewhat belatedly) taken the "linguistic turn"; indeed, a rich array of recent works in Civil War cultural history is primarily interested in *how* the story of the war has been told, recognizing that stories – not just how they are told, but who gets to tell them, and to whom they are told – are a form of cultural power. These works push us to reconsider a number of the most fundamental questions associated with any war: Who fought? Where was the war fought? How long did it last? And most importantly, how has it shaped society and culture?

All of the works discussed in this essay share a concern with the multiple *meanings* of the Civil War. But it should be said at once that Civil War cultural history is not just practiced by historians: scholars in allied disciplines such as American Studies, American literature, and American art history have also published cultural histories of the war. Moreover, many of the historians discussed here work at the intersections of social and cultural history; some might even be surprised to be included in an essay on cultural history.

But cultural history – as any reader of this volume will realize – is in fact a capacious tent that holds a wide range of approaches. An older (and still practiced) American Studies model of cultural history, for instance, primarily stresses the objects under study – whether music, art, theater, literature, and so on – employing a definition of culture that stresses primarily high culture and the fine arts. Another form of cultural history stresses ritual and the intricacies of cultural practice; such history traces its roots to the influence of anthropology on the discipline of history in the 1970s. Since the 1980s, cultural history "after the linguistic turn" has stressed the multiple and shifting meanings of language, providing new approaches to understanding the complex, layered relationships between text and context. Since the 1990s, cultural studies has provided fresh new models for interdisciplinary study as well as a sharpened focus on popular culture as a viable subject for analysis. And feminist analyses of gender and sexuality have generated new modes of understanding the social arrangements of culture, as well as the cultures of everyday domestic life, as sites where power, identity, and nationhood are constructed and contested.

These different approaches to cultural history are not, of course, mutually exclusive; instead the works reviewed in this essay utilize a wide variety of approaches not limited to those outlined above. But all of these works address larger questions of the meanings of the war. Many of them, focused on the social and political power of narratives of the war in American life, invite us to see the Civil War not as an event limited to the "Civil War Era" periodization used in college classrooms – from the Nullification Crisis in the early 1830s through the end of Reconstruction in 1877 – but as an ongoing and still unfolding event in American history.

This sense of the Civil War as a long-term event, hotly contested long after the smoke had cleared from its battlefields, pervades the influential work of David W. Blight, who has mapped out a landscape of memory in numerous essays and books, especially his prizewinning *Race and Reunion: The Civil War in American Memory* (2001). Blight clearly announces his focus on the meanings of the war: "what happened on the battlefields in the Civil War is very important," he has noted, "but the boundaries of military history are fluid; they connect with a broader social, cultural, and political history in myriad ways. In the long run, the meanings embedded in these epic fights are what should command our greatest attention" (Blight 2002: x).

In exploring the memory of the war – the ways in which its changing meanings have been embodied in a variety of physical locations, cultural practices, and forms of print culture – Blight has been inspired in part by the work of Maurice Halbwachs and Pierre Nora, whose wide-ranging studies of collective and individual memory (Halbwachs) and "*lieux de memoire*" or sites of memory (Nora), influenced numerous Europeanist historians before being taken up by Americanists. While some historians – including Stuart McConnell and Nina Silber – early joined Blight in examining the remembrance and commemoration of the Civil War in American culture and politics, others – such as William Blair and John R. Neff – have more recently responded to the first wave of work on Civil War memory. The much-mined vein of memory studies is clearly not yet tapped out.

Blight has paid particular attention to the ongoing contest for the memory of the war that occurred "beyond the battlefield" (to use Frederick Douglass's phrase) in the late nineteenth century. Despite strenuous efforts on the part of African Americans to remind the nation that the most important legacy of the Civil War was emancipation, by the turn of the century a white-dominated memory of the war had achieved hegemony. That dominant memory of the war stressed reunion and reconciliation among a white brotherhood of "brave heroes" who should put sectional differences behind them to celebrate a racialized memory of the war. This "reconciliationist" memory not only pointedly ignored the fact that close to 200,000 black soldiers had fought in the conflict, but also ignored the central outcome of the war: emancipation. The stakes in the competition between emancipationist and reconciliationist memories of the war were exceedingly high: no less than the power to define who could claim legitimate membership in the nation during the era of Jim Crow.

As is true of many of the historians discussed in this essay, Blight does not separate culture from politics; instead, he treats culture as a form of politics, by which power is contested, won, and displayed. Thus Blight's work explores a variety of cultural forms and practices with political reverberations, including the annual Civil War commemorations known as Decoration Days (the precursors to Memorial Day); the erection of monuments to Civil War heroism in small towns and large cities both North and South; the writing and publication of memoirs by Civil War soldiers; and the literary emergence of Lost Cause ideology that celebrated the myth of the "faithful slave" who had been happier as a slave than as a free person. For Blight, cultural power lies in the production and dissemination of these narratives of war, whether in the form of public monuments or widely shared fictional stories or public ceremonies of commemoration.

The politics of public commemoration is also the subject of art historian Kirk Savage's influential *Standing Soldiers, Kneeling Slaves: Race, War, and Monument in Nineteenth-Century America* (1997). Reminding us of the importance of the visual, built environment in affirming or denying citizenship, Savage teases out the racial meanings to be found in post-Civil War statues of standing soldiers erected in "hundreds of communities" across America (Savage 1997: 182). The style of these local statues evolved over time into an iconic, predictable civic art form quite different from pre-Civil War statuary of generals, leaders, or prominent civic figures. Postwar depictions of ordinary soldiers were an innovation in American public life; they democratized the American landscape, allowing common individuals to stand for collective national purpose.

But which ordinary individuals became symbols of the nation? Savage finds that "for all its novelty, the common-soldier monument was fundamentally reactionary." Its depictions of white males "worked to solidify the association between the white body and the moral duty of citizenship." Although such statues were erected during the same postwar period that African American males gained citizenship, these monuments instead gave the new nationalism "a familiar face, a white face, a likeness this nation has yet to challenge with any real determination" (Savage 1997: 182, 208).

The excision of African American experience from memories of the war did not just occur in the postwar period, of course, but was a process that began during the war itself and can be traced in the pages of an outpouring of popular Civil War literature. As I have pointed out in *The Imagined Civil War: Popular Literature of the North and South, 1861–1865* (2001), representations of black courage and manhood published during the war carried an ironic double message. After Emancipation in 1863, a number of northern popular magazines and journals published stories that prominently featured African American soldiers and celebrated black heroism. Such stories seemed to promise a new, more racially inclusive nationalism – at least in imagination. But sharply circumscribing such inclusivity was a recurrent and ironic plot device: the death of the heroic black soldier in battle. This repeated and convenient narrative strategy provided sacrificial death rather than full national citizenship as the imagined fate of African Americans in American society. A form of narrative violence that itself fed upon the violence of war, such depictions underscored the failure of American society to provide an equal place for African Americans.

Scholars have reached consensus that the exclusion of African Americans from memories of the war – whether in literature, monuments, or commemorations – was an important part of their exclusion from the national polity in Civil War and post-Civil War America. Thus culture and politics have worked hand in hand. In a culminating chapter of *Race and Reunion*, for instance, Blight explores the semi-centennial reunion of Blue and Gray at Gettysburg in 1913, a segregated gathering of some 53,000 veterans that revealed "just how much a combination of white supremacist and reconciliationist memories had conquered all others" by that year. The veterans in attendance had "come to commemorate a glorious fight; and in the end, everyone was right, no one was wrong" (Blight 2001: 387, 386). Fifty years after the war, "racial legacies, conflict itself, the bitter consequences of Reconstruction's failure to make good on the promises of emancipation, and the war as America's second revolution in the meaning of liberty and equality had been *seared clean* from the nation's memory" (ibid. 391). But that "clean narrative" of the Civil War could not "rest uncontested forever across American culture," Blight concludes, making a gesture of hope toward the Civil Rights movement; after all, he notes, "all memory is prelude" (ibid. 391, 397).

Yet that "clean narrative" – a master narrative primarily celebrating white heroism and brotherhood as the deepest meanings of the war – also had remarkable staying power throughout the twentieth century. If the semi-centennial celebrations of the war elided emancipation as a central meaning of the war, so too did the centennial celebrations of the war some 50 years later, as Jon Wiener points out. At the height of the Civil Rights movement in 1963, President Kennedy rejected Martin Luther King's proposal that he issue a Second Emancipation Proclamation, which would have explained that "the Emancipation Proclamation expresses our Nation's policy, founded on justice and morality, and that it is therefore fitting and proper to commemorate the centennial of the historic Emancipation Proclamation throughout the year 1963." Kennedy "did not consider civil rights a major issue" (Wiener 2004: 248–9). While a few state observances "firmly reasserted that slave emancipation provided the Civil War's greatest legacy," South Carolina, Alabama, and Mississippi had in 1961 "started flying the Confederate battle flag over their state capitols, ostensibly as part of the centennial observances" of the outbreak of war. The "Stars and Bars had not figured prominently as a segregationist symbol before 1961. But in 1965, when the centennial ended, none of the states took the flags down." Wiener concludes that the "continuing popularity of the Confederate flag as a symbol of white defiance of black rights remains the most significant legacy of the Civil War centennial" (ibid. 253).

Wiener is one of a number of writers who have puzzled over the continuing appeal of the Civil War – and particularly the Confederacy – within American popular culture. In *Confederates in the Attic: Dispatches from the Unfinished Civil War* (1998), journalist Tony Horwitz documents current-day nostalgia for the Confederacy in the form of reenactors, Confederate museums, and celebrations of Confederate Day (including a celebration in one town that seemed unaware it had been pro-Union during the war), among other commemorations. Among many white southerners, "remembrance of the war had become a talisman against modernity, an emotional lever for their reactionary politics" (Horwitz 1998: 386). Yet a white southern embrace of the Confederacy was not always combined with anti-modernism, as Anne Sarah Rubin shows.

In *A Shattered Nation: The Rise and Fall of the Confederacy, 1861–1868* (2005), Rubin explores the creation of a dual white southern identity – at once southern and American – immediately after the war. Influenced by the recent historiography on Civil War memory, Rubin provides a fresh examination of an old question: the "problem" of Confederate nationalism. For years historians debated whether or not a "genuine" Confederate nationalism had ever existed, given the failure of the Confederacy to build viable institutions. In *The Creation of Confederate Nationalism* (1988), Drew Gilpin Faust added an important link to this chain of argument, insisting that the debate over whether Confederate nationalism had been real or viable missed the point: historians, she urged, should "explore Confederate nationalism in its own terms – as the South's commentary upon itself – as its effort to represent southern culture to the world at large, to history, and perhaps most revealingly, to its own people" (Faust 1988: 6–7). Concentrating on the processes involved in the creation of Confederate nationalism, Faust explored national symbols and myths as well as wartime debates over slavery and societal responsibility to the poor – debates that addressed fundamental questions of paternalistic obligation and authority within southern society. She also examined southerners' self-conscious attempts to create a new national identity through cultural forms such as books, magazines, and newspapers.

Southerners who had complained repeatedly before the war of "trashy" northern literature saw the coming of war as an opportunity to "purify" their literature of Yankee influence and to create new magazines and newspapers. Yet, as I have argued in *The Imagined Civil War*, a central irony of Confederate popular literary culture was that it evolved as a close imitation of northern magazines such as *Harper's Weekly* – indeed, several times during the war Confederate magazines simply reprinted northern stories without attribution. Still, the continual assertion of Confederate difference – despite frequent evidence to the contrary – was an important performative aspect of Confederate nationalism. As Faust has noted, "the struggle for the achievement of nationalism often becomes itself the occasion of its fullest realization" (Faust 1988: 6).

Building explicitly on Faust's work, Rubin explores both the creation of Confederate identity and its continuation after the dismantling of the Confederate state. Moving from Faust's concern with ideology (influenced by anthropologist Clifford Geertz) to an interest in the "imagined community" of the nation (influenced by Benedict Anderson), Rubin defines Confederate nationalism in part as a "felt experience," a "sentimental attachment first to the Confederacy and then to its memory" (Rubin 2005: 5). By 1868, she argues, "the outlines of postwar white Southern identity had been drawn. While Southern whites wanted to be part of the American state, having full rights of political and economic participation, they self-consciously maintained an emotional and cultural connection to their Confederate past" (ibid. 246). Confederates in the post-Civil War period were not necessarily anti-modern; many embraced economic growth and enthusiastically accepted northern capital to rebuild the South. But "public accommodation and private defiance frequently coexisted, and the two strains of Southern identity need to be understood in tandem" (ibid. 247). She concludes that "national identity is not an either–or proposition," pointing out that "white Southerners could be both Southern and American" (ibid.).

Culture is at the heart of Confederate identity in Rubin's account. Confederates "disseminated their culture and values through conversation, correspondence, and a variety of printed media, including newspapers, schoolbooks, music, and literature"; they "created new rituals to bind themselves together" (Rubin 2005: 3). Rubin thus offers us the familiar materials of cultural history, reminiscent of the cultural forms and practices analyzed in Blight's *Race and Reunion*.

But one significant difference between Blight and Rubin lies in Rubin's use of a gendered analysis. Although women figure in Blight's account of the memory of the war, he is primarily interested in a politics of race that is separate from gender. Still, as Blight briefly and suggestively notes, Lost Cause ideology in the late nineteenth century expressed nostalgia for a patriarchal family structure (Blight 2001: 389). In other words, Lost Cause ideology was not only a racialized but also a gendered construct, which assumed a specific and "natural" social hierarchy in which white males would be patriarchal heads of households, with women and children as their dependents. This fundamental insight has informed the work of several Civil War historians who use gender as a category of analysis to understand the war and its aftermath, including LeeAnn Whites's *The Civil War as a Crisis in Gender: Augusta, Georgia, 1860–1890* (1995); Laura Edwards's *Gendered Strife and Confusion: The Political Culture of Reconstruction* (1997); and George C. Rable's *Civil Wars: Women and the Crisis of Southern Nationalism* (1989).

Indebted to this work, Rubin also highlights the politics of gender. As she points out, southern white male identity after the Civil War was shored up not just through the articulation of white supremacy, but also through the articulation of gender supremacy. Although women expanded their roles in wartime, moving into nursing and charity work, after the war they were "again relegated to the domestic and emotional spheres" (Rubin 2005: 209). This gender realignment was part of the racialized work of Reconstruction: white male authority rested on supremacy not just over African Americans, but over white women as well. Other historians have also made this point, stressing that it was not just men but also women who were involved in such cultural work. In *The Civil War as a Crisis in Gender*, for instance, LeeAnn Whites stresses the importance of women's participation in building memorials to wartime heroism as a means of shoring up white male identity. A number of historians agree with Rubin that in the wake of war, "reconstructing notions of appropriate masculinity and femininity allowed Southerners to feel secure in their redefined Southern identity" (ibid. 239).

Stephanie McCurry provides a brilliant elucidation of this point in *Masters of Small Worlds* (1995), her social, cultural, and political study of yeoman men and women. While hers is an antebellum study of the South Carolina Low Country, she also takes up one of the long-lived and recurring questions of Civil War historiography: Why would non-slaveholding yeomen have aligned with the Confederacy, seemingly against their own interests? On what grounds did they support a slaveholders' war? The answer lies in the identification yeomen made with slaveholders as fellow "masters." McCurry's gendered analysis stresses the importance of the household to yeoman identity: within their own households, yeomen were "masters of small worlds," whose manhood was determined by mastery and authority over their dependents – women and children. It was only through claiming such dependents that yeomen were authorized to claim manly independence in the public sphere; and it was only through manly independence that they could claim political (if not social) equality to slaveholders. Though "yeomen were not planters' equals," McCurry notes, "as freemen in a world of dependents" they shared with planters a "definition of manhood rooted in the inviolability of the household, the command of dependents, and the public prerogatives manhood conferred." Thus when they supported secession in the fall of 1860, "lowcountry yeoman farmers acted in defense of their own identity, as masters of small worlds" (McCurry 1995: 304). In contrast to Blight, who stresses the politics to be found in culture, McCurry is interested in the gendered culture attached to and constituting the practices of politics, including electoral politics.

With gender as a tool of analysis, a number of historians have opened up to view both private and public worlds in Civil War America, allowing us to see their intimate connections and their vital role in constructing power. They also challenge us to reconsider one of the most fundamental questions of any war: who fought? Gendered analysis reveals that soldiers did not fight the war alone: instead, they were involved in intricate webs of connection and received multiple forms of support – both material and ideological – from their families and others on the home front. Recognition of the close ties between battlefront and home front has recently drawn military and cultural historians into fruitful discussions of the nature and extent of "the military." While prominent military historian Gary Gallagher has called for cultural historians to study the militarization of society during the war (especially the role of the Army of Northern Virginia as a social and unifying force), gender and cultural historians have likewise called for military historians to explore more fully the permeability of boundaries between home front and battlefront, thereby expanding ideas of what legitimately qualifies as the military dimension of the war.

Most dramatically, cultural history has demonstrated that concerns of gender cannot be separated from the military outcome of the war – whether victory or defeat. According to Drew Gilpin Faust's influential (and controversial) "Altars of Sacrifice: Confederate Women and the Narratives of War" (1990), Confederate women's growing disaffection with a war that demanded unbearable sacrifices from them may have been an important factor in Confederate defeat. As Faust notes, "the way in which [women's] interests in the war were publicly defined – in a very real sense denied – gave women little reason to sustain the commitment modern war required" (Faust 1990: 1228). By early 1865, in fact, "countless women of all classes had in effect deserted the ranks," not only "refusing to accept the economic deprivation further military struggle would have required" but also "resisting additional military service by their husbands and sons" (ibid.).

At issue for Faust is not only the lived experience of the war – the deprivations and hardships it caused – but also the failure of Confederate ideology to provide women with an adequate set of justifications for their support of the war. Women were willing to sacrifice *for* their husbands and sons: "the nineteenth-century creed of domesticity had long urged self-denial and service to others as central to women's mission." But war perverted this system of meaning, transforming "women's self-sacrifice for personally significant others – husbands, brothers, sons, family" into "sacrifice *of* their loved ones" to an "abstract and intangible 'Cause'" (Faust 1990: 1209). Faust's article, a prelude to her *Mothers of Invention* (1996), not only highlights the importance of narratives in wartime to make sense of war and give it meaning, but underlines the potential cultural and social power of those narratives within women's lives.

Lyde Sizer, too, finds cultural power in women's narratives of war. But whereas Faust stresses the misfit between a larger societal "narrative" or "discourse" of patriotic sacrifice and the realities of women's lives, Sizer is more interested in focusing on the power to be found in the writings of women themselves. In *The Political Work of Northern Women Writers and the Civil War, 1850–1872* (2000), Sizer studies nine northern women writers – some of whom were famous on the eve of the war (Harriet Beecher Stowe and Lydia Maria Child), others of whom came of age as writers during the war itself (Louisa May Alcott and Elizabeth Stuart Phelps). Sizer finds that these

women, though excluded from the public sphere of electoral politics and government, were nevertheless able to perform "political work" by using "the back door of
cultural documents" such as novels, short stories, and essays in magazines (Sizer
2000: 15). Through these writings, in which women passionately addressed such
issues as slavery, women revealed their "political understanding of society" (ibid. 7).
Indeed, the war offered these "women writers the opportunity to enter into debates
of national significance" (ibid. 15). While women may not have been allowed to
speak on the floor of Congress, they could certainly debate "the meaning of the many
divisions in Northern society" in their writings, which created "an alternative history
and narrative of the war" (ibid. 13, 12). That alternative narrative featured women
as central figures in the war. "Instead of accepting their offstage relation to war, they
described the war's crucial events as happening where they were located, be it at
home well away from the fighting, in a hospital in Washington, D.C., or on the battlefield itself" (ibid. 6). And in Sizer's view, the act of telling such stories exercised a
form of social power.

    While Faust sees southern white women – including prominent writers such as
Augusta Jane Evans, author of the popular wartime novel *Macaria* – as primarily
trapped within a discourse and ideology of sacrifice, Sizer sees more varied opportunity for expression among northern women writers. To some extent this distinction
results from different methodologies: Faust's discourse analysis has the side-effect of
stressing the immersion of southern women in a dominant cultural discourse of self-
sacrifice, while Sizer tends to stress individual agency – perhaps not surprisingly, given
her choice of subjects. Trapped within the constraints of southern ideology, with its
emphasis on a rigid system of separate spheres, Faust's women had less room for
agency except at the level of resistance.

    But it is not just differences in methodology that account for the differences in
the agency of southern and northern women in these two accounts. Sizer is quick to
note that on the eve of the war, northern women writers – an outspoken, articulate
group – could draw upon the resources of a burgeoning print culture as well as a
substantial history of women's activism. In a world with a growing number of voices
reaching a diverse and widespread audience, women could hold "diverging positions
on the reigning ideologies supporting the Union war effort" (Sizer 2000: 13). Northern women as well as southern encountered the constraints of "separate spheres";
within republican ideology, women were subordinates whose voices "were not meant
to be heard in a national public context" (ibid. 12). But to some extent dominant
ideology and social reality diverged in the North: women could draw not only upon
the resources of a history of activism (from the moral reform societies that appeared
in the wake of evangelical revival, to the woman's rights movement that emerged in
tandem with abolitionism), but also upon the resources of commercial print culture.
Both gave women a "place" to speak in public.

    No wonder, then, that so many northern women claimed that the war had trans-
formed and empowered their lives. At the level of ideology there may well have been
a revolution in women's sense of themselves. Sizer argues that:

> middle-class women came to believe that they had an acknowledged stake in a national
> ordeal of overwhelming importance, a personal stake in national politics. By the end of
> the war, many believed they had a right to a place in the history books, and they

continued to believe this even after they became aware that their stories might never be written by the male scholars of the war. (Sizer 2000: 4)

Though many northern women later claimed that the war had produced a revolution in "woman's sense of herself," there was no immediate corresponding revolution in society or in material conditions; a substantial gap opened between "public rhetoric and social reality" (ibid.). Yet public rhetoric inspired and energized women – they emerged from war with a "changed understanding of womanhood and social possibility," which would sustain and inspire many in the postwar period. In short, it was at the level of culture – beliefs concerning the meanings of the Civil War for women – that northern women registered the impact of the war.

The Civil War also energized African American women writers; one of the strengths of Sizer's book is her detailed analysis of the "cultural work" of Frances Ellen Watkins Harper. Harper viewed the Civil War as "the turning point for her and her people, and she constantly reminded them of its meaning" in poems, fiction, and through lectures that underlined her commitment to an oral as well as written culture of activism (Sizer 2000: 273). But as Dickson D. Bruce, Jr. points out in *The Origins of African American Literature, 1680–1865* (2001), the venues available to African American writers for publication changed dramatically after the war. With major anti-slavery publications such as Garrison's *Liberator* discontinued in 1865, the interracial cultural arena began to narrow, and increasingly the African American press – including those papers that sought an interracial audience – had to settle for "an exclusively black readership" (Bruce 2001: 313).

Civil War cultural history has too often ignored African American women's experiences – not to mention African American experience more generally, which primarily remains the domain of slavery studies. It is telling that one of the most innovative recent studies of African American culture in wartime is Steven Hahn's *A Nation under Our Feet: Black Political Struggles in the Rural South from Slavery to the Great Migration* (2003), which explores the importance of rumor as a unifying political force among slaves. But Hahn's is primarily a political rather than a cultural history. Likewise, Leslie Schwalm's path-breaking *A Hard Fight for We: Women's Transition from Slavery to Freedom in South Carolina* (1997) provides a compelling account of slave women's experiences in wartime, but is primarily a social history.

David Blight's praiseworthy, passionate, and sustained attention to black culture during and after the war remains the exception rather than the rule in Civil War cultural history. As Jim Cullen noted in *The Civil War in Popular Culture* (1995), a study ranging in subject matter from Margaret Mitchell's *Gone with the Wind* to war reenactors: "in the twentieth century, fascination with the Civil War has been a white affair" (Cullen 1995: 198). The "most fundamental question hovering over" Cullen's book is, "Why, for whites, at least, does the Civil War continue to exert its persistent power in U.S. life?" (ibid. 199).

Cullen is not alone in his unease with Civil War cultural studies and history. Indeed, one of the most interesting trends in recent Civil War historiography has been a call by two prominent historians to reexamine the fundamental nature of our enduring fascination with the war. In "Worrying about the Civil War" (1998), Edward L. Ayers explores the recent evolution of a "progressive" narrative of the war made popular, he argues, by James M. McPherson's *Battle Cry of Freedom: The Civil War Era* (1988) and Ken Burns's PBS series *The Civil War* (1990). Ayers encapsulates what he calls these "inspiring" tales of the war as follows: "White Northerners, white Southerners, and black Americans all grow morally during the war that Burns and McPherson portray. The white North comes truly to abhor slavery; white Southerners recognize the limits of their power and the meaning of full nationhood; black Americans gain not only freedom but also heightened dignity when they take up arms for their freedom." Overall, according to Ayers, these "powerful histories tell a story of freedom emerging through the trial of war, a great nation becoming greater through suffering" (Ayers 1998: 148).

This powerful story makes Ayers nervous: "the elegance and directness with which [McPherson] and Burns tell their stories," he observes,

> can lead us to forget what a complicated event the Civil War was. It was, after all, simultaneously a war among citizens and among states, a war fought by disciplined soldier-citizens and a war that continually threatened to spin out of anyone's control, a war whose opponents were driven by hatred and yet who quickly reconciled when it became convenient, a war in which slavery died at the hands of soldiers who often fought against slavery reluctantly and even then because slavery's destruction seemed the only practical way to win.   (Ayers 1998: 149–50)

Ayers has made an important intervention in Civil War studies with these remarks, but his account of McPherson's approach to the Civil War misrepresents the complexity of McPherson's classic *Battle Cry of Freedom*. With its powerful depiction of the forces of federal power created and unleashed by war, McPherson's account gives us a strong sense of the scope, intensity, and violence of the war. And with its emphasis on the emergence of federal power and its consequences for national life, McPherson's is not simply a tidy story of progress.

Yet Ayers is right in asserting that in general we have become too complacent in our approaches to the Civil War, often making it into a "good war" without sufficient reflection. In Ayers's view a progressive narrative of the Civil War has become so dominant as to seem self-evident. We no longer remember the cynicism and irony with which historians during the 1920s and 1930s remembered the war or dared to question its violence; instead, "today's stories tend to be earnest accounts, clear and linear, with motives and emotions close to the surface." They offer familiar and therefore comfortable narratives that fit into a set of powerful cultural assumptions – derived from such disparate sources as evolutionism and the Judeo-Christian religious tradition – affirming the necessity of violence in Western culture, and accustoming us "to think of violence and blood as necessary accompaniments of progress" (Ayers 1998: 157).

Ayers acknowledges that some historians have explored the destructive violence of war. Charles Royster's *The Destructive War* (1991), for instance, not only highlights the physical violence of the war, but also examines the eagerness with which ordinary Americans sought to participate in a "vicarious war" through reading about and visualizing the war in newspapers, magazines, and countless stories. Deeply immersed in this wartime culture, spectators/participants ultimately romanticized violence, arguing that only through violence would Americans develop a higher moral character (Royster 1991: 232–95). Royster's unsentimental, often scathing view of the war is an heir to Edmund Wilson's classic 1962 account of wartime literature, *Patriotic Gore*, which condemned all "cant" about the nobility of war, on the grounds that "the wars fought by human beings are stimulated as a rule primarily by the same instincts as the voracity of the sea slug" (Wilson 1962: xi–xii).

For the most part, Ayers argues, Americans have not sufficiently questioned the violence of war. He regrets the absence in Civil War historiography of the lively historical debate surrounding comparably major historical events, such as the French Revolution (Ayers 1998: 160). Responding to these concerns, Ayers calls for a history of the war that would recognize its contingency. (Ironically, this is also a call made by McPherson, who says that "most attempts to explain southern defeat or northern victory lack the dimension of *contingency* – the recognition that at numerous critical points during the war things might have gone altogether differently" (McPherson 1988: 858).

Ayers acknowledges that "because the war ended with the survival of the Union, that survival now seems the natural outcome of the war." Likewise, "because slavery came to an end in 1865, that victory has suffused the purposes of the North throughout the war and before" (Ayers 1998: 160). But not only were wartime events contingent, "so were apparently fixed ideologies, values, personalities, and memories" (ibid. 161). He concludes that "slavery and freedom remain the keys to understanding the war – but they are the place to begin our questions, not end them." We should not be too comfortable in assuming that freedom was "driven by the machinery of modern life, achieved through cathartic violence, and embodied in a government that valued freedom above all else" (ibid. 163).

Ayers's *In the Presence of Mine Enemies: War in the Heart of America, 1859–1863* (2003) attempts to recover "the deep contingency of history," the "dense and intricate connections in which lives and events are embedded" (Ayers 2003: xix). Rich in the multiple individual stories of the war, *In the Presence of Mine Enemies* details life in two communities: Augusta County, Virginia, and Franklin County, Pennsylvania. Both social and cultural history, the book employs an array of materials including diaries, letters, official records, soldiers' records, census reports, and church records (all of which are digitized at Ayers's "Valley of the Shadow" website). It is a signal contribution to one of the most vital historiographic areas of Civil War study to emerge in recent years – community and local history.

The book starts from the premise that "Americans could not have imagined the war they brought on themselves," nor could they have known "that the most powerful slave society of the modern world, generations in the making, would be destroyed in a matter of years" – not to mention that "African Americans could so quickly rise to seize freedom from the turmoil" (Ayers 2003: xvii). It offers "a history of the Civil War told from the viewpoints of everyday people who could glimpse only parts of the drama they were living, who did not control the history that shaped their lives." It "emphasizes the flux of emotion and belief, the intertwining of reason and feeling, the constant revision of history, as people lived within history" (ibid.).

Ayers's innovation in narrative methodology is to tell numerous local individual stories, linked – or interrupted – by historical narrative providing a broader, often national, context. Thus while Ayers emphasizes the contingency of daily life during the Civil War, he does not abandon the notion of synthesis as a narrative principle.

Far from valorizing a form of historical relativism in which every story is equal, Ayers does not eschew interpretation; and his historical passages, demarcated from the rest of the text in italics, both rescue and reaffirm ideas both of narrative authority and synthesis. Indeed, to some extent that synthesis echoes the "progressive" narrative of McPherson, with its emphasis on the power of a new nationalism in American life.

Yet Ayers's language of flux, partial glimpses, and lack of control all seem appropriate to our own moment in historical time, in which historians have lost their sense that one overarching story of the Civil War could – or even should – be told. Given that the progressive story of the Civil War according to Ayers emerged during the 1960s and 1970s, arguably a time of pre-eminent American power in the world, it should not surprise us that a more fraught, postmodern story of the Civil War has emerged in the post-9/11 world.

In this new climate, at least one historian has radically questioned the whole enterprise of Civil War historiography. In " 'We Should Grow Too Fond of It': Why We Love the Civil War" (2004), Drew Gilpin Faust first acknowledges and assesses the recent growth of a "new" Civil War historiography including social history, women's history, and community history, and then steps back to consider the reasons for historians' attractions to the war as subject matter. What she finds makes her distinctly uncomfortable. We have developed a love affair with war, a deep attraction to the dramatic stories war offers. After all, war provides "a plot that imbues its actors with purpose and moves toward victory for one or another side. This is why it provides the satisfaction of meaning to its participants; this is why, too, it offers such a natural attraction to writers and historians" (Faust 2004: 382).

But what is the effect of the narratives of war constructed by historians? On the one hand, Faust notes, "writers and historians are critical to defining and elaborating the narratives that differentiate war from purposeless violence, the stories that explain, contextualize, construct, order, and rationalize – eliding from one to the other meaning of that word – what we call war." Yet that may mean that historians inadvertently contribute to what Susan Sontag called the "perennial seductiveness" of war (Faust 2004: 382). As a cultural historian, Faust is aware of the "role of war stories in mobilizing both men and women for war." As she argues, "seductive tales of glory, honor, sacrifice provide one means of making war possible." Thus the "voices of writers and storytellers have also made war possible from ancient times to the present day" (ibid. 383). But if writers and historians have helped to make war possible, Faust concludes, then "we should ask ourselves how in the construction of war's stories we may be helping to construct war itself. 'War is a force that gives *us* meaning.' But what do we and our writings give to war?" (ibid.).

Faust's question alerts us: we may be seeing only the beginning of a painful new reassessment of the entire enterprise of Civil War history. Long lagging behind other areas of Americanist historiography in embracing innovative subjects and methodologies, the broad arena of Civil War studies has begun to catch up. A field that was once dominated by narrow approaches has opened up to new voices and new subjects, and if the end result is a period of narrative uncertainty, that can only be a good thing in the quest to understand not just the American Civil War, but war itself.

REFERENCES

Ayers, Edward L.: "Worrying about the Civil War," in Karen Halttunen & Lewis Perry, eds., *Moral Problems in American Life: New Perspectives on Cultural History* (Ithaca, NY: Cornell University Press, 1998).

Ayers, Edward L.: *In the Presence of Mine Enemies: War in the Heart of America, 1859–1863* (New York: W. W. Norton, 2003).

Blair, William: *Cities of the Dead: Contesting the Memory of the Civil War in the South, 1865–1914* (Chapel Hill: University of North Carolina Press, 2004).

Blight, David W.: *Race and Reunion: The Civil War in American Memory* (Cambridge, MA: Harvard University Press, 2001).

Blight, David W.: *Beyond the Battlefield: Race, Memory, and the American Civil War* (Amherst: University of Massachusetts Press, 2002).

Bruce, Dickson D., Jr.: *The Origins of African American Literature, 1680–1865* (Charlottesville: University of Virginia Press, 2001).

Cullen, James: *The Civil War in Popular Culture: A Reusable Past* (Washington, DC: Smithsonian Institution Press, 1995).

Edwards, Laura: *Gendered Strife and Confusion: The Political Culture of Reconstruction* (Urbana: University of Illinois Press, 1997).

Fahs, Alice: *The Imagined Civil War: Popular Literature of the North and South, 1861–1865* (Chapel Hill: University of North Carolina Press, 2001).

Fahs, Alice & Waugh, Joan, eds.: *The Memory of the Civil War in American Culture* (Chapel Hill: University of North Carolina Press, 2004).

Faust, Drew Gilpin: *The Creation of Confederate Nationalism: Ideology and Identity in the Civil War South* (Baton Rouge: Louisiana State University Press, 1988).

Faust, Drew Gilpin: "Altars of Sacrifice: Confederate Women and the Narratives of War," *Journal of American History* 76 (March 1990), 1200–28.

Faust, Drew Gilpin: *Mothers of Invention: Women of the Slaveholding South in the American Civil War* (Chapel Hill: University of North Carolina Press, 1996).

Faust, Drew Gilpin: "'We Should Grow Too Fond of It': Why We Love the Civil War," *Civil War History* 50 (December 2004), 368–83.

Hahn, Steven: *A Nation under Our Feet: Black Political Struggles in the Rural South from Slavery to the Great Migration* (Cambridge, MA: Harvard University Press, 2003).

Horwitz, Tony: *Confederates in the Attic: Dispatches from the Unfinished Civil War* (New York: Pantheon Books, 1998).

McConnell, Stuart: *Glorious Contentment: The Grand Army of the Republic, 1865–1900* (Chapel Hill: University of North Carolina Press, 1992).

McCurry, Stephanie: *Masters of Small Worlds: Yeoman Households, Gender Relations, and the Political Culture of the Antebellum South Carolina Low Country* (New York: Oxford University Press, 1995).

McPherson, James M.: *Battle Cry of Freedom: The Civil War Era* (New York: Oxford University Press, 1988).

Neff, John R.: *Honoring the Civil War Dead: Commemoration and the Problem of Reconciliation* (Lawrence: University Press of Kansas, 2005).

Rable, George C.: *Civil Wars: Women and the Crisis of Southern Nationalism* (Urbana: University of Illinois Press, 1989).

Royster, Charles: *The Destructive War: William Tecumseh Sherman, Stonewall Jackson, and the Americans* (New York: Alfred A. Knopf, 1991).

Rubin, Anne Sarah: *A Shattered Nation: The Rise and Fall of the Confederacy, 1861–1868* (Chapel Hill: University of North Carolina Press, 2005).

Savage, Kirk: *Standing Soldiers, Kneeling Slaves: Race, War, and Monument in Nineteenth-Century America* (Princeton, NJ: Princeton University Press, 1997).

Schwalm, Leslie: *A Hard Fight for We: Women's Transition from Slavery to Freedom in South Carolina* (Champaign: University of Illinois Press, 1997).

Silber, Nina: *The Romance of Reunion: Northerners and the South, 1865–1900* (Chapel Hill: University of North Carolina Press, 1993).

Sizer, Lyde Cullen: *The Political Work of Northern Women Writers and the Civil War, 1850–1872* (Chapel Hill: University of North Carolina Press, 2000).

Whites, LeeAnn: *The Civil War as a Crisis in Gender: Augusta, Georgia, 1860–1890* (Athens: University of Georgia Press, 1995).

Wiener, Jon: "Civil War, Cold War, Civil Rights: The Civil War Centennial in Context," in Alice Fahs & Joan Waugh, eds., *The Memory of the Civil War in American Culture* (Chapel Hill: University of North Carolina Press, 2004), pp. 236–57.

Wilson, Edmund: *Patriotic Gore: Studies in the Literature of the American Civil War* (New York: Oxford University Press, 1962).

Chapter Nine

THE WEST

Ann Fabian

Chicago, 1893

Cultural historians working on the nineteenth-century United States have found rich material at the World's Columbian Exposition of 1893. Exposition designers created an ideal "White City" on the marshy shores of Lake Michigan, about seven miles outside downtown Chicago. They built an artificial world of some 400 neoclassical buildings where visitors marveled at the genius of American technology, gawked at the products of American industry and agriculture, and generally celebrated 400 years of post-Columbian cultural accomplishment in the Americas. The fair assured visitors, particularly its white visitors, that America could leave behind the Civil War, overcome industrial unrest, and join the world as a nation composed of culturally accomplished people.

Students looking for the American West in the cultural history of the nineteenth-century United States also do well in Chicago. Two of the West's master storytellers, historian Frederick Jackson Turner (1861–1932) and showman William F. Cody (1849–1917), appeared in Chicago that year. Turner, a 32-year-old assistant professor teaching at the University of Wisconsin, delivered his first academic paper at the inaugural meeting of the American Historical Association. Although his audience was small, the young professor took a big swing with his paper on "The Significance of the Frontier in American History," explaining to colleagues that the distinguishing feature of American history was the repeated settlement of successive American frontiers. The frontier was both the cradle of American individualism and the source of American democracy.

Cody, at the height of his fame, presided over "Buffalo Bill's Wild West Show" at a packed arena just outside the gates of the fairgrounds. We have no evidence that Cody and Turner ever met, but each of them launched a version of the American West that has had lasting influence on how we imagine the past of the region. From opposite directions – from Cody's dusty arenas and Turner's musty archives – the two men moved the West to the center of American culture, making the American frontier, with its distinctive patterns of cultural encounter, bloody conquest, and family settlement, crucial to the ways Americans imagine themselves, and the past, present, and future of the nation.

With their contrasting versions of the American West, Turner and Cody offer us different ways to think about questions cultural historians often ask about meaning and truth. The suggestion that Turner the historian offered an accurate reading of the American past while Buffalo Bill did not misses what is culturally central about each of them. The historian and the showman were co-workers in the cultural history of the American West: Turner worked with figures of speech; Cody with figures on horseback; but each man composed the metaphors that helped serious-minded students, quiet readers, and cheering audiences make sense of the world. But even though they worked the same imaginative territory, each told a partial story sure to suit the experience of some Americans better than others. Turner's heroes were yeoman farmers, plodding their way across the continent. Cody's were mounted scouts and armed cowboys, defending white families besieged by natives. As historian Richard White put it, "To see Turner as serious and significant and Buffalo Bill as a charlatan and a curiosity, to see Turner as history and Buffalo Bill as entertainment, to see one as concerned with reality and the other with myth, is to miss their common reliance on, and promotion of, the iconography of their time. Turner and Cody followed separate but connected strands of a single mythic cloth" (White 1994: 45).

For the last half-century, cultural historians have been following the threads of that mythic cloth, tracing the interplay of fact and imagination, representation and lived experience, at the heart of the nineteenth-century West. Moving Buffalo Bill and Frederick Jackson Turner together to the center of our discussion of cultural history prompts us to ask about the part the American West has played in the cultural history of the nineteenth-century United States as a whole and, taking a different tack, to investigate what the insights of cultural historians tell us about the history of the American West as a distinct region of the country. How has the American West shaped the national imagination, molding the way men and women, black and white, immigrant and native-born, European and Native American see themselves as Americans? How does the concept of culture help us to understand patterns of conflict and cooperation that mark the history of contacts among the diverse peoples who have called regions of the West home? Historians asking the first set of questions study easterners looking west and, as we shall see, it is often with easterners imagining the West with words, paint, and camera that discussions about the American West and American culture begin.

But a second set of questions about westerners themselves has become increasingly important. "The imagined West," historian Elliott West writes, "has had a profound, continuing influence on the West of reality. In the end, we cannot separate those two geographies – the Western State of Mind, and western states of Kansas, Colorado, Nebraska, and the rest" (West 1995: 131). Culture in the West can mean many things. Westerners – Euro-American and Native American – took jobs in the culture industry, playing themselves for audiences squeezed onto bleachers at Wild West shows and packed into early movie theaters. Westerners at home strutted for eastern tourists, transforming both their region and themselves. The tourist "never simply tours through the West," historian Earl Pomeroy wrote in the mid-1950s, "he changes the West when he looks at it, not only because he wears out the highway pavements, but because Westerners change the West into what they think he wants it to be" (Pomeroy 1957: vii).

More significantly, westerners of diverse ethnic and cultural backgrounds made communities along cultural fault lines, negotiating (or failing to negotiate) around deep differences in how they imagined the world and their places in it. Historians interested in culture as something more than popular representations of hardy pioneers and hard-riding cowboys employ anthropological ideas about culture and insist that the importance of the American West lies in its cultural diversity and in the persistence of the cultures of peoples whose political and economic power may have diminished.

In the American West, Native American, Hispanic, Euro-American, African American, and Asian cultures mix in complicated ways, reminding us of the region's rich history of cultural cross-fertilization. Complex cultural convergences characterize the history of the American West; groups of people used different languages and different cultural tools to express their different political and economic interests and their very different beliefs about the way the world ought to work. Elliott West described the western plains as a place where "[v]aried peoples of unequal power adapted in their own ways while contesting with each other for shrinking resources and expanding opportunities within diverse and changing environments shaped by an erratic climate" (West 1995: 11). In a world of unequal power relations, cultural exchanges were not simple, as we learn from historian James F. Brooks's history of slavery and kinship, conflict and cultural accommodation, in the southwest borderlands. A study of patterns of "cultural sharing through systems of violence and kinship," he writes, "deepens our understanding of how 'mixed' groups of peoples in the Southwest and how ethnic communities themselves were historically and culturally sorted and produced" (Brooks 2002: 37).

Brooks learned a great deal from anthropologists, and his book draws our attention to a different thread in the cloth of culture. In the early years of the twentieth century, American anthropologists worked out new definitions of culture, often among the native peoples of the American West. Again, a visit to the fair in Chicago is instructive. Many visitors took in the Exposition's serious lessons on history, progress, and the evolution of American culture. In fact, the historians Turner addressed were part of the official fair, well-educated and cultured men comfortable in the well-appointed rooms of the "White City."

Culture showed a different face along the mile of the "Midway Plaisance," an area of restaurants, carnival rides, side shows, exotic dancers, and ethnic villages. In the villages, set up under the direction of the fair's Department of Ethnology, men and women from Africa, Asia, and Europe, and families of Native Americans performed their ethnic cultures for fairgoers, male and female alike. For many visitors, the villages represented humanity's earlier stages, steps along an evolutionary pyramid of racial hierarchy that held room at its pointy top only for men and women like modern white Americans. But some also viewed these exhibits through an emerging anthropological notion of culture that acknowledged cultural differences in the ways human societies ordered their worlds and yet did not insist on seeing difference as evidence of necessary evolutionary progress from savagery to civilization.

Eastern Imaginations and American Wests

Cultural histories of the American West begin with a body of literature that looks at the ways easterners have imagined the West. Several writers have explored the role of the American West in cultural dramas played out in the minds of novelists, poets, artists, photographers, politicians, and young white men worried that their overcivilized and excessively refined lives had laid waste to their masculinity. Turner and Cody both have parts in the drama, but it was Henry Nash Smith's *Virgin Land: The American West as Symbol and Myth* (1950) that first opened the American West as territory for cultural historians.

Smith began working on eastern perceptions of the West in the 1930s when he was a graduate student in Harvard's program in American Civilization, and he stayed with the project for the next 20 years. The West might just be the place to look for answers to the most basic questions about what it has meant to be an American. In fact, Smith opens *Virgin Land* posing the question the writer St. John de Crèvecoeur asked before the American Revolution: "What is an American?" According to Smith, every American generation repeats Crèvecoeur's question, and, Smith contends, Americans of successive generations have replied that American "society has been shaped by the pull of a vacant continent drawing population westward through the passes of the Alleghenies, across the Mississippi Valley, over the high plains and mountains of the Far West to the Pacific Coast" (Smith 1950: 3). This "axiom," as he calls it, appears in writings of American pundits, politicians, statesmen, philosophers, novelists, and poets, and in images of the West produced by painters, photographers, and popular illustrators. Frederick Jackson Turner gave the myth of the West classic form in his "Significance of the Frontier in American History." Smith reads Turner's essay as an eloquent distillation of ideas about the West already deeply familiar to his audiences, if but dimly seen by them. Deep familiarity, not historical originality, gave the essay its power.

These distilled ideas, which Smith labels myths and symbols, are the subject of his classic work. *Virgin Land* is a remarkably comprehensive book, introducing readers to an enormous cast of obscure characters and the obscure products of their imaginations. Smith recovered writings of small-time journalists, journeymen politicians, hack poets, and dime novelists, and he restored complexity to the novels of James Fenimore Cooper. But for years, Smith's vague definitions of myths and symbols have troubled readers. He used the terms to distinguish literary and philosophical "products of the imagination" from "empirical fact." Products of the imagination, he wrote, "exist on a different plane. But as I have tried to show they sometimes exert a decided influence on practical affairs" (Smith 1950: xi). Smith's argument goes something like this. Images of the West lured men and women into the West and helped them imagine what they could and should do once they were there. Ideas and images were also instrumental in creating political consensus necessary to fund explorations, to wage wars against Indians and Mexicans, and to pass laws like the Homestead Act.

Of course myths and symbols were sometimes dead wrong about the worlds they pretended to describe – blinding policy makers caught up in agrarian fantasies of sturdy yeomen working well-watered farms to the needs of westerners living in cities or deserts or working in factories. Even historians were tricked; under Turner's sway they looked for the West of individualistic white pioneers, ignoring those who were racially and culturally different and minimizing the long history of government financial support that allowed so many western individuals to maintain the happy myth that they had done it all on their own. Stories of heroic pioneers were relatively harmless. At other times, however, the consequences of believing in myths and symbols and acting on them were deadly for people, plants, and animals. But, as we learn so well from Smith, empirical accuracy was not the task of myths and symbols.

Virgin Land pleased its contemporary readers, winning awards from both historians and literary scholars, who embraced the book as a contribution to the study of American character and praised Smith's insights on the intersections of politics and language. His book enriched readings of novels and poetry by exploring the historical context of literary works; enlivened economic and political history by attending to the symbolic aspects of the human imagination; and expanded the field of American studies by giving serious consideration to popular culture. In the 1950s, the book worked well in the new programs in "American Studies" taught in universities at home and sponsored by US embassies abroad.

In the 1950s, the book also appealed to readers outside the academy curious about the mix of democratic politics and popular culture that characterized "the American Century." Although Smith had begun working on the West in the 1930s, it was not until after World War II that the arguments in the book took shape when Smith began reading dime novel westerns and working on Frederick Jackson Turner's papers. Smith combined intellectual history and popular culture and presented a sketch for an intellectual history of American empire, offering readers a cultural background for the newfound dominance of the United States. Old prophecies of westward-moving empire came alive in *Virgin Land*. Expansion across the continent assured "passage to India," but once the United States had secured its continental empire, the interior became part of a vast commercial enterprise – an "empire for liberty." Smith conjures American triumph early in the book, recovering from the late eighteenth century "a humorous skit in *Lloyd's Evening Post*, to which the mid-twentieth century has lent a grim dramatic irony, pictured two Americans visiting London in 1974 and finding it in ruins like Balbec or Rome" (Smith 1950: 8).

Although Smith worked within the context of a victorious culture, his book is not triumphal. And although Smith worked over some of the territory that lent Turner's writings their optimistic tone about American democracy, his message is not entirely upbeat. He recognized that the symbolic dimension of politics was often as important as what passed for hardheaded realism, but those who entered the world of symbols sometimes checked rationality at the door. Despite the problems with Smith's casual definitions of symbols and myths, he used his history of the American imagination to remind readers who were watching wartime unity dissolve and a culture turn to the suppression of all dissent that in politics what passed as reason, learning, and experience was shaped by illogical dictates of myth. Smith's work on the "myth of virgin land" convinced him that politics could be irrational, and that empirical facts were often powerless against opinion bolstered by compelling patterns of myth.

As Smith worked on the cultural dimensions of politics, he also noticed the political dimensions of culture, describing for readers the tensions in American literature between the generic conventions of well-plotted novels and the peculiar social experience that was the United States. Could the country ever produce great literature when literary figures drawn from the key social experiences of western settlement had trouble passing as literary heroes? Reading Cooper, Smith recognized that the West could be a paradoxical source for American culture, producing good-hearted but unrefined figures for the high table of American culture. It is not surprising that

Smith turned away from *Virgin Land* and spent much of the rest of his career working on Mark Twain, a writer who knew the paradoxes of a democratic culture.

During the last half-century, critical readers have questioned Smith's broad generalizations about "Americans" and wondered at his confidence that the varied experiences of past actors could be captured in a single unifying myth. They have faulted the book for its lack of clarity about the relations between facts and the myths spun around them, and complained that the long and detailed book says very little about the native peoples who lived on the so-called virgin land and that it ignores the obvious play of gender in the language of its title. They have pointed out that Smith has too narrow a sense of American audiences, substituting a small group of readers for all of America and ignoring the fact that the myth of virgin land actually served the economic interests of railroad promoters and land speculators, narrowly, and industrial capitalists, more generally. In the end, though, as literary scholar Lee Clark Mitchell writes, Smith "forced us to consider the significance of the West in other than purely political or economic terms. He extracted a cultural meaning from the West that others have found alternately inadequate, monological, and elitist; but the important point is that he succeeded in turning us back to the study of cultural meaning" (Mitchell 1991. 265).

A notion of "cultural meaning" has proved useful to historians interested in understanding how both Turner and his frontier thesis and Buffalo Bill and his Wild West Show worked their distinctive magic on American readers and audiences. In the 1990s, to celebrate the centennial of Turner's famous paper, several historians looked back over his career, giving us a portrait of a man historian John Mack Faragher dubbed "America's first truly modern historian" (Faragher 1994: 4). To understand Turner, Faragher suggests, we need to take account of a cultural shift that granted authority to men with Turner's training and position, men with PhDs in their fields who held posts in universities.

Echoing Smith, Faragher found that the power of the "frontier thesis derived from its commitment to the study of what it meant to be American. That is the part of the Turnerian view we would do well to preserve." But there were real negative consequences to Turner's pronouncements, a dark side made more powerful by the cultural authority contemporaries granted men in positions like his. As Faragher put it,

> the Turnerian interpretation of western expansion read back into the past both the assurance and the arrogance of the victors in a centuries-long campaign of conquest. Turner made that victory seem inevitable, but the history of the American West now being written serves to remind us that there is nothing smooth about it at all – that the victory of one people was usually at the expense of another. (Faragher 1994: 241)

Turner did not see the need to calculate that expense; his position of authority, as historian Patricia Nelson Limerick has written, helped insulate him from the need to recognize that he held a distinct cultural position and that his vision of the American past might be a partial and peculiar one. Although Turner was anxious to use history to solve contemporary problems, he chose among the many kinds of problems confronting late nineteenth- and early twentieth-century Americans, picking those most explainable by the history he chose to write. He thought about the future of a society that could no longer depend on the frontier processes that made American democrats of European immigrants, for example, and not about the acts of white racial violence that cast their ugly shadows over contemporary African American communities (Limerick 1995; Klein 1997).

Buffalo Bill

Cody has fared better than Turner in recent cultural histories. Excellent books have added layers of complexity and ambiguity to Buffalo Bill, giving us a man whose cultural artistry helped shape twentieth-century mass culture and the cult of celebrity, whose shows comforted audiences anxious about industrialization, urbanization, modernization, the fate of nature, and the future of the nation. Cody was the first great celebrity of the twentieth century, the pioneer of American mass culture, the man, according to historian Joy Kasson, who forged the link between "national identity and popular culture, between Americans' understanding of their history and their consumption of spectacularized versions of it" (Kasson 2000: 8). The Wild West Show brought forward audience concerns about nature and progress and rehearsed memories of war and violence. Cody's shows (and many of the popular westerns that followed the patterns he set down), dramatized "cultural issues . . . basic to American national identity: the use of violence and conquest in the formation of the American nation, American's love–hate relationship with unspoiled nature and native peoples, gender and the meaning of heroism, and the role of the individual in an increasingly urban, industrial, and corporate society" (Kasson 2000: 269).

The shows worked because they presented audiences with imaginative solutions to real problems: the settler's cabin burned night after night, but no one died; Native Americans fired rifles into the air, but then, after the show, welcomed audiences to their campsites on the show grounds. Wild West shows, we know now, also provided a stage and living wages for Native Americans, who seized on opportunities to perform as entertainment the dances and chants prohibited on reservations. Perhaps some also took satisfaction in performing the armed raids that would have proved suicidal on the militarized frontier.

For generations, serious-minded historians working on the American West dismissed Buffalo Bill as a sort of embarrassment, one source of the region's sometimes poor intellectual or cultural standing. Buffalo Bill was too popular, too commercial, too sensational, and too much the fabulist to deserve a place in serious studies of the American West. His staged presentations distracted contemporary audiences and present-day historians alike from pressing concerns of real lives and hard facts. To keep Buffalo Bill in line, some historians set out to discover the "real" Cody operating behind the legends of Buffalo Bill, as though empirical facts were history's only goal. In textbooks on the American West, Cody's Wild West Shows often got brief mention in last chapters on the "mythic" or "imaginary" West, as though the shows' presence there as isolated afterthoughts protected discussions of real historical matters from contamination by popular fluff.

Recent work by cultural historians L. G. Moses, Joy Kasson, and Louis Warren has taught us to think otherwise. They acknowledge that Buffalo Bill's West may have been an imaginary place, but they insist, as Richard White suggested, that we are mistaken to assume that we can easily divide an imaginary West from a real one. The curious fact that Buffalo Bill Cody himself and many of those who worked with him were simultaneously theatrical and historical actors is one of the most useful insights of new cultural histories of the American West. Buffalo Bill operated in a world where imagination tangled with material reality in complicated ways. Cody is intriguing because he alternated seasons on the plains "being" himself with seasons on the stage "playing" himself, much to the delight of cultural historians schooled first by P. T. Barnum and then by postmodern cultural theorists to celebrate performance and creative play with cultural identity.

Indeed, Cody's distinctive dances of fact and imagination are typical of the new cultural history of the American West. Historians now embrace the region's curious relations with reality, following a line of inquiry that owes a great deal to Mark Twain's *Roughing It* (1872), and exploring the ironies of the American West's distinctive tangle of so-called facts and their imaginary reworkings. The West abounds in these ironic encounters, historian Patricia Limerick reminds us. In one particularly telling example, she describes Kit Carson's attempt

> to rescue a white woman, providentially named Mrs. White, who had been taken captive by the Jicarilla Apaches. When the search party caught up with the Indians, it was too late; Mrs. White had just been killed. But Kit Carson came upon a surprising souvenir. "We found a book in the camp," he reported, "the first of the kind I had ever seen, in which I was represented as a great hero, slaying Indians by the hundreds." (Limerick 1992: 167)

What, Limerick wondered, had Mrs. White been thinking as she read that dime novel? Were she and the readers who adopted her point of view imagining rescuers who would defend them from savages? Did the sufferings of captives like poor Mrs. White, so common in dime novels and Wild West shows, perform a kind of cultural work, transforming the conquest of the continent into a series of maneuvers made in defense of white families? In other words, can we discern serious matters in the popular representations of the West? Yes, cultural historians insist.

Audience fantasies have been much on the minds of those who study Buffalo Bill. Cody, of course, spun a version of the West that played into real decisions about politics and policy and into lived relations of race and gender. That the West and ideas and fantasies about the West helped construct gender relations has long been clear to historians. Several years ago, legal historian G. Edward White outlined some of the ways living in the West and imagining life in the West provided solutions to linked concerns about class and manhood. Well-educated sons of affluent easterners – men like Theodore Roosevelt, Owen Wister, and Frederic Remington – looked west for preserves of individualism and independence. Seasons spent in the western wilderness promised to restore a sense of the masculinity that life in the socially refined and overly civilized urban East threatened to destroy.

But cultural historians now look at gender as a complex set of social relationships, and the masculinity of Roosevelt, Wister, Remington, and Cody is set against changing ideas about women and families. Historian Louis Warren insists that family is crucial to understanding Cody's own life and in explaining the appeal of Buffalo Bill's presentations. Buffalo Bill showcased western virility, but the show told a story of frontier settlement that contained "virility within a framework of historical progress that culminated in household order" (Warren 2005: 215).

New work on the Wild West shows also complicates their role as nostalgic presentations. Although he was a bad investor, Cody was a successful entrepreneur of the "culture industry." He displayed a world of Indians, hunters, Army scouts, hard-riding cowboys, and struggling settlers made obsolete by the coming of railroads, corporations, and electricity. But in fact his shows were industrial enterprises that depended on the very forms they seemed to deny. At its height, the show traveled in 18 railroad cars, generated its own electricity, and moved people and animals with the skill of an efficient military operation. For historians Rob Kroes and Robert Rydell, modern industrial forms helped Cody stage "a mobile dream factory capable of producing a narrative of heroic conquest for mass audiences numbering in the millions" (Rydell & Kroes 2005: 31).

Dependence on industrial forms is only one of the Wild West shows' many contradictions. It has not escaped the notice of historians that Cody's narrative of heroic conquest called for Native Americans to play the parts of the conquered. Cody's Wild West shows were places where real westerners – cowboys and cowgirls, sharpshooters and stagehands, Native American men and women – made their lives, working their way into the twentieth-century world by performing a version of the nineteenth-century past. As historians L. G. Moses and Louis Warren have explained, Wild West shows provided Native American men and women with opportunities to perform deeds and dances banned from late nineteenth-century reservations. Some used work as "show Indians" to create places for themselves and their families in modernizing America. Working for Cody was appealing because "Buffalo Bill's Wild West celebrated the courage, honor, and character of American Indians," L. G. Moses wrote.

> Out of the Wild West show came the modern rodeo and powwow, where western skill and western artistry were displayed and rewarded. In the case of the powwow, it also became a means by which people could retain, restore, or, in certain instances, create through adaptation a modern Indian identity. The show had provided an opportunity for Indians, not so much to play a role, but simply to be themselves. (Moses 1996: 272)

However, as Louis Warren writes, what it meant to be Native American in the last years of the nineteenth century was not simple and job choices for those who went to work for Cody were few. "The truth is that Indians performed in the Wild West show because in its day it was a fine place to work. But that truth underscores an inescapable fact: there were so few other places for Indians to work and congressmen and bureaucrats were so penny-pinching, and the public so apathetic, that Indians starved to death in spite of the Wild West show" (Warren 2005: 386).

As Moses and Warren reveal, Native Americans used performances in Wild West shows to win small victories in battles to preserve cultural practices. But in the last decades of the nineteenth century, educators and reformers opened another battle on the cultural front. Plans to assimilate Native Americans into modern American culture by separating native children from their families and educating them at boarding schools, or by dividing tribal lands into individual parcels and turning Native American men into upright, individual farmers, were carried out at the expense of native cultural practices. In many cases, assimilation meant cultural death. Carlisle School founder Richard Henry Pratt put it bluntly, suggesting that it was necessary to "kill the Indian" to "save the man" (Adams 1995).

The West as America

Richard Pratt's language captures the very high stakes in some of the cultural battles set in the American West. Pratt's Native American contemporaries knew that these struggles could be matters of life and death. In recent years, the West was the scene of some fierce skirmishes in the twentieth century's culture wars. One late-century flap over an art exhibition, "The West as America," suggests that even in the 1990s, American audiences cared about the place of the West in the cultural history of the United States. The show reminds us too that visual images have played an important role in establishing the region in the American cultural imagination.

"The West as America" opened at the National Museum of American Art in the spring of 1991. It was an ambitious exhibition of nineteenth-century western American art and included paintings by Carl Bodner, Alfred Jacob Miller, John Mix Stanley, George Caleb Bingham, Emmanuel Leutze, Alfred Bierstadt, Frederic Remington, Charles Russell, and others. The choice of artists was not controversial, but the curators' labels were. Words posted on the walls beside the paintings suggested that, although images of the American West appeared to depict heroic stories of expansion, western tales actually masked darker histories of dispossession and conquest. Rather than celebrating the hard-working Americans who pioneered their way into the West, the figures central to Turner's romantic vision of the region's past, the show's organizers asked visitors to see the art of the West as part of an ideological project that served the interests of American capitalism by representing the conquest of native peoples and the destruction of natural environments as normal, natural, and inevitable. Many visitors found this version of the West disturbing.

The show and the controversy surrounding it raise several related questions for cultural historians interested in visual images of the American West. What is the cultural standing of the visual art of the American West? Should images of the West be valued as efforts at literal representation, for the information they contain about landscapes and people? Are western images, indeed, significant sources of information about the West? Or are they significant sources of misinformation that helped legitimate American expansion not by teaching people to see the real West but by helping to blind a culture to the costs of conquest? Answering "yes" to this last question got the show's organizers into trouble with conservative audiences.

The volume of essays that accompanied the show reiterated the ideological argument, as authors traced "the way artists enlisted their tales in the service of progress during the period of westward expansion in America." American artists made images to suit the interests of their eastern patrons, many of whom stood to gain from the conquest of the West. The show's organizers suggested that contemporary Americans were still paying a price for having fallen under the sway of western myths:

> That American society still struggles to adjust to limitations on natural resources, to grant
> overdue justice to native populations, to locate the contributions of ethnic minorities

within a mainstream tradition, and to resolve the conflicts between unbridled personal freedom and the larger social good tells us that we have ignored history far too long, accepting the images of the last century as reality.   (Broun in Truettner 1991: vii)

Visitors were not entirely happy with the lessons about myth and ideology, many of which the show's organizers had learned from historian Richard Slotkin. Slotkin, like Turner, recognizes that the frontier myth is one of "the primary organizing principles of our historical memory" (Slotkin 1985: 16). But in Slotkin's mind the frontier brought intolerance and violence, particularly interracial violence, and not just democracy to the heart of American culture. Settlers did not become Americans because they plowed up the plains; rather they became Americans by killing people, particularly people with red skins. As Slotkin writes in *The Fatal Environment: The Myth of the Frontier in the Age of Industrialization, 1800–1890*, "the simple fable of discovery of the new land and the dispossession of the Indians substitutes for the complexities of capital formation, class and interest group competition, and the subordination of society to the imperatives of capitalist development" (Slotkin 1985: 47).

Comments on "The West as America" suggest that many of those who turned out to view the exhibition did not want to see the sobering stories of labor, capital, and defeat read into the art of the American West. They preferred to see the iconography of cowboys and Indians in simpler terms, to read the art as a literal depiction of western scenes, a rich source of accurate information about the landscapes and peoples of the American West.

Scholars have long acknowledged a literal strain in western imagery; audiences have valued representations for the factual information they contain about landscapes and people. Painter George Catlin helped launched this trend when he decided in the 1840s that his remarkably imagined gallery of Indian portraits should be taken as "a literal and graphic delineation of the living manners, customs, character of an interesting race of people who are rapidly passing away from the face of the earth" (quoted in Goetzmann & Goetzmann 1986: 26). Indeed, as historian William Goetzmann has shown, the careers of western artists often depended on participation in scientific expeditions in the West, where a "representational and exacting scientific tradition" informed the images they made. Even if western art did not manage always to adhere to scientific standards, it "would always be an art of information – or misinformation that took on the characteristics of myth" (Goetzmann & Goetzmann 1986: xiii).

As we have seen, cultural historians suggest that information and misinformation are not always easily separated. Western artists who adopted the literal pose may have ducked the critics who placed high value on abstractions or on products of European culture. As art historian Nancy Anderson wrote, "For decades the surface realism of western art has obscured the artifice beneath. Yet it is this artifice, this conscious structuring of color and composition, that may reveal more subtle, more compelling truths about the discovered lands and invented pasts we continue to explore" (Anderson 1992: 35).

Even the most literal forms of western art – the thousands of photographs produced as the West became part of the American nation – turn out to be more interesting as inventions. As historian Martha Sandweiss writes, "[d]espite the illusive realism of the image, the role of optics and darkrooms chemistry, the photograph is not a self-evident transcription of fact. Like a memoir or a letter, it may describe events, but it inevitably does so through the lens of the recorder's own experience, ambitions, and need to convey a particular point of view" (Sandweiss 2002: 8). Photographic images carried their own powerful mix of information and misinformation. "[W]estern landscape photographs," Sandweiss writes,

> became a potent part of prevailing myths about the West as a blank slate upon which Americans could inscribe their own future. In focusing on the most dramatic features of the western landscape, in minimizing the presence of people with earlier claims to the land, in illustrating what Americans could accomplish through focused use of the West's resources, the photographs and their patrons turned their backs to the history of human conflict in the West and set their eyes squarely on the region's future. (Sandweiss 2002: 206)

Cultural historians remind us that even the most powerful mythmakers have not exercised a monopoly on meaning, and some of the most creative recent work sets out to recover alternative answers to some of the oldest questions about American culture and the American West. Historian Philip J. Deloria, for example, begins his *Playing Indian* (1998) by repeating Crèvecoeur's question, "What, then, is the American, this new man?" Deloria adds Henry Nash Smith's version of the question as an epigraph, and then he writes a book that answers it in an entirely new way. Smith, as we have seen, traced the intellectual and cultural history behind Turner's assertion that Americans were those who responded to the pull of what they imagined were empty lands in the West. And this story dominated one phase of American history writing. But what if empty land was not the principal feature of American cultural identity? What if Crèvecoeur's "new man" was born in encounters with native peoples and not with virgin land? As we know, Turner largely ignored the Native Americans who occupied the continent, but ignorance does not mean absence, and Deloria finds Indians at the very heart of American cultural identity. "As they first imagined and then performed Indianness together on the docks of Boston, the Tea Party Indians gave material form to identities that were witnessed and made real. The performance of Indian Americanness afforded a powerful foundation for subsequent pursuits of national identity" (Deloria 1998: 7). As Deloria describes it, national identity was the work of at least two populations, although his discussion of the intricate negotiations of identity might be extended to an array of ethnic groups – African American, Mexican American, Asian American, Hispanic – who have all had a hand in making the American West:

> Intricate relations between destruction and creativity – for both Indian and non-Indian Americans – are themselves in an uneasy alliance. And so while Indian people have lived out a collection of historical nightmares in the material world, they have also haunted a long night of American dreams. As many native people have observed, to be American is to be unfinished. And although that state is powerful and creative, it carries with it nightmares all its own. (Deloria 1998: 191)

And Deloria's is as useful a summary as I can find of the promises of the new cultural histories of the American West. Recent cultural histories are attuned to the interactions of the imagined and the material, attentive to the intricate dance of myth and fact that shapes lives and communities in the American West. They pay attention to the presence of Native Americans and to the persistence of native cultural forms. They acknowledge that experiences in the West helped Americans imagine gender relations in communities of the East and the West, and they teach us that cultural identity is a complex set of negotiations and an always incomplete process. They have opened territory for a new generation of explorers.

REFERENCES

Adams, David Wallace: *Education for Extinction: American Indians and the Boarding School Experience, 1875–1928* (Lawrence: University Press of Kansas, 1995).

Anderson, Nancy K.: " 'Curious Historical Artistic Data': Art History and Western American Art," in Jules Prown et al., eds., *Discovered Lands, Invented Pasts: Transforming Visions of the American West* (New Haven, CT: Yale University Press, 1992), pp. 1–36.

Brooks, James F.: *Captives and Cousins: Slavery, Kinship, and Community in the Southwest Borderlands* (Chapel Hill: University of North Carolina Press, 2002).

Broun, Elizabeth: "Introduction," in William Truettner, ed., The *West as America: Reinterpreting Images of the Frontier, 1820–1920* (Washington, DC: Smithsonian Institution Press, National Museum of American Art, 1991).

Deloria, Philip J.: *Playing Indian* (New Haven, CT: Yale University Press, 1998).

Dippie, Brian W.: *Catlin and His Contemporaries: The Politics of Patronage* (Lincoln: University of Nebraska Press, 1990).

Faragher, John Mack: " 'A Nation Thrown Back Upon Itself': Frederick Jackson Turner and the Frontier," in John Mack Faragher, ed., *Rereading Frederick Jackson Turner: "The Significance of the Frontier in American History" and Other Essays* (New York: Henry Holt, 1994).

Goetzmann, William H. & Goetzmann, William N.: *The West of the Imagination* (New York: W. W. Norton, 1986).

Kasson, Joy: *Buffalo Bill's Wild West: Celebrity, Memory, and Popular History* (New York: Hill & Wang, 2000).

Klein, Kerwin: *Frontiers of Historical Imagination: Narrating the European Conquest of Native America, 1890–1990* (Berkeley: University of California Press, 1997).

Limerick, Patricia Nelson: "Making the Most of Words: Verbal Activity and Western America," in William Cronon, George Miles, & Jay Gitlin, eds., *Under an Open Sky: Rethinking America's Western Past* (New York: W. W. Norton, 1992), pp. 167–84.

Limerick, Patricia Nelson: "Turnerians All: The Dream of a Helpful History in an Intelligible World," *The American Historical Review* 100, 3 (June 1995), 697–716.

Mitchell, Lee Clark: "Henry Nash Smith's Myth of the West," in Richard Etulain, ed., *Writing Western History: Essays on Major Western Historians* (Reno: University of Nevada Press, 1991), pp. 247–76.

Moses, L. G.: *Wild West Shows and the Images of American Indians, 1883–1933* (Albuquerque: University of New Mexico Press, 1996).

Nemerov, Alex: "Doing the 'Old America': The Image of the American West, 1880–1920," in William Truettner, ed., *The West as America: Reinterpreting Images of the Frontier, 1820–1920* (Washington, DC: Smithsonian Institution Press, National Museum of American Art, 1991), pp. 285–343.

Pomeroy, Earl: *In Search of the Golden West: The Tourist in Western America* (New York: Alfred A. Knopf, 1957).

Rydell, Robert W. & Kroes, Rob: *Buffalo Bill in Bologna: The Americanization of the World, 1860–1922* (Chicago: University of Chicago Press, 2005).

Sandweiss, Martha A.: *Print the Legend: Photography and the American West* (New Haven, CT: Yale University Press, 2002).

Slotkin, Richard: *The Fatal Environment: The Myth of the Frontier in the Age of Industrialization, 1800–1890* (Norman: University of Oklahoma Press, 1985).

Smith, Henry Nash: *Virgin Land: The American West as Symbol and Myth* (Cambridge, MA: Harvard University Press, 1950).

Turner, Frederick Jackson: *Rereading Frederick Jackson Turner: "The Significance of the Frontier in American History" and Other Essays*, ed. John Mack Faragher (New Haven, CT: Yale University Press, 1999), pp. 31–60.

Warren, Louis S.: *Buffalo Bill's America: William Cody and the Wild West Show* (New York: Alfred A. Knopf, 2005).

West, Elliott: *The Way West: Essays on the Central Plains* (Albuquerque: University of New Mexico Press, 1995).

White, G. Edward: *The Eastern Establishment and the Western Experience: The West of Frederick Remington, Theodore Roosevelt, and Owen Wister* (New Haven, CT: Yale University Press, 1968).

White, Richard: "Frederick Jackson Turner and Buffalo Bill," in James Grossman, ed., *The Frontier in American Culture* (Berkeley: University of California Press, 1994), pp. 7–65.

Chapter Ten

THE GILDED AGE

Scott A. Sandage

Mark Twain's title was far too glib to convey how profoundly the post-Civil War decades reorganized American culture – but it stuck. *The Gilded Age, A Tale of To-Day* (1873), co-authored with political journalist Charles Dudley Warner, was a *roman à clef* of grifters and grafters gone amuck. The novel itself was something of a money-making scheme: the latest thing from two hot young writers, not sold in any store – available by advance subscription only. Door-to-door salesmen showed off a "dummy" – a dozen sample pages and 20 plates in gilt-stamped bindings – to pitch *the book everyone will be talking about* to the new middle class. A status item in the growing culture of consumption, its sales were initially high but declined sharply as the Panic of 1873 gave way to a five-year depression. Behind all the ballyhoo, the best part of *The Gilded Age* seemed to be the three words encircled by a big diamond ring on its deluxe cover.

The book went into eclipse and its title entered the public domain. People quickly forgot that it took place in Washington and points west, not to Wall Street, and lampooned speculators and lobbyists, not industrialists. The title rang true in an epoch of incredulity, overrun by crooks and cranks of every sort. "This is supposed by many to be the Gilded Age, but we rather incline to the opinion that it is the cranky age," read an 1881 Kansas editorial that found the national mindset scarcely more rational than President Garfield's assassin. "One of the experts who was called upon as a witness in the Guiteau trial, declares that one person out of every five is insane" (*Daily Globe*, 1881).

The Gilded Age was born with bad press that only got worse for a hundred years. It is hard to think of a more disreputable American quarter-century, and it barely lasted that long. In textbooks the Crédit Mobilier scandal or the Panic of 1873 are prologue, but a new era cannot dawn until the defeat of Reconstruction in 1877. The presidency is a fuzzy blur – Hayes, Garfield, Arthur, Cleveland, Harrison – who had the muttonchops? Interchangeable chief executives pale beside inimitable executives: who could mistake the elfin Carnegie for the flinty Rockefeller or the bulbous Morgan? Synonymous with the Gilded Age, their chapter usually ends with the inauguration of Teddy Roosevelt and progressive reform – or the formation of the United States Steel Corporation – in 1901.

Capitalized at $1.4 billion on April Fools Day of that year, US Steel was the largest firm ever – and one of the largest metaphors for a zeitgeist defined less by gilt than by girth. People had long since begun calling it "the epoch of bigness" (*Sandusky Daily Register*, 1890). From the Statue of Liberty to the Standard Oil Trust, ward-heeler Big Tim Sullivan to gold-monger Big Jim Fisk, Edison's electric dynamo to Barnum's elephant Jumbo, America was magnifying itself. In the three post-Civil War decades, the USA admitted 20 million immigrants, added nine states, and staked imperialist claims in Samoa, Panama, Nicaragua, Hawaii, Cuba, the Philippines, Guam, and Puerto Rico. "The United States is now teaching the world what can be done by the modern organization of industry and . . . its bigness and efficiency," wrote a mid-western editor. "Abroad it is taken as positive proof of the greatness of the nation and its fitness to rule the industrial world" (*Nebraska State Journal*, 1901).

Gilded Age or "epoch of bigness" – both headings turn a pivotal era into a text-book sidebar or hazy subfield. Like "Jacksonian Democracy," another reading list formerly required of all Americanist doctoral students, "Gilded Age" has become (for non-specialists) a short detour between "Reconstruction" and "Progressivism." This treatment is unfortunate, because Gilded Age topics have long forced an uneasy but ongoing dialogue between subfields otherwise wont to ignore each other: business history and cultural history. For much of the twentieth century, scholars have often rethought the Gilded Age to ask how its legacies – the culture of business and the business of culture – shaped the modern United States.

Rather than catalog recent cultural studies of the late nineteenth and early twen-tieth centuries, this essay shows how debates about the Gilded Age shaped the growth of cultural history itself. Angry young men of the Gilded Age wrote its first histories and fixed its collective memory. With axes to grind, they honed major reinterpreta-tions of "American civilization" and helped to professionalize the study of history. Cycles of revision and reinterpretation from the 1920s to the 1960s led to a "new cultural history" in the 1980s and a "cultural turn" in business history in the 1990s. This process took a century.

Boys of Summer, 1893

Anything "gilded" is by definition bogus (or at least inferior) beneath its glint. We expect loaded words from Mark Twain, but should historians adopt them? Nineteenth-century elites turned out to be as common as pig tracks in *The Gilded Age*. But fiction shaped the truth as twentieth-century historians adopted its title and its view of "the slovenly reality beneath the gaudy exterior" – a sneer from Vernon Louis Parrington's 1927 opus, *Main Currents in American Thought*. Parrington's Gilded Age was "the Great Barbeque," a carnivorous jamboree of goldbrickers and backslappers. Monopolists prevailed in the name of individualism and plutocrats governed in the name of democracy. Such ideas colored reform clas-sics like Henry Demarest Lloyd's *Wealth Against Commonwealth* (1903) and Ida Tarbell's *History of the Standard Oil Company* (1904), but now they gained legitimacy from a new breed of professional historians (Parrington 1930, vol. 3: 10, 23).

From its Gilded Age watershed, *Main Currents* flowed inexorably from *Gemeinschaft* (community) to *Gesellschaft* (society), from virtuous tradition to venal modernity:

> The idealism of the [1840s], the romanticism of the fifties – all the heritage of Jeffersonianism and the French Enlightenment – were put thoughtlessly away, and with no social conscience, no concern for civilization, no heed for the future of the democracy it talked so much about, the Gilded Age threw itself into the business of money-getting.   (Parrington 1930: 17)

It became a Gilded Age, then, by displacing a golden age.

Parrington (1871–1929) belonged to the generation born or raised during this transformation, a cohort that would produce the first academically trained American historians. They were middle-class boys whose fathers sent them to college in the late 1880s, to learn "careers" amid rising professionalization (the American Historical Association was founded in 1884). They graduated, as Richard Hofstadter later noted, "when the great depression of the 1890s – a turning point in the development of the American mind – was at its worst." Parrington took his Harvard bachelor's degree in 1893, accepted a job teaching English at Emporia College, and went home to Kansas (and the Populist revolt) in July of that year (Hofstadter 1968: 41, 357–70).

That same month, Frederick Jackson Turner (1861–1932) addressed the American Historical Association (AHA) meeting at the Chicago World's Fair, giving his famous paper on "The Significance of the Frontier in American History." Only three years out of Johns Hopkins's new PhD program, he pondered the Census Bureau's report that western population density had finally "closed" the frontier: the font of American exceptionalism. Over the next decade, Turner refined his thesis of "frontier individualism" to refute "those captains of industry whose success in consolidating economic power now raises the question as to whether democracy under such conditions can survive" (Turner 1994 [1903]: 93).

Charles A. Beard (1874–1948) spent the summer of 1893 editing an Indiana newspaper (bought for him and a brother by their father) and a year later entered DePauw College. Graduating in 1898, he volunteered for the Spanish–American War, studied at Oxford and helped John Ruskin open a labor college, then published a book on the Industrial Revolution, all before earning his doctorate at Columbia in 1904. The original social-activist-turned-social-historian, Beard joined the "New History" movement (as did Turner) to expand the discipline beyond its staid focus on political institutions to examine society, economy, and culture. Stressing conflict and discontinuity, the New Historians embraced presentism and argued that history must be the basis of social and policy reform. Beard's provocative but paradigmatic *Economic Origins of the Constitution* (1913) notoriously probed the colonial roots of modern plutocracy.

Turner, Beard, and Parrington were disillusioned sons of the Gilded Age who defined the period (for scholars and the public) and, in the process, opened a path for modern cultural history. "Historians became more aware," Hofstadter observed, "of the wide range of subjects that they might attend to – not simply politics but the whole range of human ideas, activities, and institutions." Hofstadter dubbed them "the Progressive historians," not only for their era and their politics but for their impact on the profession. "Where the historical writing of the Gilded Age had been marked by its aloofness from if not hostility to popular aspirations," he wrote, "the historical writing of the twentieth century would be, whatever its pretensions to science, critical, democratic, progressive" (Hofstadter 1968: 40, 43). It would reveal how conflict – economic conflict in particular – had shaped the American experience. Other scholars pursued this shift, but few held such lasting academic and public sway. Turner and Beard were both elected AHA president. Turner and Parrington both won Pulitzer Prizes for history; indeed, *Main Currents in American Thought* garnered the 1928 award over a rival bestseller, *The Rise of American Civilization* (1927), co-authored by Beard and historian Mary Ritter Beard, his wife (1876–1958).

The Rise of American Civilization (1927) interpreted the Gilded Age within a sweeping, engaging synthesis of progressive historiography. It reached number two on the *Publisher's Weekly* bestseller list, despite a two-volume heft of 1,662 pages. A 97-page chapter (the work's longest) on "The Gilded Age" told how "the era of triumphant business enterprise" had enthroned "the new plutocrats." Volume one had extolled antebellum "American business men" for their "talent and initiative" and urged more historical work on business and technology. But volume two paraphrased Karl Marx: "the cash nexus pure and simple was the outstanding characteristic of social relations during the gilded age" (Beard & Beard 1927, vol. 1: 631–4; vol. 2: 383, 394, 437). The Beards' brand of economic determinism sold even better by 1934, when their names graced the dedication page of *The Robber Barons* by Matthew Josephson. Their onetime student spun a Beardian interpretation of the Gilded Age (with nods to Parrington and Turner) into a 450-page bestseller.

Great Barbeque or Great Game?

An instant classic, *The Robber Barons* took its name from anti-business slang of the 1870s and lent it to a resilient school of historiography. The Great Depression awakened new interest in the Gilded Age origins of economic and cultural crisis. Besides Josephson, public intellectuals like Lewis Mumford, Thurman Arnold, Miriam Beard, and Allan Nevins rewrote the 1870s, 1880s, and 1890s for the 1930s.

A popular biographer rather than an academic, Josephson (1899–1978) painted "an age which seemed 'gilded' or 'tarnished' or 'dreadful' or 'tragic' by turns." A Marxist of the Popular Front, he revisited Parrington's "Great Barbeque" and its "uncontrolled appetite for private profit . . . whence so much disaster, outrage, and misery has flowed." The book's villains (its Jay Gould chapter was entitled "Mephistopheles") had imposed "a new order" on capital – and on culture. Josephson cited theorists later beloved of cultural historians, including R. H. Tawney, Werner Sombart (on the "middle-class spirit"), and especially Thorstein Veblen. Using the latter's *The Theory of the Leisure Class* (1899) and *The Theory of Business Enterprise* (1904), Josephson linked Gilded Age innovations in capitalism to "new patterns or devices of consumption" (Josephson 1962 [1934]: viii, 7–8, 21, 29, 162, 180, 322, 338).

For the work of an amateur, *The Robber Barons* had a tenacious academic impact. More than 50 years after its publication (and nearly 25 years after its 1962 reissue), a business historian complained, "no study of the past is more urgently in need of revision than *The Robber Barons*" (Klein 1986: 496).

Lewis Mumford had published a similar plea three years *before* the debut of *The Robber Barons*. A friend of Josephson's and fellow protégé of Charles Beard, Mumford (1895–1990) was a largely self-educated architectural and cultural critic, urban historian, and technological theorist. In a 1931 book, he rejected Gilded Age caricatures and rechristened the 30 years after 1865. "We need a fresh name for this period, if we are to see it freshly," he wrote in *The Brown Decades*. Brown tones reflected the war-torn landscape, the faces of emancipation, "the visible smut of early industrialism," crude oil and slag heaps, stone row houses and parlors crammed with mahogany, Edison's wax-cylinder phonograph records, Roebling's bridge to Brooklyn, Richardson's edifices, Eakins's canvases, and Stieglitz's photographs (Mumford 1955 [1931]: 4, 7–9).

The Brown Decades was a slender 248 pages beside the doorstop-sized works of Parrington, the Beards, and (later) Josephson. To Mumford, these writers were not quite wrong, but they had missed something. "Beneath the crass surface, a new life was stirring in departments of American thought and culture" (architecture and art, especially) that became "a source of some of the most important elements of our contemporary culture." Seeing this awakening required seeing the era whole, not only for worse but also for better. "It is time that we ceased to be dominated by the negative aspects of the Brown Decades" to the neglect of their "creative manifestations" (Mumford 1955 [1931]: 20, 21–2). Mumford did not succeed in establishing a "fresh name" for the Gilded Age, but along with his books *Technics and Civilization* (1934) and *The Culture of Cities* (1938), *The Brown Decades* became required reading for postwar cultural historians of urban- or suburbanization, technology, public and domestic space, and other infrastructures of modernity.

Intellectuals of the 1930s like Mumford pioneered cultural analysis of the Gilded Age phenomenon of "bigness" that later consumed business historians. Five years into the Great Depression, blaming it all on the Gilded Age was too easy. In 1934, Associate Supreme Court Justice Louis D. Brandeis (1856–1941) published his collected writings under the title *The Curse of Bigness*, which seemed to say "I told you so." Twenty years earlier, in *Other People's Money and How the Bankers Use It* (1914), he had warned that bigness was a quintessentially modern evil. Seeking fresh, subtler perspectives, Mumford and others began to rethink bigness as an integral (if not inevitable) trait of modernism – culturally, economically, and even legally.

Yale Law School professor Thurman W. Arnold (1891–1969) likewise pursued iconoclastic ideas about the legacy of the Gilded Age. Its "curse" was neither the robber baron nor even "Bigness" per se. Rather, the problem was in *The Folklore of Capitalism* itself, according to the title and thesis of Arnold's 1937 bestseller. An apostle of "legal realism," he criticized old-fashioned trust-busters for not understanding that bigness had both structural and cultural implications. Rockefeller and Carnegie had embodied "the struggle of a creed of individualism to adapt itself to what was becoming a highly organized society." But instead of adapting the creed to define the merits as well as the limits of bigness, that struggle had ultimately legitimized the "personification of the corporation as an individual." In court and culture, this doctrine cloaked new companies in old ideals, paying lip service to them while actually impeding regulation. "Since the corporation was a person," this logic held, "mere bigness could not make it a bad person." The corporation and the state grew apace and grew together, like Siamese-twin Leviathans. Under the rule of corporate–capital alliances, Arnold explained, "antitrust laws became the greatest protection to uncontrolled business dictatorships" (Arnold 1937: 190, 210–12, 214).

When *The Folklore of Capitalism* came out in October 1937, Arnold was already in line for his 1938 appointment as Assistant Attorney General for the Anti-Trust Division. In a speech, he defined his job not as trust-busting but as "reconciling" two phobias: the fear of bigness and the fear of regulation. When each side claims to be "representing the ideals of a culture . . . a spiritual or psychological conflict develops" and paralyzes debate. "The neurosis continues," Arnold explained, as long as public policy is driven by irrational fears instead of pragmatic goals of "making . . . practical organizations function" (Arnold quoted in Edwards 1943: 339–40).

Arnold's interest in culture, and especially his focus on psychological strain and organizational function, owed more to the emerging sociology of Talcott Parsons (1902–79) than to the work of contemporary historians. Indeed, among the prominent writers and scholars who re-plated the Gilded Age during the 1930s, not one was a professionally trained historian. In the words of Miriam Beard, born but not schooled in the trade of her parents Charles and Mary, "The interactions of business and culture, one upon the other, form one of the least explored phases of history" (quoted in Yeager 2001: 717). Miriam Beard (1901–83) merged business and culture in *A History of the Business Man* (1938), a sweeping study of the archetype and activities of "the organizer of economic enterprise" in Europe and America from ancient to modern times. Beard's analysis of the Gilded Age as a transition from "the apogee of the Individualist" to that of "the big business man" paralleled Arnold's contest between an old creed and a new breed. This approach elicited condescension from business historians, who mostly dismissed Beard's work as "a contribution to socio-cultural history" (Gras 1938: 66). Yet few could dispute Beard's introductory remark that business history was strangely unknown and irrelevant to all but a few specialists. Despite the businessman's vital role across cultures and over time, she wrote, nevertheless "he still remains outside the main stream of history writing, and therefore is not . . . 'historified' in the popular estimation" (Beard 1938: 2).

Journalist cum scholar Allan Nevins (1890–1971) soon remedied that. His first crack at the Gilded Age, *The Emergence of Modern America, 1865–1878*, appeared in 1927 – only to be outweighed by the big books of Parrington and the Beards. Nevins then pitted doorstop versus doorstop in 1940, striking back with a two-volume, 1,500-page biography. *John D. Rockefeller: The Heroic Age of American Enterprise* renamed the years from Standard Oil's birth in 1870 to its founder's retirement in 1897. Nevins emphasized his hero's innovativeness in "the Great Game" and excused his ruthlessness: "Quite apart from this issue of ethics, the time was to come when the Standard would be praised for its pioneering qualities and for its demonstration of the useful possibilities of large-scale organization." Corporate consolidation had not simply happened as a matter of course; it was a major discovery. By means of "the huge experiment in industrial organization which he had inaugurated," history's first billionaire demonstrated that competitive individualism was obsolete – changing the fundamental calculus of American economic life. "At bottom, a question of premises was involved. Rockefeller believed in concentration; most Americans believed in unlimited competition" (Nevins 1940, vol. 1: 99–100, 683; vol. 2: 67).

The Cultural U-Turn

Nevins's emphasis on consolidation and innovation was the culmination of the first decade of a new discipline of business history, which inextricably revised interpretations of the Gilded Age. "The demonstration of the useful possibilities of large-scale organization" would preoccupy the subfield in the post-World War II era, eclipsing the "question of premises" begged by the Gilded Age. A few leading scholars, however, turned down a cultural road that promised, at first, to become the new direction of business history.

As a formal discipline, business history began on or about September 1927, when Harvard's Graduate School of Business Administration offered its first history elective, taught by Norman S. B. Gras (1884–1956). Long the turf of amateurs and muckrakers, business history had never before undergone scholarly, systematic inquiry. Gras defined the subfield as "primarily the study of the administration of business units of the past" (Gras & Larson 1939: 3). Throughout the 1930s, he collaborated with Henrietta M. Larson (1894–1983), a Columbia University PhD whose teachers had included Charles Beard (and, at the ABD stage, Gras himself). Larson eventually became the first woman appointed to a full professorship at Harvard Business School. Together, Gras and Larson pioneered the "casebook" approach to studying individual firms, invigorating the subfield yet further isolating it behind stacks of arcane monographs.

By 1940, practitioners like Harvard's Arthur H. Cole (1889–1974) grew as bored by "heroes and innovators" as by narrow studies written "wholly from the side of corporate organization." Cole began to explore the concept, practice, and social context of entrepreneurs and entrepreneurship (Gilded Age words, he noted, seldom heard in America until the 1880s). Trained as an economist, Cole interpreted American society as "an entrepreneurial *system*" but argued that this was a historical outcome, not a cause (Cole 1942: 123; emphasis in original). That is, he presented the nation's business orientation as a phenomenon that required explanation, not as a presumptive facet of human nature or a proverbial Yankee "spirit of enterprise" (Cole 1959: 271, n.13). Cole's notion of "an entrepreneurial *system*" echoed the "social systems" work of his Harvard colleague Talcott Parsons, who inspired Cole to study the social (not merely economic) functions of entrepreneurs. Although more a taxonomist than a historian, Cole pioneered the study of business as "a social-cultural area" of human interaction, rather than an administrative vacuum wherein "railroads 'were built' and banks 'were organized.'" Cole's actors were not driven by abstract managerial principles or economic laws; rather, they were shaped by "social conditioning" and "their own ideologies" of achievement – such as " 'the strenuous life' " and "the [Horatio] Alger tradition" of the Gilded Age (Cole 1959: 13, 30, 97, 132, 140).

A cultural approach to "the great business expansion after the Civil War" owed even more to Cole's protégé and colleague Thomas C. Cochran (1902–99). Besides becoming the dean of postwar business historians, Cochran had literally been present at the creation of *The Cultural Approach to History*. A ground-breaking anthology by that title, edited by Caroline F. Ware in 1940, demonstrated how historians might use the concept of culture as insightfully as sociologists and anthropologists were employing it. A volume of selected papers presented at the American Historical Association's 1939 meeting, it included Cochran's "The Social History of the Corporation in the United States." He viewed "corporateness and bigness" not only as aspects of economic or managerial innovation but also as hallmarks of powerful cultural institutions. Hence, large firms were always "both enterprising entities and political governments." But the myth of the former had concealed the growth of the latter in the form of state–industry cooperation, he argued – echoing Thurman Arnold and anticipating the 1960s New Left critique of "corporate liberalism." Legally and culturally, "the personality of the corporation as an enterprising individual" legitimated its growing power. While railroads virtually ruled California in the 1880s and 1890s, "the great company came to be personified as a kind of frontier folk hero." To scholars who naturalized or legitimized this idea, Cochran suggested cultural history as a corrective and catalyst for business history (Cochran 1940: 171–2).

In 1942, he published an interdisciplinary survey, *The Age of Enterprise: A Social History of Industrial America*, with his student William Miller (1912–92). The co-authors boldly promised "a new interpretation of the history of the United States based upon existing monographic material in American history, economics, and related social subjects." All three were necessary to historicize "our pecuniary culture" beyond the circular logic of scholars who "have interpreted [it] naïvely in terms of 'profit motive.'" Paeans to the American quest for "economic freedom" could hardly explain why "this quest has been most powerful in determining the nature of our culture." Although Cochran and Miller conceded that "we have been primarily a business people," they insisted on testing this premise by making business central to American history and culture central to business history. *The Age of Enterprise* described a long nineteenth century stretching from 1800 to 1929. Significantly, eight of 16 chapters (153 of 358 pages) covered the Gilded Age, from social Darwinism and Debsian socialism to conspicuous consumption and "how the other half lived." Cochran himself privately leaned toward socialism, and (again echoing Arnold, as well as Louis D. Brandeis) *The Age of Enterprise* often criticized "the worship of 'Bigness' in American industry and . . . the development of immense corporations." Yet the co-authors presented "industrial leaders" as the fulfillment of America's enterprising tradition, just as Nevins had done, not as a break from that past (Cochran & Miller 1942: xiii, 2, 181–2, 273, 306).

Like Nevins's *Heroic Age*, Cochran and Miller's *Age of Enterprise* pursued revision by means of reperiodization. Presenting the Gilded Age within a continuity of "business culture," they reassessed its personae and reassigned its endpoint. In the scope and titles of such books, the *Ages* of modern business history embraced industrial and corporate capitalism but orphaned their bad seed, finance capitalism. For Cochran and Miller, the problem was not bigness but big bucks: "the dramatic entrance of the investment banker as the director of the business life of the nation." Moneymen like J. P. Morgan unseated entrepreneurs and industrialists, ruling a "new oligarchy" whose only heroes were zeroes. "In the places once occupied by the Vanderbilts, McCormicks, Rockefellers, and Carnegies were bankers and bankers' sons," who raised the stakes so high as to bar the way to entrepreneurial success. "The decline of individualism" ended *The Age of Enterprise* – both the era and the book. "By 1914 most of the traditional areas for profitable enterprise were closed to all but those who had access to large amounts of investment capital, and the control of such capital had itself become concentrated in a very few hands." By distinguishing between enterprise and finance, and by equating the former to America's "business culture," Cochran and Miller made the Gilded Age its apex. Cultural betrayal came later – not by robber barons but by robber bankers (Cochran & Miller 1942: 150, 153, 194, 307, 326).

Nevertheless, Cochran pointed beyond archetypes by urging cultural analysis on business scholars apt to marginalize "the human element" without reconciling "actual human behavior and the implications of rigorous economic analysis" (Cochran 1950: 113). Cultural and economic constructs arose and must be studied together, to perceive (for example) that while Gilded Age tycoons were "creating a national market for standardized goods, they also created a national model of the successful man . . . who rose from the ranks to leadership" (Cochran & Miller 1942: 153). William Miller famously tested that model in 1949. Quantification of the socioeconomic origins of 190 turn-of-the-century corporate executives suggested that "no more than 3 per cent" had bootstraps. He concluded: "poor immigrant and poor farm boys who become business leaders have always been more conspicuous in American history books than in the American business elite" (Miller 1949: 208; and see Friedman & Tedlow 2003). Irvin G. Wyllie (1920–74) followed with a cultural study, *The Self-Made Man in America: The Myth of Rags to Riches* (1954), the first entry in what became a whole genre of American Studies critiques of success mythology. In light of social mobility findings by Miller and others, Wyllie concluded that "belief in the self-made man" persisted as "an act of faith" by hopeful Americans confronted by contradictory realities (1954: 174).

Such inquiries complemented postwar liberal sociology (like David Riesman's perennial bestseller, *The Lonely Crowd*, first published in 1950) but not the liberal "consensus school" ascendant among leading historians. Rejecting the Progressive historians' fixation on conflict, this school argued that Americans' values had converged as capitalism matured. David Potter's *People of Plenty* (1954) applied "the concept of culture" to the Gilded Age alliance of "the new corporations" and pro-business governance. Together they realized the true American dream, Potter argued, which had always meant a culture of abundance, not individualism. Before the Civil War, he wrote, individualism was merely

> the very best means of fulfilling the possibilities of abundance. When it ceased to be the best means, we modified it with a readiness alarming to people who had supposed that it was the individualism itself which was basic . . . The politics of our democracy was a politics of abundance rather than a politics of individualism, a politics of increasing our wealth quickly rather than of dividing it precisely, a politics which smiled both on those who valued abundance as a means to safeguard freedom and on those who valued freedom as an aid in securing abundance.   (Potter 1954: 36, 126)

Class conflict vanished into a cultural and scholarly consensus linking the Gilded Age and the Cold War. In 1957, Samuel P. Hays's *The Response to Industrialism, 1885–1914* was prefaced by the dean of consensus, Daniel Boorstin:

> Mr. Hays avoids presenting the age as a conflict merely between "haves" and "have-nots." The typically American variety of these groups, together with their continuing geographic and social fluidity, prevented the hardening and sharpening of class lines. This helps explain why few Americans have sought refuge in ideologies like those which had congealed in European countries during comparable eras of industrialism. (Boorstin 1957: viii)

Exceptionalism reflected social diversity and ideological uniformity, a continuity of "typically American" values and experiences. Both coalesced in the Gilded Age, according to Edward C. Kirkland (1894–1975) in his 1961 book, *Industry Comes of Age: Business, Labor, and Public Policy, 1860–1897*. "The American Standard of Living" had risen for all citizens, and "the talent for business enterprise was the source of that abundance." The book's final sentence observed, "today many nations seeking industrialization would be fortunate if they had, not so much America's resources, but the national qualities which gave birth to our industrial strength and the institutions under which these qualities flowered to achievement" (Kirkland 1961: 403, 408–9). Coming of age in the Gilded Age, "national qualities" and enduring "institutions" kept modern America prosperous and strong.

This consensus was high in the sky when Ike passed the torch to JFK, but its Gilded Age roots had been noted in 1942 by Cochran and Miller. They updated *The Age of Enterprise* in 1961, when "the continuing Cold War with Communism" inspired a new preface:

> it is the high American standard of living that is now the goad to world-wide unrest and the goal of world-wide ambition. The American standard of living has grown strikingly in the two decades since we first wrote. But its standing as a primary American "value" was firmly established during what we have called The Age of Enterprise. (Cochran & Miller 1961: x)

The Gilded Age had a new shine, as the age when the world's most capitalist country came of age, economically and ideologically. Concerned with both, Cochran's cultural approach might well have gained from the consensus school.

But in the 1950s, business historians took a different turn. "Cochran's legacy," in David Sicilia's words, was "a cultural path not taken." Entrepreneurial scholars informed by sociology, anthropology, and literary criticism ran far ahead of cultural historians and far afield of business historians. Sicilia writes: "Ideas, values, aesthetics, and other aspects of culture on the humanistic side of the discipline have proven to be far more contentious than the 'hard' facts and quantifiable phenomena on its scientific side" (Sicilia 1995: 33, 37).

Few winked at " 'hard' facts" on the path *taken*. They put marks around " 'Big Business,' " as a dated term for "the large vertically integrated, centralized, functionally departmentalized industrial organization" (Chandler 1959: 27). By charting the corporate structure and management of the modern "firm," Alfred D. Chandler, Jr. (b. 1918) set the field's dominant paradigm from the early 1960s through the 1990s – yet again repolishing the Gilded Age.

Organizational Sin Ceases

In Chandlerian terms, the age formerly known as gilded became "the years of system-building." The robber baron got replaced by "the organizational response to fundamental changes in processes of production and distribution made possible by the availability of new sources of energy and by the increasing application of scientific knowledge to industrial technology." Chandler showed how "the organizational response" limited wasteful competition through corporate consolidation and cooperation, effecting a "managerial revolution" that put administrative controls in place of market forces (Chandler 1990: 145, 376). Similar theories had been advanced by two New Dealers, legal scholar Adolph A. Berle (1895–1971) and economist Gardiner C. Means (1896–1988), in their book *The Modern Corporation and Private Property* (1933). But Chandler's historical case studies supplied hard facts to establish a full-fledged paradigm. He stated from the outset that "cultural patterns are taken as given" (as non-causal) and dismissed "cultural attitudes and values" as mere background to "the dynamic factors" of rationalization and innovation (Chandler 1959: 2).

He put those factors on the covers of a trilogy of major books, starting in 1962 with *Strategy and Structure* – a title redolent of his mentor Talcott Parsons (and of Parsons's muse, Max Weber). By the 1960s, Parsonian structural functionalism was associated with emerging theories of modernization. These influences led Chandler away from "the human element" – monographs about notable entrepreneurs, to say nothing of ordinary workers – and toward generalizing drivers of change like technology and bureaucracy. Even admirers discerned "a fair amount of subtle economic determinism" in his books (McCraw 1987: 173). If the Chandlerian paradigm was subtler than its Weberian, Turnerian, Parsonian, or Beardian forerunners, still it made the Gilded Age into a voyage to Brobdingnag: a land of giant firms instead of giant egos, an epic of modernization and inevitability.

Nonetheless, Chandler almost single-handedly made "business history" matter to "American history." Moreover, he helped recast the former as a new model for the latter. "The organizational synthesis in modern American history," as Louis Galambos dubbed it in 1970, applied new concepts of bureaucracy and modernization. Born of postwar dialogues among historians and social scientists, by the late 1960s the "organizational school" seemed to fill a paradigmatic void. With the Progressive historians defrocked as vulgar Marxists and the liberal consensus fogies besieged by the New Left, Galambos outlined a new unifying theme based on "the assumption that some of the most (if not the single most) important changes which have taken place in modern America have centered about a shift from small-scale, informal, locally or regionally oriented groups to large-scale, national, formal organizations." Historically, this trend reshaped not only business but labor, reform, and government – thus revealing important commonalities without denying conflict. Intellectually, the organizational synthesis cut "across the traditional boundaries of political, economic, and social history" (Galambos 1970: 280).

Working across disciplines, the key reinterpreter of the Gilded Age in this light was Robert H. Wiebe (1930–2000). His 1967 survey, *The Search for Order, 1877–1920*, wove a synthesis of recent scholarship into a readable story of centripetal change, from chaos to order; from a post-Civil War "distended society" of autonomous "island communities" to a post-World War I "bureaucratic system" of "new-middle-class rationality" (Wiebe 1967: 11, 111, 159, 170). On this last point, he challenged Richard Hofstadter's classic *Age of Reform* (1955), which famously construed progressivism as a backlash by old elites worried about losing status at the hands of corporatism and its assaults on individualism and democracy. Wiebe discerned a more forward-looking "new consciousness" in the loose cohort of middle managers and professionals emerging after 1895. "The heart of progressivism," he argued, "was the ambition of the new middle class to fulfill its destiny through bureaucratic means." In short, the "bureaucratic orientation" of the new middle class imbued American society with a new, middle-class orientation. Between 1877 and 1920, the managerial revolution had spawned an even more significant "revolution in values" (Wiebe 1967: 126, 133, 166, 295).

The Search for Order was a breakthrough in cultural history, notwithstanding its *Gemeinschaft*-to-*Gesellschaft* story of modernization and the "corporate liberal" undertones of the organizational school. Wiebe assessed both values and structures, bringing historical analysis to sociological hypotheses about the middle class. *The Search for Order* also resembled the "approach . . . of the cultural historian" outlined in 1965 by John Higham's seminal essay, "The Reorientation of American Culture in the 1890s."

Higham (1920–2003) surveyed sport, education, music, and other middle-class pursuits, speculating that a "new, activist mood was . . . beginning to challenge the restraint and decorum of the 'Gilded Age'" and "the constrictions of a routinized society." Pondering how scholars might pursue this apparent conflict, Higham wrote, "cultural history seeks a unifying vision." Its objects and methods come from "the institutional historian" as well as "the historian of ideas." It was imperative to examine both the structural ("levels of experience") and the cognitive ("modes of experience") aspects of culture (Higham 1970 [1965]: 75–6, 79, 85). This manifesto inspired myriad new cultural studies of the turn-of-the-century middle class, such as Burton J. Bledstein's *The Culture of Professionalism* (1976). By the late 1970s, the discovery of critical theory stimulated a new generation of scholars to look back one hundred years. Bringing cultural history into its own as the (arguably) pre-eminent approach to studying the past at the turn of the twenty-first century, they in turn prompted business historians to rethink culture.

Culture and Selfhood

The first unabashedly cultural histories of the Gilded Age benefited from the explosion of social, labor, urban, and gender history and the infusion of (anthropological and literary) theory in the 1970s. These breakthroughs suggested methods and content far beyond Higham's sketchy approach to "the reorientation of American culture." In *No Place of Grace* (1981), Jackson Lears examined "the transformation of American culture, 1880–1920" through the lives and thought of "antimodernists" like Henry Adams. Lears famously (and controversially) adapted the Marxist "concept of cultural hegemony" from Antonio Gramsci, to clarify the influence of the corporate bureaucratic state and emerging culture of consumption (Lears 1985). Alan Trachtenberg's interdisciplinary synthesis of postwar scholarship, *The Incorporation of America:*

Culture and Society in the Gilded Age (1982), viewed "incorporation" as more than a legal, industrial, or institutional phenomenon. This development changed America existentially; new modes of perception and meaning altered relationships between the culture and the individual.

Both Trachtenberg and Lears were trained in the interdisciplinary field of American studies and brought high intellectual, literary, and aesthetic perspectives to their work. Trachtenberg's first book, *Brooklyn Bridge: Fact and Symbol* (1965), exemplified what David Brion Davis later called "the first broad level of cultural history." In an important 1968 essay, Davis plotted three levels of inquiry. Level one entailed "the description of the characteristic styles, motifs, and patterns of a given period." A second level of analysis, Davis continued, may expose "tensions embedded within the culture itself as the result of an interplay between past choices and commitments and new ideas or situations." John Higham made such an argument in tracing the cultural "reorientation" of the 1890s. But Davis's "third level of cultural history, which is still the most neglected," obliged the scholar to "search out lines of intersection between the development of culture and individual personality" (Davis 1968: 697, 700, 704). Books like *The Incorporation of America* and *No Place of Grace* (Davis was Lears's dissertation advisor at Yale) succeeded on this level, as did later reappraisals like *Making America Corporate, 1870–1920*, by Olivier Zunz (1990). Of course, as Davis acknowledged, "the three levels of conceptualization are mutually interdependent" (1968: 705).

By the 1990s, cultural and business historians began to acknowledge their interdependence and common interests. Kenneth Lipartito (1995) observed that 30 years of Chandlerian study had again isolated business history from the mainstream, where quite a lot had changed. Not surprisingly, new perspectives on the Gilded Age inspired groundbreaking works such as Angel Kwolek-Folland's 1994 book, *Engendering Business: Men and Women in the Corporate Office, 1870–1930*, and Pamela Walker Laird's *Advertising Progress: American Business and the Rise of Consumer Marketing* (1998).

For much of the past century, the Gilded Age has provoked debate – and most recently, dialogue – across disciplinary lines and especially across the divide between business and cultural history. If today's dialogue continues to be as productive as yesterday's divide, all American historians will become more adept at working simultaneously on all three levels identified by David Brion Davis. He wrote: "Culture is a theoretical construct that permits us to see relationships between individuals and social groups, between concrete artifacts and abstract patterns, between literature and life. And the greatest promise of cultural history lies precisely in its potential for bridging levels and filling in gaps" (1968: 705). This is no less true of the promise of cultural history to bridge gaps between our disciplines and subfields than of its power to fill gaps in our knowledge.

REFERENCES

Arnold, Thurman W.: *The Folklore of Capitalism* (New Haven, CT: Yale University Press, 1937).

Beard, Charles A. & Beard, Mary R.: *The Rise of American Civilization*, 2 vols. (New York: Macmillan, 1927).

Beard, Miriam: *A History of the Business Man* (New York: Macmillan, 1938).

Berle, Adolph A. & Means, Gardiner C.: *The Modern Corporation and Private Property* (New York: Macmillan, 1933).

Bledstein, Burton J.: *The Culture of Professionalism: The Middle Class and the Development of Higher Education in America* (New York: W. W. Norton, 1976).

Boorstin, Daniel J.: "Editor's Preface," in Samuel P. Hays, *The Response to Industrialism, 1885–1914* (Chicago: University of Chicago Press, 1957), pp. vii–viii.

Chandler, Alfred D., Jr.: "The Beginnings of 'Big Business' in American Industry," *Business History Review* 33 (Spring 1959), 1–31.

Chandler, Alfred D., Jr.: *Strategy and Structure: Chapters in the History of Industrial Enterprise* (Cambridge, MA: MIT Press, 1962).

Chandler, Alfred D., Jr.: *The Visible Hand: The Managerial Revolution in American Business* (Cambridge, MA: Harvard University Press, 1977).

Chandler, Alfred D., Jr.: *Scale and Scope: The Dynamics of Industrial Capitalism* (Cambridge, MA: Belknap Press, 1990).

Cochran, Thomas C.: "The Social History of the Corporation in the United States," in Caroline F. Ware, ed., *The Cultural Approach to History* (New York: Columbia University Press, 1940), pp. 168–81.

Cochran, Thomas C.: "Problems and Challenges in Business History Research with Special Reference to Entrepreneurial History," *Bulletin of the Business Historical Society* 24 (September 1950), 113–19.

Cochran, Thomas C. & Miller, William: *The Age of Enterprise: A Social History of Industrial America* (New York: Macmillan, 1942); rev. ed. (New York: Harper, 1961).

Cole, Arthur H.: "Entrepreneurship as an Area of Research," *Journal of Economic History* 2 (Supplement: December 1942), 118–26.

Cole, Arthur H.: *Business Enterprise in Its Social Setting* (Cambridge, MA: Harvard University Press, 1959).

Daily Globe: Atchison, Kansas, December 14, 1881.

Davis, David Brion: "Some Recent Directions in American Cultural History," *American Historical Review* 73 (February 1968), 696–707.

Edwards, Corwin D.: "Thurman Arnold and the Antitrust Laws," *Political Science Quarterly* 58 (September 1943), 338–55.

Friedman, Walter A. & Tedlow, Richard S.: "Statistical Portraits of American Business Elites: A Review Essay," *Business History* 45 (October 2003), 89–113.

Galambos, Louis: "The Emerging Organizational Synthesis in Modern American History," *Business History Review* 44 (Autumn 1970), 279–90.

Gras, N. S. B.: "Review of *A History of the Business Man* by Miriam Beard," *American Historical Review* 44 (October 1938), 65–7.

Gras, N. S. B. & Larson, Henrietta M.: *Casebook in American Business History* (New York: F. S. Crofts, 1939).

Higham, John: "The Reorientation of American Culture in the 1890s" (1965), in *Writing American History: Essays on Modern Scholarship* (Bloomington: Indiana University Press, 1970), pp. 73–102.

Hofstadter, Richard: *The Progressive Historians: Turner, Beard, Parrington* (New York: Alfred A. Knopf, 1968).

Josephson, Matthew: *The Robber Barons: The Great American Capitalists, 1961–1901* (New York: Harcourt, Brace, 1962 [1934]).

Kirkland, Edward C.: "The Robber Barons Revisited," *American Historical Review* 66 (1960), 68–73.

Kirkland, Edward C.: *Industry Comes of Age: Business, Labor, and Public Policy, 1860–1897* (New York: Holt, Rinehart, & Winston, 1961).

Klein, Maury: *The Life and Legend of Jay Gould* (Baltimore, MD: Johns Hopkins University Press, 1986).

Kwolek-Folland, Angel: *Engendering Business: Men and Women in the Corporate Office, 1870–1930* (Baltimore, MD: Johns Hopkins University Press, 1994).

Laird, Pamela Walker: *Advertising Progress: American Business and the Rise of Consumer Marketing* (Baltimore: Johns Hopkins University Press, 1998).

Lears, T. J. Jackson: *No Place of Grace: Antimodernism and the Transformation of American Culture, 1880–1920* (New York: Pantheon, 1981).

Lears, T. J. Jackson: "The Concept of Cultural Hegemony: Problems and Possibilities," *American Historical Review* 90 (June 1985), 567–93.

Lipartito, Kenneth: "Culture and the Practice of Business History," *Business and Economic History* 24 (Winter 1995), 1–42.

McCraw, Thomas K.: "The Challenge of Alfred D. Chandler, Jr.: Retrospect and Prospect," *Reviews in American History* 15 (March 1987), 160–78.

Miller, William: "American Historians and the Business Elite," *Journal of Economic History* 9 (November 1949), 184–208.

Mumford, Lewis: *The Brown Decades: A Study of the Arts in America, 1865–1895* (New York: Dover Publications, 1955 [1931]).

Nebraska State Journal: Lincoln, January 26, 1901, p. 4.

Nevins, Allan: *John D. Rockefeller: The Heroic Age of American Enterprise*, 2 vols. (New York: Charles Scribner's Sons, 1940).

Parrington, Vernon Louis: *Main Currents in American Thought: An Interpretation of American Literature from the Beginnings to 1920*, 3 vols. (New York: Harcourt, Brace, 1930).

Potter, David M.: *People of Plenty: Economic Abundance and the American Character* (Chicago: University of Chicago Press, 1954).

Sandusky Daily Register: November 27, 1890, p. 5.

Sicilia, David B.: "Cochran's Legacy: A Cultural Path Not Taken," *Business and Economic History* 24 (Fall 1995), 27–39.

Trachtenberg, Alan: *The Incorporation of America: Culture and Society in the Gilded Age* (New York: Hill & Wang, 1982).

Turner, Frederick Jackson: "Contributions of the West to American Democracy," in *Rereading Frederick Jackson Turner: "The Significance of the Frontier" and Other Essays*, ed. John Mack Faragher (New York: Henry Holt, 1994 [1903]), pp. 77–100.

Wiebe, Robert H.: *The Search for Order, 1877–1920* (New York: Hill & Wang, 1967).

Wyllie, Irvin G.: *The Self-Made Man in America: The Myth of Rags to Riches* (New Brunswick: Rutgers University Press, 1954).

Yeager, Mary A.: "Mavericks and Mavens of Business History: Miriam Beard and Henrietta Larson," *Enterprise & Society* 2 (December 2001), 687–768.

Zunz, Olivier: *Making America Corporate, 1870–1920* (Chicago: University of Chicago Press, 1990).

Chapter Eleven

IMMIGRATION AND ETHNIC CULTURE

Hasia R. Diner

At present, the second half of the first decade of the twenty-first century, American historians concerned with ethnicity place a great deal of emphasis on a category of analysis they call "culture." This word or concept has long concerned scholars associated with ethnic and immigration history, but it has undergone a number of changes in meaning and focus.

Initially, historians employed it to refer to matters of values and beliefs. They then took that meaning of culture and applied it to the domestic and private sphere and used it when they considered the impact of certain assumed beliefs on personal and group choices. By the beginning of the new century, however, historians of ethnicity have vastly complicated what they mean by "culture" and have moved it away from the private domain of the family to an emphasis on a category of behavior that might be appropriately thought of as public culture. They have, since the 1990s, paid a great deal of attention to the ways in which the leaders of ethnic communities in America mobilized their constituents and designed public presentations of ethnicity, a departure from the earlier, more interior foci of scholarly inquiry.

The theme of culture as a preoccupation of ethnic historians has over time served a number of intellectual ends and always represented a fusion of trends within both American history and the social sciences and humanities in general. This current emphasis on public culture functions as the newest paradigm in the long involvement of historians of ethnicity with the idea of culture.

"Culture" as a concept can be – and has been – used to describe nearly anything. For many scholars who employ it, it encompasses a range of abstract and interior matters including the beliefs and values, attitudes and aspirations, fears and emotions distinctive to any particular people at specific moments in time and place. This use of culture has tended in large measure not to focus on the history of structures, institutions, and behaviors, leaving those to social historians, who have trained their lenses on the visible and measurable ways in which people – in this case immigrants and their children – acted, including how they voted, worked, went to school, organized their households, founded communal institutions, and interacted with others of different backgrounds.

In a related context, culture can be – and has been – situated for purposes of scholarly discussion in the private sphere, with scholars focusing on matters of deep emotional meaning such as ethnically distinctive family patterns and family rituals, foodways, language choices, modes of childrearing, religious rites, and, most importantly, the playing out of gender. By employing culture this way, historians of ethnicity have posited an inextricable connection between the values held dear by a group of people, the systems of meaning that inform their lives, and the ways in which they organize the patterns of their behavior.

Ethnic historians, like many of their other colleagues, came to this understanding of culture through the work of anthropologists, a group of scholars for whom "culture" had long served as the underlying justification for their field. Extending back to the late nineteenth-century work of Franz Boas, anthropologists analyzed the ways in which culture, as values and beliefs, manifested itself in the realm of the observable, including (but obviously not limited to) art, language, religion, courtship patterns, and childrearing. Culture as such came to mean not just the abstract but the tangible.

But long before ethnic historians starting reading and crediting the work of anthropology, they asserted that at the heart of their field lay the truth that when thinking about the experiences of immigrants and their descendants, culture mattered. Since as a field ethnic history has tended nearly always to concern itself with such issues as assimilation and acculturation, culture clashes, and the possibility of the retention of something assumed to be "traditional" culture, ethnic history has consistently looked to culture as a way to understand the impact of immigration on those who participated in it, and their posterity, shaped as they were by both the immigrant background and the American environment.

The long emphasis on "culture" in the historiography of ethnicity can be attributed firstly to the field's debt to the sociological writings of the 1920s produced by Robert Park, W. I. Thomas, Louis Wirth, and others of the Chicago School of Sociology. These sociologists, living in Chicago, in close proximity to one of the great immigrant cities of America, saw and concerned themselves with the fate of the immigrants as a whole and with the specific groups who lived near them, all the bearers of particular Old World baggage. Thomas, Park, and Wirth each studied the impact of those cultures on the process of adaptation to America and speculated on the different rates by which the attitudes and practices from "back home" would be replaced by American ones. In Thomas's work, *Old World Traits Transplanted*, Jewish immigrants emerged as the "winners" in the struggle for American adaptation in as much as he believed that their long history of multiple migration, institution building, and their proclivities toward commerce, education, flexibility, and cultural adaptation, equipped them to transplant more quickly and successfully to America than many of the others who had shared steerage with them on the journey across the Atlantic. These scholars placed particular emphasis on the attitudes – meaning the culture – of the Jews as opposed to those of the Italians or Poles, as they faced the demands of American modernity. The culture of the Jews in essence had predisposed them to negotiate American circumstances with greater ease. It also meant to these sociologists that the Jews would lose their traditional cultures more quickly (Thomas 1921).

These sociologists did not concern themselves with history per se, except in as much as they considered how certain aspects of the history of a particular group might facilitate or impede the process of cultural change; as environmental determinists, they believed that cultures did not stem from genetic inheritance. Culture functioned as the impress of history upon its people.

Simultaneous with the rise of the Chicago School and its underlying concern with the cultural repertoires of the immigrants as they might or might not impede Americanization – that is, the "Old World ways transplanted" – activists from within the ethnic communities also turned to culture as a way to explain, justify, and defend their group in America. The work produced by each of the various ethnic historical societies valorized the group and the values it brought to America. Regardless of whether they represented Americans of Swedish, Norwegian, German, Jewish, or Irish derivation, the writers of this kind of history held up such cultural predispositions as an intrinsic commitment to hard work, love of family, religious piety, gaiety or stoicism, and the like to present their group to itself, its American offspring, and by extension to the larger American public.

But historians followed within a decade and picked up on some of these same themes. The subfield as a whole may rightly be credited to the pioneering work of Marcus Lee Hansen, who in 1937 delivered an address, "The Problem of the Third Generation Immigrant," to the Augustana Historical Society in Rock Island, Illinois. In this essay he charted a trajectory from the immigrant generation up through the generation of its grandchildren, with a focus on how they, and the cohort in the middle, related to the "history and culture" of the places from which they came. Briefly stated, Hansen's thesis about ethnic culture propounded that immigrants brought to America fixed cultures. Their children, the "second generation," affirmatively chose to "forget" those cultural forms, embracing instead American idioms, while the next, the third generation, experienced a revival of interest and manifested an avid embrace of the culture that had been transported to the United States (Hansen, in Kvisto & Blanck 1990: 191–203).

Key works of the next two decades, like Oscar Handlin's *Boston's Immigrants* (1941) and his Pulitzer Prize-winning *The Uprooted* (1951), shaped the field of immigration and ethnic history, and structured it around the problems of culture, chiefly as embodied in the playing out of a traumatic clash between fundamental immigrant group values and the powerful ones which prevailed in America. To those the immigrants had no choice but to conform. Handlin depicted what he saw as a profound crisis of culture as experienced by immigrants. He considered this crisis to have been universally experienced by all immigrants, and this culture crisis led to the painful, but inevitable, breakdown of their families and communities. Handlin's books stated forthrightly that immigrants came to America as the bearers of definite sets of attitudes, beliefs, and values which played a – although not the only – role in how they weathered the process of uprooting. Boston's immigrants, the Irish whom he studied for his first book, came to America with a culture he deemed to be fatalistic and utterly at odds with the dominant republican culture. As a result of that misfit, according to this scholarship, a long and painfully slow process of adaptation ensued. The Irish had to accommodate to America. The crisis of the Irish achieved some resolution only when the Irish shed their fatalism and adopted American cultural values.

Like the Chicago sociologists, Handlin placed culture first and foremost in the realm of the abstract; but, like them, he measured or observed culture in the kinds of choices immigrants and their children made in their homes and in their ethnic enclaves. This reflected less an interest in the ordinary lived circumstances of their subjects than a way to see the workings out of attitudes and beliefs. Since culture functioned on the level of emotion and idea, then as scholars they needed some way to observe how it had manifested. How immigrants organized their families or used American public schools provided two examples of the kinds of overt behaviors which scholars could document and then attribute to culture.

Handlin's thesis sustained by the late 1960s a series of blows. Historians of ethnicity saw community solidarity where he saw crisis. They searched for, and found, examples of successful immigrant cultural resistance to American hegemony. Many of these historians in the 1970s and 1980s asserted in their scholarship that their subjects, immigrants to the United States, had brought with them from their pre-migration homes a set of deeply held beliefs with which they were loathe to part. Virginia Yans-McLaughlin (1977) and Tamara Hareven (1982), studying Italians in Buffalo and French Canadians in New Hampshire, fused the idea of culture as a value system and culture as lived life in the family sphere, seeking there to uncover resilience and retention, with the two immigrant cultures functioning as protective devices which sustained the immigrants from American intrusions. In these two studies, typical of 1970s and 1980s historiographic concern with the agency of ordinary people in the face of large impersonal and powerful forces, culture functioned as an effective weapon by which to resist domination. Its effectiveness derived in large measure from the fact that since it existed on the level of belief and value, it could not be changed from the outside. Italian and French Canadian culture allowed the relatively poor newcomers and their children to shape their own work practices, in particular; and the cultures which they brought from home, according to Yans-McLaughlin, Hareven, and others of this intellectual group, equipped them to set the terms of their family lives.

While they differed profoundly with Handlin over the fate of traditional culture in the American setting, they, like him, located culture in the confluence between beliefs and values and the lived inner life of the family and the ethnic enclave. But these scholars, the new generation which challenged Handlin's overarching thesis, wrote at a time when social history reigned supreme and historians considered such details of lived life – like courtship, diet, childrearing, workplace behaviors and the like – as the ends not the means of their scholarship. They did not study these behaviors in order to see culture, but rather culture served as a way to find out how workers, the poor, the "inarticulate," and the supposedly powerless shaped their own lives. Culture functioned for these historians, as for their subjects, as tools.

Indeed, an almost inextricable bond connected the post-Handlin field of ethnic history with social history. The field as a whole rose to real prominence with the efflorescence of social history in the middle of the 1960s. It grew out of the social ferment of the period and the intellectual emphasis on the idea that ordinary people could control, though not totally, the conditions of their circumstances: they had some degree of agency in the manner by which they interacted with powerful institutions and structures, schools, factories, government, among other forces supposedly beyond their control. The ethnic historians who identified strongly as social historians marshaled culture as a way to explain the patterns of resistance and not as a way to understand those cultures themselves.

Yet at the same time that students of ethnic culture used their scholarship to understand the behaviors of immigrants and their children in a social context, they also came to be influenced by the work of anthropologists, a scholarly community that foregrounded culture. At a time when the academy in general began to extol the possibilities of interdisciplinary collaboration, historians discovered the work of anthropologists. They used this work to give greater sophistication to the concept of culture.

If any one anthropologist should be cited as the scholar whose work gave ethnic historians a kind of interdisciplinary vocabulary to justify their interest in culture, it would be Clifford Geertz (1973, 1983), whose emphasis on "thick description" opened up new ways of thinking about ethnic culture. Historians directly and indirectly borrowed from his work and have been influenced by such assertions as "cultural forms can be treated as texts, as imaginative works built out of social materials," in order to analyze the contours of ethnic culture as they changed over time.

In her presidential address to the Immigration History Society, the scholarly organization of historians who study ethnicity as much as they study immigration, Kathleen Neil Conzen (1991: 12) highlighted the impact of Geertz on the emerging conceptual framework. Ethnic culture, she told her colleagues, "in a Geertzian sense," meant "the socially produced structures of meaning engendered by and expressed in public behaviors, language, images, institutions, then culture, since it inheres in the social discourse." Geertz's thinking about symbols and their constantly mutating nature, their dependence on social settings, and their evolving and lived meanings became by the 1980s and beyond a fundamental part of historical thinking about culture, with ethnic historians joining others in using his ideas to inform their interpretations.

From Geertz ethnic historians learned a new set of concepts and they joined in a broad-based academic discussion about the constructed or invented nature of ethnic tradition and practices. Immigrants, they began to say under the influence of this mode of analysis, did not bring to America a fixed and finite repertoire of beliefs and practices that they had inherited from their ancestors unchanged since earliest days of the primordial past. Rather, ethnic culture, like the practices the immigrants brought with them, had been forged over time and changed in response to constantly evolving needs and circumstances.

In America, as immigrants confronted a vast array of new situations and people, they deployed some familiar symbols and values from the past that they thought of as traditional, and marshaled them to serve their needs as they negotiated the novel circumstances in which they found themselves. The cultures which they fashioned for themselves and lived with in their new American homes involved a seemingly contradictory mélange of elements they remembered from back home, defined as traditional, and which they deemed to be fundamental and unchangeable; new practices, forms, and ideas derived from the American scene which they positively embraced; and yet others which the exigencies of life in the new place imposed upon them. The process of invention had no clear beginning or obvious end point. Rather, scholars asserted by the 1990s that ethnic cultures shifted shape, added elements derived from some part of the American setting, and discarded others, including those once thought to be absolutely fundamental. Historians of ethnicity converged on the assertion that the cultures associated with immigrant groups and their descendants went through periods of revival and reinvigoration, as leaders of these communities, and the masses who had made them the leaders, retrieved cultural practices once moribund, and created new ones which the participants in the ethnic cultural project anointed as traditional.

Whatever the particular elements that historians have focused on, they have asserted since the 1990s that ethnic cultures had not been either imported wholesale from abroad and then died out, nor did they arrive in America and remain utterly unchanged. Rather culture ought to be thought of as an evolving category, never authentic or inauthentic, fixed or depleted.

A number of books produced in the late 1980s, the 1990s, and the early years of the twenty-first century will have to suffice as exemplars of this mode. Jon Gjerde's *From Peasants to Farmers* (1985) examined in close detail how the American setting, including new forms of access to land, shaped such cultural practices among Balestrand (Norway) immigrants as naming patterns, modes of courtship, and church governance. Some of the changes involved the embrace of the new, particularly the names which parents gave their children in America, and women's work experiences; others represented the return to, or retrieval of, behaviors which had actually died out in Norway itself. The ethnic culture of the second and third generations in the Norwegian farming community of the Midwest reflected change, continuity, retrieval, and invention at one and the same time. In the same mid-to-late 1980s, writings by historians – such as Ewa Morawksa's (1985) in-depth analysis of the experiences of East European immigrants in Johnstown, Pennsylvania, Hasia Diner's (1985) writing about Irish immigrant women, Sarah Deutsch's (1987) chronicling the lives of Hispanic women and men of the American Southwest, David Hackett Fischer's (1989) extension of the discussion of ethnicity to include the earliest British settlers in seventeenth-century North America, and perhaps most notably Robert Orsi's (1985) study of Italian Harlem – all posited that ethnic culture ought not be viewed as something that came to America as a product of long, deep tradition which then either remained static and impervious to American forces or died out. These historians all asserted that ethnic culture did not confront a simple, either–or option of remaining intact or dying out. Rather, a constant process of change and negotiation constituted the best way to study ethnicity and the culture of America's ethnic communities.

Robert Orsi's *The Madonna of 115th Street* deserves a somewhat closer scrutiny as an exemplar of the ways in which ethnic historians in the aftermath of the "Geertzian revolution" wrote about ethnic culture. Orsi examined "thickly" a particular religious ritual that came to America with a group of immigrants from Genoa. In the East Harlem neighborhood they settled in they attempted to continue their devotion to Our Lady of Mount Carmel. But everything about her veneration changed as it planted itself in New York and as these immigrants confronted such new situations as a hierarchy in the Catholic Church of predominantly Irish origins, the fusion of the many "Italian" communities around them, in such proximity, in such a manner, and to an extent that had not taken place in Italy, as well as altered home spaces, gender roles, and generational relations. But the centrality of the religious ritual remained despite the vast changes which left their mark on it. The participants in the ritual practice continued to see what they did as a profound part of their ethnic cultural repertoire despite the alterations which changed it. As a form of Italian American ethnic culture it had both everything and little to do with the initial "traditional" practice.

The commitment of historians of ethnicity to the long-standing truth in the field that culture as an historical subject involved both abstract values and, in Geertz's words, the lived practices which were the "collective property of a particular people" continued into the 1990s and early years of the twenty-first century.

That "collective property" did not stand still but evolved as an essential element and by-product of the complex encounters of immigrants with both pre-migration experiences and American contexts. A group of some of America's most distinguished ethnic historians indeed participated in an international conference in Madrid in 1991 and announced the emergence of this way of thinking as the dominant paradigm. Kathleen Conzen, David Gerber, Ewa Morawska, George Pozzetta, and Rudolph Vecoli analyzed the history of the concept of ethnicity in American scholarship at the International Congress of Historical Studies, and made clear that the idea of invention offered the best and most salient way to understand it. These papers, reproduced in the *Journal of American Ethnic History* in 1992 under the title "The Invention of Ethnicity" (Conzen et al. 1992), invoked not only the transformative work of Geertz, but also that of sociologist Herbert Gans (1979: 193–220) who coined the phrase "symbolic ethnicity," and that of the literary scholar Werner Sollors (1989), whose edited volume *The Invention of Ethnicity* itself picked up on an idea popularized a few years earlier by Eric Hobsbawm and Terence Ranger (1983) in *The Invention of Tradition*.

What the scholars of immigration history discussed among themselves in the Madrid symposium and in the journal involved the usefulness of the concept of invention as a rubric for understanding ethnic culture. Did "invention" imply that immigrants had brought nothing "real" in their cultural repertoire? Could historians of ethnicity, who took as a given that different ethnic groups were the products of distinctive histories before migration, no longer assume that those actual histories had shaped the kinds of negotiations that their subjects undertook in America? For a field that had so long been wedded to social history, what value did the new thinking about culture add?

The authors of the symposium concurred on the proposition that "invention," as it referred to the "cultural construction accomplished over historical time," did not mean that historians should assume the absence of any connection between pre- and post-migration experiences. They did not have to reject the idea that ethnic cultures in America had in fact been built upon "preexisting communal solidarities, cultural attributes and historical memories," which facilitated the process by which immigrants and their children expressed their "sense of peoplehood," in large measure, "vis-à-vis outsiders." Rather they converged around a premise, offered in Kathleen Conzen's 1991 address, that for social historians, as for those who study ethnicity and immigration, culture can be used as "the publicly constructed meanings in and through which . . . life is lived" (Conzen et al. 1992: 4–5, 9, 12).

The call issued in the article by Kathleen Conzen and her colleagues continues to inspire historians in the early twenty-first century. They accept the idea that cultures involve the active assent of the people who subscribe to the symbols of group membership and that by thinking about ethnic culture scholars had to consider multiple negotiations, including those within the group, those between the group and the dominant society, and those between various ethnic groups who lived in proximity with each other.

Two examples of recent work by ethnic historians whose early twenty-first century scholarship has tackled the culture issue in a manner suggested by the 1992 *Journal of American Ethnic History* forum will have to suffice to illustrate some of the recent works operating along these lines. Dozens of other books and articles, particularly those that appeared in the *Journal of American Ethnic History* since the early 1990s, demonstrate equally well the impact of this new way of thinking about ethnic culture and the receptivity of the field to the idea of invention.

Hasia Diner (2002), for example, has studied the ways in which Irish, Italian, and East European Jewish immigrants to America brought their group-specific experiences with hunger to the United States, a place where food abounded at low cost and great variety, within the reach of the working class. Although these immigrants interacted with food very differently in America than they had "back home," and they invented new foods and food practices to take advantage of the richer ingredients (meat in particular) that they could now afford, they invested much of their new food system with the mantle of traditionalism. However, each group, since it came with different experiences and ideas about food and hunger, went through that invention process in distinctive ways.

In *Becoming Mexican American*, historian George Sanchez (1993) took the concept of invention in yet another stimulating and transformative direction. He, like a number of others of his cohort, raised questions about the very national labels which historians of ethnicity and immigration blithely used. In this new mode, exemplified here by Sanchez's work, historians suggest that such categories as "Italian," "Norwegian," "Mexican," and the like need to be interrogated because as designations of identity they do not reflect the complex regional and class make-up of the migrations. The prevailing paradigm now asserts that only after migration to America did immigrants – those women and men who left the towns and regions of the sending societies with little conception of themselves as part of some nation – adopt over time those identities. George Sanchez made this clear in this study of Los Angeles. Here, immigrants from various parts of Mexico developed a new identity and picked up a set of cultural practices which represented not only the places they came from but also the many locales that other "Mexicans" had left. In Los Angeles, as immigrants from multiple Mexican places met each other, they combined and recombined cultural practices. In addition, proximity to back home, as well as American technology, urban work patterns, and the structure of racism they confronted, all led to the process of "becoming Mexican." As such Sanchez's subjects first became Mexicans in California. The culture that they constructed, including the music, dress, food, as well as family and gender patterns, reflected the constant processes of combining and recombining idioms which together constituted the cultural landscape of Los Angeles's Mexican Americans.

Sanchez and Diner, as well as many of the historians of ethnicity writing in the 1990s and early 2000s, demonstrated in their work the emergence of the latest aspect in the historiography of ethnic culture, which asserts the importance of public culture. In the first of these two books (Diner 2002), restaurants and food shops labeled "Italian," for example, allowed immigrants from that place not only to construct a new identity, but to announce to the larger public that they had something distinctive and uniquely their own. In the second (Sanchez 1993), Mexican-owned record stores in Los Angeles not only served primarily ethnic customers, but the music blaring from the inside of the shops served to announce to anyone who passed by who owned the space. In these two cases ethnic entrepreneurs played a key role in marking off streets and neighborhoods as ethnic space.

Other historians, like Yong Chen in *Chinese San Francisco* (2000), April Schultz in *Ethnicity on Parade* (1994), Ruth Glasser in *"My Music Is My Flag": Puerto Rican Musicians and Their New York Communities* (1995), and Lon Kurashige in *Japanese American Celebration and Conflict* (2002), nudged the focus of the study of ethnic culture by changing the locus of their concern from the relatively private realm of the home to that of the more boldly obtrusive streets. In their works it can be seen that entrepreneurs, along with ethnic community leaders representing multiple factions and ideologies – as well as performers and the larger ethnic public – all collaborated to make ethnic culture public. In an array of public places, such as restaurants and food shops, music stores and clothing emporia, parks, meeting halls, saloons, and literally on the avenues and boulevards of the cities and towns where they lived, ethnic Americans performed and paraded their culture. Concerts, theatrical productions, pageants, rallies, festivals, and parades, exhibiting religious, political, and communal agendas, have come to take center stage as subjects of historical inquiry.

In all of these studies historians have shown how the immigrants and their descendants marked off, at various times, public places in and on which they could demonstrate their idealized selves. Scholars have charted the clash of visions within the ethnic communities as to the best way to perform their identities at these kinds of events. Likewise they have shown how such highly public spectacles could be used by different factions within the ethnic community for different ends, and how leaders and masses clashed over acceptable behaviors and appropriate themes.

These manifestations of ethnic public culture functioned as flashpoints of controversy within the communities and as key moments of ethnic pride. The performances, the scholarship has charted, operated in an essentially tripartite manner. First, they served a distinctly internal group purpose. Organizers staged them as identity-sustaining projects, hoping that the spectacles would solidify community bonds among the participants. Those who participated wanted to feel good about belonging, at the same time that they hoped to enjoy "traditional" music, consume distinctive foods, dress in "authentic" garb, and engage with the sounds and tropes of an imagined place called "back home." The regularity with which such public events took place meant that they began key parts of the ethnic temporality. The weekly concerts, the annual parades, the monthly theater performances, and the regular radio shows provided ethnic communities with a way to have their own group-distinctive, yet American-constructed, calendars.

Secondly, community leaders directed these public performances at their American-born progeny, hoping to show them in these events and venues the importance of the group, and the glories of its history and accomplishments. By situating them on American streets they also indirectly indicated the close fit between ethnic and American cultures.

In addition, these performances need to be understood, according to the historians who studied them, as political projects. Since these pageants, broadly defined, took place in local settings, organizers intended them to be seen by the larger

American public. In the parades and processions of ethnic culture, the participants realized that others watched. The others would assess the dignity of the events, the enthusiasm of the participants, the depth of their commitment to the group, the very distinctiveness of its symbols and styles, the quality of the music, the tastiness of the food, and ultimately the worth of the culture on display to and in America.

By turning their gaze on public performances of ethnic culture, American historians join a broad international scholarly project. In many other countries historians became fascinated with the ways that people used public space to demonstrate to themselves and to others who they were and how they wanted to be seen. In part because of the rise of postmodernism, the multidisciplinary interest in public culture inspired by the work of the theorist Jürgen Habermas, students of American ethnic life, like so many other historians around the world, shifted from the public to the private sectors.

For scholars who have turned to these performances as the focus of this newest chapter in the historiography, such highly demonstrative events offer a number of important new ways to think about ethnic culture. Analytically, to study such events scholars needed to blend concerns involving politics, aesthetics, class, power, religion, gender, and age, since those forces were constantly at work. These performances lay almost completely in the hands of the group itself. The state, the formal mechanisms of the society, had a decidedly minor role, if any, to play in making them possible. Americans as such stood on the sidelines while the members of the numerically smaller – and at times stigmatized – ethnic communities could take over the streets, albeit temporarily. These events allowed historians to see clearly how the ethnic group wanted others to see it, what it considered to fall within the bounds of acceptability, and what it thought to be the essence of its culture. Nearly all ethnic groups staged such performances, and therefore comparative studies should categorize different patterns of presentation and link them with other variables such as class, region, city size, and the degree of stigmatization endured by the ethnic communities. The parades and festivals functioned across the generations and across group lines. They invoked ideas of traditionalism and authenticity at the same time that could not possibly have taken place in "traditional" settings. As such the pageants provide historians with a lens through which to look at the process of invention. However much they had been constructed in America, they came to be considered traditional by participants, their children, and other Americans and therefore provide historians with a means by which to see the inner debates over the construction of ethnic culture.

By the beginning, then, of the twenty-first century, the study of ethnic culture has gone public. No longer relegated to the interior of the mind, to vague references to values and beliefs, nor to the intimacy of the home and private sphere of the family, it has come to be portrayed by historians as involving contested, but bold, displays of group symbols in public space. No longer does it involve an analytic polarity between the "ethnics" on one side and the Americans – that is, the larger society – on the other. Rather, immigrants and their children – and other Americans, many of them also immigrants, and their descendents – informed each other, negotiated amongst themselves, and constructed constantly changing forms which constitute ethnic cultures.

REFERENCES

Blanck, D.: *Becoming Swedish-American: The Construction of an Ethnic Identity in the Augustana Synod, 1860–1917* (Uppsala: Studia Historica Upsaliensia, 1997).

Chen, Yong: *Chinese San Francisco, 1850–1943: A Trans-Pacific Community* (Stanford, CA: Stanford University Press, 2000).

Conzen, K. N.: "Mainstreams and Side Channels: The Localization of Immigrant Cultures," *Journal of Ethnic History* 11 (Fall, 1991), 5–20.

Conzen, K. N., Gerber, D., Morawksa, E., Pozzetta, G., & Vecoli, R.: "The Invention of Ethnicity: A Perspective from the USA," *Journal of American Ethnic History* 12, 1 (Fall, 1992), 3–63.

Deutsch, S.: *No Separate Refuge: Class, Culture and Gender on the Anglo-Hispanic Frontier in the American Southwest, 1880–1940* (New York: Oxford University Press, 1987).

Diner, H. R.: *Erin's Daughters in America: Irish Immigrant Women in the Nineteenth Century* (Baltimore, MD: Johns Hopkins University Press, 1985).

Diner, H. R.: *Hungering for America: Italian, Irish and Jewish Foodways in the Age of Migration* (Cambridge, MA: Harvard University Press, 2002).

Fischer, D. H.: *Albion's Seed: Four British Folkways in America* (New York: Oxford University Press, 1989).

Gans, H.: "Symbolic Ethnicity: The Future of Ethnic Groups and Culture in America", in H. Gans, ed., *On the Making of Americans: Essays in Honor of David Riesman* (Philadelphia: University of Pennsylvania Press, 1979), pp. 193–220.

Geertz, C.: *The Interpretation of Cultures: Selected Essays* (New York: Basic Books, 1973).

Geertz, C.: *Local Knowledge: Further Essays in Interpretive Anthropology* (New York: Basic Books, 1983).

Gjerde J.: *From Peasants to Farmers: The Migration from Balestrand, Norway to the Upper Midwest* (Cambridge: Cambridge University Press, 1985).

Glasser, R.: *"My Music Is My Flag": Puerto Rican Musicians and Their New York Communities, 1917–1940* (Berkeley: University of California Press, 1995).

Handlin, O.: *Boston's Immigrants, 1790–1880: A Study in Acculturation* (Cambridge, MA: Harvard University Press, 1941).

Handlin, O.: *The Uprooted: The Epic Story of the Great Migrations That Made the American People* (Boston, MA: Little, Brown: 1951).

Hansen, M. L.: "The Problem of the Third Generation Immigrant," in P. Kvisto & D. Blanck, eds., *American Immigrants and Their Generations: Studies and Commentaries on the Hansen Thesis after Fifty Years* (Urbana: University of Illinois Press, 1990), pp. 191–203.

Hareven, T.: *Family Time and Industrial Time: The Relationship between Family and Work in a New England Industrial Community* (New York: Cambridge University Press, 1982).

Heideking, J., Fabre, G., & Dreisbach, K., eds.: *Celebrating Ethnicity and Nation: American Festive Culture from the Revolution to the Early Twentieth Century* (New York: Berghahn Books, 2001).

Hobsbawm, E. & Ranger, T., eds.: *The Invention of Tradition* (Cambridge: Cambridge University Press, 1983).

Kurashige, L.: *Japanese American Celebrations and Conflict: A History of Ethnic Identity and Festival, 1934–1990* (Berkeley: University of California Press, 2002).

Morawska, E.: *For Bread with Butter: The Life-worlds of East Central Europeans in Johnstown, Pennsylvania, 1890–1940* (New York: Cambridge University Press, 1985).

Orsi, R.: *The Madonna of 115th Street: Faith and Community in Italian Harlem, 1880–1950* (New Haven, CT: Yale University Press, 1985).

Sanchez, G.: *Becoming Mexican American: Ethnicity, Culture and Identity in Chicano Los Angeles, 1900–1945* (New York: Oxford University Press, 1993).

Schultz, April R.: *Ethnicity on Parade: Inventing the Norwegian-American through Celebration* (Amherst: University of Massachusetts Press, 1994).

Sollors, W., ed.: *The Invention of Ethnicity* (New York: Oxford University Press, 1989).

Thomas, William I.: *Old World Traits Transplanted* (New York: Harper and Brothers, 1921).

Yans-McLaughlin, V.: *Family and Community: Italian Immigrants in Buffalo, 1880–1930* (Ithaca, NY: Cornell University Press, 1977).

Chapter Twelve

CULTURAL WATERSHEDS IN *FIN DE SIÈCLE* AMERICA

Janet M. Davis

In 1907 Gertrude Stein famously remarked that she was determined to "kill" the nineteenth century and all of its florid Victorian literary norms and tightly bound cultural conventions. Amid an explosively expanding urban milieu crackling with electrification, trains, trolleys, telephones, and recorded sound, preindustrial notions of time, space, and place crumbled in the face of an increasingly compressed and motorized world. Millions of immigrants – primarily from southern and eastern Europe – arrived at Ellis Island from 1880 to 1920, swelling America's burgeoning city population and forging what historian Kathy Peiss (1986) has called a new heterosocial world of "cheap amusements," which emerged out of the industrial rhythms of work and leisure. In a nation catapulted by industrialization, new media and transportation technologies, it seemed that one could "kill" the nineteenth century and push relentlessly forward – even at a time when nostalgia was becoming a significant feature of modernity.

This essay focuses on the railroad circus, the moving picture, the car, and new ideas concerning the shift from animal power to motor power as important cultural markers of the nation's transformation from an agrarian to an increasingly urban, industrial, corporate, and consumption-oriented society. Still, it is tricky to speak definitively of wholesale cultural turning points because these transformations often intermingled with older historical conventions, ideologies, and cultural practices, oscillating between past and present. For example, as historian Lizbeth Cohen (1990) has shown, the arrival of three cultural watersheds – movies, radio, and chain stores – in Chicago's ethnic neighborhoods hardly represented an immediate and wholesale cultural breakpoint. These cultural phenomena did not instantly herald the rise of homogenous consumers and giant culture industries. Instead, movies, radio, and chain stores were initially integrated into older neighborhood economies, often in multiple languages, thereby initially preserving rather than diluting distinct ethnic identities. From a historical perspective, one sees that new cultural forms whose immediate consequences might have seemed negligible have actually exerted a significant long-term impact on the making of twenty-first-century American culture.

The American circus helped make spectacle, novelty, and ostensible educational uplift an integral part of the modern entertainment experience. As a pioneer in monopoly formation, the circus also made corporate mergers a standard practice in the amusement business. In the waning months of 1880, two veteran circus proprietors (along with a couple of other lesser-known showmen) cut a deal that transformed the circus – and arguably, the entire amusement industry. James A. Bailey, co-owner of Cooper & Bailey's Great London Circus, and P. T. Barnum, co-owner of P. T. Barnum's Greatest Show on Earth, merged their operations, opening the season in 1881 with an enormous new show, containing three rings, two stages, and an outer hippodrome track, under a canvas big top that could seat 10,000 people. By the 1890s it comprised over 1,200 performers, hundreds of animals, and scores of laborers, managers, lawyers, cooks, blacksmiths, farriers, veterinarians, musicians, animal men, and wardrobe employees. Barnum & Bailey's circus capitalized on its sprawling size as an essential feature of the show. Traveling across the entire country by railroad, the show offered consumers discounted "excursion fares" from neighboring towns to come to the circus. People scrambled out of bed before dawn to watch the spectacle of coordinated labor as workers rolled wagons off the railroad cars and set up the tents aided by horses and elephants in an era when the animal-powered economy still prevailed. Using the industrial labor principles of Frederick Winslow Taylor – the architect of industrial time–motion studies and scientific management – to increase efficiency among circus workers, Barnum & Bailey managers dictated specialized duties for each part of the labor process in erecting a virtual canvas city across nine acres on the show grounds.

Although the American circus had first emerged in Philadelphia at the turn of the previous century in 1793, this earlier cultural form bore little resemblance to Barnum & Bailey's newly merged "Greatest Show on Earth," which represented the circus at its maturation. In the early national period, circus companies containing a handful of horses, acrobatic riders, jugglers, wirewalkers, and clowns plodded their way laboriously up and down the eastern seaboard by horse and wagon, constructing wooden buildings and showing months at a time in a single city. But in the nineteenth century, transportation networks such as roads, canals, and railways, alongside new modes of travel like the steamship and train, enabled the circus to expand. This itinerant amusement complex now included a parade, a menagerie of exotic animals, and a sideshow of "human oddities" comprised of people with physical malformations, people of color (depicted as exotic "savages" in accord with contemporary ideologies of polygenesis, racial hierarchy, and white supremacy), preternatural ingestors (such as sword swallowers, glass eaters, and fire eaters), and racy "cootch" shows of nearly nude dancers (Davis 2002).

Barnum & Bailey's "Greatest Show on Earth" was born out of intense competition between rival showmen. P. T. Barnum and his Wisconsin-born partner W. C. Coup opened a successful circus in 1871 and made their show even more profitable the next year by retrofitting their wagons and equipment to travel the rails. Barnum and Coup also cut special deals with railroad companies to haul the circus at reduced rates. James A. Bailey, meanwhile, proved to be a fearsome competitor. Immersed in every aspect of circus life from mid-childhood onward (he ran away from an abusive home at age 13), Bailey became immensely adroit at managing the minutiae of circus administration. Though Bailey was intensely private, and Barnum was loquacious and media-savvy, both showmen shared a fine eye for exploiting novelties. On the eve of the merger, for example, Bailey nearly muscled Barnum out of the lucrative northeastern US circus market by marketing the birth of the first healthy captive elephant in the western world on his show. The baby elephant Columbia nursing her mother Hebe became a ubiquitous image on the thousands of posters and handbills that blanketed storefronts near upcoming show stops and trumpeted the circus's animal wonders and technological novelties: "First time of any baby elephant! First time of any electric light!" (Slout 2000: 198–204).

Against a corporate backdrop of vigorous monopoly formation in other gilded-age industries such as oil, railroads, and steel, Barnum and Bailey's merger marked the first major combination in the entertainment business. Other combinations soon followed, including the Keith–Albee vaudeville circuit, the Theatre Syndicate (run by A. L. Erlanger and Marc Klaw), and the Motion Picture Patents Company, also known as "the Trust," which was dominated by the Edison and Biograph companies from 1908 to 1918; by the 1920s, the "Big Five" motion picture companies (Metro-Goldwyn-Mayer, Paramount, RKO, Twentieth Century Fox, and Warner Brothers) held a virtual monopoly in American film production and distribution. Fred Thompson, the world's fair and amusement park showman who created Luna Park at Coney Island, denounced the octopus-like "Circus Trust," declaring that he would "wage a merry war on our three ringed opponents" as a way to preserve his other amusement interests. "Thompson could draw on Progressive rhetoric to distinguish the universal benefits and rational rates of his big business against the narrow-minded, particularistic interests of the Syndicate and circus monopolies" (Register 2001: 155). In short, the railroad circus represented a harbinger of twentieth- and twenty-first-century media conglomerates in which firms like Sony and Disney own multiple sectors in the film, music, radio, and television industries.

The merger of Barnum and Bailey also signaled the beginning of a wave of merger mania within the circus industry itself. In addition to buying other rival shows, Barnum and Bailey held substantial interests in other entertainments such as Buffalo Bill's Wild West show, which traveled by rail like the circus. Created in 1883, Buffalo Bill's Wild West show consisted of American Indian and Euro-American horsemanship, marksmanship, cattle-rustling, and historical reenactments from the recent Indian Wars. A year after James A. Bailey died in 1906, seven brothers from Baraboo, Wisconsin purchased Barnum & Bailey's Greatest Show on Earth and Bailey's financial interests in Buffalo Bill's Wild West show. In 1919, the Ringling brothers merged these separate holdings into one behemoth combination: "Ringling Brothers and Barnum & Bailey's Greatest Show on Earth." Ten years later, John Ringling (the last surviving brother) bought out the last viable rival conglomerate, the American Circus Corporation. In contrast to 1903, when nearly 100 circuses roamed the nation, by 1956 just 13 circuses remained in the United States – a long-term result of the consolidation initiated by P. T. Barnum and James A. Bailey in 1880.

Barnum & Bailey's circus monopoly embodied a culture of spectacle in which sheer bigness – corporate consolidation, the growth of massive factories, stockyards, and urbanization – was becoming a metonym for a new industrial age. The experiences of circus-goers "rubber necking" in a dazed attempt to take it all in resonated with contemporary literary representations of bewildered characters encountering city life for the first time. For example, in Theodore Dreiser's *Sister Carrie* (1963 [1900]), Carrie Meeber fled provincial Columbia City, Wisconsin by train for the excitement and opportunities of Chicago. Numbly walking the streets, Carrie tried to absorb the mammoth city:

> These vast buildings, what were they? These strange energies and huge interests, for what purposes were they? It was so with the vast railroad yards, with the crowded array of vessels she saw at the river, and the huge factories over the way, lining the water's edge. Through the open windows she could see the figures of men and women in working aprons, moving busily about. The great streets were wall-lined mysteries to her; the vast offices, strange mazes which concerned far-off individuals of importance . . . It was all wonderful, all vast, all far removed . . ." (Dreiser 1963 [1900]: 13)

Barnum & Bailey's vast, modern, three-ring railroad circus collapsed time and space in crowded canvas performances. Borrowing from the immensely popular international exposition and the titillating visual scientism of the new magazine *National Geographic* (1887), Barnum & Bailey and other railroad shows featured a huge ethnological congress of "strange and savage tribes from around the world," who performed in a separate tent alongside animals from their country of origin in popular performances of evolutionary hierarchy. The railroad circus offered patriotic spectacles reenacting scenes from the Spanish–American War, the Boxer Rebellion, and the building of the Panama Canal. Providing intimate encounters with people and animals from around the globe, the circus articulated normative ideologies concerning the body, gender, race, class, and empire for its far-flung spectators.

Alongside the circus's offerings of new technology, up-to-date spectacles of the latest foreign affairs, and a railroad-precise coordination of labor and travel, the canvas city itself was also a site of intense nostalgia. The circus was a facsimile museum-on-wheels encasing a live, preindustrial world of animal and human labor on exhibition for popular consumption. Show proprietors marketed their displays as an opportunity to catch a "last glimpse" of vanishing cultures and exotic creatures now threatened by the homogenizing march of modernization. Impresarios highlighted American Indian performers, in particular, as live artifacts of the disappearing frontier, thus echoing the federal Census Bureau, which declared in 1893 that there was no longer a distinct line between settlement and wilderness in the American West. Despite the actual diversity of Native American cultures, Plains Indians were ubiquitous at these shows and functioned as de facto representatives of all American Indians as they performed trick riding, roping, battle scenes, marksmanship, and pow-wow scenes with such verve that some assimilation-minded reformers sought to ban Native Americans from working in traveling shows altogether, out of fear that such employment encouraged cultural preservation rather than assimilation into Euro-American society (Moses 1996; Kasson 2000).

Barnum and Bailey's merger in 1880 signaled the rise of entertainment conglomerates whose success was predicated upon providing edifying, educational amusement – yet with a titillating flash of bodily display. The successors to this "propriety-with-a-wink" tradition in the film industry likewise promoted middle-class values as normative national values. Furthermore, the frenetic, colorful, exotic, too-big-to-see-at-once three-ring aesthetics of the railroad circus helped pave the way for new cultural technologies which also collapsed time and space, and would ultimately displace the circus as an entertaining source of information about the wider world.

The eventual cultural dominance of film, however, was not at all immediately apparent in the early 1890s. Thomas Edison's Kinetograph and the subsequent Kinetoscope (both invented by Edison's employee William K. L. Dickson) were "peephole" devices for recording and viewing moving images which could only accommodate one viewer at a time. The new Vitascope in 1896 could house larger audiences and consequently had broader cultural reach. (Although Edison marketed the Vitascope as his latest invention, the machine was actually a commercialized virtual replica of the Jenkins–Armat phantascope.) The Vitascope made its debut at Koster and Bial's Music Hall in March 1896 with flickering images of an umbrella dance, a scene at Dover Pier, a "burlesque" boxing match, an intricate military marching band sequence, and a color-enhanced serpentine dance. The short show received enthusiastic reviews in the local papers, such as the New York *Dramatic Mirror*: "[it] was a success in every way and the large audience testified its approval of the novelty by the heartiest kind of applause" (Musser 1990: 116). The success of the Vitascope triggered the expansion of the moving image nationwide. One year later, several hundred Vitascopes were in operation across the country and beyond, including far-flung territories like Hawaii and Arizona (ibid. 109).

Despite the Vitascope's growing national availability, its physical presence was unobtrusive because it was commonly shown alongside other amusements. For example, circus managers displayed brief films in dark sideshow tents as just one of their myriad attractions, a novelty that was often overshadowed by masses of live animals, bearded women, and other human "oddities" at the show. In addition to its place in the sideshow tent, the moving picture co-mingled with other cultural forms like department stores, saloons, railway stations, and world's fairs. With the rise of small neighborhood movie theaters in 1905, film finally found its own distinct home in these cramped, urban "cheap nickel dumps" (Sklar 1975).

Like the three-ring railroad circus, film articulated the growing currency of the visual image in American culture. Cultural historian Warren Susman once remarked that the United States at the turn of the century was fast becoming a "hieroglyphic civilization . . . a significant break for a culture that had taken form under Bible and dictionary" (Susman 1985: 111). Within 25 years after the invention of photography in 1839, middle-class Americans were eagerly collecting inexpensive *carte-de-visite* postcard photographs of stage actresses like Adah Isaacs Menken and Lydia Thompson, and freak show celebrities such as Jo-Jo the Dog-Faced Boy, and Zip . . . What Is It? in handsome photo albums on ready display in the parlor (Bogdan 1988; Allen 1991). In the 1880s, newspapers and a mushrooming magazine trade abandoned a purely textual layout in order to use halftones combining photography and the printed word. In the 1890s, the sports page took shape as a separate section of the paper, replete with halftones.

Electricity, glassy new department store windows, and the advent of indoor plumbing complete with bathroom mirrors afforded Americans ample visual opportunities for self-inspection (Brumberg 1997). Amid the hustling urban scene, masses of rushing people constituted another form of daily visual spectacle. As part of this unintentional public theater comprised of anonymous passersby, women of all classes became increasingly comfortable wearing cosmetics in a new consumer culture where standardized notions of white native-born beauty were omnipresent (Peiss 1998). But no medium to date captured the growing visualization of American life more effectively than film. Even ordinary scenes – sneezing, cockfighting, selling milk from a dogcart, frolicking in ocean waves – made up an early genre of film called actualities.

Film complemented other technologies like the railroad, which in the words of Karl Marx caused the "annihilation of space over time" (Schivelbusch 1986: xiv). As the means of transporting the vast, visually focused three-ring circus, the train also portended the rise of the motion picture. Trains were important subjects and locations for action in early motion pictures (*The Great Train Robbery* (1903) was the first film to tell a sustained story); moreover, the experience of riding on the rails also helped "train" passengers for the sensory experience of film (Kirby 1997). As passengers became acquainted with the rumbling roar of traveling faster than ever before, train windows encased the surrounding outdoors in a rhythmic, panoramic frame-by-frame view of a seemingly compressed world. Significantly, the industrialist and governor of California Leland Stanford played an important role in the development of both the railroad and film. As the co-owner of the Central Pacific Railroad, Stanford ceremoniously swung a hammer at the last spike marking the completion of the nation's first transcontinental railroad in 1869, tripping off a telegraph wire which set off simultaneous cannon fire into both the Atlantic and Pacific oceans – and thereby inaugurating the Gilded Age's version of the information superhighway wrought in iron, steel, and wood. In 1872, Stanford hired the photographer Eadweard Muybridge to help settle a $25,000 bet by proving that a horse lifted all of its feet off the ground when it galloped. Muybridge set up 24 cameras along the edge of a race track, each with a trip wire to set off the shutter when the horse passed. Muybridge's successive images of equine motion won the bet for Stanford and served as an inspiration for moving-picture innovators Etienne-Jules Marey and Thomas Edison (Musser 1990; Kirby 1997: 21). The compressed placelessness of the railroad and film ultimately served as harbingers for other media technologies such as radio, television, and the internet, thus sowing the seeds for the development of a national mass culture.

Motion pictures also accelerated a growing commercial culture of celebrity at the turn of the century. Even though fame had been an important part of American culture during the nineteenth century, it was typically the province of politicians, military leaders, and ministers. Nevertheless, amusement figures born of modest means also populated nineteenth-century media on the basis of their colorful exploits or heroic deeds. Sam Patch, an itinerant daredevil muleskinner, abandoned his trade in 1827 to become a fulltime celebrity waterfall jumper, and his fame survived him after he died in a drunken leap from Genesee Falls in 1829 (Johnson 2003). P. T. Barnum's promotional skills transformed the Swedish opera singer Jenny Lind, the Abyssinian elephant celebrity Jumbo, and the midget couple Tom Thumb and Lavinia Warren into national phenomena. But the rise of the motion picture industry triggered the development of whole media industries to support a nascent star system that was predicated not only upon charismatic exploits, but upon the growing currency of personality and likeable familiarity.

The medium of the motion picture itself did not catalyze an immediate explosion of a movie star culture in its first 15 years. Indeed, producers rigorously maintained a culture of anonymity among their actors and actresses by refusing to list these players by name in film credits. Directors at the Edison and Biograph Trust figured that named performers would be troublesome cranks with an inflated sense of entitlement, pulling greater leverage in an industry where low wages and rough working conditions were the norm. Conditions remained difficult in the 1920s with the rise of the studio and contract systems, in which a performer was required to sign on with a studio for seven years while the studio was only obligated to hire the performer for six months (Sklar 1975: 71–2, 83–5; 230–3). Some performers even preferred to remain nameless owing to the whiff of ill repute that characterized film in its early years and the desire of many actors to make it in "legitimate" theater later on (ibid. 40). But motion picture performers did not remain nameless for long (Cohen 2001). Around 1900, the Kalem Company began individuating otherwise anonymous performers by featuring specific actors and actresses – although still nameless – in photograph displays at nickelodeon lobbies; shortly thereafter companies peddled popular postcards of individual performers who were generically labeled the "Biograph Girl," the "IMP Boy," and so on. By 1910, producers were releasing the names of their performers followed by generic hyperbole. A major turning point in the development of the movie star occurred in 1909–10 when actress Florence Lawrence, previously known only as the Biograph Girl, left Biograph and signed on with IMP. The P. T. Barnumesque owner of IMP, Carl Laemmle, first spread a rumor that Lawrence had been killed by a streetcar and then happily "corrected" himself with word that she was still alive and ready to become the newest IMP Girl (Cohen 2001: 140–1). The first fan magazines, *Motion Picture Story* and *Photoplay*, were published in 1911 and were bland, flattering, industry-controlled fare that revealed little about the actual lives of such performers as Mary Pickford, Douglas Fairbanks, Theda Bara, and Charlie Chaplin (Sklar 1975: 233–4). Despite the uncritical tone and limited content of such publications, audiences eagerly consumed them. The immediate popularity of such magazines quickly made them a permanent and ubiquitous part of the American periodical scene.

Innovations within the medium of film itself in the early twentieth century were perhaps most responsible for the emergence of the movie star. Serial films (multi-part movie versions of weekly mystery or adventure newspaper serials) and special films (multi-reel movies with the same main character shown over a period of days or weeks) featured the same performer over a series of separate motion pictures, while the longer feature film provided the opportunity for the sustained and complex evolution of plots and characters (Cohen 2001: 137). The facial close-up technique was particularly significant. Although Thomas Edison's Black Maria Studios had used the close-up as early as 1893 in *Fred Ott's Sneeze*, D. W. Griffith perfected this technique in 1908 as a main vehicle for character development and narrative sustenance:

> The close-up, which [Griffith] took beyond the simple locating and reaction shot into the realm of existential exposure, caused audiences to believe they knew the actress on the screen better than she knew herself. It is the sense of such privileged knowledge – of intimacy gained by simply following the visual narrative of the face – that lies in the heart of the fanaticism and presumption of the fan. (Cohen 2001: 124)

Even though film lacked the theater's live physical proximity between audience and actor, the close-up helped breed the star system by cultivating the illusion of intimacy, familiarity, knowability, and seeming accessibility. To be sure, in a new visual age the older dictum of "appearances are deceiving" no longer held sway (ibid. 115, 129,

130). Alongside a growing media emphasis on the "personality" of the performer off-screen came an expansive new web of star trappings: product endorsements, autobiographies, celebrity self-help books, and scandal – all of which facilitated a newly self-perpetuating and permanent culture of celebrity.

These stars were uniformly white. Film, like the circus, participated in normative mass cultural constructions of racial and ethnic identity at the turn of the twentieth century. Nonetheless, as a visual medium, silent film was widely accessible to non-English-speaking immigrant groups from southern and eastern Europe. Cheap ticket prices also made silent movies available to a broad audience. Many filmmakers, such as Adolph Zukor and Carl Laemmle, were European immigrants (Cohen 2001: 17, 35). But African Americans, Asians, and American Indians were virtually absent on the silent screen, as whites performing racial caricatures took the place of actors of color. When D. W. Griffith loosely adapted Thomas Dixon's racist novel *The Clansman* (1905) for his expensive, two-and-a-half-hour-long feature film *The Birth of a Nation* in 1915, the National Association for the Advancement of Colored People mobilized nationwide protests and theater boycotts in reaction to the movie's bumbling and offensive portrayal of African Americans during Reconstruction (Sklar 1975: 58–60). Similar to the railroad circus's spectacle of "savages" from around the world, early film illustrated the racist limitations on American citizenship at the turn of the century.

Though the corporate headquarters of early film were in New York City the motion picture industry helped foster the gradual reorientation of the United States westward toward California and the sunbelt (which would flower after World War II). In 1907 motion picture companies such as the Selig Company of Chicago were drawn to Hollywood by California's sunny weather, the remarkable proximity of mountains, ocean, desert, and city, and the state's abundance of cheap land and non-union labor (Sklar 1975: 67–9). But Hollywood's rapid rise in the film industry was bitterly contested. Film producers in other states such as Florida fought vigorously to promote their own companies, demonstrating the ubiquity of the moving image throughout the country in the early twentieth century (Frick 2005).

The popularity of the motion picture and the railroad circus rested in part upon their shared ability to destroy temporal and physical boundaries in a culture increasingly defined by speed. The automobile also represented the dizzying pace of change in *fin de siècle* America – despite early speeds that we in hindsight find unimpressive. Sponsored by early automakers as a way to advertise their products, the first American automobile race was held in Chicago on Thanksgiving Day, 1895, and it was a laborious affair: out of 83 entrants, only six cars were able to start. Only two automobiles completed the 55-mile race and the top average speed clocked in at an underwhelming 8 miles per hour (Flink 1988: 23). Despite the inauspicious beginnings of the automobile age, the car quickly embodied a complex matrix of cultural transformations that promulgated the arrival of the nation's modern mass consumer culture.

Automobiles represented an individuated mode of travel – a striking departure from mass transportation technologies like the railroad and streetcar. The popularity of the bicycle hastened the rise of the car, an odd nexus from the vantage of the twenty-first century when cyclists and motorists often despise each other. Many early motorcar makers such as Opel in Germany, Peugeot in France, Rover in Great Britain, and the Americans Charles and J. Frank Duryea and William Knudsen were bicycle engineers who based their primitive automobiles on bicycle prototypes. With the advent of the moderately priced, mass-produced "safety bicycle" in 1885 (so called because of its reliable brakes, steel-tube tires, chain drive, pneumatic tires, and differential gearing), Americans entered the age of the "bicycle craze." Frances Willard, the president of the Woman's Christian Temperance Union, became an enthusiastic cyclist, while Americans across the nation began lobbying for better cycling roads. Cyclists formed the National League for Good Roads in 1893, advocating that road construction and maintenance be funded by county and state taxes (Flink 1988: 5). Ultimately, the bicycle created an enormous demand for individualized, long-distance transportation in a nation with huge, open spaces. As cars became faster, more reliable, and less expensive, they eventually became an optimum technology for satisfying these cultural needs (ibid. 6).

But automobiles at the turn of the century were expensive and generally unreliable. Henry Ford, a machine-shop apprentice, engineer, and tinker from the Dearborn, Michigan area, created the Ford Motor Company in 1903, desiring to build a reliable car for the "great multitude." In 1908, Ford unveiled his vastly improved new car, the Model T. Besieged with orders for this reliable, simple, and easy-to-fix-it-yourself car, Ford opened a new 62-acre plant in Highland Park, Michigan in 1910, where he perfected the use of the moving assembly line as a way to simplify and segment the labor process according to Taylorist time–motion principles. Although cultural observers like Woodrow Wilson worried that the high cost of the automobile (the Model T cost $825.00 in 1908) would incite class warfare and make the United States a socialist country, Henry Ford wanted to make his Model T more affordable over time through increasingly efficient production techniques and through vertical integration (Susman 1985: 135). Ford controlled all aspects of the production process, buying rubber plantations in Brazil, iron mines and lumber mills in Michigan, coal mines in West Virginia and Kentucky, railroad interests, and a fleet of ships (Flink 1988: 57–9). Consequently, the price of the Model T fell to $290.00 when the car was finally retired in 1927 (ibid. 37–8). In contrast to his competitors at General Motors who were already cultivating the concept of planned obsolescence as a way to sell cars in perpetuity, Ford resolutely refused to offer new automotive models, bowing to pressure from the industry only in 1927 when he finally introduced a new car, the Model A.

Along with falling prices, installment buying plans made cars accessible to growing numbers of consumers. The Singer Sewing Machine Company was the first American business to cultivate credit purchases successfully in the 1850s, but the widespread growth of installment buying came of age only with the rise of the automobile. Formalized in 1915 by a group of Toledo, Ohio automobile dealers who wanted to increase sales by allowing customers "to enjoy while you pay" and "buy now, pay later," installment buying became a common part of the automobile economy (Flink 1988: 190–1). By 1925 a majority of American families owned a car, and by 1926 three-quarters of all cars sold in the United States were purchased on installment buying. The bank depositor was no longer the hero of American civilization, as consumers zealously embraced cars, credit, and instant gratification (Susman 1985: 111).

Still, it is important to remember that the rise of the car did not signal an instant, radical reorientation of consumer spending. Older spending patterns still persisted at the dawn of the automotive age. In 2004, Alice Osborne, a keen 95-year-old, recalled that after her father opened his Buick dealership in tiny Palmyra, Wisconsin in 1905, customers used to barter for their Buicks, supplying Osborne's father with scores of horses, other livestock, land, and diamonds (interview with Janet M. Davis, 2004). The rise of automobility, then, did not indicate a neat, wholesale shift into consumer credit; an older barter economy persisted for at least a few years into the twentieth century.

As an architect of welfare capitalism, Henry Ford envisioned his workers as good consumers. Ford's mandate on labor efficiency and low production costs meant that the average time required to build the Model T fell from 14 hours to an hour and a half in 1914. In the routinized world of the moving assembly line, the work was boring and turnover was high. Forecasting the relentless movement of the assembly line in Charlie Chaplin's film, *Modern Times* (1936), one Ford worker observed that, "You could drop over dead, and they wouldn't stop the line." Moreover, company spies patrolled the line while workers were hired and fired with impunity. But in 1914 Ford cut the workday to eight hours and instituted the "$5.00 Day" as the minimum standard for any kind of work. In exchange for a shorter workday and higher pay, employees had to adhere to rigid standards of comportment. Ford's new Sociology Department (later renamed the Education Department) taught workers how to manage their financial affairs, maintain their homes, look after their hygiene, and stay sober (Green 1980: 108–12; Flink 1988: 120–3). Ford's competitors soon copied many of his methods, resulting in a 255 percent gain in productivity in the auto industry during the 1920s – at a time when other manufacturers increased productivity by only 64 percent (Green 1980: 111). Even though the seasonal production cycles in the automobile industry mitigated against substantive wage gains, Ford's pioneering and profitable forays into welfare capitalism helped mold the behavior and values of his workforce in order to maximize their potential as car buyers (Susman 1985: 137).

The automobile age also transformed American courtship rituals. In the late nineteenth century, middle-class Americans typically engaged in an elaborate web of courtship conventions known as the "call system," whereby a young woman's parents would invite a prospective suitor to "call" at their home under watchful parental supervision. Middle-class women's magazines such as *Ladies Home Journal* and *Good Housekeeping* enumerated the complex rules concerning the timing of the call, refreshments to be served, and more. By contrast, many urban, working-class teenagers engaged in a new courtship practice called "dating" (a term first used by turn-of-the-century prostitutes who referred to their customers as "dates"), in which unmarried teenagers would meet at amusement sites outside the workplace (Bailey 1988: 13–24).

But starting in the 1910s the automobile helped homogenize American courtship. In the aptly titled *From Front Porch to Back Seat*, historian Beth Bailey demonstrates that the rise of the car contributed to the growth of dating as a national social practice, particularly in rural and suburban areas, as young adults relished the autonomy and privacy afforded by automobility (Bailey 1988: 19, 86–7). "Cars fulfilled a romantic function from the dawn of the auto age. They permitted couples to get much farther away from front porch swings, parlor sofas, hovering mothers, and pesky siblings than ever before . . . Courtship itself was extended from the five-mile radius of the horse and buggy to ten, twenty, and fifty miles and more . . ." (Lewis 1983: 123). Fearful municipalities passed "parking" laws to prevent backseat intimacy in parks and newly christened "lovers' lanes," while Henry Ford reportedly designed his Model T with a particularly short seat to dissuade young lovers from using the car for sexual activity. Nevertheless in the 1920s automakers tacitly promoted the automobile as a space for youthful sexual autonomy by offering new technologies such as heaters, tilt steering wheels, and even Jewett's fold-down bed and bed-conversion model in 1925. Auxiliary entertainments such as drive-in restaurants (Royce Hailey's Pig Stand in Dallas was the first in 1921) and drive-in movies became an integral part of twentieth-century youth culture (ibid. 124–8). After World War II, automobility (in tandem with federally subsidized mortgage loans) hastened the rise of the suburbs and fast-food restaurants such as Carl's Junior and McDonalds (Schlosser 2001: 13–25).

The arrival of the automobile in the 1890s was cause for immediate meditation about the future of the nation's animal-powered economy and, more broadly, the place of animals in American society. A sampling of headlines from the *New York Times* demonstrates this early awareness of the automobile's cultural power: "To Run Without Horses," "The Passing of the Horse," "The Future of the Horse." One writer argued that automobiles were an inexpensive alternative to the ever-hungry horse, positing that petroleum was cheaper than oats: "Steam and electricity have begun to supersede [the horse] for public transportation, the bicycle has smitten him sorely in his capacity as a means of locomotion for exercise or pleasure, and the perfection of the horseless carriage will render him useless with respect to several of his remaining functions . . . Petroleum produces more horse power for the money than oats" ("The Horseless Carriage," *New York Times*, September 22, 1895: 4). Other contemporary writers posited that automobiles represented an environmentally cleaner alternative to the horse, whose copious manure and urine were a constant urban sanitation problem (Flink 1988: 135–40; Jones 2002). A *New York Times* editorial in 1895 argued that the horse was now obsolete: "When, like pigs and cows, he is relegated to his place outside the purlieus of urban residence by the ceasing of that necessity, there may be comfort and health as well as pleasure and zest in dwelling in cities. The horse should go" ("Horses in the Streets," *New York Times*, May 16, 1895: 16). Through the end of the nineteenth century, American cities were home to dense populations of domestic animals: not only horses, but cows and hogs and chickens. The automobile helped hasten a cultural reconsideration of rural and urban environments and ultimately contributed to a more rigidly defined distinction between the two, as domestic animals gradually disappeared from the urban scene.

The horseless carriage helped crystallize an increasingly nostalgic and sentimental treatment of animals and nature at the turn of the century. Animal welfare activists focused on the humane promise of the nation's transition from animal to motor power, arguing that automobiles would ultimately eliminate the use of the horse as a beast of burden, thereby allowing horses to live comfortably in a state of bucolic, pastoral "nature" apart from the urban environments in which they had labored for centuries. In an effort to hasten this transition, George Angell, founder of the Massachusetts Society for the Prevention of Cruelty to Animals (1868), initiated work-horse parades in 1903 as a way to acknowledge equine labor and simultaneously celebrate its passing. Meanwhile, a raft of writers such as Ernest Thompson Seton and William Long were writing wildly popular anthropomorphic stories about charismatic and noble wild animals, in which they affirmed the Darwinian interconnectedness of people and animals while simultaneously rejecting Darwin's and Spencer's bleak, amoral vision of natural selection. The "new nature writers," as they were called in the popular press, envisioned a peaceful natural world imbued with moral and spiritual order, filled with intelligent animals that acted wisely and rationally, not instinctively. Diverse audiences – from the preservationist John Muir to William T. Hornaday, the director of the New York Zoological Society – enthusiastically received this vision of an animal kingdom governed by cooperation rather than struggle (Mighetto 1991: 17–24). Yet in 1903, the publication of William Long's article, "Animal Surgery," created a major controversy. Contending that wild animals possessed the ability to heal their injuries, the piece was met with immediate outrage from the scientific community. Even President Theodore Roosevelt weighed in on what he called "nature fakers," vigorously decrying Long as a "yellow journalist of the woods" whose animals were "storybook beasts" (ibid. 18).

The participants in the nature faker controversy of 1903, however, did share a common concern: sentimentalists and scientists alike were alarmed at the rapid loss of wilderness habitat and animal life in the booming industrial age. In 1893, the US Census Bureau declared that the frontier had closed because there was no longer a distinct line between settlement and wilderness. In addition, extractive mining for silver, iron, copper, coal, lead, zinc, and tin destroyed ecologically diverse habitats across the nation. From Quebec to Texas the skies no longer darkened and rumbled from the annual migration of the passenger pigeon. Once numbering in the billions, the passenger pigeon was extinct by 1913 when the lone survivor, "Martha" – whose very naming denoted the new attitudes towards nature – died at the Cincinnati Zoo (Price 1999). Egrets, bison, and cod, among other animals, also faced the threat of extinction (Doughty 1975; Kurlansky 1997; Price 1999; Isenberg 2000).

In this milieu of vanishing wilderness and the simultaneous rise of motor power, two distinct approaches to environmental policy emerged: conservation and preservation. Conservation became the rallying cry of President Roosevelt and his Secretary of the Interior, Gifford Pinchot. Conservationists argued that America's natural resources could be sustained by applying Progressive principles of "scientific management," regulation, and "wise use" to environmental policy. As president, Roosevelt established the National Forest Service (1905), five new national parks, and 16 national monuments (Vickery 1986: 98). Starting with Yellowstone in 1872, the creation of national parks was, in part, animated by preservationist ideologies. John Muir became a leading architect of this viewpoint, asserting that wild spaces were sacred and should be set aside and preserved – as opposed to being subject to suspiciously industry-friendly "wise use" policies. Muir energetically promoted the creation of natural parks, believing in a strict separation of wild spaces from the built environment (Dizard 1999: 18–21). Despite their differences, Roosevelt and Muir both believed that the wilderness was a site of manly rejuvenation in a modern, urban age when men were going "soft" from excess brainwork. Millions of ordinary Americans agreed: camping, canoeing, the advent of the Boy Scouts and Girl Scouts, and the rise of physical culture all became interlocking cultural manifestations of a distinctly modern and nostalgic sensibility about nature and its dialectical counterpoint, the urban environment.

The railroad circus, the motion picture, the automobile, and the new sensibility about animals and nature represent complementary cultural watersheds at the turn of the twentieth century. All helped define a modernizing nation. The circus, film, and automobile participated in the rise of big business and monopoly formation, and the growth of consumerism. Moreover, each resonated with a cultural nostalgia for a pastoral ideal while simultaneously quickening the formation of an increasingly kinetic, modern visual culture, one whose compression of time and space percolated into every realm, including the fine arts through the development of Impressionism, Cubism, and more. With its powerful ability to represent the world in nitrate and celluloid, film ultimately superseded the circus – an artifact of a live entertainment tradition that transmogrified the world into live spectacle under canvas – only to be superseded in its turn by the growth of a suburbanized television culture, which owed a debt to the movies. As the chief symbol of the nation's transition from animal power to motor power, the car, or horseless carriage, accelerated the cultural turn toward nature nostalgia – which has become a hugely profitable artifact of contemporary American consumer culture.

The privilege of historical hindsight makes clear the enduring cultural influence of the railroad circus, the moving picture, the car, and the rise of nature nostalgia. With the exception of the car, however, the arrival of these cultural watersheds was at first unremarkable. The merger of Barnum and Bailey's circus operations in 1880 received modest media attention, while the cultural profile of early film was limited by the physical location of the Vitascope inside railroad depots and crowded sideshow tents, among other jam-packed locales. Although the sentimental new nature writers were harbingers of modern attitudes toward nature, they were roundly dismissed at the turn of the century. Even though the earliest cars represented a slow, unreliable mode of transportation whose hefty cost placed it out of the reach of most Americans, cultural observers still recognized the future implications of the automobile. Each of these cultural watersheds was also deeply tied to older conventions and ideologies. The circus borrowed freely from previous cultural forms like the menagerie and museum. The subject matter of early film often documented those popular live amusements that the moving picture would soon supersede – including the circus and vaudeville. People made sense of the new automobile by evoking the older world of animal power in the emergent lexicon of the motorized economy – thus "horse power" and the "horseless carriage" have become reminders of a passing age. In all, the act of defining a cultural watershed is an historical balancing act in which one recognizes the long-term significance of specific cultural breakpoints without losing sight of the historically contingent and often unremarkable ways in which these cultural forms emerged.

REFERENCES

Allen, Robert: *Horrible Prettiness: Burlesque and American Culture* (Chapel Hill: University of North Carolina Press, 1991).

Bailey, Beth L.: *From Front Porch to Back Seat: Courtship in Twentieth-Century America* (Baltimore, MD: Johns Hopkins University Press, 1988).

Bogdan, Robert: *Freak Show: Displaying Human Oddities for Amusement and Profit* (Chicago: University of Chicago Press, 1988).

Brumberg, Joan Jacobs: *The Body Project: A Social History of American Girls* (New York: Vintage, 1997).

Cohen, Lizbeth: *Making a New Deal: Industrial Workers in Chicago, 1919–1939* (New York: Cambridge University Press, 1990).

Cohen, Paula Marantz: *Silent Film and the Triumph of the American Myth* (New York: Oxford University Press, 2001).

Davis, Janet M.: *The Circus Age: Culture and Society under the American Big Top* (Chapel Hill: University of North Carolina Press, 2002).

Dizard, Jan E.: *Going Wild: Hunting, Animal Rights, and the Contested Meaning of Nature* (Amherst: University of Massachusetts Press, 1999).

Doughty, Robin W.: *Feather Fashion and Bird Preservation: A Study in Nature Preservation* (Berkeley: University of California Press, 1975).

Dreiser, Theodore: *Sister Carrie* (New York: Bantam Books, 1963 [1900]).

Flink, James J.: *The Automobile Age* (Cambridge, MA: MIT Press, 1988).

Frick, Caroline: "Restoration Nation: Motion Picture Archives and 'American' Film Heritage," dissertation, University of Texas at Austin, 2005.

Green, James R.: *The World of the Worker: Labor in Twentieth-Century America* (New York: Hill & Wang, 1980).

Isenberg, Andrew C.: *The Destruction of the Bison* (New York: Cambridge University Press, 2000).

Johnson, Paul E.: *Sam Patch, the Famous Jumper* (New York: Hill & Wang, 2003).

Jones, Susan D.: *Valuing Animals: Veterinarians and Their Patients in Modern America* (Baltimore, MD: Johns Hopkins University Press, 2002).

Kasson, Joy S.: *Buffalo Bill's Wild West: Celebrity, Memory, and Popular History* (New York: Hill & Wang, 2000).

Kirby, Lynne: *Parallel Tracks: The Railroad and Silent Cinema* (Durham, NC: Duke University Press, 1997).

Kurlansky, Mark: *Cod: A Biography of the Fish that Changed the World* (New York: Penguin Books, 1997).

Lewis, David L.: "Sex and the Automobile: from Rumble Seats to Rockin' Vans," in David L. Lewis & Laurence Goldstein, eds., *The Automobile and American Culture* (Ann Arbor: University of Michigan Press, 1983), pp. 123–33.

Mighetto, Lisa: *Wild Animals and American Environmental Ethics* (Tucson: University of Arizona Press, 1991).

Moses, L. G.: *Wild West Shows and the Images of American Indians, 1883–1933* (Albuquerque: University of New Mexico Press, 1996).

Musser, Charles: *The Emergence of Cinema: The American Screen to 1907* (Berkeley: University of California Press, 1990).

Peiss, Kathy: *Cheap Amusements: Working Women and Leisure in Turn-of-the-Century New York* (Philadelphia: Temple University Press, 1986).

Peiss, Kathy: *Hope in a Jar: The Making of America's Beauty Culture* (New York: Owl Books, 1998).

Price, Jennifer: *Flight Maps: Adventures with Nature in Modern America* (New York: Basic Books, 1999).

Register, Woody: *The Kid of Coney Island: Fred Thompson and the Rise of American Amusements* (New York: Oxford University Press, 2001).

Rooks, Noliwe: *Hair Raising: Beauty, Culture, and African American Women* (New Brunswick: Rutgers University Press, 1997).

Schivelbusch, Wolfgang: *The Railway Journey: The Industrialization of Time and Space in the 19th Century*, rev. ed. (Berkeley: University of California Press, 1986).

Schlosser, Eric: *Fast Food Nation: The Dark Side of the All-American Meal* (Boston, MA: Houghton Mifflin, 2001).

Sklar, Robert: *Movie-Made America* (New York: Random House, 1975).

Slout, William L.: *A Royal Coupling: The Historic Marriage of Barnum and Bailey* (San Bernardino: An Emeritus Enterprise Book, 2000).

Susman, Warren: *Culture as History: The Transformation of American Society in the Twentieth Century* (New York: Pantheon, 1985).

Vickery, Jim Dale: *Wilderness Visionaries* (Merrillville, IN: ICS, 1986).

Part III

THE TWENTIETH CENTURY

Chapter Thirteen

CONSUMER CULTURE AND MASS CULTURE

Charles F. McGovern

In the century after the Civil War, the United States steadily urbanized. American cities swelled from the massive influx of new generations of foreign immigrants, along with transplants from the countryside. Industrialization and mass production transformed the economy, which came decisively to rest on the mass circulation and consumption of an ever-increasing array of commodities. Unevenly but inexorably, Americans became dependent on getting and spending for their daily living. Social relations changed as well, with new institutions and values centered on spending. Mass production and distribution fostered commodification of personal and communal experiences, rituals, and emotions. As a modern capitalist nation, the United States in these years saw the birth of what we know as "mass culture" and "consumer culture." These cultures arose from mass circulation of commodities and have always been intimately linked.

During the twentieth century Americans embraced consuming as a significant index of national well-being and an important activity in daily life. In a nation with long-standing suspicions of ostentatious wealth and display, and a political heritage that placed production and labor at the center of democratic politics and civic membership, Americans came to accept spending and accumulation as markers of their national culture and rituals of citizenship. Long before World War II, mass culture pervaded daily life: consumption defined the US political economy and shaped American culture. Entering the twenty-first century, corporations purveying mass culture led the economy. This essay traces the entwined advent of mass culture and consumption (sometimes called "commercial culture"), outlining key issues of their influence. Although their impact has only increased over time, this essay will primarily consider commercial culture in the years of its emergence, 1880–1930.

Coming to Terms

The nature, influence, and meanings of mass entertainment and spending have long been contested in debates which have generated considerable attention. Throughout the twentieth century, critics and pundits have argued that the American society and economy was structured by mass consumption, but only within the past generation have historians given sustained attention to it. Warren Susman most famously argued that the twentieth century inaugurated a "culture of consumption" that replaced an older "culture of production" (Susman 1984). Though scholars have since challenged the argument, his contention that mass consumption entailed a distinct way of life built around spending remains a critical starting point in understanding the historic specificity of modernity (Simmel 1990 [1907]; Leach 1993; Lears 1994). Over the century many observers – economists, businessmen, social theorists – celebrated the expansion of consumer abundance, which they argued would spread luxury and leisure throughout society. The United States would become a wealthier, freer, more peaceful society. But there were consequences: ever-increasing numbers and kinds of goods, unevenly distributed wealth, and the burgeoning corporate and commercial influence generated political and social commitments to a seemingly limitless market system that drove – and in turn was driven by – consumption. Alarmed critics of mass consumption emerged alongside its celebrants. Drawing on long-standing critiques of wealth and excess, they decried the moral and material harms of widespread spending. They viewed the consumer regime above all as wasteful, harming the natural environment, and coarsening everyday life. For them, the consumer regime did not reinforce, but eroded democracy by promoting invidious social competition (Veblen 1899; Horowitz 1985). The debate between mass consumption's proponents and critics has resurfaced periodically as new crises have generated new social movements. From Progressive era boycotts to current-day anti-globalization crusades, these movements contest the market system's dominance of politics and society, even as they inevitably question the cultural consequences of consumer capitalism.

Mass consumption generated debate: mass culture touched off controversy. Generally, commentators have understood mass culture as art, amusements, or expressions produced along industrial principles for large markets that are usually distinct from communities that cohere within discrete social or geographic borders. Intellectuals, activists, critics, historians, artists, and audiences have debated, often bitterly, distinctions among "popular," "mass," "folk," "high," and "low" culture, but have most consistently heaped scorn upon mass culture. Some scholars have sought the differences along chronological lines. Historian Michael Kammen, for instance, insists that popular culture held sway in the United States from 1870 to 1915, and shared dominance with an emerging mass culture through 1945. With the inauguration of the television age, mass culture has since reigned unchallenged (Kammen 1999). Historian Lawrence Levine has argued that the critical difference has been between so-called "high" and "low" culture, a distinction he argues arose in the late nineteenth century as elites sought to distance themselves from the very immigrants and workers who were transforming American society (Levine 1988).

But most significant and durable have been the critical debates castigating and defending mass culture. For many commentators, mass culture in turn was both intellectually debased and inert. It bred passivity and reflected the alienated conditions of mass society (Macdonald 1962; Horkheimer & Adorno 1972; Gorman 1996). For the advocates of this long-lived and influential argument, mass culture debased its audiences by feeding them an unending diet of formulaic, degrading, and simple-minded entertainment that neither enlightened nor relieved its audiences. Mass culture's unrealistic and escapist fare not only glorified the worst of human excess – violence, greed, lust, narcissism – but, by crippling their critical faculties, it rendered people unable to assess their social conditions or their rulers. In such a manner, mass culture actually debased both morality and the civic fabric of society. Still others defended mass culture, arguing that audiences could distinguish between reality and escapism, and charging that critics desired more to insult the public than understand its culture.

For many critics, mass culture's commodity status threatened the privileged status of the realm of art or "high" culture, which had long been viewed as art that represented the "best" of a civilization (Storey 2003). Mass culture blurred the boundaries of art. Other critics believed that such mass culture embodied modernity, commerce, and mass society itself. They feared the disappearance or pollution of supposedly pure folk expressions by commercial culture's encroachments. While "mass" and "popular" have been used interchangeably by some, especially since the 1930s, others denounced the blurring of the two.

This essay distinguishes mass culture less by form than by framework: historically, "mass culture" has addressed and constituted broad audiences through the supple medium of the commodity form, usually in tandem with means of mass communication. Such audiences may not necessarily share the same social conditions and consciousness as more localized communities that shape and embrace popular culture. Yet the mass cultural commodity reviled by critics has often served as an essential element in a vibrant localized popular culture. Mass culture's signature ability to convene broad groups, along with its unabashed commodity status, distinguishes it at times from popular culture.

Over the twentieth century, clear-cut distinctions between mass and popular have lost their historic relevance. Even as debates about the effects of mass culture proliferated, new material conditions eroded its meaning. Michael Denning asserts that since the ending of the Cold War, the West has witnessed "the end of mass culture," that is, an era in which mass culture's sway and meanings have been contested. He argues that in contemporary times, no other form of cultural organization can compete with mass culture (Denning 2004). The mass-produced commodity is ubiquitous, common to civilizations around the globe even as local societies adopt them differently. Ultimately, the world now hosts a global commodity culture increasingly untethered from strict national boundaries through transnational capitalism, yet heavily implicated in local cultures (Appadurai 1996). Mass culture is everywhere, although its meanings are always in flux.

Mass culture's contentious history reveals continuous struggle. As Stuart Hall and others have argued, struggles over culture have arisen with social crises challenging a ruling order's dominance. These crises engender attempts to police and contain the particular communities that create or embrace specific cultural forms; not coincidentally, these are the groups that threaten the rulers (Hall 1981; Levine 1988). I would further argue that, far from representing the antithesis of engaged citizenship or national cohesion, mass culture and consumption both have been integral in making the modern United States by fostering and embodying national identity. Throughout American history, ascriptive definitions of citizenship have entrenched political and economic inequality and disenfranchisement. Citizenship has never been full or equal (Smith 1997; Glenn 2002; Ngai 2004). Commercial culture has continually figured in popular struggles to secure justice, to reimagine democracy, and to redefine national identity. People without power used culture to make claims and forge identities as Americans when law and custom denied them equality or freedom.

Antebellum Origins

Many Americans of means had been purchasing manufactured goods (especially from England) since the eighteenth century, but Revolutionary America and the early republic were hardly full-fledged consumer economies or cultures. While commercial culture does not significantly appear until the late nineteenth century, its basis took shape in the years before the Civil War. The contemporary ascendance of P. T. Barnum, blackface minstrelsy, and mass publishing laid the foundations for the later mass and consumer culture industries. Barnum's pursuit of publicity and marketing laid the foundations both for advertising and for a celebrity culture. Minstrelsy left a legacy of entertainment built on racial stereotyping and oppression that embodied the emotional longings of a normative white audience. Mass publishing's appropriation of the public sphere through sentiment and sensation insured that Americans would both expect ready access to cultural goods and associate public issues with entertainment. Minstrelsy, Barnum's exploits, and mass publishing all critically shaped commercial culture. Their international success made clear that American mass culture and consumption would be global from the outset (DeGrazia 2005; Rydell & Kroes 2005).

The Making of Consumer Culture

Commercial culture emerged as an element in the late nineteenth-century maturation of modernity, a moment film scholar Ben Singer identifies as "modernity at full throttle" (Singer 2003: 19). Although many scholars argue that the intertwined development of capitalism and modernity had been underway since the seventeenth century, the second industrial revolution of the late nineteenth century saw a convergence of trends that set this moment apart (Giddens 1990). Industrial capitalism not only produced the infrastructure of the modern city and the thousands of goods of its economy; it also spread waves of migration and displacement as people left villages and towns for new urban lives and jobs; in those cities these people encountered unprecedented circulation and association of people and things (Simmel 1990 [1907]). Older ways of life once firmly rooted in local authority, community, and religion now receded in influence. Capitalism generated, in Singer's description, "[A] social order, and frame of mind, shaped by an economic life based on universal competition, a money economy, contractual relations, wage labor, the commodification of goods and services and a profit-motivated system of exchange among totally independent and self-interested parties" (Singer 2003: 33). In the United States, the new consumer culture itself was a production of modernity.

Mass production, new technologies, and urbanization all fostered the appearance and adoption of commodities and habits in daily life. Most critical were the successful deployment of technologies of production and distribution. Antonio Gramsci dubbed the American system "Fordism" after its most visible and famous innovator, automobile manufacturer Henry Ford (Gramsci 1971). Fordism involved highly specialized, repetitive tasks performed on assembly lines by a largely unskilled labor force according to rigid standards without variance or individual freedom. Ford regulated his workforce within the factory through divisions of labor, and beyond its gates through restrictive, rigorously enforced codes of personal behavior. These practices aimed to produce a disciplined but disposable labor force. Ford in turn was able to cut his production and sales costs in half between 1908 and 1914, in effect enabling his workers to become his customers. This American system depended on such workers not only to produce but to consume, and "Fordism" culturally represented regimes of inflexible mass production and of regularized mass consumption. The company instituted the highly touted "$5 day" wage not just to guarantee fair pay for workers but to enable them in effect to afford Ford cars (Watts 2005). If Ford and similar American industries produced goods, Fordism turned workers into consumers.

Americans created a mass consumer *culture* only with widespread access to such goods. Between 1880 and 1930 powerful new institutions and methods of mass distribution and communication brought an expanding array of goods to all corners of the nation. Mail order retailers Montgomery Ward and Sears, Roebuck found eager customers for their wares throughout remote rural areas as well as cities: by the early twentieth century, their catalogs, known as "wish-books," regularly reached 800 densely packed pages of items from thimbles to complete houses (Boorstin 1973). Mail order introduced thousands of standardized goods into the routines of daily life, insuring not lock-step experiences but common exposure to similar things, habits, and technologies. Federal subsidies in the form of favorable "second class" rates for magazines and newspaper delivery (1885), rural free delivery (1896), and parcel post (1913), all enabled the postal system to deliver billions of pieces of goods and advertising throughout the nation.

Revolutions in retailing established two pillars of the new culture: department and chain stores. Combining a limitless variety of goods with in-house manufacturing and custom production, such department stores as Marshall Field, Macy's, John Wanamaker's, and Filene's won the trade of a burgeoning middle class. Highlighting fashion, modernity, variety, and service, department stores offered this new class both endless goods and attractive rituals and settings for acquiring them. They purveyed entertainment and service along with their wares: orchestras, concert organs, and choirs regularly performed; many stores also featured art exhibitions, pageants, theatricals, and lectures (Leach 1993). Providing even more goods to a greater array of Americans were the chain stores. Spearheaded by F. W. Woolworth, "5 & 10s" brought an array of inexpensive manufactured items to small towns and cities alike. The chains offered discounted prices on limited lines of wares, thus spreading the mass consumption economy to folks of modest means (Strasser 1982). Chains such as A&P (groceries), United Drugs/Rexall (pharmaceuticals), and General Cigar (tobacco) penetrated nearly every city and hamlet in the United States. Today, led by Wal-Mart, chain stores dominate American retailing more than ever.

Key to the new consumer culture was national print media, the most significant being new, commercially oriented magazines. Heavily subsidized by advertising, these weekly and monthly publications addressed the new urban middle and business classes, particularly their female homemakers (Scanlon 1995; Ohmann 1996). In a form of literary Fordism, publishers Frank Munsey and Cyrus H. K. Curtis filled their magazines with ever-increasing advertising space; the advertising income enabled them to publish at a much lower retail price. That won the magazines a vast and growing number of readers that older, Victorian-era genteel periodicals did not reach. This readership, now quantified and dubbed as "circulation," was resold in turn to other prospective advertisers as distinct and desirable "markets." While this system established a successful business model – expanding profits by lowering unit prices and production costs – standards of success ensued that measured success solely through readership size. Circulation – the aggregate number of consumers or audience – became the dominant if not sole arbiter of success for the culture industries.

The linchpin of mass consumption was the trademarked brand name. Between 1880 and 1930, the American economy became a brand-name system. Manufacturers, wholesalers, and retailers all clashed over who would dictate what goods would reach consumers; put differently, they competed to control and restrict the numbers and kinds of goods consumers would choose. The battle over distribution centered upon supplying the retailer (Strasser 1989; Laird 1998). Manufacturers allied with an increasingly powerful professional group – advertisers – to reach consumers without the intercession of independent wholesalers or jobbers. Teaching consumers to identify and request a specific manufacturer's product from an array of competitors became advertisers' principal service to business. Formerly brands designated an individual artisan or producer; they now stood in for corporate manufacturers producing goods at a far remove from their customers. Supplanting the face-to-face relationships between the maker and customer characteristic of preindustrial commerce, brands now offered a different authority – the distant, large, anonymous corporation (Marchand 1985, 1998).

Brand names, distinctive packaging, visually distinctive logos, and trade marks became the identifying face of both goods and their firms. By the Great Depression branding had taken such a strong hold in American life that few consumer products in everyday life were sold without them. Brand names not only were an economically profitable means to establish proprietary claims upon commonplace technologies or goods; they also assumed cultural significance as a modern iconic vocabulary, a set of signs visible not only on store shelves but throughout everyday life, including media, the built environment, and, indeed, entertainment and language. If goods were the bricks of consumer culture, the brand name was their mortar.

Brands also amplified the importance of consumers. Cultivating consumer preference and loyalty became the techniques of selling to the mass markets (Strasser 1989; Laird 1998; Friedman 2004). Just as they had rationalized manufacturing and planning, by World War I American firms were producing customers with similar precision and efficiency. Firms identified specific groups within the populace with possible interests in their wares, and then deployed a variety of means to reach that specific group. Advertisers offered to those potential consumers distinct ideas and images about themselves. Advertisers and media then packaged the purported characteristics of such groups, now called "markets," and sold them to business clients. Circulating images of people and products, advertisers sold stereotypes about groups to business, and sold consumers stereotypes about products, society, and themselves (Marchand 1985; Lears 1994; Leiss et al. 2004). Promoting consumption, marketers urged people above all to think of themselves as consumers. In spending to create their everyday lives, Americans made a consumer culture. That culture in turn originated in a series of entertainments, spectacles, and diversions – mass culture.

The Ascendance of Mass Culture

Mass culture appeared in a series of industries that produced entertainment and leisure experiences for national and far-flung audiences. Just as the rational organization of capital and labor produced the mass consumer system, aspects of late nineteenth-century modernity were critical to the new appearances of mass culture. The disruptions of this era were amplified by a series of new technologies and forms. The new technological systems of electricity were perhaps most far-reaching. Electric lighting and power extended the hours of the day, thus altering centuries-old work and living rhythms (Nye 1990). Railway, automobile, and later air travel transformed experience of time, space, and distance. New communications technologies, beginning with the telegraph and later the telephone, the photograph, the phonograph, and motion picture, further annihilated traditional experiences of place, distance, and time (Kern 1983). All these innovations fostered sensory and perceptual dislocations of time, space, and causality. In effect they insured that subjectivity itself – the manner and mode of individual experience – would change. The fragmentary nature of individual perception and social experience became most noticeable in the detachment, alienation, and spectatorial behaviors associated with modern urban life (Simmel 1990 [1907]; Benjamin 1999).

The cities offered a veritable theater of continual performances on the streets and in shop windows. To be an urbanite was to reside and take part in a continual pageant. In the city, mass society visually observed and experienced itself *as* mass society. Yet modernity's new bureaucratic, social, and commercial organizations enhanced both isolation and connection. People were simultaneously severed from familiar, sustaining communities and, curiously, more linked to complete strangers (Giddens 1990). This spectacular, theatrical and yet distant and alien environment encouraged people to become viewers, passers-by to become spectators, and citizens to become audiences. The results were ripened appetites for a plethora of entertainments that we know as mass culture.

The numerous forms of mass culture that came to prominence in the late nineteenth century were notable for both their variety and the rapidity with which they gained national favor. The motion picture, the phonograph, wild west shows, the railroad circus and medicine shows, world's fairs, comic strips, cheap mass-circulation magazines, dance halls, amusement parks and midways, roller rinks, along with mass spectator sports (professional baseball, college football, auto racing), all found national acceptance between 1880 and 1920 (Nasaw 1993). Although reliable figures are scarce, all plausible evidence demonstrates that vast numbers of Americans took part in mass culture. The continued expansion of these industries indicates that purveyors of mass culture had found success. Mass culture created mass audiences, who in turn sought more mass culture.

Commercial amusements found national acceptance during the 1890s, a moment when the socioeconomic arrangements of the new were undermining the didactic, self-consciously moral norms of Victorian America (Susman 1984). Restraint, sobriety, and frugality – bedrock traits of bourgeois respectability – met newer, competing values. Amusement for its own sake challenged the probity and "useful" recreation of Victorianism; gratification overtook virtuous self-denial, while youth and novelty overshadowed long-standing veneration of age and tradition. Americans of course did not simply discard an older set of values or moral codes for another. The advent of mass culture often provoked conflicts between these two outlooks, battles that were also taking place in the realms of economics, social class, and politics. Underlying them all were a series of social crises – the prolonged "labor question," the possibility of socialism and revolution, the rights of women, the oppression of African Americans with the reversal of Reconstruction, the consequences of monopoly and entrenched economic power. These crises arose in conflicts between immigrants and natives, capital and labor, plain people and authorities, the middle class and cultural pundits, women workers and male family members or bosses, and citizens and corporations. They took place not only in the factory, street corner, town square, and courthouse, but in the sites of mass culture. Mass culture's protean forms insured that these fights would continue well beyond the initial years in which commercial culture took firm hold.

Success and Contest: Two Cases

We can discern broader patterns of mass culture's acceptance and controversy in the rise of amusement parks and the motion picture. Amusement parks overturned conventional Victorian morality by allowing adults to indulge in hedonism and play, and to experience forbidden, sexually charged physical proximity to others. From the outset in the 1890s these parks were a success, and by 1907, over 400 were in operation (Register 2001: 98). New York's Coney Island and its many imitators amplified the sensory and social dimensions of markets, village festivals, and highly populated neighborhoods through a mix of stimulation, kinetic sociability, and spectacle. These attractions immersed their patrons in a wash of noise, an abundance of artificial light, an array of scents, and dense physical crowding. Entrepreneur Fred Thompson filled Coney's Luna Park with attractions summoning exotic locales and orientalist fantasies. Spectacular architectures – exotic, mammoth, fantastic – evoked otherworldly splendor. Pageants and shows enacted famous battles or bygone imperial opulence. The rides, of course, gave patrons temporary dangers and thrills, titillation, and simulated risk (Kasson 1978). A chance to take "A Trip to the Moon" or careen against a romantic companion on "The Tickler," offered a steady stream of otherwise illicit contact.

Such parks achieved a kind of Fordist perfection: millions entered their turnstiles every year, taking their place on an assembly line of amusement. Marvels of mechanical modernity, roller coasters, Ferris wheels, tilt-a-whirls, and carousels linked the achievements of the machine age to outsize fantasies of childhood. Most telling, they efficiently processed hundreds of people in attractions every few minutes. Amusement parks were mechanized factories of fun.

They also manufactured class and promoted sex. Catering to the business-class families, parks often sought to limit the presence of working-class patrons and alcohol. Nonetheless, millions of young workers went to the parks to court and socialize. Working women often found men to pay their way in return for companionship and occasional limited sexual favors. Such "treating" became a complex ritual allowing women independence from familial authority, middle-class rebuke, and indeed their own suitors (Peiss 1986; Enstad 1999). Thus the amusement parks offered respite and freedom from their everyday lives to both middle- and working-class visitors, yet the stakes differed for each group. For the middle class, amusement parks enabled the overthrow of the probity expected of them at all times. For working-class women, the parks offered amusement and agency, a place to define themselves against the expectations of others.

The overwhelming success of the movies in everyday life offers a different story. Cultural authorities attempted to control movie going, but different audiences proved resolutely determined to use the movies according to their own needs and aspirations. Revealing the utopian appeals of mass culture, these conflicts also demonstrated the flaws in critics' perpetual arguments that mass culture imposed a uniform level of mediocrity on a supposedly homogeneous mass populace. The movies' fitful but inexorable movement from nickelodeon to picture palace, working-class neighborhood to affluent downtown, sideshow attraction to national institution, revealed and indeed prolonged battles over the uses of mass culture.

Americans first witnessed moving pictures in the early 1890s; in 1904 Pittsburgh businessman Harry Davis opened the first downtown space dedicated specifically to showing projected films. Like Woolworth's "5 & 10," such "nickelodeons" advertised the price in their name; within a few years they had mushroomed throughout the ethnic neighborhoods of the USA (Nasaw 1993). Their successes enabled a generation of ethnic businessmen and -women to enter the culture industries: many of the great Hollywood studios were founded by immigrant nickelodeon and arcade operators.

Finding such favor with working-class patrons, nickelodeons almost immediately attracted attention from those determined to regulate the new mass society. Social workers, reformers, politicians, civic officials, and critics attacked the nickel shows as unsanitary, dangerous, and debased. A *Moving Picture World* critic in 1910 offered a scathing portrait that reflected the elite attitude toward the working class:

> The audience also sat still for one or two high-class films without any fuss, although we are sure they didn't understand what they were looking at any more than they would a Chinese opera. . . . I would have been more comfortable on board a cattle train than where I sat. There were five hundred smells combined in one. . . . But what is hardest to swallow is that the tastes of this seething mass of human cattle are the tastes that have dominated, or at least set, the standard of American moving pictures. (Quoted in Bowser 1990: 3–4)

Moreover, critics charged that in theaters women endured unwanted sexual advances from predatory men, and that couples used the theaters as an illicit space for intimacy. The critics' worst fear was that the movies' knowing allusions to, and vivid portrayals of, sexual desire, crime, adultery, and disrespect for authority would poison social order. Reformers fought the "immorality" of movies by closing theaters, extending blue laws, and enforcing building safety codes. They also established local and national censorship groups, most prominently the National Board of Review (1909) to police both content and audience (Grieveson 2004). The Board scrutinized plots and scenes and encouraged "higher-class" films. By the decade's end nickelodeons were on the defensive and soon gave way to newer theater spaces that catered to middle classes, even as shorter films exhibited there were replaced by narrative feature films (Kozarski 1990; Bowser 1990).

One reason critics declared these audiences in need of regulation was the threat the movies seemed to pose to parental authority and traditional mores. Again, young women were a principal target. The furor increased through the 1910s as concern over "movie-struck girls" – film's first true "fans" – blossomed. Yet these women flocked to the shows for good reasons. As New Women inhabiting the streets as well as the workplace, they sought entertainment that addressed their lives. Independent, working-girl heroines of serials such as *The Perils of Pauline* (1914) appealed to viewers who themselves labored. Cross-promoted in cheap papers and dime novels, these serials were meaningful stories for workers themselves braving hostile environments in the workplace and the limiting demands of family and society (Enstad 1999; Singer 2003). Indeed, these female viewers helped lay the groundwork for the star system, Hollywood's brand-name regime (DeCordova 1990). Despite reform efforts to promote more decorous films and to purify the theaters, young women used movie going according to very different lights; they sought leisure that fitted them for independence and role models very different from proper and passive Victorian ladies.

While attempts to curtail the overall influence of the movies were bound to fail, the censors attained significant victories and pervasive influence. Progressive-era local censorship boards were followed by the creation of the Hays Office to regulate morality in the movies. There followed in the 1930s the Motion Picture Production Code (1934), written with significant input from Roman Catholic officials; and the Payne Fund Studies privately supported research geared to prove that movies and mass media exerted harmful effects upon children (Black 1994; Jowett et al. 1996). This unending stream of moral crises pointed both to the movies' central significance in American life, and to the determination of many groups to make their own meanings and to evade the overt control of authorities. Stuart Hall rightly reminds us that the "popular" has traditionally meant those without power (Hall 1981); the movies especially remind us that such people still held significant agency in making their daily lives. That agency and the vitality of such groups have continually made their lives a target in the ongoing battles over mass culture.

Mass Culture, Consumer Culture, and Nation

Commercial culture's myriad forms of entertainment and goods proved integral in making the American nation in the modern era. Lisa Lowe (1996) reminds us that, "It is through the terrain of national culture that the individual subject is politically formed as the American citizen." In the United States, that training took the form of participation in commercial cultures. Mass culture and commodities offered a common experience in an otherwise diverse and fragmentary society. People have used the products and rituals of commercial culture to fashion themselves as full citizens and to reshape a social order that recognizes them. These two dynamics of nationalization and naturalization deepened the influence of commercial culture.

Elites drew upon commercial culture for nation making and citizenship. National corporate advertisers, for example, used explicitly political language, patriotic images, and nationalist ideas to educate buyers to be consumers (McGovern 2006). Portraying spending as voting, freedom as marketplace choice, and manufactured material abundance as the distinct exceptional American heritage, advertising explicitly linked Americanness with spending. From the late nineteenth century through World War II, corporations, marketers, and media fought to establish consumption as social membership. When the Depression's economic collapse established that the consumer was integral to the economy's survival, the civic dimensions of consumption became unmistakably clear. The economy depended on consumers, and the need to enhance their purchasing would influence government and economic planning for the future (Brinkley 1995; Cohen 2003).

Commercial culture reinforced nation and patriotism through other means as well. Mass culture producers trafficked in spectacles with nationalist themes and implications. For example, the fledgling movie industry presented war as patriotic entertainment, repeatedly documenting both the Spanish–American war in Cuba and Pancho Villa's Mexican Revolution in the borderlands. Similarly, from the outset films often focused upon narratives of nation, history, and belonging. The most celebrated early American film, *The Birth of a Nation* (1915), established the feature film as the dominant narrative in movies. Southern-born director D. W. Griffith transcribed Thomas Dixon's novel *The Clansman*, a Confederate revenge fantasy whose racist repudiation of Reconstruction rewrote a central moment of American national history, the remaking of the Union.

Elites also utilized the instruments of mass communication to forge a new national citizenry through rituals and symbols. The same media that offered entertainment could now readily provide a steady stream of patriotic images and nationalist rhetoric. In 1892 Francis Bellamy campaigned to make the Pledge of Allegiance a daily ritual through the national children's magazine *Youth's Companion* (O'Leary 1999). During World War I, the federal government extensively used mass-produced posters and movies to advertise the war effort. The much-celebrated "Four-Minute Men" gave brief speeches to millions to fund the war's Liberty Loans. Indeed, training in mass culture became one index of civic fitness. During the 1910s, the Army Intelligence Tests, which screened potential servicemen, examined recruits' familiarity with advertising slogans, brand names, and mass culture to assess overall mental aptitude and intelligence (Lears 1994).

In the 1920s, the advent of commercial broadcast radio would accelerate interest in the nation-making possibilities of media. Radio's entertainment forms – adapted from vaudeville, tent shows, minstrelsy, and comic strips – enabled Americans to imagine a nation far beyond the borders of their own daily lives. This imagined nation enabled listeners and broadcasters to conceive of their membership in a larger social body, and to exclude those who were undesirable. It also allowed listeners to consider themselves members of a radio public that broadcasters needed to consult as well as respect. Through the 1940s, listeners would hold radio accountable for its civic relationship with the public (Douglas 1999; Newman 2004; Razlogova 2006).

The listeners' determination to hold broadcasters to a social compact reflected the citizenship of mass culture. Audiences and consumers frequently and fiercely made use of the tools of mass culture to make civic claims, gain political power, and seek full social equity in custom along with law. Critics of mass culture have long complained that it encouraged a passive, apolitical outlook. But mass culture and consumption in fact have provided both a utopian promise and vocabulary for claims to civic rights and social membership. The history of African Americans bears this out.

African Americans linked their struggle for political and social freedom to the cultural resources of the mass market and entertainment. African American cultural figures – performers and celebrities – along with clergy, emerged as critical leaders in black life, particularly in the years before the national civil rights movement. With celebrity came political opportunities, and prominent black performers often pressed for African American rights and critiqued racism and oppression by whites. Pioneering filmmaker Oscar Micheaux, song publisher W. C. Handy, record company owner Harry Pace, Negro baseball entrepreneur Rube Foster, along with numerous others, built careers and businesses creating mass culture specifically by and for African Americans. Micheaux and other black filmmakers of the time explicitly contested the racist stereotypes of silent cinema, most notably *Birth of a Nation*, while portraying black everyday life from complex political, reformist, and middle-class perspectives (Bowser et al. 2001; Stewart 2005). Black theatrical productions portrayed African American history, heritage, and social life. These cultural productions made clear that African American cultural producers claimed the forms of mass entertainment to represent themselves and narrate their own lives, a form of agency routinely denied them under slavery and then Jim Crow (Sotiropoulos 2006).

Both African Americans and radio audiences participated in commercial culture determined to shape its meanings and offerings to their interests. They saw the political and national implications of commercial culture, and showed it was possible for citizens to reshape the national prescriptions of the culture industries to their own very different uses and ends. In so doing, they fashioned a critique of the assumptions of national unanimity and cohesion produced in commercial culture. They revealed the determination of Americans to use commercial culture to enhance their citizenship.

Conclusion

Throughout the twentieth century, commercial culture has formed the vocabulary of powerless people for justice and equality. Workers, women, immigrant groups, and people of color encountered similar opportunities and barriers. Mass culture has long provided opportunities for communities to envision themselves as communities, and to speak to issues beyond local boundaries. They have provided joy, release, comfort, and self-expression in lives that often held few pleasures and great struggle. The venues – theaters, dance halls, department stores – facilitated for women especially a public presence previously taboo in conventional Victorian morality. The new media – from magazines and dime novels to radio and movies – offered workers the means to narrate or participate in stories that spoke to their experiences and aspirations. The new commodities gave ethnic workers a common connection where older ties of ancestry or language might have proven a barrier. Yet at every turn they faced industries that held considerable power and that were often allied with the state. Mass culture and material abundance have long been identified with the American nation and the promise of American life (McGovern 2006). But their history has been complex. The utopian promise of entertainment and abundance has too often gone unfulfilled, and Americans have become acutely aware over time of what these realms cannot provide. But as long as the United States continues to produce mass culture and remains a consumer society, scholars will need to study the relationships of commercial culture to the American nation.

REFERENCES

Appadurai, Arjun: *Modernity at Large: Cultural Dimensions of Globalization* (Minneapolis: University of Minnesota Press, 1996).

Benjamin, Walter: *The Arcades Project* (Cambridge, MA: Belknap Press of Harvard University Press, 1999).

Black, Gregory D.: *Hollywood Censored: Morality Codes, Catholics and the Movies* (New York: Cambridge University Press, 1994).

Boorstin, Daniel J.: *The Americans: The Democratic Experience* (New York: Random House, 1973).

Bowser, Eileen: *The Transformation of Cinema, 1907–1915* (New York: Scribner, 1990).

Bowser, Pearl, Gaines, Jane, & Musser, Charles, eds.: *Oscar Micheaux and His Circle: African-American Filmmaking and Race Cinema of the Silent Era* (Bloomington: Indiana University Press, 2001).

Brinkley, Alan: *The End of Reform: New Deal Liberalism in Recession and War* (New York: Alfred A. Knopf, 1995).

Cohen, Lizabeth: *A Consumer's Republic: The Politics of Mass Consumption in Postwar America* (New York: Alfred A. Knopf, 2003).

DeCordova, Richard: *Picture Personalities: The Emergence of the Star System in America* (Urbana: University of Illinois Press, 1990).

DeGrazia, Victoria: *Irresistible Empire: America's Advance through Twentieth Century Europe* (Cambridge, MA: Belknap Press, 2005).

Denning, Michael: *Culture in the Age of Three Worlds* (New York: Verso, 2004).

Douglas, Susan J.: *Listening In: Radio and the American Imagination from "Amos 'n' Andy" and Edward R. Murrow to Wolfman Jack and Howard Stern* (New York: Times Books, 1999).

Enstad, Nan: *Ladies of Labor, Girls of Adventure: Working Women, Popular Culture and Labor Politics at the Turn of the Twentieth Century* (New York: Columbia University Press, 1999).

Friedman, Walter A.: *Birth of a Salesman: The Transformation of Selling in America* (Cambridge, MA: Harvard University Press, 2004).

Giddens, Anthony: *The Consequences of Modernity* (Stanford, CA: Stanford University Press, 1990).

Glenn, Evelyn Nakano: *Unequal Freedom: How Race and Gender Shaped American Citizenship and Labor* (Cambridge, MA: Harvard University Press, 2002).

Gorman, Paul R.: *Left Intellectuals and Popular Culture in America* (Chapel Hill: University of North Carolina Press, 1996).

Gramsci, Antonio: *Selections from the Prison Notebooks*, ed. and trans. Quintin Hoare & Geoffrey Nowell Smith (New York: International Publishers, 1971).

Grieveson, Lee: *Policing Cinema: Movies and Censorship in Early Twentieth-Century America* (Berkeley: University of California Press, 2004).

Hall, Stuart: "Notes on Deconstructing the Popular," in Raphael Samuel, ed., *People's History and Socialist Theory* (London: Routledge & Kegan Paul, 1981), pp. 227–40.

Horkheimer, Max & Adorno, Theodor: *Dialectic of Enlightenment* (New York: Herder & Herder, 1972).

Horowitz, Daniel: *The Morality of Spending: Attitudes Toward the Consumer Society in America, 1875–1940* (Baltimore, MD: Johns Hopkins University Press, 1985).

Horowitz, Daniel: *Anxieties of Affluence: Critiques of American Consumer Culture, 1939–1979* (Amherst: University of Massachusetts Press, 2004).

Jowett, Garth S., Jarvie, Ian C., & Fuller, Kathryn H.: *Children and the Movies: Media Influence and the Payne Fund Controversy* (New York: Cambridge University Press, 1996).

Kammen, Michael: *American Culture, American Tastes: Social Change and the Twentieth Century* (New York: Alfred A. Knopf, 1999).

Kasson, John F.: *Amusing the Million: Coney Island at the Turn of the Century* (New York: Hill & Wang, 1978).

Kern, Stephen: *The Culture of Time and Space, 1880–1918* (Cambridge, MA: Harvard University Press, 1983).

Kozarski, Richard: *An Evening's Entertainment: The Age of the Silent Feature Picture, 1915–1928* (New York: Charles Scribner's Sons, 1990).

Laird, Pamela Walker: *Advertising Progress: American Business and the Rise of Consumer Marketing* (Baltimore, MD: Johns Hopkins University Press, 1998).

Leach, William: *Land of Desire: Merchants, Power and the Rise of a New American Culture* (New York: Pantheon, 1993).

Lears, T. J. Jackson: *Fables of Abundance: A Cultural History of Advertising in America* (New York: Basic Books, 1994).

Leiss, William, Kline, Stephen, Jhally, Sut, & Botterill, Jackie: *Social Communication in Advertising: Consumption in the Mediated Marketplace*, 3rd ed. (New York: Routledge, 2004).

Levine, Lawrence: *Highbrow/Lowbrow: The Emergence of Cultural Hierarchy in America* (Cambridge, MA: Harvard University Press, 1988).

Levine, Lawrence: "The Folklore of Industrial Society: Popular Culture and Its Audiences," *American Historical Review* 97, 5 (December 1992), 1369–99.

Lowe, Lisa: *Immigrant Acts: On Asian American Cultural Politics* (Durham, NC: Duke University Press, 1996).

Macdonald, Dwight: "Masscult and Midcult," in Dwight Macdonald, *Against the American Grain* (New York: Random House, 1962), pp. 3–75.

Marchand, Roland: *Advertising the American Dream: Making Way for Modernity, 1920–1940* (Berkeley: University of California Press, 1985).

Marchand, Roland: *Creating the Corporate Soul: The Rise of Public Relations and Corporate Imagery in American Big Business* (Berkeley: University of California Press, 1998).

McGovern, Charles F.: *Sold American: Consumers, Citizenship, and Culture, 1890–1945* (Chapel Hill: University of North Carolina Press, 2006).

Musser, Charles: *The Emergence of Cinema: The American Screen to 1907* (New York: Scribner, 1990).

Nasaw, David: *Going Out: The Rise and Fall of Public Amusements* (New York: Basic Books, 1993).

Newman, Kathy: *Radio Active: Advertising and Consumer Activism 1935–1947* (Berkeley: University of California Press, 2004).

Ngai, Mae: *Impossible Subjects: Illegal Aliens and the Making of Modern America* (Princeton, NJ: Princeton University Press, 2004).

Nye, David E.: *Electrifying America: The Social Meanings of a New Technology, 1880–1940* (Cambridge, MA.: MIT Press, 1990).

Ohmann, Richard M.: *Selling Culture: Magazines, Markets, and Class at the Turn of the Century* (New York: Verso, 1996).

O'Leary, Cecilia Elizabeth: *To Die For: The Paradox of American Patriotism* (Princeton, NJ: Princeton University Press, 1999).

Peiss, Kathy Lee: *Cheap Amusements: Working Women and Leisure in New York City, 1880 to 1920* (Philadelphia: Temple University Press, 1986).

Razlogova, Elena: "True Crime Radio and Listener Disenchantment with Network Broadcasting, 1935–1946," *American Quarterly* 58, 1 (2006), 137–58.

Register, Woody: *The Kid of Coney Island: Fred Thompson and the Rise of American Amusements* (New York: Oxford University Press, 2001).

Rosenzweig, Roy: *Eight Hours for What We Will: Workers and Leisure in an Industrial City, 1879–1920* (New York: Cambridge University Press, 1983).

Rydell, Robert W. & Kroes, Rob: *Buffalo Bill in Bologna: The Americanization of the World, 1869–1922* (Chicago: University of Chicago Press, 2005).

Scanlon, Jennifer: *Inarticulate Longings: The* Ladies' Home Journal, *Gender, and the Promises of Consumer Culture* (New York: Routledge, 1995).

Simmel, Georg: *The Philosophy of Money*, 2nd enlarged edn., trans. Tom Bottomore & David Frisby (New York: Routledge, 1990 [1907]).

Singer, Ben: *Melodrama and Modernity: Early Sensational Cinema and Its Contexts* (New York: Columbia University Press, 2003).

Smith, Rogers M.: *Civic Ideals: Conflicting Visions of US Citizenship in History* (New Haven, CT: Yale University Press, 1997).

Sotiropoulos, Karen: *Staging Race: Black Performers in Turn of the Century America* (Cambridge, MA: Harvard University Press, 2006).

Stewart, Jacqueline Najuma: *Migrating to the Movies: Cinema and Urban Black Modernity* (Berkeley: University of California Press, 2005).

Storey, John: *Inventing Popular Culture: From Folklore to Globalization* (Malden, MA: Blackwell, 2003).

Strasser, Susan: *Never Done: A History of American Housework* (New York: Pantheon, 1982).

Strasser, Susan: *Satisfaction Guaranteed: The Making of the American Mass Market* (New York: Pantheon, 1989).

Susman, Warren I.: *Culture as History: The Transformation of American Society in the Twentieth Century* (New York: Pantheon Books, 1984).

Watts, Stephen M.: *The People's Tycoon: Henry Ford and the American Century* (New York: Alfred A. Knopf, 2005).

Veblen, Thorstein: *The Theory of the Leisure Class* (New York: Macmillan, 1899).

Chapter Fourteen

MODERNISM

Joel Dinerstein

Modernism has always been a contentious term and remains more a cultural field than a historical period. For more than two generations, it was a relatively stable category defined by literary (and artistic) works between 1910 and 1940 that featured radical experimentation with language, multiple points of view, and innovative narrative structures, all unified solely by the artist's aesthetic vision. This traditional artistic modernism emerged as both a critique of conformist bourgeois life and an inquiry into the subjective nature of reality employing Freud's keys for unlocking the layers of consciousness. American modernism has long since been decentered and pluralized along lines of class and identity; in just the past few years, it has been variously approached as "border modernism," "primitivist modernism," "diasporic modernism," "pulp modernism," and "Machine-Age modernism."

International modernism, by contrast, suffers no such identity crisis. Surveys of Eurocentric modernism still provide a sweeping portrayal of modernist thought and culture, but focus almost exclusively on Europe; the United States plays only a small but vital role. For example, William R. Everdell's *The First Moderns* (1997) begins in Vienna and depicts that city's intellectual ferment in the fields of literature, architecture, physics, psychology, and mathematics, before following key figures to Paris, London, and Berlin. Modris Eksteins's *Rites of Spring* (1989) picks up the thread in 1913 Paris, and immediately establishes the concurrent modernisms of art, technology, and politics just before World War I exposed German nationalism and the shock of modern warfare. In the dynamic physical display of Russian ballet, the spatial reorientation of Cezanne and the Cubists, the Futurists' embrace of machine technology, and the rage for ragtime dances, Eksteins reveals the diffuse desires of those attempting, in Gertrude Stein's term, to "kill off the nineteenth century." In these histories, the USA provides the innovations and inventions of industrial capitalism and its responsive cultural forms: skyscraper cities, assembly lines, sleek powerful cars, jazz rhythms, and African American kinesthetics (physical movement).

The analogous texts on American modernism are two anthologies. One maps the impact of technology across the spectrum of the arts, from George Antheil's *Ballet Mecanique* to Busby Berkeley's musicals (Ludington 2000); the other explores race, class, and gender responses to the quicksilver shifts in markets and production, equating modernism with the embrace of mobile identities (Scandura & Thurston 2001).

Both works focus on individual negotiations of the massive social changes in the half-century between 1890 and 1940: the demands of the industrial workplace; immigration and urbanization; ethnic consciousness and labor rebellion; adaptations of the body to machines; the emergence of a national media culture. Such experiential modernism registers "the simultaneous disenchantment and reenchantment of the world . . . both anaesthesia and shock, boredom and exhilaration" (Stewart 2001: 22).

Before the late 1980s, three generations of scholars treated artistic modernism as the leading edge of necessary cultural rebellion, featuring a heroic individual Euro-American rising up against both the middle-class materialism of Victorian society and the standardization of mass, industrial society (Crunden 2000). That nearly every scholar and artist still seems attracted to the modernist mantle of self-liberation, autonomous creativity, and cultural rebellion has created a scholarship of inclusion under various hyphenated modernisms. Only with the emergence of postmodernism did it become possible to critique modernism (Ross 1986; Harvey 1989; Jameson 1991).

Philosopher Robert B. Pippin reduced modernism to the question of "autonomy," as first theorized by Kant and expanded by Nietszche (Pippin 1991). Being modern involved the challenge of establishing one's own beliefs through introspection and reflection, and crafting an identity without recourse to family background, religious precepts, or social convention. Such an ethos of individualism was at odds with Victorian notions of "order" that valued hierarchy and stability, utility and rationality, tradition and social progress. As late as 1910, the dominant artistic values of Euro-American white elites could be summed up as the pursuit, in Matthew Arnold's famous aphorism, of "the best that has ever been thought." This intellectual master narrative assumed a seamless connection back to the works of antiquity, and offered individuals either self-mastery through wisdom or the reward of Heaven.

To be modern was to reject the wisdom of the ancients for self-authorization through experience. For such mid-nineteenth-century figures as Whitman, Baudelaire, Nietzsche, and Dostoevski, an objective, transcendent ideal of beauty gave way to a relativist notion of the sublime (Calinescu 1987). Exposing one's self to the world – unaccompanied, unprotected – became the objective of the artistic (or intellectual) life; experiences became the equivalent of deeds. The self-conscious modern artist came into being as a seeker after new truths – a rebel, a path breaker, the avant-garde of an army-not-yet-born.

Certainly the novelists of Stein's Lost Generation – Hemingway, Fitzgerald, and Dos Passos, among others – conceived of themselves in these terms. Their canonical works narrated the search of self-conscious bohemians for a floating community of cosmopolitan freethinkers; their drunken adventures validated a free-spirited lifestyle achieved through engaging the dark side of life spurned by bourgeois Victorian society (sexuality, transience, criminality, substance abuse, poverty). Hemingway's *The Sun Also Rises* became a handbook for young (white) Americans, a bohemian romance whose characters' absurd conversations mitigate their deferral of middle-class life. Valorizing unproductivity was an exemplary strategy for disaffected modernist youth and the novel's reception sheds light on the generation gap between Victorian and modern. Its characters "begin nowhere and end in nothing," wrote one critic; it was a "most unpleasant" reading experience; "the lives of a group of people [are] laid bare, and . . . it does not matter to us" (Wagner-Martin 1998). For Victorian-era literati, the disaffected moderns were adjudged as immoral rebels without cause or purpose.

By way of contrast, the same ethos of autonomy has turned modernist female artists such as O'Keeffe, Kahlo, and Stein into contemporary icons of liberation; concurrently, feminist theory, studies of sexuality, and recuperative work on H.D., Amy Lowell, and Marianne Moore have liberated individual female artistic projects from once male-dominated canons (Scott 1990; Rabinowitz 2001). Christine Stansell has shown that the prototype urban bohemia, Greenwich Village, was first settled by female intellectuals from across the nation, creating a café society animated by a love of talk, sexual freedom, and socialist politics (Stansell 2000). At the level of popular culture, modern feminism had "theatrical roots" in the iconic actresses, dancers, and singers who performed the spirited self-sufficiency denied by society, from Sarah Bernhardt to Isadora Duncan to chorus girls. The chorus girl in particular has received attention as an agent mediating the rationality of modernization, mass production, sex, and hedonism for both men and women (Mizejewski 1999; Glenn 2000).

Scholars have achieved no consensus on what modernism is, when it began, what methods its artists shared (beyond self-conscious experimentation), or what role American modernists played in international modernism. Some argue that American modernism was simply constructed out of the self-promotion of its artists, critics, scholars, and camp followers (Poirier 1978); others that it is a *habitus*, a structural field equivalent in importance to Victorianism or the Enlightenment (Hoffman & Murphy 1992). While many scholars understand the 1950s and 1960s as a continuation of modernism (or "high modernism") via the Beats, Abstract Expressionists, and Black Mountain artists, others – myself included – argue that the events of 1945 marked the birth of *post*modernism. Beckett differs from Joyce and Pynchon from Stein because artistic responses to the failure of technology, progress, and rationality between 1890 and 1940 must be distinguished from later responses to the Holocaust, Hiroshima, and the arms race.

Four themes mark a distinctively American modernism: the opposition of urban, cosmopolitan culture to the perceived repression of small-town society; the artistic tension between cultural nationalism, self-actualization, and ethnic and gender consciousness; the emergence of popular cultural expressions that mediate modernity, from film to the blues; and, finally, the dialogic relationship of technological "speed-up" and African American culture. Narratives of modernism now revolve as much around the broader incorporation of Americans into modern society as around specific literary figures.

Modernism, Modernity, Modernization

Marshall Berman first aligned modernism with "modernity" and "modernization" in his landmark meditation, *All That Is Solid Melts into Air: The Experience of Modernity* (1982), and this matrix remains a fruitful mode of inquiry. *Modernization* concerns rapid technological change in industrial society. Conceptually, new inventions and networks challenge the idea that human life is static and produces concrete objects that compel individuals to "keep up with the times"; further, man-made improvement weakens the religious enterprise. New technologies are alternately thrilling – as when they serve leisure and consumption – and terrifying, as when they disrupt traditional aspects of human life. The Italian Futurists were the first intellectuals to celebrate technology and considered "the beauty of speed" in trains and cars the first new modern aesthetic experience, which added to "the world's splendor." Humans would acquire a "new mechanical sense," they believed, and enjoy "a fusion of instinct with the efficiency of motors" (Marinetti 1909: 21) In more mundane fashion, the owner-ship and handling of an automobile gave Americans a sense of control concerning industrial transformation. As Sinclair Lewis wrote of his emblematic middle-class American materialist, "To George F. Babbitt . . . his motor car was poetry and tragedy, love and heroism" (Lewis 1922: 24).

On the one hand, machines replaced human labor, resulting in "technological unemployment," and an identity crisis for men in particular (Smith 1993). The "control revolution" subjugated the average worker to alienated, repetitive work, the invasive supervision of efficiency managers, and corporate surveillance (Beniger 1986; Kanigel 1997). Yet the American hunger for "the technological sublime" brought crowds to world's fairs and technological expositions, to railroad fairs and skyscraper sites and air shows (Nye 1994). In the wake of World War I's destruction, Europe found in American culture a fast-paced, machine civilization and new forms of indus-trial organization (Fordism) and efficiency (Taylorism). What the French called "Americanisme" in the 1920s, Thomas P. Hughes has called "the second discovery of America" (Hughes 1989).

Many scholars date the emergence of modernism according to Virginia Woolf's cryptic reflection, "In 1910, human nature changed." The more useful declaration came six years later from Henry Ford, the representative figure of the era: "History is more or less bunk." Raised in the Midwest within Victorian ideals of utility, ratio-nality, and progress, Ford created the means to destroy that mindset by doubling the wages of his workers and building an affordable car. The Model T virtually created contemporary American society and its car culture: its suburbs, fast food, and mobility; its teenaged rebellion, rituals for adulthood, and sexual mores. "Fordism" may have been the global model of vertical corporate integration, yet by the mid-1920s, Ford himself was nostalgic for the stability of his childhood: he built a museum and a model small town to encourage Americans to return to the alleged virtues of small-town life while publishing pro-fascist, anti-Semitic rants and moving toward fascism. Ford stood at the crossroads of modernism and "anti-modernism," Jackson Lears's term for the nostalgic yearnings of upper-class elites for the order and spirituality of small-town pastoralism and exotic religions (Lears 1981; Susman 1984).

Modernity, then, concerns the individual experiences of the transformation from an agrarian society into an urban, mass society. The shift entailed a gradual loss of secure identities previously embedded in local social institutions: church and religion, family and community, class and geography. Individuals became just another element in the flow of industrial society, as much as capital, raw materials, or mass-produced goods. The grounds for identity shifted to new forms of popular culture, such as dime novels, radio dramas, films, mass consumption, and the urban, industrial landscape.

Modernity further signifies the sensory (and cognitive) adjustment to new experiences of space and time, speed and movement, self and other (Kern 1983). Bodies adjusted to fast, impersonal transportation networks (rail, auto, air), to communication networks that separated the message from the sender (telegraph, telephone), and to new visual regimes rendered through film, aerial perspectives, or abstract art. The so-called "speed-up" of modern life produced apocalyptic fears of sensory overload, and the "shocks" of these new experiences were theorized by sociologists such as Karl Marx, Georg Simmel, Thorstein Veblen, and Walter Benjamin (Adams 1931; Frisby 1986). With such radical shifts in sensoryscapes, work, leisure, personal contact, and the rate of change, the individual consciousness could hardly remain trapped in nineteenth-century ways of seeing.

Modernism applies to the artistic and intellectual representation of the experiences of modernity and modernization, the search for "new aesthetic vocabularies" to represent "the innovative terms of industrial life" (Kasson 2000: 154). To be "modern" is to undergo perpetual change. And because the modern self has been battered and moved about, modern artists and writers break words and images into fragments (Cubism, *The Waste Land*), creating art and literature that demand constant attention to produce coherence. Shifts in daily rhythms, sensory perception, and the speed of information led to shifts in conceptions of time, the self, and the nature of experience.

Until recently, modernism was configured primarily through literature for a number of reasons: the prestige of literature in the humanities; the historical significance of the 1920s for the emergence of the United States as a world power; the cultural changes of the 1920s, as reflected in novels that maintain their cachet in high school and college curricula (*The Great Gatsby*, *The Sun Also Rises*, *The Sound and the Fury*, Dos Passos' *USA* trilogy); the built-in ending to the "roaring twenties" with the crash of 1929; the romantic self-promotion of the Lost Generation through memoirs and novels; a kinship between writer, critic, and scholar through cultural rebellion and "the virtues . . . of difficulty" in teaching inaccessible texts (Poirier 1978). Malcolm Cowley first codified the mythology of the Lost Generation of writers in *Exile's Return* (1934): born between 1891 and 1905, their education focused on European history and literature; but after World War I, "civilization" became a pejorative term, and they took refuge in cosmopolitan bohemia in protest against the "Babbitry" (Lewis's term) or the "booboisie" (H. L. Mencken's).

Hugh Kenner's *A Homemade World* (1975) was a landmark work. First, he identified the styles, influences, and formal intentions of the best modernist poets (Marianne Moore, William Carlos Williams, Wallace Stevens, Ezra Pound, T. S. Eliot) and prose stylists (Hemingway, Faulkner, Fitzgerald). Second, he identified their common intention of liberating words from their technical function (i.e., signifier from signified) in order to "reconstellate" them on the page. Third, he invoked technology as an equivalent form of artistic creation, calling the discovery of flight by two bicycle mechanics a modernist act of creative transformation. In fact, Lindbergh's solo flight over the Atlantic excited Europeans more than any single cultural event of the 1920s (Eksteins 1989), and linked the "homemade world" of American vernacular technological innovation with the "homemade" poetics of Hemingway and Faulkner.

Invention and self-invention travel hand in modern glove. In fact, modernism involves a dialectic between technological development and self-development;

technology was the driving force of the European avant-garde's call for an anarchic vision of a new society. This dialectic became entrenched in World War I, the first modern war: modern in its mass slaughter, its use of transportation networks across Europe (in trains, cars, and planes), its communications networks (radio, telegraphs, telephones), and its technological development of new weapons (machine guns, hand grenades, chemical warfare) (Fussell 1975; Kern 1983). The Great War thus brought together modernization (technological change and adaptation), modernity (new sensory experiences of time and space), and modernism (aesthetic reflections upon these changes), and disillusioned a cadre of American modernist writers who served in the war. Yet the modernism of literary salons, the Lost Generation, the "little magazines" (e.g., Harriet Monroe's *Poetry*), and the Harlem Renaissance still maintains a stronghold on the discourse. Ann Douglas's *Terrible Honesty* (1995) attempted to synthesize the concurrent revolutions of modernism and modernization in a panoramic exploration of the "mongrel Manhattan" of the 1920s. Ranging over a hundred modern lives, Douglas showed that immigrants, women, and urbanized Americans aspired to an energized personality in order to compete with New York's technological displays and its sped-up, jazzed-up tempo of life.

The totemic mechanical agent of liberation was the train, and from 1900 to 1920, literary characters – in *Sister Carrie* (1900) and *Winesburg, Ohio* (1919), for example – leave town by train to become modern, acquiring a mobile identity and aspiring toward autonomy. Those who stay behind remain stuck in traditional lives governed by church, family, community, sexual repression, and bitterness. Similarly, the immigrant's experience is modernist in as much as the process of claming an American identity requires self-transformation and a break with the past. Ezra Pound's artistic appeal to "Make it new!" reflects relentless social and global change that makes every *person* anew, and not solely by artistic means.

Self and Subjectivity

The making of the modern individual involved a radical shift in the experience of time, as theorized by William James and Henri Bergson. Time itself was one of the first industrial commodities, divided into minutes and sections, appended to the human body by chain and pocket, imposed on all Americans by a de facto act of the railroads in 1883. In various cultural forms, artists depicted protagonists taking their bodies back from clocks, factories, and the rationalization of industrial life. For each person to have a separate, subjective consciousness – the core of Bergson's *durée* or Jamesian "flux" – meant that "reality" itself might be plural and not objective, might be determined by agency as much as social role, and might include the irrational and unconscious as constant (and even useful) elements of consciousness.

Stephen Dedalus's prototypical modernist statement in the opening chapter of Joyce's *Ulysses* (1922) speaks to this sense of time: "History is a nightmare from which I am trying to awake." *History* was an ideological foundation of the Victorian social order, an evolutionary narrative that moved from primitive to civilized societies through the Enlightenment idea of "progress." History narrated the triumph of science and rationalism over superstition and emotionalism, setting up the dualism of white European male rationality against the natural, emotional "Others" of women and the darker races. Dedalus's one-liner illuminates the modernist turn to self-awakening through the rejection of social definition, the embrace of subjectivity, and the potential for ethical individuality. As mirrored in a letter home from a British soldier – "the whole of the past, as far as I can make out, is down the drain" – the nightmare of history led to a postwar embrace of immediate sensory experience wherein "the 'I' became all important" (Eksteins 1989: 211).

Contrast modernism to realism, the dominant literary mode of the late nineteenth century, as it reflected the hopes for stability of an empowered middle class. Realism features an omniscient narrator with moral authority, characters that worry more about fitting into the social order than finding themselves, and an audience with an assumed dualistic moral sense. James's concept of "stream of consciousness" destabilized that objective, external observer and its stable social order by elevating interior consciousness; his concept was carried to Europe by his student Gertrude Stein, who from her Paris salon influenced James Joyce and others (Crunden 1993). Stream of consciousness precludes the authority of a third-person narrator and disrupts the rational thought process depicted in proper grammar and syntax. The external observer for a bourgeois society based on rationality and productivity gives way to a map of the interior consciousness marked by a constant flow of desires, sense perceptions, impulses, memories, and fantasies, mirroring Freud's theories of the unconscious.

Faulkner wrote *The Sound and the Fury* and *As I Lay Dying* after reading *Ulysses*, novels informed by the ideas of Bergson and James (according to Faulkner), and inconceivable within a realist framework: there is no narrator, no morality, no judgment of character, no point. In *As I Lay Dying*, reality can only be constructed by the reader's collation of the characters' responses to the last days of Addie Bundren. Each character's internal monologues contain local history, personal memory, identity and projection, unspoken and thwarted desires; each chapter adds to the reader's knowledge of region, clan, and county. Faulkner's method is kaleidoscopic: a single action is split into a mosaic of experience. "My ambition is to put everything into one sentence," Faulkner once wrote, "not only the present but the whole past on which it depends and which keeps overtaking the present, second by second" (quoted in Kenner 1975: 198). By rendering the internal monologue in vernacular language, Faulkner validates the oral storytelling traditions and rural southern white dialect he inherited and transmuted into his own artistic language.

In applying Sherwood Anderson's advice to engage his "postage stamp of native soil," Faulkner captured the spirit of cultural nationalism in American literary modernism. In similar fashion, Zora Neale Hurston, Langston Hughes, Hemingway, and Stein attempted to honor vernacular language, oral traditions, ethnic and regional cultures (Pavlic 2002). However, the relationship between writer, race, and geography – and the nightmare of history – translated differently for ethnic groups. When African American songwriters Fats Waller and Andy Razaf crafted "What Did I Do to Be So Black and Blue?" they asked a modernist question from a modernist position: self-referential, detached, outside of stable traditions, buffeted by forces, injured by the nightmare of history that has bruised you black and blue. What are you going to do, now that you're black and blue? Sing it out of your system, show the forces acting upon your life as a roadmap for others, sing it so it becomes part of everybody's system.

This is, more or less, the history of this song. It was originally a lament sung by a dark-skinned woman about internal color bias within African American communities, as performed by Ethel Waters in a 1929 Harlem revue entitled *Hot Chocolates*. Seemingly overnight, it became a vehicle for dozens of black performers and a signature song for the young Louis Armstrong. Armstrong dropped the verse about color bias and made it a self-affirming plaint for all African Americans. Twenty years later, the narrator of Ralph Ellison's *Invisible Man* (1952) invokes the song in the novel's prologue as a catalyst for his rebellion, claiming "this music demanded action." Ellison regarded Armstrong as a trickster (or shaman) for the African American community, and his deft mixture of deference and empowerment – Uncle Tomming on stage but sending out coded resistance – suggests an alternative modernist route than those of middle-class Euro-Americans (Appel 2002; Dinerstein 2003). Similarly, James Baldwin singled out Billie Holiday as a poet who guided audiences through the processes of what Toni Morrison calls "re-memory": "When I say poet . . . I'm not talking about literature at all. I'm talking about the recreation of experience, you know, the way that it comes back. Billie Holiday was a poet. She gave you back your experience" (quoted in Pavlic 2002: 257). Holiday's best work invoked tones, textures, cadences, and phrases that inflected the English language to serve as coded markings of African American past and possibility.

Arguably, Holiday's contemporary global popularity depends upon the grain of a voice that captures the underlying tensions of modernity: the loss of cohesion and stability balanced by the promise of autonomy and the thrill of self-liberation. In consciously attempting to synthesize Bessie Smith's vocal power and Louis Armstrong's subtle phrasing, Holiday's work illustrates how African American artistic subjectivity first emerged in the blues, a form that has only begun to receive its due as a modernist expression in the past generation (Baker 1984). First, the vernacular artistically formalized in "the blues" consciously defied "Standard English," cultural elites, assimilationist rhetoric, and the Christian themes of the spirituals. Second, blues functions almost entirely through lyrics focused on "the all-important 'I,'" through blunt talk of sexuality, oppression, and transgression. Third, along with the jazz soloist, blues marked the emergence of both an introspective African American artistic consciousness and African American music itself as a "counterculture of modernity" (Gilroy 1993).

Modernism and the Other

American modernism marks the intersection of conflicting histories difficult to synthesize. In *The Modernist Nation* (2004), Michael Soto ambitiously attempts to unite the objectives of the Lost Generation, the Harlem Renaissance, and female modernist writers and artists around the concepts "generation" and "renaissance." Soto presents four unifying, intertwined narratives for modernist artists: rejection of one's philistine upbringing and symbolic rebirth for purposes of self-definition; the creation of a formulaic "bohemian narrative" that naturalizes (and nationalizes) cultural rebellion; the valorization of the artistic imagination against the rational planning of a utilitarian, industrial society; the search for models of cultural nationalism in other colonized or emergent literatures (e.g., such as Irish and Russian). For the purposes of rebirth and rebellion, the language of American modernism is jazz: it provides the new rhythms, the slang, the improvisational method, the subculture of performance (in dance), and the sense of being modern or at least "hip to the [new] lingo" (Soto 2004).

In the 1910s, a generation of young Euro-American elites rejected the waltz, quadrille, and European dances for ragtime dances such as the turkey trot, the grizzly bear, the fox trot, and the buzzard lope. The formal, public performance of these dances made Vernon and Irene Castle national icons and international stars (Erenberg 1981). Their bestselling book of dance and refined manners diluted African American kinesthetics and marked the first "white-facing" of African American modernist cultural production. When Henry May identified the first stage of American modernism in the five-year period from 1912 to 1917, he correlated the significance of the kinesthetic revolution implicit in these dance crazes with more familiar artistic and intellectual influences (James, Freud, Veblen, and Frank Lloyd Wright), singling out the shimmy, a dance that later gave Mae West her first national success (May 1959). In effect, the shimmy gave the lie to the civilizing process, especially as the Castles and Mae West committed classic acts of "love and theft": stealing African American expressive culture while dishonoring their artistic producers (Lott 1993).

European social dance and kinesthetics were repudiated and have not returned; whether this was an act of primitivism or modernism remains an ongoing debate, but the answer seems obvious – it's both – when speaking of a popular revolution both with regard to the aesthetics of movement and in the recognition of sublime response to propulsive rhythmic music. Music and dance of the African diaspora broke down set forms of European pattern dances such as the waltz, liberated parts of the body for individual creative expression, encouraged a playful eroticism, and brought a new sense of spatial orientation to self-awareness. The rhetoric of "getting primitive" protected Americans from honoring non-white cultural production and functioned as a conduit for Euro-Americans to imagine a different relationship to their bodies (Torgovnick 1997). Ragtime and jazz dances paralleled the influential work of Franz Boas's *The Mind of Primitive Man* (1911), which disrupted nineteenth-century dualism: Boas argued that "primitive" cultures indeed practiced logic and reason, and had their own systems of ethics and aesthetics; conversely, "modern" Europeans practiced tribal rites and customs, and rationalized violence and superstition through irrational beliefs.

Yet a lively debate remains regarding whether the Harlem Renaissance marked the advent of a "New Negro" artistic formation – an ethnic literary aesthetic – that successfully broke down ingrained ideas of African American artistic ability or intellectual equality (Lewis 1981). Did it transform the white gaze of African Americans, destroy plantation stereotypes, and move Euro-Americans closer to believing in social equality? Yes. Did it produce literary and artistic work that stands alongside the best Euro-American cultural production as modernist work? Yes. Did it leave a legacy that has provided a corrective in the modernist discourse? Yes. Houston Baker has grouped blues, literature, and minstrelsy all together as cultural acts of "maronnage" (after "maroon" societies of runaway slaves) that resist dominant social codes and reinscribe resistant ideas in both popular and highbrow cultural forms (Baker 1989).

The second major site of "primitivist modernism" was Mexico. As a contact zone for modernists from O'Keeffe, D. H. Lawrence, and Mabel Dodge Luhan to the Beats, Mexico presented writers and artists with images both to critique a runaway technological society and to imagine an Edenic preindustrial innocence (Crunden 1993). In Mexico and New Mexico, artists believed they could still find a sense of place, community, stable rituals, and unselfconscious behaviors, while maintaining a distance of exoticism. Such projections took almost no account of the cultural production of Mexican and Mexican American modernists, and scholars have returned the voice of "the Other" to a "border modernism," pairing primitivist texts of D. H. Lawrence, Hemingway, and Willa Cather with "native" voices such as Americo Paredes (Schedler 2002).

Such questions would seem to point to a debate about defining American culture, but the term "culture" has become so contentious within the humanities that questions of identity nearly always override it. The definition of culture shifted during the modern period from cultivation through arts and education – classical music, ballet, philosophy – to patterns and behaviors in everyday life transmitted intergenerationally (Hegeman 1999). Boas provided the ethnographic model that brought about the emergence of cultural relativism through the work of his influential students (such as Margaret Mead, Ruth Benedict, and Zora Neale Hurston), and anthropology became the first intellectual field in which women participated as near-equals (Deacon 1997).

Scholars have recently called for a remapping of "American literature" toward a postcolonial, postnationalist "literature of the Americas." A major aspect of that project would be Hispanic modernism, a six-stage model mirroring the European cultural arc from 1890 to 1940 (Calinescu 1987), including Diego Rivera's monumental murals of Ford's River Rouge plant and Frida Kahlo's self-reflexive paintings of Mexican identity; the illustrations of Miguel Covarrubias and Marius de Zayas, along with the polyethnic cosmopolitan community around Alfred Stieglitz's 291 group (and in Harlem); Americo Paredes's ethnography on South Texas and its legacy in borderlands studies. It would also include major postmodern Latin American writers such as Marquez, Borges, and Llosa, who were indebted to Faulkner for bringing the modernist interplay of time, memory, identity, and geography to peripheral, insulated communities (Cohn 1999).

Technology and the Body

"The machine" (so called) remains a complex, contradictory metaphor at the heart of modernity. All at once, "the machine" was an artistic model of efficient creativity, a metaphor for relentless, impersonal forces, and an invasive system of surveillance and repression. Francis Picabia painted human figures as machines or mechanical principles, such as *The Picture of an American Girl*, which was a spark plug. Technology is the Other of modernism in such representative works as Fritz Lang's *Metropolis* (1927), Charlie Chaplin's *Modern Times* (1936), and Huxley's *Brave New World* (1932). Yet William Carlos Williams defined a poem (positively) as "a small (or large) machine made out of words"; Le Corbusier defined a house as "a machine built for living"; and Margaret Bourke-White created an aesthetic grammar of machine beauty. Alfred Stieglitz's photograph *The Hand of Man* gets to the heart of this tension: it depicts a train rounding a bend at full steam, juxtaposing human physical labor in a natural landscape to the vitality of machines in an industrial landscape.

The train was the prime mover of modernity, "the primary metaphor of modernity and its metonym" (Scandura & Thurston 2001: 25). The modern American tempo of life arguably derives from train rhythms and its embodiment of machine aesthetics as both object and network (and thus the introduction of terms such as traffic, flow, precision, and efficiency). For rural Americans, the "metropolitan corridor" of every small town was the train station, telegraph shack, and factory warehouse districts on the outskirts of town (Stilgoe 1983). Every major American poet celebrated the colonization of the landscape by train and Whitman granted it pride of place in modernity: "Type of the modern – emblem of motion and power – pulse of the continent" (Whitman 2002 [1892]).

The experience of looking at landscapes from a train window helped create a new visual regime for the camera eye, framing fast-moving landscapes and a plethora of images into a modern flux without sensory overload. Riding the train also provided precedent for the consumer society: a passenger is both a parcel carried by a train and a consumer staring at a constant stream of new objects from a safe vantage point. As commodity and consumer, the train provides the conditions for a debased relationship to nature. This experience trained audiences to watch films, the primary medium by which Americans adjusted to the shocks of modernity. The train itself was the biggest action star in silent film, framed not only for its power and speed, but as the vehicle for the hero's arrival; *The Big Train Robbery* (1903) taught directors cinematic technique for capturing a moving object (Kirby 1997). Railway passengers of the 1830s frightened by speeds of 20 miles per hour clearly had a different relationship to their bodies than Americans who now drive at 80 miles an hour while eating a sandwich and listening to heavy metal.

In the late nineteenth century, the prevalent metaphor of the body shifted from organic and religious models to "the human machine" (Rabinbach 1990). Mirroring the industrial division of labor, the body was seen as an aggregation of separate parts in an interlocking system. Early research on the body-as-machine came from British studies of the laboring body under duress, and studies of human and animal bodies-in-motion. Electricity in particular – the machine as energy network – became a metaphor for energizing the body, as early as Whitman's "I Sing the Body Electric"; sexual devices such as electric belts (for male virility) and the first vibrators date from the late nineteenth century (de la Pena 2003). The electric landscape of Manhattan, Chicago, and Coney Island was the cultural ground of modernism: it elevated advertising into the sky, celebrated technology for pleasure and awe, and trained the eye to revel in simultaneity, fragmentation, and montage, instead of rejecting such visual cacophony as chaos (Nye 1997).

Modernism involved the adaptation of all bodies to technological society, a process theorized usefully in Sara Danius's *The Senses of Modernism* (2002). Danius argues that new machines and inventions extend the capabilities of the human body not only through *prosthesis*, but also through *aisthesis*, the "interiorization" of technological modes of perception. In the first volume of *Remembrance of Times Past*, Marcel hears his beloved grandmother's voice on the phone for the first time and has a disturbing epiphany: he hears some old woman, her voice wracked with pain and age. Until the telephone, there was no voice without presence, no message without embodiment; previously, whenever Marcel heard his grandmother, his perceptions were informed by love, devotion, history, and memory. Marcel assumes there's an impostor in his grandmother's body and rushes to her house, where he finds her engrossed in the newspaper. But his perception of his grandmother has already been irrevocably altered; before him sits an old woman. Here is the human eye in the process of becoming a "camera eye": more efficient at gathering sense data but sundered from the organic experience; now just one sense among many within a new division of perceptual labor.

Such ambivalence toward machines was mediated through spectacle, such as watching planned train wrecks or turning gearwheels into Ferris wheels. At Coney Island, the pressures of industrial change were transmuted into titillating pleasure: coal carts and tracks became roller coasters; electricity lit up a phantasmagoric skyline; speed and torque created a hedonistic sense of disorientation that bordered on the psychedelic (Kasson 1978). New terminology reflected mechanical metaphors for action, emotion, and cognition: a person got "steamed up" or "off-track" or "in gear" (all originally references to trains) (Tichi 1987). In silent film, Charlie Chaplin, Buster Keaton, and Harold Lloyd functioned as scapegoats of modernity. Their manic antics and metropolitan meanderings reflected their own modern disorientation as they negotiated machines, crowds, and authorities; victims of social and technological forces, they were constantly in motion (Basalla 1981). In these ways, individuals engaged technology abstractly through what art historians call "machine aesthetics": speed, flow, power, drive, repetition, and precision (Smith 1993).

In jazz, blues, and swing, African American music and dance captured the pace and power of the industrial soundscape and assimilated machine aesthetics into dynamic forms of popular culture. American college students of the 1920s and female laborers pressed jazz and its dances into service for their own cultural rebellion, rejecting the concept of "sin," especially as it related to sex and the body (Peiss 1986). Whether in ragtime dances, the Charleston (1920s), tap dance, or the lindy hop (the 1930s), African American dance was a participatory modernist art form. The rhythmic drive of all jazz until 1945 came from the "techno-dialogic," an artistic engagement with machine rhythms and industrialization, as African American musicians developed a musical grammar through "locomotive onomatopoeia" (i.e., the rhythms and sounds of trains) (Murray 1976; Dinerstein 2003). Since the function of social dance in African American culture is the integration of music, movement, culture, and social forces into "participatory consciousness," black culture became a global lingua franca, reproducing new musical idioms, slang, fashion, and generational identity throughout the past century (Keil & Feld 1994).

Finally, modernism involved a crisis of cultural authority heightened by the emergence of the first national advertising agencies, which filled the mediascape with sophisticated imagery for national brands that continually stimulated desire and consumption (Marchand 1985; Leach 1993; Lears 1994). Concurrent to artistic modernism, consumerism advanced a paradigm shift in the modal self, from Victorian "character" to modern "personality" – the self as commodity in the urban marketplace (Susman 1984). As images of success, beauty, pleasure, and even piety were drawn from popular culture and generated for commercial ends, the "mediated self" comes into being via mass culture (Gabler 1998). The modernist ethos of rebellion became entrenched in contemporary consumer culture, and what began as adversarial combat with history and tradition has since become rhetorical sloganeering for multinational corporations. Autonomy, choice, rebellion – these terms register as a permanent ideological matrix of consumer society.

Coda: Modernism and Postmodernism

What cohesive set of Western or American values could remain after the Holocaust and the dropping of the atomic bombs – even to rebel against? In the immediate aftermath of World War II, American intellectuals and writers embraced existentialism while the first postmodern writers – Beckett, Borges, and Nabokov – created labyrinthine narratives centered less on self and subjectivity than on the inadequacy of language to represent postwar reality.

In *The Post-modern Condition* (1984), Lyotard theorized that all European modernism worked within four underlying narratives, all of which were secularized Christian myths of redemption: (1) the Enlightenment ideal of linear progress through knowledge leading to the good society; (2) the goal of autonomy, after introspection and inquiry into the dark recesses of the self; (3) the Marxist promise of the revolutionary struggle of the proletariat; (4) the capitalist narrative of the good society through market forces, enlightened self-interest, and global economic harmony (Lyotard 1984; Calinescu 1987). The capitalist narrative retains its power and influence (Fukuyama 1992) and Marxist analysis still informs modernist scholarship in the humanities (Jameson 1991), but no sense of universalism frames postmodernism. Instead, all sets of values are assumed to be rationalizations of power, and stability is always relative, whether of self, language, or society (Harvey 1989).

In Brian McHale's elegant distinction: whereas modernism concerned epistemology, postmodernism is about ontology (McHale 1987). The artist is no longer a guide towards authentic self-knowledge but an assembler of forms into pastiche, its meaning left to the consumer to interpret. In the architecture of Frank Gehry, hip-hop musical collage, and the "media assemblages" of Pynchon, artists mix high, low, and pop culture, seed their works with genres and cultural quotations, and celebrate irony, camp, gaudiness, and self-reflexivity. In postmodernism, rebellion was simply one pose among many, no more or less valuable than cynicism, stoicism, or romanticism (Hassan 1971). Randomness and instability were celebrated as agents of change – in chaos theory, in self-experimentation, in the pursuit of novelty – and, therefore, the antithesis of self and society became moot. Postmodernism reflected a more playful engagement between artistic production and popular culture, and art was no longer envisioned as a privileged critical vantage point.

Perhaps the most significant failed project of modernism was that of the authentic self. Modernist artists saw themselves as guides to a future unburdened by the chains of the past and redolent with sex, pleasure, and meaningful introspection. Such transgression against Victorian morality and order is now the rhetoric of self-actualization as it is used to fuel consumerist ideology; its familiarity reflects the unintended triumphs of modernism. From the vantage point of *post*modernism, the goal of autonomy without consequent attachment to community or politics seems self-indulgent, hedonistic, or simply performative. Postmodern critics accuse modernist artists of lacking politics, promulgating a naïve idea of progress, and supporting a vague humanism and universalism that indirectly supported colonialism (Ross 1986;

Williams 1989). The challenge of understanding the legacy of American modernism now turns upon the debate over its success or failure in creating large-scale social change.

REFERENCES

Adams, James Truslow: *The Tempo of Modern Life* (New York: A. & C. Boni, 1931).

Apollonio, Umbro: *Futurist Manifestos* (New York: Viking, 1970).

Appel, Alfred, Jr.: *Jazz Modernism: From Ellington and Armstrong to Matisse and Joyce* (New York: Alfred A. Knopf, 2002).

Baker, Houston A., Jr.: *Blues, Ideology, and Afro-American Literature* (Chicago: University of Chicago Press, 1984).

Baker, Houston A., Jr.: *Modernism and the Harlem Renaissance* (Chicago: University of Chicago Press, 1989).

Basalla, George: "Keaton and Chaplin: The Silent Film's Response to Technology," in *Technology in America* (Cambridge: MIT Press, 1981), pp. 192–201.

Beniger, James R.: *The Control Revolution: Technological and Economic Origins of the Information Society* (Cambridge, MA: Harvard University Press, 1986).

Berman, Marshall: *All That Is Solid Melts Into Air: The Experience of Modernity* (New York: Simon & Schuster, 1982).

Bradbury, Malcolm & McFarlane, James: *Modernism, 1890–1930* (New York: Penguin, 1976).

Calinescu, Matei: *The Five Faces of Modernity* (Durham, NC: Duke University Press, 1987).

Cohn, Deborah N.: *History and Memory in the Two Souths* (Nashville: Vanderbilt University Press, 1999).

Cowley, Malcolm: *Exile's Return: A Literary Odyssey of the 1920s* (New York: W. W. Norton, 1934).

Crunden, Robert: *American Salons: Encounters with European Modernism, 1885–1917* (New York: Oxford University Press, 1993).

Crunden, Robert: *Body and Soul: The Making of American Modernism* (New York: Basic Books, 2000).

Danius, Sara: *The Senses of Modernism: Technology, Perception, and Aesthetics* (Ithaca, NY: Cornell University Press, 2002).

Davis, Angela Y.: *Blues Legacies and Black Feminism* (New York: Pantheon, 1998).

Deacon, Desley: *Elsie Clews Parsons: Inventing Modern Life* (Chicago: University of Chicago Press, 1997).

Dinerstein, Joel: *Swinging the Machine: Modernity, Technology, and African-American Culture between the World Wars* (Amherst: University of Massachusetts Press, 2003).

Douglas, Ann: *Terrible Honesty: Mongrel Manhattan in the 1920s* (New York: Farrar, Straus, & Giroux, 1995).

Eksteins, Modris: *Rites of Spring: The Great War and the Birth of the Modern Age* (Boston, MA: Houghton Mifflin, 1989).

Ellison, Ralph: *Invisible Man* (New York: Random House, 1952).

Erenberg, Lewis: *Steppin' Out: New York Nightlife and the Transformation of American Culture, 1890–1930* (Westport: Greenwood Press, 1981).

Everdell, William R.: *The First Moderns* (Chicago: University of Chicago Press, 1997).

Frisby, David: *Fragments of Modernity: Theories of Modernity in the Work of Simmel, Kracauer, and Benjamin* (Cambridge, MA: MIT Press, 1986).

Fukuyama, Francis: *The End of History and the Last Man* (New York: Free Press, 1992).

Fussell, Paul: *The Great War and Modern Memory* (New York: Oxford University Press, 1975).

Gabler, Neal: *Life, the Movie: How Entertainment Conquered Reality* (New York: Alfred A. Knopf, 1998).

Gilroy, Paul: *The Black Atlantic: Modernity and Double Consciousness* (Cambridge, MA: Harvard University Press, 1993).

Glenn, Susan A.: *Female Spectacle: The Theatrical Roots of Modern Feminism* (Cambridge, MA: Harvard University Press, 2000).

Harvey, David: *The Condition of Postmodernity* (New York: Blackwell, 1989).

Hassan, Ihab: *The Dismemberment of Orpheus: Towards a Postmodern Literature* (New York: Oxford University Press, 1971).

Hegeman, Susan: *Patterns for America: Modernism and the Concept of Culture* (Princeton, NJ: Princeton University Press, 1999).

Hoffman, Michael J. & Murphy, Patrick D.: *Critical Essays on American Modernism* (New York: G. K. Hall, 1992).

Hughes, Thomas P.: *American Genesis: A Century of Invention and Technological Enthusiasm, 1870–1970* (New York: Viking, 1989).

Huxley, Aldous: *Brave New World* (London: Chatto & Windus, 1932).

Huyssen, Andreas: *After the Great Divide: Modernism, Mass Culture, Postmodernism* (Bloomington: Indiana University Press, 1986).

Jameson, Fredric: *Postmodernism, or The Cultural Logic of Late Capitalism* (Durham, NC: Duke University Press, 1991).

Joyce, James: *Ulysses* (London: Egoist, 1922).

Kanigel, Robert: *The One Best Way: Frederick Winslow Taylor and the Enigma of Efficiency* (New York: Viking, 1997).

Kasson, John F.: *Amusing the Million* (New York: Hill & Wang, 1978).

Kasson, John F.: "Dances of the Machine in Early Twentieth-Century America," in Townsend Ludington (ed.), *A Modern Mosaic: Art and Modernism in the United States* (Chapel Hill: University of North Carolina Press, 2000), pp. 153–74.

Keil, Charles & Feld, Stephen: *Music Grooves* (Chicago: University of Chicago Press, 1994).

Kenner, Hugh: *A Homemade World: The American Modernist Writers* (New York: Alfred A. Knopf, 1975).

Kern, Stephen: *The Culture of Time and Space, 1880–1918* (Cambridge, MA: Harvard University Press, 1983).

Kirby, Lynne: *Parallel Tracks: The Railroad and Silent Cinema* (Durham, NC: Duke University Press, 1997).

Leach, William: *Land of Desire: Merchants, Power, and the Rise of a New American Culture* (New York: Pantheon, 1993).

Lears, T. J. Jackson: *No Place of Grace: Anti-Modernism and the Transformation of American Culture, 1880–1920* (New York: Pantheon, 1981).

Lears, T. J.: *Fables of Abundance: A Cultural History of Advertising in America* (New York: Basic Books, 1994).

Lemke, Sieglinde: *Primitivist Modernism: Black Culture and the Origins of Transatlantic Modernism* (New York: Oxford University Press, 1998).

Lewis, David Levering: *When Harlem Was in Vogue* (New York: Alfred A. Knopf, 1981).

Lewis, Sinclair: *Babbitt* (New York: Harcourt, Brace, 1922).

Lott, Eric: *Love and Theft* (New York: Oxford University Press, 1993).

Ludington, Townsend, ed.: *A Modern Mosaic: Art and Modernism in the United States* (Chapel Hill: University of North Carolina Press, 2000).

Lyotard, Jean François: *The Postmodern Condition* (Minneapolis: University of Minnesota Press, 1984).

Marchand, Roland: *Advertising the American Dream* (Berkeley: University of California Press, 1985).

Marinetti, Filippo: "The Founding and Manifesto of Futurism," (1909) in Umbro Apollonio, ed., *Futurist Manifestos* (New York: Viking, 1970), pp. 19–24.

May, Henry: *The End of American Innocence: A Study of the First Years of Our Time, 1912–1917* (New York: Alfred A. Knopf, 1959).

McHale, Brian: *Postmodernist Fiction* (New York: Methuen, 1987).

Mizejewski, Linda: *Ziegfeld Girl: Image and Icon in Culture and Cinema* (Durham, NC: Duke University Press, 1999).

Murray, Albert: *Stomping the Blues* (New York: McGraw-Hill, 1976).

Nye, David E.: *The Technological Sublime* (Cambridge, MA: MIT Press, 1994).

Nye, David E.: *Narratives and Spaces: Technology and the Construction of American Culture* (Cambridge, MA: MIT Press, 1997).

Pavlic, Edward M.: *Crossroads Modernism* (Minneapolis: University of Minnesota Press, 2002).

Peiss, Kathy: *Cheap Amusements: Working Women and Leisure in Turn of the Century New York* (Philadelphia: Temple University Press, 1986).

de la Pena, Carolyn: *The Body Electric: How Strange Machines Built the Modern American* (New York: NYU Press, 2003).

Pippin, Robert B.: *Modernism as a Philosophical Problem* (Cambridge, MA: Blackwell, 1991).

Poirier, Richard: "The Difficulties of Modernism and the Modernism of Difficulty," *Humanities in Society* 1, 1 (1978), 271–82.

Rabinbach, Anson: *The Human Motor: Energy, Fatigue, and the Origins of Modernity* (New York: Basic Books, 1990).

Rabinowitz, Paula: "Great Lady Painters, Inc.: Icons of Feminism, Modernism, and the Nation," in Jani Scandura & Michael Thurston, *Modernism, Inc.: Body, Memory, Capital* (New York: New York University Press, 2001), pp. 193–218.

Ross, Andrew: *The Failure of Modernism* (New York: Columbia University Press, 1986).

Scandura, Jani & Thurston, Michael: *Modernism, Inc.: Body, Memory, Capital* (New York: New York University Press, 2001).

Schedler, Christopher: *Border Modernism: Intercultural Readings in American Literary Modernism* (New York: Routledge, 2002).

Scott, Deborah Kime: *The Gender of Modernism* (Bloomington: Indiana University Press, 1990).

Smith, Terry: *Making the Modern: Industry, Art and Design in America* (Chicago: University of Chicago Press, 1993).

Soto, Michael: *The Modernist Nation: Generation, Renaissance, and Twentieth-Century American Literature* (Tuscaloosa: University of Alabama Press, 2004).

Stansell, Christine: *American Moderns: Bohemian New York and the Creation of a New Century* (New York: Metropolitan, 2000).

Stewart, Kathleen: "Machine Dreams," in Jani Scandura & Michael Thurston, *Modernism, Inc.: Body, Memory, Capital* (New York: New York University Press, 2001), pp. 21–8.

Stilgoe, John R.: *The Metropolitan Corridor: Railroads and the American Scene* (New Haven, CT: Yale University Press, 1983).

Susman, Warren I.: *Culture as History: The Transformation of American Society in the Twentieth Century* (New York: Pantheon, 1984).

Tichi, Cecilia: *Shifting Gears: Technology, Literature, Culture in Modernist America* (Chapel Hill: University of North Carolina Press, 1987).

Torgovnick, Marianna: *Primitive Passions* (New York: Alfred A. Knopf, 1997).

Wagner-Martin, Linda: *Ernest Hemingway: Seven Decades of Criticism* (East Lansing: Michigan State University Press, 1998).

Whitman, Walt: "To a Locomotive in Winter," in *Leaves of Grass* (New York: W. W. Norton, 2002 [1892]).

Williams, Raymond: *The Politics of Modernism* (London: Verso, 1989).

Chapter Fifteen

POLITICS AND CULTURE IN THE 1930S AND 1940S

Julia L. Foulkes

The noted historian Warren Susman once suggested that Mickey Mouse was more crucial to understanding the 1930s than Franklin D. Roosevelt (Susman 1984: 197). Provocation in place, cultural historians since have sought to prove, embellish, and modify that idea. An animated mouse with a heft stronger than a president gave cultural history real weight, an enticing proposition for historians studying pubs, dance halls, movies, sports, and all genres of the arts. Cultural historians have long worked to establish complex meanings for social and intellectual activities, but Susman's formulation accorded broad significance in addition to meaning. And his formulation seemed readily convincing in the case of the "red decade" of the 1930s, with its John Reed Clubs devoted to using literature to foster proletarian revolt, rancorous debates amongst critics in the *Partisan Review,* and the direct involvement of government in the arts through the Works Progress Administration (WPA). For historians seeking to uncover the political influences and ramifications of culture, the years of the 1930s and World War II offer ripe possibilities.

The 1930s began with examinations of the era just passed. The stock market crash of 1929 dramatized a moment when the recent past looked markedly different from the present. Although not nearly as drastic as it has become in memory, the stock market crash did accelerate changes already under way and a number of books published between 1929 and 1931 focused on the social and cultural changes that underlay the more dramatic economic and political ones. Books such as *Recent Economic Changes in the United States* (1929), *Recent Social Trends in the United States* (1933), Lynd & Lynd's *Middletown: A Study in American Culture* (1929), and the more colloquial *Only Yesterday* (1931) by Allen surveyed contemporary American society with the aim of understanding the daily lives of "average" Americans in all their habits. They employed new techniques and goals pioneered by sociologists and anthropologists, turning an eye to native rather than foreign lands and furthering a "scientific" approach to understanding society. These books serve as exemplary texts of Progressive-era thought in their use of quantitative methods, emphasis on change, and moral tone. They also reveal a society attuned to changes in the roles of men, women, immigrants, and African Americans; the relationship between government and its citizens; the increasingly visible economic and social importance of consumption; and the role of culture in shaping behavior and values. Young women bobbed their hair, washing machines appeared in more and more homes, and Ford's Model T represented the freedom and technological wizardry of a young nation beginning to take its place as a powerful economic and political player on the world stage.

Both overtly and more subtly, the books also revealed the issue around which many of the others whirled: the divisions of class. The dramatic economic ups and downs of the 1930s and 1940s marked the era. Americans have often worked hard to muddy class divisions with the rhetoric of American opportunity and a commitment to the possibility of "pulling yourself up by your own bootstraps." While this rhetoric remained strong during the era, it was inadequate to cover up the unprecedented bare poverty of the Great Depression. The struggles of the poor and the working classes, the appeal of socialism and communism, and the continued striving to become part of the middle class in the face of even greater obstacles dominated cultural activities.

The Red Decade

At the beginning of the era, hope lay in an unabashed embrace of communism. The John Reed Clubs, begun in 1929 by the Communist Party in the USA (CPUSA), captured the idealism and commitment to broad social change that had motivated John Reed in his short life to travel around the world and immerse himself in the Mexican and Russian revolutions. The clubs captivated young artists and intellectuals, providing a platform for young writers such as Richard Wright and an audience for more established writers such as Kenneth Burke. Many intellectuals and artists concerned with these ideas spent part of the 1920s in exile in Europe and returned to the USA in the late 1920s and early 1930s imbued with the possibilities of revolution. This particular brand of revolution, though, featured fewer marches and more novels and paintings than the recent Mexican and Russian revolutions. The John Reed Clubs launched the era's determination to find ways to use art and culture as weapons in a revolutionary class struggle (Cowley 1934; Aaron 1961; Pells 1973).

This determination resulted in novels about the struggles of workers, paintings that depicted oppressed peoples, and dances that showed masses moving in unison. Tillie Olsen's novel *Yonnondio* (first written in the early 1930s and added to and published in 1974) chronicled the impoverished life of men and women moving from a mining town to a farm and then to a city next to a slaughterhouse; Reginald Marsh's painting *Why Not Use the L?* (1930) featured a homeless man sleeping in the subway; and Helen Tamiris's *Revolutionary March* (1929) was a dance of defiance, a group of women with heads lifted and fisted arms piercing the air. Classes on political theory accompanied classes on dance technique at the Workers Dance League, and publications like the *New Masses* and *The Daily Worker*, the newspaper of the CPUSA, provided criticism that weighed the political impact of an artwork in addition to its aesthetics. Michael Gold, a novelist and editor of *The New Masses*, played a critical role in this movement through his popular novel *Jews without Money* (1930), his unremitting commitment to Marxism, and his ruthless focus on the political purposes of artworks. *Jews without Money* excoriated capitalism in its unvarnished depiction of ghettos as places of crime, disease, forced prostitution, and bitter unhappiness. And by incorporating Jews into this larger struggle, Gold demonstrated his belief in the diminishing importance of ethnicity in the face of the more inclusive and more urgent battle between class-based ideologies (Aaron 1961; Pells 1973; Denning 1997; Corn 2000).

In founding *The New Masses*, Gold pushed to print the literary work produced by workers rather than that of bourgeois liberals with leftist leanings. At the same time, unions promoted cultural activities for their members, such as participation in dance and theatrical events. As a weapon in the class struggle, seeing workers as artists was a recognition of the empowering nature of the arts. Not only could workers experience different roles for themselves beyond factory work and manual labor, but their products, the artworks themselves, would glisten with the authenticity of workers' voices. This strategy would insert the workers themselves in the process of production – in this case the making of art – and their artistic product would serve as a promotion of the quality and talent of workers' broad abilities (Denning 1997; Graff 1997).

But this effort received less attention and had less impact beyond individual workers' transformations than the political efforts of artists. Edith Segal, born on the Lower East Side to Russian Jewish parents and trained in dance at Henry Street Settlement House, choreographed *The Belt Goes Red* (1930) for the Lenin Memorial performance sponsored by the Communist Party at Madison Square Garden in 1930. Recreating an assembly line with dancers in stiff, calibrated movements representing the machine, the dance ended triumphantly as the dancers overtook the machine and covered it with a red cloth. Segal envisioned workers owning the product of their labors. Charlie Chaplin's *Modern Times* (1936), produced a few years later, offered a humorous, but trenchant, critique of the mechanization of human labor that did not end so optimistically. Based on his tour of the Ford automobile plant in the early 1920s, Chaplin's "dance of the machines" dramatized the sacrifices – inhuman, in his opinion – that factories demanded of their workers, as Chaplin's Tramp worked himself to the point of lunacy rather than triumph (Graff 1997; Ludington 2000: 153–74).

The attention to workers' issues went beyond utilizing that specific content in artworks, however. In the ferment of change at the end of the 1920s, as the economy boomed and then crashed, artists seized the opportunity to define a new role for the arts. *Revolt in the Arts* (Saylor 1930), a compendium of manifestoes by representatives of theater, film, dance, music, literature, and painting, advanced the idea that a refiguring was taking place across the arts. In creation, distribution, and appreciation of the arts, the essayists described a chaotic moment that manifested a revolution so complete that it introduced not just a new set of values and attitudes about the arts, but a new understanding of life itself. This tumult stirred up debates about the utility of the arts and artists tackled these questions that had been pushed into the public arena by the growing appeal of communism and socialism: Whom did the arts serve? What was their proper function in society? What was the relation between content and form? Were certain genres of the arts more effective than others in relaying political messages? What relation did an artist have to a factory worker? (Denning 1997; Foulkes 2002).

These questions mattered in a more tangible way when economic desperation and homelessness lurked around every corner. The economic realities of the Depression and the political failings of Presidents Coolidge and Hoover reinforced artists' and intellectuals' embrace of communism and socialism in the late 1920s and early 1930s. By 1934, however, ever-worsening economic troubles tested the idealism in political theories and the possibilities of the arts. Strict devotion to communism and socialism waned – while remaining an undercurrent in these debates – as artists and intellectuals such as the dancer Martha Graham and literary critic Philip Rahv pursued new ideas about the relations between individual and community and, in particular, how individuals could be linked to communities in beneficial ways. More abstract than the revolutionary rhetoric of Marxism, the work of these artists incorporated ideals of modernism in their stripping to essentials of form. Analogously, the particularities of class struggles morphed into a more general debate about the individual's relation to society. Moving beyond the autonomous, inward-looking, autocratic–individual strain of modernism, artists such as the painter Thomas Hart Benton and the writer John Steinbeck, influenced by the political questions of the day, tried to find ways to preserve the sanctity of the individual without succumbing to insularity (Aaron 1961; Pells 1973; Doss 1991; Corn 2000; Ludington 2000).

The common theme of the individual-in-the-group surfaced in novels and plays, such as Thornton Wilder's *Our Town*, which eulogized Americans' ability to establish communities of quirky individuals in both life and death. Paintings and murals by the regionalist school featured heroic collective scenes of workers and pioneers, such as Thomas Hart Benton's "Steel," which placed workers at the center of production in the mural *America Today* (1930). A new theatrical initiative of the era, The Group Theater, enacted its name, making collaborative productions often on political issues, such as Clifford Odets's *Waiting for Lefty* (1935). But the fullest formal exposition of this theme of the individual-in-the-group was in live performances of jazz and dance. Led by bandleaders like Benny Goodman and Duke Ellington, jazz orchestras in performance pushed at the limits of this theme with the improvisations of soloists melded into the swinging harmonies and sounds of the full group. Even more important, most jazz bands and the dance halls in which they performed were places of unprecedented racial integration. Barriers remained, particularly on tour when white and African American players were required to use different hotels and club entrances, but in the transitory performance of music or dance the theme of the fundamental reciprocity between individual and group became a lived reality. Solos allowed for individual expression, but instruments merged together again into the full orchestra – just as dance partners returned to each other after a breakaway moment of individual movement (Doss 1991; Stowe 1994; Erenberg 1998).

This ubiquitous characteristic of the cultural activities of the era – the dominance of the group – has been interpreted by scholars as evidence of the overt joining of politics and culture. Emerging from the more specific debate over class-based ideologies in the early years of the 1930s, the group continued to carry the political overtones of those debates. The purpose of a collective may no longer have been militant revolution but the belief in working together toward social change remained. The permutations of the joining of politics and culture, its meanings and ramifications, however, have inspired continued debate then and now. The dominant question in the scholarship has been: how deeply committed to leftist politics were these artists and intellectuals? Part of the reason for the dominance of that question arose in response to the withering attack of the first look back at the period, enduringly titled *The Red Decade* (1941). Journalist Eugene Lyons condemned artists for their devotion to the CPUSA, which, he believed, was ruled by the Soviet Union in an effort to influence US foreign policy. Artworks, then, were just another means of infiltration. As an earlier believer in much of what Russia epitomized, Lyons was typical of the fierce betrayal that many felt in the face of Stalin's increasing power and the signing of the Nazi–Stalin Pact of 1939. That perspective continued to inform the prevailing view of the decade during the McCarthy era, when critics assailed the misspent radicalism of the 1930s from the vantage point of the consensus-driven 1950s (Lyons 1941; Aaron 1961).

Daniel Aaron's *Writers on the Left* (1961) attempted to rectify the dismissal by Lyons of writers of the 1930s, not by agreeing with their communist sympathies but by exploring writers' attraction to and opinions of communism. Aaron promoted the idea of "fellow travelers" – those people who were influenced by the idea of communism or socialism but not necessarily Communist Party members or devotees of the Soviet Union. In Aaron's rendering, fellow travelers were not driven ideologues, and could not be categorized as having the blinding fervor of CPUSA members. Their cultural activities, then, deserved attention rather than dismissal. The spate of scholarly literature that followed Aaron's lead tended to acknowledge the political edge to these writers' work, neither embracing the political elements nor investigating the ramifications and meanings of the attention to politics too closely. Warren Susman, however, reckoned with the politics of the era in his essay, "Culture and Commitment," offering an interpretation that incorporated the radicalism by diluting it (Susman 1984: 184–210). Susman argued that politics itself was less important to most Americans – and even most writers and artists of the time – than the act of commitment to a cause. In the devotion to communism he saw commitment to a group, an action that provided meaning and purpose in desperate times. For him, the turn to American content and subject matter in the era proved this less fervid embrace of the politics of communism and socialism; nationalism, he argued, was the dominant ideology (Aaron 1961; Pells 1973; Susman 1984).

The American Way

"The American Way," a popular term of the era, captured the quest to find and define what made the United States unique. Although not new, this quest gained momentum with the proliferation of anthropology, which upheld the idea that different societies had distinct habits and values that made up a particular worldview. Two bestselling works – *Patterns of Culture* (1934) by Ruth Benedict and *American Humor* (1931) by Constance Rourke – exemplified this urge to explain the country to itself. Benedict looked at Native American cultures to determine a leading characteristic of the group, finding in Zuni Pueblos, for instance, a calming devotion to ritual; Rourke investigated literature for constant characters that conveyed humor, such as the bravado and exaggeration of the backwoodsman's tall tales. Comparative work on the Americas reinforced the effort to define America to itself. Stuart Chase's *Mexico: A Study of Two Americas* (1931) depicted the northern part of the Americas as dominated by technology, in contrast to the thriving folk traditions of the southern part of the hemisphere. Mexican muralist Diego Rivera painted this contrast in *Pan-American Unity* (1940) and suggested that each America could benefit from the patterns of the other. In these works, culture served not only as an explanatory tool but as an affirmation. Altering the meaning of culture from the elite arts to habits and values accorded culture broader power as a force that affected all people's lives. So the broader idea of culture, as well as the quest to define a distinctively American culture, as Susman argued, offered a way to unify Americans in their search for harmony and hope (Susman 1984; Fleischhauer & Brannan 1988: 15–42).

Changes in the policies of the CPUSA in the middle of the 1930s began to align the more radical political ideas of the early part of the decade with the growing efforts to define the American Way. In 1935 the Congress of the Communist International called for a Popular Front to combat the rise of fascism. Seeking to embolden communist parties within nations (and make more friendly those nations' relations with the Soviet Union), the Popular Front took a broader approach to doctrinaire communist policies. The Popular Front fostered an Americanization of communism with an emphasis on cultural questions and issues rather than party policy and discipline. Echoing the Popular Front strategy, artists and intellectuals with radical or proletarian sympathies shifted their attention from international revolution to American culture. The Popular Front reconceptualized the traditional Marxist theory of a world-wide struggle between classes into one refracted through nations (Pells 1973; Susman 1984).

This new cultural effort manifested itself in the formation of various congresses – a grouping together of artists of a particular genre. In May 1935 the first National Writers Congress met; in February 1936 the first American Artists Congress convened in New York City; and the first National Negro Congress met in Chicago. Instead of joining explicitly political organizations, such as the cultural branches of the Communist Party, artists formed organizations defined by their art form or race and worked for the betterment of their status. Sometimes this goal included specific political issues. The first National Writers Congress spoke out against discrimination of African American and minority groups, supported the labor movement, and, most strongly, denounced imperialism, fascism, war, and censorship. But it did not specify any specific political affiliation beyond these precepts. Though this strategy departed from strictly propagandist notions of using art only to relay a political message, it nevertheless demonstrated the extent to which social and political awareness was still incorporated within artists' missions (Aaron 1961; Denning 1997; Foulkes 2002).

European fascism prompted many artists to fuse nationalism with leftist political ideologies. The Spanish Civil War, in particular, sparked both political action – in the form of benefit performances, petitions, and political committees – and artwork with expressly political content. The dancer Anna Sokolow's *Excerpts from a War Poem* (1937), for instance, contained no battle scenes or pacifist polemic, but its five sections, organized around lines from a poem by the Italian poet F. T. Martinetti, contrasted the heroics celebrated in the poem with the chaos, despair, and suffering caused by war. Dancers moved spasmodically, crumpled by pain, frantic in chaos. In the face of fascism in Spain, Germany, and Italy, artists held up America and its version of democracy as the ideal by showing that fascism was nationalism gone awry. Radical political statements that highlighted class struggles faded as attention to nationalism grew in the volatile situation of world affairs, and trumpeting America's democratic tradition became the most common political position (Susman 1984; Graff 1997; Foulkes 2002).

New Deal Culture

The Americana impulse of the era received a significant boost from the federal government, particularly with the passage, in 1935, of the Works Progress Administration, which involved a $4.8 million appropriation for federal arts programs in Art, Music, Writers, and Theatre. Like many of the programs of the New Deal, the WPA was immediately pressured to build up its bureaucracy, hire people off the relief rolls to provide a weekly paycheck, and produce results within a few months. These programs were the first to provide the arts with the support and oversight of the federal government, and, given the enormous scale and the rapid timetable of the mission, they were quite successful. Within a few months of the bill's passage, writers began putting together guides to states and cities; painters were creating murals in post office buildings; musicians offered free concerts and classes; and actors staged productions based on headlines from the daily newspapers (Flanagan 1940; Marling 1982; Park & Markowitz 1984; Melosh 1991; Foulkes 2002).

If the first years of the 1930s began with workers becoming artists and unions offering their members ways to express themselves through the arts, the middle years of the decade were about artists becoming workers. A weekly paycheck buoyed struggling artists, providing a kind of stability previously unknown to their risky vocation. The question of who was worthy of this regular government paycheck, however, caused continuous rancor. Many argued that those artists who were on relief rolls were there because they lacked talent, not work. These artists, according to critics, should not be encouraged to produce work that would be considered representative of the USA and given public notice because of the prominence of the WPA. Established artists argued that they should be considered eligible for government aid by virtue of their talent, which qualified them to take part of this endeavor to create artworks for the public at large. The WPA struggled to mediate between these conflicting demands, often designating a percentage of workers that did not have to come from relief rolls so that well-known artists – such as Federal Theatre Project directors John Houseman and Orson Welles – could participate (Flanagan 1940; Melosh 1991).

Artists' overriding concern, however, was the risk of censorship by the federal government. They worried that if they accepted public monies, the government would dictate what they could and could not create. This concern was most evident – and most well placed, as it turned out – in the work of the Federal Theatre Project (FTP). Hallie Flanagan, the director of the project, immediately tested the issue with the formation of the Living Newspapers, theatrical events that pieced together a play from the stories of the daily papers. These productions relied on sparse sets, dramatic music, lights, movement, and impassioned actors. The first production, *Ethiopia*, scheduled for February 1936, depicted the recent invasion of Italy, using the words and recorded voices of Roosevelt, Mussolini, and Haile Selassie. In response to an order from Harry Hopkins, who oversaw the WPA, not to use actual recordings, the New York head of the project invited critics to see an unrevised preview performance of the production; the next day, the play's debut, he cancelled the entire production and resigned. The Living Newspapers continued, however, with *Triple-A Plowed Under* (1936), which dramatized the plight of farmers, and *One-Third of a Nation* (1938), which took words from Roosevelt's second inaugural address to highlight the extensiveness of poverty and need. But censorship issues dogged all the arts projects. Artists protested in front of WPA offices to decry censorship; then immediately turned around to protest budget cuts of their programs. Concerns about censorship warred with the need and desire to continue working and creating, an emblematic battle of government sponsorship of the arts (Flanagan 1940; Melosh 1991).

Perhaps least contentious were those projects that hewed closely to the commitment to revivify the country by offering visions of unity and accomplishment, uplifting the nation by piecing together its parts into a stronger whole. To that end, many of the projects advocated a close look at local and regional traditions. Murals in government buildings, which utilized this strategy, were one of the most successful efforts, pursued under the US Department of Treasury's Section of Painting and Sculpture, later renamed the Section of Fine Arts. Competition to pick the painter was a local affair, open to artists throughout the country but judged by regional juries, and the content of the mural usually focused on local history. *From Such Beginnings Sprang the Country of Lake, Indiana* (1938), by George Melville Smith in the post office of Crown Point, Indiana, depicted the encounter of Native Americans and white pioneers as the settling of the area; *Hauling Water Pipe Through Antelope Valley* (1941) by Jose Moya del Pino in the Lancaster, Calilfornia post office, dramatized the geographical realities of settling in that region (Marling 1982; Park & Moskowitz 1984).

Such regional work stimulated an exaltation of folk traditions. The most comprehensive study of American folk traditions occurred under the Federal Music Project in its recording of folk songs. Led by musicologist Alan Lomax, researchers found musicians, interviewed and photographed them, recorded their songs, compiled radio programs, and created the Archive of American Folk Song. Similarly, the Federal Arts Project initiated the Index of American Design, which employed over 300 artists to make hand copies of 22,000 objects that were considered American crafts. Not only did this project expand the category of art to include folk art, it also promoted the distribution of these images to a wider audience through purchase for personal display (Fleischhauer & Brannan 1988: 15–42; Doss 1991; Saab 2004).

During the years of the WPA, the national government became the largest and most significant patron of the arts and, in doing so, exposed the desperation, hopes, and contradictions of the era. In its attempts to create a national culture, the government reinforced local and regional distinctions. In its broad embrace of artists and artworks, it sanctioned an "official" New Deal culture. And in its advocacy of the democratizing powers of the arts, it revealed the internal contradictions of that effort: whereas art rested on the distinctiveness of individual creativity, skill, and special insight, democracy promoted the equality of all. Because of these contradictions – as well as the effort to continue despite them – the WPA projects have left a lasting and significant legacy as an initial foray into public art.

Documentation

The WPA gave the federal government a voice in the arts, but the artistic weapon that the government most often wielded was photography. New Deal agencies used photography more than any other genre to document social conditions, actions taken, and the ensuing results. While most branches of the government employed photographers in some capacity, the photographers of the Farm Security Administration (FSA) – including Walker Evans, Dorothea Lange, and Gordon Parks – stand out because of their talent and the vast range of their documentation. From 1935 until 1943, photographers working for the Resettlement Administration, Farm Security Administration, and then the Office of War Information, initially set out to capture government efforts to help farmers by securing loans and to settle migrants in planned suburban communities. Photographers then followed sharecroppers and the migration of agricultural workers from the South and Midwest to the West. The final years of the project focused on the growing war build-up and the movement of workers to cities. The photographs reveal a country on the move, from rural to urban, from wandering to settled, from desperation to hope. Unparalleled in scope and public access (the online catalog is available at www.loc.gov), the photographs provide a visual journey through the era (Stott 1973; Susman 1984; Fleischhauer & Brannan 1988).

The photographs do not, however, present unvarnished truth. Alan Trachtenberg has written insightfully on the FSA project (Trachtenberg 1988) by investigating the photographs themselves, the governmental oversight of the photographers, and the archival treatment of the photos. Taken together, these elements of the project embodied the prevailing beliefs in progress, universality, and objectivity. The project demonstrated the joining of two roles into one person: of the photographer and the social scientist, the artist and the activist. The manager of the project, for example, crafted a shooting script for the photographer before entering the field. The photographer, then, created a caption for each print and a report on each shoot. The words offered an alternative story to the photographs, which was sometimes dissonant, sometimes compatible. The archiving of the photos, too, revealed the twin goals of documentation and artistry. The administrators of the project created the blandest of descriptive categories to organize the photographs, first by geographical place and then by titles such as "Abandoned Building." This exposed the universalizing and objective stance of the overall project. The administration, however, also kept the photographers' rolls intact, showing the sequence of photographs on a particular shoot, which allowed viewers to construct another kind of narrative, one that betrayed more of the intentions and assumptions of the photographers (Fleischhauer & Brannan 1988: 43–73).

As with other New Deal projects, the FSA set out to affirm presumably American values that were rooted in a nostalgic view of rural America as separate from the world of commerce, a self-sustaining world that derived democratic and individualistic sovereignty from a close relationship to the land. That rural America was ending, and the FSA intended to capture its passing; the "truth" of pictures was a way to hold onto it. The valorization of pioneer and agricultural life was part of the attempt to inspire hope by manufacturing a continuity of images if not realities. The 1920 census had shown that more Americans lived in cities than in rural areas for the first time since the nation's founding, and the Depression only hastened the exodus from agricultural and town life to the city. Given that cities remained a place of fear, full of strangeness and strangers, the perceived simplicity and familiarity of rural life soothed many (Fleischhauer & Brannan 1988).

Documentation was the common way to convey these tangled needs. "Documentation" rather than "creation" pointed out what was already there, perhaps buried but idling, awaiting rediscovery. William Stott, in *Documentary Expression and Thirties America* (1973), expanded upon this theme of the era, recognizing that the documentary impulse dignified the ordinary and leveled the extraordinary. Documentation lent to commonplace subjects and topics a profundity usually attributed to art; it leveled social inequities by inspiring human empathy. As Trachtenberg's work on the FSA project has shown, however, documentation was far more calculating – with its cropped photographs, scripted narratives, staged scenes – than widely acknowledged. Documentation served as yet another stable belief, another anchor, in unsettled times. If somehow the "truth" could be revealed on a broad scale, the photographers believed, then surely solutions must follow (Stott 1973; Susman 1984; Fleischhauer & Brannan 1988).

A more critical look at this faith in documentation prompted some of the most trenchant works of the era, particularly at the end of the 1930s and in the early 1940s. Two works stand out for their perceptiveness in the nuances, difficulties, and hazards of documentation: the film *Sullivan's Travels* (1941) and the book *Let Us Now Praise Famous Men* (1941). *Sullivan's Travels*, written and directed by Preston Sturges, explored the desire to depict – and know – human suffering during the Depression. The plot concerned a filmmaker known for his popular comedies who sets out to make a movie about suffering. To do so, he becomes a bum so as to experience the real conditions of people in such dire straits. In a twisted case of mistaken identity, he is jailed for murder and on a rare night of entertainment for prisoners, he is awakened to the need for comedy in people's lives. He eventually returns to his privileged life more convinced of his usefulness as a filmmaker of comedies, giving up his intention to document the suffering of his fellow citizens. While the film appears to support the idea that movies provided escape during troubled times, it actually provides a more subtle commentary on the difficulty of portraying suffering. The character's walk through the lives of the homeless as a bum himself is one of the more effective parts of the movie, played against music with no dialogue, and portraying both destitution and fecklessness. Poignant as those minutes are, they are surrounded by scenes demonstrating the distance between the privileged and the poor, and the ultimate inability of the privileged few to change the lives of the many (Bergman 1971; Stott 1973; May 2000).

The complex issues raised by observation and documentation received closer and more insightful analysis from James Agee in *Let Us Now Praise Famous Men*, with photographs by Walker Evans. Agee framed the book around the ambiguous relation between photographs and their subjects, between reporters and the people reported upon, between writers and their words. The book serves as a long meditation on both the necessity and the limits of art and documentation. Agee is strenuously conscious of the ways in which he and Evans inevitably changed the scenes that they observed and described, and Agee wrote of that tension most evocatively in a passage about asking directions of an African American couple in the countryside. What was, from the documenters' point of view, a seemingly innocent request for directions was interpreted by the couple as a threat, vague but real enough to compel them to run through the woods (Agee & Evans 1941: 35–9). This kind of analysis framed the bulk of the text, which featured long and layered descriptions of clothing, furniture, work, houses, and family relations. The book revels in conjunctions between tortured analysis of the self as documenter and detailed description of objects. Agee attempted to both articulate and show the hypocrisy of documentation, particularly of a privileged person observing a poor one, and the inevitable failure to convey human complexity. If Agee and Evans fall on the side of idealism, a full-hearted endorsement of the dignity and good of humans and avoidance of the possibility of evil, they did so as a conscious and considered choice (Stott 1973; Susman 1984; Fleischhauer & Brannan 1988).

Whose America?

The urge to document captured many realities of the era, some unintentionally. If a search for the American way prompted both the attempts to record and to create, the resulting documentaries demonstrated the variety of people left out of many definitions of America. Certainly public attention shifted to the poor in the midst of the Depression, and recognition of the divisions between classes generated new understandings of the lack of opportunities that shaped many people's lives. The light shed on this inequality led to newly configured responsibilities of the government to its citizens. While the development of a larger welfare system may be the most long-lasting political achievement of the New Deal, the focus on inequalities also opened up debates about who did and did not participate fully in the possibilities of the USA. Women, African Americans, gay men and lesbians, Jews, Latino/as, Asians, political radicals and conservatives: whose America was it?

Warren Susman argued that the white middle classes deserved close scholarly attention in this era because it was they who experienced the greatest shock of the Depression, going from relatively prosperous, optimistic times to radically narrowed opportunities. His examination of the middle classes convinced him that the idea of commitment proved more significant than the specific ideas and activities to which people committed; politics was less important than community. Scholars since Susman have focused on variations within the middle classes – such as gender – or alternatively on other social classes, and come to varying conclusions. In a thorough look at New Deal art and theater, Barbara Melosh in *Engendering Culture* (1991) furthered Susman's view by arguing that these works presented a domesticated version of pioneer life, with women cast as pacifist mothers, and the complementarity of male and female figures as an expression of genial collectivity. Research on modern dance, for example, has countered those images, presenting confrontational women and much more conflicted gender relations (Susman 1984; Melosh 1991; Graff 1997; Foulkes 2002).

Susman's interpretation has drawn more criticism than support, particularly from scholars who have looked beyond the white middle classes. Lewis Erenberg in *Swingin' the Dream* (1998) and David Stowe in *Swing Changes* (1994), for example, demonstrate the bridge that jazz music provided for racial integration, a bridge constructed by people such as record producer and promoter John Hammond whose radical politics reinforced his artistic choices. Most of the major jazz musicians of the day, including Count Basie, Benny Carter, Artie Shaw, Sidney Bechet, and Duke Ellington, played at benefits for the *New Masses* and rallies for the defendants in the Scottsboro trial. Similarly, Lary May in *The Big Tomorrow* (2000) finds that movies of the era inflected with political radicalism also conveyed a social radicalism in their diverse portrayals of America that featured more African Americans, women, and ethnic groups. In the figure of Will Rogers, May sees an emblem of the pluralism at the heart of characterizations of the USA during this period, exemplified by Rogers's trumpeting of his Native American and working-class heritage. Lizabeth Cohen's research on the development of a workers' culture from the 1920s to the 1930s in *Making a New Deal* (1990) traces a relocation of working-class affinities from local organizations such as employers' welfare programs and ethnic organizations to a growing, national commercial culture that consolidated in the 1930s. This more national culture, best exemplified in movies and radio, she argues, allowed workers to overcome ethnic fragmentation and stage more unified and effective political action in the 1930s (Cohen 1990; Stowe 1994; Erenberg 1998; May 2000).

Michael Denning's *The Cultural Front* (1997) expands Cohen's argument into the most thorough response to Susman's claim. Denning replaces Mickey Mouse as the reigning symbol of the era with the Congress of Industrial Organizations (CIO), categorizing the era as the "laboring" of American culture. In Denning's view, neither conservative commitment nor a simple adherence to the Communist Party characterized the cultural politics of the 1930s. Instead, he sees fellow travelers, not as weaker adherents to Communist Party policy, tagging along with others without coherent purpose, but as all-important advocates of a more expansive leftist orientation of US culture, reflected in a pervasive infusion of the symbols and ideas of radical political ideologies, unionism, and striving for workers' rights. Denning thus moves beyond other scholars' fixation on Party membership and control of cultural policy, to uncover a broader move leftward (Denning 1997).

Denning substantiates his argument by detailing the simultaneous development of the Popular Front with the rise of "cultural apparatus," the structural and institutional elements of state and commercial cultural industries (Denning 1997: 38–50). The resulting Cultural Front assumed a variety of forms: a proletarian avant-garde that created little magazines, art schools, and workers' theater; the educational, artistic, and recreational initiatives of labor unions and the Communist Party; the formation of state agencies, primarily the arts projects of the WPA, that gave institutional power to working-class concerns; and the rise of the film, radio, and music industries that not only employed more and more workers but also incorporated and disseminated many of the views of more radical artists and intellectuals. The Cultural Front, then, was marked by its infiltration into all aspects of US culture, and by the variety of people who mobilized it, from labor feminist writer Elizabeth Hawes to singer Billie Holiday, Filipino writer Carlos Bulosan, and activist Ernesto Galarza.

If Denning and others restore the importance of radical politics to the culture of the1930s, they do not reaffirm the charges of "un-Americanness" that dominated earlier views of the decade's radical politics. Instead, recent scholars redefine the American Way: not as the collective commitment of the white, conservative middle classes, but as a contentious debate of a pluralistic, politically engaged, broad range of intellectuals, artists, workers, and audiences that altered US culture for decades to come. By continuing to focus on how red the "red decade" really was, scholars are reinforcing the centrality of that question for an understanding of the era.

At War

The debate also continues about whether the radicalness of the 1930s extended into the years of World War II. The war often serves as a facile way for historians to mark significant social and cultural changes, and the decline of radicalism in the face of impending war is a primary example of this tendency. But even the short life of the New Deal programs demonstrates the inexact marker that the war provides. Throughout the 1930s, the WPA was constantly attacked, its budget cut, and its politics investigated. The hearings of the Dies Committee on the Federal Theatre Project in 1937 fomented the beginnings of anti-communism that would end in the McCarthy hearings in the early 1950s. Despite the congressional rescinding of money for the FTP in 1939, other WPA projects were only slowly squeezed of funding until the formal end of the initiative in June 1943. Even then, the Office of War Information continued some projects, particularly the employment of photographers to document the home front and war-production industries (Lipsitz 1994; Erenberg & Hirsch 1996; Denning 1997).

In many ways, the war reinforced those representations of pluralism that cultural ventures of the 1930s had promoted. In movies, music, radio programs, and dance, however, that pluralism was no longer a contentious struggle centered on working-class concerns. Instead, pictures flourished of a harmonious and unified pluralism in support of the war effort. One of the most notable examples of this new emphasis was changing images of women. Smiling Rosie the Riveter reveling in her strength replaced Dorothea Lange's resignedly suffering "Migrant Mother." While both images granted women a strength not seen in the conventional role of pliant housewife, the Migrant Mother, haunted by the father's absence, suggested the instability of family life in the midst of poverty and migration; whereas Rosie the Riveter provided a more direct support of men, and presaged the more powerful image of the nuclear family that would triumph after the war. During the Depression, women often found ways to support the family through small jobs outside of the agricultural or factory economy, and endured public warnings not to emasculate their men. The rise of the war industry not only provided men with purposeful, important duties, but offered women factory jobs in support of men on the battlefields (Erenberg & Hirsch 1996; Foulkes 2002).

In the 1940s, more celebratory pictures of America replaced earlier visions that had criticized the government, appealed for greater economic and racial justice, and called for a more combative democratic tradition. Musicals that centered on entertaining troops, such as *This Is the Army* (1943), presented comic visions of the USA that stressed the unity of its people and the freedoms of its democracy. Films like *Bataan* (1943), according to Lary May, showed that American military strength came from its diverse platoon of soldiers, including African Americans and Mexican Americans. Lewis Erenberg finds the "sweet" jazz of Glenn Miller soothed the edges of improvisation in jazz and orchestrated the big band into a melodious whole swinging together rather than a more stratified melding of individual instrumental voices (Black & Koppes 1987; Berube 1990; Erenberg 1998; May 2000).

Miller's music and band, in fact, retreated from the racial integration that was so notable in jazz in the 1930s. In contrast to Miller, African American musicians in the 1940s delved further into improvisation and developed the style of be-bop. The place of African Americans in the cultural work of the war demonstrated both the persistence of segregation and a renewed determination to strive for civil rights which would explode into activism in the 1950s. Alan Brinkley has argued that the strengthening of liberalism that occurred through the New Deal and the war effort resulted in a diminishing of class and gender concerns and a growing attention to racial and ethnic issues (Erenberg & Hirsch 1996: 313–30). In his view, the politics of race and ethnicity became the radical issues of the day during – and especially after – the war. The triumph of New Deal liberalism ensured the weakening of class-consciousness and struggle that synthesized the social issues of the 1930s; racial and ethnic justice overwhelmed arguments for economic redistribution and gender equality in the 1940s. Other scholars, most notably Denning, have countered that class-consciousness was embedded in all of these issues to a much greater extent than has been recognized. In fact, the war years have suffered from comparatively little scholarly attention, perhaps because of the tendency to use decades as markers and to set the war off as a distinctive experience untied to what came before or after. Following some of the benchmarks that Denning provides, such as closer investigations of the ties between state and commercial cultural industries and uncovering the local-level connections between workers rights' activists and artists, should lead to more specificity about the effects of the war on cultural production (Erenberg & Hirsch 1996; Denning 1997; May 2000).

Whether emphasizing cultural continuity or discontinuity from the 1930s into the war years, scholarship on the 1940s illuminates the distinctiveness of the previous decade. The years of the Great Depression and New Deal have captured a great deal of scholarly attention and debate – and secured a place in the cultural history of the USA as one of the few periods of undisputed politicization of cultural and artistic activities. The economic disaster of the Great Depression unsettled so much that arts and culture flourished with unparalleled intensity and importance. The cultural activities of the decade offered both ways to escape those realities, and ways to face, conquer, and reimagine social problems. Men, destitute but famous in Agee's eyes; women, resigned and strong, from Dorothea Lange's "Migrant Mother" to Rosie the Riveter; African Americans, resolute in the face of oppression, lindy hoppin' to the wailing of Louis Armstrong's trumpet and the beat of Chick Webb's drums; and Mr. Smith going to Washington and reviving democracy for all: these are iconic images of Americans, forged in a time of fear and hopelessness. Mickey Mouse may not fully succeed in displacing Franklin D. Roosevelt as the most critical figure of the era, but the cacophony of sounds, images, texts, movements, and spectacles created a cultural surge that expressed the political laborings of the era and has given American culture the undeniable, and enduring, force of a nation struggling to overcome economic collapse, fight a world war, and emerge more powerful than ever.

REFERENCES

Aaron, D.: *Writers on the Left: Episodes in American Literary Communism* (New York: Harcourt, Brace & World, 1961).

Agee, J. & Evans, W.: *Let Us Now Praise Famous Men* (New York: Houghton Mifflin, 1941).

228 JULIA L. FOULKES

Allen, F. L.: *Only Yesterday: An Informal History of the 1920s* (New York: Harper & Brothers, 1931).

Benedict, R.: *Patterns of Culture* (New York: Houghton Mifflin, 1934).

Bergman, A.: *We're in the Money: Depression America and Its Films* (New York: New York University Press, 1971).

Berube, A.: *Coming Out Under Fire: The History of Gay Men and Women in World War II* (New York: Free Press, 1990).

Black, G. & Koppes, C.: *Hollywood Goes to War: How Politics, Profits and Propaganda Shaped World War II Movies* (Berkeley: University of California Press, 1987).

Chase, S.: *Mexico: A Study of Two Americas* (New York: Macmillan, 1931).

Cohen, L.: *Making a New Deal: Industrial Workers in Chicago, 1919–39* (New York: Cambridge University Press, 1990).

Corn, W.: *The Great American Thing: Modern Art and National Identity, 1915–35* (Chicago: University of Chicago Press, 2000).

Cowley, M.: *Exile's Return* (New York: W. W. Norton, 1934).

Denning, M.: *The Cultural Front: The Laboring of American Culture in the Twentieth Century* (New York: Verso, 1997).

Doss, E.: *Benton, Pollock, and the Politics of Modernism: From Regionalism to Abstract Expressionism* (Chicago: University of Chicago Press, 1991).

Erenberg, L.: *Swingin' the Dream: Big Band Jazz and the Rebirth of American Culture* (Chicago: University of Chicago Press, 1998).

Erenberg, L. & Hirsch, S., eds.: *The War in American Culture: Society and Consciousness during World War II* (Chicago: University of Chicago Press, 1996).

Flanagan, H.: *Arena* (New York: Duell, Sloan and Pearce, 1940).

Fleischhauer, C. & Brannan, B. W., eds.: *Documenting America, 1935–43* (Berkeley: University of California Press in association with the Library of Congress, 1988).

Foulkes, J. L.: *Modern Bodies: Dance and American Modernism from Martha Graham to Alvin Ailey* (Chapel Hill: University of North Carolina, 2002).

Fraser, S. & Gerstle, G., eds.: *The Rise and Fall of the New Deal Order, 1930–1989* (Princeton, NJ: Princeton University Press, 1989).

Gold, M.: *Jews Without Money* (New York: H. Liveright, 1930).

Graff, E. *Stepping Left: Dance and Politics in New York City, 1928–1942* (Durham, NC: Duke University Press, 1997).

Lipsitz, G.: *Rainbow at Midnight: Labor and Culture in the 1940s* (Urbana: University of Illinois Press, 1994).

Ludington, T., ed.: *A Modern Mosaic: Art and Modernism in the United States* (Chapel Hill: University of North Carolina Press, 2000).

Lynd, R. & Lynd, H.: *Middletown: A Study in American Culture* (New York: Harcourt, Brace, 1929).

Lyons, E.: *The Red Decade: The Stalinist Penetration of America* (Indianapolis: Bobbs-Merrill, 1941).

Marling, K. A.: *Wall-to-Wall America: A Cultural History of Post Office Murals in the Great Depression* (Minneapolis: University of Minnesota Press, 1982).

May, L.: *The Big Tomorrow* (Chicago: University of Chicago Press, 2000).

Melosh, B.: *Engendering Culture: Manhood and Womanhood in New Deal Public Art and Theater* (Washington, DC: Smithsonian Institution Press, 1991).

Olsen, T.: *Yonnondio: From the Thirties* (New York: Delacorte Press, 1974).

Park, M. & Markowitz, G. E.: *Democratic Vistas: Post Offices and Public Art in the New Deal* (Philadelphia: Temple University Press, 1984).

Pells, R.: *Radical Visions and American Dreams: Culture and Social Thought in the Depression Years* (New York: Harper & Row, 1973).

President's Conference on Unemployment: *Recent Economic Changes in the United States* (New York: McGraw-Hill, 1929).

President's Research Committee on Social Trends: *Recent Social Trends in the United States* (New York: McGraw-Hill, 1933).

Rourke, C.: *American Humor: A Study of the National Character* (New York: Harcourt Brace, 1931).

Saab, A. J.: *For the Millions: American Art and Culture between the Wars* (Philadelphia: University of Pennsylvania Press, 2004).

Saylor, O.: *Revolt in the Arts* (New York: Brentano's, 1930).

Stott, W.: *Documentary Expression and Thirties America* (New York: Oxford University Press, 1973).

Stowe, D.: *Swing Changes: Big Band Jazz in New Deal America* (Cambridge, MA: Harvard University Press, 1994).

Susman, W.: *Culture as History: The Transformation of American Society in the Twentieth Century* (New York: Pantheon Books, 1984).

Trachtenberg, A.: "From Image to Story: Reading the File," in C. Fleischhauer & B. W. Brannan, eds., *Documenting America, 1935–43* (Berkeley: University of California Press in association with the Library of Congress, 1988), pp. 43–73.

Chapter Sixteen

THE 1950S AND 1960S

Daniel Belgrad

Cultural historians have begun to recover the complexity of a period that for many years was seen only in the mirrors of its self-celebration and self-critique. From "affluence" and "anxiety" to "conformity" and "counterculture," the words we still use to map the era are often relics of the social and cultural changes they purport to describe. We cling to them in part because the cultural struggles they represent continue into the present.

The fight against world communism nurtured a culture of "political realism" that had developed in America during World War II (Craig 2003). Americans imagined themselves as an idealistic people prone to naïveté. This was understood to be the lesson of Pearl Harbor as well as the lesson of American communism (as presented in *The God That Failed*, a collection of essays by ex-communists, edited by Richard Crossman, 1950). As reiterated in numerous private-eye, western, and war movies of the period, the world envisioned by political realists was a harsh one in which people betrayed others to get what they needed and the wisest course was not to trust anyone too quickly. The heroes of such genre films were "hard-boiled" men like Humphrey Bogart's Philip Marlowe in *The Big Sleep* (1946), who buried their ideals beneath savvy and invulnerable exteriors (Palmer 1994; Coyne 1997). The most enduring icon of this type in westerns and war movies was John Wayne.

America's international assertiveness in the postwar world was not, however, fundamentally a conservative position. It was championed by an array of centrists or "corporate liberals" who grasped the possibility to remake the postwar world in America's image. Luce's influential call for an "American century" in the pages of *Life* magazine (1941) was repeated in many variations over these decades, including the traveling USIA (United States Information Agency) photographic exhibit *The Family of Man* (Sandeen 1995). It added an ethnocentric note to a universalist doctrine: all people wanted the same things in life, and America demonstrated how to get them. Liberals believed in the benefits of advanced technology, the economic relations of corporate capitalism, and the separation of church and state. This cultural and economic package was exported to the developing nations of Latin America, Africa, Asia, and the Middle East. By the mid-1950s, however, it was evident that Third World leaders had become adept at playing the superpowers against each other for maximum benefit (Karabell 1999).

The frustrations of American foreign policy were a major source of anxiety. The atomic bomb's promise of omnipotence quickly decayed once the Soviet Union developed atomic weapons and locked horns with the USA in a pattern of "mutually assured destruction" (Winkler 1993). Civil defense films, several of which have been collected in the documentary video *The Atomic Café* (1982), suggest that the saccharine mood of the era, lampooned by later generations, was recognized by contemporaries as contrived, but still served as a psychological defense against anxiety. Scares over toxic radioactive fallout (detected in tuna fish, wheat, milk, and mother's breast milk in the mid-1950s and measured euphemistically in "sunshine units") epitomized the nature and causes of this anxiety: fallout was everywhere and its effects were unknown. The dilemma involved in poisoning Americans in order to protect them gave rise to the first major political movement of dissent from the Cold War consensus: the "Ban the Bomb" marches of the late 1950s. Backyard fallout shelters concretized a fantasy of sheltering one's near and dear from the anticipated general apocalypse through sacrifice, preparedness, and the moral resolve to shut the door against importunate neighbors (Oakes 1994).

Anxiety and moral conflict also suffused the postwar "Red Scare." Americans interviewed by the FBI (Federal Bureau of Investigation) or called to testify before Congressional committees were forced to choose whether or not to "name names" – that is, to prove their patriotism by offering the investigators other possible targets of investigation (Navasky 1980). Historians debate the degree of threat posed by actual communist espionage. But the scope of the anti-communist investigations and the lack of due process in the compilation of "blacklists" cut a broad and damaging swath through American intellectual and cultural circles (Fariello 1995). In the early 1950s, leftist writers and artists traded coded salvos over the rightness or wrongness of the anti-communist cause – most famously, Arthur Miller's *The Crucible* (1953) and Elia Kazan's response *On the Waterfront* (1954).

Though originating in anxiety, the drama of the space race ultimately unfolded as a reassuring spectacle of American supremacy. During World War II the Germans had used rockets to deliver bombs; Wernher von Braun surrendered to the Americans in 1945, and his V-2 rocket became the basis of the Atlas missile and Mercury space programs. In the mid-1950s, von Braun teamed up with Walt Disney to convince Americans that space exploration was more reality than fantasy; Disney produced a series of television specials on the benefits of space exploration, and von Braun's rocket design became the centerpiece of Disneyland's Tomorrowland (McCurdy 1997). The Soviet launch of Sputnik in 1957 induced massive Congressional appropriations for NASA and the National Defense Education Act; as a result, space exploration became a potent symbol of the technocratic vision that Kennedy described as the "New Frontier." The astronaut joined the cowboy as an American icon. As opposed to the cowboy's mythical self-sufficiency, the astronaut faced his frontier supported by an army of technicians and computers, inside a spacesuit that transformed him visually into a cyborg symbolizing the possibilities of human integration with high technology. Science fiction provided a venue for debating the wisdom of delegating decision-making power to technocrats and their machines (Seed 1999).

The economic theories of John Maynard Keynes pointed to federal spending during the war years as the main reason for the end of the Great Depression. Cold War military spending and foreign aid helped to create a "permanently mobilized"

economy and avert a postwar recession (Lipsitz 1982). Other elements of the permanently mobilized economy included the Taft–Hartley Act of 1947 (which effectively
extended the wartime "no-strike pledge" of organized labor) and research-and-
development funding for military technologies with commercial applications. William
Levitt, for instance, solved the postwar housing shortage by applying the mass-
production techniques he had learned building Navy bases in the Pacific to the creation of suburban "Levittowns." Almost one-third of the population would eventually
live in the 20 million suburban homes created by Levitt and his imitators. The federal
government subsidized the suburbanization of America through tax breaks for home
owners, mortgage insurance that allowed affordable payment plans, and a new inter-
state highway system (Jackson 1985). Ultimately, the engineered affluence of "mass
middle-class" suburbia came to symbolize the rewards of the American way of life, as
the Nixon–Khrushchev "kitchen debate" of 1959 attested (Hine 1986).

After the social dislocations of Depression and war, suburban Americans were
eager to return to domestic normalcy, and their fantasy of it tended to be exaggerated, with parents and children assuming clearly demarcated roles (Weiss 2000). Dad
was to be the breadwinner; Mom, the homemaker; childhood was sentimentalized
(Coontz 1992). Television situation comedies helped suburbanites distance themselves from their urban and rural pasts and acculturate to the new suburban lifestyle
(Lipsitz 1990). Television's aura of intimacy made it uniquely compatible with the
sentimental ideal of the 1950s family (Spigel 1992). In 1952, Richard Nixon saved
his position as Eisenhower's running mate by making a sentimental appeal to American television viewers invoking the family dog, "Checkers."

Design and fashion in the 1950s echoed the themes of space-age optimism and
suburban sentimentality. The "New Look" in women's fashions emphasized femininity, exaggerating the narrowness of shoulders and waists and the wideness of breasts
and hips (Steele 1997). The resulting "hourglass figure" was popularized by such
period icons as Marilyn Monroe, Walt Disney's Sleeping Beauty, and Mattel's Barbie.
The promise of advanced technology to improve the everyday lives of individuals (in
the famous slogan of the Du Pont corporation, "Better living through chemistry")
was manifest in the bright colors and easy-care instructions of synthetic fabrics like
acrylic and polyester. A revolution in plastics spawned linoleum and fiberglass, which
were celebrated as harbingers of the high-tech "world of tomorrow" (Meikle 1995).
This futuristic narrative was reinforced by design elements that included geometric
shapes, starbursts, atomic orbitals, boomerangs, and fins. From its epicenter in Southern California, a futuristic architecture spread across the American landscape, most
fully realized in the Theme Building at the Los Angeles airport (1961) and the Seattle
Space Needle (1962), but integrated into the American vernacular through countless
motels, fast-food restaurants, and roadside signs in a style that has come to be called
"googie" (Hess 1986). Googie employed starbursts, boomerangs, and upswept
entrances to catch the eyes of passing motorists on the roadside "strip." The "golden
arches" of McDonald's restaurants and the blinking arrow of the Holiday Inn sign
are among its best-known examples.

While googie invoked a space-age future, "tiki" fed fantasies of primitive paradise
(Klein 2003). Rumors of tropical Polynesian islands brought back by returning
servicemen were seconded by James Michener's Pulitzer prize-winning bestseller
Tales of the South Pacific (1948), which was adapted into a popular Rodgers and

Hammerstein musical. In addition, Thor Heyerdahl's quasi-scientific Kon-Tiki expedition, intended to prove that the islands of the South Pacific had been peopled by Native Americans and not by Asians, fed Americans' proprietary interest in the Pacific islands and gave the annexation and statehood of Hawaii an aura of poetic justice. The Trader Vic's restaurant chain was foremost in codifying the vocabulary that came to signify "Polynesian paradise," replete with invented "exotic" cocktails like the Mai Tai (which was introduced by Trader Vic's to Hawaii in 1953). The mystique of Tahiti and Honolulu could be brought home through simple props like tiki torches, leis, and Hawaiian shirts, transforming a backyard barbecue into a luau. The bikini bathing suit, though it alluded to the atomic bisection of Bikini atoll, was more tiki than googie.

Backyard barbecues, lawn work and the do-it-yourself movement that turned countless suburban garages into amateur carpenters' workshops gave suburban men opportunities to exercise and confirm their masculinity, as if to compensate for the changing nature of middle-class jobs in American society. The creation of the mass middle class was accompanied by a multiplication of the number of men working in large, bureaucratically managed corporations. The Taft–Hartley Act paved the way for the incorporation of blue-collar workers into the suburban ranks, under the condition that they forego strikes in favor of protracted negotiations – an arrangement that maximized productivity but deprived workers of the "manly" satisfaction of standing up to the boss (Geoghegan 1991). Moreover, the increase of management positions meant that many other men were entering white-collar jobs for the first time; it was difficult for them to feel manly doing work that did not involve sweating or manual labor. For those already established in the middle class, the concentration of economic power fostered by the permanently mobilized economy meant an end to small, independently owned businesses; those who associated masculinity with autonomy and self-sufficiency had to adjust to working in the corporate bureaucracy (Lipsitz 1982). David Riesman's seminal study *The Lonely Crowd* (1950) chronicled the emergence of a new character type that he termed "other directed": as opposed to the "inner directed," self-made man of a previous era, the new white-collar man was highly attuned to the needs and opinions of others. Although Riesman's analysis was not pejorative, popular portrayals emphasized the erosion of masculinity. In *White Collar* (1951), C. Wright Mills wrote that such workers sold their personalities as well as their time and energy: they had to be charming (traditionally a feminine attribute) in order to succeed. The fictional protagonist of Sloan Wilson's *The Man in the Gray Flannel Suit* (1955) no longer commanded the respect of his wife and children. William Hollingsworth Whyte's *Organization Man* (1956) portrayed the new white-collar worker as a personality type ripe for totalitarianism: a conformist who wanted to be told what to do and who was above all else loyal to the organization. As Jack Lemmon lamented in the film *The Apartment* (1960), "I'm the kind of guy who can't say no."

Some explanations for the perceived crisis of masculinity blamed American women rather than the workplace. Men were weak, it was argued, because their women were domineering. Women who had learned independence during the war years were seen as a threat to American manhood and a violation of the natural order. Philip Wylie's classic statement of "momism," *A Generation of Vipers* (1942), was reissued in 1955. The dime-novel detective fiction of Mickey Spillane reveled in thinly veiled sadism directed against assertive females, while the movie *The Manchurian Candidate* (1962) effectively linked momism to totalitarianism through the image of "brainwashing." Another version of the misogynist myth vilified homemakers as manipulative opportunists who saddled their men with debts and children. This was the premise of Hugh Hefner's *Playboy* magazine (1953), which offered men an alternative to the traditional "breadwinner" path to social status by constructing a masculinity based on connoisseurship and casual sex (Ehrenreich 1983). An image of masculinity similar to that of the playboy was promulgated by the "rat pack" trio of Frank Sinatra, Dean Martin, and Sammy Davis, Jr. Their milieu of Las Vegas nightclubs, black tuxedos, mixed drinks, and womanizing represented a white-ethnic ideal of masculine sophistication – Sammy Davis Jr.'s skin color notwithstanding (Pugliese 2004).

The rise to prominence of the "white ethnics" – particularly Irish and Italian Catholics, and Jews – was a defining feature of postwar American culture, as those descendants of nineteenth-century immigrant groups challenged the historical ascendancy of the white Anglo-Saxon Protestant (WASP) elite. In 1955, Will Herberg published *Protestant–Catholic–Jew*, in which he described mid-century America as a "triple melting pot" where ethnic distinctions among those of European origin were discarded in favor of these equally liberal and equally American religious categories. In retrospect, Herberg's work reads as wishful thinking on the part of an assimilated Jew: in fact, the mutual acceptance of WASPs and white ethnics was only skin-deep, and old prejudices surfaced regularly in politics and literature, universities and country clubs. Bestselling novels about World War II – including Norman Mailer's *The Naked and the Dead* (1947), James Jones's *From Here to Eternity* (1951), and Harriette Arnow's *The Dollmaker* (1954) – portrayed both the battlefield and the home front as sites of internecine ethnic rivalries. An ethnic dimension also colored the fight between the federal government and organized crime, which pitted the FBI's all-American "G-men" against the "un-Americanism" of crime syndicates and local political machines associated in the public imagination – and often in fact – with Irish, Italian, and Jewish ethnic groups. As America's first Catholic President, John F. Kennedy felt compelled to distance himself from the political baggage of his white-ethnic past – his father had ties to the Chicago gangster Sam Giancana (Pugliese 2004). White-ethnic rivalries were also played out through anti-communism: for if organized crime was the skeleton in the closet of Catholic politics, past communist affiliations were the albatross of the Jews (Bloom 1986). Joseph McCarthy built on a heritage of Catholic anti-communism bequeathed by the anti-Semitic Depression-era radio priest Father Charles Coughlin (Fisher 1997). Whittaker Chambers, a Jew, grasped his opportunity to prove himself a repentant ex-communist by fingering Alger Hiss, a prominent WASP, in 1948; in his memoir *Witness* (1952), Chambers compared his patriotism to his religious faith. Finally, "triple melting pot" dynamics entered into the "quiz show" and "payola" scandals of the late 1950s and early 1960s. In the former, WASP English professor Charles Van Doren of Columbia University was brought low for cheating at a television game show by two Jews, Herbert Stempel and Richard Goodwin (Goodwin later wrote the script for the 1994 film *Quiz Show*, which acknowledged both the ethnic dimension of the scandal and its parallels to McCarthyism). In the payola scandal, Alan Freed, the Jewish disc jockey who brought Negro rock and roll to the attention of white teenagers, bore the brunt of a Congressional investigation into corruption in the music industry.

Sometimes intersecting with this cultural power struggle among WASPs and white ethnics was one between "highbrows" and "middlebrows." While the general affluence of the postwar period obscured class divisions, the proliferation of mass culture that accompanied it prompted a reinscription of social distinctions in cultural terms, as a cultural elite defended its "higher" tastes, whether modern or genteel, against the onslaught of the new mass culture. Highbrows and middlebrows each represented their particular canon of taste as the necessary basis of American democracy, with the former championing subtlety, and the latter, accessibility. As the GI Bill encouraged the expansion of the American university system, the highbrow position was institutionalized in academia (Jacoby 1987), most explicitly in the cultural criticism of such theoretical sociologists as Dwight Macdonald, C. Wright Mills, Marshall McLuhan, and members of the Frankfurt School (including Erich Fromm, Theodor Adorno, and Herbert Marcuse). Highbrows condemned middlebrow media like television, popular music, and mass-circulation magazines for encouraging conformity, sadomasochism, and poor reasoning, thereby transforming America's citizenry into "cheerful robots" (Gorman 1996). In response, middlebrow advocates like journalist Russell Lynes and painter Norman Rockwell satirized highbrow culture as antidemocratic and purposely obscure (Belgrad 1998).

The discourse of analytical psychology was powerful enough to transcend the highbrow/middlebrow divide. From Alfred Hitchcock's *Spellbound* (1945) to Perls et al.'s *Gestalt Therapy* (1951), multiple sources fed Americans' excitement over the potential of the unconscious mind to shape lived experience. The ability of neo-Freudian psychotherapy to address contemporary issues as diverse as "brainwashing," criminality, and homosexuality gave it considerable popular authority (Herman 1995). This psychotherapeutic authority was liberal: its impulse was to understand and cure rather than enforce and punish; and it thus challenged older, more conservative forms of social authority. This conflict was represented formulaically in the plot triangles of numerous B-movies, which pitted psychologists against police in the pursuit of justice, or scientists against soldiers in encounters with aliens (Biskind 1983). In childrearing, the neo-Freudian approach focused on the quality of the emotional relations between parent and child: Benjamin Spock's bestselling *Common Sense Book of Baby and Childcare* (1946) advised parents to communicate with their children and respond to their needs rather than enforce strict discipline.

Despite – or perhaps because of – this new vision of emotionally intimate family life, the problem of juvenile delinquency developed into a national preoccupation in the mid-1950s (Gilbert 1986). Jeans, boots, and leather jackets were adopted as the dress code of defiant young men, encouraged by Marlon Brando's performance in *The Wild One* (1954). Public concerns that the minds of youth were vulnerable to bad influences led to voluntary censorship codes in the television and comic-book industries. Adults also worried about youth gangs in public high schools, as portrayed in *Rebel Without a Cause* and *Blackboard Jungle* (both in 1955). To a large extent, these fears encoded class issues: public high schools were one of the few social venues where middle-class white adolescents were compelled to mingle with lower-class whites, blacks, and Hispanics, who were then finishing high school in record numbers. Their "bad influence" on their middle-class peers included blue jeans and T-shirts, rock and roll music, disrespect for authority, and a casual attitude towards future job prospects. Although delinquency among lower-class youths was typically framed as a sociological problem requiring official intervention, middle-class delinquency was seen as a psychological issue susceptible to the right kind of parental attention (Devlin 1998).

Rock and roll music epitomized the image of youth culture as "out of control." A synthesis of R&B, jump, and doo-wop influences pioneered by black dance-band leaders like Johnny Otis and Hal Singer in the late 1940s, rock and roll became a national phenomenon through late-night radio broadcasts for teenage jitterbug enthusiasts. By 1954, enough white teenagers were buying rock and roll records that they began to appear on the white pop charts. A rock and roll industry developed, which cultivated its teen market with songs that addressed their concerns and life-styles. White pop musicians imitated hits by black rock and roll bands, often outselling the originals because of their "cleaner" timbre (cf. Pat Boone's 1955 cover of Little Richard's "Tutti Frutti"). Rock and roll's integration of musical styles included white-southern country-western music (Lange 2004), creating the "rockabilly" phenome-non Elvis Presley. Its aura of uninhibited dancing and racial mixing fomented a protest movement that included Congressional investigations (Martin & Segrave 1988); but Dick Clark's popular television show *American Bandstand* helped to assuage fears by presenting rock and roll in a cleaned-up context. *American Band-stand* also fostered short-lived "dance crazes" identified with particular performers, like Chubby Checker's "twist" and Dee Dee Sharp's "mashed potato." At the turn of the decade, white and black rock and roll assumed separate tracks: in southern California, a sound was developing within the surfer subculture, represented by Dick Dale and the Beach Boys, that became the soundtrack for youthful white fun; mean-while, a new infusion of black gospel music, related to the prominence of spirituals in the Civil Rights movement, led to the "soul" sound of musicians like Ray Charles and the Isley Brothers, and, in Detroit, Barry Gordy's black "Motown" sound fostered "girl groups" like the Marvelettes and the Supremes (Greig 1989; Smith 1999).

Rock and roll songs celebrated displays of emotion and temporary abdications of self-control, behaviors whose cultural validity in the 1950s was not restricted to adolescents. Hollywood icons like Marlon Brando and Marilyn Monroe, trained in the Stanislavski "method" acting technique, played characters who were vulnerable and childlike and who responded to those qualities in other adults (McCann 1993; Churchwell 2005). As Monroe's natural woman was innocent and sexy (her "naughty girl" became the prototype *Playboy* bunny), Brando's natural man was sensitive, virile, and suddenly violent. Contrasted to the gender role models once provided by Hum-phrey Bogart and Lauren Bacall, Brando and Monroe evinced less self-inhibition, less self-sufficiency, and greater volatility. A bit of wildness was also encouraged by the neo-Freudian prescription of sexual intimacy as key to a successful marriage. Birth control was becoming more readily available, in the form of IUDs, the diaphragm, and the pill (introduced in 1961). The Kinsey reports, *Sexual Behavior in the Human Male* (1948) and *Sexual Behavior in the Human Female* (1953), also encouraged sexual experimentation by offering scientific evidence that the sexual practices of white, middle-class, college-educated Americans were more wide-ranging than almost anyone had previously acknowledged (Reumann 2005).

At the same time, certain needs and desires were classified as "deviant" behaviors that fell outside the limits of the socially acceptable. The liberal discourses of psychotherapy and American universalism combined to make a powerful ideological statement about what was natural and good – and by extension, what was unnatural and therefore bad. Women without domestic ambitions were demeaned as unfeminine and unnatural (Breines 1992; Harvey 1993). Dissatisfied and frustrated women were ostracized as depressive anomalies, as described by Sylvia Plath in her autobiographical novel *The Bell Jar* (1963). There, Plath also described her sense of alienation from her own feminine image, her anger at the sexual double standard, her attempted suicide, and her subsequent electroshock therapy. The ideology of the suburban homemaker was systematically debunked by Betty Friedan in *The Feminine Mystique* (1963), which helped inspire a new era of political feminism.

Gays and lesbians also lived beyond the pale of tolerance. Conservatives considered homosexuality a crime and a sin, while liberals dubbed it a psychological illness. McCarthyism targeted gays and lesbians in the State Department and the military. Subjected to legal and extralegal persecution (random violence against gays was condoned in most communities), gays and lesbians lived "closeted" lives (Kennedy & Davis 1993; Howard 1999). The gay community could represent itself only in encrypted form, giving rise to a style known as "camp" in which homosexuality was the subject of a double entendre perceived only by those in the know (as in the dance number "Ain't There Anyone Here for Love" in the 1953 movie *Gentlemen Prefer Blondes*). Camp typically exaggerated or parodied the conventional codes of gendered behavior to reveal their nature as performances rather than natural categories. After the Kinsey report suggested that gays and lesbians constituted a sizeable fraction of the population, support groups with secret membership lists were established – the Mattachine Society and the Daughters of Bilitis – that took the first step towards gay and lesbian liberation (D'Emilio 1983). This "homophile" movement included an important literary dimension, as James Baldwin (who had expatriated to Paris) published the autobiographical *Giovanni's Room* (1956) about a gay love affair, and Allen Ginsberg (reclaiming the homoerotic legacy of Walt Whitman) celebrated gay sex in the poem "Howl" (1955). The obscenity trial of *Howl and Other Poems*, which was seized by postal inspectors in 1957, resulted in Ginsberg's vindication and a new self-awareness among the gay community. In 1963, the first gay picket line was organized by the Homophile League of New York, to protest the army's habitual "outing" of those who had been found unfit for military service on the basis of their sexuality. The Stonewall riot of 1969, in which drag queens fought back against police harassment, brought political assertiveness to an even broader contingent of gays and lesbians.

In an era given to sentimentality, the gothic mode (historically the inverse of the sentimental) enlisted tropes of insanity, incest, monstrosity, and entrapment to mark what was repressed by cultural consensus. As the dark antithesis of the suburban ideal of family togetherness, incest commanded attention in bestselling pulp fictions like Grace Metalious's *Peyton Place* (1956) and real-life dramas like that of Marilyn Van Derbur, the 1958 Miss America (Coontz 1992). The literary subgenre termed "Southern gothic" (pioneered by William Faulkner during the inter-war period) employed gothic elements to tell the story of the South's imperfect adaptation to the American mainstream. A generation of southern gothic writers coming of age in the postwar era – including Truman Capote, Tennessee Williams, Carson McCullers, and Flannery O'Connor – peopled their narratives with grotesque misfits to dramatize their mixture of regional inferiority complex with condescending ambivalence towards secular liberal modernity.

Satirical stand-up comedy and "underground comics" mocked the self-satisfaction of Cold War America from a different angle. In 1955, E. C. Comics began regular publication of *Mad* magazine, whose poster child Alfred E. Neuman and his refrain of "What, me worry?" parodied the sheltered suburban ideal. In 1962, the creator of *Mad*, Harvey Kurtzman, brought his irreverent talents to Hugh Hefner's *Playboy* with a comic entitled *Little Annie Fannie*; in the late 1960s, his work would inspire a generation of underground cartoonists including R. Crumb (Rosenkranz 2002). Hefner bankrolled the careers of several underground satirists of the era, including stand-up comedians. The premier nightspot for satirical stand-up was the "hungry i" in San Francisco, which had introduced Mort Sahl in 1953. Sahl's groundbreaking style of improvisational monologue in response to the daily newspaper relied more on a general attitude of cynicism than on the delivery of one-liners. Lenny Bruce took this form to another level (sometimes called "sick" humor), intended to shock the audience as well as amuse them; Bruce was arrested for obscenity 19 times in the early 1960s (Nachman 2003).

The bohemian "Beat" subculture, informally headquartered in the coffeehouses and jazz clubs of Greenwich Village and San Francisco, constituted another group of self-identified cultural outsiders. From the Beat perspective, exemplified in the writings of Jack Kerouac and Allen Ginsberg, the affluence of the American century was not worth the cost it exacted in personal freedom. The Beats admired the "algebra of need" (William Burroughs's phrase from *Naked Lunch*, 1959) that lent authenticity to the acts of those living on the social margins. Their fascination with the cultures of America's black, Native American, and Latino minorities has been variously interpreted as a key moment in the development of American multicultural-ism and as a reinscription of colonialist primitivism (Martinez 2003). The Beats experimented with drugs like marijuana and peyote in search of spiritual insight and an "honest" style of writing, sometimes courting madness. They celebrated modern jazz, whose forms they emulated in their writings and in literary performances like "jazz poetry" (Belgrad 1998; MacAdams 2001).

The Beat subculture took some of its values from existentialism, a loose-knit philosophical movement that came to the USA from Europe after World War II, most notably through the works of Jean-Paul Sartre (Cotkin 2003). Existentialism emphasized the individual's quest for significance in a potentially absurd universe, asserted that freedom lay in refusing to let choices be dictated by the expectations of others, and introduced terms like "anxiety" and "authenticity" into general usage. The existentialist vision of the embattled self had many applications in postwar America, and was incorporated into discourses as diverse as the highbrow critique of "mass man" and Kennedy's appeal for space exploration. It had particularly wide influence in intellectual circles, where it seemed to fill the metaphysical vacancy left by Marxism; its impact registered almost everywhere, from the psychology of Rollo May to the literary criticism of Cleanth Brooks and the art criticism of Harold Rosenberg. In literature, existentialist thinking informed Ralph Ellison's *Invisible Man* and Ernest Hemingway's *The Old Man and the Sea* (both of 1952) – as well as the works of Joseph Heller, Saul Bellow, J. D. Salinger, Philip Roth, and Kurt Vonnegut. As a reference to French existentialism, the black beret became a fashion statement adopted by many bohemians, including the bebop jazz pioneer Dizzy Gillespie.

Bebop was understood by both aficionados and critics as a musical analog of existentialism, as suggested by John Clellon Holmes's novel *The Horn* (1958) and Norman Mailer's essay "The White Negro" (1957). Bebop had developed during the war years as a reaction against the regimentation of "big band" swing. As such, it featured solo and group improvisations, made more challenging by its characteristically fast pace and complex harmonies. The improvised solos and uneven phrasings of bebop emphasized the qualities of polyphony and prosody (musicians' "talking" through their instruments), which Leroi Jones in *Blues People* (1963) identified as "Africanisms" within the American musical heritage (Belgrad 1998). In 1949, Miles Davis articulated a countercurrent of "cool" jazz, with slower rhythms that declined to share in bebop's edgy energy (Rosenthal 1992; Meadows 2003). Cool jazz was generally more popular with white musicians and audiences, particularly the "West coast" variation exemplified by Paul Brubeck. In the late 1950s and early 1960s, modern jazz underwent a further permutation known as "free jazz," characterized by atonality and improvised time signatures.

Aesthetically, bebop jazz was linked not only with Beat literature but also with Abstract Expressionism, which synthesized Cubist and Surrealist influences to produce the first widely acclaimed style of modern art in America. Painters including Jackson Pollock, Adolph Gottlieb, and Robert Motherwell, who during the war years were preoccupied with Jungian archetypal symbols, broke through in the postwar period to heroic-sized "contrapuntal" paintings in which gestural markings combined to create "an energetic field of force" (in Motherwell's terminology). Abstract Expressionists built on a visual vocabulary that alluded to the "ideographic" representations of Amerindian art; but art historians are divided as to whether the resulting style of painting embodied radical or imperialist constructions of sociality and selfhood (Leja 1993; Belgrad 1998).

Native Americans during this period were for the most part able to exert little control over the way their histories and cultures were interpreted by white Americans. Various stereotypes prevailed: in westerns, they were the "savages"; to bohemians, they were the keepers of an esoteric wisdom; to the hundreds of thousands who traversed Route 66 during summer vacations, they were the creators of souvenir handicrafts. To the federal government, they represented a challenge to the ideology of American universalism: many Indians, like many citizens of the Third World, preferred not to adopt the "American way of life" wholesale; instead, they adapted its technologies selectively to their own cultural value systems, as satirized in Dan Cushman's novel *Stay Away, Joe* (1953). In 1953, the Eisenhower administration embarked on a policy of "Termination" intended to end the special status accorded to Indian tribes by treaty. In response, Native Americans developed the first significant inter-tribal political organizations. In 1969, the American Indian Movement emerged, modeled on the Black Power and Chicano movements (Wilkinson 2005).

Latino culture in the USA during this period was defined primarily by three ethnic groups: Puerto Ricans, Cubans, and Mexicans. The hybridities represented by the Latino presence (whether Mexican "mestizaje" or Caribbean "creole") belied the racial binaries that traditionally structured American society. Predominantly Catholic, these groups nevertheless preserved distinct cults of the saints, syncretizing

Catholicism with Amerindian or African religions, such as the Virgin of Guadalupe among Mexicans and *santeria* among Afro-Cubans. A wave of Puerto Rican immigration transformed New York City neighborhoods in the postwar decade, as rendered fancifully in the Leonard Bernstein/Stephen Sondheim musical, *West Side Story* (1958), and more realistically in memoirs like Piri Thomas's *Down These Mean Streets* (1967) and Esmeralda Santiago's *Almost a Woman* (1998). Afro-Cuban culture made a national impact with the mambo, which emanated from the nightclubs of Havana to become the ballroom alternative to rock and roll; the Palladium ballroom in New York City, where Tito Puente presided, was known as the "temple of mambo" (Loza 1999). After the Cuban revolution of 1959, Cuban immigration was given a new social meaning by a flood of anti-communist exiles. The cultural impact of Mexican Americans was concentrated in the southwest. As distinct from the African heritage of Caribbean cultures, Mexican "mestizo" culture was partly Amerindian, as evidenced by foodways like corn tortillas and tamales. The Mexican musical heritage was also distinct: an amalgamation of *corrido* and polka which gave rise to *ranchera* or "Tex-mex" music (Tejeda and Valdez 2001). In the late 1960s, following Cesar Chavez's successful organization of the United Farm Workers union, a new era of political assertiveness known as the Chicano movement developed among Mexican Americans, with cultural heroes like poet "Corky" Gonzales and performance artist Luis Valdez (Belgrad 2004).

The cultural impact of the black Civil Rights movement during this era was extremely far-reaching, because it served as a model for other political identity movements including the Chicano movement, the American Indian movement, feminism, and gay rights. Most immediately, however, it exploded the two most common myths about blacks in white America: first, that blacks were content with their place in American society as a segregated servant class – a myth encapsulated in the television show *Beulah* (1950–3); and second, that blacks would be assimilated individually into white society as they merited social acceptance – captured in the *Nat King Cole Show* (1957) (Riggs 1991). Black authors in the 1950s also dared to challenge another myth: that of the black rapist of white women. From the "Scottsboro boys" case to Richard Wright's *Native Son* (1940), arguments of the previous decade had challenged particular versions of the myth, but not the myth itself. Postwar black authors replaced it with its inverse: the image of the white woman who seduced and destroyed the black man, symbolizing the double bind of blacks in white society – as in Ralph Ellison's "Battle Royal" and Chester Himes's *Lonely Crusade* (both of 1947). LeRoi Jones, who began his literary career as a Beat bohemian, made this image the core of his play, *Dutchman* (1964). Elijah Muhammad's Nation of Islam popularized a different inversion of the myth, replacing the image of the raped white woman with that of the black slave woman raped by the master. Through Malcolm X, this teaching gained influence as the Civil Rights movement was radicalized; the liberal phase of the movement waned in the mid-1960s, as passage of the federal Voting Rights Act coincided with the Student Nonviolent Coordinating Committee's rejection of King's leadership. After 1965, momentum lay with the more radical Black Power movement, which discarded King's integrationist objective in favor of black nationalism. Cultural elements of the Black Power movement included Africanized names and fashions, the afro hairstyle, and funk rock (Ogbar 2004).

Partly as a result of the Civil Rights movement, Americans in the early 1960s reawakened to the problem of poverty within the United States. Television documentaries like Edward Murrow's *Harvest of Shame* (1960) and sociological studies like Michael Harrington's *The Other America* (1961) and the Moynihan Report (1965) outlined a "culture of poverty": a vicious cycle of low-paying jobs, poor health, poor education, and transience that kept the poor impoverished for generation after generation. The liberal solution adopted by the Kennedy and Johnson administrations emphasized federal programs and a strengthening of organized labor. The more radical "New Left" movement championed grassroots democracy and claimed to represent "the people" against the corporate–liberal "establishment," which they distrusted as a legitimating mask of the "military–industrial complex." The Students for a Democratic Society articulated its critique of the establishment in the *Port Huron Statement* (1962). It criticized universities in particular for their collaboration in this oppressive structure of "desensitization." After 1964, as America's military involvement in Vietnam drastically increased, the New Left stressed anti-war activism and organized draft resistance, "teach-ins," protest marches, and sit-ins. Norman Mailer's *Armies of the Night* chronicled its 1967 march on the Pentagon in an emotionally engaged style that was called the "new journalism."

The folk music revival accompanied the birth of the New Left. Folk music was historically linked to political protest through a legacy represented by Woody Guthrie's group, the Weavers (later featuring Pete Seeger). The annual Newport Folk Festival began in 1959 and featured such acts as the Kingston Trio, Joan Baez, Odetta, and Peter, Paul and Mary. In the early 1960s, folk music eclipsed modern jazz as the music of the Greenwich Village coffeehouses, and college students came from across the country to Washington Square Park in the heart of the Village to play "hootenannies." Bob Dylan, who joined the folk revival as a freshman at the University of Minnesota in 1959, debuted at the Newport Folk Festival in 1963 and scandalized it in 1965 by appearing onstage with an electrically amplified guitar (Cohen 2002). Bob Dylan and the Beatles helped to propel a fusion of folk music and rock and roll known as "folk-rock" (and later simply as "rock") that became the soundtrack of the late-1960s youth counterculture.

Historians debate the extent and significance of linkages between the New Left and the hippies. The hippie counterculture developed a style of cultural radicalism that centered on the use of psychedelic drugs. Slogans like "make love, not war" and "flower power" reflected its holistic, romantic worldview. Critical observers saw in it the solipsistic culmination of the middle-class baby-boomers' overindulged childhoods. The hippies proposed to liberate themselves from the psychological patterns and physical behaviors imposed by mainstream culture (Rossinow 1998). Following in the footsteps of the Beat generation, they gravitated to Golden Gate Park and the Haight–Ashbury district of San Francisco, where they celebrated the "summer of love" in 1967. Many who attended the Woodstock music festival of 1969 believed that it demonstrated what an alternative social reality based on hippie precepts would be like. To assist those interested in founding rural communes, *The Whole Earth Catalog* (1968) compiled a list of the tools available for living "off the grid" of corporate–liberal society.

Environmentalism was a common cause of radicals and liberals in the 1960s, from Buckminster Fuller's "spaceship earth" to Ladybird Johnson's "highway beautification" – an intersection marked by Edward Abbey's *Desert Solitaire* (1968). Abbey, who had worked for the National Park Service, became an advocate of ecoterrorism directed against billboards and dams. Less radically, the Sierra Club, led by environmental activist David Brower, organized effectively to stop the government from building more dams in the Grand Canyon, aided by the nature photography of Ansel Adams, Philip Hyde, and Eliot Porter (Rothman 2000). Rachel Carson's *Silent Spring* (1962) fostered another public outcry that led to a ban on the pesticide DDT. On a more abstract plane, Gregory Bateson proposed ecological feedback dynamics to be the basis of intelligent systems – an insight that generated the field of cybernetics.

Like environmentalism, feminism in the 1960s developed both liberal and radical agendas. Liberal feminism, led by Friedan's National Organization for Women, focused on creating legislation to eliminate structural barriers to women's equality; its issues included professional opportunity, equal pay for equal work, socialized childcare, and planned parenthood. Liberal feminism's de-emphasis of gender differences corresponded to the eclipse of 1950s women's fashions in favor of the straight lines of the "day dress." Radical feminists, paralleling their counterparts in the Black Power movement, rejected the notion of equality within a society whose very language, pastimes, and organization bespoke the values of male supremacy – a condition that they named "the patriarchy." The *Redstocking Manifesto* of 1969 articulated a strategy of radical subjectivity aimed at challenging patriarchal assumptions in all aspects of life, encapsulated in the slogan "the personal is political" (Davis 1991).

In the 1970s, the notion that the identities people embrace are contingent on the context from which they emerge and are open to radical redefinition led to a popular perception of selfhood as performative – as evident in the personae adopted by glam and punk rockers. The roots of this phenomenon lay in the 1960s – not only in the quasi-political performativity of identities like Black Power, Chicano, hippie, and queer (Martin 2004), but also as championed in the Pop art movement. Pop art undercut the heroic posture of high modernist painting styles like Abstract Expressionism with its mimicry of mass-produced Americana. Jasper Johns's sculpture of two beer cans, Andy Warhol's Campbell's soup cans, and Roy Lichtenstein's comic-book enlargements all partook of the concept of the simulacrum: the paradox of the copy with no original. Warhol's quadruple print of Marilyn Monroe (1962) implied that the simulacrum was an inescapable condition at the heart of her identity (Whiting 1997). Undermining the notions of a "natural" and "authentic" order that had underpinned so much of 1950s and 1960s culture, this vocabulary of "simulacra" and "performativity" prefigured the postmodern sensibility of the coming era.

REFERENCES

Belgrad, Daniel: *The Culture of Spontaneity: Improvisation and the Arts in Postwar America* (Chicago: University of Chicago Press, 1998).
Belgrad, Daniel: "Performing *lo chicano*", *MELUS* 29, 2 (Summer 2004), 249–64.
Biskind, Peter: *Seeing is Believing: How Hollywood Taught Us to Stop Worrying and Love the Fifties* (New York: Pantheon, 1983).
Bloom, Alexander: *Prodigal Sons: The New York Intellectuals and Their World* (New York: Oxford University Press, 1986).

Breines, Wini: *Young, White, and Miserable: Growing Up Female in the Fifties* (Boston, MA: Beacon Press, 1992).

Chambers, Whittaker: *Witness* (New York: Random House, 1952).

Churchwell, Sarah: *The Many Lives of Marilyn Monroe* (New York : Metropolitan Books, 2005).

Cohen, Ronald: *Rainbow Quest: The Folk Music Revival and American Society, 1940–1970* (Amherst: University of Massachusetts Press, 2002).

Coontz, Stephanie: *The Way We Never Were: American Families and the Nostalgia Trap* (New York: Basic Books, 1992).

Cotkin, George: *Existential America* (Baltimore, MD: Johns Hopkins University Press, 2003).

Coyne, Michael: *The Crowded Prairie: American National Identity in the Hollywood Western* (New York: St. Martin's Press, 1997).

Craig, Campbell: *Glimmer of a New Leviathan: Total War in the Realism of Niebuhr, Morgenthau, and Waltz* (New York: Columbia University Press, 2003).

Crossman, Richard, ed.: *The God that Failed: Six Studies in Communism* (New York: Harper, 1950).

Davis, Flora: *Moving the Mountain: The Women's Movement in America since 1960* (New York: Simon & Schuster, 1991).

D'Emilio, John: *Sexual Politics, Sexual Communities: The Making of a Homosexual Minority in the United States, 1940–1970* (Chicago: University of Chicago Press, 1983).

Devlin, Rachel: "Female Juvenile Delinquency and the Problem of Sexual Authority in America, 1945–1965," in Sherrie Inness, ed., *Delinquents and Debutantes: Twentieth-Century American Girls' Cultures* (New York: New York University Press, 1998).

Ehrenreich, Barbara: *The Hearts of Men: American Dreams and the Flight From Commitment* (Garden City, NY: Anchor Books, 1983).

Fariello, Griffin: *Red Scare: Memories of the American Inquisition: An Oral History* (New York: W. W. Norton, 1995).

Fisher, James: *Dr. America: The Lives of Thomas A. Dooley, 1927–1961* (Amherst: University of Massachusetts Press, 1997).

Friedan, Betty: *The Feminine Mystique* (New York: W. W. Norton, 1963).

Geoghegan, Thomas: *Which Side Are You On? Trying to Be for Labor When It's Flat on Its Back* (New York: New Press, 1991).

Gilbert, James: *A Cycle of Outrage: America's Reaction to the Juvenile Delinquent in the 1950s* (New York: Oxford University Press, 1986).

Gorman, Paul: *Left Intellectuals and Popular Culture in Twentieth-century America* (Chapel Hill: University of North Carolina Press, 1996).

Greig, Charlotte: *Will You Still Love Me Tomorrow? Girl Groups from the '50s On* (London: Virago Press, 1989).

Harvey, Brett: *The Fifties: A Women's Oral History* (New York: HarperCollins, 1993).

Herberg, Will: *Protestant, Catholic, Jew: An Essay in American Religious Society* (New York: Doubleday, 1955).

Herman, Ellen: *The Romance of American Psychology: Political Culture in the Age of Experts* (Berkeley: University of California Press, 1995).

Hess, Alan: *Googie: Fifties Coffee Shop Architecture* (San Francisco: Chronicle Books, 1986).

Hine, Thomas: *Populuxe* (New York: Alfred A. Knopf, 1986).

Howard, John: *Men Like That: A Southern Queer History* (Chicago: University of Chicago Press, 1999).

Jackson, Kenneth: *Crabgrass Frontier: The Suburbanization of the United States* (New York: Oxford University Press, 1985).

Jacoby, Russell: *The Last Intellectuals: American Culture in the Age of Academe* (New York: Basic Books, 1987).

Karabell, Zachary: *Architects of Intervention: The United States, the Third World, and the Cold War, 1946–1962* (Baton Rouge: Louisiana State University, 1999).

Kennedy, Elizabeth & Davis, Madeline: *Boots of Leather, Slippers of Gold: The History of a Lesbian Community* (New York: Routledge, 1993).

Klein, Christina: *Cold War Orientalism: Asia in the Middlebrow Imagination, 1945–1961* (Berkeley: University of California Press, 2003).

Lange, Jeffrey: *Smile When You Call Me a Hillbilly: Country Music's Struggle for Respectability, 1939–1954* (Athens: University of Georgia Press, 2004).

Leja, Michael: *Reframing Abstract Expressionism: Subjectivity and Painting in the 1940s* (New Haven, CT: Yale University Press, 1993).

Lipsitz, George: *Class and Culture in Cold War America: "A Rainbow at Midnight"* (South Hadley, MA: Bergin & Garvey Publishers, 1982).

Lipsitz, George: *Time Passages: Collective Memory and American Popular Culture* (Minneapolis: University of Minnesota Press, 1990).

Loza, Steven: *Tito Puente and the Making of Latin Music* (Urbana: University of Illinois Press, 1999).

MacAdams, Lewis: *Birth of the Cool: Beat, Bebop, and the American Avant-Garde* (New York: Free Press, 2001).

Martin, Bradford: *The Theater is in the Street: Politics and Performance in Sixties America* (Amherst: University of Massachusetts Press, 2004).

Martin, Linda & Segrave, Kerry: *Anti-Rock: The Opposition to Rock and Roll* (Hamden, CT: Archon Books, 1988).

Martinez, Manuel: *Countering the Counterculture: Rereading Postwar American Dissent from Jack Kerouac to Tomás Rivera* (Madison: University of Wisconsin Press, 2003).

McCann, Graham: *Rebel Males: Clift, Brando, and Dean* (New Brunswick: Rutgers University Press, 1993).

McCurdy, Howard: *Space and the American Imagination* (Washington, DC: Smithsonian Institution Press, 1997).

Meadows, Eddie: *Bebop to Cool: Context, Ideology, and Musical Identity* (Westport, CT: Praeger, 2003).

Meikle, Jeffrey: *American Plastic: A Cultural History* (New Brunswick: Rutgers University Press, 1995).

Mills, C. Wright: *White Collar: The American Middle Classes* (New York: Oxford University Press, 1953 [1951]).

Nachman, Gerald: *Seriously Funny: The Rebel Comedians of the 1950s and 1960s* (New York: Pantheon, 2003).

Navasky, Victor S.: *Naming Names* (New York: Penguin, 1980).

Oakes, Guy: *The Imaginary War: Civil Defense and American Cold War Culture* (New York: Oxford University Press, 1994).

Ogbar, Jeffrey: *Black Power: Radical Politics and African American Identity* (Baltimore, MD: Johns Hopkins University Press, 2004).

Palmer, R. Barton: *Hollywood's Dark Cinema: The American Film Noir* (New York: Twayne, 1994).

Perls, Frederick S., Hefferline, Ralph F., & Goodman, Paul: *Gestalt Therapy: Excitement and Growth in the Human Personality* (New York: Bantam Books, 1977 [1951]).

Pugliese, Stanislao, ed.: *Frank Sinatra: History, Identity, and Italian American Culture* (New York: Palgrave Macmillan, 2004).

Reumann, Miriam: *American Sexual Character: Sex, Gender, and National Identity in the Kinsey Reports* (Berkeley: University of California Press, 2005).

Riesman, David: *The Lonely Crowd: A Study of the Changing American Character* (New Haven, CT: Yale University Press, 1970 [1950]).

Riggs, Marlon: *Color Adjustment* [videorecording] (San Francisco: California Newsreel, 1991).

Rosenthal, David: *Hard Bop: Jazz and Black Music, 1955–1965* (New York: Oxford University Press, 1992).

Rossinow, Douglas: *The Politics of Authenticity: Liberalism, Christianity, and the New Left in America* (New York: Columbia University Press, 1998).

Rothman, Hal: *Saving the Planet: The American Response to the Environment in the Twentieth Century* (Chicago: Ivan R. Dee, 2000).

Rosenkranz, Patrick: *Rebel Visions: The Underground Comix Revolution, 1963–1975* (Seattle: Fantagraphics Books, 2002).

Sandeen, Eric: *Picturing an Exhibition: The Family of Man and 1950s America* (Albuquerque: University of New Mexico Press, 1995).

Seed, David: *American Science Fiction and the Cold War: Literature and Film* (Chicago: Fitzroy Dearborn, 1999).

Smith, Suzanne: *Dancing in the Street: Motown and the Cultural Politics of Detroit* (Cambridge, MA: Harvard University Press, 1999).

Spigel, Lynn: *Make Room for TV: Television and the Family Ideal in Postwar America* (Chicago: University of Chicago Press, 1992).

Spock, Benjamin: *The Common Sense Book of Baby and Childcare* (New York: Duell, Sloan & Pearce, 1946).

Steele, Valerie: *Fifty Years of Fashion: New Look to Now* (New Haven, CT: Yale University Press, 1997).

Tejeda, Juan, & Valdez, Avelardo, eds.: *Puro Conjunto: An Album in Words and Pictures* (San Antonio, Texas: CMAS Books, 2001).

Weiss, Jessica: *To Have and to Hold: Marriage, the Baby Boom, and Social Change* (Chicago: University of Chicago Press, 2000).

Whiting, Cecile: *A Taste for Pop: Pop Art, Gender, and Consumer Culture* (New York: Cambridge University Press, 1997).

Wilkinson, Charles: *Blood Struggle: The Rise of Modern Indian Nations* (New York: W. W. Norton, 2005).

Winkler, Allan: *Life Under a Cloud: American Anxiety about the Atom* (New York: Oxford University Press, 1993).

Chapter Seventeen

THE GLOBALIZATION OF AMERICAN CULTURE

Petra Goedde

In 2004 Lynn Hirschberg of the *New York Times* sounded an unexpected warning: globalization was undermining American film. Hollywood was still exporting movies all over the world, but their cultural content was no longer distinctly American. "While other countries have interpreted globalism as a chance to reveal their national psyches and circumstances through film," Hirschberg contended, "America is more interested in attracting the biggest possible international audience" (Hirschberg 2004: 89). Popular films such as *Shrek 2, Troy* (both shown at the Cannes Film Festival in 2004), and *Van Helsing* derived from European myth and folktales and were not situated in a recognizably American milieu. Could it be, Hirschberg implied, that the globalization of the American movie was now eroding American culture itself? Was American culture in danger of losing its heart and soul to the global marketplace?

While Hirschberg might have prematurely lamented the loss of authenticity in American film, she alluded to a fundamental truth about America's global influence: the proliferation of American culture abroad affects the production of culture in the United States itself. Yet, few, if any, historical treatments of the globalization of American culture have acknowledged this reciprocal effect (Hoganson 2006). From the earliest works on Americanization to the most recent studies of globalization, historians' focus has been on America's influence abroad rather than the impact of globalization on American culture.

The reasons for this omission lie primarily in the scholarly domains of those who have shaped the literature of Americanization. For a field of study that takes American culture as its subject, it has been curiously devoid of American cultural historians. Instead, it has been shaped primarily by area specialists from disciplines such as anthropology, sociology, political science, and diplomatic history. These specialists looked outward from the USA, uncritically assuming the existence of a single national culture at home. While these cultural internationalists took the existence of a single American culture for granted, US cultural historians were focusing predominantly on local, regional, and ethnic cultures. Their understanding of the complexity of the American cultural landscape made it ever harder to justify writing about American culture in the singular.

Cultural internationalists not only posited the existence of a single American culture, but also assumed its power and influence on a global scale. After World War

II such an assumption evolved in tandem with the projection of American economic and military power abroad. At the height of the Cold War with the Soviet Union, the deliberate exportation of American culture became an integral part of America's foreign policy. The origins of America's cultural diplomacy date to 1938 when the State Department created the Division of Cultural Relations to foster intellectual cooperation with other countries. In 1946, Congress established the Office of International Cultural Affairs and the International Press and Publication Division, which in turn became the United States Information Agency (USIA) in 1953 (Hixson 1997). The agency set up information centers all over the world, sent cultural representatives on global publicity tours, and directed broadcasts of the Voice of America into areas under communist control.

The myth of a unified American culture and the programmatic use of American culture as a Cold War weapon were hardly coincidental. America's international cultural offensive was complemented by the Cold War era state's unprecedented exercise of power over the lives of individuals, restricting the political, personal, and sexual freedoms of its citizens, all in the name of national security and the fight against communism. Just as the USA fostered a conformist, homogeneous image of American culture and society at home, it projected a homogeneous image abroad.

The civil rights movement and the social upheavals of the 1960s challenged this myth of conformity. They put into sharper relief the cultural rifts and contradictions within American society, and destroyed the image of a unified national culture that the American government had cultivated meticulously throughout World War II and into the Cold War. As a result, in the international arena America represented both model and nemesis. Students in Eastern and Western Europe, Latin America, and Asia embraced the civil rights and anti-war movements in order to condemn American imperialism in Latin America and Southeast Asia. These developments coincided with the questioning of America's cultural influence abroad among scholars of Americanization. Inspired in part by African American, women's, and ethnic studies, area specialists and foreign scholars not only criticized America's cultural foreign policy, but also began to investigate closely the ways in which indigenous cultures adapted to and resisted American cultural imports. They often found that American cultural products, rather than overwhelming and displacing indigenous cultures, blended into domestic cultural trends (Iyer 1988: 358; Appadurai 1996: 7).

In recent years, the discussion of America's global cultural influence has fused with debates in other fields about transnational history, globalization, and the internationalization of American history (Thelen 1992, 1999; Bender 2002; Fishkin 2005). Scholars have introduced new questions and new problems of definition concerning cultural hegemony, cultural imperialism, imagined national and international communities, creolization, and hybridization (Anderson 1983; Hannerz 1992). Taken together, scholars have concluded that globalization does not necessarily mean homogenization or Americanization but can instead encourage the localization of cultures (Appadurai 1996: 17–19; Thelen 1999; Geertz 2000). For instance, new developments in media and electronic communications allow Indian expatriates in New York to receive local Indian television and stay in touch with their native culture on a daily basis. Such cultural communities are no longer bound by physical space, but are increasingly deterritorialized (Appadurai 1996).

How has the field evolved since the late 1940s from the presumption of a single national culture transmitted outward only, like a Voice of America radio signal, to the current fractured, multidirectional, deterritorialized paradigm? The transformation has followed the trajectory of American culture at home over the past six decades. The first wave of scholars emerged in the first two decades of the Cold War when the nation state wielded unprecedented power. They treated Americanization as an integral part of America's Cold War foreign policy and a vital element of national security. Some saw the remaking of the world in America's image as the best path toward global peace and prosperity; others saw it as the cultural complement to America's economic and military expansionist policies. The second wave of scholars, writing in the aftermath of the Vietnam War and the social protest movements of the 1960s, when the power of the state was contested both domestically and internationally, asked how American culture had been received abroad. They identified Americanization as a historically constructed term used by particular groups to advance a political argument. They redefined Americanization as modernization, a process that was not exclusive to the USA but occurred simultaneously in countries experiencing rapid industrialization. The third wave of scholars, beginning in the 1990s, embedded American history in the broader debates about globalization (Thelen 1992, 1999; Bender 2002). For these scholars, America was only one of many agents of change, and was both engine and product of globalization. While still in an evolutionary stage, this third approach promises to restore to center stage the idea of a reciprocal flow of cultural influence without obliterating the centrality of power in the process. Each of these three schools of thought merits discussion in its own right.

Americanization

Debates about America's cultural influence abroad originated long before the end of World War II. As early as 1902, the British journalist and editor W. T. Stead wrote *The Americanisation of the World* with the prophetic subtitle *The Trend of the Twentieth Century*. In Europe the concept of Americanism and Americanization received wide currency in the 1920s and was subject to heated debate, especially among intellectuals. Europeans were both drawn to American popular culture and its economic innovations, and appalled by its apparent materialism and conformity. Germans looked toward the United States as their own country's future. They did so with optimism as well as dread, regarding Americanism simultaneously as promising and dangerous, liberating and confining (Nolan 1994: 5, 12). In France a similar but more pessimistic debate ensued. Writers such as Georges Duhamel and André Siegfried derided the superficiality of American popular culture and the materialism of the American business world (Siegfried 1927; Duhamel 1930; Kuisel 1993: 2). As American businesses and business culture swept European markets in the inter-war period, cultural conservatives lamented the loss of Europe's cultural identities (Rosenberg 1981; Nolan 1994).

Ironically, as Europeans feared the influx of American materialism and popular culture, Americans feared the influx of European and Asian peoples. In the 1920s, "Americanism" in the domestic context came to be identified with the effort of conservative groups to limit immigration and narrowly define America as white, Protestant, and native-born. Since the turn of the century, urban progressives had used the term "Americanization" to describe their efforts to assimilate immigrants into American society. Rather than contemplating America's influence in the world, social progressives and public intellectuals were preoccupied with assessing the potential dilution of American culture by Southern and Eastern European as well as Asian immigrants. In the 1920s, advocates of this form of Americanization had as yet little interest in spreading the American dream abroad.

World War II dramatically changed that mindset. By the end of the war, few Americans challenged their government's involvement in world affairs. The war also brought about the institutional exportation of American culture. America's growing military, political, and economic dominance in the world was accompanied by a rush of cultural exports. As millions of American GIs made their way into just about every corner of the world, they took with them American popular music, food, and consumer goods. At the same time, the US State Department launched its own cultural diplomacy to advance its political and economic interests abroad. By the 1950s USIA sponsored a variety of international cultural programs, including student exchanges, foreign radio broadcasts, publication and dissemination of American literature abroad, and international tours of American musical entertainers (Hixson 1997; von Eschen 2000, 2004). Germany and Japan, the two primary enemies during the war, became test cases for America's postwar cultural mission abroad. Occupation officials reasoned that the rebuilding of Germany and Japan could succeed only if the process of denazification and demilitarization was accompanied by a rigorous program of democratization and re-education (Tent 1982; Dower 1999; Gienow-Hecht 1999). The US military government set up libraries stacked with what it deemed "wholesome" American literature – deliberately leaving out works critical of the government, such as John Steinbeck's *The Grapes of Wrath*. The democratization campaign even included a youth activities program, which featured baseball as a tool to impart democratic values to Germany's future generation (Goedde 2003: 144). The apparent success of the programs in Germany and Japan gave rise in the early Cold War years to a full-scale cultural foreign policy aimed at the containment of communism throughout the world.

The first group of scholars to explore the expansion of this cultural foreign policy in the aftermath of World War II included many former government officials. The State Department launched its own series of historical monographs on the early history of America's cultural diplomacy (Fairbank 1976; Espinosa 1977; Kellermann 1978). These works concentrated on the institutional mechanisms of the Cultural Affairs Division. In their assessment of the policies the authors drew almost exclusively on US government documents, often painting a favorable picture of the effects of US cultural policies abroad (Kellermann 1978: 243). These works revealed one core shortcoming of early studies of Americanization: the assumption that the flow of influence was exclusively uni-directional, from the United States to other nations. The object of study was to trace the influence of American cultural diplomacy – with only limited scrutiny of its reception, rejection, or adaptation abroad.

In recent years, however, scholars have begun to deconstruct the cultural programs of the State Department during the Cold War (Hixson 1997; Pells 1997; von Eschen 2000, 2004). New research on the State Department-sponsored tours of jazz musicians showed that performers in the early Cold War found ways to subvert the official American cultural message. In 1962, for instance, Louis Armstrong and Dave and Iola Brubeck performed a musical revue called *The Real Ambassadors* in which they openly satirized the State Department's cultural mission and exposed the glaring inequalities suffered by African Americans in the American South (von Eschen 2000: 168; 2004: 79).

American scholars continued the debate begun in the 1920s about the influence of US businesses abroad. Following in the footsteps of W. T. Stead, they argued that American companies were transforming the European business world. Americaniza-tion thus did not mean the "takeover of Europe by essentially American ideas, atti-tudes, and prejudices" so much as the "development and spread of American or American-like products, techniques, and organizations throughout Europe" (McCreary 1964: 8). Even though American companies had been active in the Euro-pean market since the turn of the century, US investment in Europe expanded exponentially in the first two decades after World War II (ibid. 4). Along with the influx of money came the proliferation of America's business culture, advertising techniques, and consumer products. American companies dispatched business execu-tives to Europe, where they often found themselves opposite an American-educated business elite, well versed in American business culture. Europeans had already real-ized that the future of business lay in the American model. Jean-Jaques Servan-Schreiber, editor of the French magazine *L'Express*, soon articulated this sentiment from a distinctly European perspective. He strongly advocated the adoption in Europe of American corporate culture, not because Europe was powerless against American economic predominance, but because such an adoption represented the only way to preserve Europe's independence vis-à-vis America. Only by taking up this "American challenge" could Europeans hope to compete with the transatlantic colossus (Servan-Schreiber, 1967).

Historians further developed these arguments in the 1970s and 1980s, looking at the ways in which American economic policy aided the recovery of Western Europe and East Asia after World War II. The two most spectacular cases of economic revival were West Germany and Japan. Because these two countries had been subject to the most direct political, economic, and cultural influence from the United States during the postwar occupation, evidence seemed to suggest that their economies had been substantially rebuilt in the American image. In 1948, the United States launched the Marshall Plan, which provided economic aid to West Germany and other Western European nations. In Japan, the United States launched the Foreign Operations Administration in 1953 and later the International Cooperation Administration, which gave technical and financial assistance to Japan. Several monographs have explored the effects of the Marshall Plan on Europe's economy (Mayer 1969; Mee 1984; Hogan 1987; Kipping and Ove 1998) and the role of the United States in reviving and Americanizing West Germany's and Japan's economies (Berghahn 1986; Gordon 1993; Shiomi 1995). Rarely did these works stray from business into culture to explore the connections between America's economic predominance and its cul-tural exports.

As US government and business institutions strove to export business and popular culture, a different form of cultural transfer was underway that often occurred outside and at times in direct contradiction to America's official cultural mission: the dissemination of American popular music and movies to receptive audiences abroad. Jazz and Hollywood movies had already spread to the European continent in the 1920s, but in the postwar era America's popular entertainment culture achieved global recognition. The unprecedented international success of American popular culture after World War II renewed the debate of the 1920s about the benefits and perils of Americanization. Yet the nature of the debate changed, particularly in Europe. Economically devastated after World War II, most European nations welcomed the influx of American capital and business in the 1950s. But the same people often grew concerned about protecting their countries' cultural identities.

Coca-Cola became one of the lightning rods that ignited heated debates in Europe over America's cultural hegemony. The debates were exacerbated by the flamboyant style of James Farley, the Chairman of the Board of the Coca-Cola Export Corporation. A shrewd marketer and ardent anti-communist, Farley combined advertising with political messages as he promoted the drink in Europe (Kuisel 1991: 99). For the 1952 Olympic games in Helsinki, Finland, he rebuilt a World War II landing craft and shipped 30,000 cases of Coca-Cola to the games. The symbolic meaning of the move was obvious to all participants. Finland was following a precarious policy of neutrality in the early Cold War; it hosted Soviet troops on its territory and had concluded a security treaty with the Soviets in 1948. Farley's invasion of a country on the fault line between capitalism and communism – even if armed only with a soft drink – suggested the close association between military and cultural weapons in the Cold War.

Opposition to these informal invasions was strongest among the European left. In 1950, the French parliament debated a proposal brought forth by the Communists to ban Coca-Cola from France, because, as leftist parliamentarians warned, the drink posed a potential health threat. In France, as in the USA and elsewhere, Coca-Cola maintained a strict policy of secrecy concerning its ingredients, thus leaving much room for speculation as to the nutritional composition of this strange potion. The debate in parliament as well as amongst the public exposed French fears of America's commercial and cultural invasion as a potential threat to France's distinctive culinary identity (Kuisel 1993: 52–69).

Scholars exploring the informal transfer of American culture paid more attention than their State Department predecessors to the way in which cultural exports were transmitted to other countries. Most of them were neither American cultural historians, nor historians of American foreign relations. Instead, they were specialists in areas that had been the recipients of America's cultural expansion. Most of them found serious deficiencies in the concept and terminology of Americanization. One critic noted that Americanization represented a highly charged argument in domestic political debates about the ownership of national culture, reflecting deep-seated concerns about cultural change. Cultural traditionalists often used the term to charge their opponents with undermining their own cultural, and by extension national, identity (Bigsby 1975: 6). In addition, there was no objective way to measure the degree of Americanization in various countries (Forgacz 1996: 83). Another critic asserted that opponents of Americanization have wrongly looked upon the process of US cultural influence as a zero-sum game in which "any degree of Americanization [implies] an equal degree of de-Europeanization" (Kroes 1996: xi). These critiques suggested that Americanization, rather than being a historical process, was in fact a historically constructed and contextualized concept expressing local fears about foreign domination at particular moments of vulnerability in each nation's history. Despite its shortcomings, however, Americanization remains an integral part of the scholarly debate about America's global role. Some scholars use the term for want of a better one, others because they still feel it most accurately captures the nature of US global cultural influence and power (Kuisel 2000: 510).

Debates about the existence and limits of Americanization extended to Asia as well. Japan, in particular, came under scrutiny because of America's direct political and economic role in Japan's postwar reconstruction. Yet, here too, scholars found that despite an unmistakable American imprint, Japanese culture remained distinct. Japanese obsession with baseball, for instance, seemed to represent an unmistakable sign of Americanization. But upon closer scrutiny, the differences between Japanese and American baseball became obvious (Iyer 1988: 328). The game had been popular in Japan long before the American occupation after World War II. Evolving from its roots in the latter part of the nineteenth century, baseball was well established as a national sport by the 1930s. According to one American observer, the Japanese version exhibited the same values of personal discipline, hard work, and perfectionism that had made Japan a successful industrial giant. In America, baseball represented "good clean fun," he noted. In Japan, it was "deadly serious" (Iyer 1988: 328, 327). Similar phenomena emerged elsewhere in Asia: *Rambo* was a blockbuster hit in Indonesia; the Vietnamese were listening to Bruce Springsteen's "Born in the USA"; and residents of Manila ate pizza while listening to Sinatra. In all these places, one could detect local twists to the ways American cultural artifacts and expressive forms were incorporated into the indigenous culture. The Asian world was not being Americanized; American culture was being localized in Asia (ibid. 358).

Modernization

As some scholars began to redefine the concept of Americanization, others questioned its usefulness altogether, arguing that the term obscured more than it revealed. First, Americanization implied cultural imperialism or hegemony, both of which require a measure of force. The USA undoubtedly utilized its superior military and economic power to influence other countries, but did this power extend to the cultural realm? Were foreign cultures subjected to Americanization against their will? Were they powerless against the American commercial onslaught? When investigated from the vantage point of the recipients, skeptics concluded, Americanization appeared to be superficial. A change in habits, customs, and patterns of consumption did not necessarily demonstrate a deeper transformation in cultural values.

Second, the term "Americanization" implied the existence of a territorially bound, monolithic national culture, and assumed that culture's agency. Yet American culture was not homogeneous, nor were its exports orchestrated from a single source (Wagnleitner & May 2000). In fact, advances in communication technology, particularly the international dissemination of movies, music, and other cultural artifacts, blurred national boundaries as well as national proprietorship of cultural products. While still produced within a particular national framework, the products took on a life of their own outside national venues. Roland Barthes argued that any cultural product that is widely distributed is by its very nature ambiguous (Barthes 1957: 157). The ambiguity seemed apparent at both ends of the process, at the point of production in the USA as well as the point of consumption abroad.

These problems were so fundamental, critics asserted, that the term "Americanization" was no longer analytically useful. Some called the concept a myth, and argued that what had been identified as Americanization was in fact modernization (Pells 1997; Fehrenbach and Poiger 2000: 81). In the European context their view is supported by writings of intellectual observers from the 1920s, who had identified Americanism as a European myth created in response to the cultural upheavals and processes of modernization in the aftermath of World War I. The German writer Rudolf Kayser asked in 1925 whether America was "not a new orientation to being, grown out of and formed in our European destiny?" (Kayser 1994 [1925]). The emergence of popular or mass culture was seen as an integral part of the process of modernization. As the leading producer of modernity, America had become spatially identified with a process that was, in fact, territorially unbound.

In the twentieth century, mass culture became artificially separated from "high" culture, the former defined as entertainment, the latter as art. Mass culture was also intimately connected to the processes of industrialization, commercialization, and consumption. In the 1930s, the German philosopher Walter Benjamin had argued that through new techniques of mechanical reproduction, art was losing its "aura," which he identified as its "presence in time and space, its unique existence at the place it happens to be." Through the process of mechanical reproduction, a work of art could be transferred in time and place and thus become "reactivated" in a vastly different context. This transfer, Benjamin concluded, represented a "tremendous shattering of tradition," commodifying but at the same time democratizing art by making it accessible to a broader audience. From this critical perspective, the transfer of products of popular culture, especially film, from their place of original production in the United States to places of consumption anywhere in the world, stripped them of their "authenticity," their uniqueness in time and space. They became symbols of the generic nature of modern consumer culture. No matter where one was in the world, one could see the same movies, consume the same food, and buy the same clothes. They ceased to be American, and became global symbols of modernization (Benjamin 1968 [1936]).

Benjamin's analysis sheds light on European intellectual battles over modernization since the 1920s. On one side were those who saw it as a tale of progress. Since industrialization, they argued, people had produced more, lived longer and in greater comfort, and known more. In cultural terms, modernization was associated with a better-informed public, greater political participation (Benjamin's democratization), and greater equality of the sexes (Inglehart & Baker 2000: 21). On the other side were those concerned about the loss of what Benjamin had called "aura" or authenticity. They saw in modernization the depersonalization of production in the machine age, the loss of individualism in an increasingly technocratic and bureaucratic society, and the predominance of materialism and consumerism in people's lives. Spearheaded by the Frankfurt School in the 1920s and 1930s, this view became a major critique of Western industrialized society in the period after World War II and helped spark the protest movements of the 1960s. These critics warned that the forces of modernization would create universal cultural conformity. The overwhelming power of the capitalist system would crush indigenous cultures and replace them with modern consumerist icons such as the golden arches of McDonald's, or Disney's cartoon characters (Dorfman & Mattelart 1975).

While this critique of modernity originated on the intellectual left, Europe's conservative elites in the 1920s were also growing concerned about the popular embrace of American mass culture, and were eager to defend "Europe's traditions against subversion by modernism" (Woodward 1991: 83). Anti-Americanism in inter-war Europe especially expressed an "aristocratic disdain for the emerging realities of mass-produced popular culture." The same critique of modernism resurfaced in the 1990s, "dividing the Europeans and evoking in some of them – opinion makers, writers, commentators, 'intellectuals' – many of the Old World's most characteristic anti-Americanist reflexes" (Ellwood 2000: 33). Modernism and anti-modernism thus remained inextricably linked to debates about Americanization.

Because of this close association, many scholars began to write about Americanization as a historically specific construct utilized by particular groups of people at particular moments in time in an effort to make sense of the structural and cultural changes brought about by modernization. French attitudes toward America after World War II were intimately linked to the process of modernization (Kuisel 1993: ix). As Raymond Aron had postulated in 1959, at the height of the Americanization debate in France, the battle was "not so much against Americanism as against the universalizing of phenomena linked to the development of material civilization" (ibid. 114). Rob Kroes later argued that it was "a common fallacy in much of the critique of Americanization to blame America for trends and developments that would have occurred anyway, even in the absence of America." Even though much of the expansion of capitalism occurred under American tutelage, the process was one of "modernization, ranging from the impact of capitalism to processes of democratization of the political arena or the rise of a culture of consumption" (Kroes 2002: 298). Other scholars redefined Americanization as the emergence of a modern consumer culture, "the pursuit of happiness as the pursuit of consumption" (Wagnleitner 1994: 6–7; Hoganson 2006). As the most advanced consumer society in the world, the USA served as both prototype and antitype in European debates about capitalism and modernity.

Yet most of these scholars also hinted at the particular ways in which local populations adapted American symbols of consumerism and popular culture to their own specific situations. The spread of McDonald's restaurants throughout East Asia did not automatically signify the cultural Americanization of the region. Instead, they became part of the indigenous social and cultural fabric and served different functions in different settings (Watson 1997). Viennese branches of McDonald's catered to local tastes by offering beer and a pork-based Big Mac on their menus; one restaurant even offered a typical Viennese breakfast and newspapers on hangers, common staples of Viennese cafés (Thurnher 2004: 31). Scholars increasingly emphasized cultural idiosyncrasies over cultural homogeneity, drawing on examples of the transformation of American cultural elements within a nationally specific context. For instance, the Argentine novelist Manuel Puig in his 1976 novel *Kiss of the Spider Woman* drew on American film noir as a narrative tool. The book is set in a prison cell near Buenos Aires in the mid-1970s, where the homosexual Molina bides his time retelling plots of cheap American movies from the 1930s and 1940s to his fellow inmate, the

THE GLOBALIZATION OF AMERICAN CULTURE

revolutionary activist Valentin. Puig uses these plotlines to frame the relationship between the two characters. The protagonist's reading of American film serves a specific function within the Argentinian context unlike the American original (Rollin 1989: 62).

Another example is the reception of the 1978 NBC mini-series *Holocaust* in the United States and West Germany. National history and cultural heritage produced different readings of the American production in these two countries. In the USA, the series reinforced Americans' positive image of themselves. In the wake of the Vietnam War and the Watergate affair, Americans felt comforted by the memory of their role as liberators in World War II (Rollin 1989: 98). In Germany, where the series was shown in 1979 to record TV audiences, the broadcast reignited national debates about the origins of National Socialism and the question of Germany's collective guilt. While, on a personal level, the film encouraged Germans to identify with the Jewish victims, on a political level it cast them, as members of the German national community, in the role of perpetrators. The mini-series did not represent the Americanization of the Holocaust, as some critics had charged, but instead produced nationally specific readings of a single historical subject. Taken together, these examples demonstrate that Americanization did not necessarily or even typically mean homogenization or the loss of cultural identity.

In fact, as postwar critics of Americanization warned against the increasing homogenization of national cultures, young people often enlisted American popular culture as a weapon against cultural conformity in their own communities. West Germany's youth in the 1950s embraced American cultural symbols as a form of protest against the deeply conservative culture of their parents' generation (Maase 1992). Jazz, rock and roll, blue jeans, cigarettes, and chewing gum became universal symbols of postwar youth rebellion (Wagnleitner 1994; Poiger 2000). In Great Britain, "Rock Around the Clock" became "a teenage national anthem" (Melling & Roper 1996: 166). Rather than identifying with a particular regional or national culture, postwar youth in the industrialized world created a separate generational culture that pitted them against the traditionalism of their elders. Americanization for them meant emancipation, modernization, and ultimately democratization. Most youth perceived their embrace of American pop culture not as cultural homogenization but as rebellion against the cultural conformity and authoritarianism of their parents and the state (Hixson 1997). America thus became an integral part of internal national battles over cultural dominance and cultural emancipation.

Globalization

By the mid-1990s, the debates about modernity and Americanization fused with contemporary debates about globalization. Although no consensus exists about the meaning of globalization, it has been closely associated with the extent of – and resistance to – America's influence abroad. Cultural globalization forms but one element of a far broader process of economic, political, and military globalization. The economic aspects of globalization have elicited by far the greatest measure of public attention, as young protesters battled the police outside economic summit meetings at the turn of the millennium. These protesters drew on old ideas to wage new battles. In their eyes globalization meant little more than Western, primarily American, economic and cultural imperialism. It crushed indigenous economic development and self-sufficiency, created new postcolonial dependencies, and threatened the "diversity of socio-cultural practices" (Wimmer 2001: 436). Though these arguments echoed earlier critiques, it would be misleading to label opponents of globalization anti-modernists or traditionalists. Their concerns remained closely associated with the preservation of cultural and economic independence on the periphery against the overwhelming power of the metropole.

Yet assumptions about loss of cultural identity had by that time already been called into question by both the recent scholarship on modernization/Americanization and the new scholarly literature on globalization. In the early 1990s, historians began to speak of creolization or hybridization when exploring cultural transfers. Developed first by anthropologists, creolization and hybridization meant the blending of the global/foreign with the local/indigenous (Hannerz 1992; Appadurai 1996; Wimmer 2001). These twin concepts allowed scholars to emphasize both the domestication of foreign cultural impulses and the reciprocal nature of cultural influence. They rejected cultural imperialism and cultural hegemony and assumed a more even playing field for cultures changing and adapting in response to outside influences (Minganti 2000: 148). Creolization emphasized the transformation of the cultural message itself as it came into contact with the indigenous culture – for instance, the localization of baseball in Latin America and Japan, or the meaning of American music and film in different national contexts. It assumed the reciprocal flow of influence and the active participation of indigenous people in the adaptation of foreign elements into domestic cultures (Kroes 1996; Pells 1997; Bell & Bell 1998; Thelen 1999; Husted 2001).

The idea of reciprocity was also central to Charles Bright and Michael Geyer's postulations on globalization. Scholars should approach globalization, they argued, as a process "in which flows of peoples, ideas, and things accelerate and the networks of worldwide interconnectivity become ever denser, facilitated in part by the increasing speed of communication and ease of transportation" (Bright & Geyer 2002: 67; 1995). What distinguishes globalization from Americanization is the flow of people, ideas, and things not only from the USA to the world, but also from the world to the USA. For instance, the Argentinian novel *Kiss of the Spider Woman* was in 1985 made into an American motion picture starring William Hurt and Raul Julia. Ironically, the flow of cultural influence was presumed by nineteenth-century thinkers to be exclusively from Europe to the USA, until Frederick Jackson Turner pioneered the creolization theory with his thesis that American culture was essentially a hybrid of earlier European influences with the frontier experience (Turner 1893).

Bright and Geyer challenged two fundamental assumptions about globalization: that it led to homogenization, and that it generated a universal global consciousness (Bright & Geyer 2002: 68). They rejected the idea prevalent in modernization theory that globalization of American culture involved a struggle between the forces of modernity and traditionalism. Instead, the process of interaction created new segmentation and diversity along new social and cultural fault lines. Hence "difference is reproduced locally, not as an assertion of traditional meanings or practices, but as a product of engagement with the global processes of change that are played out in everyday life." A universal global consciousness has yet to emerge. To the contrary:

"The world is much better known, yet people have trouble finding themselves in it. Subjectivities become less fixed and more fluid as people assemble meanings and identities from everywhere (and nowhere)" (ibid. 70). Bright and Geyer call into question the general assumption of America's cultural hegemony in the world: American culture's meanings are fluid, its boundaries are continually redrawn and resegmented, and its message to the world is unclear and often contradictory.

Taken to its logical conclusion, the argument seems to suggest that globalization should be understood as localization, leading to more, not less, diversity as people create new imaginary deterritorialized communities (Appadurai 1996: 17). Mass migration and the development of new electronic media have blurred the boundaries between and within cultural entities, and deterritorialized the idea of national communities. The anthropologist Arjun Appadurai explicitly rejected the use of the term "culture" as a noun because it implied "that it is some kind of object, thing, or substance, whether physical or metaphysical" (ibid. 12). Instead, he preferred the use of "cultural" as an adjective because it acknowledges its "contextual, heuristic, and comparative dimensions and orients us to the idea of culture as difference, especially difference in the realm of group identity" (ibid. 13). Following Benedict Anderson's definition of nations as imagined communities (Anderson 1991), Appadurai argued that in the age of global migration and new technologies of communication, people create imagined communities over vast distances, bypassing the territorial and political confines of the existing nation state and identifying themselves with new communities of people defined by such characteristics as class, gender, religion, occupation, and age. While predictions of the nation state's demise are highly premature, the argument points to the evolution of multiple levels of identity or community consciousness, of which the national is only one, and not necessarily the most important.

Samuel Huntington took the idea of cultural difference to its extreme with his thesis of the "clash of civilizations" (1993, 1996). He argued that, "a de-Westernization and indigenization of elites is occurring in many non-Western countries at the same time that Western, usually American, cultures, styles and habits become more popular among the mass of the people." Huntington separated the economic process of Americanization and Westernization from the cultural process, arguing that the world was divided into eight civilizations based largely on religious traditions, and that a clash of these civilizations will be "the latest phase in the evolution of conflict in the modern world" (Huntington 1993: 22). Thus, instead of increased homogenization, he saw increased cultural segregation and the potential for violent conflict in the future.

While Huntington's thesis remains highly controversial, its emphasis on cultural difference has echoed other scholars and forms part of our understanding of the globalization of American culture. It refocuses attention on the role of power in cultural interactions. Inequities of power in cross-cultural encounters privilege one group over another. Historians have warned against overemphasizing the ability of the periphery to resist the cultural onslaught of the metropole. They argue that America remains central to the process of globalization, even if the products of American culture become indigenized within local contexts (Kroes 1996: 163–5; Kuisel 2000: 209). Yet even if we take into account differences in power, there is growing evidence that America's cultural hegemony was and is far less pervasive than many scholars had previously assumed. Concerns over the loss of cultural identity ironically appear to be far greater in countries, such as France, whose cultural traditions proved relatively strong, and whose economic and political power was comparatively great, than in countries that had experienced successive colonizations.

In the current intellectual environment of postmodernist and poststructuralist theories, scholars concerned with the global reach of American culture increasingly ask the question: how *American* was American popular culture "if many of those who created its most popular forms were the underdogs and outsiders in America? And what makes these forms of popular culture *American* if those who consumed and reproduced them in other countries could make them their own?" (Wagnleitner & May 2000: 2). In other words, American culture is not necessarily synonymous with American power or American capital. While Hollywood and McDonald's (and more recently Starbucks) undoubtedly had the backing of huge financial enterprises in their global expansion, musical forms such as the blues, jazz, rock and roll, and rap were initially as marginal and culturally embattled in the United States as abroad. In fact, in the 1950s, the meaning of America was itself contested in the very exports of American culture (von Eschen 2000: 164; 2004). Both the message and the reception of America's cultural exports were ambiguous and contested (Wagnleitner & May 2000).

The Globalization of Cultural Studies

Globalization, like Americanization and modernization, is a historically configured process whose dimensions have shifted constantly over time. Globalization emerged before the ascendancy of American power in the twentieth century and will continue after the decline of the American empire (Armitage 2004). More importantly, American culture itself has become subject to global influences (Hoganson 2006). The movie industry is no longer spatially tied to Hollywood; production of some of the biggest blockbusters in recent years has occurred outside the United States. Hollywood studios are owned by foreign or multinational corporations. Sushi now competes with pizza, hamburgers, and hot dogs for the attention of international fast-food gourmands. Even the media, once considered American, are increasingly in the hands of non-American corporate giants (Tunstall 1977). Bright and Geyer point to this change as one of the most striking developments of the past three decades. American civil society itself has been incorporated into what they call a "trans-nation," one that is independent and distinct from the territorial nation (Bright & Geyer 2002: 89).

The future of the study of the globalization of American culture thus increasingly points back to the study of American culture itself. Following the challenge posed by a former editor of the *Journal of American History* (JAH) to internationalize American history, US historians have paid increasing attention to foreign scholarship on the USA, to comparative approaches, and to global historical processes as they intersect with domestic US history (Thelen 1992, 1999; Bender 2002; JAH forum September 1999, December 1999). Scholars in coming years will have to explore how the global expansion of American culture has affected America's cultural identity at home; put more poignantly by Bright and Geyer, they have to figure out "where in the world is America[n culture]?" Just as nation states look increasingly fragile and fragmented at the beginning of the twenty-first century, so too does American culture (Thelen 1999: 965). American cultural historians have to reconnect the local cultures they have been investigating over the past three decades to the transnational cultures of the world. Studying the interconnectedness of these cultures and the processes of transfer from the local to the global and back again will enrich our understanding of the globalization of American culture. The concept of the nation state is still alive and well, but the concept of national culture may be disintegrating before our eyes; or maybe it has been dead for a while and nobody noticed.

REFERENCES

Anderson, Benedict: *Imagined Communities: Reflections on the Origin and Spread of Nationalism* (London and New York: Verso, 1983).

Appadurai, Arjun: *Modernity at Large: Cultural Dimensions of Globalization* (Minneapolis: University of Minnesota Press, 1996).

Appadurai, Arjun, ed.: *Globalization* (Durham, NC: Duke University Press, 2001).

Armitage, David: "Is there a Pre-History of Globalization?," in Deborah Cohen & Maura O'Connor, *Comparison and History: Europe in Cross-National Perspective* (New York and London: Routledge, 2004).

Barthes, Roland: *Mythologies* (Paris: Éditions du Seuil, 1957).

Bell, Philip & Bell, Roger, eds.: *Americanization and Australia* (Sydney: University of New South Wales Press, 1998).

Bender, Thomas, ed.: *Rethinking American History in a Global Age* (Berkeley: University of California Press, 2002).

Benjamin, Walter: "The Work of Art in the Age of Mechanical Reproduction" (1936), in *Illuminations*, ed. and intr. by Hannah Arendt, trans. by Harry Zohn (New York: Harcourt, Brace & World, 1968).

Berghahn, Volker: *The Americanisation of West German Industry, 1945–1973* (Leamington Spa: Berg, 1986).

Bigsby, Chris W. E., ed.: *Superculture: American Popular Culture and Europe* (Bowling Green, OH: Bowling Green University Popular Press, 1975).

Bischof, Günter & Pelinka, Anton: *The Americanization/Westernization of Austria*, Contemporary Austrian Studies, vol. 12 (New Brunswick: Transaction Publishers, 2004).

Bright, Charles & Geyer, Michael: "World History in a Global Age," *American Historical Review* 100, 4 (October 1995), 1034–60.

Bright, Charles & Geyer, Michael: "Where in the World is America? The History of the United States in the Global Age," in Thomas Bender, ed., *Rethinking American History in a Global Age* (Berkeley: University of California Press, 2002).

De Grazia, Victoria: *Irresistible Empire: America's Advance through Twentieth-Century Europe* (Cambridge, MA: Belknap Press, 2005).

Dorfman, Ariel & Mattelart, Armand: *How to Read Donald Duck: Imperialist Ideology in the Disney Comic* (New York: International General, 1975).

Dower, John: *Embracing Defeat: Japan in the Wake of World War II* (New York: W. W. Norton, 1999).

Duhamel, Georges: *Scènes de la Vie Future* (Paris: Mercure de France, 1930).

Ellwood, David W.: "Comparative Anti-Americanism in Western Europe," in Heide Fehrenbach & Uta G. Poiger, eds., *Transactions, Transgressions, Transformations: American Culture in Western Europe and Japan* (New York: Berghahn Books, 2000).

von Eschen, Penny: 'Satchmo Blows up the World': Jazz, Race, and Empire during the Cold War," in Reinhold Wagnleitner & Elaine Tyler May, *"Here, There, and Everywhere:" The*

Foreign Politics of American Popular Culture (Hanover, NH: University Press of New England, 2000).

von Eschen, Penny: *Satchmo Blows Up the World: Jazz Ambassadors Play the Cold War* (Cambridge, MA: Harvard University Press, 2004).

Espinosa, J. Manuel: *Inter-American Beginnings of US Cultural Diplomacy, 1936–1948* (Washington, DC: Government Printing Office, 1977).

Fairbank, Wilma: *America's Cultural Experiment in China, 1942–1949* (Washington, DC: US Government Printing Office, 1976).

Fehrenbach, Heide & Poiger, Uta G., eds.: *Transactions, Transgressions, Transformations: American Culture in Western Europe and Japan* (New York: Berghahn Books, 2000).

Fishkin, Shelley Fisher: "Crossroads of Cultures: the Transnational Turn in American Studies – Presidential Address to the American Studies Association, November 12, 2004," in *American Quarterly* 57, 1 (March 2005), 17–57.

Forgacz, David: "Americanisation: the Italian Case, 1938–1954," in Phil Melling & Jon Roper, eds., *Americanisation and the Transformation of World Cultures: Melting Pot or Cultural Chernobyl?* (Lewiston, NY: Edwin Mellen Press, 1996), pp. 81–96.

Geertz, Clifford: "The World in Pieces: Culture and Politics at the End of the Century," in *Available Light: Anthropological Reflections on Philosophical Topics* (Princeton, NJ: Princeton University Press, 2000).

Gienow-Hecht, Jessica: *Transmission Impossible: American Journalism and Cultural Diplomacy, 1945–1955* (Baton Rouge: Louisiana State University Press, 1999).

Gienow-Hecht, Jessica: "Shame on US? Academics, Cultural Transfer, and the Cold War – a Critical Review," *Diplomatic History* 24, 3 (Summer 2000), 465–94.

Goedde, Petra: *GIs and Germans: Culture, Gender, and Foreign Relations, 1945–1949* (New Haven, CT: Yale University Press, 2003).

Gordon, Andrew, ed.: *Postwar Japan as History* (Berkeley: University of California Press, 1993).

Hannerz, Ulf: *Cultural Complexity: Studies in the Social Organization of Meaning* (New York: Columbia University Press, 1992).

Hirschberg, Lynn: "What is an American Movie Now?," *New York Times Magazine*, November 14, 2004.

Hixson, Walter L.: *Parting the Curtain: Propaganda, Culture, and the Cold War, 1945–1961* (New York: St. Martin's, 1997).

Hogan, Michael J.: *The Marshall Plan: America, Britain, and the Reconstruction of Western Europe, 1947–1952* (Cambridge and New York: Cambridge University Press, 1987).

Hoganson, Kristin: "Stuff It: Domestic Consumption and the Americanization of the World Paradigm," *Diplomatic History* 30, 4 (September 2006), 571–94.

Huntington, Samuel P.: "The Clash of Civilizations?," *Foreign Affairs* 72, 3 (Summer 1993), 22–49.

Huntington, Samuel P.: *The Clash of Civilizations and the Remaking of World Order* (New York: Simon & Schuster, 1996).

Husted, Bryan W.: "Cultural Balkanization and Hybridizaton in an Era of Globalization: Implications for International Business Research," Instituto Tecnológico y de Estudios Superiores de Monterrey, http://egade.sistema.itesm. mx/ investigacion/documentos/ documentos/ 8egade_husted.pdf, January 2001.

Inglehart, Ronald & Baker, Wayne E.: "Modernization, Cultural Change, and the Persistence of Traditional Values," *American Sociological Review* 65, 1 (February 2000), 19–51.

Iriye, Akira: "Culture and International History," in Michael J. Hogan & Thomas G. Patterson, eds., *Explaining the History of American Foreign Relations* (Cambridge: Cambridge University Press, 1991).

Iriye, Akira: *Cultural Internationalism and World Order* (Baltimore, MD: Johns Hopkins University Press, 1997).

Iyer, Pico: *Video Night in Kathmandu: And Other Reports from the Not-So-Far East* (New York: Alfred A. Knopf, 1988).

Journal of American History Forum: "Rethinking History and the Nation-State: Mexico and the United States as a Case Study: A Special Issue," *Journal of American History* 86, 2 (September 1999).

Journal of American History Forum: "The Nation and Beyond: Transnational Perspectives on United States History: A Special Issue," *Journal of American History* 86, 3 (December 1999).

Kaplan, Amy & Pease, Donald E., eds.: *Cultures of United States Imperialism* (Durham, NC: Duke University Press, 1993).

Kawai, Kazuo: *Japan's American Interlude* (Chicago: University of Chicago Press, 1960).

Kayser, Rudolf: "Amerikanismus," *Vossische Zeitung* 458 (September 27, 1925), cited in *Weimar Republic Sourcebook*, ed. Anton Kaes, Martin Jay, & Edward Dimendberg (Berkeley: University of California Press, 1994), pp. 395–6.

Kellermann, Henry J.: *Cultural Relations as an Instrument of US Foreign Policy: The Educational Exchange Program between the United States and Germany, 1945–1954* (Washington, DC: US Government Printing Office, 1978).

Kipping, Matthias & Bjarnar, Ove, eds.: *The Americanisation of European Business: The Marshall Plan and the Transfer of US Management Models* (London and New York: Routledge, 1998).

Kroes, Rob: *If You've seen One You've Seen the Mall: Europeans and American Mass Culture* (Urbana: University of Illinois Press, 1996).

Kroes, Rob: "American Empire and Cultural Imperialism: a View from the Receiving End," in Thomas Bender, ed., *Rethinking American History in a Global Age* (Berkeley: University of California Press, 2002), pp. 295–313.

Kuisel, Richard F.: "Coca Cola and the Cold War: The French Face of Americanization, 1948–1953," *French Historical Studies* 17, 1 (Spring 1991), 96–116.

Kuisel, Richard F.: *Seducing the French: The Dilemma of Americanization* (Berkeley: University of California Press, 1993).

Kuisel, Richard F.: "Americanization for Historians," *Diplomatic History* 24, 3 (Summer 2000), 509–15.

Maase, Kaspar: *Bravo Amerika: Erkundungen zur Jugendkultur der Bundesrepublik in den fünfziger Jahren* (Hamburg: Junius, 1992).

Mayer, Herbert Carleton: *German Recovery and the Marshall Plan, 1948–1952* (Bonn and New York: Edition Atlantic Forum, 1969).

McCreary, Edward A.: *The Americanization of Europe: The Impact of Americans and American Business on the Uncommon Market* (Garden City, NY: Doubleday, 1964).

Mee, Charles L., Jr.: *The Marshall Plan: The Launching of the Pax Americana* (New York: Simon & Schuster, 1984).

Melling, Phil & Roper, Jon, eds.: *Americanisation and the Transformation of World Cultures* (Lampeter, UK: Edwin Mellen Press, 1996).

Minganti, Franco: "Jukebox Boys: Postwar Italian Music and the Culture of Covering," in Heide Fehrenbach & Uta G. Poiger, eds., *Transactions, Transgressions, Transformations: American Culture in Western Europe and Japan* (New York: Berghahn Books, 2000).

Nolan, Mary: *Visions of Modernity: American Business and the Modernization of Germany* (New York: Oxford University Press, 1994).

Pells, Richard: *Not Like Us: How Europeans have Loved, Hated, and Transformed American Culture Since World War II* (New York: Basic Books, 1997).

Poiger, Uta: *Jazz, Rock, and Rebels: Cold War Politics and American Culture in a Divided Germany* (Berkeley: University of California Press, 2000).

Rollin, Roger, ed.: *The Americanization of the Global Village: Essays in Comparative Popular Culture* (Bowling Green, OH: Bowling Green State University Popular Press, 1989).

Roper, Jon, ed.: *Americanisation and the Transformation of World Cultures: Melting Pot or Cultural Chernobyl* (Lewiston, NY: Edwin Mellen Press, 1996).

Rosenberg, Emily S.: *Spreading the American Dream: American Economic and Cultural Expansion, 1890–1945* (New York: Hill & Wang, 1981).

Schaller, Michael: *The American Occupation of Japan: The Origins of the Cold War in Asia* (New York: Oxford University Press, 1985).

Servan-Schreiber, Jean-Jacques: *Le défi Americain* (Paris: Denoël, 1967).

Shiomi, Haruhito, ed.: "Postwar Revival and Americanization," *Japanese Yearbook on Business History* 12 (1995).

Siegfried, André: *Les Etats-Unis d'Aujourd'hui* (Paris: A. Colin, 1927).

Slater, David & Taylor, Peter: *The American Century: Consensus and Coercion in the Projection of American Power* (Oxford: Blackwell Publishers, 1999).

Stead, W. T.: *The Americanization of the World: The Trend of the Twentieth Century* (New York and London: H. Markley, 1902).

Stephan, Alexander: *The Americanization of Europe: Culture, Diplomacy, and Anti-Americanism after 1945* (New York: Berghahn Books, 2006).

Tent, James F.: *Mission on the Rhine: Reeducation and Denazification in American-Occupied Germany* (Chicago: University of Chicago Press, 1982).

Thelen, David: "Of Audiences, Borderlands, and Comparisons: Toward the Internationalization of American History," *Journal of American History* 79, 2 (September 1992), 432–62.

Thelen, David: "The Nation and Beyond: Transnational Perspectives on United States History," *Journal of American History* 86, 3 (December 1999), 965–75.

Thurnher, Armin: "The Americanization of Vienna," in Günter Bischof & Anton Pelinka, *The Americanization/Westernization of Austria*, Contemporary Austrian Studies, vol. 12 (New Brunswick: Transaction Publishers, 2004), pp. 29–37.

Tomlinson, John: *Cultural Imperialism: A Critical Introduction* (Baltimore, MD: Johns Hopkins University Press, 1991).

Tunstall, Jeremy: *The Media Are American* (New York: Columbia University Press, 1977).

Turner, Frederick Jackson: "The Significance of the Frontier in American History," American Historical Association *Annual Report* (1893), 199–227.

Wagnleitner, Reinhold: *Coca-Colonization and the Cold War: The Cultural Mission of the United States in Austria after the Second World War* (Chapel Hill: University of North Carolina Press, 1994).

Wagnleitner, Reinhold & May, Elaine Tyler, eds.: *"Here, There, and Everywhere:" The Foreign Politics of American Popular Culture* (Hanover, NH: University Press of New England, 2000).

Watson, James, ed.: *Golden Arches East: McDonald's in East Asia* (Stanford, CA: Stanford University Press, 1997).

Willett, Ralph: *The Americanization of Germany, 1945–1949* (London: 1989).

Wimmer, Andreas: "Globalizations *Avant la Lettre*: a Comparative View of Isomorphization and Heteromorphization in an Inter-Connecting World," *Comparative Studies in Society and History* 43, 3 (July 2001), 435–66.

Woodward, C. Vann: *The Old World's New World* (New York: Oxford University Press, 1991).

Part IV

THEMATIC AND METHODOLOGICAL APPROACHES

Chapter Eighteen

CULTURAL THEORY, DIALOGUE, AND AMERICAN CULTURAL HISTORY

George Lipsitz

It is then impossible to carry through any serious cultural analysis without reaching towards a consciousness of the concept itself: a consciousness that must be, as we shall see, historical.

Raymond Williams, *Marxism and Literature*, p. 11

The truth is, history is always theoretical.

Laura Briggs, *Reproducing Empire*, p. 193

At the end of Willa Cather's *My Antonia*, the novel's narrator, Jim Burden, muses wistfully about the paradoxical nature of the past. Returning as an adult to his childhood Nebraska home, he finds the old main road that he remembers has been plowed under and paved over. Progress has virtually erased all visible signs of the processes that produced it. Yet the struggles of the past have left a mark on the present, even though most people cannot see it.

In a half-mile stretch within a fenced-in pasture, Burden detects the remains of the open trail that "used to run like a wild thing across the open prairie." In this isolated spot most of the tracks made in the ground by the wagons of the first settlers have grown faint, virtually disappearing. Yet in places where the original road traversed a draw, the deep cuts of wooden wagon wheels created channels that later filled with rainwater, resisting new sod. "A stranger would not have noticed them," Burden observes. His memories, however, position him perfectly to see that these small gashes in the ground are in fact the material remains of the journeys made years earlier by farm wagons lurching "up out of the hollows with a pull that brought curling muscles on the smooth hips of the horses" (Cather 1977: 371). The same landscape that appears unremarkable to the eye of the uninformed newcomer provides a transparent window into a richly sensuous past for the viewer with knowledge of the past who knows where – and how – to look.

Yet the past remains out of reach for Jim Burden, appearing more as a spectral presence than a proximate reality. The history that he "reads" from the ruts in the road is irreparably over. He has returned to a Nebraska very different from the one he left. He is no longer the youth whose experiences he recalls. His friend Antonia Shimerda is an adult, not the young girl he used to know. The Nebraska road that they once traveled on together has taken them to different destinations. That journey cannot be undone. Even telling the tale does not satisfy fully, because something escapes in the telling. Burden's memories produce pangs of unfulfilled longing. For him, historical memory becomes little more than aesthetic compensation for actual personal loss. In the novel's final sentence, Burden mourns the adult life together that he and Antonia have never experienced and now never will, consoling himself with the thought, "Whatever we had missed, we possessed together the precious, the incommunicable past" (Cather 1977: 372).

Cather's detailed, evocative, and poignant descriptions of nineteenth-century Nebraska give us ample reason to honor Burden's view of the past as precious. But his evocation of the past as incommunicable seems anomalous in a novel that devotes 372 pages to precisely that communication. Burden's perception of the past as both precious and incommunicable speaks, however, to powerful currents in Western thought. The cycles of creative destruction that characterize capitalist modernity proceed relentlessly, destroying the places, objects, and optics of previous generations. Cather's Burden, like Goethe's Faust, makes his way in the world with nostalgic reverence for the very places and people he had once fought to leave, and which his work helped to destroy. The past becomes more precious the more it seems out of reach; history appears incommunicable because it provides us with only oblique references and tangential clues to what Marshall Berman calls "little worlds emptied out" – the sensuous intersubjectivity of communities erased by progressive change over time (Berman 1982: 23).

Like so much else in *My Antonia*, Jim Burden's ruminations about the ruts in an abandoned Nebraska road contain powerful allegorical significance for historians. We attempt to recreate the infinitely diverse, plural, and polysemic life of the past by sifting through the infinitesimally small fragments, remnants, and traces of it that remain available to us as evidence. We believe that knowing where to look and how to look can make the past speak to us in important ways. Yet we know all too well the limits of our own enterprise, that the accumulated legacy of historical actions, events, and ideas exceeds our capacity to communicate them accurately and adequately. There is always more to be known, more to be said, more to be learned about the past than we can convey in our writing.

For cultural historians, Jim's "burden" is especially relevant. Political, military, and economic historians generally come to consensus quickly about the authority of written documents in identifiable archives in their fields. Cultural historians, however, debate a more elusive "record." The study of culture addresses both the broadly social and the proximately personal. It encompasses works of artistic expression, the development and enrichment of human faculties, systems of meaning, publicly proclaimed and privately held values, personal practices, religious beliefs, and family patterns (Williams 1990: 13–14).

These broad fields have no single privileged archive, epistemology, or ontology. Studying them requires us to look for significance in unexpected and often overlooked places. Evidence about political, economic, and military matters generally comes from official documents, records, and pronouncements. These sources announce themselves as important; they exist because individuals and institutions crafted them to tell an official story. Cultural history, on the other hand, often focuses on sources that did not intend to become sources, on evidence that does not announce itself as important, on information that becomes evidence only after the fact. These sources do not speak *for* themselves or even *about* themselves, but they reveal complex dimensions of human experience when interpreted properly.

The work of cultural historians resembles Jim Burden's ruminations on the ruts in a Nebraska road. The record of westward expansion lies in an unexpected place, in the gashes on the ground in a fenced-in pasture. Burden could have found evidence about his youth by visiting the courthouse and perusing written records detailing land transactions or registries of marriages, births, and deaths. He could have looked at collections of old newspapers, or inquired about the existence of archived or privately held diaries, letters, and memoirs. All would have yielded important historical information, but they might not have evoked the experiences of settlement and their senescence in the same way as his discovery of the empty spaces in the sod where the first road used to exist.

The affective dimension of the concluding passages of *My Antonia* also illuminates the practices of cultural history. Cultural historians study the role of cultural products and processes as forces within history, but they also examine the ways in which different eras and societies generate their own understandings of historical change. Raymond Williams reminds us that the concept of culture has changed over time, acquiring different meanings in different eras. "Culture" once referred exclusively to the cultivation of plants and animals. Later it took on new connotations – as the development, enrichment, and refinement of human skills and abilities, as a signifier for shared values, beliefs, and practices, as an achieved state of civilization or a state that might be lost without due vigilance (Williams 1990: 13–15).

Researching and writing any kind of history entails cultural activity *about* cultural activity. It generates affect *about* affect. The narratives of cultural historians can be especially effective in identifying, evoking, and analyzing subjectivities and states of affect from the past, while at the same time producing them in the present. Plotting linear chronologies about events that take place in bounded spaces entails innumerable choices and decisions. Producing historical narratives requires representation, depiction, and portrayal.

The problems of narrative often serve as provocation for theoretical inquiry by cultural historians. Laura Briggs observes that historical writing necessarily entails authorial decisions about what belongs in a narrative and what does not, about how parts of a narrative work together, about what is important and what is unimportant, about who speaks and who is silenced (Briggs 2002: 194). These problems of representation stem from the inevitability of representation, from the fact that all written accounts of the world translate experience into texts via mediation and interpretation. Marxist literary critic Fredric Jameson poses the conundrum clearly when he explains that while history is *not* a text, "it is inaccessible to us except in textual form" (Jameson 1981: 35).

The wistful melancholy evoked in Jim Burden's words about the precious and incommunicable past tells us more about the performance of affect in the time when Cather wrote the book than it does about the inner world of pioneers in the time her book describes. Yet Cather's book also reveals the ways in which popular and professional expressions about the past inevitably take on aesthetic dimensions in modern industrialized societies permeated with anxieties about change over time. Cultural history enables us to explore the inner worlds, feelings, aspirations, and disappointments of people in the past, but it also helps constitute the historical record it purports to discover. As Melanie McAlister explains with illuminating precision, "if culture is central to the worlds we regard as political and social, it is not only because culture is part of history, but also because the field of culture is history-in-the-making" (McAlister 2001: 276).

Cultural historians turn to cultural theory in order to learn where and how to look for the past. Just as the ruts in an abandoned Nebraska road reveal evidence about early patterns of settlement for the investigator armed with the proper tools, seemingly ordinary and insignificant sites and practices can be sources of historical insight for theoretically informed cultural historians. They make use of theoretical work by scholars who come from fields other than history, some of them expressly hostile to history's conventions, presumptions, and methods, but whose work contains great relevance and utility for asking and answering historical questions.

During the last three decades of the twentieth century, cultural historians benefited from an efflorescence of scholarship about culture across the disciplines. Immanuel Wallerstein and his colleagues on the Gulbenkian Commission on Restructuring the Social Sciences report that the study of culture has been particularly popular among literary scholars, anthropologists, and "among persons involved in the new quasi-disciplines relating to the 'forgotten' peoples of modernity (those neglected by virtue of gender, race, class, etc.), for whom it provided a theoretical ('postmodern') framework for their elaborations of difference" (Wallerstein et al. 1996: 65). Robin D. G. Kelley's brilliant book *Freedom Dreams* explains that these quasi-disciplines emerged within the academy as an indirect reflection of the egalitarian social mobilizations of the mid-twentieth century – movements which frequently called attention to culture as a site of contestation and a vehicle for opposition (Kelley 2002).

In anthropology, Michel Rolphe-Trouillot and Johannes Fabian have raised important questions about time and memory. Michael M. J. Fischer, Emily Martin, George Marcus, and Ruth Behar have examined the textualization of ethnographic scholarship and the role of social position and subjectivity among author/observers. Arjun Appadurai and Nestor Garcia Canclini have explored how the rapid movement across the globe of images, ideas, products, and people in contemporary life undermine traditional understandings of the relationships between culture and place.

Literary criticism by Jacques Derrida and Gayatri Spivak has focused attention on the instability of language and its relationship to relations of unequal power. The cultural and literary critiques of Raymond Williams have been especially valuable to cultural historians because of their attentiveness to time, history, and memory. Sociological studies by Stuart Hall and Pierre Bourdieu have revisited traditional distinctions in the discipline between culture and social structures as well as between social structure and agency.

Feminist studies scholars Judith Butler, Donna Haraway, Teresa de la Lauretis, and Angela Davis have offered generative analyses of identity, power, and performativity that demonstrate key links between ways of knowing and ways of being. The new interest in culture provoked by these scholars has also led to renewed interest in older work on culture by Antonio Gramsci, Walter Benjamin, T. W. Adorno, and Herbert Marcuse.

Michel Foucault has been tremendously influential because of his understandings of the relationships between power and knowledge, his emphasis on how power becomes decentralized throughout society in small sites and practices, and his arguments about how seemingly emancipatory struggles construct oppressive normative regimes of knowledge and behavior. The view of nations as imagined communities articulated by Benedict Anderson has informed an astounding range of studies about national cultures and national histories. Homi Bhabha's concepts of colonial mimicry and "third space" provide an important alternative to models of social struggle built around binary oppositions between oppression and resistance. The view of deviant, dirty, and despised individuals as socially peripheral but symbolically central advanced in the work of Peter Stallybrass and Allon White has guided important studies of sexuality and popular culture. Michel de Certeau's critiques of the tactics and strategies of everyday life open up new definitions of the nature of politics, while the Third World US Women of Color feminism of Chela Sandoval presents a new understanding of political subjects and subjectivity through the concept of differential consciousness.

Cultural historians have drawn especially useful frameworks from Michel Foucault and Raymond Williams. In his Foucauldian study of Chinese immigrants in nineteenth-century San Francisco, Nayan Shah demonstrates how societies sometimes produce the kinds of non-normativity they purport to police. In order to discourage Asian settlement and inhibit the formation of nuclear families in the USA, anti-Asian immigration restrictions limited the number of women allowed entry into the USA from China. These policies produced a Chinese American community with many more men than women. Anti-miscegenation laws prohibited Chinese males from marrying white women. As a result, Chinese settlement in San Francisco took the form of largely bachelor communities that created unconventional forms of household units. Shah refers to these as forms of "queer domesticity" – not only because they included homosexual as well as homosocial attachments, but also because the community consisted of extended "families" across gender lines of "kin" who were not necessarily blood relations. Though these arrangements represented a logical response to white supremacist regulations and exclusion, they were used by Nativists to justify additional discrimination by portraying the Chinese as deviant and non-normative (Shah 2001).

Shah shows how discourses of deviance often entail associating despised populations with disease. Psuedo-scientific discussions about disease control played a central role in anti-Chinese sentiment, rendering people *with* problems as themselves the problem. Dwelling in unclean tenements that they did not own, relegated to neighborhoods with numerous health hazards, and deprived of the sanitation facilities routinely available to white immigrants, the Chinese were blamed for the diseases they contracted as a result of white callousness and greed. More than a matter of metaphor, the link between "foreign" substances in the body and "foreign" populations in the body politic helped make racially exclusionary and discriminatory practices seem natural, necessary, and inevitable.

In response, Chinese American community leaders campaigned for public housing by presenting their community as composed of normative nuclear families imbued with Victorian values and the Protestant work ethic. By the 1930s, these discourses succeeded in securing access to public housing for some families. This victory depended, however, on disowning and disavowing the community's non-normative members, especially the male bachelor communities that had emerged out of necessity because of the ways in which the Page Act and other immigration laws created a largely male Chinese American population. Shah shows that in turning hegemony on its head through dialogue with dominant discourse, Chinese Americans in San Francisco betrayed the possibilities of the "queer domesticity" mentioned earlier – the amalgam of living arrangements and affective relations that actually predominated in the community beneath the façade of stable nuclear family units (Shah 2001).

The processes Shah illumines so well for nineteenth-century Chinese immigrants to San Francisco appear in many other cultural histories. Clyde Woods shows how low wages, labor migration, and the prison system impeded family formation among black workers in the plantation South. White supremacists then used those conditions to blame blacks for not forming and maintaining traditional nuclear families (Woods 1998). Woods emphasizes the importance of culture by showing how blues music emerged as an ethno-racial and ethno-spatial epistemology generated in the Mississippi Delta in response to the power of the plantation aristocracy. Woods observes that the Union troops stationed in the South to enforce the principles of emancipation and abolition democracy were described as "the blues" because of the color of their uniforms. Their removal from the South as a result of the Compromise of 1877 enacted a terrible blow against the newly freed black men and women of the region. Yet, as Woods explains, when "the blues" (the soldiers) left the area, "the blues" (the music) appeared to express, nurture, and defend the freedom dreams of the era of abolition democracy (Woods 1998). Similarly, Linda Maram reveals how gendered immigration restrictions, alien land laws, and anti-miscegenation statutes combined to produce a self-assertive masculine culture of display among Filipinos in California in the 1930s. Anti-Asian racists then demonized Filipino men as hyper-masculine, predatory, and threatening, on the one hand, and feminized, docile, and childlike, on the other (Maram 1998).

Although not always credited for his influence, Raymond Williams has provided historians with particularly useful tools with his concepts of dominant, residual, and emergent forces (Williams 1990). Williams argues that at any given moment of hegemonic domination, the floating equilibrium that makes up the dominant historical bloc consists of residual elements from the past that have not yet disappeared and emergent forms of the future that have not yet arrived. Robert Lee uses this concept to show how stereotypical and negative portrayals of Asians and Asian Americans in US culture over two centuries have done more than provide negative images of a despised social group. These portrayals have also served the function of arbitrating and negotiating changing relations between residual and emergent forces. Thus an anti-Asian film like Cecil B. DeMille's *The Cheat* (1915) did not use its anti-Asian stereotypes randomly, but instead mobilized them to displace onto "foreigners" anxieties about the threats posed by new social roles for women and the rise of consumer society. Lee explains that judges deciding legal cases about the eligibility of Asian immigrants for naturalized citizenship often relied on the images and stereotypes that originated in motion pictures and popular fiction (Lee 1999). Similarly, Philip Deloria shows how changing images of Native Americans have responded to anxieties and disruptions in society at large, not just to the changing relations between indigenous people and the groups that dominate, marginalize, and oppress them (Deloria 2004, 1998).

Critical theory enables historians to interrogate paradigms inherited from the past, not merely to add on to them. Theoretical training encourages scholars to question taken-for-granted categories. Cultural histories influenced by theoretical debates challenge the meaning and cognitive mapping of the local, the national, and the global as fixed and finite entities. They question the work performed by periodization and mechanistic models of historical causation. They examine the ideological origins and effects of claims about objectivity and universality. Perhaps most importantly, cultural theory elevates a dialogic conception of historical understanding over the monologic practices traditionally favored by the discipline. The concept of dialogism comes from the literary criticism of Mikhail Bakhtin. It provides especially important tools for cultural historians. Of course, Bakhtin is not the only, or even necessarily the most important, cultural theorist utilized by cultural historians. Yet a close analysis of Bakhtin's writings provides the best single introduction to how scholars synthesize cultural theory and cultural history in productive and generative ways.

Bakhtin argues that no monologue can exist in culture; that every act of expression engages in a dialogue already in progress. Rather than isolating discrete statements as facts that stand alone, Bakhtin emphasizes relations and interactions among diverse voices (Bakhtin 1984; 1986: 69, 91). Because every utterance responds to a previous statement, and anticipates a future response, every articulation has to be studied relationally and comparatively. Juxtaposition and counterposition can reveal unexpected affinities between discourses, practices, and institutions that might first appear to be unconnected (Bakhtin 1984: 28).

Bakhtin's emphasis on dialogue promotes an appreciation of contradiction, conflict, and contestation. Rather than telling one story from one point of view, dialogic criticism encourages appreciation of "interrelationships in the cross-section of a single moment." Because of the pervasive power of dialogue, "the word in language is half someone else's" (Bakhtin 1981: 293). Individuals and groups make words their own by appropriating and accenting speech they inherit from others. Yet ownership in this sense remains partial, provisional, and permeated by the presence of one's interlocutors.

Bakhtin does not view societies as unified totalities, but rather as sites where opposing social camps and voices collide and transform one another. Doing most of his work within the context of Stalinist rule in the Soviet Union, he paid special attention to the covert qualities of cultural expressions, to their capacities for remembering the blasted hopes of the past and for preserving emancipatory desires for the future. Bakhtin lauds Dostoevsky "for hearing the dialogue of his epoch," noting that "he heard both the loud, recognized, reigning voices of the epoch, that is, the reigning dominant ideas (official and unofficial), as well as voices still weak, ideas not yet fully emerged, latent ideas heard yet by no one but himself, and ideas that were just beginning to ripen, embryos of future world views" (Bakhtin 1984: 27, 90).

Dostoevsky's ability to hear more than "the loud, recognized, and reigning voices" of an epoch informs much of Bakhtin's own work as well. He recognized remnants of popular carnival traditions designed to ridicule and "uncrown" power in the humorous sections of writings by François Rabelais. By analyzing the recurrence of key tropes in widely different contexts, Bakhtin explains how seemingly innocent and innocuous plot devices like a journey down a road, which appear again and again in different kinds of novels, provide a widely understood shared social language signaling significant circumstances. The road is not just a road, Bakhtin explains with insight relevant to the concluding passages of *My Antonia*; the road is also a trope for "events governed by chance" (Bakhtin 1981: 236–42, 244).

Culture is both collective and cumulative for Bakhtin. Yet rather than viewing history as a linear progression through time that creates unbridgeable gaps between the past and the present, Bakhtin advances a conception of history as an endlessly recombinant dialogue within and across time periods. Past meanings are not fixed and stable, but rather they take on new qualities each time they are invoked in the present. "Nothing is absolutely dead: every meaning will have its homecoming festival," he writes (Bakhtin 1986: 170). In the spirit of Paul Ricoeur's assertion that "the temporal distance separating us from the past is not a dead interval but a transmission that is generative of meaning," Bakhtin treats slippages between times and places as enabling rather than disabling (Ricoeur 1988: 221). His concept of heteroglossia presumes an inevitable tension between texts and contexts, because every word that is uttered reflects both the uniqueness of the historical context in which it was first articulated, as well as the complex and dynamic social forces that shape its expression and reception in subsequent times and places (Bakhtin 1981: 428).

Cultural historians of the USA in recent years have drawn directly and indirectly on the concepts advanced in Bakhtin's writings. The aggressive festivity and sensuous celebration of carnival contains strong affinities with many of the practices of commercial popular culture, and Bakhtin's ideas about carnival have permeated performance studies and cultural studies scholarship about popular music, dance, theater, speech, and style. While attending to anthropological questions about the uses and effects of culture, cultural historians have insisted on the distinctly historical dimensions of the artistry, ingenuity, and ritualistic practices of aggrieved groups in dialogue with the "loud, recognized, and reigning" voices of their epic. Choosing to foreground previously undervalued research objects, and to interpret them as participants in a broader social dialogue, cultural historians have emphasized how seemingly ordinary sites can register, reflect, and shape monumental historical changes in significant ways. Their work focuses on the ways in which diverse voices constitute complex historical moments, how competing social groups appropriate and accent each other's words, and how cultural expressions encode complex temporal and spatial mappings.

The practices and processes of popular culture frequently provide cultural historians with opportunities for demonstrating the dialogic nature of social life. Nan Enstad interprets the creative appropriations of commercial fiction and fashion by working-class women during the early years of the twentieth century, considering these appropriations as a consequence of dialogue between capitalism's promises of universal inclusion and working women's experiences of differentiated exclusion (Enstad 1999). Vicki Ruiz reveals how young Mexican American women in Los Angeles in the 1920s and 1930s took on complex roles as consumers of commercial culture and still dutiful family members, in the process creating hybrid forms of cultural coalescence that enabled them to remain faithful to their families yet still act effectively in the outside world (Ruiz 1998).

Joe Austin demonstrates how dominant discourses about New York City by local elites during the 1970s and 1980s presented a mortal challenge to the interests and identities of inner-city youths – who responded by creating graffiti art to speak back to power (Austin 2001). Tricia Rose explains the aesthetics of hip-hop as a dialogic response to the disruption and delocation enacted in inner-city black neighborhoods during the 1980s by deindustrialization, capital flight, urban restructuring, and reversals for the egalitarian civil rights agenda of the 1960s (Rose 1994). Helena Simonett shows that the popularity of Mexican *banda* music in southern California in 1993 and 1994 functioned to express the experiences and defend the dignity of a new generation of immigrant workers facing particularly virulent forms of exploitation and exclusion (Simonett 2001).

Bakhtin's insistence on connecting culture with power enables cultural historians to delineate the ways in which competing social groups find themselves imbricated in each other's words, stories, and ideas. Emma Perez demonstrates how the "colonial imaginary" against which radical Chicano historians rebelled inadvertently shaped their work to the detriment of the Chicano community. Drawing on cultural theory by Judith Butler, Homi Bhabha, Teresa de Lauretis, and Chela Sandoval, Perez argues for a "dialectics of doubling": in her view, the limits of the radical Chicano position inaugurated a process producing a radical Chicana feminist critique that did not replicate the colonial imaginary, even though it emerged out of dialogue with it (Perez 1999).

Similar dynamics appear in historically conscious studies by Deborah Wong, of contemporary Asian Americans making music, and by Juana Rodriguez, of queer Latino/a activists combating the frames used to interpret the AIDS epidemic in contemporary San Francisco (Wong 2004; Rodriguez 2003). Both projects display a strong sense of dialogism in narrating how aggrieved groups turn hegemony on its head by tactically inhabiting the identities designed to oppress them, but for oppositional ends. To make their cases, Wong and Rodriguez invoke Judith Butler's important arguments about how embracing identities tactically and critically can help reveal their constructedness and call them into question. Butler notes that "these terms we never really choose are the occasion for something we might still call agency, the repetition of an imaginary subordination for another purpose, one whose future is partly open" (Wong 2004: 6; Rodriguez 2003: 44).

Yet while hegemony can be turned on its head, so can counter-hegemony. The dialogic nature of social relations means that groups attempting to fool their enemies sometimes fool themselves. Kevin Gaines explores the powerful logic behind the African American "culture of uplift" that emerged as a dialogic response to Jim Crow segregation with its attendant ideological and cultural assaults on the decency and dignity of black people in the period between 1890 and 1945. Seeking control over one of the few spheres left to them by segregation, black male leaders successfully urged the community to perform normativity to disarm its enemies: to embrace puritanical norms of abstinence, thrift, sobriety, and piety. Gaines demonstrates that this strategy won little, if anything, from the community's enemies, but instead imposed onerous and destructive patriarchal restraints on black women and children, while dividing the black bourgeoisie from the black working class at a time when unity was desperately needed (Gaines 1996).

The dynamics of dialogism play a central part in Michael Miller Topp's history of Italian anarchists in the United States in the early twentieth century. Topp shows how Italian immigrant male workers interpreted their class subordination as a gendered injury, an insult to their manhood. In response, they crafted a masculinist discourse of opposition based on manly courage, physical violence, and patriarchal privilege. Although logical and effective in turning negative ascription into positive affirmation, this masculinist discourse trapped the anarchists in a form of gendered solidarity that made it impossible for them to mobilize the members of their class who were women. Moreover, the vehicle of masculine self-assertion originally crafted to advance the cause of anarchist revolution eventually became an end in itself. When Italy's fascist dictator Benito Mussolini ordered his troops to invade Italy, many of the US-based Italian anarchists cheered him on, even though their anarchism should have precluded such nationalist and fascist fervor (Topp 2001). The aggressive masculinity that emerged as the vehicle for advancing anarchist ideas had become more important to them than the ideas themselves.

James Kyung-Jun Lee's examination of the rise of multicultural literature in the United States during the 1980s demonstrates yet another case of dialogic entrapment. Responding to the monocultural literary canon and its emphasis on unified and homogenous "American" experiences and identities, authors from aggrieved communities created literary works that revolved around the dynamics of difference rather than the solidarities of sameness. Works published in the 1970s and early 1980s by Toni Morrison, Maxine Hong Kingston, Toni Cade Bambara, Leslie Marmon Silko, Gloria Anzaldua, Cherie Moraga, and others placed resistance at the center of "multicultural" literature. Yet the very success of their writings with critics and consumers created the preconditions for very different kinds of writings by authors from previously underrepresented groups. Lee argues that publishers and academic institutions worked to disconnect multicultural literature from anti-racist resistance and struggle. They welcomed, rewarded, and promoted authors who turned unease about the possibility of resistance into aesthetic pleasure, who concentrated on the unequal representation of communities of color in literature as they deflected attention away from their unequal representation in the rewards, benefits, and opportunity structures of society. Lee argues that this co-optation produced works of fiction that "teach us how to abandon people even as they cling to hopes this might not come to pass" (Lee 2004: 28). Part and parcel of the process that turned anti-subjugation laws like the Fourteenth Amendment into anti-discrimination warrants, that portrayed struggles to end racist practices as racist themselves because they acknowledged the existence of race, these literary works advanced the fortunes of ethnic authors at the expense of the communities they purported to represent.

Bakhtin's emphasis on the dialogic relationships that link together different voices "at the cross section of a single moment" informs the work of cultural historians who make effective use of seemingly unlikely and even inappropriate juxtapositions. Rachel Buff finds that the very different racially exclusionary definitions of citizenship that confront Native Americans in Minneapolis and Afro-Caribbean immigrants to Brooklyn produce the guiding logic and affective power of both powwows and "pan" festivals (Buff 2001).

Josh Kun shows that precisely because the production and performance of popular music has often served as a central site for the creation of a univocal and homogenous understanding of national identity in the United States, musical works have also functioned as privileged places for the production of identities that pluralize and diversify understandings of citizenship and social membership (Kun 2005). In a similar vein, Eric Porter explains how the role of music instruction within black

communities and jazz music's location within the social, commercial, and even industrial matrices of US society forced its leading practitioners to go beyond the pursuit
of economic sustenance and career success to develop critical, contemplative, and
creative responses to institutionalized racism and white supremacy (Porter 2002).
Matt Garcia finds powerful evidence of inter-ethnic anti-racism in the social interactions played out in rock and roll dances at the El Monte American Legion Stadium
in suburban Los Angeles in the 1950s (Garcia 2001).

Dialogic relations are often spatial as well as temporal and cultural. Laura Briggs
demonstrates how US colonial power in Puerto Rico legitimated itself through discourses about family, reproduction, and sexuality that eventually came back to the
mainland through punitive policies against powerless and non-normative groups
(Briggs 2002). Clyde Woods reveals how the political power of the plantation aristocracy and the unresolved contradictions of class and race in small counties in
Mississippi have been externalized onto the entire nation and the world in present-
day policies about welfare, criminal justice, and agriculture that originated in the
Magnolia State (Woods 1998).

Melanie McAlister presents an exemplary blend of cultural history and cultural
theory in *Epic Encounters* (2001). Her sophisticated study reveals how Hollywood
films, museum exhibits, reliance on oil-driven automobile transportation, and religious concerns have combined to help make the Middle East not only an important
area of concern for national foreign policy but also a crucial location for the production of individual and group identities within the United States. *Epic Encounters* –
probably the only scholarly work ever to combine references to Captain Lou Albano's
The Complete Idiot's Guide to Professional Wrestling with references to works of cultural theory by Edward Said, Etienne Balibar, Arjun Appadurai, Walter Benjamin,
Benedict Anderson, Pierre Bourdieu, and Fredric Jameson – offers an inventory of
unexpected affiliations that link works of expressive culture to national identities.
Although McAlister does not cite Bakhtin directly, her work presents a fully theorized
and fully realized dialogic analysis of encounters "fraught with tension and ripe with
possibility" across national boundaries among people who never meet (McAlister
2001: 1).

Consistent with the trajectories in recent cultural theory that combine temporal
and spatial relations, *Epic Encounters* explains how nineteenth-century panoramas of
Bible scenes and twentieth-century biblical epic films both "frame and claim history"
and influence the assumptions and presumptions of twenty-first century foreign
policy. The book reveals how perceptions of US failures during the war in Vietnam
promoted increased attachment to Israeli military victories among Jewish neo-
conservatives and fundamentalist Christians. It explains how the 1991 Gulf War dia-
logically responded to the 1979 Iranian hostage crisis, and how the theology that
Elijah Muhammad articulated as leader of the Nation of Islam during the 1940s
helped shape popular African American attitudes toward the Arab world in the 1960s
and 1970s. McAlister's text details how the exhibition of the treasures of King Tut-
ankhamen by art museums in the 1970s served as an unlikely site for the negotiation
and arbitration of emerging forms of consumer, gender, and racial identities. In addition, the book shows how idealized portrayals in works of expressive culture of idealized, properly gendered, and heterosexual nuclear families serve as constant symbols
of normative order in American culture.

McAlister's book makes important contributions to cultural history. Rather than separating culture from politics or relegating different cultural forms to their own hermetically sealed autonomous spheres, she demonstrates the utility of looking at culture as a confluence of convergences and coincidences shaped by self-interested and self-aware social agents. Building especially on writings by Etienne Balibar and Benedict Anderson, McAlister shows that nations construct through culture the "people" they purport to represent; that cultural texts function as producers of meaning in history, not merely as reflections of realities produced elsewhere.

Perhaps most importantly, *Epic Encounters* shows that while cultural history can profit from exposure to cultural theory, cultural theory also desperately needs empirically grounded and theoretically sophisticated historical analysis. The great strength of McAlister's work lies not only in its impressive theoretical breadth and depth, but even more so in its insistence on historical specificity. Her engagement with Edward Said's undeniably useful concept of Orientalism proves that the theory only works in specific historical cases, that it cannot be applied successfully to the US context without substantial revision. Moreover, she shows that understanding *any* text requires understanding of the full discursive field from which it emerges, especially the broader social and historical texts from which it emerges and which it helps shape.

Cultural theory enables cultural historians to do better work, but it also helps remind us that historical thinking and writing are quintessentially cultural processes. From this perspective, Jim Burden's concluding rumination in Willa Cather's *My Antonia* reveals little about history, but a great deal about culture. Burden realizes that his visit to his childhood home has been a disappointment. Most of the people he knew well have either died or moved away. Subsequent settlers have cut down the stately trees he recalls fondly in his memory. Yet when he takes a walk past the settled parts of the city, he becomes reinvigorated and feels "at home" again. The long red grass strikes him as "the grass of early times." The blue autumn sky, dun-shaded river bluffs, pale gold cornfields, and grey plumes of goldenrod fill his mind with pleasure and enable him to escape "the curious depression that hangs over little towns" (Cather 1977: 369–70). To the narrator, and to the inscribed and implied maximally competent reader of the novel, the virtues of timeless nature have triumphed over the corruptions of historical time. Yet this is not so much a description of history as it is a performance of a specific cultural text.

This opposition between nature as virtuous and timeless and human society as corrupt and time-bound goes back to the republican ideology of Machiavelli in the Renaissance. As David W. Noble explains, this idea became institutionalized within the national culture of the United States through the writings of transcendentalists, the visual art of the Hudson River School, and the evocations by historians of the frontier as a unique source of regeneration (Noble 2002). Noble shows that belief in a redemptive American landscape as a refuge from the corruptions of European "time" performed important cultural work necessary for the construction of the USA as an imagined community before 1945. Long before Willa Cather put the words into Jim Burden's mouth, bemoaning the corruptions of time and mourning the lost virtue of nature had already been well established as a cultural trope in the national imaginary. Thus the pairing of "precious" and "incommunicable" expresses more of a connection than a contradiction. For Cather and the national tradition she carried on, in order to be precious, the past must remain incommunicable, mysterious, and finished.

For cultural historians educated after 1945, when the vision of a redemptive national landscape became eclipsed by faith in boundless global markets as the true space of America, the past is precious *and* eminently communicable. Jim Burden's wistfulness about the elusiveness of the past does not seem like liberation to theoretically informed cultural historians, but rather like the small-town life that he complains about in the novel. "This guarded mode of existence was like living under a tyranny," he narrates. "People's speech, their voices, their very glances, became furtive and repressed. Every individual taste, every natural appetite, was bridled by caution" (Cather 1977: 219).

For theoretically informed cultural historians, the antidote to the cultural romance of timeless space is self-reflexive historical specificity. Dialogic interaction across times and spaces frees these furtive and repressed voices of the past and present, allowing them to speak in all their rich and contradictory complexity. Melancholy for lost objects is understood not as the inevitable frame through which history must be viewed, but rather just another historically specific cultural performance. As Bakhtin writes:

> There is neither a first nor a last word and there are no limits to the dialogic context (it extends into the boundless past and the boundless future). Even *past* meanings, that is, those born in the dialogue of past centuries, can never be stable (finalized, ended once and for all) – there will always be change in the process of subsequent future development of the dialogue. (Bakhtin 1986: 170)

That is why cultural theory counts; because it helps us to see not only how history happens, but also how it happens to get recorded, interpreted, and changed by historians.

REFERENCES

Austin, Joe: *Taking the Train* (New York: Columbia University Press, 2001).

Bakhtin, Mikhail: *The Dialogic Imagination: Four Essays by M. M. Bakhtin* (Austin: University of Texas Press, 1981).

Bakhtin, Mikhail: *Problems of Dostoevsky's Poetics* (Minneapolis: University of Minnesota Press, 1984).

Bakhtin, Mikhail: *Speech Genres and Other Late Essays* (Austin: University of Texas Press, 1986).

Berman, Marshall: *All That is Solid Melts into Air* (New York: Simon & Schuster, 1982).

Briggs, Laura: *Reproducing Empire: Race, Sex, Science, and US Imperialism in Puerto Rico* (Berkeley: University of California Press, 2002).

Buff, Rachel: *Immigration and the Political Economy of Home: West Indian Brooklyn and American Indian Minneapolis, 1945–1992* (Berkeley: University of California Press, 2001).

Cather, Willa: *My Antonia* (Boston, MA: Houghton Mifflin, 1977).

Deloria, Philip J.: *Playing Indian* (New Haven, CT: Yale University Press, 1998).

Deloria, Philip J.: *Indians in Unexpected Places* (Lawrence: University Press of Kansas, 2004).

Enstad, Nan: *Ladies of Labor, Girls of Adventure: Working Women, Popular Culture and Labor Politics at the Turn of the Twentieth Century* (New York: Columbia University Press, 1999).

Gaines, Kevin K.: *To Uplift the Race: Black Leadership, Politics, and Culture in the Twentieth Century* (Chapel Hill: University of North Carolina Press, 1996).

Garcia, Matt: *A World of Its Own: Race, Labor and Citrus in the Making of Greater Los Angeles, 1900–1970* (Chapel Hill: University of North Carolina Press, 2001).

Jameson, Fredric: *The Political Unconscious: Narrative as a Socially Symbolic Act* (Ithaca, NY: Cornell University Press, 1981).

Kelley, Robin D. G.: *Freedom Dreams* (Boston, MA: Beacon, 2002).

Kun, Josh: *Strangers Among Sounds* (Berkeley: University of California Press, 2005).

Lee, James Kyung-Jun: *Urban Triage: Race and the Fictions of Multiculturalism* (Minneapolis: University of Minnesota Press, 2004).

Lee, Robert G.: *Orientals: Asian Americans in Popular Culture* (Philadelphia, PA: Temple University Press, 1999).

McAlister, Melanie: *Epic Encounters: Culture, Media, and US Interests in the Middle East, 1945–2000* (Berkeley: University of California Press, 2001).

Maram, Linda: "White Trash and Brown Hordes," in Joe Austin & Michael Nevin Willard, *Generations of Youth: Youth Cultures and History in Twentieth-Century America* (New York: New York University Press, 1998).

Noble, David W.: *Death of a Nation: American Culture and the End of Exceptionalism* (Minneapolis: University of Minnesota Press, 2002).

Perez, Emma: *The Decolonial Imaginary: Writing Chicanas into History* (Bloomington: Indiana University Press, 1999).

Porter, Eric: *What is This Thing Called Jazz? African American Musicians as Critics, Artists, and Activists* (Berkeley: University of California Press, 2002).

Ricoeur, Paul: *Hermeneutics and Human Sciences* (New York: Cambridge University Press, 1988).

Rodriguez, Juana Maria: *Queer Latinidad: Identity Practices, Discursive Spaces* (New York: New York University Press, 2003).

Rose, Tricia: *Black Noise* (Hanover: Wesleyan/University Press of New England, 1994).

Ruiz, Vicki L.: *From Out of the Shadows: Mexican Women in Twentieth-Century America* (New York: Oxford University Press, 1998).

Shah, Nayan B.: *Contagious Divides: Epidemics and Race in San Francisco's Chinatown* (Berkeley: University of California Press, 2001).

Simonett, Helena: *Banda: Mexican Musical Life across Borders* (Middletown, CT: Wesleyan University Press, 2001).

Topp, Michael Miller: *Those Without a Country: The Political Culture of Italian American Syndicalists* (Minneapolis: University of Minnesota Press, 2001).

Wallerstein, Immanuel et al.: *Open the Social Sciences: Report of the Gulbenkian Commission on the Restructuring of the Social Sciences* (Stanford, CA: Stanford University Press, 1996).

Williams, Raymond: *Marxism and Literature* (Oxford and New York: Oxford University Press, 1990).

Wong, Deborah: *Speak It Louder: Asian Americans Making Music* (New York: Routledge, 2004).

Woods, Clyde: *Development Arrested: The Blues and Plantation Power in Mississippi* (New York: Verso, 1998).

Chapter Nineteen

SITUATING VISUAL CULTURE

Sally M. Promey

In conversations and classrooms in universities and colleges all over the United States, interest in "visual culture" is running high. "Things seen" have moved from more marginal positions to center stage of scholarly exchange and investigation, even in fields traditionally occupied with words rather than images. Academics in many disciplines – from history to anthropology, sociology to art history, American studies to literature and languages, art criticism to gender and women's studies, religious studies to psychology, and film studies to philosophy – are focusing attention on some aspect of visual culture. When viewed from the vantage of the mid-1990s, so remarkable was this redirection of energy that W. J. T. Mitchell, a scholar of texts and pictures, characterized the "explosion of interest in visual culture" as a "revolution" in higher education (Mitchell 1995a: 7).

At least to some degree, the pervasiveness and magnitude of concern have been functions of media-saturation in the present age. Among rather newly privileged visual forms, photography, film, television, the internet, and related or supporting visual technologies have ranked high. The proper subjects of investigation have also included graffiti, tattoos, broadsides, posters, advertisements, maps, book and newsprint illustrations, cartoons, pornography, festivals and parades, as well as painting, sculpture, and architecture, and images seen with an interior "eye" like the products of visionary experience and imagination. To the proverbial question, "But is it art?" the answer would have to be: sometimes, and for these particular audiences, and under these specific historical and contextual circumstances.

For many scholars of visual culture, including those principally invested in "vernacular visuality," interest in "fine" or "elite" or "high" art is not necessarily diminished by this expansion of subject, but fine art no longer defines the set of parameters marking out legitimate avenues of investigation (Mitchell 2002: 247). Aiming to operate outside the hierarchies of taste and value resident in fine art, a visual culture approach views these hierarchies as social constructions, themselves the legitimate objects of scrutiny as artifacts of Western culture, bound in time and place to particular moments and audiences. "What visual culture denies, then, is not a discourse of art but rather a definition of art" (Holly & Moxey 2002: xv). "Masterworks," for example, remain an appropriate visual cultural subject of study, but visual culture's approach foregrounds historical analysis and critique of the systems of valuation and canon formation that secure their cultural capital *as* masterworks in a particular time and place. (In this case the gendered term of appraisal – *master*works – as well as other historical measures of "value" would elicit investigative attention.) The scholarship of visual culture, furthermore, while acknowledging and analyzing distinctions between and among different visual and artistic forms, discourages the rigid or premature separation or partitioning of one sort of visual experience or production from another.

From Mitchell's 1995 perspective, the new study of visual culture constitutes not a discrete scholarly discipline – a coherent branch of knowledge or learning with fairly fixed institutional locus and apparatus – so much as a "hybrid *interdiscipline*" (Mitchell 1995b: 541, italics added). This relatively fluid framing of the field, its subject, and its practices asserted for the study of visual culture an apparently permanent in-betweenness in disciplinary situation. A decade later this in-betweenness endures, anchored by the disciplinary inter-location remarked by Mitchell as well as by a healthy lack of consensus about nomenclature and about what, precisely, visual culture is and what its study entails.

Internationally, a multidisciplinary set of possibilities for the study of visual culture has inflected its programmatic sources and institutional homes. In England the study of visual culture carries its heaviest debts to cultural studies; in France, and elsewhere in continental Europe, semiotics and communication theory have figured most prominently. The scholarship of a small constellation of European individuals exercises considerable authority. A core list would surely include the works of Roland Barthes, Walter Benjamin, Guy Debord, and Michel Foucault. In the United States, where the study of visual culture originated in, and in relation to, the discipline of art history, a modest-sized group of scholars is principally engaged in theorizing the field – and many more have contributed to its practice (Elkins 2003: 9–14). Six authors whose recent publications have been especially helpful in navigating the shifting American terrain include, in addition to Mitchell, Margaret Dikovitskaya (2005), James Elkins (2003), Michael Ann Holly and Keith Moxey (2002), and David Morgan (2005).

Visual culture remains an unsettled field of investigation. Discussion and debate about the term and its claims focus on three closely related questions. First, what nomenclature or terminology most accurately describes the interests and activities of those who study visual culture? Second, what is the disciplinary status of this entity called visual culture? And third, what is its subject of study?

Nomenclature and Terminology

In scholarly conversation there are moments when it seems critical to coin new terms, to invent new categories and vocabularies, to find new spaces, to describe and make possible the study of subjects obscured (deliberately or accidentally) by earlier definitions and approaches. Sometimes these new terms achieve intellectual clarity and popularity very rapidly; sometimes they begin rather quietly, taking up residence in the scholarly literatures and discussion almost unnoticed, inserting themselves into self-conscious academic awareness only over time. "Visual culture" made its first appearances in this latter, more circumspect manner, initially carrying with it only some of the meanings it now asserts. A brief historiographic account will help to provide context for this discussion of the selection and significance of terms.

Caleb Gattegno's *Towards a Visual Culture: Educating through Television* (1969) represents the term's first documented use in a manner at least distantly relevant to its current configuration (Walker & Chaplin 1997: 6, n. 2). Three years later, art historian Michael Baxandall employed "visual culture" in *Painting and Experience in Fifteenth-Century Italy* (1972: 141). He did so as a means of articulating his notion of a social historical "period eye" (ibid. 29) or "cognitive style," by which he meant the skills and categories of interpretation, the "model patterns and the habits of inference and analogy" that belong to perception in a particular moment and place (ibid. 30). By the time Baxandall's disciplinary colleague Svetlana Alpers extrapolated on this subject with respect to seventeenth-century Dutch "visual culture" in her *Art of Describing* (1983), and certainly by the mid-1980s, ideas and approaches that would loosely coalesce around the study of visual culture were beginning to occupy considerable air space as topics of discussion in some quarters of the academy.

In the mid-1980s and early 1990s, for many scholars in the discipline of art history and elsewhere, choosing to situate "visual culture" as the subject of study promised to infuse new vitality into the examination of images and objects and thus to refocus and refine both interdisciplinary and disciplinary inquiry. Initially the novel constellation represented a moment of intellectual liberation in at least two ways: first, it suggested the possibility of moving beyond the overly formalistic and obsessively high-cultural dead-ends that many, within art history and outside it, believed to hinder much contemporary art historical investigation; and second, it offered a viable alternative to exclusively text-based analyses in other disciplines that were, just around this time, appropriating the modifier "visual" to specify this newly important aspect of their own disciplinary inquiry: visual anthropology, visual geography, visual sociology, or visual archaeology, for example.

In the 1950s and 1960s, and for a variety of often political and ideological reasons, art history's set of methodological possibilities had focused largely on formalist aesthetics and connoisseurship, with their watchwords of genius, innovation, quality, and "transcendence." Though this had not always been the case, during these two decades the practice of art history sustained relatively little real interaction with other disciplines. Formalism, characterized by its close attention to the "purely" visual and material qualities of works of art, effectively divorced art objects from cultural and social practices and contexts.

Beginning in the 1970s with new social histories of art, and increasingly in the 1980s with the "cultural turn" (see Bonnell & Hunt 1999), scholars insistently reintroduced questions of context and interpretation and provided an opportunity and even necessity for more intimate art historical engagement with developments in other fields. In particular, the influential cultural anthropological works of Clifford Geertz reasserted a fundamental orientation toward discerning meaning in art and other products of human culture. It was in this context of disciplinary openness and exchange that the term "visual culture" came into usage as a proper subject of scholarly investigation. As has become increasingly clear (Holly 1984), however, this moment represented a return to interdisciplinarity in art history rather than a new engagement. As Mitchell observes, early art history

was closer to what I call visual culture, as can be seen in the work of [Alois] Riegl,
[Erwin] Panofsky, and Aby Warburg. The Warburg school of art history was interested
in general iconography and in nonartistic modes of representation. Panofsky also made
it clear that in order to study iconology one has to go beyond the masterpieces and
engage with vernacular forms of visual representation like cinema. [Ernst] Gombrich
was a pioneer of visual culture in his resolute insistence on studying "everyday seeing"
and the psychology of visual perception. So visual culture in some ways comes directly
out of a certain tendency in art history . . . Many of the more ambitious art historians
have always been interested in areas beyond the traditional boundaries of the fine
arts.   (Mitchell quoted in Dikovitskaya 2005: 240–1)

From its beginning, the growing scholarly interest in visual culture and the move
in the academy toward its study had special significance for Americanists, including
scholars in the young discipline of American Studies (the work of John Kasson, Joy
Kasson, and Karal Ann Marling, for example, figured importantly here). The academic embrace of visual culture offered new legitimation to the arts of colonial
America and the United States, objects that had failed to measure up on an earlier
scale of valuation geared to European high-cultural standards. The simultaneous
emergence of the newly positive climate for American art and material histories and
of academic interest in visual culture was not simply coincidental. The same preoccupations with formalism, connoisseurship, innovation, and quality that had hampered much "traditional" art history had created especially formidable barriers for
the study of American arts. In broadening attention to the full range of pictures and
images that people make and live with, investigations of visual culture facilitated
scholarly examination of things American. This inclusiveness rendered visual culture
an easier and earlier match for Americanists, who breathed a collective sigh of relief
when the new constellation of visual culture opened a way out of the Eurocentric
"quality" impasse.

   As a descriptive label, the term "visual culture" was applied to a particular configuration of intellectual commitments, many of them already emerging even before the
term came into use. Important among these were inclinations toward an interdisciplinary approach, a focus on everyday practices, and a reconceptualization of the
cultural geography of "margins" and "centers" (Promey 2003: 593). The multiplicity
and hybridity represented in visual culture's ascendancy have continued to characterize its practice. In selecting the modifier "visual," most scholars meant to signify the
field's engagement not just with images and objects – George Roeder's "things seen"
(1998: 275) – but also with culturally and historically specific ways of seeing and
modes of representation – and in relation to peoples as well as the things they produce
(Brown 2004). In choosing the subject "culture," these scholars also indicated a
commitment to the constructed nature of experience, to understanding the ways
people make their worlds and make their worlds work (see Bryson et al. 1994: xvi,
xxix). The adoption and application of the name "visual culture" modifies not just
what historians and other scholars look at but also the ways they construe these subjects and the questions they ask of them. Visual culture is not just a subject matter,
but also the shape of scholarly inquiry in relation to it.

   Scholarly nomenclature with respect to visual culture is still unfixed, often impre-
cise or inconsistent across authors or even within a single author's work. For Margaret
Dikovitskaya "visual culture" and "visual studies" are one and the same thing

(Dikovitskaya 2005: 1). Mitchell, on the other hand, has preferred the phrasing "visual culture" to "visual studies" because he wishes to communicate his commitment to the subject's "contructedness, its symbolic and imaginal formations" (Mitchell in Dikovitskaya 2005: 243–4). David Morgan (Morgan 2005: 32) agrees with Mitchell and others in foregrounding the "constructivist emphasis" and also in subtly shifting the punctuation from artists and objects to *practices* of image production and reception (Promey 1993, 2005; Morgan & Promey 2001; Mitchell 2002). In Morgan's recent study, "visual culture is what images, acts of seeing, and attendant intellectual, emotional, and perceptual sensibilities do to build, maintain, or transform the worlds in which people live." For Morgan, "the study of visual culture is the analysis and interpretation of images and the ways of seeing . . . that configure the agents, practices, conceptualities, and institutions that put images to work" (Morgan 2005: 33).

Mitchell and Elkins would like the study of visual culture to expand beyond the humanities (Elkins 1999; 2003: 7), to embrace, for example, scientific images, topographical charts, and mathematical figures and graphs. Elkins recommends the "study of visual practices across all boundaries." Mitchell is likewise committed to "the general study of images across the media" (1995b: 540). Elkins explicitly distances himself, however, from Mitchell's anthropological understanding of culture, where visual culture is "the study of the social construction of visual experience" (Mitchell 1995b: 540). Elkins, while he uses "visual culture," "visual studies," and "image studies" as synonyms, prefers "visual studies" precisely for its divorce from Mitchell's anthropological constructivist models. Elkins argues that, "It is exactly that apparently unconstricted, unanthropological interest in vision that I think needs to be risked" (2003: 7). More recently, Mitchell has adopted the term "visual studies" to signify "the study of visual culture," thus distinguishing the subject of study – visual culture – from the practice of studying it (Mitchell 2002: 232; Herbert 2003: 452). The yoked term "visual culture studies" also enjoys some currency (e.g., Todd 2005: 13).

Disciplinary Status

Some scholars of visual culture (Herbert 2003: 452; Mirzoeff in Dikovitskaya 2005: 225) ideally imagine disciplinary standing for their subject. Indeed, the development of a number of near-disciplinary and proto-disciplinary structures, like academic programs and curricula and the publication of textbooks, readers, and an historiographic dissertation gives substance to their claims (e.g., Bryson et al. 1994; Jenks 1995; Mirzoeff 1998, 1999; Dikovitskaya 2001). It is presently the case, however, that the study of visual culture in North America most often finds its place as an "interdiscipline"; and that many practitioners are satisfied with this arrangement (see, e.g., Morgan 2005: 27). The conversation is still fluid enough that the various contributors to most edited single volumes on visual culture represent fairly distinct points of view. One recent example (Holly & Moxey 2002: ix–x) both maintains and refutes the notion of a teleological genealogy of disciplines concerned with visual matters and labeled "aesthetics" (eighteenth century), "art history" (nineteenth century), and "visual studies" (twenty-first century). "Is it [visual culture] a field at all or simply a moment of interdisciplinary turbulence in the transformations of art history, aesthetics, and media studies?" asks Mitchell (in Holly & Moxey 2002: 231).

Though very few would assent to an actual merger with any single established discipline, most agree that visual culture operates as an interdiscipline while maintaining special relations with art history. These familial connections are marked, on the one hand, by art history's prior expertise in and claims to the study of "visual" dimensions of human creativity, experience, and practice; and, on the other hand, by the critique of art history implicit for many in the early formation and configuration of visual culture. In defining a new arena of investigation and new investigatory rubrics and questions, the study of visual culture took aim at "traditional" art history's preoccupations with style and subject matter, with artistic genres and aesthetic hierarchy, with the elevation of "masterworks" and with the focus on "art" itself. It is important to remember, however, that art historians themselves most frequently leveled this critique; it came from within the discipline even more insistently than from without.

In the United States, as the study of visual culture sought to locate itself on an academic institutional map defined by disciplinary boundaries and practices, it landed for the most part on territory at the interface of art history and something(s) else (literature, history, film studies, or anthropology, for example) – and always at the meeting point(s) of at least two disciplines. At the University of Chicago in the early 1990s, Mitchell organized an undergraduate course in "Visual Culture" as a revisionist enterprise in conversation with the art history department's introductory "Art 101." The new course was "not an introduction to the history of art but rather an introduction to the study of visual culture, the way people see the world, how they mediate the world through various forms of representation, and how images come into being, how they circulate." Mitchell, whose own doctoral training was in the field of English literature, set out to teach a kind of visual inquiry with conceptual recourse to art historian Joshua Taylor's classic *Learning to Look* (1957). "Suppose you ask yourself the question," Mitchell suggested, "'How do I learn to look?' without restricting it to painting or sculpture" or other fine art forms (interview with Mitchell, 2001, in Dikovitskaya 2005: 242). Undergraduate courses in visual culture have proliferated over the last decade and more.

While Mitchell is generally credited with offering the first undergraduate course in "visual culture," in the years prior to the introduction of this course other scholars had raised similar questions. Some were in active dialogue with Mitchell on this subject. In the mid-1980s, University of Chicago art historian Linda Seidel had already used Taylor to some of the same ends in her own teaching of Art 101. At the time, Seidel was a participant in the interdisciplinary Laocoon Group of faculty and graduate students for which Mitchell was an organizing figure. For some decades, moreover, the University of Chicago's degree-granting interdisciplinary graduate committees (the Committee on History of Culture, for example) had made possible the study of subjects located "on the margins" of two or more disciplines, facilitating the study of visual culture in the years before formal consolidation of the subject.

The two earliest graduate programs in the study of visual culture adopted "visual studies" as a formal descriptor of their activity. Both also took shape in relations of some intimacy and complexity with the discipline of art history. The Graduate Visual and Cultural Studies Program at the University of Rochester (1989) and the

Graduate Program in Visual Studies at the University of California, Irvine (1998), began in academic institutional contexts of limited or diminishing resources for art history. Rochester supported an undergraduate art history program, but not graduate study in the discipline. The Visual and Cultural Studies graduate program is currently housed in the art history department at the University of Rochester. In its genesis, UC Irvine's visual studies program represented a creative regrouping after the California state system turned down a proposal to establish an art history graduate program. In neither case does this background make the study of visual culture any less compelling, nor interdisciplinarity any less desirable from an intellectual perspective. It does, however, significantly complicate the institutional situation and explain some of the turf wars over visual culture, and especially its institutionalization. The defensive tone and posture of the 1996 "Visual Culture Questionnaire" and the responses to it that appeared in the journal *October* are best accounted for in some relation to this "competitive" context.

To return to the matter of disciplinarity, according to Margaret Dikovitskaya, who interviewed Rochester and UC Irvine faculty in 2001 for her dissertation and the book it became, *Visual Culture: The Study of the Visual after the Cultural Turn* (2005), the Rochester program uses interchangeably the terms "visual culture" and "visual studies" and situates the subject that the terms represent as an "interdisciplinary research field" rather than a disciplinary constellation. The UC Irvine faculty, in contrast, understands "visual studies" to describe "the academic discipline that studies visual culture" (ibid. 97), offering an early disciplinary version of Mitchell's more recent interdisciplinary arrangement of the two.

To summarize, it might be said that in the American academy and among other things "visual culture" is what happened in and to art history after the cultural turn. The prefatory pages in the 1994 *Visual Culture* volume edited by Norman Bryson, Michael Ann Holly, and Keith Moxey state this position quite explicitly: "visual culture" is a product of applying contemporary theory to the discipline of art history (Bryson et al. 1994: xiii). Some have construed art history to be a subdivision of visual culture. Others see the study of visual culture as operating entirely within the domain of art history, with visual culture constituting a new subset of scholarly practices within the older discipline. Still others construe "visual culture studies" or "visual studies" to represent a discipline of scholarly endeavor all its own. Mitchell's "interdiscipline," where visual culture is always engaged in some interstitial relation between disciplines, seems most closely to describe the current situation. Art history, in large part because of its own history of expertise in the analysis of visual form, expression, communication, and exchange, is often one among the disciplinary conversation partners.

Subjects of Study

The activity of framing what qualifies as the subject of study is fundamental to scholarly investigation. In the last 25 years, visual culture has constituted a new subject of study, or at least a new way of configuring the subject of study. As with many fields, new and old, the study of visual culture sustains mutual, sometimes contradictory, definitions and understandings. Though no real consensus has emerged, and though definitions proliferate, there are several discernible directions in scholarly practice. Each frames and characterizes visual culture differently. Together they provide four ways of identifying and parsing the subject of study; together they address both "representational practices" and "modes of observation" (Schwartz & Przyblyski 2004: 7). None stands entirely alone for the whole. All have fluid boundaries with respect to the others. Each intersects the other at various points, has implications for the other, enlivens and enriches the other. Each shares the commitment of cultural studies to issues of power and identity, especially as concerns race, ethnicity, gender, and sexualities. The important study of the visual construction of race, for example, takes place within each of these categories of scholarly practice. The four overarching dimensions of current visual culture studies include the history of images; the study of visuality; the history and theory of representation; and investigation of "hypervisuality" in contemporary media and experience.

The *history of images* as a description of the subject of study, articulated in contrast to a *history of art* by Bryson et al. (1994: xvi), accentuates both terms: history and images. Scholars pursuing this approach to the study of visual culture are concerned with images, and their relations, in historical time; they deal with the past as well as the present. This trajectory for visual culture studies might be seen to include most art history within its expanded purview. The rationale for this approach is fairly straightforward: while not all images are art, all art objects present as images of one sort or another. From this perspective, the histories of art and of images seem perfectly compatible, but the visual cultural expansion of the subject of study decisively tempers and delimits "the art historical taste for the exceptional and unique, rather than the quotidian and broadly representative" (Schwartz & Przyblyski 2004: 6). Perhaps because of its apparent continuities with respect to earlier historical scholarship, this category of research and publication has received relatively little attention in the explicitly visual cultural literature. Generally speaking, this latter focused body of writing has invested more energy in theorizing the study of visual culture than in tracking and interpreting visual practices over time (see Elkins 2003: 34–7, on the presentist bias in historiographies of visual culture). Despite relative lack of attention from those charting the rise of the study of visual culture, the scholarship of the history of images is rich and diverse. Some important recent works include Joshua Brown, *Beyond the Lines: Pictorial Reporting, Everyday Life, and the Crisis of Gilded Age America* (2002); Rachael DeLue, *The Struggle of Vision: George Inness and the Science of Landscape Painting* (2005); Patricia Johnston, *Seeing High and Low Seeing: Representing Social Conflict in American Visual Culture* (2006); Anthony Lee, *Picturing Chinatown: Art and Orientalism in San Francisco* (2001); Michael Leja, *Looking Askance: Skepticism and American Art from Eakins to Duchamp* (2004); Richard Meyer, *Outlaw Representation: Censorship and Homosexuality in Twentieth-Century American Art* (2002); David Lubin, *Shooting Kennedy: JFK and the Culture of Images* (2003); David Morgan, *The Sacred Gaze: Religious Visual Culture in Theory and Practice* (2005); Kirk Savage, *Standing Soldiers, Kneeling Slaves* (1997); and Ellen Wiley Todd, "Photojournalism, Visual Culture, and the Triangle Shirtwaist Fire" (2005).

Visual culture scholarship in this historical vein not only embraces new sorts of images but also, and importantly, poses new questions of its expanded subject, shifting and augmenting the locus of inquiry along the way. Scholarly practitioners trace the histories of not just pictures and visually designed objects, but also their reception over time, what people *do* with objects and images, the ways people understand, interpret, and use them, think and speak about them, organize and categorize them. Studies of this sort encourage avenues of scholarly interrogation that facilitate highly textured encounters with images and objects and their social and cultural work, their engagement with lived experience in practice, performance, and ritual. This notion of the "work" that images do has been usefully explored by a number of scholars (e.g., Freedberg 1989; Bryson et al. 1994, esp. pp. xvi and xxix; Morgan & Promey 2001; Roeder 1993, esp. p. 286; Morgan 2005; and Promey 2005). It historicizes, contextualizes, and reconfigures earlier critiques of utilitarian and instrumental value as well as philosophical notions of aesthetics as a domain of transcendence and disinterested reflection. Interest in the work of images in human life-worlds helps to account for the fact that some of the earliest deliberately visual cultural scholarship in the American field is emphatically interdisciplinary, exploring the work of images as it falls under rubrics generally assigned to such other subjects as, for example, religion or consumerism or both, and race, ethnicity, gender, and sexualities (see, e.g., Promey 1993; Bogart 1995; McDannell 1995; Schmidt 1995; Morgan 1996; Bloom 1999; Doss 1999; Smith 1999).

A second substantial category of visual culture scholarship directs attention away from the object and its immediate relations, towards visuality, opticality, the physiologies of perception, and ways of seeing. In this rendering, visual studies exceeds the boundaries of most past art and image histories (works by Rudolph Arnheim, John Berger, and Ernst Gombrich constitute obvious exceptions here) in the sense that it invests in the "biological and cultural processes that render our visual experience comprehensible" (Holly & Moxey 2002: xiv). Jonathan Crary's studies (1990 and 1999) of the activities and situation of the observer and theories of spectatorship figure prominently here, as does a widespread interest in relations between visuality and emerging technologies. John Berger's *Ways of Seeing* (1972), Norman Bryson's *Vision and Painting: The Logic of the Gaze* (1983), Hal Foster's *Vision and Visuality* (1988), Martin Jay's *Downcast Eyes: The Denigration of Vision in Twentieth-Century French Thought* (1993), James Elkins' *The Object Stares Back: On the Nature of Seeing* (1996), Ian Heywood and Barry Sandywell's *Interpreting Visual Culture: Explorations in the Hermeneutics of the Visual* (1999), and Marita Sturken and Lisa Cartwright's *Practices of Looking: An Introduction to Visual Culture* (2001) contribute to this literature. Given that ways of seeing are products of acculturation, and that visuality is "a cultural practice of everyday life" (Mitchell 1994: 20) that implicates artifacts of various kinds, this second version of visual culture studies is closer to the first, more object-oriented, category of histories than might initially seem to be the case.

If the first approach to visual culture has more to do with "visual" objects and the life-practices they engage or provoke, and the second sets its sights on visualities and ways of seeing, the third focuses attention on the history and theory of representation. Here, for example, the more historically minded work of Robert Blair St. George on a multimedia "poetics of implication" in colonial New England and the more theoretically inclined publications of W. J. T. Mitchell number importantly. The "expansion" of the field of study in this third category has to do with the incorporation of not just images but texts, the imagination (in the sense of "pictures" produced in the mind's or soul's eye), and even perhaps other signifying "marks" and traces like sounds and smells. When scholars talk about a "pictorial turn" (Mitchell 1992) or a "visual turn" (Jay 2002) in everyday life and in contemporary scholarship, they are engaging systems of representation.

In 1994 Mitchell expanded the definition of his pictorial turn, locating pictures as a "point of peculiar friction and discomfort across a broad range of intellectual inquiry." At the juncture Mitchell charted, pictures claimed a place at the center of "discussion in the human sciences in the way that language did: that is, as a kind of model or figure for other things (including figuration itself) . . ." (Mitchell 1994: 13). Mitchell's pictorial turn is a "postlinguistic, postsemiotic *rediscovery* of the picture as a complex interplay between visuality, apparatus, institutions, discourse, bodies, and figurality. It is the realization . . . that visual experience or 'visual literacy' might not be fully explicable on the model of textuality" (1994: 16, italics added). Instead of concluding that all images are texts to be read, a fair assessment now seems to be that all texts are images to be seen. Conceptually, however, this "move" suggests a thought pattern that might most usefully be considered additive rather than substitutionary, introducing the opportunity to hold both ideas together, to toggle quickly back and forth between them as well as to consider the two possible sets of relations as sequential developments. This approximates, in fact, what Patricia Crain claims for letters in *The Story of A*: "As an object of representation, the alphabet is an androgyne, moving back and forth between text and image" (2000: 7). Mitchell wishes to assert the same kind of motion for relations between the "social construction of the visual field" and the "visual construction of the social field" he posits as its conversation partner (Mitchell 2002: 238). It is important to note that Mitchell's pictorial turn is a "rediscovery"; his shift "is a trope, a figure of speech that has been repeated many times since antiquity" (ibid. 240).

The scholarship of Nicholas Mirzoeff charts a fourth use of "visual culture," this time as a contemporary transnational mass-media phenomenon. Mirzoeff's visual culture position accentuates genealogical relations with film and digital media studies. Human existence today, he argues, is characterized by an apparently unlimited proliferation of images under which modern/postmodern living is essentially subsumed. This accounting situates this sort of "hypervisual" culture as a synonym for contemporary life itself: "Modern life takes place onscreen. . . . In this swirl of imagery, seeing is much more than believing. It is not just a part of everyday life, it is everyday life" (1999: 1). Visual culture here depends not on objects, images, or pictures but on the "modern tendency to picture or visualize experience" (1998: 6). Mirzoeff's position is linked to his sense of a "massive cultural change arising from the development of digital technologies, which has given the visual a preeminent place" in daily living (Mirzoeff in Dikovitskaya 2005: 225). In this rendering, visual culture becomes the "study of the hypervisuality of contemporary everyday life and its genealogies" (2003: 7). While the focus on "everyday life" would seem to add up to a democratization of interests, David Morgan (2005: 29) points out that Mirzoeff's position (re-)inscribes a new sort of aesthetic avant-gardism in its presentist emphasis on the disruptive break with the past represented in modern and postmodern hypervisuality. Postmodernity, for Mirzoeff, stands apart as a period when meaning is most fundamentally created in pictures rather than in written words (1999: 3–4).

In response, Mitchell moved to clarify the distinction between Mirzoeff's position and his own "pictorial turn." For Mitchell, the

> pictorial or visual turn, then, is not unique to our time. It is a repeated narrative figure that takes on a very specific form in our time, but which seems to be available in its schematic form in an innumerable variety of circumstances. . . . The mistake is to construct a grand binary model of history centered on just one of these turning points, and to declare a single "great divide" between the "age of literacy," for instance, and the "age of visuality." (Mitchell 2002: 241)

Location/Relocation: Whither Visual Culture?

Scholarly terminologies are time-bound. They offer ways out of conceptual difficulties inherent in earlier constellations and then play differently constraining roles when the configurations shift. The politics of the "new" (and the consequently "newly old") is only one of the engines that powers this dynamic. Terms are part of a conversation; ideally their availability furthers study rather than confining or directing it. As new terms take shape and come into currency, there are equally moments when the limitations of those terms and categories become obvious, when the agendas they chart become inadequate, when the horses scholars had hoped to corral elude capture. Though it would be premature (not to mention naïve) to consider discarding the nomenclature of "visual culture," it is not too soon to reflect on the label's terrain and to identify just a few of the problems with its present location.

Visual culture, as an "alternative" to older forms of image studies like art history or aesthetics, suggested in the moment of its coining an expansiveness that promised intellectual and material escape from more restricted configurations of the visual subject and the hierarchies constructed around it. The focus on the *visual*, however, introduced a constraint of its own. Constance Classen calls this constraint the "visualist regime of modernity" (1998: 1); Thomas Crow draws attention to "modernism's fetish of visuality" (Crow in "Visual Culture Questionnaire," 1996: 35). The question of how to successfully investigate "visual" practice when vision might be most fruitfully approached as fully engaged in a rounder human sensorium is a matter that deserves attention. From the perspective of human being and activity, images do not exist apart from objects, practices, and performances that invoke or involve a range of sensory experiences. While imagination, memory, and other cognitive functions may abstract pictures from such moorings, images-in-time are part of the larger fabric of things that tangibly circulate within human life-worlds and in relation to human bodies. The study of visual culture in the United States has so far proved more adequate to the experience of pictures passing by in visual profusion, than to the multisensory operations of designed and manufactured objects/images and human encounters with them.

The split in the American academy between visual culture studies and material culture studies can be ascribed to different institutional and disciplinary genealogies. The two take shape independently but also in opposition to each other in a manner that is arbitrarily and institutionally determined. The division, moreover, serves to reinvent old sensory hierarchies, to reinforce an imperialism of the eye, lifting the visual from the richer constellation of human senses and claiming for "sight" a higher plane in relation to the "lower" senses of smell, taste, and touch, with hearing occupying a middle register (Classen 1998: 10). Classen further points out that "men have traditionally been associated with the 'higher,' 'spiritual' senses of sight and hearing, while women have been associated with the 'lower,' 'animal' senses of taste, touch, and smell" (ibid. 6). Conventional sensory genderings, such as these, and racialized ascriptions to sensory codes further complicate the situation for visual culture and its claims to democratic expansiveness. Speaking of visuality and the "visual" in visual culture requires attention to materiality and sensory reception, and their social, political, and cultural construction, as well.

The *culture* in visual culture, furthermore, has also produced its own limitations by tending in some directions rather than others. "Visual culture" might well have elicited studies broadly and deeply sensitive to transnational concerns and *cultures* (plural) within and without national borders; it might well have produced work that regularly thinks across geographic and chronological boundaries in new ways. Instead, with some exceptions, visual culture studies have largely concerned Western modernity and especially mechanically reproduced imagery (photography, film, the internet, and their respective genealogies). Surprisingly, "visual culture studies" has brought little illumination thus far to such charged and inadequate historical categories as "folk" art in the United States, a label initially applied as nineteenth-century European elites, in the midst of imperialism and colonialism, were inventing their own rural, ethnic, and geographically provincial cultures as the "primitive within."

Finally, much of the theoretical visual culture literature to date has been preoccupied with situating its subject within or without art history (the sort of "is it or isn't it" debate that this essay has itself engaged). While these efforts to discern and define the substance of visual culture studies are useful in some ways, they seem rather futile in others. The problems stem in part from the rhetorical use of disciplines as though they were static phenomena. Mitchell, for example, maintains that "art history is not sufficient because it is focused – quite appropriately – on the history of art" (Mitchell in Dikovitskaya 2005: 240). Disciplines, however, like scholarly terminologies, are in constant process of refinement and change. Few art historians, for their part, would agree that art history is now exclusively occupied with "art," or consumed by questions of style and iconography, or indeed that it ever was. Disciplinary shape is moving and indefinite: there never was *one* art history any more than there is *one* visual culture. Disciplines exist in fairly fluid relations with their most immediate conversation partners; visual culture has been a constant and creative conversation partner inside and outside art history's boundaries for some 25 years.

In the introduction to their recent *Nineteenth-Century Visual Culture Reader*, Vanessa Schwartz and Jeannene Przyblyski propose "interdisciplinarity as the best roadmap for how visual culture studies and the history of visual culture will be written in the future. Likewise . . . visual culture studies is constituted less by its topical repertoire and more to the degree that it produces a discursive space where questions and materials that have been traditionally marginalized within the established disciplines become central" (2004: 4), and where disciplinarity itself is subject to interrogation (see also Herbert 1995: 539–40). Importantly, situating visual culture studies as an interdiscipline usefully focuses attention on the degree to which it is a *relational* enterprise, calling its various constituencies to provide space for exchange.

This interdisciplinarity also has the distinct advantage of locating the subject(s) of visual culture "in between" other things. Considered from this perspective, visual culture occupies a fluid discursive domain of interactions among artifacts, viewers, sensory perceptions, and contextual worlds. Relational models of vision and culture invite research built around strategies of multiplication and accumulation rather than simple replacement or substitution. The scholar of visual culture is challenged not so much, for example, to shift concern away from objects and images and toward visual practices as to attend, rather, to practices *and* visual artifacts, *and* their producers *and* processes and contexts of production, *and* viewers and audiences, *and* ways of seeing and interpreting things seen. Together, these provide a more faithful picture of the range of human interactions with images and objects in daily practice and experience. Visual culture, while unsettled, is ideally situated to elicit this highly textured scholarship of visual and material life-worlds.

REFERENCES

Alpers, Svetlana: *The Art of Describing: Dutch Art in the Seventeenth Century* (Chicago: University of Chicago Press, 1983).

Baxandall, Michael: *Painting and Experience in Fifteenth-Century Italy* (Oxford: Oxford University Press, 1972).

Berger, John: *Ways of Seeing* (London: BBC; Harmondsworth: Penguin Books, 1972).

Bloom, Laura, ed.: *With Other Eyes: Looking at Race and Gender in Visual Culture* (Minneapolis: University of Minnesota Press, 1999).

Bogart, Michele H.: *Artists, Advertising, and the Borders of Art* (Chicago: University of Chicago Press, 1995).

Bonnell, Victoria & Hunt, Lynn, eds.: *Beyond the Cultural Turn: New Directions in the Study of Society and Culture* (Berkeley: University of California Press, 1999).

Brown, Bill: *A Sense of Things: The Object Matter in American Literature* (Chicago: University of Chicago Press, 2004).

Brown, Joshua: *Beyond the Lines: Pictorial Reporting, Everyday Life, and the Crisis of Gilded Age America* (Berkeley: University of California Press, 2002).

Bryson, Norman: *Vision and Painting: The Logic of the Gaze* (New Haven, CT: Yale University Press, 1983).

Bryson, Norman, Holly, Michael Ann & Moxey, Keith, eds.: *Visual Culture: Images and Interpretations* (Hanover and London: Wesleyan University Press, 1994).

Cartwright, Lisa: *Screening the Body: Tracing Medicine's Visual Culture* (Minneapolis: University of Minnesota Press, 1995).

Classen, Constance: *The Color of Angels: Cosmology, Gender, and the Aesthetic Imagination* (London and New York: Routledge, 1998).

Crain, Patricia: *The Story of A: The Alphabetization of America from* The New England Primer *to* The Scarlet Letter (Stanford, CA: Stanford University Press, 2000).

Crary, Jonathan: *Techniques of the Observer: On Vision and Modernity in the 19th Century* (Cambridge, MA: MIT Press, 1990).

Crary, Jonathan: *Suspensions of Perception: Attention, Spectacle, and Modern Culture* (Cambridge, MA: MIT Press, 1999).

DeLue, Rachael: *The Struggle of Vision: George Inness and the Science of Landscape Painting* (Chicago: University of Chicago Press, 2005).

Dikovitskaya, Margaret: "From Art History to Visual Culture: the Study of the Visual after the Cultural Turn," PhD dissertation, Columbia University, New York, 2001 (UMI Number: 3028516).

Dikovitskaya, Margaret: *Visual Culture: The Study of the Visual after the Cultural Turn* (Cambridge, MA: MIT Press, 2005).

Doss, Erika: *Elvis Culture: Fans, Faith, and Image* (Lawrence: University of Kansas Press, 1999).

Doss, Erika, ed.: *Looking at Life Magazine* (Washington, DC: Smithsonian Institution Press, 2001).

Elkins, James: *The Object Stares Back: On the Nature of Seeing* (New York: Simon & Schuster, 1996).

Elkins, James: *The Domain of Images* (Ithaca, NY: Cornell University Press, 1999).

Elkins, James: *Visual Studies: A Skeptical Introduction* (New York: Routledge, 2003).

Evans, Jessica & Hall, Stuart, eds.: *Visual Culture: The Reader* (London: Sage, 1999).

Foster, Hal: *Vision and Visuality* (New York: New Press, 1988).

Freedberg, David: *The Power of Images: Studies in the History and Theory of Response* (Chicago: University of Chicago Press, 1989).

Friedberg, Anne: *Window Shopping: Cinema and the Postmodern* (Berkeley: University of California Press, 1993).

Gattegno, Caleb: *Towards a Visual Culture: Educating through Television* (New York: Outerbridge & Dienstfrey, 1969).

Geertz, Clifford: *The Interpretation of Cultures* (New York: Basic Books, 1973).

Geertz, Clifford: *Local Knowledge: Further Essays in Interpretive Anthropology* (New York: Basic Books, 1983).

Harris, Michael: *Colored Pictures: Race and Visual Representation* (Chapel Hill: University of North Carolina Press, 2003).

Herbert, James D.: "Masterdisciplinarity and the 'Pictorial Turn,'" *Art Bulletin* 77 (December 1995), 537–40.

Herbert, James, D.: "Visual Culture/Visual Studies," in Robert S. Nelson & Richard Shiff, eds., *Critical Terms for Art History*, 2nd ed. (Chicago: University of Chicago Press, 2003), pp. 452–64.

Heywood, Ian & Sandywell, Barry, eds.: *Interpreting Visual Culture: Explorations in the Hermeneutics of the Visual* (London and New York: Routledge, 1999).

Hoffer, Peter Charles: *Sensory Worlds in Early New England* (Baltimore, MD: Johns Hopkins University Press, 2003).

Holly, Michael Ann: *Panofsky and the Foundations of Art History* (Ithaca, NY: Cornell University Press, 1984).

Holly, Michael Ann & Moxey, Keith, eds.: *Art History, Aesthetics, Visual Studies* (Williamstown, MA: Sterling and Francine Clark Art Institute, 2002).

Jay, Martin: *Downcast Eyes: The Denigration of Vision in Twentieth-Century French Thought* (Berkeley: University of California Press, 1993).

Jay, Martin: "That Visual Turn: The Advent of Visual Culture," *Journal of Visual Culture* 1, 1 (2002), 87–92.

Jenks, Chris, ed.: *Visual Culture* (London and New York: Routledge, 1995).

Johnston, Patricia, ed.: *Seeing High and Low Seeing: Representing Social Conflict in American Visual Culture* (Berkeley: University of California Press, 2006).

Kibbey, Ann: *The Interpretation of Material Shapes in Puritanism: A Study of Rhetoric, Prejudice, and Violence* (Cambridge and New York: Cambridge University Press, 1986).

Lee, Anthony W.: *Picturing Chinatown: Art and Orientalism in San Francisco* (Berkeley: University of California Press, 2001).

Leja, Michael: *Looking Askance: Skepticism and American Art from Eakins to Duchamp* (Berkeley: University of California Press, 2004).

Lubin, David: *Shooting Kennedy: JFK and the Culture of Images* (Berkeley: University of California Press, 2003).

McDannell, Colleen: *Material Christianity: Religion and Popular Culture in America* (New Haven, CT: Yale University Press, 1995).

Meyer, Richard: *Outlaw Representation: Censorship and Homosexuality in Twentieth-Century American Art* (Oxford: Oxford University Press, 2002).

Mirzoeff, Nicholas, ed.: *The Visual Culture Reader* (London and New York: Routledge, 1998).

Mirzoeff, Nicholas: *An Introduction to Visual Culture* (London: Routledge, 1999).

Mirzoeff, Nicholas: "A Conversation with Nicholas Mirzoeff," *CAA News* 28, 4 (July 2003), 1 and 7.

Mitchell, W. J. T.: "The Pictorial Turn," *Art Forum* 30 (March 1992), 89–94.

Mitchell, W. J. T.: *Picture Theory: Essays on Verbal and Visual Representation* (Chicago: University of Chicago Press, 1994).

Mitchell, W. J. T.: "What is Visual Culture?" in Irving Lavin, ed., *Meaning in the Visual Arts: Views from the Outside* (Princeton: Institute for Advanced Study, 1995a), pp. 207–17.

Mitchell, W. J. T.: "Interdisciplinarity and Visual Culture," *Art Bulletin* 77 (December 1995b), pp. 540–4.

Mitchell, W. J. T.: "Showing Seeing: A Critique of Visual Culture," in Michael Ann Holly & Keith Moxey, eds., *Art History, Aesthetics, Visual Studies* (Williamstown, MA: Sterling and Francine Clark Art Institute, 2002), pp. 231–50.

Morgan, David, ed.: *Icons of American Protestantism: The Art of Warner Sallman* (New Haven, CT: Yale University Press, 1996).

Morgan, David: *Protestants and Pictures: Religion, Visual Culture, and the Age of American Mass Production* (New York: Oxford University Press, 1999).

Morgan, David: *The Sacred Gaze: Religious Visual Culture in Theory and Practice* (Berkeley: University of California Press, 2005).

Morgan, David & Promey, Sally M., eds.: *The Visual Culture of American Religions* (Berkeley: University of California Press, 2001).

Mulvey, Laura: *Visual and Other Pleasures* (Bloomington: Indiana University Press, 1989).

Nochlin, Linda: *The Politics of Vision* (New York: Harper & Row, 1989).

Promey, Sally M.: *Spiritual Spectacles: Vision and Image in Mid-Nineteenth-Century Shakerism* (Bloomington: Indiana University Press, 1993).

Promey, Sally M.: "The 'Return' of Religion in the Scholarship of American Art," *Art Bulletin* 85 (September 2003), 581–603.

Promey, Sally M.: "Seeing the Self 'in Frame': Early New England Material Practice and Puritan Piety," *Material Religion* 1 (March 2005), 10–47.

Prown, Jules David: "Mind in Matter: An Introduction to Material Culture Theory and Method," *Winterthur Portfolio* 17 (Spring 1982), 1–19.

Rigal, Laura: *American Manufactory: Art, Labor, and the World of Things in the Early Republic* (Princeton, NJ: Princeton University Press, 1998).

Roeder, George H., Jr.: *The Censored War: American Visual Experience during World War II* (New Haven, CT: Yale University Press, 1993).

Roeder, George H., Jr.: "Filling in the Picture: Visual Culture," *Reviews in American History* 26, 1 (1998), 275–93.

St. George, Robert Blair: *Conversing by Signs: Poetics of Implication in Colonial New England Culture* (Chapel Hill: University of North Carolina Press, 1998).

Savage, Kirk: *Standing Soldiers, Kneeling Slaves: Race, War, and Monument in Nineteenth-Century America* (Princeton, NJ: Princeton University Press, 1997).

Schmidt, Leigh Eric: *Consumer Rites: The Buying and Selling of American Holidays* (Princeton, NJ: Princeton University Press, 1995).

Schwartz, Vanessa R. & Przyblyski, Jeannene, eds.: *The Nineteenth-Century Visual Culture Reader* (New York: Routledge, 2004).

Smith, Shawn Michelle: *American Archives: Gender, Race, and Class in Visual Culture* (Princeton, NJ: Princeton University Press, 1999).

Stafford, Barbara Maria: *Visual Analogy: Consciousness as the Art of Collecting* (Cambridge, MA: MIT Press, 1999).

Sturken, Marita & Cartwright, Lisa: *Practices of Looking: An Introduction to Visual Culture* (Oxford: Oxford University Press, 2001).

Taylor, Joshua Charles: *Learning to Look: A Handbook for the Visual Arts* (Chicago: University of Chicago Press, 1957).

Todd, Ellen Wiley: "Photojournalism, Visual Culture, and the Triangle Shirtwaist Fire," *Labor Studies in Working Class History of the Americas* 2, 2 (2005), 9–27.

Ulrich, Laurel Thatcher: *The Age of Homespun: Objects and Stories in the Creation of an American Myth* (New York: Alfred A. Knopf, 2001).

"Visual Culture Questionnaire," *October* 77 (Summer 1996), 25–70.

Walker, John A. & Chaplin, Sarah: *Visual Culture: An Introduction* (Manchester: Manchester University Press, 1997).

Wexler, Laura: *Tender Violence: Domestic Visions in an Age of US Imperialism* (Chapel Hill: University of North Carolina Press, 2000).

Chapter Twenty

MATERIAL CULTURES

J. Ritchie Garrison

In 1839 Godey's *Lady's Book* published a bit of light fiction titled "A Reverie." As the story opens, a woman visits the home of an acquaintance and discovers that the mistress is away. Ushered into a drawing room to wait, she rests on a soft ottoman and falls into a half slumber during which she dreams that the various items of furniture in the room argue over their relative importance to the household. One by one, they talk about their distinct purposes in the family's cultural life. Some complain about their misfortunes – the carpet whines that it has to support everyone and is always getting walked on. Other more favorably situated furnishings express pride of place. The center table claims happily that "my mistress sets a great deal by me, and leans upon me very much," and the solar lamp observes that "when my master sits down of an evening to read his papers, he never pretends to see into the writer's meaning without bringing the matter to me." Masked by the light-hearted punning and inverted reality is a critical set of dilemmas for material culture scholars: to what extent can objects be treated as cultural texts, and how do we assay their meaning in the absence of their words?

The basic questions concerning material culture are easily articulated: why do things look the way they do, how did they get that way, and what do they mean? The answers prove more difficult, and require an exploration of various personal, institutional, and disciplinary approaches to material culture as they have evolved over the past two centuries of American history.

Material Culture Studies before the 1960s

Contemporary scholars of material culture are indebted to generations of antiquarian collectors and the various institutions they created, including museums and historical societies, government-sponsored projects, philosophical societies and libraries, and preservation efforts both private and public. Well before the emergence of modern academic disciplines, a wide range of American antiquarians were assiduously collecting, classifying, researching, and interpreting material objects, and often exhibiting them to a public eager to view them.

Preservation efforts and museums laid the foundations for American material culture scholarship, beginning in the late eighteenth century. David Brigham (1995) has written a fine overview of early museums with a focus on Charles Willson Peale's museum and its audience. Charles Hosmer offers a sweeping, two-volume survey of the preservation movement from the first state historical societies and house museums to the establishment of the National Trust in 1949 (1965, 1981). Peale experimented with many of the programming and exhibition strategies that modern museums use, and helped shape public expectations of how museums should gather and display objects for the public's benefit. But financing these early efforts remained a problem. Peale tried in vain to persuade the federal government to establish and support a national museum; he and his children had to charge admission, and, when that strategy failed, the museum's valuable collections had to be sold and dispersed.

By the mid-nineteenth century, however, the federal government was beginning to play a critical role in collection and research, especially in the area of Native American cultures. Exploring parties, government agents and contractors, and military servicemen collected material objects, recorded information, and sometimes systematically studied native cultures. A number of the government-sponsored collections and images were deposited in the Smithsonian Institution (established in 1846), the Library of Congress, and other institutions where archaeologists, ethnographers, and anthropologists could study them. Some of these collections became the foundations that later generations of historians and anthropologists would depend upon for their research.

The Smithsonian Institution was an exception. By the mid-nineteenth century, there were several models for museums and cultural institutions. Antiquarians and collectors had formed private libraries, historical societies, and art collections. Entrepreneurs such as P. T. Barnum and artists such as Frederic Edwin Church organized exhibits to profit from customers anxious to see curiosities and spectacular artworks. And great cultural fairs such as the Crystal Palace Exhibition in England and the Centennial Exhibition in the United States attracted throngs of people who came to see new technologies and objects from foreign lands. These models ensured that twentieth-century cultural institutions would consider how to balance scholarly and entertainment goals for public audiences.

The growth of industrial capitalism generated large personal fortunes among a wealthy elite, many of whom became deeply interested in material culture scholarship and thus invested in it. Some used their fortunes to collect books, manuscripts, artworks, and historical artifacts that became the nucleus for great museum and library collections. Wealthy and middle-class collectors supported the operating costs of cultural institutions, subsidized research on their collections, and endowed chairs in academic departments. The great collectors believed in the power of objects to Americanize immigrants, entertain, and elevate public taste; they promoted access to their collections through public programming.

Few efforts in the twentieth century had a greater impact on material culture scholarship and the burgeoning field of cultural tourism than John D. Rockefeller, Jr.'s restoration of Williamsburg, Virginia. Rockefeller commanded the financial means to sustain decades of research in archaeology, architectural history, historic crafts, historic furnishings, landscapes, and social and political history. The Williamsburg staff established a tradition of careful planning, field research on objects that remained in their original context, and sharing information across disciplines.

They sought to recreate the material, political, and cultural history of eighteenth-century Virginia, and used their research to guide public interpretation (Hosmer, Jr. 1981). It is possible to admire their achievements without glossing over their distortions and omissions, especially on the subject of slavery and institutionalized racism.

The Depression era further contributed to the development of material culture scholarship as the federal government increased its role in cultural research by hiring scholars for government-financed projects. Several archaeologists from the Williamsburg excavations moved south to dig into colonial Jamestown. Simultaneously, the National Park Service that had long administered the big western parks expanded its role by creating historical parks such as Gateway Park in St. Louis and Independence National Historical Park in Philadelphia; Park staff helped initiate the Historic American Building Survey in 1933, to preserve information on the nation's historic structures and landscapes. The goal of these efforts was to promote preservation and restoration by assembling reliable architectural and historical information at the local and regional level, so that managers and contractors could properly care for their historic resources. But until the 1950s, most museum and preservation-related scholarship focused on the founding fathers.

After World War II, museum officials and philanthropists grew increasingly concerned over the lack of systematic academic training for museum professionals. Most had acquired their expertise through a form of apprenticeship. Many had been collectors, a few held doctoral degrees in related disciplines, and some had started in artistic, business, or various professional careers. In 1952, The Henry Francis duPont Winterthur Museum collaborated with the University of Delaware on a graduate program that paired the museum's extensive collections of American decorative arts with university courses in early American culture. In 1964, the New York State Historical Association in Cooperstown, New York followed suit, establishing a program with the State University of New York that was devoted to folklore and history-museum training. These and other programs that followed had a seminal impact on material culture scholarship, training many of the museum professionals and academic scholars who would shape the field in the second half of the century. They also promoted the study of objects that did not fit the criteria for "high" art (generally thought of as European), for ethnographically significant objects, or for classical antiquities.

Most professional historians before and after World War II remained skeptical of this persistent fascination with material objects. Their doubts were articulated by William Hesseltine at a meeting of the American Association for State and Local History in 1957: professional historians, he declared, depended upon documents, and would continue to do so, because they could not subject material objects to the same critical techniques they used on documents. Objects were best remanded to the role of illustrations for ideas gleaned from written texts. His essay encapsulated an enduring debate among material culture scholars: in what ways, if any, are objects useful to historians, and what methodologies might render them meaningful forms of evidence rather than illustrations?

For their part, material culture scholars in the 1950s and early 1960s were busy developing new methodologies for material culture study, and cataloging collections to professional standards. Charles Montgomery, who had been an antiques dealer before joining the Winterthur staff in 1949, emphasized the value of learning directly from the objects. His essay, "Some Remarks on the Practice and Science of Connoisseurship" (1982 [1961]), set down his own approach to material culture and its interpretation. His years selling antiques had given him experience with collectors who often sought historical information, not just status markers. His approach was contextual, emphasizing the necessity of looking carefully at things and situating them in time and place; but he also understood that humans respond to things on an emotional and aesthetic level. Montgomery's rigorous approach fused concepts employed by art historians, historians, anthropologists, and archaeologists, but he rarely won approbation from scholars, who disliked the connotation of elitism that the term "connoisseur" held. Yet his emphasis as a teacher on careful research (sometimes using scientific analysis of materials), attention to detail, and individual agency in the production and consumption of objects has remained critical to the study of objects.

At Cooperstown, Louis Jones and Bruce Buckley approached material culture from the perspective of folk life. Both valued rigorous fieldwork and a bottom-up approach to understand cultural behavior, although their own training pre-dated the fluorescence of the new social history. Influenced by cultural geography, sociolinguistics, and folklore's emphasis on traditional culture, they treated the rural landscape around Cooperstown as a laboratory, sending students out to document buildings, landscapes, craft, foodways, ghost stories, leisure, music, and other aspects of folk culture. The program also taught field skills such as drafting, oral history, photography, and systematic record keeping.

The museum-training programs that were pioneering new methodological approaches to object study continued to operate outside the orbit of conventional disciplines in the 1960s. But students of the era were beginning to challenge academic and political canons, and to embrace the possibilities of interdisciplinary knowledge. In an era of civil rights and existential angst, many believed that the study of popular culture and marginalized social groups might help restore justice and equality. And the study of the decorative arts, visual culture, folklore, and material culture seemed to offer a way of understanding popular culture and marginal groups who were often underrepresented in documentary records. Material culture scholars borrowed methods and ideas from archaeologists (object seriation and stratigraphy), cultural anthropologists (ethnography and structuralism), geographers (patterns of spatial diffusion), and folklorists (oral and social performance and linguistics). Objects were not just works of art; they were symbols situated in historical contexts.

The New Social History

In the 1960s and 1970s, as many professional historians set out to explore the lives of non-elites and understudied groups – women, slaves, the poor, a variety of ethnic groups – they turned to sources that they had once relegated to antiquarians and genealogists. Material culture evidence, they discovered, could contribute to a more thorough understanding of the past. Fernand Braudel's enormously influential *Capitalism and Material Life, 1400–1800* (1967) made a case for studying everyday life – the "enormous mass of history barely conscious of itself" (p. 7) – across the *longue durée*, and demonstrated how material objects expressed the contributions of people left out of standard histories, marked the boundaries of spatial diffusion, opened up and closed off social possibilities in human landscapes, and located human behavior in the stratigraphy of time. Three years later, John Demos registered Braudel's influence by offering chapters on housing, furnishings, and clothing in his study of family life in Plymouth Colony (1970). Material culture studies were now part of a larger tool kit for historians asking new questions about the past. Federal funding began to foster collaborative, cross-institutional research. Museum professionals and academicians could work together to address such issues as housing and standards of living, fertility and family life, social rituals and consumer behavior, and other topics drawing the attention of the new social historians.

At the same time, material culture scholars began to borrow theoretical approaches from other disciplines, such as Claude Lévi-Strauss's theories of structuralist anthropology and Clifford Geertz's calls for an ethnography of "thick description" (1973). They applied them to data amassed by generations of collectors and preservationists, and findings from field research. Few scholars in the 1960s and 1970s had a greater impact on the links between theory and field evidence than folklorist Henry Glassie. *Pattern in the Material Folk Culture of the Eastern United States* (1968) used evidence gathered from an enormous geographical area to suggest how traditional forms of cultural behavior persisted across time; by contrast, *Folk Housing in Middle Virginia: A Structural Analysis* (1975) used a limited area in Louisa and Goochland Counties, Virginia, to draw sweeping conclusions about *mentalité* and cultural change in the Anglo-American world. *Folk Housing* generated considerable controversy, because of Glassie's use of linguistic theory and structuralist anthropology to argue that traditional housing in a small section of the Upper South could stand in for a larger unit of analysis. He attempted to reconstruct the generative grammar used by folk builders in designing dwellings by measuring and analyzing house forms, much as an anthropologist might break cultural myths into constituent parts to visualize a metanarrative. Though many historians found his analysis confusing or implausible, Glassie, who had worked with noted geographer Fred Kniffen and at Cooperstown with folklorist Bruce Buckley, modeled the importance of linking careful field methods to theory and interpretation.

Another scholar interested in the implications of structuralism and linguistics for material culture study was Robert Trent. His published catalog of Connecticut folk chairs from 1720 to 1840 (1977) used the ideas of Henri Focillon to justify the importance of studying ordinary objects as artistic achievements, and took a structuralist approach to understanding the proportioning and construction systems encoded in the chairs. Several years later, Jules David Prown published "Mind in Matter: An Introduction to Material Culture Theory" (1982), urging scholars to bridge the interpretive gap between "vernacular" and "high style" objects. In Prown's view, objects were intentional products that encoded cultural behavior, and scholars should make "affective contact" with the sensibilities of people in the past. Uniting these two essays was the conviction that it was possible to interpret cultural behavior by studying object patterns.

Segmentation

While the enthusiasm for interdisciplinarity and shared theoretical approaches tended to hold together the scholarship of material culture in the 1960s and early 1970s, the field began to segment in the 1970s and 1980s into such subspecialties as vernacular architecture, historic archaeology, consumer studies, decorative arts, and visual culture. Some formed their own interest groups, held annual meetings, and published newsletters or journals. The Vernacular Architecture Forum, for example, started out as a group of friends who shared an enthusiasm for architectural field research. They used the term "vernacular" to distinguish their approach from mainstream architectural historians who studied elite buildings and architects. Even as they sought a distinctive interpretive stance and method, they broadened their scope to include a much larger universe of structures and landscapes that were largely ignored, embracing "fishing shacks" as opposed to Frank Lloyd Wright's "Falling Water," in one scholar's formulation. Members shared a fondness for field research, and at their annual meetings typically spent two days looking at area buildings for every day they listened to papers in hotel conference rooms (Carter & Cromley 2005). This emphasis on field- (or collection-) based study has remained important to many material culture scholars, who can distinguish between those who understand objects from close study, and those who frame arguments about material life that are untested by object study.

Some subspecialties of material culture form within the disciplines, which shape both the questions and intellectual uses of the resulting scholarship. For geographers concerned with spatial patterns, material culture can demarcate regional and ethnic behavior. To study the diffusion of the Pennsylvania German bank barn (Ensminger 1992) or *flürkucken* house (Weaver 1986) was to follow the movement of people from a continental hearth to a colonial hearth and thence to the backcountry. For historical archaeologists, trash pits, potshards, and soil stains reveal human actions in specific associational relationships. The objects that James Deetz recovered at Plymouth, Massachusetts, and "Flowerdew Hundred" plantation (1977, 1993), that Ivor Noël Hume studied from "Martin's Hundred" (1982), or that Lyle Stone examined from Fort Michilimackinac (1974) represented vicariously the men, women, and children, whites and blacks, free people and slaves, rich and poor, savants and idiots who all left their marks in time as ghosts in the dirt, akin to the shadows on Plato's cave walls. No matter the care with which archaeologists measured and recorded the past, they could only see the shadows, not the actions that had made them. The stories they told had to conform to the boundaries of the available evidence and reasonable interpretation.

The plethora of public and private documents for long-lived early New Englanders made the study of family and community life in that region very fruitful even before historians resorted to historic archaeology (although such institutions as Historic Deerfield, Plimoth Plantation, and the Society for the Preservation of New England Antiquities had conducted important archaeological work). Further south, however, archaeology played an indispensable role in the study of colonial life. Seventeenth-century Virginia's and Maryland's documentary records were scarcer than New England's, but the archaeological excavations funded for over 40 years by private foundations and federal, state, and local governments found new applications in the 1970s and 1980s. In the late 1950s, Colonial Williamsburg had reinvigorated its archaeological program under the direction of Ivor Noël Hume, who recovered a huge collection of objects from Williamsburg sites, then excavated Wolstenhome Towne in the 1970s and 1980s (1982, 2001). Further north, Mark Leone and his students had dug sites in Annapolis, and Henry Miller and a group of professional historians had embarked on an interdisciplinary study of St. Mary's City (Leone 2005; Miller 1989). Elsewhere in the Tidewater region, archaeologists studied a number of other plantation sites – some famous (Mount Vernon and Monticello), and others obscure (Flowerdew Hundred and Kingsmill Plantations) (Deetz 1993; Kelso 1984).

This archaeological research was collaborative, inter-institutional, interdisciplinary, and, because it was so expensive and labor-intensive, government-funded. It was also fruitful. The artifacts recovered from these excavations, when combined with the work of demographers, historians, architectural historians, and curators, reshaped Tidewater historiography. The cultural life of seventeenth- and early eighteenth-century Southerners proved more complicated than most scholars had previously realized, and seemed almost an inversion of New England patterns. Until the mid-seventeenth century, the majority of Tidewater homes were impermanent post-in-the-ground houses, while most New England dwellings built within a few years after settlement were of solid timber-frame construction on foundations. In the first half of the century, gender imbalance and high mortality were endemic to the Chesapeake region, while New Englanders enjoyed comparatively good health and rapid population growth from high fertility rates. Datable artifacts from the seventeenth-century South are comparatively rare, while New England furnishings and artifacts have survived in some abundance. Nevertheless, Southerners, including some slaves, had a richly textured material life, and were important consumers of English goods traded throughout the Atlantic world. The dig at Martin's Hundred, for example, uncovered European armor, silver threads from clothing, leaded window glass, inlaid cutlery, and Rhenish stoneware – objects that told a story of cultural consumerism (Noël Hume 2001).

The topic of consumerism has energized material culture scholarship over the past 25 years. While scholars in a variety of disciplines had long debated the timing and implications of capitalism, much of the discussion had focused on production – changing labor, technology, and business practices and their resonance throughout the world – and studies of consumerism had followed Veblen's theory of status envy (1912), or Simmel's concept of social-boundary maintenance grounded in social structures (1904). Comparatively few scholars had examined the cultural changes wrought by consumer demand. But in 1982, Neil McKendrick, John Brewer, and J. H. Plumb's *The Birth of a Consumer Society* contested the notion that English consumer behavior largely postdated industrialization. Preindustrial consumers had different consumption habits than their descendants, but they helped establish an Atlantic world economy that circulated people and commodities within a remarkably sophisticated understanding of aesthetics, production strategies, costs, and profits. Eighteenth-century families – including some Native Americans and other non-elites – drank imported beverages, wore professionally tailored clothing of imported fabrics, peed in imported chamber pots, ate off English pewter plates, used Sheffield and Birmingham tools, and depended on an array of powders and pomades to maintain proper deportment (Noël Hume 2001). Some of these items made their way into the middens of colonial America.

As professional historians became more interested in consumer behavior, some began to examine more closely the sorts of things people bought. Pots emerged as a key marker of human action, mapping imperial power outward from the confines of London, Liverpool, and Staffordshire, and signifying the shifting boundaries of political and ideological relationships as people started switching from pewter to ceramic plates. Pewter was the archaeologist's "missing artifact"; though it could survive in the ground, it had significant value to recyclers, and thus was rarely discarded. Ceramic plates, by contrast, became a datable horizon line in the expansion of capitalism around the Atlantic world (Martin 1989; Noël Hume 2001). Consumer demand in British colonial America was driven by the needs of a nation of immigrants whose mobility distanced them from their native communities. For the colonists, consumer behavior and deportment communicated social intentions and values to those around them (Carson 1994). The evidence in the ground yielded information about individual sociability as people responded creatively to the prescriptions of the dominant cultural system.

These studies that trace the consumer revolution to the colonial era are based on a deep understanding of objects by material-culture specialists. By contrast, most historical studies that attribute mass consumerism to advanced industrialization rely primarily on the textual and visual evidence of advertising, as well as the impact of mass production on the quantity and price of consumer goods. While Robert and Helen Lynd's famous study *Middletown* (1929) does include information about what people were purchasing, many key works on mass consumption focus on the marketing strategies developed by businesses to persuade consumers to buy their products. Roland Marchand's *Advertising the American Dream* (1985) examined the world of ad men through thousands of advertisements, rather than the consumers who received their messages. Susan Strasser's *Satisfaction Guaranteed* (1989) and Richard Tedlow's *New and Improved* (1990) also relied heavily on advertisements, though they disagreed on the effects of mass marketing: while Tedlow argued that mass consumption expanded the range of products available to people of limited means, Strasser emphasized a darker side of mass merchandizing in which corporations shaped public buying habits to their own ends.

The richness of this scholarship on advertising, and its participation in contemporary arguments about capitalist ideology and policy, are compelling, but the methodological differences between document- and object-based research are analogous to the distinctions between writers and readers. As Michel de Certeau observed in *The Practice of Everyday Life* (1984), writers inscribe their view of the world in texts, while readers appropriate selective readings of texts to their own tactical ends. Whereas documentary research on advertising reveals vigorous efforts by powerful people to impose their hegemony over others, field research in housing and archaeological sites often uncovers the ways in which people selectively interpreted and used the manufacturers' and marketers' products. William Rathje provides an example of the complex relationships between material culture, marketing, ideology, and politics in *Rubbish!: The Archaeology of Garbage* (1992), a report on the University of Arizona's long-term excavation of a modern landfill to discover patterns of late twentieth-century consumption.

Another sector of material culture study has focused on issues of race and ethnicity, within two broad categories: research on ethnic history and material life, and a fascination with surviving traditions of art, craft, and aesthetics. Studies of Latino, Asian American, Caribbean, Jewish, and Inuit material cultures are growing, particularly in areas of the country where population densities are large and cultural traditions are most visible. The challenge of this research is to work through the ways in which the dominant national culture absorbs and effaces ethnic traditions over time, as well as the means by which ethnic populations resist total assimilation. The largest body of literature considers African Americans.

Early studies of African American artifacts concentrated on making the case for including them in the canon of American arts. In 1943, James Porter argued in *Modern Negro Art* that enslaved African Americans had made many important contributions to American art, some of which had their roots in African cultures brought to the "new" world by slaves. More recently, Richard J. Powell's *Black Art: A Cultural History* (2003) surveys key figures in African American art and the contexts in which they worked. But the best starting point for students seeking an introduction to this field remains Theodore C. Landsmark's "Comments on African American Contributions to American Material Life" (1998), which reviews the historiography and surveys a broad range of objects including decorative and fine arts.

Mainstream southern historians have long considered various aspects of slave material life – usually through the lens of written documents. Thus, Eugene Genovese's *Roll Jordan Roll: The World the Slaves Made* (1972) included sections on housing, gardens, and clothing, based largely on written texts. Charles Joyner engaged a wider range of material culture topics in *Down By the Riverside: A South Carolina Slave Community* (1984), focusing on the task system employed at rice plantations along the Waccamaw River, and uncovering the ways in which slaves became agents in shaping their own material worlds. More recently, Philip D. Morgan's magisterial *Slave Counterpoint: Black Culture in the Eighteenth-Century Chesapeake and Lowcountry* (1998) included an entire chapter on slave material life that addressed slave housing, dress, and diet. One of the problems associated with the study of slave material culture, however, is distinguishing the ambiguous boundary between master and slave, between standards of living imposed from above and those actively created by slaves and free blacks in the interstices of a world dominated by whites.

It is not difficult to find evidence of hard usage and ill treatment in the material lives of slaves; it is more challenging to understand from an emic perspective how African American families creolized the world of objects, preserving some traditions of ethnic sensibility while acculturating to an initially alien culture. In *Uncommon Ground: Archaeology and Early African America, 1650–1800* (1992), Leland Ferguson illuminates how slaves in the Lowcountry of South Carolina expressed their own cosmology through symbolism inscribed on the bottoms of pots that were then broken and hidden under water. Such distinct forms of expression were, however, comparatively rare in everyday life. Though collectors seek out objects such as pots or quilts that they associate with African American artistry, most African American families lived with and desired the same sorts of objects owned by whites. In the Valley of Virginia, to cite one example, black workers used overtime wages to buy the clothing accessories and domestic wares common to both white and black families in the region (Dew 1994).

Museums have sponsored important research on African American material folk culture. John Michael Vlach's well-known study *The Afro-American Tradition in the Decorative Arts* appeared first as a museum exhibition in 1978, and was reissued as a book in 1990. In it, he discusses the persistence of African culture and sensibilities in objects such as shotgun houses, sweet grass baskets, ironwork, and pottery. In 1991, the Museum of the Confederacy sponsored an exhibition and catalog, *Before Freedom Came: African American Life in the Antebellum South*, that explored themes of African American history and material life (Campbell, Jr. 1991). More recently, scholars have studied the quilts and quilters of Gee's Bend, a community formed by ex-slaves after the Civil War that has maintained a tradition of expressive quilt making (Beardsley et al. 2002). These volumes catalog and interpret important objects and share data that scholars will continue to build upon.

Decorative arts scholarship has also grown vigorously and has further sub-divided into areas of specialty associated with particular genres of collecting and connoisseurship – visible in such publications as the Chipstone Foundation's serial, *American Furniture* (1993–present), and *Ceramics in America* (2001–present), or the Costume Society of America's *Dress* (1975–present). These serials complement a number of important exhibition catalogs on specific private and museum collections. But with a few important exceptions, cultural historians have tended to ignore this scholarship, which seems removed from the scholarly conversations to which they are accustomed.

Yet this work often provides valuable information on material objects, and challenges cultural historians to come up with more sophisticated interpretations of subjects such as aesthetics, art, commodification, craft habits, social customs, and patronage. Linda Baumgarten's study of "the language of clothing" in early America (2002), written for an exhibition at Colonial Williamsburg, pairs well, for example, with Richard Bushman's chapter on "Bodies and Minds" in his *Refinement of America: Persons, Houses, Cities* (1992), because Baumgarten unpacks the visual and material culture of fabric and design, now obscure, that once shaped the posture and position of men and women throughout the Anglo-American world. Similarly, Ken Ames's *Death in the Dining Room and Other Tales of Victorian Culture* (1992) amplifies C. Dallett Hemphill's *Bowing to Necessities: A History of Manners in America, 1620–1860* (1999). Ames shows the complex meanings and behaviors encoded in decorative arts objects, while Hemphill demonstrates how manners simultaneously liberated and ensnared Americans in codes of conduct rooted in aristocratic European conventions. Etiquette could stultify social relationships through ritual, but it could also mask rank for those who learned what the codes meant and how to manipulate them through objects.

Decorative arts scholars also ask questions about the sensations evoked by objects. Thus, Katherine C. Grier examined the development of spring-seat upholstery and the physical sensations that redefined middle-class notions of comfort in *Culture and Comfort: People, Parlors, and Upholstery, 1850–1930* (1988). Her study examined the canonical objects of middle-class domesticity, but she also included how people of lesser means adapted found materials to selectively embrace cultural norms. Jonathan Prown and Richard Miller explored how themes of sexuality were covertly encoded into furniture in "The Rococo, the Grotto, and the Philadelphia High Chest" (1996), emphasizing that all objects convey mixed messages. The historical challenge of such visual analysis of art is to strike a proper balance between the concerns of the present and the people in the past who created and used these objects.

Decorative arts scholarship encompasses many different objectives and consumers: from the trained scholars who spend years piecing together the life and work of Duncan Phyffe, to the devotees of *Antiques Roadshow* eager to learn whether a family heirloom is worth a small fortune at auction. Knowledge of the decorative arts is not restricted to academic conversation; it can affect both demand and market value in a realm where objects are commodities.

Although the study of visual culture is often associated with the work of art historians, it is as much an interpretive approach as a scholarly discipline. As the new cultural turn gained traction in the 1980s, many material culture scholars set out to explore contested ideological boundaries, seeking to reveal the ways in which ideas fixed in society's superstructure a canonical rendering of the world deployed by the powerful against the weak or uninformed. By unmasking hegemonic ideas expressed through objects, scholars could recover the politics of social control. A controversial exhibition at the National Museum of American Art, *The West as America*, explored the visual imagery of the West as a tool in America's politics of manifest destiny (Truettner & Anderson 1991). Similarly, Angela Miller's *Empire of the Eye: Landscape Representation and American Cultural Politics, 1825–1875* (1993) considered American landscape paintings as complex ideological expressions of regional and nationalist identities and hegemonies. Visual culture was polyvocal, and layered with symbolism and metaphors that competing groups employed as they jostled for power and position.

Subsequent efforts modified the determinism implicit in these efforts by reconstructing the dense network of social relationships that influenced aesthetic production and circulation. Objects helped organize the public sphere by shaping personal identity and social exchange. The elite women whose "salon culture" Susan M. Stabile recovers in *Memory's Daughters: The Material Culture of Remembrance in Eighteenth-Century America* (2004) used objects to communicate social bonds, intellectual aspirations, and taste. Most recently, Margaretta Lovell explored the linkages between portraiture, artists, and artisans in *Art in a Season of Revolution: Painters, Artisans, and Patrons in Early America* (2005). She considers art and material culture as "the residue of the intentions and collaborations of dozens, even hundreds of people making individual decisions, making them in an enormous network of intended and unintended actions and consequences . . . " (2005: 267–8). Culture shapes the strategies of human expression, but individuals adjust tactically and creatively to the situations they confront.

Interpretation

Material culture scholars sometimes make sense of what they see by trying to reconstruct relationships: between producers and consumers and sometimes everyone who has used the object in the years since it was created. In *Reading the Past: Current Approaches to Interpretation in Archaeology* (1986), Ian Hodder noted that interpretation involves a process of testing in which scholars evaluate ideas for consistency – ideas must make sense – and congruency – arguments should be grounded in evidence rather than rhetoric. Sound interpretation demands that researchers pass both tests. But even when an interpretation passes these tests, material culture scholars are captive to their own and their subjects' modes of communication. In studying houses, for example, they measure and map plans and landscapes to record systematically human and spatial relationships; but they understand that the floor plans they draw to record the information are conventions that stand in for what they observed. Living people do not experience life in the form of floor plans; they encounter it as a set of articulated spaces through which they move. As they do, their perspective constantly shifts as portions of the material world appear or recede. Thus, the information they command is redundant, overlapping, chaotic, contingent, and episodic by turns and simultaneously, depending on how people sort it. It is culture that helps them decode and assign significance.

Viewed from afar, cultural patterns often seem more salient than individual variation, but scholars who walk a historical landscape or examine closely a piece of furniture can sometimes gain understanding of the idiosyncratic decisions made by individuals and groups coping with particular contingencies anchored in sequences of time. How does one account for or theorize about human idiosyncrasy and taste? Culture is strategic, rooted in shared values, beliefs, and manners; individual behavior is tactical, connected to the contingencies that people encounter in everyday life. Cultural history is a mixture of the two.

As critical theory reshaped cultural history, material culture scholars seized the notion that culture was contextual and mutable, discursive rather than fixed. Robert B. St George's *Conversing by Signs: Poetics of Implication in Colonial New England* (1998), for example, used objects to uncover the unspoken but visible assumptions English men and women and New Englanders used to make meaning in their world. Moving across time and space, he examines a series of objects and stories that implicate beliefs and values – a farmstead in Connecticut, the relationship of the body to buildings, attacks on houses, the paintings of Ralph Earl, and the tensions between commerce and faith. Dell Upton's *Holy Things and Profane: Anglican Parish Churches in Colonial Virginia* (1986) examined the relationships of secular and religious life by first cataloguing Virginia's colonial Anglican churches, and then exploring how they expressed both religious faith and social rank before a community. Finally, Bernard Herman reassembled the meanings of housing, landscape, and family life in the great cedar swamp of southern Delaware in *The Stolen House* (1992). His methodology is a version of archaeological cross mending (akin to the process of re-assembling the fragments of a pot scattered about a site) in which he uses a detailed court case and a careful study of buildings and landscapes to situate intention and meaning in a place where the value of land is lodged in the timber growing on it. Whereas removing the timber degrades the value of the land by eliminating its most valuable commodity, leaving it uncut squanders the heirs' return on their capital. The meaning of court testimony is made visible through the linkage of objects and texts. Objects are not just illustrations of litigious exchanges; they are freighted with symbolic weight.

While thinking about objects as a form of text predisposes scholars to conceptualize culture as a semiotic system, the material in most material culture imposes a burden of tangibility in which words do not fully stand in for things. As Grant McCracken pointed out in *Culture and Consumption: New Approaches to the Symbolic*

Character of Consumer Goods and Activities (1990), the ability to combine a small number of sounds and symbols into words, sentences, and paragraphs is a far more flexible way to communicate than making an artifact. People create objects from a wide range of materials in an endless parade of styles and forms, but the communicative power of these objects rests in their conformity to – or violation of – cultural expectation. The meaning of an ambiguous artifact cannot be decoded through simple analogies to shared experience. Thus, objects are at their most powerful when conveying relatively simple messages that resist change over time. The fenced yard in front of the Miles Brewton house in Charleston, South Carolina sends a clear message that the owners will defend their domain. The top of the fence, made of iron *cheveaux-de-fries* – used by eighteenth- and nineteenth-century armies to break up charges on battle lines or trenches – lays bare the vulnerability of slave owners and the potential for violence in a society filled with latent insurgents. Brewton's use of a military device in his fence symbolized his connections to political instruments of coercion and rendered the consequences of an attack brutally clear.

If postmodern theory has exposed the ways in which ideological and political systems can shape cultural behavior, it has also helped illuminate the various ways individuals and organizations redefine expectations and standards to their own ends. Objects are laden with pattern and ambiguity. Ambiguity cedes power to individuals or groups by conveying the opportunity or even the right to experiment with alternatives. The process is visible in Jack Crowley's history of the word "comfort" in *The Invention of Comfort: Sensibilities and Design in Early Modern Britain and Early America* (2001). Originally denoting a tradition of moral support, "comfort" gradually became identified with physical comfort and social progress on the ambiguous moral and political ground between luxury and poverty. Industrialization complicated the debate about cultural values by simultaneously increasing the gap between the rich and the poor *and* raising material standards of living for almost everyone during a brief moment in time – a theme Ruth Schwartz Cowan explored in *More Work for Mother: The Ironies of Household Technology from the Open Hearth to the Microwave* (1983). The majority of Americans – rich and poor – went from chamber pots and privies to flush toilets, from candles and oil lamps to the electric light bulb, and from letters and face-to-face chat to the telephone, in less than a century. Material life was not a zero-sum game in which the rich got richer and the poor got poorer. It was more often confusing and paradoxical as changing technologies and costs led to debates about what was necessary, possible, or desirable.

The recursive relationship of individuals and their objects complicates cultural interpretation because all objects have an aesthetic dimension that material culture scholars and cultural historians struggle to understand and theorize. Reading a recipe for apple pie is not the same as eating it to learn how it tastes. Some people's pies taste better than others; some manufacturers succeed and others fail because consumers' judgments are based on a host of variables that are difficult to quantify or even express. Thus, power is not lodged inevitably in the political asymmetries of a culture's superstructure or in the metanarratives of social relationships; people artfully lead their everyday lives in the midst of objects that can either open up or constrain their possibilities. The author of "A Reverie" uses witty dialogue to teach readers about the function of objects in parlor culture, but words alone cannot capture the complex and often ambiguous meanings of lamps and center tables. At some level, all humans who explore their world by reaching out to touch it are scholars of material culture.

REFERENCES

Ames, Kenneth L.: *Death in the Dining Room and Other Tales of Victorian Culture* (Philadelphia, PA: Temple University Press, 1992).

Baumgarten, Linda: *What Clothes Reveal: The Language of Clothing in Colonial and Federal America* (Williamsburg, VA: Colonial Williamsburg Foundation in Association with Yale University Press, 2002).

Beardsley, John et al.: *Gee's Bend: The Women and Their Quilts*, intr. by Alvia Wardlaw (Atlanta: Tinwood Books, Houston: The Museum of Fine Arts, 2002).

Braudel, Fernand: *Capitalism and Material Life, 1400–1800* (New York: Harper & Row, 1973 [1967]).

Brigham, David R.: *Public Culture in the Early Republic: Peale's Museum and Its Audience* (Washington, DC: Smithsonian Institution Press, 1995).

Bushman, Richard L.: *The Refinement of America: Persons, Houses, Cities* (New York: Alfred A. Knopf, 1992).

Campbell, Jr., Edward D. C. with the assistance of Rice, Kym S.: *Before Freedom Came: African American Life in the Antebellum South* (Richmond. Published for the Museum of the Confederacy by the University Press of Virginia, 1991).

Carson, Cary: "The Consumer Revolution in Colonial British America: Why Demand?" in Cary Carson, Ronald Hoffman, & Peter J. Albert eds., *Of Consuming Interests: The Style of Life in the Eighteenth Century* (Charlottesville: Published for the United States Capitol Historical Society by The University Press of Virginia, 1994).

Carter, Thomas & Cromley, Elizabeth Collins: *Invitation to Vernacular Architecture: A Guide to the Study of Ordinary Buildings and Landscapes* (Knoxville: University of Tennessee Press, 2005).

de Certeau, Michel: *The Practice of Everyday Life* (Berkeley: University of California Press, 1984).

Chipstone Foundation: *American Furniture* (Hanover: University Press of New England, published for The Chipstone Foundation, 1993 to present).

Chipstone Foundation: *Ceramics in America* (Hanover: University Press of New England, published for The Chipstone Foundation, 2001 to present).

Costume Society of America: *Dress* (1975 to present).

Cowan, Ruth Schwartz: *More Work for Mother: The Ironies of Household Technology from the Open Hearth to the Microwave* (New York: Basic Books, 1983).

Crowley, John E.: *The Invention of Comfort: Sensibilities and Design in Early Modern Britain and Early America* (Baltimore, MD: Johns Hopkins University Press, 2001).

Deetz, James: *In Small Things Forgotten: The Archaeology of Early American Life* (New York: Anchor Press/Doubleday, 1977).

Deetz, James: *Flowerdew Hundred: The Archaeology of a Virginia Plantation, 1619–1864* (Charlottesville: University Press of Virginia, 1993).

Demos, John: *A Little Commonwealth: Family Life in Plymouth Colony* (New York: Oxford University Press, 1970).

Dew, Charles B.: *Bond of Iron: Master and Slave at Buffalo Forge* (New York: W. W. Norton, 1994).

Ensminger, Robert F.: *The Pennsylvania Barn: Its Origin, Evolution, and Distribution in North America* (Baltimore, MD: Johns Hopkins University Press, 1992).

Ferguson, Leland G.: *Uncommon Ground: Archaeology and Early African America, 1650–1800* (Washington, DC: Smithsonian Institution Press, 1992).

Geertz, Clifford: *The Interpretation of Cultures: Selected Essays* (New York: Basic Books, 1973).

Genovese, Eugene D.: *Roll Jordan Roll: The World the Slaves Made* (New York: Vintage Books, 1972).

Glassie, Henry: *Pattern in the Material Folk Culture of the Eastern United States* (Philadelphia: University of Pennsylvania Press, 1968).

Glassie, Henry: *Folk Housing in Middle Virginia: A Structural Analysis* (Knoxville: University of Tennessee Press, 1975).

Grier, Katherine C.: *Culture and Comfort: People, Parlors, and Upholstery, 1850–1930* (Rochester, NY: The Strong Museum, dist. by the University of Massachusetts Press, 1988).

Hemphill, C. Dallett: *Bowing to Necessities: A History of Manners in America, 1620–1860* (New York: Oxford University Press, 1999).

Herman, Bernard L.: *The Stolen House* (Charlottesville: The University Press of Virginia, 1992).

Hesseltine, William B.: "The Challenge of the Artifact," in Thomas J. Schlereth, ed., *Material Culture Studies in America* (Nashville: American Association for State and Local History, 1982), pp. 93–105.

Hodder, Ian: *Reading the Past: Current Approaches to Interpretation in Archaeology* (Cambridge: Cambridge University Press, 1986).

Hosmer, Charles B.: *Presence of the Past: A History of the Preservation Movement in the United States Before Williamsburg* (New York: Putnam, 1965).

Hosmer, Jr., Charles B.: *Preservation Comes of Age: From Williamsburg to the National Trust, 1926–1949* (Charlottesville: Published for the Preservation Press, National Trust for Historic Preservation in the United States, by the University Press of Virginia, 1981).

Joyner, Charles: *Down By the Riverside: A South Carolina Slave Community* (Urbana: University of Illinois Press, 1984).

Kelso, William M.: *Kingsmill Plantations, 1619–1800: Archaeology of Country Life in Colonial Virginia* (Orlando, FL: Academic Press, 1984).

Landsmark, Theodore C.: "Comments on African American Contributions to American Material Life," *Winterthur Portfolio* 33, 4 (1998), 261–82.

Leone, Mark P.: *The Archaeology of Liberty in an American Capital: Excavations in Annapolis* (Berkeley: University of California Press, 2005).

Lovell, Margaretta M.: *Art in a Season of Revolution: Painters, Artisans, and Patrons in Early America* (Philadelphia: University of Pennsylvania Press, 2005).

Lynd, Robert & Lynd, Helen: *Middletown: A Study in Contemporary American Culture* (New York: Harcourt, Brace, 1929).

Marchand, Roland: *Advertising the American Dream: Making Way for Modernity, 1920–1940* (Berkeley: University of California Press, 1985).

Martin, Ann Smart: "The Role of Pewter as Missing Artifact: Consumer Attitudes Towards Tablewares in Late 18th Century Virginia," *Historical Archaeology* 23, 2 (1989), 1–27.

McCracken, Grant: *Culture and Consumption: New Approaches to the Symbolic Character of Consumer Goods and Activities* (Bloomington: Indiana University Press, 1990).

McKendrick, Neil, Brewer, John, & Plumb, J. H.: *The Birth of a Consumer Society: The Commercialization of Eighteenth-Century England* (Bloomington: Indiana University Press, 1982).

Miller, Angela L.: *The Empire of the Eye: Landscape Representation and American Cultural Politics, 1825–1875* (Ithaca, NY: Cornell University Press, 1993).

Miller, Henry M. with contributions by Morrison II, Alexander H. & Stone, Gary Wheeler: "A Search for the 'Cittie of Saint Maries': Report on the 1981 Excavations in St. Mary's City Maryland" (St. Mary's, MD: Saint Mary's City Commission, 1989).

Montgomery, Charles F.: "Some Remarks on the Practice and Science of Connoisseurship," in Thomas J. Schlereth, ed., *Material Culture Studies in America* (Nashville: American Association for State and Local History, 1982 [1961]), pp. 143–52.

Morgan, Philip D.: *Slave Counterpoint: Black Culture in the Eighteenth-Century Chesapeake and Lowcountry* (Chapel Hill: Published for the Omohundro Institute of Early American History and Culture by the University of North Carolina Press, 1998).

Noël Hume, Ivor: *Martin's Hundred* (New York: Alfred A. Knopf, 1982).

Noël Hume, Ivor: *If These Pots Could Talk: Collecting 2000 Years of British Household Pottery* (Hanover: Published by the Chipstone Foundation, dist. by the University Press of New England, 2001).

Noël Hume, Ivor & Noël Hume, Audrey: *The Archaeology of Martin's Hundred* (Philadelphia: University of Pennsylvania Museum of Archaeology and Anthropology, and Williamsburg: The Colonial Williamsburg Foundation, 2001).

Porter, James A.: *Modern Negro Art* (Washington, DC: Howard University Press, 1992 [1943]).

Powell, Richard J.: *Black Art: A Cultural History* (London: Thames & Hudson, 2003).

Prown, Jonathan & Miller, Richard: "The Rococo, the Grotto, and the Philadelphia High Chest," *American Furniture 1996* (Hanover: Published by the Chipstone Foundation, dist. by the University Press of New England, 1996).

Prown, Jules D.: "Mind in Matter: An Introduction to Material Culture Theory," *Winterthur Portfolio* 17, 1(1982), 1–19.

Rathje, William L.: *Rubbish!: The Archaeology of Garbage* (New York: HarperCollins, 1992).

St. George, Robert B.: *Conversing by Signs: Poetics of Implication in Colonial New England* (Chapel Hill: University of North Carolina Press, 1998).

Simmel, Georg: "Fashion," *International Quarterly* 10, (1904), 130–55.

Stabile, Susan: *Memory's Daughters: The Material Culture of Remembrance in Eighteenth-Century America* (Ithaca, NY: Cornell University Press, 2004).

Stone, Lyle M.: *Fort Michilimackinac, 1715–1781: An Archaeological Perspective on the Revolutionary Frontier* (East Lansing, MI: Museum, Michigan State University, in cooperation with the Mackinac Island State Park Commission, Mackinac Island, 1974).

Strasser, Susan: *Satisfaction Guaranteed: The Making of the Mass Market* (New York: Pantheon Books, 1989).

Tedlow, Richard S.: *New and Improved: The Story of Mass Marketing in America* (New York: Basic Books, 1990).

Trent, Robert F.: *Hearts and Crowns: Folk Chairs of the Connecticut Coast, 1720–1840 as Viewed in the Light of Henri Focillon's Introduction to Art Populaire* (New Haven, CT: New Haven Colony Historical Society, 1977).

Truettner, William H. ed., with contributions by Anderson, Nancy K.: *The West as America: Reinterpreting Images of the Frontier, 1820–1920* (Washington, DC: Published for the National Museum of American Art by the Smithsonian Institution Press, 1991).

Upton, Dell: *Holy Things and Profane: Anglican Parish Churches in Colonial Virginia* (Cambridge, MA: MIT Press, 1986).

Veblen, Thorstein: *The Theory of the Leisure Class* (New York: Macmillan, 1912).

Vlach, John Michael: *The Afro-American Tradition in the Decorative Arts* (Athens: University of Georgia Press, 1990 [1978]).

Weaver, William Woys: "The Pennsylvania German House: European Antecedents and New World Forms," *Winterthur Portfolio* 21, 4(1986), 243–64.

Wertenbaker, Thomas Jefferson: *The Puritan Oligarchy: The Founding of American Civilization* (New York: Charles Scribner's Sons, 1947).

Chapter Twenty-One

PERFORMANCE AND DISPLAY

M. Alison Kibler

Looks can be deceiving; and looking conveys power. These are the central themes of the cultural history of performance and display in the United States. Cultural historians have deconstructed the claims of authenticity, enlightened science, and the apparently transparent truth of the body. They have uncovered the staging of seemingly objective displays, the layers of disguise within social interaction, and the artifice of identity. Racial masquerades, for example, have been central to the construction of national identity, and manners have been crucial to the production of what was once seen as "natural" class identities. Cultural historians have also examined the power dynamics or politics of performance and display. Their themes include the motivations for masquerade (who has the authority to imitate others?), the empowerment of looking and the disempowerment of being on display (who has the privilege of looking at "others"?), and the transgressive potential of performance (what kinds of performances challenge the status quo?).

Historians have explored performance, power, and social difference in three main ways: performance as a means to economic or political advancement; performance as a tool for disparagement and discrimination; and performance as identity construction. First, scholars have illuminated how a wide range of performances – either as professional careers or as amateur entertainment – have offered space for subcultural expression and the advancement of marginalized groups. Second, scholars have examined the ways certain performance styles have maligned and displaced subordinate groups. Much of this research focuses on the guilty pleasures of such denigration, and the class or racial cohesion that spectators may experience. Finally, scholars have focused on how identities are created through performance. In this vein of criticism, social groups do not just advance or decline through roles in theater, dance, and film; they are made. This essay explores how these three analytical tracks have evolved historically in the performance and display of race, gender, ethnicity, and sexuality.

American Performance Anxiety

Prior to the early nineteenth century, theatrical performances were largely taboo. Few population centers were large enough, or wealthy enough, to support a permanent theater (Allen 1991: 46). However, New England's Puritan settlers established fines to punish actors who tried to offer any public stage performance; and the founder of Pennsylvania also penalized anyone who tried to produce a play. "Colonial anti-theatricalism," as historian Robert Allen explains, "was not, in the main, prompted by a particular instance of an immoral performance . . . but rather by a deeply held fear of the very notion of theatricality itself" (Allen 1991: 47). Puritans objected to the theatrical performance because mimicry and spectacle violated their theological values. Masquerade was considered to be both deceitful and politically dangerous. And the spectacle of theater was believed immodest because the actor produced nothing; he just showed off. In some parts of the colonies, the objections to the theater dissipated enough so that amateur plays and advertisements for a touring company did not prompt criminal charges. But even after the American Revolution, the Continental Congress banned traveling shows in 1774, in an effort to foster republican virtue (Davis 2002). These moral doubts about the theater were particularly intense for women on stage; into the nineteenth century, female performers were associated with prostitutes because they "sold" their bodies on stage and sometimes offered sexually expressive performances; and the theater venue was linked with prostitution, because prostitutes and their customers often occupied its upper gallery (Johnson 1984).

Theatrical performance did, however, gain more acceptance in America in the nineteenth century, first as an eclectic mixture of performances directed at all social classes, and later as a bifurcated form appealing to either high or low culture. A key theme in the history of nineteenth-century performance is thus the shifting cultural order of performances: what qualified as high and low, and when did cultural ordination change? In the early 1800s, the theater audience in America was a diverse crowd; the upper classes joined manual laborers, and African Americans (though restricted to the upper balcony) joined white patrons to watch a variety of attractions, from Shakespeare to tumbling. Opera, for example, often combined with variety acts like jugglers and blackface comedians, attracted a diverse crowd. But this mingling of social groups and theatrical genres gradually gave way to a division between art and popular culture. Elites defined "arts" as separate from a marketplace of entertainment, set standards of contemplative spectatorship, and often hoped that a canon of great works would uplift the masses. In the second half of the nineteenth century, many highbrow cultural institutions emerged, including art museums, symphony orchestras, and foreign opera. The heterogeneous audience was divided into separate, homogenous classes, and bourgeois manners replaced unruly activities in the finer theaters. Works designated as "art" were isolated not only from working-class, immigrant audiences but also from popular material on stage. By the late nineteenth century, opera had been separated from other forms of entertainment, divided into high and low culture, with English-language opera remaining popular, and foreign-language opera attracting a narrower, more elite audience. Historians have shown that these new venues of high culture were, in large part, a means of conferring social power and defending a particular social order. They helped provide an escape for urban elites from the disruptions of the day, such as immigration and labor unrest.

Middle-class white women held the key for theater entrepreneurs eager to establish a respectable reputation for their houses. The rising reputation of theater depended upon a "regendering" of theatrical space, including a demasculinization of audiences (Butsch 2000). Bourgeois women, according to Victorian conventions, were the moral and spiritual guides of their families. Beginning in the 1840s, theater managers promoted their fare as educational, uplifting, and family-oriented. They silenced much of the audience's traditional combativeness and reduced the number of prostitutes in their theaters by requiring that women be admitted only with male escorts. Often finding the new atmosphere stifling, many men sought other forms of entertainment – like the minstrel show or the concert saloon – where they could enjoy drinking and lewd performances away from female moralism.

Just as Americans expressed anxiety about the professional theater in the nineteenth century, they were also concerned about theatricality offstage, in everyday interaction. In the early to mid-nineteenth century, middle-class Americans were worried about the possibility of hypocrisy and duplicity in social life. The figures of the confidence man and the painted woman, who passed as respectable, threatened the Victorian ideals of sincerity and candor. Partly in response to the new industrial city in which strangers freely intermingled, middle-class Americans developed a set of rituals and manners – a "genteel performance" – to signal their identity. These behaviors, however, were supposed to be effortless and natural. It was indeed contradictory to practice "self-conscious and theatrical forms of bourgeois etiquette – in the avowed interest of transparent sincerity" (Halttunen 1981: 93). All signs of its artifice – putting on or removing gloves, for instance – needed to be hidden from the primary stage (the parlor) and conducted instead in dressing rooms or halls. The cultural history of the theatricality of everyday life is indebted to sociologist Erving Goffman (1959), who argues that the "presentation of self in everyday life" – a theatrical construction of the self for others – has particular importance in societies with significant social mobility. He holds that these societies are divided into front and back areas. The front region requires control over bodies and expressions, while the back region allows relaxation: the front is for performance, the back for preparation of and respite from performance. Access to back regions allowed people to maintain the high standards of social control in the front.

Human Exhibits for Science and Amusement

Showman P. T. Barnum played a prominent role in unraveling American "performance anxiety" by making popular performances acceptable to the middle class, drawing racial boundaries in American popular entertainment, and pioneering the display of live human beings for profit. After purchasing his first dime museum in New York City in 1841, Barnum established a formula for success that entertainment entrepreneurs copied throughout the nineteenth and twentieth centuries. He appeased those who were critical of theatrical amusements on moral and religious grounds by touting the educational benefits of his museum; he eliminated drinking from his establishment along with lewd remarks on stage so he might attract women and children; and by offering diverse entertainment (and frequently changing his exhibits of curiosities), he recruited patrons of varied backgrounds, many of whom attended again and again.

Over his long career, from the dime museum through the three-ring circus, Barnum pioneered the display of live humans in his freak shows. At its heyday in the mid-nineteenth century, the freak show combined the "drama and costuming of the theater with the more sober conventions of the scientific exhibit" (Adams 2001: 29). As Rachel Adams has observed, "Debates over the propriety of human exhibition often bring community standards into conflict with the rights of marginalized constituencies to support themselves financially" (Adams 2001: 13). On one hand, "freaks" could find financial independence in entertainment; freak shows made some human oddities rich and famous. Charles Stratton, the legendary "General Tom Thumb," owned a yacht and a house in Bridgeport, Connecticut. On the other hand, these careers were often grim: managers often manipulated the performers' private lives (arranging marriages between incongruous pairs of freaks, for example) and enforced grueling work schedules as well.

Many scholars have argued that a freak is not a given quality, but a "performative identity" produced through "gesture, costume, and staging" (Adams 2001: 5), which varies depending on the particular context. "Freakishness is a historically variable quality, derived less from particular physical attributes than the spectacle of the extraordinary body swathed in theatrical props, promoted by advertising and performative fanfare" (ibid. 5). Early theories about the cultural work of freak shows argued that spectators saw themselves as beautiful when they looked at unseemly freaks. Freak shows "built self-esteem; people left freak shows feeling more at ease with their lot in life" (Dennett 1997: 318). But more recent work has posited a more complicated relationship between the identity of the spectator and the freak. While freaks reassured some viewers of their normality, they may have encouraged others, especially those from marginalized groups, to see themselves as freaks also (Adams 2001: 31).

Significantly, freak shows often involved displaying people of color to white audiences. In 1835, Barnum began to tour with an African American woman, Joice Heth, whom he marketed as the oldest living human and as George Washington's nurse. Heth's display as a human oddity was contradictory. While her connection to Washington elevated her stature and "ostensibly marked [her] inclusion in the civic life of the nation," her performance highlighted her marginality as an African American woman. Though her tour among white audiences was largely based on her adherence to stage conventions of blackness – including coarse, comical speech and the deferential demeanor of a servant (Reiss 2001: 66) – sometimes she pierced audience expectations with her stare and wit. In her final theatrical role, however, she was deprived of all power to shape audience response. For after Joice Heth died, Barnum arranged for an autopsy to be performed at a New York theater, and 1,500 people paid 50 cents each to watch. This anatomical spectacle was not unprecedented: when the South African woman known and exhibited across Europe as the "Hottentot Venus" died in 1815, a French zoologist dissected her body, preserved her genitals in a jar, and sent her skin to England, where her remains were put on display. These examinations of Sartje Baartman's and Joice Heth's dead bodies were part of the growing inquiry into the biological differences between the races. In the mid-nineteenth century, for example, the American School of Anatomy began to study the physical features of "racially typed specimens" to prove their distinctiveness and inferiority (ibid. 131).

The display of freaks, especially racialized freaks, had much in common with anthropological museum exhibits in the late nineteenth century. Both practices blended claims to enlightenment and science with entertainment; the exhibits were often non-white and non-Western; and notions of national and racial hierarchies – seemingly visible on specimens' bodies – framed these exhibits. The emphasis on physical signs of race (including the equation of disfigurement with racial categories) was widespread around the turn of the twentieth century. Social Darwinists conducted many experiments, measuring skulls and brains, for example, to compile proof of Europeans' presumed evolution far beyond the current status of Africans and Asians. At museums and anthropological exhibitions at world's fairs, human beings of non-Western origin became the objects of a new ethnographic gaze in the late nineteenth century. Spanning science and entertainment, the ethnographic gaze constructed modernity, and Western superiority, by scrutinizing the primitive other.

Although nineteenth-century scholars promoted their ethnographic displays as objective surveys of racial evolution, historians today point to several axes of power framing these exhibits. Challenging their subjects' understanding of race as apparent in the body, cultural historians have analyzed ethnographic displays as "Orientalized performances" of racial stereotypes. One journalist observed that Barnum's circuses transformed "an unassuming and quiet-appearing citizen" into a "wild warrior of the desert plains . . . or perhaps a dark-hued Nubian" (Adams 1997: 191). The new discipline of anthropology did not simply discover biological racial differences; it actively constructed them within a framework of colonialism. Studies of the "politics of exhibition" have also focused on the inequality of looking and being looked at. White Americans affirmed their cosmopolitan identity when they gazed upon non-Westerners, regarding them as dying races and primitives. Following Foucault's insights, this assessment of visibility has broader implications for the production of knowledge and imperial power relations. These ethnographic displays produced a certain understanding about non-Western populations that called for Western imperial action in the form of regulation. The practice of looking at "others" (savage, poor, or sick) steered spectators towards the question of what to do with them (Lidchi 1997: 195).

Barnum was a major player in the exhibition of non-Westerners in international racial exhibitions. In 1884, his Ethnological Congress, of the Barnum and London Circus, advertised "100 UNCIVILIZED, SUPERSTITIOUS, AND SAVAGE PEOPLE" (Adams 1997: 175). Barnum identified racial types by physical disfigurement: he set Hindu dwarves alongside "short-headed Buddhist priests" and the "Hairy Family of Burmah [sic]" (ibid. 185). Cultural critics have suggested a contradictory reading of these exhibits. The live exotic exhibits were violent, yet gentle; and the extermination of non-Westerners was regarded simultaneously as a form of progress and a regrettable loss. One advertisement of Barnum's non-Westerners nostalgically proclaimed, "[L]ike most of the ancient people of the world, the GLORY OF THE ANCIENT HINDOO HAS DEPARTED And is now a dream of the past before the aggressive stride of civilization" (ibid. 189). Scholars have thus posed a dynamic tension between identification and Othering in the contradictory representation of the exotic in Barnum's show. "The circuses exploited the non-Westerner not simply as the decadent Other of their images of potent white manhood, but also as the vehicle of an implicit critique of Western rationality, science, and capitalism" (ibid. 186). This interpretation of performance and display recurs throughout American cultural history. As this essay shows, this theme runs through the histories of the minstrel show and the representation of American Indians.

The popularity of the Midway Plaisance – a row of restaurants, rides, and theaters next to the White City at the World's Columbian Exposition in 1893 – was a watershed event in the history of American performance and display. It demonstrated the legitimation of performance for amusement, and perfected the Orientalist framework for displaying non-Western peoples. The Midway included a Ferris wheel and a series of ethnological villages (Dahomeyans, Egyptians, and Algerians), drawing specifically on Barnum's ethnological shows. At first, the fair's organizers carefully kept Barnumesque entertainment quarantined in the Midway, away from the highbrow "White City," with its neoclassical architecture and dignified, orderly atmosphere. But to recoup financial losses, they decided to bring Midway performers into the White City for concerts, athletic contests, and dances. Though contemporary critics condemned this shift as "barnumising the Fair" (Adams 1997: 195), future world's fairs continued the trend. Fairs became more than exhibitions of scientific progress and artistic innovation; they were sites of new popular amusements, like the roller coaster. Many genteel writers invoked Barnum when they decried the general decay of American culture in the late nineteenth century. Barnum, it seemed, was responsible for American superficiality, boastfulness, immorality, and coarse taste. In other words, Barnum had contributed significantly to the creation of a world of fakery, immodest spectacle, and popular performance.

The display of "exotic" peoples played a significant role in world's fairs, museums, circuses, and freak shows. By the early twentieth century, such performances were also becoming central to tourism. Tourists expected to enjoy contact with "primitives" in colonial "pleasure zones" (Desmond 1999: 37). Hawaii, for example, began to rely on "cultural tourism" – meaning the presence and performance of "natives" – to represent Hawaii as a tropical destination, compared to other island locations. Between 1900 and 1930, native Hawaiian culture increasingly became "commodified and enacted through dance shows." In short, the "hula girl" became the definitive symbol of Hawaiianness (ibid. xxii). By the early twentieth century, however, freaks were no longer treated as part of anthropology, medicine, or respectable entertainment. The freak show had fallen into disfavor because society had become more sensitive concerning disabilities, and medicine had " 'demystified' many of nature's mutations" (Dennett 1997: 318).

Playing Indian and Blacking Up

Freak shows, museum exhibits, ethnological displays at world's fairs, and tourism all provide evidence of Western fascination with racial "primitives." While claiming to showcase "real" non-Western peoples, these human exhibitions have actually involved layers of performance and imitation. American performances of Indianness and blackness have worked in similar ways, prompting cultural historians to explore the role of racial disguise in the establishment of national, class, and racial identity. White actors have used racial disguises as a mode of protest, a precondition of whiteness, and a "primitive antidote to modernity" (Deloria 1998: 5). These racialized performances have been riddled with ambivalence: white Americans have been both attracted to and disgusted by Indians and African Americans, who symbolize freedom and nature, on the one hand, and savagery and violence, on the other. Playing Indian and blacking up thus demonstrate fascination with and desire for these racial others; yet they still occur in the context of racial dispossession and segregation.

White men's "playing Indian," as Philip Deloria has shown, has been a powerful force in creating a new American identity, particularly during the Revolutionary era and the late nineteenth-century response to modern, urban, industrial life. The new American incorporated the noble Indian who figured the North American landscape as part of his non-British self. But at the same time, he blended his own civilized identity with that of the Indian as savage Other in an effort to control the threat of savagery. The liberating and constructive aspects of playing Indian were limited to white men, who dominated this performance tradition along with broader claims to American citizenship. At the Boston Tea Party, in December 1773, the protesters used disguises as Mohawk Indians to fuel their political and economic protest. Borrowing from anthropology, some historians have argued that American performances in various disguises, including Indian dress and makeup, have been liminal experiences. Liminality is a part of a rite of passage, a period of suspense or "unpredictable potential," which can express rebellious discontent at particular historic moments. Playing Indian, in Deloria's view, was a small-scale liminal experience within the larger rite of passage – the Revolution. Americans constructed new ideas of themselves as rebels and citizens from old notions of "Indian and Briton" (Deloria 1998: 36). Deloria links the open, unfinished definition of American – its liminality – to the contradictory status of the Indian. Americans continued to identify with the Indian as native North American, not British, and also separated themselves from Indian savagery.

Peaking in popularity in the mid-nineteenth century, the minstrel show offered blackface fun for the common man. The minstrel show has been both reviled by scholars for its racism, including its exploitation of black culture, and celebrated as the first indigenous form of American popular culture. The blackface minstrel, like the independent and patriotic Yankee and the manly and robust backwoodsman, served as an expression of American identity in defiance of European elitism; all three of these stock characters of nineteenth-century drama and literature undermined pretentious and immoral aristocrats with their wit. In the first section of the basic three-part minstrel show, a pompous interlocutor stood at the center of a semi-circle of performers made up in blackface (burnt cork or greasepaint), with two unruly end men, Brudder Tambo and Brudder Bones (named for the instruments they played), who were usually the stars of the show. Dressing in grotesque costumes and gesturing wildly on stage, they exchanged malapropisms, riddles, and one-liners, often insulting the interlocutor with their comic barbs. The second part of the show featured variety acts, while the final segment was a one-act sketch, usually set in a plantation. Playing sentimental images of contented slaves in the South off against negative images of rebellious and incompetent free blacks, the minstrel show clearly denigrated African Americans. But its depiction of slavery was also ambivalent, particularly prior to 1850, when minstrel shows featured black tricksters who outwitted masters and sometimes even criticized the cruelty of slavery.

Historians have argued that the minstrel show produced complicated feelings among its primary fans, who were northern working-class men. It helped these workers unite through a sense of shared racial superiority over blacks, encouraged a defiant stance toward elites and moral authority, and offered a temporary escape from their dreary daily lives through fantasy. Through the libidinous, carefree black performer, the minstrel show provided an outlet for spectators' longings for a preindustrial, rural past – a way to counter the discipline and dislocation of urban, industrial life. In his influential study of the antebellum minstrel show, *Love and Theft* (1993), Eric Lott argues that the fans of the minstrel show were not just denigrating African Americans: they also identified with them as a subjugated class, and identified with the childish fun they enacted on stage. The enjoyment of the minstrel show, then, involved an ambivalent mixture of white men's contempt and desire for African Americans.

African American Performance and Protest

Recently, historians have begun to explore African Americans' use of "whiteface." Prior to the ascendancy of blackface, African American actors put on whiteface, which lacked the popularity and cultural authority of blackface, and played prominent Shakespearean roles (McAllister 2003). In the early nineteenth century, impresario William Brown established a racially integrated theater, not in the degraded, mixed-race neighborhood of Five Points, but in white Manhattan's backyard. Brown's African American actors used whiteface minstrelsy primarily to mock white society, but also to insult the Irish and southern blacks. White critics charged that the Shakespearean productions at Brown's theater were politically dangerous; they were sources of African American pride and expressions of African American cultural aspirations, in opposition to presumed white superiority. One critic of Brown's theater warned that if African Americans excelled at Shakespearean drama, they might want to extend their political roles offstage. Such fears no doubt persuaded the police, in January 1822, to arrest Brown's company, and release them only when "they promised never to act Shakespeare again" (McAllister 2003: 139). Later that year, white New York patrons physically assaulted black actors and ripped off their costumes, which they perceived as a sign of black arrogance. The attackers responded to racial integration at Brown's theater and the power of black actors who "took command of social space" (ibid. 65).

Cultural historians have focused on two dilemmas in the history of African American performance. They have explored how white standards constrained African American performances, but have also found significant signs of African American protest in theater and dance. In addition, scholars have searched for authentic African American culture amidst the fluid mixtures of African and European cultural forms. For example, the history of the cakewalk, a popular dance in the minstrel show and then a craze in the 1890s, shows complex borrowing across racial lines as well as the possibility for resistance to racism through popular performance. The cakewalk contained a mocking view of white society dating to the origins of the dance under slavery. Slaves are believed to have developed the dance by observing and then imitating the style of their owners. "They did a take-off on the high manners of the white folks in the bighouse," according to dance historians Marshall and Jean Stearns, "but their masters, who gathered around to watch the fun, missed the point" (Stearns & Stearns 1994: 123). Even as the cakewalk brought fame to African American performers, and provided them with an opportunity to parody white society, white audiences continued to regard this dance as simply an expression of natural black talent and "racial heritage."

Between 1890 and 1915, African American performers found unprecedented success in American theater. Bert Williams and Sissieretta Jones defied the stereotypes of lazy "darkeys" and pursued serious roles and opera, not just the comedy and dance that many whites considered their natural gift. Williams, the star of many musical comedies written and performed almost entirely by African Americans, blacked up to play a bumbling, shiftless character, but he revised the degrading stereotype in other ways. Instead of playing the conventional minstrel show instruments – the banjo and tambourine – he appeared in a production of *In Dahomey* with a tuba. Scholars suggest that Williams's careful and nuanced performances transcended racial cliché. Sissieretta Jones was part of a vogue of African American prima donnas who were novelties on the concert stage in the 1890s. When white audiences tired of this trend, opera singers like Jones had to look beyond highbrow music for their livelihoods. So Jones added popular ballads to her repertoire, and surrounded herself with black comic dancers and singers in her touring company, Black Patti's Troubadours.

But African Americans had to temper their rejection of performance traditions, under the supervision of white managers and audiences who carefully monitored their acts. As George Walker, Williams's partner for many years, wrote: "We noticed that colored men had to be comedians and athletic comedians at that. Head stands, flip flaps and such" (Walker 1908: 4). One vaudeville theater manager wrote to his colleague about an African American vocal group, the Golden Gate Quintette: "Like most colored entertainers, after they get a bit of standing, they want to do the 'neat' work more suited to white people and in that way, lose the darkey personality. At the points where they did comedy work it was exceedingly well accepted" (Report Book 6: 150, Keith/Albee Collection, University of Iowa).

Staging Ethnicity

Influenced by the cultural history of performance, historians of ethnicity and immigration have begun to understand ethnicity, not as a set of innate characteristics, but as a performance. Werner Sollors, for example, argues (over the protests of some ethnic communities) that ethnicity is not "eternal or essential," but rather "pliable and unstable" (Sollors 1984: xiv). William Boelhower (1987) has similarly characterized ethnicity as a process of interaction and interpretation, a way of seeing oneself in opposition to and comparison with others. Ethnic identity is thus unstable, dependent on performance and surveillance.

This insight helps explain the importance of ethnic theater as an expressive form for various immigrant groups. Yiddish theater, for example, flourished between 1890 and 1910, during the period of immigration from southern and eastern Europe. Disdained by assimilated Jews of German descent, these theaters were important gathering places for eastern European Jewish immigrants on the Lower East Side. Yiddish plays frequently explored Jewish experiences in the ghetto. The audience for Yiddish theater, as Richard Butsch has argued, resembled the working-class theater audience of the early nineteenth century. Yiddish theatergoers went to plays to see their friends, often moving around the theater and talking to acquaintances during the play, and they also interjected into the action on stage, hissing at villains or warning characters of impending danger in plays the audience knew very well (Butsch 2000: 135).

If immigrants enjoyed their own theatrical traditions, they also suffered from the derisive caricatures of the mainstream theater. Between 1880 and 1910, no vaudeville bill was considered complete without at least one act of rambunctious ethnic comedy; and many shows included several ethnic comedians. The German character, often played by Joe Weber or Lou Fields, was a rotund heavy drinker. For his portrayal of an Irishman ready to drink and fight, Thomas J. Ryan dressed in ragged clothes and wore a red wig and whiskers. Actress Kate Elinore, a rare woman in the rough field of ethnic comedy, portrayed a drunken Irish widow who bumbles through high society and shocks suitors with her ugly face. The stock Jewish character was stingy, greedy, and vengeful. These ethnic caricatures sometimes displayed a softer side, and occasionally outwitted superiors with their common sense, but they remained over-whelmingly unruly and uncouth.

The cultural history of ethnic stereotypes has generated a prominent debate about who actually controls performance: performers, theater managers and producers, or audiences? Around the turn of the twentieth century, Jewish influence in show business had become "unmistakable" (Erdman 1997). In 1896, six Jewish theater entre-preneurs created the Theatrical Syndicate to control bookings around the country, and eight major motion-picture companies were created by Jewish businessmen. This power fueled anti-Semitic charges of cultural decay at the hands of immoral Jewish capitalists. Jewish producers may have also helped soften the Jewish caricature on stage; they turned to the representation of other groups more often, and promoted the ideal of the "melting pot" on stage.

Race and ethnicity were interwoven in the racial disguises of those immigrant groups – including Italians and Jews – who were considered non-white upon their arrival in the USA. Blackface minstrelsy in particular left an important legacy to Hollywood, especially with respect to the role of film in Americanizing immigrants. Jewish film stars in blackface, such as Al Jolson in *The Jazz Singer* (1927), constructed new, "white," American identities as they displaced African Americans on stage and screen. Just as the original minstrel show had contributed to the nascent nationalism of the white working classes, Hollywood blackface helped construct an American "melting pot" for white ethnics only.

Performing Gender and Sexual Desire

Historians of gender and sexuality have paid attention to the history of performance as an "enactment of sexuality and gender" (Desmond 2001: 6). They have been strongly influenced by Judith Butler's work, which challenges the cultural matrix in which heterosexual desire naturally follows gender identity; and gender appears to follow biological sex. She argues that gender is not the cultural overlay to an immu-table given called sex: rather, "gender must also designate the very apparatus of pro-duction whereby the sexes themselves are established" (Butler 1990: 7). For Butler, then, "There is no gender identity behind the expressions of gender; that identity is performatively constituted by the very 'expressions' that are said to be its results" (ibid. 25).

Gay men and lesbians practiced a variety of expressive forms to explore the performative quality of gender identity. In the 1890s, they began to organize drag balls, drawing on the tradition of masquerade balls in which people from different classes mingled in disguise. Thus, gay men did not invent drag balls; they adapted a pre-existing cultural form to their own subculture. At drag balls, which reached their peak of popularity in the 1920s, men dressed in women's clothes and danced with each other. These events helped solidify the gay community and expressed the importance of "gender inversion" to this culture (Chauncey 1994: 297). Drag queens often expressed a camp sensibility – an exaggeration and mockery of dominant gender norms. At the same time, female impersonators in the popular theater were increasingly identified as homosexuals. Female impersonator Julian Eltinge was popular with gay men, though he publicly asserted his own heterosexual virility in the press. In contrast, Bert Savoy, another female impersonator, used feminine pronouns to identify himself, and included slang from gay male subculture in his routine.

Gay men's flamboyant appropriation of femininity – the tradition of camp – has been the subject of theoretical debates. While some scholars have identified camp as a negative gay stereotype built on the misogynist representation of women, others have argued that camp was a strategy for coming out, publicizing gay identity, and building a foundation for political confrontation. Another reading of camp is that it undermines the naturalness of gender; within this interpretation, the display of female excess serves as a tactic of resistance, not just a stereotypical representation of women. Feminist theorists have equated drag with "performative status of gender identity" (Robertson 1996: 11). Butler explains that "in imitating gender, drag implicitly reveals the imitative structure of gender itself" (1990: 137). But if feminists widely see the subversiveness of drag and camp performances, they also acknowledge its limits. The humorously surprising quality of camp, for example, depends on spectators' understanding that the person in costume is really the opposite gender.

Although lesbian subculture was not as clearly and publicly defined as gay male subculture, lesbians were becoming increasingly visible on stage in the early twentieth century. Several male impersonators of the late nineteenth century had romantic relationships with women, but their private lives were not well known to theater audiences. By the 1920s, however, such performers' offstage relationships were part of their star personae. Lesbians on stage were one of the many attractions of Harlem in the 1920s. Male impersonator Gladys Bentley wore men's clothes on stage and on the street, and was married (dressed in a tuxedo) to a woman in a civil ceremony in New Jersey.

In modern dance, leading performers like Ted Shawn (who concealed his own same-sex relationships) both celebrated love between men, and tried to dispel the perceived link between dance and homosexuality. To negotiate this tension, Shawn promoted an ideal of masculine virility in dance, avoiding such conventional signs of homosexuality as limp wrists and skipping, and cultivating a dance style that deliberately countered the characterization of gay men as sissies or "gender inverts." Some critics have argued that Shawn simply affirmed dominant heterosexual norms, but dance historian Julia Foulkes (2002) points out that Shawn also "idealized male homosexuality" on stage, a theme that audiences often discussed.

Feminists have taken two distinct approaches to the cultural history of women's performance. The first draws on Bakhtin's analysis of carnival to explore unruly, often comic performances and displays by women, which often served as strategies for disrupting male authority. The second develops Laura Mulvey's analysis of the "male gaze" as the key dynamic in a passive form of female sexual spectacle designed for men's viewing pleasure.

Early modern European carnivals, as Bakhtin has shown, upset the official language and hierarchy of the day by featuring grotesque bodies and the inversion of usual relationships, thus opening up transgressive opportunities for marginalized and disempowered groups. Feminist critics and historians have drawn on Bakhtin's treatment of carnival with primary attention to women's transgressions of gender norms. In particular, Natalie Zemon Davis's definition of the "woman on top" has been important to historical considerations of women's comic performances. "The female sex," Davis observes,

> was thought the disorderly one par excellence in early modern Europe. . . . Her womb was like a hungry animal; when not amply fed by sexual intercourse or reproduction, it was likely to wander about her body, overpowering her speech and senses. . . . The lower ruled the higher within the woman, then, and if she were given her way, she would want to rule over those above her outside. (Davis 1975: 125)

Women who seized the opportunity of carnival to become "woman on top" could carry over their transgression into "everyday 'serious' life" and thus widen their options in both family life and politics.

Within Bakhtin's theory, the grotesque body is one of the unsettling aspects of carnivalesque. Bearing the imprint of social structure, the grotesque body emphasizes the lower bodily functions (such as eating, defecating), in contrast to the classical body, which focuses on the higher functions (thinking, seeing). The grotesque body emphasizes the body in connection with the world and in process – giving birth or dying, for example. Bakhtin noted that women, particularly mothers, were primarily associated with the lower body. Feminist critics such as Mary Russo have elaborated on this idea to find transgressive female performers in the grotesque tradition, identifying a variety of female performers – from Miss Piggy to Roseanne Barr – as "unruly women" who want to "make a spectacle" of themselves rather than become passive, erotic objects of the male gaze (Russo 1994: 53).

In the last third of the nineteenth century, burlesque was a potent theatrical form for women performers who found freedom and authority through its enlistment of the grotesque. Beginning with Lydia Thompson's first season of burlesque in 1868, this performance genre blended female sexual display with impertinent verbal banter. In the late nineteenth century, before burlesque became "strip tease," these female performers offered a "leg show" – with dyed blonde hair and flesh-colored tights – along with male impersonation and a parody of bourgeois culture. Burlesque was sexually titillating and "anti-authoritarian"; and "[n]o form of American commercial theatrical entertainment before or since has given the stage over to women to a greater degree" (Allen 1991: 147, 137). In an effort to contain the threat of these female performers, critics identified them as monsters and prostitutes. The body of the burlesque performer became a symbol of disease and decay threatening the

social "body." She was identified as a "low other" – working-class, coarsely prominent – in opposition to bourgeois femininity – ethereal and delicate. The bourgeoisie, according to Peter Stallybrass and Allon White (1986), exclude the low other
with a social leer, but also depend on and desire it. The burlesque performer
remained popular and attractive, but was marginalized from middle-class theaters.
Middle-class men could freely enjoy watching her only because the class distance
between performer and spectator was reinforced by the moral distance between the
abject performer and the "respectable" wives and daughters of the men in the
audience.

Even more conventional female performers have been seen as a "proto feminist
vanguard" in the late nineteenth century (Glenn 2000: 6). Thirty years before the
emergence of feminism offstage, women in the theater were powerful symbols and
advocates for two feminist principles: women's right to sexual expression and to the
development of individual personalities. Many actresses also supported women's suffrage, sometimes merely to enhance their own publicity, and chorus girls spoke up
for women's rights in the Actors Equity strike of 1919. Female performers during
this period shaped the New Woman with their unconventional behavior. When they
struggled to achieve or maintain top billing, they offered a rare image of women's
public competitiveness. White women sometimes sacrificed beauty to become grotesque comedians, and, by the early twentieth century, some female comedians left
the self-deprecating role behind, establishing that women could be both funny and
attractive. Female vaudeville mimics participated in the emergence of modernist social
thought. These "actress intellectuals" – women who copied the personalities of other
stars – defended this style of imitation as a creative act. This line of argument paralleled developments in psychology that elevated personality as performance over an
outdated notion of immutable character, and thus placed imitation at the center of
identity formation. Perhaps these female performers had more influence over the
shape of modern life than the social scientists.

Beginning in the late 1970s, film theorists brought a new line of interpretation to
women's performance when they began to discuss the "gaze" that was structured by
the apparatus (rather than solely the text) of cinema. Film, they argued, was significantly more restricted and less reciprocal than live performance. Though theater
spectators could train a powerful, sexual gaze on women performers, live performers
always commanded the power to look back. Building on Jacques Lacan's theory of
the "mirror phase," Laura Mulvey argued that both film plots and cinematic structures were built around the pleasure of an imagined male spectator. The distinction
between the active male and the passive female is embedded both in the film's narrative – in which men control the looks and move the storyline forward – and in the
apparatus of cinema – the editing and sequencing of shots. As Mulvey concludes, "In
their traditional exhibitionist role, women are simultaneously looked at and displayed,
with their appearance coded for strong visual and erotic impact so that they can be
said to connote to-be-looked-at-ness" (Mulvey 1999 [1975]: 62).

Scholars debated Mulvey's thesis in several ways. Some critics questioned the psy-
choanalytic framework as ahistorical and exclusively focused on gender. Jane Gaines,
for example, explains how black male looking is frustrated in film, in favor of white
male characters' perspectives. She identifies several relevant historical structures – the
lynching of black men falsely accused of raping white women, and black women's

vulnerability to white men's sexual violence – to show that sexual looking is tied to "racial taboos" (Gaines 1999 [1988]: 301). She urges a more materialist analysis of film history to explain "how some groups have historically had the license to 'look' openly while other groups have 'looked' illicitly" (ibid. 302). Other critics have noted that African American men have been "feminized" in their own performances and displays. Photographic portraits of Paul Robeson, as Richard Dyer explains, fit within the tradition of classical female nudes whose bodies were represented as "calm still-ness" (Dyer 1986: 122). This pattern of "passive beauty" extended to Robeson's performances as well: critics called him a natural beauty and a natural actor and praised his performances as "unproduced" (ibid. 125). In the 1920s and 1930s, Robeson was often treated as "little more than a body and voice. In this regard, his treatment is typical of the treatment of black people, female and male, in Western culture" (ibid. 138).

Cultural historians have also looked beyond the cinema's construction of a male spectator to focus on women in the "social audience." Early cinema objectified women at the same time that it offered space for social experimentation. Vaudeville, amusement parks, and nickelodeons all marketed "open displays of female sexuality"; their development was thus based in part on women's "spectacularization." These urban amusements thus offered new opportunities for female patrons to explore greater sexual independence, while at the same time transforming women into "objects of consumption" (Rabinovitz 1998: 10, 145). Miriam Hansen argues that classical cinema's privileging of a male perspective actually emerged as a "defense" against women's emergence as public consumers, as film fans, in the early twentieth century (Hansen 1991: 122).

The cultural history of performance and display illuminates controversial psycho-logical and social dramas of the American past – from racial conflict and imperialism to women's rights. Scholars have shown that performance and display offer oppor-tunities for visibility and affirmation to marginalized groups. They have traced the protests imbedded in African American performances, the nascent feminism of some female performers, and the importance of drag balls to the development of a gay male subculture. The history of American performance and display is also the story of deception and exploitation: entertainment masquerading as science; white working-class Americans blacking up and playing Indian; and women's exhibitionist role in film. Historians have shown how various groups perform, impersonate, and watch, but they have also deconstructed social groups by showing how identities are con-tingent and constructed. Imbedded in social hierarchies and saturated with guilty attractions and rejections across social divides, performance and display have indeed been central to America's multicultural history.

REFERENCES

Adams, Bluford: *E Pluribus Barnum: The Great Showman and the Making of US Popular Culture* (Minneapolis: University of Minnesota Press, 1997).

Adams, Rachel: *Sideshow USA: Freaks and the American Cultural Imagination* (Chicago: University of Chicago Press, 2001).

Allen, Robert: *Horrible Prettiness: Burlesque and American Culture* (Chapel Hill: University of North Carolina Press, 1991).

Bakhtin, Mikhail: *Rabelais and His World*, trans. Helene Iswolsky (Cambridge, MA: MIT Press, 1968).

Boelhower, William: *Through a Glass Darkly: Ethnic Semiosis in American Literature* (New York: Oxford University Press, 1987).

Butler, Judith: *Gender Trouble: Feminism and the Subversion of Identity* (New York: Routledge, 1990).

Butsch, Richard: *The Making of American Audiences: From Stage to Television, 1750–1990* (Cambridge: Cambridge University Press, 2000).

Chauncey, George: *Gay New York: Gender, Urban Culture, and the Making of the Gay Male World, 1890–1940* (New York: Basic Books, 1994).

Davis, Janet: *The Circus Age: Culture and Society under the Big Top* (Chapel Hill: University of North Carolina Press, 2002).

Davis, Natalie Zemon: "Women on Top," in *Society and Culture in Early Modern France* (Palo Alto, CA: Stanford University Press, 1975), pp. 124–51.

Davis, Susan: *Parades and Power: Street Theatre in Nineteenth-century Philadelphia* (Philadelphia, PA: Temple University Press, 1986).

Deloria, Philip J.: *Playing Indian* (New Haven, CT: Yale University Press, 1998).

Dennett, Andrea Stulman: *Weird and Wonderful: The Dime Museum in America* (New York: New York University Press, 1997).

Desmond, Jane: *Staging Tourism: Bodies on Display from Waikiki to Sea World* (Chicago: University of Chicago Press, 1999).

Desmond, Jane, ed.: *Dancing Desires: Choreographing Sexualities On and Off Stage* (Madison: University of Wisconsin Press, 2001).

Dyer, Richard: *Heavenly Bodies: Film Stars and Society* (New York: St. Martin's Press, 1986).

Erdman, Harley: *Staging the Jew: The Performance of an American Ethnicity* (New Brunswick: Rutgers University Press, 1997).

Foulkes, Julia: *Modern Bodies: Dance and American Modernism from Martha Graham to Alvin Ailey* (Chapel Hill: University of North Carolina Press, 2002).

Gaines, Jane: "White Privilege and Looking Relations: Race and Gender in Feminist Film Theory," in Sue Thornton, ed., *Feminist Film Theory: A Reader* (New York: New York University Press, 1999 [1988]), pp. 293–306.

Glenn, Susan: *Female Spectacle: The Theatrical Roots of Modern Feminism* (Cambridge, MA: Harvard University Press, 2000).

Goffman, Erving: *The Presentation of Self in Everyday Life* (Garden City, NY: Doubleday Anchor Books, 1959).

Halttunen, Karen: *Confidence Men and Painted Women: A Study of Middle-class Culture in America, 1830–1870* (New Haven, CT: Yale University Press, 1981).

Hansen, Miriam: *Babel and Babylon: Spectatorship in American Silent Film* (Cambridge, MA: Harvard University Press, 1991).

Johnson, Claudia: *American Actress: Perspectives on the Nineteenth Century* (Chicago: Nelson Hall, 1984).

Kasson, John: *Amusing the Million: Coney Island at the Turn of the Century* (New York: Hill & Wang, 1978).

Kibler, M. Alison: *Rank Ladies: Gender and Cultural Hierarchy in American Vaudeville* (Chapel Hill: University of North Carolina Press, 1999).

Lidchi, Henrietta: "The Poetics and Politics of Exhibiting Other Cultures," in Stuart Hall, ed., *Representation: Cultural Representations and Signifying Practices* (London: Sage Publications, 1997), pp. 151–208.

Lott, Eric: *Love and Theft: Blackface Minstrelsy and the American Working Class* (New York: Oxford University Press, 1993).

McAllister, Marvin: *White People Do Not Know How to Behave at Entertainments Designed for Ladies and Gentlemen of Colour: William Brown's African and American Theater* (Chapel Hill: University of North Carolina Press, 2003).

Mulvey, Laura: "Visual Pleasure and Narrative Cinema," in Sue Thornton, ed., *Feminist Film Theory: A Reader* (New York: New York University Press, 1999 [1975]), pp. 58–69.

Rabinovitz, Lauren: *For the Love of Pleasure: Women, Movies, and Culture in Turn-of-the-Century Chicago* (New Brunswick: Rutgers University Press, 1998).

Reiss, Benjamin: *The Showman and the Slave: Race, Death, and Memory in Barnum's America* (Cambridge, MA: Harvard University Press, 2001).

Robertson, Pamela: *Guilty Pleasures: Feminist Camp from Mae West to Madonna* (Durham, NC: Duke University Press, 1996).

Rogin, Michael: *Blackface, White Noise: Jewish Immigrants in the Hollywood Melting Pot* (Berkeley: University of California Press, 1996).

Russo, Mary: *The Female Grotesque: Risk, Excess and Modernity* (New York: Routledge, 1994).

Sollors, Werner, ed.: *The Invention of Ethnicity* (New York: Oxford University Press, 1984).

Stallybrass, Peter & White, Allon: *The Politics and Poetics of Transgression* (Ithaca, NY: Cornell University Press, 1986).

Stearns, Jean & Stearns, Marshall: *Jazz Dance: The History of American Vernacular Dance* (New York: Da Capo Press, 1994).

Turner, Victor: *Dramas, Fields, and Metaphors: Symbolic Action in Human Society* (Ithaca, NY: Cornell University Press, 1974).

Walker, George: "Bert, Me, and Them," *New York Age*, December 24, 1908, p. 4.

Chapter Twenty-Two

GENDER AND SEXUALITY

Jane H. Hunter

The terms "gender" and "sexuality" are relatively new. As recently as the 1960s, "gender" was most commonly a grammatical term applying to nouns in Romance languages. Only recently has it become a critical half of a "sex/gender" system, in which "gender" refers to the social expectations and social roles that are attached to biological sex. "Sexuality" has a longer heritage in its present meaning, appearing in the *Oxford English Dictionary* in the nineteenth century as "the quality of being sexual or having sex." Within the past several decades, however, it has come to embrace a spectrum of sexual differences rather than an implicit heterosexuality. The rich and ever-expanding literature dealing with both gender and sexuality testifies to their centrality to today's understanding of structures of power and meaning in the American past.

Writing about both gender and sexuality initially emerged in the field of Women's History, a major effort to recover the perspective of over half the population by bringing the background into the foreground, and discovering the difference it made. As the marked category, women were conventionally the "other," the forces for community, kinship, or propriety accompanying the rugged American individualist on his journey west; the Aunt Polly who set off Mark Twain's American original Huck Finn. In the history of gender and sexuality, however, women were often the first points of reference, the subjects of inquiry whose experience brought new questions back to the study of men. Informed by that approach, scholars have increasingly embraced the relational aspect of any study of women, exploring the ways that womanhood or womanliness was often defined in comparison with masculinity or manhood, and vice versa. Women's history interweaves throughout the remarks to come but, given spatial limitations, I have chosen to highlight two themes. The first is the American history of femininity and masculinity, changing ideas about how to think about and enact one's biological sex. The second is the history of attitudes and practices surrounding reproduction, romantic love, sexual desire, and sexual identity. Among the many subcultures created within different class, racial, and ethnic groups, there were inevitable differences in the ideology of gender and sexuality. Yet, with the rise of the publishing industry in the nineteenth century, a national media helped to shape a dominant or hegemonic ideology of gender and sexuality, which is the focus of this essay.

Common Law and Commensurability

Ideas about sex difference in the premodern period emphasized commensurability, the idea that male and female sex organs marked different stages of evolution on a common continuum. In half the population, the theory went, sex organs never descended and fully matured outside the body, but instead remained arrested inside, trapped as uterus and ovaries. From this principle of femininity as incomplete masculinity stemmed many premodern ideas about the differences between the sexes. It suggested women's imperfection, but also women's fundamental similarity to men as sexual and economic beings. Women shared men's passions, though with weaker powers of self-control. And when men were absent or ill, wives stepped in as "deputy husbands." Just as they might exercise authority in the family, they might represent their family when necessary in legal and economic transactions. Women (at least in the northern colonies) learned to see their highest good in their accord with their role in the hierarchy of the patriarchal family as "good wife" (Ulrich 1982; Laqueur 1990).

The colonial approach to sex was reproductive, as families moved to populate the "new" land with offspring and a labor force, producing large families to compensate for the losses to infant mortality. By 1800, the birth rate in the United States had become the highest in the world, at 7.04 children for each native-born woman. In the colonial world of the Northeast, married couples were obliged to love their partners as two mates yoked together to pursue the shared labors of this world. Despite injunctions promoting chastity, the practice of bundling and the close quarters of frontier dwellings enabled a premodern and pragmatic attitude towards sexuality, especially in the late eighteenth century, as documented by high bridal pregnancy rates. Communities anxious to avoid the support of bastards required midwives to ask women giving illegitimate birth the name of their impregnators, in the belief that under the duress of childbirth, the mother could not lie. If a marriage could be arranged, or a patrimony secured, the state proved reluctant to prosecute for unlawful fornication (D'Emilio & Freedman 1988: 3–55; Ulrich 1990).

The structure for the sexual system of the colonial period echoed the premises of the common law imported from Britain, especially in the religious colonies of the North, where families arrived together. In the Tidewater and southern colonies, gender relations were initially more fluid if more exploitative. Female indentured servants and slave women together provided domestic, agricultural, and some reproductive labor. Efforts to formalize patriarchy in the South coincided with the codification of slavery in the late seventeenth century and the imposition of restrictions on wives and daughters. The resulting gender hierarchy also regulated race, distinguishing white "good wives" from black "nasty wenches" (Brown 1996).

The Revolution and the Market

The Enlightenment of the Atlantic World provided the vocabulary for a challenge to the common law, as well as British tyranny. Scientific inquiry subjected sex differences between male and female to empirical investigation and allowed elite women to question the "natural" hierarchy of the sexes. The natural-rights under-pinnings of the American Revolution opened opportunities for women as republican mothers equipped to train their sons for the higher virtues of citizenship. Although Thomas Jefferson never meant to include women in his famous formulations that "all men" were created equal, women from Abigail Adams to modest farm wives learned their abilities through the necessity of men's war absences, and some also learned a new vocabulary with which to express their desires for power (Norton 1980).

But the economic dislocations of the Revolutionary and Indian Wars of the late eighteenth century increased vulnerability rather than power for many women. The rural economy offered few means of support for solitary women, who often migrated to the city to seek work as seamstresses and shop girls. As unaccompanied women or as the equally exposed wives and daughters of seafaring men who were away from port for months and even years at a time, women were at risk (Stansell 1986). The journey from shop girl to prostitute could be short, and the risks high, result-ing in a number of high-profile rape and murder cases. The new penny press seized on these lurid tales of sex and scandal, which played to broader cultural concerns about the rise of the impersonal city and the breakdown of traditional moral order. A number of exemplary historical studies have explored these moral parables. Amy Srebnick (1995) uses the death of cigar-seller Mary Rogers as a window into social history, a subject for poet Edgar Allan Poe, an episode in early criminology, and a revealing case study in the history of abortion; Patricia Cline Cohen (1998) examines the celebrated murder case of Helen Jewett as both a crime story and a cultural prism, demonstrating that the power of romantic fiction extended beyond the parlor into farm girls' imaginative scripts for their lives.

Separate Spheres and Gender Difference

At the same time that anatomical research was raising questions about the fundamen-tal commensurability of men and women, ministers in the established denominations of the Northeast came to question the established view that women were simply lesser versions of men. Confronting their largely female congregations, and pondering the souls of their absent male parishioners, they began to reconsider the relative virtue of men and women. Preaching from the pulpit and contributing to the proliferating new advice literature, the clergy joined women writers to suggest women's special moral stature – more angelic or heavenly than their godless husbands, but also fun-damentally *different*. Increasingly, they allied the future of the republic with women and the hearth. As men left their homes for the counting houses, shops, and factories of northeastern cities, women found a separate empire of their own in the homes that they claimed as their sphere. Among those helping to construct this sphere were such women as Catharine Beecher, teacher and essayist, and her sister, Harriet Beecher Stowe, whose anti-slavery writings, like those of other radical abolitionists, extended some, but not all, of the protections of women's sphere to African American slaves. As conceptualized in this early generation of women's history, separate spheres meant separate qualities attributed to men and women, a "femininity" of love, nurture, and care counterposed with a competitive "masculinity" of struggle, strength, and leadership in both the geographic and commercial frontiers of American life (Sklar 1973; Cott 1977).

The increasing geographic mobility of the nineteenth century required a new code of sexual morality to accord with the vulnerabilities of young women and men now released without parental supervision in the cities. A newly discovered female purity joined piety and domesticity as idealized characteristics of woman's sphere. Historians have debated the meaning of this dominant theme in the prescriptive literature of the mid-nineteenth century. Nancy Cott (1978) has argued the strategic benefits women might gain from claiming "passionlessness," using their purity and supposed lack of desire as a form of birth control or power brokering in the home. Such findings were also enabled by new scientific studies which disputed traditional ideas about the physiology of conception, noting that contrary to popular belief, female orgasm was unnecessary for procreation (Laqueur 1990). More recently, Helen Horowitz (2002) has asked us to texture this presumption of female passionlessness, seeing it as only one theme in a diverse discourse of sexuality in the nineteenth century. However women understood bodily desire, the statistics suggest a downward revolution in native-born fertility over the course of the century, from 7.04 births per adult woman in 1800 to 3.56 in 1900. Janet Brodie (1994) gives us the most comprehensive survey of the prescriptive literature that attempted to help women in the project of "family limitation." Effective birth control was not yet available – beyond the misunderstood rhythm method – so matrons and others seeking to control their fertility also took advantage of nostrums advertised as abortifacients, and medical abortions often performed by so-called "irregulars" – midwives and homeopaths. Though never fully respectable, abortions were fairly common in urban areas before the Civil War (D'Emilio & Freedman 1988).

The same economic developments that encouraged the articulation of separate men's and women's spheres contributed in different ways to the creation of new personal opportunities for men and women. In subsistence farm economies, men required wives, and women husbands, to supply and process food and clothing. As Michel Foucault (1978) observed, the early modern world punished illicit sexual acts, including sodomy, but did not recognize diverse sexual *identities*, in keeping with the economic and social imperative that all men and women marry. (More recently, Richard Godbeer (2002) challenges this idea with his description of a figure, the Sodomite, who often appeared before colonial courts.) The introduction of wage labor for both men and women and the move beyond a subsistence economy allowed for the possibility of different kinds of lifetime choices, including decisions not to marry (D'Emilio & Freedman 1988: 109–30).

The most influential historiographic debate about nineteenth-century same-sex relationships, however, concerned bourgeois women, often married, who inhabited the separate emotional sphere of the home. In one of the founding articles of women's studies, Caroll Smith-Rosenberg in 1975 proposed a new way of looking at sexual identity based on her research in letters among middle-class women. In contrast to the prevailing binary model of sexuality, she offered a continuum, suggesting that women inhabiting a shared separate sphere often looked to each other for intimate and romantic friendships which existed well within any spectrum of the "normal." In retrospect, Smith-Rosenberg's article can be seen as an early entry into a new history of sexuality, however controversial her argument. Since its first appearance, Smith-Rosenberg's article has drawn abundant criticism from historians challenging her claim that bourgeois heterosexual marriage lacked romantic intimacy. From the Revolutionary era on, elite parents had accorded children marital choice, reflecting an acknowledgment that the "pursuit of happiness" often led into private life. Over the course of the nineteenth century, as Darwinian science challenged a God-centered universe, the celebration of a distinctively human romantic love evolved among the bourgeois classes to provide life's most precious meaning. This belief in the blessed communion between two souls reached its apotheosis in a sexualized marriage (Lystra 1989).

Many scholars have considered the consequences of this hegemonic, oversimplified tale of gender difference. The development of separate spheres coincided with industrialization, and the replacement of domestic with factory production. As described by Jeanne Boydston (1990), when manufacturing moved outside the home, and its workers were paid, the unwaged household duties still performed by women in the home were increasingly redefined as distinct from productive labor. In fact, domestic ideology suggested that home duties were scarcely work at all, so effortless were they to the true woman. Idealized femininity featured a domestic angel, who rarely broke a sweat but nonetheless provided a restorative haven in a heartless world for all who crossed its threshold. The result (still evident today) is that generations of Americans (both men and women) have ignored and mystified women's housework, remaining blind to its economic value, strenuousness, and contribution to an entire range of men's capitalist and other social endeavors.

Women's Reform, State Regulation

The presumption of women's superior morality helped encourage their participation in religious voluntary societies from mid-century on. Because women were considered more "disinterested" than men, their efforts were considered purer, and their influence more benign, with women's culture influencing men's and women's collective efforts at benevolence. Although initially women tended to form auxiliaries supplementary to men's, by the Civil War and thereafter, women began to found organizations, schools, and colleges that played to what was often portrayed as a uniquely female view of the world. From the Women's Christian Temperance Union to female missionary societies, organized women spoke with a recognizably "feminine" voice. Although still economically dependent on men, middle-class woman, empowered by the moral dimensions of their "sphere," contributed to a "feminized" American Victorian culture (Douglas 1978; Ginzberg 1990).

The ideology of romantic love notwithstanding, the late nineteenth century lived with a double standard. Despite the efforts of such reformers as the New York Female Reform Society, which in the 1840s attempted to shame the men of the upper and middle classes from "ruining" the nation's daughters, in the postbellum period men patronized prostitutes, including many widows and daughters from the defeated South (Smith-Rosenberg 1985). The efforts of Christian reformers made some inroads in encouraging the state to involve itself in the regulation of sexual practices. One such effort was initiated by a former YMCA (Young Men's Christian Association) secretary, Anthony Comstock, who succeeded in persuading Congress to pass "an act for the suppression of trade in and circulation of obscene literature and articles of immoral use." The Comstock Act interfered with the circulation of information about birth control from 1873 well into the twentieth century. Women reformers succeeded in raising the age of consent from as low as 10 (in the state of Delaware), to 16 and 18, triggering a debate among feminist historians about the appropriate agency of teenaged girls and the authority of parents who sometimes made use of statutory rape laws to control their children (Odem 1995; Ullman 1997). The newly organizing medical profession was largely responsible, after the Civil War, for state laws restricting access to abortion. Explanations for these new laws range from efforts to put "irregular" medical practitioners out of business to efforts to curb the freedoms of matrons demanding control of their own fertility and their own lives. At the turn of the century, this declining birth rate among the native-born, in conjunction with a "new" immigration from southern and eastern Europe, would cause concerns about "race suicide," and an interest in eugenics among Progressive reformers (D'Emilio & Freedman 1988: 165–6; Reagan 1997).

New Women and Embattled Masculinity

The doctrine of the spheres defined masculinity and femininity in mainstream culture for much of the nineteenth century, but the natural rights ideology of the Revolutionary era did have some proponents. Early women's rights advocates had little impact on conventional ideas of femininity, and were often considered an unseemly and radical minority. Yet as women expanded their activities in accord with their newly discovered sense of social and moral obligation, they developed more respect for themselves, and a corresponding desire for equal voice in the public and the political mainstream. Public high schools opened in substantial numbers following the Civil War, enrolling consistently more girls than boys, and bringing both sexes into contact and competition with each other – a competition that girls often won. Colleges and universities, too, opened for women, encouraging girls to engage with the questions of the world, and to seek more than could be found at home thereafter. Although male voters refused to enfranchise women at the national level until 1920, women made formative contributions in the fields of education, social work, and medicine well before then. Altogether these developments encouraged a new cultural ideal, a more public and active New Woman in the 1890s and after, who was educated, independent, and sometimes employed. By the turn of the century, helped along by the popular art of Charles Dana Gibson, the New Woman had become the alluring Gibson Girl, striding through the streets, pedaling a bicycle, and demonstrating a more athletic and assertive feminine style (Muncy 1991; Stansell 2000; Hunter 2002).

If femininity at first acknowledged women's economic dependence, masculinity all along required independence, a "manly" and republican ability to stand alone – increasingly difficult to acquire in the context of the consolidation of the means of production over the course of the nineteenth century. The open lands of the American West provided an ongoing opportunity for some to live independently, luring men and sometimes reluctant wives to take up homesteads far from the schools, churches, and voluntary societies with which middle-class women marked their gains.

For men left behind, secret societies provided a way of mediating new moral and economic constraints with traditional masculinity. Among the working classes, many of the new immigrant men entering the Northeast worked for others in factories and on labor gangs building canals, railroads, and, later, streetcars. Immigrant and working-class men congregated in saloons and bars, and enacted their masculinity through an expressive and competitive masculine leisure culture, which featured among other contests "the manly art" of boxing (Rosenzweig 1983; Gorn 1986; Clawson 1989).

The centralization of the economy created desk jobs for managers and owners and by the late nineteenth century, as New Women arrived in public, the masculinity of that class was in question, especially in contrast with the well-muscled working classes. The product of smaller families, and less burdened mothers, the sons of the elite increasingly grew up in privilege and comfort, and were considered soft. The most famous such son was asthmatic Theodore Roosevelt, who went west and remade himself as a gentleman cowboy at the beginning of his political career, later urging "the strenuous life" on men of his circumstances. Roosevelt left a job as assistant secretary of the Navy to lead a brigade of "Rough Riders" in the Spanish–American War, a decision best understood in terms of a gender crisis for the native-born elite (Hoganson 1998). Indeed, the era's near-obsession with the desire for "manliness" meant that a range of projects, from crusades against lynching to campaigns for the advance of a racialized "civilization," used this term to argue their cases (Bederman 1995).

Inscribing Heterosexuality

New Women were less dependent on men than earlier feminine prototypes, and those who continued to pursue careers were less likely to marry. The custom of romantic friendships with schoolmates continued into the new century for many girls. In later life, women authors, settlement workers, and others sometimes formed lifetime partnerships with other women as they pursued their public lives. Sometimes referred to as "Boston marriages," these relationships largely remained within the realm of respectability suggested in Smith-Rosenberg's analysis of earlier patterns, and have been detailed in a number of biographies (Cook 1992; Horowitz 1994). Of course, this respectability both at the time and in the historical record came at a cost, named in a brief but powerful essay by Blanche Wiesen Cook, "The Historical Denial of Lesbianism" (1979). It challenges any decision not to use 1970s terminology for lifetime same-sex partnerships, with or without genital "proofs." She writes, "Women who love women, who choose women to nurture and support and to form a living environment in which to work creatively and independently, are lesbians." Although sympathetic to Cook's perspective, Estelle Freedman (1998) disagrees with Cook's conclusion in a useful article, "'The Burning of Letters Continues': Elusive Identities and the Historical Construction of Sexuality."

In the context of an embattled masculinity, the arrival of New Women on the scene, and concerns about race suicide, medical authorities began to raise questions about the meaning of same-sex relationships. British sexologist Havelock Ellis followed Austrian Richard von Kraft-Ebbing in raising questions about the gender choices of working-class female "inverts," who dressed in a masculine manner and rejected the norms of femininity. Later physicians made a connection between unconventional gender behavior and the choice of sexual object, bringing scrutiny to once blameless "Boston marriages" (Smith-Rosenberg 1985; D'Emilio & Freedman 1988). Observers of men involved in homosexual relations also found gender role more determinative of root identity than object choice. Men who took the active, "masculine" role in homosexual relations did not risk a loss of traditional masculinity. Those "fairies" who took the passive role did. In any case, by the early twentieth century, physicians cataloguing the range of human normalcy trained their gaze on human sexuality, inscribing a newly named heterosexuality, and proscribing other variations (Chauncey 1994).

Sexual Liberalism, Consumerism, and the City

The work of Sigmund Freud especially encouraged American intellectuals and champions of the "modern" to reject Comstockery and advocate a more affirming and open approach to heterosexuality. Urban bohemia and radical politics approvingly regarded the efforts of Emma Goldman and Margaret Sanger to educate the working classes about birth control as a way to deprive capitalists of workers. This same cohort of writers and feminists also came to reject claims of women's special purity, and to argue women's equal claims to pleasure, ideas which spread among some prewar intellectuals and artists around the country (Stansell 2000).

In some ways, bohemian claims for sexual freedom followed the mores of popular culture in the immigrant city. As the lure of the American cash economy drew rural and immigrant girls and youth into urban jobs, Old World and distant rural parents had less ability to enforce traditional gender expectations. Despite the persistence of a "family economy," in which the labor of sons and daughters was often essential to the family's livelihood, working youth often held on to a portion of their earnings, and patronized the vaudeville and dance halls proliferating in the bustling city. Young women, as well as men, found in the urban labor market a degree of personal and sexual autonomy that they could not find at home (Peiss 1986).

Changes in sexual mores coincided with a gradual transformation in the economy to create the beginnings of a "modern" culture. As production moved out of home workshops and into factories, women from all walks of life increasingly provisioned their families through shopping rather than home manufacture. In the Gilded Age, elite matrons frequented well-stocked department stores, which were designed to entice as well as supply them. Working girls, too, were attracted by the shops, and spent precious wages needed at home on bits of fashion or finery offered by the consumer culture. Historians have debated the meanings of consumerism for immigrant girls and women, wondering how it changed them, and whether it oppressed or affirmed them. The recent emphasis has been on the latter, with Nan Enstad (1999) showing the ways in which treating oneself to a hat raised self-esteem, and contributed to the self-advocacy of labor activism. Together, consumerism and sexual expression contributed to a cultural shift towards indulgence and experience rather than denial and abstinence, summed up by cultural historian Warren Susman (2003) as a transition from a culture of "character" to one of "personality."

The ferment in gender roles at the turn of the century emerged in popular culture. The social freedoms of urban living were reinforced by the spread of a new mass culture modeled more on working-class than polite sensibilities. While much popular literature of the nineteenth century offered sentimental treatments of virtuous womanhood, the new mass film industry looked for inspiration to popular vaudeville, which had long offered the working classes a broader kind of entertainment. In the early twentieth century, the fledgling film industry created the humorous figures of the old maid and the respectable matron, thus exposing to ridicule the middle-aged women who had staffed women's reform efforts. This new mass culture also indulged in the celluloid sale of female sexuality – if only through revealing an occasional ankle (Ullman 1997). Historians have differed on how to interpret these various "female spectacles," with some seeing objectification, others empowerment. Diverse audiences adored female impersonators as well as female stars as long as they presented appropriately masculine personae elsewhere. In big cities in the early century, even "fairy boys" could enjoy their own culture, if not achieve respectability (Chauncey 1994).

If bohemians and the working classes provided the vanguard, by the 1920s, mainstream, middle-class Americans had rewritten some of the sexual rules. College youth threw off the traces, courting couples moved "from the front porch to the back seat," and Margaret Sanger rewrote her argument for birth control to appeal to a middle class seeking greater pleasure in marriage. (The American Birth Control League also brought business to "doctors only" – the only ones allowed to prescribe birth control devices.) The 1920s saw a broad-based mainstream rebellion against Comstockery, sexual repression, and domestic restraint, and introduced a more indulgent, sexualized, and consumer society (Bailey 1988; Chesler 1992).

National Crisis, "Traditional" Roles, and Consensus Sexuality

The 1930s and 1940s brought two decades of crisis and a drop in the marriage and birth rates. The war mobilized the American population for public ends, setting quests for private happiness to the side. After the Japanese attack on Pearl Harbor, the nation's mobilization of young men created immediate labor shortages in the armaments, aircraft, and shipbuilding industries. The radio and print media cooperated in recruiting women to fill what had formerly been men's jobs in heavy industry. "Rosie the Riveter," a media creation, demonstrated that women could do men's high-paying industrial jobs, and even that some of the skills of women's work were transferable. Representations of "Rosie" in overalls, sporting a bandanna, ranged from conventionally feminine to hyper-masculine, suggesting the temporary fluidity of gender identities. Although for the first time many married women joined the workforce, the absence of a broad-based public commitment to providing day-care for young children signaled the temporary nature of support for women's work. As wartime industries demobilized, women workers lost their jobs and new consumer industries hired returning veterans (Gluck 1987).

The wartime massing of Americans in the same-sex cultures of the military, however, introduced many small-town youth to alternative sexualities. When the war ended, many such soldiers remained in ports of discharge such as San Francisco and

New York, expanding gay subcultures. When McCarthy-led anti-communists routed
many homosexuals out of the military and government as security risks, gay professionals formed the Mattachine Society and the Daughters of Bilitis, advocacy groups
for homosexual men and women which provided advice for survival in an age of
conformity (D'Emilio & Freedman 1988: 288–95; Bérubé 1990).

Following two decades of public crisis and delayed families, according to popular
wisdom, Americans greeted the end of the war as an opportunity to marry, procreate,
and rediscover a domesticated, private happiness. Although many married women
went back to work, and most did not achieve suburban prosperity, there is some
truth to this image. The popular literature glorified family life as a counterpoint to
the all-embracing Soviet state, and contrasted "warm hearth" with the Cold War in
a nuclear age. The mean age of marriage lowered, and the American birth rate spiked
in a "baby boom" peaking in 1957 at 3.2. The United States emerged from the war
with infrastructure intact, and access to many of the world's resources. Renewed
prosperity encouraged restored respect for American capitalist culture (challenged
during the Great Depression), and successful husbands donned white collars, and
commuted from newly constructed suburbs to corporate jobs as "organization men"
(May 1988).

Housewives left behind at home found themselves swaddled in a "feminine mystique," which assured them that their material prosperity and freedom to invest in
their homes, husbands, and children made them the most fortunate women of all
time. Many housewives of the middle classes were not so sure, stranded in a new
"separate sphere" beyond the political and professional mainstream. Unlike the separate women's moral sphere of the mid-nineteenth century, however, the "feminine
mystique" explored by journalist Betty Friedan (1963) based women's uniqueness
on a Freudian idea of a sexualized femininity. When Friedan asked middle-class
women why they were discontented, they imagined that she was inquiring about their
sex lives. In search of solutions, they were more likely to turn to psychoanalysis than
social analysis.

Sexual Liberation, Gender Revolution

Few men or women felt free to challenge head-on the polarized sex roles of this
conforming age. Yet just as Friedan prophesied a female revolt against the housewife
ideal, so did bohemian Beats such as Jack Kerouac and Allen Ginsberg anticipate a
male revolt against the straitened role of the male breadwinner (Ehrenreich 1983).
It was not until the 1960s, however, and the popularization of the Civil Rights
crusade and the student campaign against the Vietnam War, that the postwar gender
system was seriously challenged. Modeling themselves on the example of black
nationalist youth, who temporarily rejected integration to celebrate Black Power,
women students who found themselves marginalized in the student movement also
withdrew to explore and understand gender oppression. Feminist consciousness-
raising groups spread from beyond student groups to many different sectors of
American life, as women in the company of friends considered the impact of gender
ideology in their own lives and relationships (Evans 1980). Radical feminism offered
a plethora of alternatives, ranging from equal rights feminism to a cultural feminism

which celebrated women's fundamental "difference" from men. One of the most important frontiers of the gender revolution was sexuality itself and all the social practices resulting from women's role as child-bearers. The 1950s had seen a continuation of the sexual liberalism ventured in the 1920s, and the flowering of a sexualized teen culture nourished by music and the advertising industry (Douglas 1994). But the double standard, which bound women to more restrictive sexual codes than men, remained intact. The student counterculture challenged it, arguing that women's liberation meant freeing women from its hypocrisies. Indeed, early understandings of "women's lib" emphasized a new sexual freedom for women enabled by the availability of more reliable birth control (in the form of the birth control pill) and easier access to abortion, with the Supreme Court's decision in *Roe* v. *Wade* (1973) restricting state control over pregnant women's bodies. Advocates for women's full autonomy won important gains as American civil rights law was applied to women's status as sexual agents (and victims of rape), child-bearers, and workers (Rosen 2000).

Some radical feminists, however, located the site of male oppression within heterosexual practice itself. Declaiming that "feminism is the theory, lesbianism is the practice," radical feminists encouraged women newly enlightened to gender oppression to consider challenging the heterosexual imperative, renouncing men, and embarking on a separatist sexual existence. These political recruits joined women who identified as lifelong lesbians to create an important same-sex culture within American feminism and American society (Echols 1989).

If the emergence of lesbian culture within American feminism was gradual, the arrival of the broader gay rights movement in the United States was linked with a particular moment – a riot at the Stonewall Inn, a gay bar in New York, which, like many gay bars in cities around the nation, was routinely subjected to harassment by local police and alcohol enforcement authorities. The last weekend of June, 1969, however, the working-class patrons fought back, giving rise in the aftermath to the celebration of Gay Power, as male and female homosexuals joined together, challenged themselves to come out of the closet, claim their identity and fight social discrimination (Carter 2004). Launched by Stonewall in the 1960s, in the intervening decades other sexual minorities too have organized, disputed the "sexual binary," and inspired new works in cultural and social history. The histories of intersexed individuals and those who self-identify with the opposite gender (transsexuals) are important in their own right, but also as their experiences illuminate our entire sex–gender system, helping to construct a complex model for contemporary sexuality (Meyerowitz 2002).

The overturning of traditional gender and sexual orthodoxies in the 1970s and thereafter has not gone unchallenged. Any cultural history of gender and sexuality must take account of a powerful backlash, dating from the 1970s and gaining force in the recent past. Cultural conflict over abortion is only one of the many arenas of conflict, in which traditional ideas of feminine role conflict with new claims for women's empowerment, often breaking down over class lines. Debate over sex education in schools has been another arena contextualized by historians. The cultural empowerment of women and the rise of movements to end discrimination based on sexual orientation are at the heart of the rise of the New Right, a voting block with a conservative political agenda, which has used such "hot button" issues as a way to mobilize a citizenry for conservative causes. Especially in a competitive economic climate, in which many unskilled men are losing precarious holds on livelihoods, the economic and political gains of educated women, and the claims to equality of gay and lesbian men and women, have been exploited to aggravate deeply felt vulnerabilities – often expressed in the restatement of "traditional" ideas of femininity and masculinity (Luker 1984; Faludi 1991, 1999).

It is hard to know just now how far this retreat from the sexual and gender revolutions of the past decades will go. Diverse constituencies do seem to be reconsidering some of the most important innovations of the 1970s and thereafter. Christian men's groups are urging their membership to commit to being reliable breadwinners to regain their standing as heads of families. These "Promise Keepers" propose a traditional exchange – sexual fidelity and economic support in return for feminine subordination and service. Even at elite universities, where the gender revolution began, some female students are said to be planning for occupations as housewives rather than for careers. Within the religious right, there are some who are challenging sexual liberalism itself – arguing against the use of contraception even within marriage, because of their belief that copulation should only be in the service of reproduction. Yet despite these efforts to roll back the developments of the past 30 years, the divorce rate has only been rising, suggesting no fundamental changes in long-term trends. Historian Estelle Freedman is probably accurate in the prediction announced in a recent book title, *No Turning Back* (2002). Freedman argues that the power of feminism has fundamentally altered both the nation and the world, and that despite the accompanying backlash its insights are here to stay. Whether or not she is right about the ideological directions of the future, it seems unlikely that historians will soon lose their interest in charting the evolving American sex/gender system – one of the most volatile dimensions of modern life.

REFERENCES

Bailey, Beth L.: *From Front Porch to Back Seat: Courtship in Twentieth-Century America* (Baltimore, MD: Johns Hopkins University Press, 1988).

Bederman, Gail: *Manliness and Civilization: A Cultural History of Gender and Race in the United States, 1880–1917* (Chicago: University of Chicago Press, 1995).

Bérubé, Allan: *Coming out under Fire: The History of Gay Men and Women in World War Two* (New York: Free Press, 1990).

Boydston, Jeanne: *Home and Work: Housework, Wages, and the Ideology of Labor in the Early Republic* (New York: Oxford University Press, 1990).

Brodie, Janet Farrell: *Contraception and Abortion in Nineteenth-Century America* (Ithaca, NY: Cornell University Press, 1994).

Brown, Kathleen M.: *Good Wives, Nasty Wenches, and Anxious Patriarchs: Gender, Race, and Power in Colonial Virginia* (Chapel Hill: University of North Carolina Press, 1996).

Carter, David: *Stonewall: The Riots That Sparked the Gay Revolution* (New York: St. Martin's Press, 2004).

Chauncey, George: *Gay New York: Gender, Urban Culture, and the Makings of the Gay Male World, 1890–1940* (New York: Basic Books, 1994).

Chesler, Ellen: *Woman of Valor: Margaret Sanger and the Birth Control Movement in America* (New York: Simon & Schuster, 1992).

Clawson, Mary Ann: *Constructing Brotherhood: Class, Gender, and Fraternalism* (Princeton, NJ: Princeton University Press, 1989).

Cohen, Patricia Cline: *The Murder of Helen Jewett: The Life and Death of a Prostitute in Nineteenth-Century New York* (New York: Alfred A. Knopf, 1998).

Cook, Blanche Wiesen: "The Historical Denial of Lesbianism," *Radical History Review* 20 (Spring/Summer, 1979), 60–5.

Cook, Blanche Wiesen: *Eleanor Roosevelt* (New York: Viking, 1992).

Cott, Nancy F.: *The Bonds of Womanhood: "Woman's Sphere" in New England, 1780–1835* (New Haven, CT: Yale University Press, 1977).

Cott, Nancy F.: "Passionlessness: An Interpretation of Victorian Sexual Ideology, 1790–1850," in Judith W. Leavitt, ed., *Women and Health in America: Historical Readings* (Madison: University of Wisconsin Press, 1978).

D'Emilio, John & Freedman, Estelle B.: *Intimate Matters: A History of Sexuality in America* (New York: Harper & Row, 1988).

Douglas, Ann: *The Feminization of American Culture* (New York: Avon Books, 1978).

Douglas, Susan J.: *Where the Girls Are: Growing up Female with the Mass Media* (New York: Times Books, 1994).

Echols, Alice: *Daring to be Bad: Radical Feminism in America, 1967–1975* (Minneapolis: University of Minnesota Press, 1989).

Ehrenreich, Barbara: *The Hearts of Men: American Dreams and the Flight from Commitment* (Garden City, NY: Anchor Press, 1983).

Enstad, Nan: *Ladies of Labor, Girls of Adventure: Working Women, Popular Culture, and Labor Politics at the Turn of the Twentieth Century* (New York: Columbia University Press, 1999).

Evans, Sara: *Personal Politics: The Roots of Women's Liberation in the Civil Rights Movement and the New Left* (New York: Vintage Books, 1980).

Faludi, Susan: *Backlash: The Undeclared War against American Women* (New York: Crown, 1991).

Faludi, Susan: *Stiffed: The Betrayal of the American Man* (New York: W. Morrow, 1999).

Foucault, Michel: *The History of Sexuality* (New York: Pantheon Books, 1978).

Freedman, Estelle B.: "'The Burning of Letters Continues': Elusive Identities and the Historical Construction of Sexuality," *Journal of Women's History* 9, 4 (Winter 1998).

Freedman, Estelle B.: *No Turning Back: The History of Feminism and the Future of Women* (New York: Ballantine Books, 2002).

Friedan, Betty: *The Feminine Mystique* (New York: W. W. Norton, 1963).

Ginzberg, Lori D.: *Women and the Work of Benevolence: Morality, Politics, and Class in the Nineteenth-Century United States* (New Haven, CT: Yale University Press, 1990).

Gluck, Sherna Berger: *Rosie the Riveter Revisited: Women, the War, and Social Change* (Boston, MA: Twayne Publishers, 1987).

Godbeer, Richard: *Sexual Revolution in Early America: Gender Relations in the American Experience* (Baltimore, MD: Johns Hopkins University Press, 2002).

Gorn, Elliott J.: *The Manly Art: Bare-Knuckle Prize Fighting in America* (Ithaca, NY: Cornell University Press, 1986).

Hill, Patricia Ruth: *The World Their Household: The American Woman's Foreign Mission Movement and Cultural Transformation, 1870–1920* (Ann Arbor: University of Michigan Press, 1984).

Hoganson, Kristin L.: *Fighting for American Manhood: How Gender Politics Provoked the Spanish–American and Philippine–American Wars* (New Haven, CT: Yale University Press, 1998).

Horowitz, Helen Lefkowitz: *The Power and Passion of M. Carey Thomas* (New York: Alfred A. Knopf, 1994).

Horowitz, Helen Lefkowitz: *Rereading Sex: Battles over Sexual Knowledge and Suppression in Nineteenth-Century America* (New York: Alfred A. Knopf, 2002).

340 JANE H. HUNTER

Hunter, Jane H.: *How Young Ladies Became Girls: The Victorian Origins of American Girlhood* (New Haven, CT: Yale University Press, 2002).

Laqueur, Thomas Walter: *Making Sex: Body and Gender from the Greeks to Freud* (Cambridge, MA: Harvard University Press, 1990).

Luker, Kristin: *Abortion and the Politics of Motherhood.* California Series on Social Choice and Political Economy (Berkeley: University of California Press, 1984).

Lystra, Karen: *Searching the Heart: Women, Men, and Romantic Love in Nineteenth-Century America* (New York: Oxford University Press, 1989).

May, Elaine Tyler: *Homeward Bound: American Families in the Cold War Era* (New York: Basic Books, 1988).

Meyerowitz, Joanne J.: *How Sex Changed: A History of Transsexuality in the United States* (Cambridge, MA: Harvard University Press, 2002).

Muncy, Robyn: *Creating a Female Dominion in American Reform, 1890–1935* (New York: Oxford University Press, 1991).

Norton, Mary Beth: *Liberty's Daughters: The Revolutionary Experience of American Women, 1750–1800, with a New Preface* (Ithaca, NY: Cornell University Press, 1980).

Odem, Mary E.: *Delinquent Daughters: Protecting and Policing Adolescent Female Sexuality in the United States, 1885–1920*, Gender & American Culture series (Chapel Hill: University of North Carolina Press, 1995).

Peiss, Kathy Lee: *Cheap Amusements: Working Women and Leisure in Turn-of-the-Century New York* (Philadelphia, PA: Temple University Press, 1986).

Reagan, Leslie J.: *When Abortion Was a Crime: Women, Medicine, and Law in the United States, 1867–1973* (Berkeley: University of California Press, 1997).

Rosen, Ruth: *The World Split Open: How the Modern Women's Movement Changed America* (New York: Viking, 2000).

Rosenzweig, Roy: *Eight Hours for What We Will: Workers and Leisure in an Industrial City, 1870–1920* (New York: Cambridge University Press, 1983).

Sklar, Kathryn Kish: *Catharine Beecher: A Study in American Domesticity* (New Haven, CT: Yale University Press, 1973).

Smith-Rosenberg, Caroll: "The Female World of Love and Ritual: Relations between Women in Nineteenth-Century America," *Signs* 1, 1 (Autumn 1975).

Smith-Rosenberg, Caroll: "The New Woman as Androgyne: Social Disorder and Gender Crisis, 1870–1936," in *Disorderly Conduct: Visions of Gender in Victorian America* (New York: Oxford University Press, 1985).

Srebnick, Amy Gilman: *The Mysterious Death of Mary Rogers: Sex and Culture in Nineteenth-Century New York* (New York: Oxford University Press, 1995).

Stansell, Christine: *City of Women: Sex and Class in New York, 1789–1860* (New York: Alfred A. Knopf, 1986).

Stansell, Christine: *American Moderns: Bohemian New York and the Creation of a New Century* (New York: Metropolitan Books, 2000).

Susman, Warren: "'Personality' and the Making of Twentieth-Century Culture," in *Culture as History: The Transformation of American Society in the Twentieth Century* (Washington, DC: Smithsonian Institution, 2003).

Ullman, Sharon R.: *Sex Seen: The Emergence of Modern Sexuality in America* (Berkeley: University of California Press, 1997).

Ulrich, Laurel: *Good Wives: Image and Reality in the Lives of Women in Northern New England, 1650–1750* (New York: Alfred A. Knopf, 1982).

Ulrich, Laurel: *A Midwife's Tale: The Life of Martha Ballard, Based on Her Diary, 1785–1812* (New York: Alfred A. Knopf, 1990).

Chapter Twenty-Three

RACE AND ETHNICITY

Eric Avila

Historian Matthew Frye Jacobson's observation that "to write about race in American culture is to exclude virtually nothing" (1998: 11) aptly sums up the standing of race in the field. For if cultural history is essentially the history of stories that people tell, and the analysis of how those stories anticipate the creation and evolution of social identities, then race is ubiquitous within the cultural milieu of American history. Within the historiography of the United States, of course, race and ethnicity have remained ongoing preoccupations, but the key question for the purposes of this brief survey of the cultural history of race and ethnicity in the United States is: what can cultural historians say about the significance of race and ethnicity in the American past that other kinds of historians cannot? The body of scholarship that has been amassed on the subject, which had its formative years during the 1970s, constitutes an important and distinctive avenue by which to comprehend the predicaments and possibilities of being "of color" in American history.

As the subject of historical inquiry, culture played a paradoxical role in the maintenance and subversion of racial and ethnic hierarchies in the United States. Even as it legitimized the ongoing subordination of racialized peoples, it also provided an important channel of resistance and assimilation by racial and ethnic minority groups. Over the past 30 years, cultural historians have illuminated the ambiguous uses of culture among generations of upwardly mobile, geographically restless, and racially diverse Americans. Their work demonstrates that cultural history, with its emphasis upon values, meanings, and myths, its attention to the significance of the word and the image, and its engagement with broader social theories about the nature and construction of identity, provides a unique window for understanding the salience of race and ethnicity in the American past.

What distinguishes the cultural history of race and ethnicity, first and foremost, is its refusal to take the core concepts of "race" and "ethnicity" for granted, as previous historians had done. During the 1960s, the Civil Rights Movement among African Americans, and its parallel social movements among other minority groups, asserted an invigorated set of separate and distinct racial identities, inspiring historians, in turn, to take up the subjects of "black history," "Chicano history," and so forth. "Race relations" also became a subject of historical inquiry, and social historians initially used that term unselfconsciously, documenting the shifting numbers and concentrations of the so-called "races" over time. While this mode of writing history shed unprecedented light upon a previously unknown record of racial interaction and conflict, and called important attention to the broader history behind the racial conflicts that wracked 1960s America, it generally rested upon an unproblematized assumption that race was something internal and fixed, and constituted an essential component of one's being. For a moment, this concept of race provided a broader foundation for social scientists from various disciplines, including history, to launch an array of investigative studies that measured and mapped shifting racial populations across time and space.

In the following decades, however, the "cultural turn" within the humanities and social sciences disrupted these efforts to empirically portray the historically evolving geography of race and ethnicity in the United States, and historians, like other social scientists, learned that their categories were not as fixed and self-evident as they had presumed. On the contrary, social identities such as race, gender, and sexuality were increasingly understood as constructions of language and representation – which became reified through the arenas of law, politics, and the economy – and less as something indelibly marked upon human bodies. As scholars from various disciplines interrogated and dismantled the concept of race itself, exposing its construction through language and discourse, historians could no longer suppose essentialist notions of race in history, and cultural historians in particular assumed the important task of identifying the historical construction of racial categories and their implications for American social relations. It is this very attention to the creation and evolution of racial identity that distinguishes the cultural history of race and ethnicity from other modes of historical research. What follows is a chronological overview of some of the major works in the cultural history of race and ethnicity, paying close attention to both the cultural genres that codified the formation of various racial identities, and to the different interpretations of race and ethnicity and their various meanings in the American past.

The social climate of America in the 1960s proved conducive for historical investigations of race, racial conflict, and racial identity. While the civil rights movement of the preceding decade drew attention to the legacy of racial inequality in the United States and pressed the need for integration, the 1960s witnessed the explosion of more particularized social movements that galvanized around a set of essentialized racial and ethnic identities. The Black Power Movement and the Chicano Movement, to name two examples, asserted essentialized versions of racial identity as a strategy towards group solidarity and political empowerment. Moreover, the explosion of "race riots" in American inner cities – incited by joblessness, police brutality, and invasive urban renewal and highway construction programs – generated intensified concern about the nation's racial problems, and prodded experts in the universities and in government to investigate the specific causes of these disturbances.

In the midst of this turmoil, historians undertook a concerted effort to add historical perspective to the nation's racial crisis by emphasizing the history of race and race relations in the United States. Slavery thus emerged as a timely historical question: How and why did it develop? What were its structural features? And perhaps most important for the day, what was its legacy? How had it shaped subsequent patterns of socioeconomic relations in the United States? Drawing upon the energy of the civil rights movement, and responding to a need to recover a sense of black history against the disorienting effects of slavery and segregation, American historians sought answers to these poignant questions by producing an enormous body of historical monographs on slavery and the slave system in the United States. Kenneth M. Stampp's *The Peculiar Institution: Slavery in the Ante-Bellum South* (1956), Eugene D. Genovese's *Roll, Jordan, Roll: The World the Slaves Made* (1974), and George P. Rawick's, *From Sundown to Sunup: The Making of the Black Community* (1972) became landmarks in the historiography of slavery; and they underscored a key paradox that Edmund S. Morgan articulated in his classic study, *American Slavery, American Freedom: The Ordeal of Colonial Virginia* (1975): that American independence from colonial rule depended upon the elaboration and maintenance of a vast system of slave labor. While these scholars added their own unique insights to the historical portrait of slavery and black–white relations, they shared a common emphasis upon conventional source material – slave and slave-owner narratives, tax records and appraisal inventories, newspapers, advertisements, diaries – in their effort to render an objective portrait of social interaction in the slave-owning South.

One book, however, earned distinction for its novel approach to the subject. In 1968, Winthrop Jordan published his landmark study *White over Black: American Attitudes Towards the Negro, 1550–1812* (1968), which anticipated the "cultural turn" within the historiography of race and ethnicity in the United States. What distinguished this book from other histories of slavery was its attention to racial "attitudes," and its exploration of the subjective dimensions of racial identity. As both citizens and immigrants, the English maintained a cultural predisposition to enslave Africans on the basis of their unfavorable associations with the color black. Jordan identified these associations through a meticulous reading of forms of evidence that other historians generally shunned. For example, *White over Black* incorporates Shakespearean drama into its analysis, demonstrating how *Othello* and *The Tempest* revealed an acute color-consciousness that conditioned English perceptions of Africans from the first stages of contact between Europe and Africa. Jordan also considered scientific ideas about race and racial difference that emerged within the evolving disciplines of anatomy and anthropology in eighteenth-century Europe and America, which created a well of stereotypes and prejudices that informed the elaboration of the slave system. By emphasizing ideas, language, and discourse, Jordan set his study apart from other histories of slavery in the United States and directed attention to the ways in which Anglo-Americans affirmed their own identity in contrast to the negative qualities of "black" Africans, as well as the social attitudes that shaped social circumstances and practices.

Jordan's groundbreaking look at the history of slavery shed new light upon the real effects of racial ideas and concepts, and generated a broadening awareness of how popular impressions and expressions of racial difference shaped actions and policies towards non-white racial groups. Shortly after the debut of *White over Black*, George M. Fredrickson enlarged this awareness with *The Black Image in the White Mind: The Debate on Afro-American Character and Destiny, 1817–1914* (1971), which presented an intellectual history of white racism towards blacks in nineteenth-century America. Drawing upon literary, scientific, and philosophical tracts, Fredrickson emphasized the elaboration of racial concepts, theories, and categories that confirmed white suspicions of black degeneracy and showed how these developments worked in tandem with the ongoing subordination of African Americans.

Through a common emphasis upon the centrality of ideas, perceptions, and attitudes, Jordan and Fredrickson added a new inflection to the historiography of slavery in the United States, and expanded the methodological parameters of Afro-American history. Other historians followed their example throughout the 1970s, bringing other racial and ethnic groups into the analytic fold. In the aftermath of the Vietnam War, and amidst pervasive concerns about the abuse of government and the global exertion of American hegemony, scholars such as Michael Rogin, Richard Slotkin, and Robert F. Berkhofer constructed a historical narrative about the expansionist ambitions of the United States during the nineteenth century, and illuminated the degree to which Indians fell victim to those efforts. Michael Rogin, for example, took a novel approach in *Fathers and Children: Andrew Jackson and the Subjugation of the American Indian* (1975), which synthesized Marxist analysis with Freudian psychology to illustrate the "infantilizing discourse" (1975: 209) about Indians in the culture of Jacksonian America. By closely reading two staples of cultural history – newspapers and literary fiction – and scrutinizing the political speeches of Andrew Jackson himself, Rogin located a "familial language" (ibid. 12) in official discussions of Indian removal and identified a "paternalist" ethos (ibid. 241) in official policies towards Indian peoples.

Rogin's interest in ethos and language, which fell squarely within the parameters of cultural history, also infused the historical writings of two contemporary historians of the American West. Richard Slotkin's *Regeneration Through Violence: The Mythology of the American Frontier, 1600–1860* (1973) excavates the discourse of westward expansion to identify a series of "cultural myths" about conquering heroes and savage Indians. This study surveyed a variety of popular stories that circulated in the colonies and in the early republic, including Puritan narratives of King Philip's War, the captivity narrative of Mary Rowlandson, the cult of Daniel Boone, and the epic tales of Thoreau and Melville. In these texts, Slotkin identifies a central myth that racial violence against Indians purifies and regenerates its perpetrators. This myth of "regeneration through violence" became, according to Slotkin, "the structuring metaphor of the American experience" (1973: 5). In 1978, Robert F. Berkhofer followed with *The White Man's Indian: Images of the American Indian from Columbus to the Present*, which singled out the role of culture in the construction of a monolithic notion of "the Indian" that obliterated the cultural and geographical diversity of indigenous peoples in North America. Berkhofer compiles an historical array of scientific and literary tracts about, as well as artistic images of, Indians to discern the "perceptual constructs and conceptual categories" (1978: xv) that white Americans created in order to justify their policies and actions against Indians. Not unlike Winthrop Jordan's study of Anglo-American conceptions of Africans and African Americans, *The White Man's Indian* emphasizes the role of images and words in the subjugation of Indian peoples.

The emphasis upon "structuring metaphors," "paternalist language," and "perceptual constructs" in the work of Jordan, Rogin, Slotkin, and Berkhofer signaled a new culturalist approach to understanding the salience of race in the historic project of making a new nation. Other historians of the 1970s took a similar approach, but expanded their scope to include other "Others" as well. Reginald Horsman's *Race and Manifest Destiny: The Origins of American Racial Anglo-Saxonism* (1981), for example, presented a study of changing racial attitudes in the United States from the late eighteenth to the mid-nineteenth centuries, as manifest in various aspects of nineteenth-century culture. Horsman demonstrated how these evolving racialist attitudes made Indians, blacks, and Mexicans permanent candidates for subjugation on the basis of their supposed innate inferiority. Through a close reading of literary and scientific tracts, Horsman traces the origins of a myth of Anglo-Saxon racial superiority that originated in England and was popularized in the expanding United States. Similarly, in *Iron Cages: Race and Culture in Nineteenth-Century America* (1979), Ronald Takaki surveys the words and ideas of the leading "culture makers" (1979: 11) of the nineteenth century – Benjamin Rush, Thomas Jefferson, Andrew Jackson, Oliver Wendell Holmes, George Custer, Bret Harte, Henry George, and others – to identify a deeply rooted cultural pathology that assigned to blacks, Mexicans, Indians, and the Chinese the negative values and qualities that whites repressed within themselves. Like Jordan's *White over Black*, and Slotkin's *Regeneration Through Violence*, Takaki's study is focused upon what whites, and white elites in particular, said and wrote about people of color. Although *Iron Cages* is not about the experience and consciousness of allegedly inferior racial groups, the book demonstrates how race can provide a primary category of analysis in the historical study of nineteenth-century American culture. Blacks, Indians, Mexicans, Chinese, and Japanese appear in the text not as social beings, but as cultural referents that preoccupied the white imagination. This is by design, as Takaki remains concerned with how ideas about these racial groups provided raw material for the historic project of making a white racial and national identity, providing an intellectual basis for a subsequent strand of cultural history, discussed towards the end of this essay, which considered the evolution of a white racial identity.

By illuminating the historic ways in which various strands of racial thinking shaped the emergence of racial hierarchy and inequality in the United States, the new cultural histories of race and ethnicity in the 1970s provided an alternative approach to the history of race relations in the United States. These historians distinguished themselves by their willingness to engage cultural texts and discourses as evidence, and by their emphasis upon the making of race and racial hierarchy through words and images. Yet, for all this analytic insight and methodological innovation, this new generation of historians shared a somewhat narrow focus upon the few noteworthy individuals whom Takaki identified as the "culture makers": those men of science, religion, literature, and politics who commanded the authority and expertise necessary to create and disseminate ideas that shaped popular conceptions about the superiority of some racial groups, and the inferiority of others. Their research suggested the historical emergence of a top-down model of racist ideology in the United States, in which elites generated and disseminated ideas about white supremacy and non-white inferiority. Left out of that model, however, was the extent to which the racist words and images of the culture makers circulated among expanding concentrations of consumers and spectators, who, for a variety of reasons that a subsequent generation of historians would elaborate upon, developed their own variants on ideas of racial hierarchy.

Cultural history flourished during the 1980s as more historians directed their attention towards the mid-nineteenth-century origins and subsequent development of American popular culture. As a new area of historical inquiry, popular culture provided a means of reconstructing the values, attitudes, and desires of historically inarticulate groups, including workers, families, and women. Some historians brought questions of race and ethnicity to this new interest in the history of American popular culture. Robert W. Rydell, for example, in his 1984 study of world fairs and expositions at the turn of the century, emphasized the degree to which race and racism emerged as central themes within the representational schema of the world's fairs. In an age marked by global expansion, rapid industrialization, and scientific advancement, the ubiquitous display of Borneo's "wild man," African pygmies, giant Patagonians, and scalp-dancing Indians at world's fairs constituted a form of "white supremacist entertainment" (1984: 6) in which the spectacle of the Other, in his visibly primitive state, provided a racial marker by which the fairs' creators and visitors could celebrate the achievements of an ascendant national power.

In a similar vein, the filmmaker Marlon T. Riggs produced the historical documentary *Ethnic Notions* (1986), which catalogued the variety of racial stereotypes leveled against African Americans in mainstream popular culture from the 1820s to the civil rights era. Although a documentary film might seem anomalous in a historiographic essay, the very title of Riggs's project captures the essence of the cultural history of race and ethnicity, which is first and foremost concerned with changing conceptions of race across time. The creators of *Ethnic Notions* were meticulous in their collection and organization of historical artifacts, and filmed the commentary of two experts in the field of Afro-American history: George L. Fredrickson and Lawrence W. Levine. These efforts produced an extensive catalog of black stereotypes that had elicited the amusement, humor, nostalgia, and sometimes even envy of generations of white Americans. Rife with Loyal Toms, carefree Sambos, faithful Mammies, grinning Coons, savage Brutes, and wide-eyed Pickaninnies, *Ethnic Notions* demonstrates how African Americans have been viewed through the refracting lenses of cartoons, feature films, popular songs, minstrel shows, advertisements, folklore, household artifacts, and even children's rhymes, and suggests the ways in which those images worked to reproduce the disempowerment of generations of African Americans.

As a documentary, *Ethnic Notions* marked an exception to the historical role of film as a powerful perpetrator of racial and ethnic stereotypes, a subject of historical inquiry taken up by Thomas Cripps. In *Slow Fade to Black: The Negro in American Film, 1900–1942* (1977), Cripps considers the role of blacks in Hollywood up through World War II. While much attention is given to the negative portrayals of African Americans in such films as D. W. Griffith's *The Birth of a Nation* (1915) and David Selznick's *Gone with the Wind* (1939), Cripps's study is not a straightforward story of how Hollywood churned out vicious misrepresentations of black Americans. While these films had an enormous influence upon the way Americans perceived African Americans – as treacherous opportunists lusting after white women, or as happy, docile servants of decadent white masters – Cripps also considers efforts to establish an autonomous sphere of "black underground cinema" (1977: 3), citing the films of the black director Oscar Micheaux, as well as the campaign of the NAACP (National Association for the Advancement of Colored People) to make Hollywood filmmakers more sensitive to the cinematic image of African Americans.

Cripps develops further this dialectical emphasis upon the on- and offscreen role of blacks in *Making Movies Black: The Hollywood Message Movie from World War II to the Civil Rights Era* (1993). World War II, he argues, inaugurated a new era in Hollywood's attitude towards African Americans. As the film industry deepened its engagement with the war effort, it cast a new integrationist vision that emphasized interracial camaraderie and loyalty among whites and blacks. Under the auspices of what Cripps identified as "conscience liberalism" (1993: ix), Hollywood largely abandoned its old stock of pernicious stereotypes to embrace a more complex portrayal of African Americans, which endured through the dawning civil rights era and reached an apotheosis in the career of Sidney Poitier. But Poitier's box office success did not mark a Hollywood ending to the saga of representing race onscreen, for even as the film industry posited a kinder vision of racial integration, it did so on the dominant group's terms, denying black actors the multidimensional characters that whites portrayed.

Cripps's documentation of images of African Americans in Hollywood film followed the lead of earlier cultural histories of race and ethnicity in cataloguing the degrading racial stereotypes that motion pictures perpetrated throughout much of film history, and in examining how whites regarded blacks in and through film. And yet, by emphasizing the efforts of black activists through such institutions as the NAACP to eradicate such stereotypes, Cripps also ascribed a modicum of agency to African Americans to resist the cultural power of the film industry. And agency is precisely what had been missing from the work of earlier historians who had mined political discourse and popular culture for racial and ethnic stereotypes. For while they revealed the important role that images and ideas played in the historical formation of racial hierarchy, they said little about the capacity of African Americans and other racial minorities to resist and/or subvert powerful cultural stereotypes, either through conventional political strategies or through cultural expression. In other words, while much had been written about blacks, Indians, and Chinese immigrants as the passive objects of domination and racist representation, very little consideration, if any, had been given to their role as active historical subjects of creative thought and action.

This role, however, garnered attention from growing numbers of cultural and social historians who sought to create inclusive histories of those groups largely left out of the dominant historical narrative. As early as 1977, Lawrence W. Levine was adding a new dimension to the cultural history of race and ethnicity with the publication of *Black Culture and Black Consciousness: Afro-American Folk Thought from Slavery to Freedom*. Here, Levine concentrates upon black folk thought and expression from the antebellum period to 1950, as manifest in slave songs, folktales, animal trickster stories, gospel songs, black secular music and work songs, the blues, black humor, the "dozens," and black hero figures – materials "without which it is impossible to understand the history and culture of the bulk of black Americans" (1977: xi). Levine's emphasis upon black cultural expression dispelled a pervasive view among culturally tone-deaf social scientists that North American slavery had stripped African Americans of all aesthetic creativity and forced them to "borrow" culture wholesale from whites. It also countered a dominant tendency in the social sciences, including history, to characterize the black experience in America as an "unending round of degradation and pathology" (ibid. x–xi). By exposing a shared legacy of intense cultural creativity among African Americans, *Black Culture and Black Consciousness* exposed the multidimensional complexity of the black experience in American history, and demonstrated how cultural expression allowed African Americans to articulate bitter feelings within themselves, perpetuate tradition, derive aesthetic pleasure, preserve values, and "say what they felt" (ibid. 297).

Black Culture and Black Consciousness established African American culture as a legitimate field of historical inquiry and foreshadowed subsequent investigations of black experience and identity through the lens of cultural production. Notable examples of this genre of cultural history include Robin D. G. Kelley's *Race Rebels: Culture, Politics and the Black Working Class* (1994) and Shane and Graham White's *Stylin': African American Expressive Culture from Its Beginnings to the Zoot Suit* (1998). Kelley's study emphasizes the subversive potential of black cultural production, drawing inspiration from the writings of intellectuals such as W. E. B. DuBois and C. L. R. James, who emphasized the independent will and creative autonomy of black people. Like Levine, Kelley considers a historical range of black cultural production, but he is explicitly concerned with the political implications of such activity, laying out a theoretical framework for ascribing a more central role to culture in the history of black political struggle. Drawing upon the ideas of the anthropologist James C. Scott, who argues that the bulk of political struggle among subordinate groups is often necessarily disguised or invisible, Kelley argues that certain expressions of black culture constituted a form of "infrapolitics" (1994: 8) that marked a veiled yet conscious resistance to white racist oppression. During the 1940s, for example, in urban centers across the nation, the exaggerated stylings of the zoot suit were not an ostentatious cry for attention among young black and Chicano men, but rather a cultural sign that working-class men of color were able to subvert the social mores of the dominant society by reappropriating the signature garb of white bourgeois masculinity while circumventing the demanding and often degrading routines of conventional wage labor. Likewise, the explosion of hip-hop and rap music during the late 1970s and early 1980s generated broader consciousness of the historical predicament of black people in the United States and heightened demands for empowerment in both implicit and explicit ways.

Shane and Graham White also examine black agency and empowerment, but they do not emphasize the oppositional politics embedded within that culture. They seek instead to illustrate how such cultural expressions as clothing, hairstyle, and dance allowed African Americans to specify their presence in the transition from slavery to freedom, as well as from rural to urban (1998: 17, 64). What distinguishes their study from previous works is that they also consider variations in black expressive culture across class lines, demonstrating that members of the black middle class often forged their own unique cultural expressions in an effort to distance themselves from the bulk of working-class African Americans, especially through such rituals as beauty pageants, debutante balls, and fashion shows. Still, common denominators tied together the disparate array of black cultural expressions. Through the emphasis upon exaggeration and bright hues, the privileging of spontaneity, humor and irony, as well as the adoption and reappropriation of European cultural forms, African Americans forged a distinctive cultural presence that marked a unique synthesis of European preferences and African inspirations.

Right down to the early years of the twenty-first century, the cultural history of race and ethnicity in the United States has taken shape around a key paradox. On the one hand, beginning with Winthrop Jordan's *White over Black*, cultural historians have demonstrated the extent to which cultural expressions of racial difference and racial hierarchy – found either in the writings and oratory of elites, or in the alluring spectacles of popular culture – provided a means of enforcing and justifying the subjugation of people of color: whether through the enslavement and segregation of African Americans, the displacement and dispossession of Indians and Mexicans, or the violence leveled against Chinese and Japanese immigrants in the far West. On the other hand, since the publication of Lawrence W. Levine's *Black Culture and Black Consciousness*, cultural historians have emphasized the history of cultural production within racial minority communities, and its uses as a strategy towards building collective consciousness and achieving political empowerment. If some historians have emphasized that culture could provide a means of enforcing racial domination, others have shown that it could also engender communal consciousness and solidarity among oppressed groups, as well as provide important strategies of resistance. Despite this central tension in historians' views of culture and its significance to racial stratification in the United States, cultural historians have illustrated the vital role of culture in shaping the way Americans think and have thought about race.

Those same methods of cultural history that have revealed the contested meanings of being "black" have also been used – in a recent twist of the hierarchies illuminated by the "new social history" of the 1970s and 1980s – to reveal what it has meant to be "white." The 1990s brought a decisive twist in the history of race and ethnicity in the United States, as historians undertook a sustained investigation of the normative racial category of whiteness, seeking to understand how and why certain groups became identified as "white," and what consequences those identities have entailed for the historical development of a multiracial, multiethnic society. Inquiry into the history of white racial formation followed a more general pattern in the 1990s, in which historians began to explore the cultural construction of not marginal, but normative social identities. Whereas the new social history, for example, had sought to recover the hidden role of women in the narrative of US history, the new cultural history generated subsequent interest in the historical construction of masculinity and the cultural processes by which "men" are produced. Similarly, the project of excavating the history of homosexuality in the United States was now prompting investigations of the history of heterosexuality as a dominant social category, and the means by which people came to identify as "straight." Thus, the history of white racial formation emerging in historical scholarship during the 1990s was part and parcel of a broader effort to turn historians' analytic gaze upon the dominant categories of identity that conferred privilege in a society historically stratified not only by class, but also by race, gender, and sexuality.

Cultural history provided an important avenue for considering the history of white racial formation. Like their forerunners in the 1970s, historians who turned to this topic discerned the prominent role of language, discourse, and other elements of the broader culture in the construction of whiteness as a dominant and normative racial category. "Whiteness studies," a term many use to designate the growing body of scholarship on white racial formation, had its origins in the discipline of history, particularly with the publication of Alexander Saxton's *The Rise and Fall of the White*

Republic: Class Politics and Mass Culture in Nineteenth-Century America (1990),
which stressed the centrality of white racism to nineteenth-century American politics
and culture. Like an earlier generation of cultural historians who recognized the
power of values and ideas in precipitating the emergence of racial hierarchy, Saxton's
project explores the relationship "between white racial domination in the United
States and ideas and attitudes about race" (1990: 1). But Saxton takes this relationship one step further by considering the role of racial ideology within the development of American capitalism. Analyzing blackface minstrel performance, novels such
as Owen Wister's *The Virginian* (1902), vernacular folk heroes such as Kit Carson,
and the journalistic enterprises of the artisan radical George Wilkes, Saxton emphasizes how notions of racial identity tied together with political ideas as well as
economic and social practices to form a coherent worldview that sanctioned the
development of a class structure in nineteenth-century America.

Though Saxton's work foreshadowed the rise of "whiteness studies" in history, it
was David Roediger's 1991 groundbreaking book *The Wages of Whiteness* that
launched a small cottage industry around the topic. Writing squarely within the tradition of the "new labor history," founded upon E. P. Thompson's assertion of the
agency of workers in the process of class formation, Roediger sought to reveal how
American workers fashioned a working-class identity that suited the imperatives of
urban industrial development during the early and mid-nineteenth century. What
distinguishes *The Wages of Whiteness* from other examples of the new labor history is
its insistence upon the centrality of race in the process of class formation. Racial
consciousness and hierarchy were not imposed upon workers by elites, nor were they
part of a divide-and-conquer strategy to assert capitalist control over an unwieldy
industrial economy. Deftly maneuvering away from the classic conundrum of "race
or class?" in American history, Roediger argues that workers acquired a sense of the
value of their whiteness by virtue of their increasing subordination at the workplace,
as well as the proximity of free and enslaved blacks in a slave-owning republic.

Language, discourse, and cultural representation played an important role in this
process, and Roediger took careful measures to demonstrate their centrality to the
creation of a white working-class consciousness. The linguistic categories for work
and workers, for example, underwent a profound transformation in the decades
between the American Revolution and the Civil War. As workers grew anxious over
their increasing dependence upon an exploitative and highly disciplined wage-labor
system, they developed a language that drew sharp distinctions between the white
worker and the black slave. During the antebellum period, for example, workers
exhibited a preference for euphemisms such as "boss" to replace the term "master,"
which maintained disturbing associations with slave owners (Roediger 1991: 63).
And terms such as "work like a nigger" and "white slavery" (ibid. 68) were deployed
to protest the mistreatment of workers under the new factory system, and to enforce
an unambiguous distinction between white workers (whether men, women, or children) and black slaves. Labor exploitation, this new lexicon implied, was appropriate
for blacks, who were considered inherently unworthy of the freedoms and privileges
conferred by republican ideology and government, but wholly unacceptable for a
growing pool of wage workers who increasingly saw themselves as "white."

What provided white workers with the opportunity to refine the sense of their
own whiteness was the minstrel show. The most popular arena of nineteenth-century

urban culture, that renowned exhibition of racial masquerade dramatized the power-ful appeal of applying burnt cork to white skin. Perhaps more than any other popular cultural practice in US history, blackface minstrelsy commands a persistent fascination among historians, who have produced a number of monographs on the subject. The minstrel show affords a prismatic glimpse into the intersections of race, class, and gender in nineteenth-century America. For Roediger, the minstrel show's particular allure for white workers was its capacity to simultaneously transgress and reinforce emerging racial boundaries. On the one hand, the minstrel show provided an arena for cross-racial desire, inviting white workers to indulge in a momentary release from an oppressive industrial discipline by discovering a nostalgic affinity with characteriza-tions of "coons," "sambos," and "pickaninnies," who embodied a more carefree, preindustrial morality that white workers sorely missed. On the other hand, the very act of "blacking up" made the distinctions between whiteness and blackness more transparent, and further consolidated a shared sense of whiteness among an ethnically diverse audience of working men.

Thus Roediger, far more than other practitioners of the "new labor history," demonstrated a willingness to engage the methods and approaches of cultural history in his effort to understand the history of white racial formation. His attention to blackface minstrelsy, in particular, debuted alongside far more detailed histories of blackface performance, which also enriched the scholarship on white racial formation. Most notably, Eric Lott's *Love and Theft: Blackface Minstrelsy and the American Working Class* (1993) places minstrelsy within the context of emerging working-class formations in the urban industrializing North, and complicates standard interpreta-tions of that cultural practice as a straightforward example of racial domination. Through close textual analysis, combing minstrel song sheets and books, performance bills, burlesque skits and plays, reviews, literary representations and allusions, as well as contemporary illustrations, Lott sketches a historical dialectic between black cul-tural forms and their appropriation by white blackface performers, and characterizes the ambivalent relationship between white working-class audiences and African Amer-ican culture as one of "love and theft." Thus, white use of black cultural forms entailed more than the familiar story of racial domination and aversion. It also sig-naled the lesser-known aspects of cross-racial desire and appropriation in nineteenth-century America, loaded with "envy as well as repulsion, sympathetic identification, as well as fear" (1993: 8).

Michael Rogin, already an established voice in the cultural historiography of race and ethnicity, further developed Lott's insights on the minstrel show by demonstrat-ing its extended appeal among movie audiences during Hollywood's golden age of film production. Looking back to the nineteenth-century popularity of the minstrel show, and noting its virtual ubiquity within the output of the studio system at the peak of its power, Rogin broadens blackface as a cultural category and sees the burnt-cork sensibility as the foundation of American cinema in particular, and American culture in general. In doing so, he places race relations at the center of twentieth-century mass politics and culture, and emphasizes the role of Jews in reigniting the appeal of blackface among twentieth-century film audiences. By tracing the careers of popular Jewish entertainers and closely reading the meanings of films such as *The Birth of a Nation* (1915), *The Jazz Singer* (1927), and *Gone With the Wind* (1939), Rogin argues that Hollywood became a melting pot for Jewish immigrants, who applied and applauded the conventions of blackface to gain their own access to American national identity. What's missing from Rogin's analysis is what Roediger and Lott stress emphatically in their accounts of blackface minstrelsy: the ambivalence about black culture that sometimes achieved the status of "sympathetic identification" (Rogin 1996: 51). For Jews in Hollywood's melting pot, according to Rogin, the act of blackening up was not a means of expressing solidarity with African Americans (though he acknowledges the linkages between blacks and Jews in the history of civil rights struggle), but rather part of an implicit strategy to exclude blacks' involvement in their own representation.

By looking specifically at the role of Jews in the twentieth-century adaptation of the blackface ritual, Rogin revealed the implicit connections between race and ethnicity lurking behind the mask of burnt cork. Upon their arrival in cities like turn-of-the-century New York, Jews occupied a marginal position in a society obsessed with Anglo-Saxon racial purity. So they utilized available cultural practices, as Rogin illustrates through the cinematic careers of Al Jolson and Eddie Cantor, to find inclusion within a dominant national identity predicated upon whiteness, suggesting the ways in which distinctive ethnic identities are subsumed within the racial matrix that defines the broader social landscape. Roediger traces a similar dynamic in the minstrel show of antebellum New York. There, blackface was most popular among working-class Irish men, who patronized minstrel shows en masse and often took to the stage in blackface caricature. Like Jews, the Irish were subject to vicious nativist attacks upon their arrival to the United States (and they were likened particularly to blacks in nineteenth-century print media). Despite their racial victimization, however, Irish Americans often adopted a virulent racism towards blacks and found political inclusion within a white supremacist Democratic Party. Still, uprooted from their native land, subject to familial disintegration, and forced into the disciplinary regimes of industrial wage labor, the Irish working class extracted from the blackface performance a "pornography" (Roediger 1991: 96; he is drawing on Rawick 1972: 132) of their former life, symbolized through the caricatured bodies of lazy, carefree, and lascivious African Americans.

The process by which ethnic identities become subsumed within broader racial categories is the subject of Matthew Frye Jacobson's *Whiteness of a Different Color* (1998), which traces the "vicissitudes of race" (1998: 7) as manifest in the racial odysseys of non-WASP immigrant groups from Europe, especially the Irish, Italians, and Jews. By analyzing the texts of federal documents such as the 1790 Naturalization Act and the Immigration Act of 1924, documenting the ongoing revision of racial and ethnic categories in Congress and courts of law, and scrutinizing the changing meanings of racial categories like "Caucasian," Jacobson demonstrates the changing taxonomy of racial and ethnic groups, and the discursive processes by which "Celts," "Slavs," "Hebrews," "Latins," and "Iberics" eventually shed the racial stigma assigned to them by the dominant white society upon their arrival. Jacobson also ventures into the language of nineteenth-century science, exposing the ways in which the classifications and constructs developed by scientists reflected the reigning wisdom about race and racial difference. By looking closely at the circulating discourses of science and law in nineteenth-century America, Jacobson reaffirms the now-dominant scholarly understanding of race: that it is not immutable or fixed in biology, but rather fluid, historically relative, and socially constructed.

In writing the history of white racial formation, Saxton, Roediger, Lott, Rogin, and Jacobson drew heavily upon the methods and insights of cultural history, paying close attention to the role of words and images in codifying a broad sense of whiteness that eventually enveloped even those groups that came to the United States as racially suspect. Their work set the precedent for subsequent treatments of the history of white racial formation, which have added their own inflection to the subject. Grace Elizabeth Hale's *Making Whiteness: The Culture of Segregation in the South, 1890–1940* (1998), for example, locates the regional contours of white racial formation by focusing specifically on the South in the age of Reconstruction. She considers popular literary constructions of the "Old South" and the ways in which texts such as *The Clansman* (1905) and the Uncle Remus stories reified a regional sense of whiteness. She also identifies regional cultural practices that conferred a shared sense of whiteness upon a community fragmented along class and gendered lines, analyzing in particular such "deadly amusements" as lynching as a basis for the creation of regional white unity (1998: 199). And unlike other histories of white racial formation, *Making Whiteness* also pays close attention to the gendered dynamics of white racial formation. In particular, Hale scrutinizes the role of the mammy. As a pervasive literary and visual icon in cultural representations of the South, the mammy provided an important symbolic link between the Old South and the New. She stood as the protector, nurturer, and teacher of white children, and marked an important signifier of membership in the white southern middle class. And yet her very real presence in the homes of white southern families underpinned the whiteness of her employers. In both the Old and the New Souths, Hale asserts, "being white meant having black help" (ibid. 103).

While the overwhelming majority of written histories on whiteness have emphasized the centrality of African Americans to the construction of a white racial identity, other historians have shown how that process implicated other racialized groups as well. In Philip J. Deloria's *Playing Indian* (1998), for example, Indians occupy a central role in the construction of a racialized national identity. Deloria, who writes within a familial tradition of studying the role of Indians in American history, commands a sweeping analysis of American history from the Boston Tea Party to Grateful Dead shows to emphasize the recurring presence, indeed the centrality, of the Indian in the most important stories white Americans have told about themselves. Like Berkhofer's *White Man's Indian*, Deloria pays close attention to the connections between the image of the Indian and the construction of national identity, but his analysis goes further by drawing upon recent theoretical insights about the processes and practices of constructing identity. The result is a fresh interpretation of the importance of Indians to generations of white Americans who developed a range of cultural practices – particularly the use of costume and disguise – to recreate and experience aboriginal "authenticity" amidst the most disruptive aspects of nineteenth- and twentieth-century modernity (Deloria 1998: 101). Thus, the same ambivalence towards the racial Other that Roediger and Lott emphasized in their studies of white racial formation is present in Deloria's narrative. For even as white Americans conquered and displaced the bodies of American Indians, they elaborated and appropriated a set of cultural images of those bodies to articulate their own struggle to define themselves as a nation and as individuals. Mindful of the challenges implicit within the effort to write the history of cultural interactions between white and non-white social groups, Deloria also accounts for the ambiguous role that Indians themselves played in the process. Throughout history, Indians have supported, challenged, exploited, and conformed to the performative traditions of "playing Indian" (ibid. 8).

Matthew Jacobson's observation concerning the ubiquity of race in the cultural history of the United States, with which I began this essay, should now be clear. From the first imaginings of African bodies in Elizabethan England to the reenactment of powwows at Grateful Dead shows, images of race and racial difference have permeated the temporal expanse of American culture. The cultural history of race and ethnicity implicates the agency and experience of diverse racial and ethnic groups, even – if not especially – those not "of color." It encompasses a diverse array of cultural practices and technologies. Cultural historians of race and ethnicity have mined literature, drama, art, photography, film, television, newspapers, and advertising to identify the ways in which ideas about race and racial difference have shaped popular conceptions of both the Other and the self. And they have demonstrated the complex and often contradictory uses of culture in the creation of racial hierarchy. Culture has worked to reproduce existing social hierarchies, even as it has also provided an important avenue for challenging and subverting those hierarchies.

Using the methods of cultural history to assess the saliency of race and ethnicity in the American past promotes a greater awareness of the fundamental linkages between structure and culture. Too often, scholarly analyses of culture ignore historical context, leaving aside the social, political, and economic issues that underlie cultural production and consumption. Race may well be a fiction of our collective imagination, and may lack a discernible basis in human physiology, but the concept itself, as it has evolved over centuries of human history, has delivered structural causes and real effects. Within the context of American history, cultural stories about Indians, Africans, Mexicans, "Orientals," and "whites" precipitate, as well as perpetrate, the economic, social and political structures of racial hierarchy that have evolved across four centuries of American history; and it is the task of the historian to return those stories to their proper historical context. Each of the works cited above emphasizes the social, political, and economic structures surrounding disparate representations, linking those representations to the empowerment and disempowerment of diverse Americans along racial lines.

REFERENCES

Berkhofer, Robert F.: *The White Man's Indian: Images of the American Indian from Columbus to the Present* (New York: Alfred A. Knopf, 1978).
Cripps, Thomas: *Slow Fade to Black: The Negro in American Film, 1900–1942* (New York: Oxford University Press, 1977).
Cripps, Thomas: *Making Movies Black: The Hollywood Message Movie from World War II to the Civil Rights Era* (New York: Oxford University Press, 1993).
Deloria, Philip J.: *Playing Indian* (New Haven, CT: Yale University Press, 1998).
Fredrickson, George M.: *The Black Image in the White Mind: The Debate on Afro-American Character and Destiny, 1817–1914* (New York: Harper & Row, 1971).

Genovese, Eugene D.: *Roll, Jordan, Roll: The World the Slaves Made* (New York: Pantheon Books, 1974).

Hale, Grace Elizabeth: *Making Whiteness: The Culture of Segregation in the South, 1890–1940* (New York: Pantheon Books, 1998).

Horsman, Reginald: *Race and Manifest Destiny: The Origins of American Racial Anglo-Saxonism* (Cambridge, MA: Harvard University Press, 1981).

Jacobson, Matthew Frye: *Whiteness of a Different Color: European Immigrants and the Alchemy of Race* (Cambridge, MA: Harvard University Press, 1998).

Jordan, Winthrop: *White over Black: American Attitudes towards the Negro, 1550–1812* (Chapel Hill: Published for the Institute of Early American History and Culture at Williamsburg, by the University of North Carolina Press, 1968).

Kelley, Robin D. G.: *Race Rebels: Culture, Politics and the Black Working Class* (New York: Free Press, 1994).

Levine, Lawrence W.: *Black Culture and Black Consciousness: Afro-American Folk Thought from Slavery to Freedom* (New York: Oxford University Press, 1977).

Lott, Eric: *Love and Theft: Blackface Minstrelsy and the American Working Class* (New York: Oxford University Press, 1993).

Morgan, Edmund S.: *American Slavery, American Freedom: The Ordeal of Colonial Virginia* (New York: W. W. Norton, 1975).

Rawick, George P.: *From Sundown to Sunup: The Making of the Black Community* (Westport: Greenwood., 1972).

Riggs, Marlon T.: *Ethnic Notions* [videorecording] (San Francisco: California Newsreel, 1986).

Roediger, David R.: *The Wages of Whiteness: Race and the Making of the American Working Class* (New York: Verso Press, 1991).

Rogin, Michael: *Fathers and Children: Andrew Jackson and the Subjugation of the American Indian* (New York: Random House, 1975).

Rogin, Michael: *Blackface, White Noise: Jewish Immigrants in the Hollywood Melting Pot* (Berkeley: University of California Press, 1996).

Rydell, Robert W.: *All the World's a Fair: Visions of Empire at American International Expositions, 1876–1916* (Chicago: University of Chicago Press, 1984).

Saxton, Alexander: *The Rise and Fall of the White Republic: Class Politics and Mass Culture in Nineteenth-Century America* (New York: Verso Press, 1990).

Scott, James C.: *Domination and the Arts of Resistance: Hidden Transcripts* (New Haven, CT: Yale University Press, 1990).

Slotkin, Richard: *Regeneration Through Violence: The Mythology of the American Frontier, 1600–1860* (Middletown, CT: Wesleyan University Press, 1973).

Stampp, Kenneth M.: *The Peculiar Institution: Slavery in the Ante-Bellum South* (New York: Alfred A. Knopf, 1956).

Takaki, Ronald: *Iron Cages: Race and Culture in Nineteenth-Century America* (New York: Alfred A. Knopf, 1979).

Thompson, E. P.: *The Making of the English Working Class* (New York: Pantheon Books, 1963).

White, Shane & White, Graham: *Stylin': African American Expressive Culture from Its Beginning to the Zoot Suit* (Ithaca, NY: Cornell University Press, 1998).

Chapter Twenty-Four

POPULAR CULTURE

Nan Enstad

"Jazz" is only a word and really has no meaning. To keep the whole thing clear, once and for all, I don't believe in categories of any kind.
Duke Ellington, in Lawrence W. Levine, *Highbrow, Lowbrow*, p. 244

When the brilliant bandleader and composer Duke Ellington wanted to give his highest praise to another musician, he would call them "beyond category." As one of the most successful musicians of the twentieth century, Ellington made his mark in the marketplace as well as in people's hearts. This gained him a great deal of attention from people who wanted to categorize his work for marketing or aesthetic purposes – often both at once. Was Ellington an itinerant bandleader playing the profane music of the masses, a spokesperson for "the people," or a great avant-garde composer? Should his music be marketed solely to the masses, or also to elites? Ellington understood that categories enabled others to profit from his creative success and he tried to evade all such labels, for himself and for others he respected. Words like "swing" and "jazz" had emerged as a way to talk about a powerful new energy in music, but even these terms had become marketing categories, and Ellington could not control how they would be deployed. Ellington's struggle epitomizes the volatility of popular culture in the US marketplace, as well as the challenge of finding a historical language that can address its complex relationship to capital, critics, and quotidian formations.

I am going to follow the Duke's lead and say, "popular culture" is only words, and they really have no meaning. That is, "popular culture," like "jazz," is laden with conflicting meanings, each harnessed to somebody's struggle to shift cultural and monetary capital more to their liking. Sometimes denigrated, sometimes validated, "popular culture" is always part of a larger story, in historical studies no less than in the wider society. Perhaps we should abandon a term with such a complicated history and so many contradictory and problematic meanings. Why categorize culture at all? But just as "jazz" dogged Duke Ellington, "popular culture" is too entrenched in ongoing classification projects for us simply to wish it away. Instead, we need to understand the emergence of competing meanings of popular culture over the twentieth century as a story of cultural struggle that shaped the boundaries of historical discourse.

Popular culture has occupied a denigrated status in historical study. Until recently, historians largely abdicated the study of certain kinds of popular culture – particularly commercial and media-based popular culture – to other disciplines. The result has been an impoverished understanding of the history of the United States. Thus, this essay studies the barriers as well as the advances in the historical study of popular culture. Popular cultural studies emerged in an interdisciplinary context, and most historians of popular culture tool themselves in interdisciplinary methods. This essay acknowledges this influence, but focuses on historians' particular trajectory. Despite the discipline of history's original mission to study "high culture," historians influenced by labor unrest and popular front activism of the 1930s began to consider commercial popular culture as a window into non-elites' histories. However, during the Cold War era, US historians backed away from this approach; their theory that commercial culture solely reflected capitalist logics would continue to influence some historians for decades. Nevertheless, the rise of social history in the 1960s and 1970s led historians back to the culture of non-elites. By the 1980s, close study of leisure practices prompted some historians to take commercial popular culture seriously. They queried whether popular culture should be seen as an oppressive product of culture industries or as quotidian practices that could be resistant to capitalism. By the 1990s, historians explored popular culture as a window into complex dynamics of power and the construction of hierarchies and identities. In recent years, historians of popular culture have expanded the fields they engage, indicating that popular culture study is currently at a new moment of blossoming.

The category of popular culture emerged in the early twentieth century out of contested cultural hierarchies as a means to challenge the notion of "lowbrow" forms. Cultural historians have studied the emergence of an articulated division between "highbrow" and "lowbrow" culture in the nineteenth century, as entrepreneurs increasingly marketed cultural forms such as story papers and sensational exhibitions, and a heterogeneous commercial public culture expanded in urban spaces like saloons and popular theaters (Denning 1987; Levine 1988; Cook 2001). Middle-class constructions of "highbrow" and "lowbrow" betrayed unease about the increased role of the market in creative life. By constructing "high" culture as free from market forces and "low" leisure practices as market driven, the emerging white middle class persuaded itself that it had protected one channel of culture from market interests. According to this view, because "low" forms responded only to market forces, they were sensational and devoid of meaningful content. "High" culture, in contrast, was independent and could therefore carry forward the best traditions of American expression and further the nation's progress. Of course, the capitalist market did shape high-culture institutions, albeit sometimes in different ways than popular forms.

This bifurcated view of culture was rooted in processes of racialization, engendering, and class formation and, by the end of the nineteenth century, amplified the saliency of culture as a location for the constructions of difference. Indeed, the terms "highbrow" and "lowbrow" came from the racializing work of phrenology in the late nineteenth century: "highbrow" referred to the supposedly high foreheads of Western Europeans who were declared to be the apex of the evolutionary ladder. At the bottom of the evolutionary chain, with the lowest brows, were Africans, Asians, and the indigenous Americans (Levine 1988). Naturalized divisions between high and low became an idiom through which other differences could be constructed and contested. "Lowbrow" culture appealed invariably to "low" people, who therefore required regulation, reform, or rescue by those trained in high culture. Though this categorization was a construction, it had material impact on how different cultural forms were funded, regulated, promoted, and consumed. By the late nineteenth century, some middle-class people saw "low" culture such as story papers, dime novels, and burlesque shows not only as empty of value, but as deviant and in need of regulation or censorship. Different laws and a vastly different discourse came to surround popular forms such as print media and, by 1909, motion pictures. For reformers like Anthony Comstock or the Board of Censorship of Motion Pictures such forms endangered America because producers' goals were to proliferate and profit on people's most prurient desires, rather than to ennoble and uplift, as high culture was assumed to do (Sklar 1975; Peiss 1986).

Historians are part of this story because the modern discipline of history arose in the late nineteenth century concurrently with bifurcated notions of culture, and historians pursued a mission to narrate the nation's evolution to higher planes of human achievement in government, economy, and culture. Culture became particularly important when historians searched for a distinctive "American" ethos that might distinguish it from Europe. Since historians initially saw "high" culture as the only culture capable of conveying significant values to the next generation, they reinforced its status as normative. Whether nineteenth-century historians saw "low" culture as deviant and dangerous or simply as meaningless, they were unlikely to see it as consequential for the story they were telling. Indeed, history as a discipline was consolidated in part by what it did not study about the daily grind of human experience: it did not study the low, the marginal, or the deviant. Historians' originary emphasis on people with institutionalized power and on high culture reinforced the conflation between forms of culture and their presumed audiences, and the binary between high and low.

The term "popular culture" emerged from opposition to the highbrow/lowbrow dichotomy. In the Progressive era, those reformers affiliated with the labor or settlement-house movements did not refer to working-class people's cultural practices as "lowbrow," but used the less derogatory term, "popular amusements." Progressives did not, however, typically utilize the term popular *culture* or *art*. "Culture," originally an agricultural term, indicated certain levels of cultivation and refinement and even the progressives saw most popular forms as too new, too linked to new media technologies like the motion picture, and too mired in the market, to have a cultivating function. Indeed, this was the source of their concern. So, the progressives utilized the term "popular," but accepted a binary between "high" and "popular," associating "popular" with the working classes.

The 1930s Popular Front challenged the notion that "culture" should not apply to working-class activities. Even in the 1920s, some scholars had begun to consider whether commercial forms could be considered "culture." A diverse range of activists and scholars in the 1930s, such as Mike Gold, Dorothy West, Tillie Olsen, Carter Woodson, and Merle Curti, were influenced by the Great Depression, domestic labor unrest, and international workers' movements, including communism, to assess and take seriously the culture of working people. Many radicals deplored commercialized culture, assuming it to be a tool of capitalism leading only to conformity. Some became interested in promoting "popular arts," by which they meant literature, sculpture, or painting created by radicals that would replace commercial culture for a politicizing working class. Still others looked among working people to see what their own "popular arts" were, including commercialized forms (Denning 1996; Gorman 1996; Fitzpatrick 2002). The shift from "amusements" to "arts" is significant. By considering popular forms in the realm of art, some Popular Front scholars and activists challenged the value distinction between high and low, though they continued to conflate cultural forms with class categories: the "popular arts" always emanated from or aimed at the working class.

Some historians actively participated in this movement. When workers' practices came to be seen as "culture" they entered the purview of historians, who responded by inaugurating a fascinating revision of the purpose of history. In 1937, Merle Curti published an article entitled "Dime Novels and the American Tradition," which argued that though dime novels were not created by the "plain people of America," and were "designed to fill the pockets of both author and publisher," dime-novel audiences "made them their own." The dime novel, argued Curti, "is the nearest thing we have had in this country to what is now so much discussed, a true 'proletarian' literature" (1937: 761). When he made dime novels, long the focus of reformers' ire, a legitimate subject of research into "the development of class consciousness," Curti incorporated the insights of the Popular Front into the discipline of history (ibid. 778).

Curti was part of a larger movement of cultural history. In 1940, Caroline Ware published an edited collection of articles on cultural history that grew out of a series of panels at an American Historical Association (AHA) annual conference. The volume was interdisciplinary and filled with Popular Front thinkers, including musicologist Charles Seeger who wrote about the possible uses of popular music in historical study. While the volume does not utilize the term "popular culture," it does call for the study of commercialized forms. According to Ware, historians had begun to realize that "whereas they had considerable information about rulers and how they had exercised their power, they had little or none about the ruled and how they had responded. They knew something of the literary and artistic highlights, but little of the mass culture from which these highlights stood out" (Ware 1940: 8). For Ware, "mass culture" was not a derogatory term. Her usage derived from Marxism, and referred to the culture of the many, or the proletariat, the potential source of revolutionary change. She thus positioned "mass culture" as a subject of pressing interest to historians. From these beginnings, it might have been expected that the 1940s and 1950s would see a flowering of histories of the cultural practices of non-elite people, including their consumption of commercialized popular culture. This flowering, however, did not happen.

Instead, after World War II, the red scare made the Popular Front rhetoric endorsed by many at the 1939 AHA newly suspect. In history as well as other humanities and social science disciplines such rhetoric faded from view. Meanwhile, scholars reeling from totalitarianism and the atrocities of the Holocaust sought to explain how an unjust state secures popular acquiescence to a repressive and violent agenda. This question in turn led them to explore overtly commercialized culture, particular "mass" media. Marxist scholars from the Frankfurt School contributed an important element of this conversation. Forced by the Holocaust to flee to the USA, Frankfurt School scholars were interested in how people become wrapped up in spectacle or narrative, and how ideology is conveyed through popular media. Unlike nineteenth-century reformers, the Frankfurt School did not associate popular culture with deviance, but saw it as normative in its capacity to secure an individual's acquiescence with the status quo. The culture industry, then, was validated as an object of study because it was a central part of the capitalist system. Crucially, some Frankfurt School scholars paid attention not only to media "messages," but to pleasure, for they believed that the appeal of spectacle and narrative needed to be understood in order to comprehend the workings of ideology.

While the Frankfurt School's scholarship was quite diverse and complex, US scholars in the postwar era focused on its condemnation of "mass culture," a term that took on a new meaning. Such thinkers were not necessarily Marxists, but they did critique capitalism. The term "popular culture," which had become common in journalism and the social sciences, receded in usage. In 1953, author and editor Dwight Macdonald revised his 1944 article, "A Theory of Popular Culture," and gave it the new title, "A Theory of Mass Culture," which he said better indicated his view that these forms had no redeeming value. Macdonald explicitly accepted the nineteenth-century notion that the capitalist market had influenced only some cultural production: "For about a century, Western culture has really been two cultures: the traditional kind – let us call it 'High Culture' – that is chronicled in the textbooks, and a 'Mass Culture' manufactured wholesale for the market." While Ware had used the term "mass culture" only a decade before as a potentially positive reference to the cultural practices of non-dominant people, Macdonald saw "mass culture" as a totalitarian threat to democracy, and equated mass culture in the USA with state-sponsored culture in the Soviet Union. Thus, Macdonald's critique of capitalism was made in Cold War, rather than Popular Front, rhetoric. Popular Front-influenced scholars in the 1930s questioned whether media culture could be workers' culture, but scholars like Macdonald argued that "mass culture" replaced the "culture of the common people," which he termed "Folk Art." While folk art could be seen as beneficial, even innocent (he referred to it as "their private little garden"), mass culture parasitically fed on and homogenized the true creativity in high culture. For Macdonald, the only solution lay in "restoring the old class lines . . . [for] all the great cultures of the past were elite cultures."

In the decade following this "mass culture" critique, the term "popular culture" gradually accrued the new meanings of mass culture: its associations with proletarian practices receded (though they did not entirely disappear) and it increasingly referred to mass-produced and -distributed media culture, consumed by both working- and middle-class people. The term "popular culture" also gained associations from emerging "pop art" and "pop music" phenomena in the 1950s and 1960s, both of which evoked the mass-replicated nature of media culture. "Popular culture," sometimes now called "pop culture," gained a renewed connotation of triviality associated with emergent teen cultures.

The widely distributed Cold War critique of mass culture had two major effects on the historical study of popular culture. First, it buttressed the traditional historical imperative to chart the "high" cultural heritage of the country. While the wider debates of the 1930s had brought "popular culture" closer to the historians' trade, the debates of the 1950s amplified the stigma of the category by resuscitating a notion of "low" culture (meaningless or deviant) and revising it with the concept of "mass" culture (normative and tending towards totalitarianism). Such debates once again distanced most non-elite culture from historians' purview, until the emergence of "history from below" in the 1960s and 1970s. The second, and longer lasting, effect of the Cold War critique of mass culture was the theory of culture held in the 1960s by non-Marxist and Marxist historians alike: the theory that commercial culture functioned solely to reconcile people to capitalist relations. Any participation in mass culture thus had an exclusively homogenizing impact, making workers identify with the middle class and accept the political status quo. The staying power of this theory slowed empirical studies about the social relationships that developed around commercialized forms. Because historians believed overtly commercialized forms could only lead to conformity, they assumed that resistance required an autonomous culture untouched by market relations.

Social historians of the 1960s and 1970s did, however, ask crucial questions about the culture of non-elites, and that inquiry would lead historians back to questions about commercial popular culture. E. P. Thompson's *The Making of the English Working Class* (1963) established the significance of culture in class formation and ensured that cultural questions would be central to history from below. While Thompson saw "class experience" as emerging materially from relations of production, he saw "class consciousness" as "the way in which these experiences are handled in cultural terms; embodied in traditions, values, systems, ideas, and institutional forms." Thus, turning to ordinary people's culture was crucial to the project of the new labor history. In the United States, Herbert G. Gutman picked up on Thompson's innovations and argued that industrialization required a transformation not only in work patterns, but in "whole cultures" (Gutman 1973: 540). Drawing on cultural anthropology, Gutman argued that premodern cultural traditions became crucial resources in the cultural struggle between industrial workers and employers. Also influenced by Thompson, George Rawick argued that slaves' cultural practices "from sundown to sunup," including African traditions, became resources for adapting to a new and oppressive setting (Rawick 1972). He asserted that racism developed in tandem with capitalism. Like new industrial workers, slaves engaged in a cultural struggle to resist being subjugated to the needs of capital. In a path-breaking work in women's history, Nancy Cott (1977) argued that the idea of "women's sphere" also emerged with industrialization: as men's work changed to fit industrial production and the time clock, the enduringly "premodern" nature of most women's work both encouraged bonds between women and contributed to their increased marginalization. Collectively, this work implicitly challenged Macdonald's view of "folk culture" as a "private garden": cultural conflict and struggle took center stage as social historians raised questions of class, race, and gender formation.

In thus valuing their subjects' utilization of *premodern* popular cultural forms to resist capitalist logics, these historians tacitly implied the eventual triumph of those logics once market-driven culture had replaced premodern forms. (Historians have since challenged the presumption that preindustrial cultural forms were free of market influence.) By looking backward in time for such cultural resources, historians could evade vexing questions about the commercialization of culture. For example, despite the fact that factories were the marketplace of labor, historians studied workplace culture as though it were independent of market forces. Likewise, although slaves themselves were commodities, and white commercial performers obsessively

mimicked slaves' music and dance, historians studied slaves' culture without considering the market. Lawrence Levine's brilliant and path-breaking study *Black Culture
and Black Consciousness* (1977) examined African American songs, folktales, and jokes
from slavery's end to World War II, but ignored the circulation of these forms
through commercial theater, print culture, and early sound recordings. As a result,
this body of work also implied that ordinary people's culture was autonomous,
authentic, and resistant, standing outside of the workings of power rather than emerging from and engaging them.

By the early 1980s, studies of work and culture had generated a growing interest
in histories of leisure, which led historians to confront the inextricable relationship
between the market and ordinary people's culture. Scholars noted that the consolidation of industrial capitalism resulted in a more rigid division of the workday from
leisure time. Leisure offered clues to how people experienced, and potentially resisted,
capitalist control. Historians followed their subjects after the working day was done
to saloons, dance halls, vaudeville shows, motion picture shows, circuses, and other
commercial sites of leisure. There, despite mass culture theory, historians found
resistance to capitalist logics, and struggled to account for it.

Roy Rosenzweig's path-breaking *Eight Hours for What We Will* (1983) interrogated commercialized leisure during the transition to industrial capitalism, and found
that workers maintained an autonomous culture despite market relations. Workers
formed bonds of mutuality in saloons that resisted capitalist individualism. Through
the practice of treating – taking turns paying for drinks – workers pooled resources
and honored each other, utilizing market spaces for an egalitarian practice. Rosenzweig opened up a dramatic new historical inquiry into commercial leisure as a productive site of meaning-making and new, cross-ethnic bonding, rather than simply
of conformity. He complicated but did not fully challenge the notion that commercialization would lead to the eventual demise of workers' culture. "Although the
saloon was a commercial enterprise, its ethnic working-class customers still decisively
shaped its ritual and character. Somewhat paradoxically, they infused the saloon with
a set of values that differed from those of the dominant industrial capitalist society
that had given rise to the saloon in the first place" (1983: 36). The ethic of mutuality, Rosenzweig noted, was "probably strongest in the least commercialized saloons
and drink places" (ibid. 60).

The "paradox" that Rosenzweig identified (an autonomous, resistant culture
within, but strangely independent of, a capitalist, commercial space) would eventually
cease to hold. A key challenge came from studies of gender and race hierarchies within
working-class cultures. Kathy Peiss's *Cheap Amusements* (1986) built upon Rosenzweig's argument with its exploration of the sexual economy of treating between
working-class men and women. Men's treating of women came with an expectation
of sexual repayment that women found a range of ways to negotiate or subvert. Peiss
crucially demonstrated that leisure culture not only resisted or accommodated, but
also produced, social hierarchies. Nevertheless, much like Rosenzweig, Peiss emphasized that popular amusements become a location for women's relatively autonomous
culture – in this case a culture increasingly freed from familial control. As long as
historians construed resistant working people's culture as autonomous, they would
not rethink the relationship between culture and the market in producing social
practices and ideologies. Historians studied the experience of movie-going, for

example, but rarely rigorously examined the content and impact of the motion pictures themselves. Nevertheless, scholarship on leisure established that people did not simply capitulate to capitalist imperatives when participating in commercial leisure, and that the cultures they created were themselves productive of social hierarchies. The mass culture theory and its counterpart, the utopian notion of autonomous workers' cultures, began to strain under the weight of new findings. Four historians leveraged critiques of both concepts and inspired a wealth of scholarship in the 1990s that explored the construction of identities and hierarchies utilizing sophisticated notions of power.

In "Encountering Mass Culture at the Grassroots: The Experience of Chicago Workers in the 1920s" (1989), Lizabeth Cohen directly challenged the mass culture theory that most historians had held since the 1950s. Like Rosenzweig, Cohen argued that workers' culture could coexist with commercial culture, but took this idea further in two ways. First, she showed people shaping commercial culture to their own ends: ethnic and African American workers participated in "mass culture" (meaning mass-distributed commercial culture) but in "their own stores, in their own neighborhoods, and in their own way" (1989: 12). Workers used the new phonographs and radios, for example, not simply to participate in mainstream American culture, but to listen to Polish- and Italian-language music records or radio shows that helped them maintain ethnic identities. People integrated "mass culture" into local culture with a variety of effects, none of which could have been guessed before conducting rigorous empirical research. Cohen acknowledged that she studied a transitional moment, and that commercial culture became more standardized and less neighborhood-responsive over time. Her second key innovation, however, was to resist a story of declension tied to participation in mass culture: "[G]rassroots control over mass culture did diminish during the thirties. But the extent to which this more national mass culture in the end succeeded in assimilating workers to middle-class values remains an open question" (1989: 26). Indeed, Cohen suggested that market segmentation might have been an effort to respond to widely different popular culture practices entrenched in regional, ethnic, racial, and gender differences. In other words, Cohen suggested that the relationship between ordinary people and the market may be two-way. Cohen, thus, demonstrated that the "mass culture" theory lacked an empirical basis, and opened the door to richly contextualized studies of popular culture.

George Lipsitz's collected essays, *Time Passages* (1990), argued that scholars should not look for autonomous workers' or ethnic cultures untainted by capitalism, but rather see popular culture as a site of struggle in which people utilized the imperfect resources available to them in order to engage, and sometimes resist, oppressive power structures. Lipsitz argued that the nineteenth-century transition to industrial capitalism did increase capitalist control over communications, but also created "new possibilities" (1990: 8). The telegraph and newspaper "detach[ed] culture from tradition," shaping it to the needs of business, but also expanded communication over space. For example, Lipsitz explored how 1950s television ethnic sitcoms such as *The Goldbergs* positioned individual consumption as the solution to unmet needs based in structural problems. At the same time, however, the show evoked and validated needs and longings – as well as extended-family and ethnic ties – that could challenge the 1950s consumer ideal. Lipsitz rejected both the mass culture theory and the autonomous culture thesis, and argued that both tyranny and resistance were possible in people's engagement with popular culture. Because Lipsitz saw commercial culture as a site of struggle rather than inevitable cooptation, he could shift historiographic attention from the nineteenth and early twentieth centuries to the mid- and late twentieth century, when commercial culture undeniably had saturated life in the USA, and make heretofore denigrated forms a legitimate focus of inquiry. In *Time Passages*, Lipsitz published path-breaking analyses of post-1945 television, popular music, film, and carnival. Because his questions engaged both use and ideology, he sought methods that would allow him to analyze the production, content, and circulation of popular forms. He was one of the first scholars to introduce the theories and methods of interdisciplinary cultural studies into history. Lipsitz drew upon a wide range of theoretical approaches, including those emerging from the Birmingham School of Cultural Studies, literary and film theories, and deconstruction and post-structuralism, demonstrating that popular forms could be interpreted by the historian with theoretical nuance and rigorous contextualization.

David Roediger, in *The Wages of Whiteness* (1991), dismantled the autonomous culture thesis by construing popular culture as a site where ordinary people – not just capitalists – constructed hierarchies. Combining Gutman's commitment to understanding workers' culture in the transition to industrialization with Rawick's analysis of the role of culture in the structure of racism, Roediger argued that blackface minstrelsy in the 1830s and 1840s constructed a "popular sense of whiteness" that helped consolidate the emerging working class. "[Workers'] consensus," he argued, "derived from the idea that blackness could be made permanently to embody the preindustrial past that [white industrial workers] scorned and missed" (1991: 97). White workers, then, while attempting to resist capitalist devaluing of their labor, became architects of the capitalist racial system. Like Peiss, Roediger examined how workers' attempts to build a common identity produced exclusions and investments in hierarchies. Unlike Peiss, however, he did not center his study in an argument about resistance or an autonomous workers' culture. Rather, popular culture was a location in which hierarchies take shape in daily lives. Interestingly, unlike Cohen and Lipsitz, Roediger ignored the market. He did not discuss the fact that minstrelsy was embedded in the market and that performers responded to and helped construct perceived market "demands." Rather, he treated the performances of whites in blackface as expressions springing, unmediated, from workers' interests as industrial wage laborers.

Robin D. G. Kelley's *Race Rebels* (1994) examined popular culture as a positive site of African American political identity formation. Kelley's goal was to envision an African American oppositional history that included the many people who did not participate in formal organizations. Like Lipsitz, Kelley drew on cultural studies theories to explore denigrated popular forms previously neglected by historians. Kelley's reinterpretation of Malcolm X's political development demonstrated the potential of such an approach. Rescuing Malcolm X from historical deification, Kelley revealed how Malcolm X's ordinary but pivotal participation in hipster culture and style, including wearing the zoot suit, shaped his later radicalism. He argued that historians could look to contemporary rap artists for a similar, informal resistance, based in popular culture, that held radical potentials.

After the publications of Cohen, Lipsitz, Roediger, and Kelley, popular culture histories expanded dramatically and construed power in dynamic terms. As the critique of mass culture weakened, historians began to study popular culture forms that were clearly embedded in market relations, often making the nature of those market relations a point of inquiry rather than a foregone conclusion. Rather than trying to identify cultures that remained autonomously free from the reach of capital, historians undertook, first, to explore the political potentials and liabilities of culture that is not separable from capitalist relationships; and second, to examine the ways people build investments in identities, sometime oppressive and hierarchical, through popular culture practices. In addition, emerging histories emphasized rigorous contextualization: the effects of popular culture practices could be understood only through empirical study of daily life, rather than through a priori assumptions about the impact of commercial capitalism. Because popular culture could now be at once a way into the construction of hierarchies and resistance to them, scholars in the 1990s transformed the historical study of labor and the working classes, sexuality, US imperialism, women and gender, African Americans, Native Americans, Latinas/os, Asian Americans, and whiteness. Three contributions in just one field, Native American history, illuminate the creative ferment in popular cultural history and its achievements over the next decade. Work on the construction of "Indianness" reveals the potential of popular cultural analysis for understanding not only the construction of imperial identities and the role of the capitalist market in shaping and proliferating such forms, but also the significance of cultural practices in engaging and resisting these processes.

Philip J. Deloria's book *Playing Indian* (1998) demonstrated that popular practices of racial disguise could be read historically in order to reveal that the "Indian" has been at the center of "American" identity. "From the colonial period to the present," wrote Deloria, "the Indian has skulked in and out of the most important stories various Americans have told about themselves." Deloria linked his project to Roediger's *Wages of Whiteness* and others that traced the formation of whiteness through racial masquerades of African Americans, but Deloria did not focus on how people defined themselves racially as white. Rather, Deloria asserted that "Americans – particularly white Americans – have been similarly fixated on defining themselves as a nation" (1998: 5). Deloria's project, then, interrogated popular culture practices in order to reveal ideology taking shape historically in daily life. He argued that whites "played Indian," first, to articulate a revolutionary nationalism in the late eighteenth and nineteenth centuries, and then to claim an anti-modern authenticity in the twentieth. Playing Indian was more complex than simply identifying with a text: "The donning of Indian clothes moved ideas from brains to bodies, from the realm of abstraction to the physical world of concrete experience" (ibid. 184). Whites who played Indian created a hybrid identity, a fantasy of being "in between" that allowed them to preserve stability while indulging in a supposedly "aboriginal" anarchic freedom. Deloria's project was centrally concerned with hierarchy, because this identity "rested fundamentally on asymmetrical relations of power . . . [i]n every instance playing Indian represented, evaded and perpetuated those relations" (ibid. 186). Indeed, Deloria noted that whites regularly rewarded native people for matching white constructions of "authenticity" and playing Indian themselves. Thus, Deloria revealed that categories of identity that historians had taken for granted in the past – white American and Indian – were themselves historical constructions that took on lived, creative resonance through popular practices.

Joy Kasson's *Buffalo Bill's Wild West* (2000) explored similar themes of national identity through explicitly commercial popular practices. She argued that Wild West shows in the late nineteenth century gained enormous popularity by selling whites an idea of the frontier and the "Indian." The Wild West show featured such spectacles as Indian attacks on a white frontier cabin being vanquished by Buffalo Bill and his cowboys, and a reenactment of Custer's Last Stand. Combined with extensive publicity campaigns, these shows served to make Buffalo Bill one of the nation's first modern celebrities and this version of the Wild West a foundation of national identity. Rooted in the burgeoning leisure market, Wild West shows had a long-lasting impact on whites' ideas of "authentic" and "traditional" Indian culture. Indeed, native people employed by Buffalo Bill to perform in the Wild West shows had to "play Indian" themselves by performing in Plains costumes and conforming to scripts designed to appeal to whites' imaginations. Both Deloria and Kasson noted that whites' fascination, while lethal in its dependence on Indians as a "vanishing race," sometimes gave individual indigenous people opportunities to gain social power. Kasson noted that Wild West shows proved a lucrative employment option for people whose prior economies had been systematically destroyed, and Deloria showed that people from hobbyists to hippies often hired Native American people to help them approximate "authentic" Indian play. While Deloria's study acknowledges that playing Indian intertwined with economies in print media, and "Indian" crafts and costumes, Kasson's study more directly engaged the capitalist market's role in shaping the national imaginary. Indeed, the ubiquitous nature of the Wild West narrative in film and television may partially account for the proliferation, and particular qualities, of playing Indian in the twentieth century.

While Deloria and Kasson took different approaches to asking ideological questions about the construction of Indianness and national identity, Rachel Buff's *Immigration and the Political Economy of Home* (2001) examined native people's own cultural practices of powwow in Minneapolis since World War II, in comparative context with West Indian carnival in Brooklyn. Buff argued that the Native American powwow circuit of the post-World War II era functioned as a response to the US government's termination policy, which prompted the migration of many native people from reservations to urban centers. In the wake of relocation, powwows shifted from being celebrations of particular home spaces to being places for Native Americans to respond to migration and shape new, urban identities. Buff argued that powwows were not worlds apart, but profoundly hybrid spaces in which native people encountered and negotiated notions of Indianness promulgated by whites. Indeed, Buff asserted that even some of the powwow's central features were "traditions" invented in the Wild West shows. For Buff, powwow performances were not tainted by these elements: rather, they "imaginatively reconfigure a mass-mediated universe" (Buff 2001: 38). For example, Buff pointed out that the powwow's "Master of Ceremonies is likely derived from the imperialist spectacle provided by Buffalo Bill Cody, but today he is also likely to talk about red power and rallies for treaty rights" (ibid. 36). The powwow was resistant, but not autonomous, not untouched by capital or the ideological maneuvers of whites. Configuring identity as hybrid, she did not search for "authentic" native cultural practices, nor measure resistance with an "assimilation" model. Rather, her comparative ethnic history, like the work of Lipsitz and

Kelley, deeply contextualized cultural practices in order to reveal their political meanings.

The works of Deloria, Kasson, and Buff demonstrate that the construction of imperial identities, the role of the market, and the development of resistant cultural forms, while the focus of different specialized inquiries, are necessarily part of the same story of popular culture. Collectively, they demand that historians reassess how they configure the "American Indian" in their historical research, paying attention to ideology and pleasure, the mass market, and the interlocking histories of identity formation. These scholars were not alone: historians in a wide variety of subfields made popular culture a focus for inquiries into the complexities of power in people's daily lives. There is now a particularly fertile field for future work. Lacunas in scholarship due to the long-lasting barriers to historians studying popular culture remain. At present, historians are expanding the topics, questions, and methods for popular culture history, demonstrating that we have only begun to imagine where this inquiry might lead.

The effects of decades of neglect of twentieth-century media-based popular culture in historical study are still acute. As historian Barbara Savage notes, few would disagree that the media has been a "defining aspect of American political and cultural life," particularly in the twentieth century, and yet, "there has been relatively little . . . [historical] exploration of its full dimensions and implications" (Savage 1999: 5). Indeed, considering its centrality to twentieth-century human experience, shockingly little work has been done by historians on radio, television, film in the sound era, and popular music, not to mention newer media forms. Likewise, historians are only now beginning to explore the transnational circulation of commercial popular culture. Because of this neglect, studies of diverse and dramatic changes in twentieth-century political and social experience have yet to be integrated into our historical understandings, and the possibilities for future work are many. Two examples of recent work demonstrate the ways that popular culture history is expanding into new topics, questions, and methodologies.

Barbara Savage's *Broadcasting Freedom* (1999) writes political history through the lens of radio, tracing the development of early radio's race discourse in the interaction between African American activists, government agencies, and radio entrepreneurs and advertisers. Black political strategies, she showed, must be accounted for in the context of what could be said in the mass media. In 1934, the federal government established the private, commercial ownership of radio, but advocates of public ownership won one concession: a requirement for all stations to broadcast educational or civic programming. The Radio Education Project at the federal Office of Education was formed in order to create such programming and became an "institutional home" for African Americans who wished to intervene in radio's soundscape (Savage 1999: 14). The networks, however, rejected public programming proposals they feared would offend powerful southern white advertisers. But World War II strengthened the activists' hand. The government demanded "positive programming" in an effort to sustain black patriotism and soften racist responses to black soldiers and war workers. Radio still was not an avenue for free expression, but activists did air new narratives of African Americans in US history, and even criticized the federal government. Savage's methodologies included not only textual and audience-response analysis, but also traditional political history methods of tracking government

agencies and their policies. She demonstrated that our understanding of the long civil
rights movement has yet to reckon fully with the politics of the media.

Eric Avila's *Popular Culture in the Age of White Flight* (2004) writes urban history
through the lens of a spatial analysis of popular culture in order to reveal the relationship between shifting geographies in Los Angeles in the postwar era and emerging
political alignments. The urban popular culture of the turn of the twentieth century
was characterized by ethnic, racial, and gender heterogeneity, yet ordered by segregation, regulation, and censorship. Avila argued that this pattern gave way after 1945
to a new order, which mapped racialization, largely through popular culture, onto
the urban/suburban divide. This process fostered a fantasy of an inclusive, safe, white
suburb, and occluded class and ethnic differences as it highlighted race. Avila's analysis of Dodger Stadium and the freeway demonstrates that urban entrepreneurs and
planners orchestrated how people moved through the city, and this process built
personal geographic maps that rendered certain aspects of urban life alien: to be traveled over but not dwelled within. Meanwhile, spaces like Disneyland replaced heterogeneous leisure spaces like Coney Island with a carefully ordered experience. The
spatial geographies people experienced with their bodies were imaginatively reinforced through film noir screen images that presented dark, dangerous urban centers.
Such a bifurcated racial imagination, Avila argued, provided a foundation for emerging political identities, including both the New Right, and black and brown power
movements.

Avila and Savage both build on established historical questions about the role of
culture in the production of power and identity, but go further to show that popular
culture can be an avenue into accounting historically for a wide range of social phenomena such as the emergence of political discourses and alignments. The result is
an increasingly sophisticated rendering of power and the production of cultural texts,
experiences, and subjectivities that indicate a central role for popular culture inquiry
in future work.

The recent and ongoing creative ferment in popular culture history might seem
to suggest that the stigma on "popular culture" has lifted. Is there still a reason to
invoke the problematic term "popular culture?" The term encodes a tacit binary,
implicating us in past distinctions and hierarchies, most notably the highbrow vs.
lowbrow dichotomy. Furthermore, popular culture's additional connection to the
mass vs. high culture debate invites a dismissal in the name of radical critique. Clearly,
anything that we might term "popular culture" could also be termed "culture." And
indeed, not all of the historians reviewed here explicitly invoke the term. Why not
move beyond category?

We should not abandon or avoid the term "popular culture" because the stigma
on media-based cultural forms has not entirely lifted in the discipline of history, and
furthermore, the very paradoxes and stigma that make the term problematic also
endow it with creative potential. The term "popular culture" remains prevalent in
both scholarly and non-scholarly contexts, and continues to be part of the discursive
terrain historians must navigate in choosing and legitimating their studies. Historians
still need to embrace the term precisely in order to prop open the door to a wider
range of sources and topics that have been sorely neglected. In addition, social and
cultural historians know from the past 40 years that historians often learn the most
when they embrace and interrogate stigmatized categories, and "popular culture"

contains a compelling paradox. For some, it refers to capitalist, commercialized culture, while for others it has meant the people's culture. While these poles are misleading – scholars have convincingly challenged the notions of cultural manipulation and of cultural autonomy – the paradox can remind historians that the inextricable relationship between people's creativity and the culture industries is historically constituted, intricate, and a source of insight into diverse historical inquiry.

Lastly, we do well to maintain the term "popular culture" because it links us to a long and honorable tradition of activists and historians who, however imperfectly, have insisted that historians must take seriously ordinary people and their expressive cultural experiences. From Progressive era labor and settlement activists, to Popular Front activists and scholars, to historians of the 1960s, 1970s, and 1980s committed to history from below, to the large community of scholars who have explored popular culture since the turn of the 1990s, this tradition insists that we grapple with the sources of injustice, and ask questions about how people make meaning in their lives. As globalization and war turn historians to renewed focus on economic policy and diplomatic powerbrokers, it is particularly important that popular culture, as the interface between large culture industries and daily expressive practices, remains a location significant to historical explanation. The past 90 years of activist and scholarly work endow us with sophisticated tools for analyzing unexpected sources of historical change, tools that can sidestep both utopianism and hopelessness. It is a tradition that, to echo Duke Ellington, is beyond category.

REFERENCES

Avila, Eric: *Popular Culture in the Age of White Flight: Fear and Fantasy in Suburban Los Angeles* (Berkeley: University of California Press, 2004).

Buff, Rachel: *Immigration and the Political Economy of Home: West Indian Brooklyn and American Indian Minneapolis, 1945–1992* (Berkeley: University of California Press, 2001).

Cohen, Lizabeth: "Encountering Mass Culture at the Grassroots: the Experience of Chicago Workers in the 1920s", *American Quarterly* 41 (1989), 6–33.

Cook, James W.: *The Arts of Deception: Playing with Fraud in the Age of Barnum* (Cambridge, MA: Harvard University Press, 2001).

Cott, Nancy: *Bonds of Womanhood: "Woman's Sphere" in New England, 1780–1835* (New Haven, CT: Yale University Press, 1977).

Curti, Merle: "Dime Novels and the American Tradition," *The Yale Review* 26 (1937), 761–78.

Deloria, Philip: *Playing Indian* (New Haven, CT: Yale University Press, 1998).

Denning, Michael: *Mechanic Accents: Dime Novels and Working-Class Culture in Nineteenth-Century America* (New York: Verso, 1987).

Denning, Michael: *The Cultural Front: The Laboring of American Culture in the Twentieth Century* (New York: Verso, 1996).

Fitzpatrick, Ellen: *History's Memory: Writing America's Past, 1880–1980* (Cambridge, MA: Harvard University Press, 2002).

Gorman, Paul R.: *Left Intellectuals and Popular Culture in Twentieth-Century America* (Chapel Hill: University of North Carolina Press, 1996).

Gutman, Herbert G.: "Work, Culture and Society in Industrializing America, 1815–1919," *American Historical Review* 78 (1973), 531–88.

Kasson, Joy S.: *Buffalo Bill's Wild West: Celebrity, Memory, and Popular History* (New York: Hill & Wang, 2000).

Kelley, Robin D. G.: *Race Rebels: Culture, Politics, and the Black Working Class* (New York: Free Press, 1994).

Levine, Lawrence W.: *Black Culture and Black Consciousness: Afro-American Folk Thought from Slavery to Freedom* (New York: Oxford University Press, 1977).

Levine, Lawrence W.: *Highbrow, Lowbrow: The Emergence of Cultural Hierarchy in America* (Cambridge, MA: Harvard University Press, 1988).

Lipsitz, George: *Time Passages: Collective Memory and American Popular Culture* (Minneapolis: University of Minnesota Press, 1990).

Macdonald, Dwight: "A Theory of Mass Culture" (originally published in 1953 in the journal *Diogenes*), in B. Rosenberg & D. W. White, eds., *Mass Culture: The Popular Arts in America* (New York: Macmillan, 1957), pp. 59–73.

Peiss, Kathy: *Cheap Amusements: Working Women and Leisure in Turn-of-the-Century New York* (Philadelphia, PA: Temple University Press, 1986).

Rawick, George P.: *From Sundown to Sunup: The Making of the Black Community* (Westport: Greenwood, 1972).

Roediger, David R.: *The Wages of Whiteness: Race and the Making of the American Working Class* (New York: Verso, 1991).

Rosenzweig, Roy: *Eight Hours for What We Will: Workers and Leisure in an Industrial City, 1870–1920* (New York: Cambridge University Press, 1983).

Savage, Barbara Diane: *Broadcasting Freedom: Radio, War, and the Politics of Race, 1938–1948* (Chapel Hill: University of North Carolina Press, 1999).

Sklar, Robert: *Movie-made America: A Cultural History of American Movies* (New York: Random House, 1975).

Thompson E. P.: *The Making of the English Working Class* (London: Victor Gollancz, 1963).

Ware, Caroline, ed.: *The Cultural Approach to History* (New York: Columbia University Press, 1940).

Chapter Twenty-Five

HISTORY AND MEMORY

David Glassberg

Examining popular representations of the past has been an especially fruitful avenue for the study of American culture. Throughout history, Americans have employed images of the past in art, literature, and public ceremonies as a medium for expressing their present-day concerns and communal identities. Not only has the content of American historical imagery changed over time to incorporate new events, but the social organization of American historical practices has changed as well, incorporating new media and reflecting new social, political, and economic relationships.

In recent years, cultural historians have called their analyses of popular images and uses of the past the study of "memory." While memory is conventionally understood to be solely an individual phenomenon, the product of personal experience and psychological disposition, cultural historians have emphasized its social dimension. How have popular ideas about the past been created, institutionalized, disseminated, and understood among various social groups and at various levels of American society? What consequences have these ideas had for American politics? How have they changed over time? What is the relationship of popular memory to the historical profession? What is distinctive about American memory practices compared to those of other nations?

At first glance, the study of memory seems a new field, but in fact historians have long been interested in tracing how ideas about history change over time. Since the turn of the twentieth century, historians have taught the history of what professional historians have thought about history and called it historiography, making its study central to training future generations of professionals. Literary critics and art historians have analyzed the often idiosyncratic historical imagery present in the works of artists and writers, while folklorists have investigated the historical tales of less prominent groups. In the 1930s, historian Carl Becker (1932) challenged his fellow members of the American Historical Association to consider how ordinary Americans thought about history. While few colleagues took up this study at the time, it became an important area of research in the 1950s and 1960s when American Studies scholars such as Henry Nash Smith (1950), Richard Hofstadter (1955), and Robert Bellah (1967) analyzed historical imagery in everything from dime novels to presidential speeches to the ideology of political movements such as populism and progressivism as the myths and symbols that formed the basis of regional identities and a national civil religion.

What distinguishes the new scholarship on "memory" from the old is not subject matter but approach. While earlier studies primarily sought to characterize a single group's or institution's beliefs about its past, the new studies primarily seek to understand the interrelationships between different versions of the past in public. They investigate how various versions of the past were communicated in society through a multiplicity of institutions and media, including school, government ceremonies, popular amusements, art and literature, stories told by families and friends, and landscape features designated as historical either by governmental edict or popular practice. The new memory scholarship expands the types of institutions and ideas that historians customarily examine, and assesses how various versions of the past competed for public influence in particular places and times.

With this change in approach, scholars have focused not only on how widely disseminated cultural memories were produced, but also on how they were understood. Earlier approaches assumed that everyone who encountered a historical image more or less understood it in the same way. New approaches, by contrast, emphasize the many different meanings that could be derived from the same historical representation. The meaning of a historical book, film, or display was not intrinsic, determined solely by the intention of its creator, but constructed by various audiences actively reinterpreting what they saw and heard by placing it in alternative contexts derived from their diverse social backgrounds and past experiences. But if every person was his or her own historian, creating idiosyncratic versions of the past that made sense to them based on their personal situation and experiences, then how can cultural historians make meaningful generalizations about an "American" memory?

The Problem of Scale: Memory and Collective Identity

Among the biggest challenges historians of memory face is that of scale. Much of the new scholarship on memory examines communication about the past only at the most intimate of scales: autobiographical memory and reminiscence. Oral historian Alessandro Portelli (1991) observes that individuals in recalling the past form a coherent personal identity and sense of self. They tell stories about the past that place themselves at the center of historical events, combining recollections of the events with judgments concerning how history should have turned out. But following the early insights of French sociologist Maurice Halbwachs (1951), historians of memory have explored how individual memories were not solely produced by idiosyncratic recollection, but were also established and confirmed through social interaction. An individual memory was shaped by group communication, intimately linked to the "collective" memory of the community. Through conversations with family and friends, individuals learned about a past before their own experience and shared versions of that past with others. Much of the new scholarship on memory looks at group experience and face-to-face interaction, the way that stories about the past were communicated among family and friends and passed down through generations.

Taking their analysis to the next level, cultural historians have generalized about the collective memory of ethnic groups, religious groups, racial groups, women's groups, groups organized around sexual orientation, and working-class groups. Since the 1960s, the study of collective memory has been inextricably intertwined with the study of collective identity. Historian Lawrence Levine took this approach in his pioneering volume *Black Culture and Black Consciousness* (1977), examining the evolution of tradition among African Americans in slavery and freedom. Historians Roy Rosenzweig and David Thelen (1998), surveying American attitudes toward the past in the 1990s, discovered significant differences in historical consciousness among predominantly white and Mexican American, Native American, and African American communities. W. Fitzhugh Brundage's exemplary study *The Southern Past* (2005) carefully traces the emergence in the South of separate black and white versions of southern history, structured by the local segregation of schools, churches, newspapers, and other media of communication, and their eventual collision in the decades after World War II.

Memories and collective identities were shaped by more than the intersection of personal experience with local stories and conversation. They were also influenced by historical images and stories from outside the community available in print and other mass media. The first European settlers in North America saw a "wilderness" to be improved into a garden because they viewed the environment in terms of the Bible stories they remembered. In the late eighteenth century, the Founding Fathers recalled the ancient empires of Greece and Rome in their arguments about the need to separate from the corruption of the British Empire. By the mid-nineteenth century, mass communication of historical images grew wider and faster with the development of chromolithography and the steam printing press, a trend greatly accelerated in the twentieth century with the invention of motion pictures, radio, television, and the internet. Clearly, the cultural historian of memory must account for what Americans learned about the past not only from their neighbors, but also from afar. This realization has led cultural historians to focus less on the workings of memory at the local level and more on the widely available versions of the past that circulated in public at the national or even global scale.

The most productive area for future historical studies of memory and collective identity lies in the effort to integrate local and global approaches by exploring the interpenetration of various scales, as local, regional, national, and transnational historical imagery intersected with traditions of ethnic group, family, and friends in various places and times. Memory in America has always been a transnational phenomenon, as generations of immigrants to America remained in touch with family and friends back home, combined memories and traditions from their home countries with those of neighbors in their new locales, and encountered larger political and economic institutions.

This leads to a second question, one that has been at the core of much of the recent historical scholarship on memory: with all the possible versions of the past that circulated in society, at various scales, how did particular accounts of the past get institutionalized and disseminated as the public one? How was this public version accepted as true? What opportunities did dissenting voices have to get their version out in public? Much of the scholarship on memory has focused on politics, and the struggle between official versions of the past and alternative views in the establishment of war memorials, civic celebrations, and public institutions such as museums, archives, and historic sites.

The Politics of Public Memory

The vast majority of scholarly studies of American memory over the past 20 years consider the ways that pasts have been "invented," "imagined," institutionalized, disseminated, and contested in national political culture. Indeed the development of historical scholarship on memory in recent years has been closely intertwined with the historical scholarship on nationalism. One approach to this study considers public historical imagery as supplying the myths and symbols that held diverse groups in political society together. In the words of Benedict Anderson (1991), a shared history – elements of a past remembered in common as well as elements forgotten in common – was the crucial element in the creation of an "imagined community" through which disparate individuals and groups envisioned themselves as members of a collective with a common present and future. These were the "mystic chords of memory" that political leaders such as Lincoln sought to articulate, an overarching, broadly shared civic or national faith that could transcend particular ethnic, class, and sectional loyalties. For much of the nineteenth century, the separation of church and state did not prevent the essentially religious notion of Americans as a chosen people with a unique destiny from permeating July 4th orations, public school textbooks, and other venues in which the history of the nation was recited. While Americans were deeply divided by the Civil War, as well as wars in the West against Mexico and native peoples, historian David Blight (2001) has shown that within a generation the memories of those conflicts in national political culture were subordinated to the politics of race, reunion, and westward expansion. In this respect memory and forgetting in American political culture shared much with other societies around the world that fought wars of national unification or displaced native populations.

Cognizant of those conflicts, recent approaches to the politics of memory depict the public practices and representations of history as instruments in the political struggle for power among various social groups. In this view, historical imagery disseminated by government and mass media advanced the imagined community of the nation while suppressing authentic local and group memories and collective identities. Studies such as John Bodnar's *Remaking America* (1992) sharply distinguish between an official history that government agencies such as the military and the National Park Service (and increasingly, their corporate underwriters) employed to maintain the political status quo, and a multiplicity of vernacular memories that ordinary citizens employed to sustain ties of family and local community.

While a civil religion approach that emphasizes history's role in holding political society together tends to overlook conflicts between competing versions of the past, a conceptual framework pitting official history versus vernacular memories also oversimplifies the play of forces shaping American memory. As historian Michael Kammen (1991) has shown, it appears that until the mid-twentieth century, the United States government exercised a relatively light hand in shaping national memory compared to the governments of France and other European nations. Most historical monuments that referred to the nation were the products of local initiatives and private fundraising, including the preservation of George Washington's home in Mount Vernon and the room where the Declaration of Independence and Constitution were signed in Philadelphia. There was no federal support for elementary and secondary education, no national university, and no national museum of American history. Kammen notes that the federal government did step up its efforts to disseminate a particular version of the nation's history in the mid-twentieth century, but never to the extent of authoritarian regimes in Nazi Germany, the Soviet Union, or communist China.

Rather than viewing the creation of national histories as strictly a top-down phenomenon, communicated from an elite to the masses, we should understand the process from the bottom up as well. There were multiple official histories as well as multiple vernacular memories. Americans interpreted national history through the lens of their family and local community histories. Public officials appropriated and transformed local memories into their official civic and national histories, even as the official imagery they employed acquired diverse meanings from the local contexts in which they were displayed. Public historical representations simultaneously reproduced the unequal political relationships of American society, through the relative power of groups to have their version of history accepted as the public history, and served as instruments through which those relationships were transformed, through the interaction of that public history at the local level with the other versions of the past that circulated among ethnic, fraternal, and labor organizations, as well as among family and friends.

The new historical scholarship analyzing the politics of public memory illuminates an important difference between professional history and public memory. Historians' efforts to provide an original interpretation of the past or to translate the latest professional scholarship for a popular audience inevitably entered a world of competing political forces. The product of compromise and negotiation, public historical representations such as a museum exhibit, war memorial, or commemorative ceremony were often deliberately ambiguous to satisfy competing factions. Unlike a historian's monograph, public memorial sites such as the Vietnam Veterans Memorial in Washington brought (and continue to bring) discrete and often conflicting memories to converge as dialogue in a common space.

Memory and Popular Culture

The dialogical nature of public memory is especially evident from cultural historians' examinations of historical imagery in commercial mass media and tourist attractions, representations of the past shaped less by politics and the desire to communicate an official ideology or a sense of collective identity, than by the marketplace and the desire to appeal to large numbers of people in their leisure hours. Much new scholarship on memory has employed critical theories of mass communication to analyze historical imagery that appeared in popular film, music, and tourist attractions. Historian George Lipsitz (1990) observes that Americans neither passively received nor actively challenged the historical imagery they saw and heard in popular television docudramas, music, film, novels, and tourist attractions; rather, they "negotiated" between the mass-media versions of the past and the versions they had already encountered in their own particular subcultures. To appeal to the widest possible audience, popular historical representations, like other pop culture forms, incorporated a wide variety of possible characters and themes with which Americans could identify their particular concerns. Embedded within even the most commercial and mass-produced representations of the American past, Lipsitz insists, were elements reflecting the historical experience of various subcultures; through close analysis, scholars can recover the hidden meanings and memories that were encoded in these narratives. Popular films and television programs did not impose a single view of history on the masses, but rather communicated a multiplicity of submerged alternative visions, each accessible to those with the particular social background to decipher them.

Looking at popular history, historian Allison Landsberg (2004) identifies a trend in mass culture through the twentieth century toward simulating on some physical level a past that one never experienced personally. Living-history museums, historical reenactments, and popular films invite the audience to identify emotionally with particular historical characters. In these popular entertainment venues, historical imagery has been more likely to refer to everyday life sometime in the past than to specific and potentially controversial historical events. This focus on everyday life has been employed in particular when elements of the past are adapted for global popular culture in settings such as Disney's Main Street USA and Cinderella Castle.

While approaches to the study of memory as popular cultural texts emphasize the multiplicity of possible meanings for each historical image, a productive area for future historical research is to discover what meanings actually surfaced in particular places and times. Cultural historians of memory can examine popular historical representations not only as created by their authors, but also as reshaped by the institutional bureaucracies that presented them, and reinterpreted by the various groups that saw and heard them. If the meaning of a historical fact was not intrinsic but changed with context, then historians can investigate closely the successive contexts created by the author, the mass media, and the public, tracing the path through each particular place where knowledge about the past was communicated.

Memory and Environment

The scholarly trend toward tracing the communication of memory among particular groups and settings has led cultural historians to investigate the relationship between memory and environmental perception. Memories provide meaning to places. Televised images of a Civil War battlefield and designated local historic sites or districts, for example, connect stories of past events to a particular physical setting. What cognitive changes occurred when an environment became considered as "historical," either by government designation or popular practice, or when a civic organization such as the local chamber of commerce created maps and historical atlases that recognized some historical places but not others? How have the American historical experience of geographical mobility, dramatic upheaval in the physical environment, and new electronic forms of communication from the radio to the internet affected the way that its citizens have formed memories and attachments to their local environment?

Paralleling the development of historical scholarship on popular memory, scholarship in other disciplines such as environmental psychology, folklore, and cultural geography has emerged that investigates the making of "sense of place."

Environmental psychologist Clare Cooper Marcus (1992) has explored how children bond emotionally with places as they develop, and how memories of these special childhood places remain a crucial anchor for their personal identity in adulthood. The social networks they participate in as adults also can further develop and reinforce their sense of place; the longer they live in a place, the more likely they are to associate local environmental features with memories of their significant life experiences with family and friends. Psychologists have also explored the emotional consequences when the bonds between people and places are broken: the grieving for a lost home that occurs among the elderly or exiles forcibly deprived of their familiar environment and memory sites.

Environmental memories loom large not only in personal recollections, but also in the collective memory of communities. Conversations among family and friends about past local characters, about the weather, about work, transform ordinary environments into storied places. In writing about sense of place, Wallace Stegner (1992) notes, "No place is a place until the things that have happened in it are remembered in history, ballads, yarns, legends, or monuments." Folklorists have observed the often conflicting meanings for the same environment communicated among different groups, and how representations of a collective sense of place, like that of a collective history, reflect the often unequal power relations between various local groups and interests. The meanings established for a place, and the land-use decisions that stem from those meanings, are shaped by the social, economic, and political relationships among the various residents of a town or neighborhood, as well as by local residents' relationships with the outside world.

In applying these insights concerning memory and environment to the study of the past, historians can examine the extent to which Americans' high degree of geographical mobility undermined their ability to identify with distinctive places and local histories. I have suggested elsewhere (Glassberg 2001) that the experience of geographic mobility socialized Americans to form attachments in memory to multiple locales. Among the distinctive memory practices that developed in nineteenth-century America were Pioneer Societies celebrating the first (white) settlers in a town, Old Home Week and periodic reunions of former residents, and the formation of social organizations in distant places based on members' attachment to where they used to live, such as the Sons of New England in California. Much of the local-color literature popular in late nineteenth-century America consisted of memoirs written by authors who had long departed the places they wrote about. A nation of immigrants on the move, Americans seemed to be always remembering a home somewhere else, either in another part of the United States or overseas, or else remembering a past local environment dramatically different from that of their present. In the twentieth century, the sentiment for remembered places fueled the emergence of museum villages, historic preservation, and heritage tourism. J. B. Jackson charged in his provocative essay "The Necessity for Ruins" (1980) that in America the historical was always somewhere else, that Americans seldom saw any continuity between the historical places they visited and the non-historical places where they lived their everyday lives. But this phenomenon merits future study by cultural historians.

Some of the best new scholarship on memory and environment has appeared under the heading of cultural landscape studies. Gail Lee Dubrow (2000) has examined Asian American imprints on the landscape of the Pacific Northwest, investigating how

ethnic group memories were embedded in landscape features. More explicit conceptualization of the relationship of memory and environment has also appeared in new
histories of the historic preservation movement, such as the anthology edited by Max
Page and Randall Mason (2004). Lying at the scholarly intersection of cultural and
environmental history, studies of memory and environment have proven a productive
avenue of inquiry for historians of American culture.

What's American about American Memory?

Cultural historians have found the concept of memory useful in investigations of
Americans' individual, group, local, regional, and national identities and political
ideologies; in the analysis of mass media and popular culture products; and in the
examination of the meanings that Americans have attached to the built and natural
environment. A future direction is to study these aspects of memory comparatively.
David Lowenthal (1996) has demonstrated the essential similarity in how nations
throughout the world adopted the Western use of the term "heritage" in the late
twentieth century. Historian Charles Maier (1993) noted a "surfeit" of memory as
various groups made claims to distinctive cultural identities based on past traumas.
But to what extent has the relationship between grassroots memories and invented
public histories differed across cultures as well as over time? Or the relationship of
the historical profession to the other groups that practice history in public? Or the
kinds of events that reenactors have chosen to reenact? Why, for example, did reenacting the American Civil War become popular in Australia, or the Wild West in
Germany? The process of creating memorials in the wake of traumatic events such
as wars and natural disasters seems to have followed similar patterns worldwide in
the early twentieth century, with World War I memorials in the United States following those of Europe in depicting mourning rather than victory as their major
theme. But does the pattern that historian Edward Linenthal (2001) described in his
study of the American memorialization of the Oklahoma City bombing of 1995 hold
true for the way that other nations have memorialized terrorist acts? In a model study,
James Young (1993) compares the memorialization of the Holocaust in Germany,
Poland, Austria, the United States, and Israel, demonstrating how each nation's
version of the Holocaust was shaped by its political culture and incorporated into its
national identity. To what extent have memory and forgetting in American political
culture shared much with other "settler" societies around the world that fought wars
of national unification or displaced native populations? With the movement of populations around the world, have the ways of relating memory and place and the development of translocal memories and identities that developed from the American
experience of geographic mobility in the nineteenth century become more common
elsewhere?

Memory and Historians

The study of memory offers historians of American culture not only new
research questions, but also new understandings of their place in society, and new

opportunities for sharing their scholarship with the public. In an influential essay, historian Pierre Nora (1989) argues that history all but eradicated popular memory and oral tradition in the modern period. But clearly forms of what historian Raphael Samuel (1994) describes as "unofficial knowledge" of the past have continued to survive alongside formal historical institutions and scholarship. The organization of tradition in society has a history; and understanding this history, and the memory practices Americans have inherited from the past, can help cultural historians to understand the institutional contexts in which they operate as well as the presuppositions about history with which the public approaches their work. In different times and places, professional historians have been more or less influential in shaping popular memory. Through studying the history of this interaction, contemporary historians might learn ways to communicate their ideas concerning the American past more effectively.

REFERENCES

Anderson, Benedict: *Imagined Communities: Reflections on the Origins and Spread of Nationalism* (New York: Verso, rev. ed. 1991).

Becker, Carl: "Everyman His Own Historian," *American Historical Review* 37 (1932), 221–36.

Bellah, Robert: "Civil Religion in America," *Daedalus* 96 (Winter 1967), 1–21.

Blight, David: *Race and Reunion: The Civil War in American Memory* (Cambridge, MA: Harvard University Press, 2001).

Bodnar, John: *Remaking America: Public Memory, Commemoration, and Patriotism in the Twentieth Century* (Princeton, NJ: Princeton University Press, 1992).

Brundage, W. Fitzhugh: *The Southern Past: A Clash of Race and Memory* (Cambridge, MA: Harvard University Press, 2005).

Dubrow, Gail Lee: "Asian American Imprints on the Western Landscape," in Arnold R. Alanen & Robert Z. Melnick, eds., *Preserving Cultural Landscapes in America* (Baltimore, MD: Johns Hopkins University Press, 2000), pp. 143–68.

Frisch, Michael: *A Shared Authority: Essays on the Craft and Meaning of Oral and Public History* (Albany, NY: SUNY Press, 1990).

Glassberg, David: *Sense of History: The Place of the Past in American Life* (Amherst: University of Massachusetts Press, 2001).

Halbwachs, Maurice: *The Collective Memory* (New York: Harper & Row, 1980 [1951]).

Hofstadter, Richard: *The Age of Reform: From Bryan to FDR* (New York: Alfred A. Knopf, 1955).

Jackson, J. B.: "The Necessity for Ruins," in *The Necessity for Ruins and Other Topics* (Amherst: University of Massachusetts Press, 1980), pp. 89–102.

Kammen, Michael: *Mystic Chords of Memory: The Transformation of Tradition in American Culture* (New York: Alfred A. Knopf, 1991).

Landsberg, Allison: *Prosthetic Memory: The Transformation of American Remembrance in the Age of Mass Culture* (New York: Columbia University Press, 2004).

Levine, Lawrence: *Black Culture and Black Consciousness* (New York: Oxford University Press, 1977).

Linenthal, Edward T.: *The Unfinished Bombing: Oklahoma City in American Memory* (New York: Oxford University Press, 2001).

Lipsitz, George: *Time Passages: Collective Memory and American Popular Culture* (Minneapolis: University of Minnesota Press, 1990).

Lowenthal, David: *Possessed by the Past: The Heritage Crusade and the Spoils of History* (New York: Free Press, 1996).

Maier, Charles: "A Surfeit of Memory? Reflections on History, Melancholy, and Denial," *History and Memory* 5 (Fall 1993), 136–52.

Marcus, Clare Cooper: "Environmental Memories," in Irwin Altman and Setha Low, eds., *Place Attachment* (New York: Plenum, 1992), pp. 87–112.

Nora, Pierre: "Between Memory and History: Les Lieux de Mémoire," *Representations* 26 (Spring 1989), 7–25.

Page, Max & Mason, Randall, eds.: *Giving Preservation a History: Histories of Historic Preservation in the United States* (New York: Routledge, 2004).

Portelli, Alessandro: *The Death of Luigi Trastulli and Other Stories: Form and Meaning in Oral History* (Albany, NY: SUNY Press, 1991).

Rosenzweig, Roy & Thelen, David: *Presence of the Past: Popular Uses of History in American Life* (New York: Columbia University Press, 1998).

Samuel, Raphael: *Theatres of Memory* (New York: Verso, 1994).

Smith, Henry Nash: *Virgin Land: The American West as Symbol and Myth* (Cambridge, MA: Harvard University Press, 1950).

Stegner, Wallace: "The Sense of Place," in *Where the Bluebird Sings to the Lemonade Springs: Living and Writing in the West* (New York: Random House, 1992), p. 202.

Young, James: *The Texture of Memory: Holocaust Memorials and Meaning* (New Haven, CT: Yale University Press, 1993).

Part V

THE CULTURAL TURN IN OTHER FIELDS

Chapter Twenty-Six

CULTURALIST APPROACHES TO INTELLECTUAL HISTORY

Casey Nelson Blake

Long before other historians took "the cultural turn," American intellectual historians put questions of value, meaning, and interpretation at the center of their inquiry. The challenge of placing the history of ideas and intellectuals in a broader context – be it political, social, institutional, or cultural – has likewise preoccupied such scholars for many decades. And the recent interest in "internationalizing" the study of United States history comes as old news to intellectual historians who have long examined American liberalism, religion, and modernism (among other subjects) from a trans-atlantic perspective. That said, the scholarship in intellectual history has changed significantly over the last 30 years, largely in response to critiques from social historians, literary theorists, and advocates of cultural studies. The result has been a re-invigoration of a field that, as recently as the 1970s, stood accused of elitism and methodological incoherence.

The most influential historians of American thought and culture of the post-World War II era were, in fact, more sophisticated in their approach, more skeptical of dominant traditions in US ideology, and more wide-ranging in their subject matter than subsequent critics have often allowed. Richard Hofstadter and Louis Hartz, the pre-eminent political historians of their day, were determined to expand the scope of political history to include systematic ideology (or the lack thereof), popular conceptions of a democratic society, and the political aspirations and practices of different social groups. They also subjected mainstream American liberal ideals to a degree of analytical scrutiny that far exceeded that of their Progressive-era predecessors in its philosophical sophistication and cosmopolitan scope. The "Lockean synthesis" has been widely criticized and revised since Hofstadter and Hartz advanced it as a framework for understanding US political ideology more than a half-century ago; but no sensitive reader can claim that their arguments endorsed mainstream American political assumptions or restricted the range of political ideas to a handful of rarified tracts.

The same might be said of the "myth-and-symbol" scholarship of the American Studies movement in the 1950s and early 1960s. Now widely derided as triumphalist in its embrace of American exceptionalism, the best of this work combined cultural history and cultural criticism to indict national assumptions about nature, agrarianism, and urbanism as inadequate responses to industrial capitalism and world war. Books such as Henry Nash Smith's *Virgin Land* and Alan Trachtenberg's *Brooklyn Bridge* also prefigured contemporary efforts to embed the history of ideas in larger developments in cultural production, placing canonical works of art, literature, and criticism in dialogue with dime novels, political pamphlets, technology, and material culture. Perry Miller's magisterial studies of the "New England mind" were primarily concerned with the consolidation and subsequent unraveling of a coherent Puritan worldview, an orientation that reflected Miller's determination to refute the easy debunking of "Puritanism" by modernists. Yet, like his postwar colleagues in American Studies, Miller probed connections between different realms of historical experience. The Puritans' "covenant theology," in his telling, had implications for the rise of democratic politics in the United States. Moreover, Miller joined historical inquiry to a critique, however implicit, of contemporary liberal culture that had much in common with the Protestant "realism" of Reinhold and H. Richard Niebuhr.

Many intellectual historians of the postwar period initiated an inquiry into the social position of intellectuals that continues until this day. Classic works like Hofstadter's *Anti-intellectualism in American Life* (1963) and Christopher Lasch's *The New Radicalism in America* (1965) explored the history of intellectuals as a social group and sought to understand the institutional and ideological conditions for the emergence of a secular intelligentsia in the United States at the end of the nineteenth century. That inquiry, in turn, impelled a discussion of the relationship between intellectuals and the middle class, with historians and sociologists teasing out the complex linkages between the intelligentsia, the professions, and the so-called "new class" of managers and experts. These early discussions carried on debates about the "responsibility of intellectuals" that had preoccupied critics for decades, while at the same time anticipating later controversies about the fate of "public intellectuals" and the relationship between academic knowledge and civic life that still preoccupy historians and cultural commentators.

Perhaps most importantly, intellectual historians provided a counter to the positivism of the social-scientific mainstream in the postwar academy. At a time when all disciplines felt pressure to imitate the "hard" sciences in their methodology, intellectual historians remained proud generalists who took the messy subject of human consciousness as their domain. Not surprisingly, then, the reorientation of the social sciences in the 1960s and 1970s went hand in hand with a retrieval of earlier social theorists, whose engagement with idealist philosophical traditions was made newly available by intellectual historians of the turn of the twentieth century. Just as Raymond Williams's *Culture and Society* (1958) and H. Stuart Hughes's *Consciousness and Society* (1958) were reconstructing alternatives to positivist social theory in European thought, Morton White's *Social Thought in America: The Revolt against Formalism* (1949), Henry May's *The End of American Innocence* (1959), and Lasch's *New Radicalism* (1965) kept alive traditions of philosophy, social theory, and cultural criticism that the postwar academy had marginalized or forgotten. The "cultural turn" in scholarship is more than a little indebted to the intellectual history of the late 1950s and early 1960s.

Nonetheless, the postwar scholarship in intellectual history came under sustained, often justified, criticism, beginning in the early 1970s. Social historians condemned intellectual historians for their alleged elitism, arguing that an emphasis on canonical texts and the ideas of educated Euro-American men neglected the experiences of the vast majority. Those committed to writing "history from below" in the 1970s added to that charge the claim that intellectual historians promoted a homogeneous portrait of American culture at the expense of diversity. Such criticisms had particular significance for the field of American Studies, which subsequently turned its back on the "intellectual-history synthesis" of the field's foundational works and abandoned the "myth-and-symbol" approach. The social-historical critique presented its greatest challenge when it moved beyond populist polemics to methodological issues. Taking its cue from new developments in cultural anthropology (particularly the work of Clifford Geertz), the neo-Marxist historiography of E. P. Thompson, Christopher Hill, Williams, and other British scholars, and the study of collective *mentalités* by the French Annales school, many social historians criticized intellectual historians for failing to ground ideas in social reality. The "weightlessness" of the history of ideas – the abstraction of consciousness from institutions, political economy, and social conflict – became a familiar complaint.

A new literature examining the history of intellectuals and ideology in the context of class, economics, and social movements quickly followed this critique. Eric Foner's *Tom Paine and Revolutionary America* (1976) was an early example of such work, setting Paine's emergence as a political pamphleteer in the tumultuous milieu of late eighteenth-century Philadelphia. Foner's synthesis of intellectual and social history has been followed by other significant work in this genre: Nancy Cohen's study of modern liberalism; James Livingston's books on political economy; Daniel H. Borus's social history of literary realism and the publishing history; Rosalind Rosenberg's work on feminist social science in the academy; and studies of reformist intellectuals by Kathryn Kish Sklar, David Levering Lewis, and Leon Fink. In a similar vein, the recovery in the 1970s and 1980s of the "critical theory" of the Frankfurt School and Italian Marxist Antonio Gramsci's concept of "cultural hegemony" led many historians to identify transformations in culture and ideology as integral to the consolidation of bourgeois dominance in the nineteenth century. David Brion Davis's *The Problem of Slavery in the Age of Revolution* (1975) and T. J. Jackson Lears's *No Place of Grace* (1981) are influential examples of Gramscian intellectual and cultural history. Alan Trachtenberg's second book, *The Incorporation of America* (1982), deployed Gramscian ideas to reconfigure traditional concerns of American Studies scholarship. The American assimilation of Michel Foucault's studies of disciplinary institutions has also influenced intellectual historians. Michael Meranze's *Laboratories of Virtues* (1996), a history of the intellectual underpinnings of the early penitentiary, is one example of a Foucauldian approach to power and liberal ideology in the United States.

A more sustained and ultimately more consequential critique of postwar work in intellectual history came in the 1970s and 1980s from poststructuralist literary and cultural studies that bore the influence of Jacques Derrida, Foucault, and other Continental theorists. The work of European intellectual historians such as Hayden White, Dominick LaCapra, and Mark Poster, as well as the "New Historicism" of Stephen Greenblatt, Walter Benn Michaels, and other literary scholars, advanced arguments about the entanglement of ideas and language, the ever-shifting meanings of texts, and the inability of historians and other inquirers to transcend their own cultural location to achieve an objective view of the past. The belief that historical texts were clear windows onto the intentions of their authors, or even that historians could locate a stable set of meanings in texts, came under attack. Stanley Fish and other theorists of "reader-response" criticism shifted the search for meaning in texts from the intentions of their producers to the uses and interpretations made of them by different audiences. The "creative misreading" of texts, in Harold Bloom's phrase, became as much an object of inquiry as their original meaning. Indeed, postmodernist currents in philosophy rejected the search for definitive meanings altogether. The quest for an Archimedean perspective on the past gave way to self-consciously pro-visional histories that borrowed liberally from narrative techniques in literature and vernacular traditions of popular memory and storytelling. "Textualist" sensitivity to the complexities of language, rhetoric, and narrative came to be essential to the study of what was once understood as "context." Historical actors, the institutions that shaped their thought and experience, and subsequent interpreters in the academy were all creatures and creators of intricate systems of representation.

A conference held in 1977 at Racine, Wisconsin represented the first concerted effort by intellectual historians to respond to the challenges from social historians and poststructuralists. Published as *New Directions in American Intellectual History* (Higham & Conkin 1979), the papers from the conference initiated myriad "textual-ist" and "contextualist" strategies for reconceptualizing the history of ideas and intellectuals. This volume led immediately to the launching of a new annual publica-tion, the *Intellectual History Newsletter* (*IHN*), which, under the successive editorship of Thomas Bender, David D. Hall, Richard Wightman Fox, and Casey Nelson Blake and Howard Brick, sponsored important debates on theory and methodology, reli-gious history, women and intellectual history, pragmatism and liberalism, the rise of cultural studies, and the arts and intellectual life, among other subjects. By 2002, the *IHN* had come to resemble a journal more than a newsletter, and was succeeded in 2004 by *Modern Intellectual History*, edited by Charles Capper, Anthony J. La Vopa, and Nicholas T. Phillipson. Together, these developments signal an engagement with new theoretical developments in literary and cultural interpretation that have signifi-cantly reoriented scholarship in the field.

The consequences of poststructuralist theory for US intellectual history are most evident in scholarship on the early period, perhaps because so much of the European-ist scholarship in this vein addressed topics in early modern history. The study of a nascent American political ideology is noteworthy for its engagement with textualist and culturalist themes, and for rich interdisciplinary exchanges between literary schol-ars and intellectual historians. Traditional histories of political thought continue to shape debates about the founding ideas of the republic. The early work of Bernard Bailyn, Gordon Wood, J. G. A. Pocock, and Joyce Appleby on the republican and liberal strains in American political philosophy remains central. But more recent studies of print culture, literary voice, oratory, performance, and public ritual by Michael Warner, Jay Fliegelman, Robert Ferguson, Kenneth Cmiel, and David Wald-streicher have profoundly shifted the frame of analysis of American political thought by demonstrating the interplay between ideology, cultural context, and multiple venues of cultural expression in the Revolutionary period. Rather than simply docu-menting how political philosophy "influenced" cultural practices, or vice versa, these scholars have argued for the constitutive role of language – both printed and spoken – in enabling the very idea of a democratic public and enacting a new national identity.

Michael Warner's *The Letters of the Republic* (1990) and Jay Fliegelman's *Declaring Independence: Jefferson, Natural Language, and the Culture of Performance* (1993) exemplify the ambition and interdisciplinary reach of the new culturalist approach to American political ideology. Warner draws heavily on Jürgen Habermas's philosophical writings on the "public sphere" in analyzing the liberation of eighteenth-century print media from their customary usage as instruments of particular social interests. Once colonists distinguished the language of newspapers, pamphlets, and other broadsides as an impersonal medium, they could make use of the printed word as a site for the creation of independent judgments on the public realm. The "publicness" of print generated an abstract ideal of citizenship for white, propertied men, who in turn constituted themselves as a democratic public. Fliegelman, by contrast, insists on oral culture and performance as the primary media for Revolutionary politics. He recaptures the Declaration of Independence as a text meant for public declaration, and locates its author's political career in the shifting terrain of eighteenth-century understandings of rhetoric and public voice. Jefferson and his contemporaries found themselves pulled in opposite directions as performers of a new national politics. On the one hand, the Protestant tradition of plain speaking, the natural rights tradition in political philosophy, and the Scottish "common sense" Enlightenment all promoted the ideal of a "natural language" that articulated "self-evident" truths in a rhetoric accessible to all listeners. On the other, an "oratorical revolution" with echoes in theater, portraiture, and music emphasized sincerity and the revelation of private feeling as instruments of persuasion. That such persuasion deployed theatrical techniques to reveal the orator's "true" self only added to the epistemological and political complexities of Revolutionary oratory. Natural language and the oratory of sincerity each claimed the mantle of authenticity and promised a public speech appropriate to democratic citizenship. Yet each contained internal contradictions that frustrated legibility and public accountability. Their collision in the late eighteenth century further confounded the search for fixed understandings of self, citizen, and nation.

Warner and Fliegelman have drawn criticism from historians who chafe at what they perceive as linguistic determinism. Fliegelman in particular has been faulted for reasoning by analogy, instead of making causal connections between his dazzling array of sources. Yet, more traditionally minded scholars have shared the belief that democratic politics in the Revolutionary and early national periods was bound up with new understandings of public language. Robert Ferguson's studies of law, literature, and the American enlightenment (1984, 1997) have demonstrated the indebtedness of early American writers – many of whom were trained as lawyers – to Ciceronian and other classical orators. Kenneth Cmiel's *Democratic Eloquence* (1990) similarly joins the history of public speech and the evolution of civic philosophy, examining how conflicting notions of appropriate language were inseparable from disagreements over the scope of political participation. Fights over how public actors spoke were also fights over who could speak (and act) in public. David Waldstreicher's study of patriotic celebrations, *In the Midst of Perpetual Fetes* (1997), examines how the politicization of public rituals in the post-Revolutionary period furthered a unified nationalist ideology.

These studies have in no way swept aside studies of political ideology, strictly defined, by intellectual historians, political theorists, and philosophers. But they represent an expansion of the scope of political history to include varied forms of expressive culture, and an insistence on the political consequences of language and communication that have dramatically transferred the history of political ideology. Ruth Bloch's work on gender and American politics (2003) likewise bears the imprint of this culturalist shift. Bloch's examination of popular literature, religion, and depictions of love and marriage shows how representations of gender relations transcended the stark dichotomy between civic republicanism and liberalism that has dominated many accounts of the American founding. In a very different context, Robert Westbrook's ambitious essays on liberalism and the problem of political obligation during World War II (2004) examine posters, cartoons, pinups, film, and social criticism for evidence of how democratic theory was lived and understood by ordinary citizens in their encounters with popular culture.

The history of American Protestantism, another field of long-standing significance for the early period in North American history (and after), has witnessed a transformation in its methodology and subject matter that parallels recent developments in the study of political ideology. Perry Miller's foundational writings on the Puritans' reconstruction of Calvinism in New England continue to inspire work on the history of theology. His arguments have been refined and challenged over the last four decades by such scholars as Alan Heimert, Andrew Delbanco, Michael McGiffert, E. Brooks Hollifield, and Stephen Foster. Among other innovations, this recent work gives greater weight to the continuities between European and North American Reformed theology.

The culturalist tendencies in historical writing that drew on developments in post-structuralist theory have inspired a more far-reaching orientation in the study of early American Protestantism. Literary historian Sacvan Bercovitch's influential book *The American Jeremiad* (1978) explored the ideological implications of the Puritans' sermonic tropes and considered the subsequent political consequences of the jeremiad tradition in American oratory. For Bercovitch, the very structure of the jeremiad – with its condemnation of the fallen present in the name of past prophecy, followed by a call for the restoration of traditional ideals on a new basis – fostered an ideological insularity that disabled radical social criticism. David D. Hall's *Worlds of Wonder, Days of Judgment* (1989) also directed historians' attention from theology to other aspects of Puritan life. Hall placed devotional practice, reading, ritual, and magic at the center of Puritan experience, but deliberately avoided a simple dichotomy between "high" and "low" religious cultures. Congregational practice joined clergy and laity, formal sermons and vernacular rituals in a complex set of negotiations that embedded religious doctrine in everyday activities.

The treatment of other aspects of American Protestantism also reflects this new attentiveness to language and popular practice. Histories of African American Protestantism, during and after slavery, have been enriched by consideration of the syncretism of African and Christian beliefs and practices, and slaves' interpretations of the biblical narratives learned from their masters. In the work of Eugene Genovese, Albert Raboteau, Lawrence Levine, and Eddie Glaude, African American Protestantism emerges as a distinctive strain of prophetic religion with its own understanding of the relationship between sacred and secular history. The Exodus is at the forefront of these accounts, with African American preachers' interpreting the flight from Egypt as a prophetic narrative that embodied congregants' own histories, hurts, and hopes.

African Americans' recuperation of Exodus militated against a simple otherworldly religion and made biblical prophecy the vehicle for racial identity.

New England's religious transformation from Puritanism to theological liberalism – long a feature of historical studies from Miller onwards – has also been a subject for historians of a culturalist bent. Karen Halttunen's *Murder Most Foul* (1998) traces the shift from a Calvinist morality to the humanitarian sensibility of the nineteenth century by examining the transformation of murder narratives from execution sermons to murder-trial transcripts, press accounts, detective stories, and other examples of a nascent Gothic imagination. While the seventeenth-century execution sermon implicated its audience in the state of human sinfulness that included the condemned killer, these later narratives constructed the murderer as a moral monster beyond the reach of human recognition. Halttunen deepens our understanding of the pervasiveness of this shift in American Protestants' understanding of sin and evil in human nature by her use of unconventional sources, but her greatest methodological achievement may be her rewriting the evanescence of Calvinism as a transformation in the form and structure of the stories Americans told themselves about murder.

Richard Wightman Fox's history of the famous Beecher–Tilton affair, *The Trials of Intimacy* (1999), shares with Halttunen's work an interest in narrativity – in this case, the legal, fictional, and autobiographical narratives that surrounded the mystery of the allegations of adultery between Henry Ward Beecher and Elizabeth Tilton. Fox takes an iconoclastic approach to historical narration, writing the history of the affair backwards, from the death of its main protagonists through the adultery trial and back to the origins of the friendships linking Beecher, Tilton, and her husband. The result is a deliberate confounding of the detective genre that this history-in-reverse most resembles. Fox argues that no definitive evidence supports or counters the alleged affair, and that the historical significance of the relationship lies in the stories told about it. Much like Halttunen, Fox makes an argument about the history of liberal Protestantism that moves from theology to lived experience. Whatever else it may have been, the relationship between Beecher and Tilton was part of the romantic gospel of love that swept through middle-class congregations in the wake of Calvinism. Long caricatured as a banal doctrine suitable for the complacent Gilded Age bourgeoisie, Beecher's romantic Protestantism emerges in Fox's book as a counter-cultural force that threatened marriage and other conventions in the name of true love and intense spirituality. This is a history of theology as lived, felt, and interpreted experience.

Many intellectual historians who write about the late nineteenth and twentieth centuries have argued for a "contextualist" approach that represents another response to the dual challenges of social history and poststructuralist literary studies. Since the 1980s, David A. Hollinger has been the foremost advocate of the contextualist position, which has drawn on the efforts of pragmatist philosophers to ground truth-claims in the provisional consensus of particular communities of inquirers. In a series of highly influential articles, Hollinger has urged intellectual historians to make the history of discourse their primary area of study and to place ideas in the context of "communities of discourse." Discourse, in this view, is as much a collective, socially constructed activity as labor, economics, or politics and thus represents an answer to those who have condemned intellectual history for examining ideas as abstract, disembodied phenomena. "Discourse is a social as well as an intellectual activity," in Hollinger's view; "it entails interaction between minds, and it revolves around something possessed in common." What holds a discursive community together is not unanimity on fundamental principles, or the participation of intellectuals in the cultural hegemony of a particular social class, but shared questions that may generate as much controversy as consensus. "Questions are the points of contact between minds, where agreements are consolidated and where differences are acknowledged and dealt with; questions are the dynamisms whereby membership in a community of discourse is established, renewed, and sometimes terminated" (Hollinger 1985: 132). Communities of discourse preoccupied with the relationship between scientific method and religion, the consequences of ethno-racial diversity for national identity, and the moral implications of literary modernism – three subjects that Hollinger himself has explored – have a history that scholars can trace through the rise and fall over time of common questions.

Given the indebtedness of this contextualist position to a pragmatist epistemology, it is perhaps not surprising that some of the best recent work in this tradition examines the history of the progessive intelligentsia at the turn of the last century. James Kloppenberg's *Uncertain Victory* (1986) and Daniel Rodgers's *Atlantic Crossings* (1998) – two magisterial studies of progressive and social-democratic intellectuals on both sides of the Atlantic – Robert B. Westbrook's *John Dewey and American Democracy* (1991), George Cotkin's *William James, Public Philosopher* (1990), Thomas Haskell's work on professionalism and social science, Dorothy Ross's *The Origins of American Social Science* (1991), and Hollinger's writings are all examples of contextualist scholarship on pragmatist and progressive ideas. Each author has set particular works and figures in the context of a discursive community preoccupied with questions of democracy, civic life, and American exceptionalism. Likewise, one of the most influential recent books on historical objectivity, *Telling the Truth about History*, by Joyce Appleby, Lynn Hunt, and Margaret Jacob (1994), uses the precedent of the pragmatist search for a position "beyond objectivism and relativism" in its defense of the practices of an open scholarly community.

Such historians have come under fire in the last two decades from poststructuralist scholars who charge the contextualists with a reductionist approach to historical texts. In an important debate with Kloppenberg in the pages of the *Intellectual History Newsletter*, European intellectual historian Dominick LaCapra charged the contextualists with imposing "closure" on interpretation, and of "lumping" texts together, at the expense of the close reading demanded by contemporary literary theory (LaCapra 1988). David Harlan has seconded LaCapra's critique in his stinging polemic, *The Degradation of American History* (1997). "The contextualist (or historicist) imperative that has dominated intellectual and literary history for the past thirty years," Harlan charges, "has become an elaborate mechanism for reducing complex texts to the status of documents. It is essentially a restraining apparatus, a device designed to shackle the text, to restrict and repress its suggestive powers while the historian cuts it open to examine its historical origins" (Harlan 1997: 192). For Harlan, intellectual history remains a dialogical inquiry in which scholars should acknowledge the contemporary interests they bring to their reading of works from the past: "*Our* questions, derived from *our* needs, couched in *our* terms" (ibid. 30). Harlan endorses the deliberately presentist orientation of John Patrick Diggins's work on Thorstein

Veblen, and of Hayden White's excavations of the literary tropes at work in historical writing, as examples of the historian's "right to fool around with the past, to assemble its materials in whatever impromptu configuration seems to work at the moment" (ibid. 88).

Harlan's critics have contended that he would align historical writing too closely to cultural criticism, in the manner of Richard Rorty and Stanley Fish, and that his objections to the neo-pragmatism of the contextualists caricatures their epistemological position as a covert objectivism. Unlike their counterparts in European history, historians of modern American intellectual history have largely kept their distance from the textualism of the poststructuralists. Few works of scholarship in the United States have followed the historiographic lead of LaCapra and Harlan. Yet even contextualists have given more attention to language and literary interpretation in recent years, with context itself understood increasingly as formed by the deployment of particular language, rhetorics, and literary conventions. The work of neo-Marxist cultural theorists such as Raymond Williams, Pierre Bourdieu, and Frederic Jameson has left its imprint on much current scholarship.

Neo-Marxist theory has likewise impelled the cultural studies movement, which began in Britain in the 1960s and has since inspired new programs throughout the United States. Although much work in cultural studies is preoccupied with the politics of popular culture, Andrew Ross and Bruce Robbins have written about the social position of intellectuals from a perspective that contradicts many of the assumptions of the modern intelligentsia and its historians. Writing in the 1960s, Hofstadter and Lasch kept alive a discourse about the public responsibility of intellectuals that once produced symposia in the *Partisan Review* and other journals of opinion. Such concerns continue to inspire the writings of Thomas Bender, Russell Jacoby, and Cornel West, among others, who seek to revivify the civic mission of generalist intellectuals through a combination of history and criticism. Cultural studies scholars, by contrast, have drawn on Foucault and Bourdieu in their critiques of the very idea of a generalist intellectual, arguing that such a conception is complicit with an Enlightenment ideological project that marginalizes difference and dissent in the service of a false universalism. In this view, intellectuals compete with other social actors in the pursuit of public authority or "cultural capital"; hence the persistent condemnation by modern intellectuals of "mass" and "middlebrow" culture.

The differences between intellectual historians and cultural studies scholars were evident in a 1996 symposium in the *IHN* on "Intellectual History in the Age of Cultural Studies." That exchange, however, has done little to change the positions of scholars on either side of this divide. One possible explanation may be the fundamentally different approaches the two groups take to the idea of culture itself. Whereas many, if not all, intellectual historians remain committed to an inquiry that combines reconstruction of the past with a recovery of the moral, political, and intellectual resources of texts for contemporary debate, the cultural studies movement views cultural production and reception as a terrain of struggle between different social groups. The historical study of intellectual culture, from this perspective, is part of a larger project of identifying how race, class, and gender fracture the "cultural field." This is not to say that there have been no efforts to bring together such approaches. Joan Shelley Rubin's history of middlebrow culture (1992) and Michael Denning's book on the 1930s "cultural front" (1996), however different in approach, both give full weight to the dual role of intellectuals as civic actors and arbiters of cultural taste.

The debates between textualists and contextualists, the challenges of social history and cultural studies, and the ongoing concern with the social position of intellectuals have more recently invigorated scholarship that crosses the boundaries between intellectual and expressive culture, often by way of work on the history of cultural criticism. In many respects, such work represents a renewal of the original American Studies project – now informed by more recent theoretical developments – and an elaboration in the US context of the landmark work of Carl Schorske on art and ideas in *fin de siècle* Vienna. Casey Nelson Blake, Rochelle Gurstein, Michael Kammen, and Joan Shelley Rubin have written books on modern cultural criticism that have reconstructed the historical relationship between the modern intelligentsia and new developments in the arts. In literary studies, Andrew Delbanco, David Reynolds, and Ross Posnock have taken the lead in reconstructing the moral, political, and philosophical settings for contacts between leading American literary figures and other intellectuals. Scholars of American women have also worked at the intersection of literary and intellectual history, particularly in the nineteenth century, when sentimental fiction and advice literature often served as the primary vehicles of expression for women intellectuals. Here, Mary Kelley's *Private Woman, Public Stage* (1984) is an exemplary work of how literary analysis, collective biography, and the history of gender ideology may open up fictional texts for insights into the intellectual contradictions that plagued the lives and works of a generation of women writers. Examining a dozen of the most popular "literary domestics" of the mid-nineteenth century, Kelley's study explores how the writing of sentimental novels both enabled women to break with prevailing understandings of women's sphere and reinforced those understandings. Such women largely wrote in secret, under pseudonyms, and thus inhabited "divided selves" – private women working on the public stage of literary culture – that could never be reconciled.

Literary culture is not the only site of artistic endeavor that has attracted the interest of intellectual historians. Heirs to the pioneering work of Neil Harris on the artist in American society, Daniel Belgrad and Richard Candida Smith are among a growing group of scholars conversant with the history of the visual arts who have demonstrated how visual culture has functioned both as an object of intellectual discourse (in art theory and criticism) and as a vehicle for the elaboration of ideas about self, culture, and place. Their work finds a resonance in new scholarship by art historians that examines artists and art objects in specific ideological settings: Alan Wallach's work on Thomas Cole (Cole 1994), Angela Miller's work on nationalism and nineteenth-century landscape painting (1993), Andrew Hemingway's history of the 1930s artistic left (2002), and Michael Leja's study of Abstract Expressionism (1993) are leading examples of this strain in art-historical writing. New work on the history of dance, music, theater, and other artistic genres follows a similar pattern.

Culturalist approaches have helped transform intellectual history, broadening its scope of study and deepening practitioners' understanding of the complexity of interpreting texts and contexts from the past. By the same token, intellectual history has remade other branches of historical scholarship and much of the humanities besides. Literary scholars, art historians, and philosophers have all taken historicist and contextualist turns that demand approaches to the history of ideas and ideology that intellectual historians often recognize and find congenial. Political, social, and diplomatic historians increasingly ask questions about meaning and interpretation that once preoccupied intellectual historians alone. Perhaps it is time to speak of an "intellectualist turn" in all the humanities. After decades of isolation, scholars in the field might well have reason to boast: we are all intellectual historians now.

REFERENCES

Appleby, Joyce O., Hunt, Lynn, & Jacob, Margaret: *Telling the Truth about History* (New York: W. W. Norton, 1994).

Belgrad, Daniel: *The Culture of Spontaneity: Improvisation and the Arts in Postwar America* (Chicago: University of Chicago Press, 1998).

Bercovitch, Sacvan: *The American Jeremiad* (Madison: University of Wisconsin Press, 1978).

Blake, Casey Nelson et al.: "Intellectual History in the Age of Cultural Studies," *Intellectual History Newsletter* 18 (1996), 3–69.

Bloch, Ruth H.: *Gender and Morality in Anglo-American Culture, 1650–1800* (Berkeley: University of California Press, 2003).

Borus, Daniel H.: *Writing Realism: Howells, James, and Norris in the Mass Market* (Chapel Hill: University of North Carolina Press, 1989).

Cmiel, Kenneth: *Democratic Eloquence: The Fight over Popular Speech in Nineteenth-century America* (New York: William Morrow, 1990).

Cohen, Nancy: *Reconstruction of American Liberalism, 1865–1914* (Chapel Hill: University of North Carolina Press, 2002).

Cole, Thomas: *Landscape into History*, ed. William H. Truettner and Alan Wallach (New Haven, CT: Yale University Press; Washington, DC: National Museum of American Art, Smithsonian Institution, 1994).

Cotkin, George: *William James, Public Philosopher* (Baltimore, MD: Johns Hopkins University Press, 1990).

Davis, David Brion: *The Problem of Slavery in the Age of Revolution, 1770–1823* (Ithaca, NY: Cornell University Press, 1975).

Denning, Michael: *The Cultural Front: The Laboring of American Culture in the Twentieth Century* (New York: Verso, 1996).

Ferguson, Robert A.: *Law and Letters in American Culture* (Cambridge, MA: Harvard University Press, 1984).

Ferguson, Robert A.: *The American Enlightenment, 1750–1820* (Cambridge, MA: Harvard University Press, 1997).

Fink, Leon: *Progressive Intellectuals and the Dilemmas of Democratic Commitment* (Cambridge, MA: Harvard University Press, 1997).

Fliegelman, Jay: *Declaring Independence: Jefferson, Natural Language, and the Culture of Performance* (Stanford, CA: Stanford University Press, 1993).

Foner, Eric: *Tom Paine and Revolutionary America* (New York: Oxford University Press, 1976).

Fox, Richard Wightman: *Trials of Intimacy: Love and Loss in the Beecher–Tilton Scandal* (Chicago: University of Chicago Press, 1999).

Glaude, Eddie S., Jr.: *Exodus! Religion, Race, and Nation in Early Nineteenth-Century Black America* (Chicago: University of Chicago Press, 2000).

Hall, David D.: *Worlds of Wonder, Days of Judgment: Popular Religious Belief in Early New England* (New York: Alfred A. Knopf, 1989).

Halttunen, Karen: *Murder Most Foul: The Killer and the Gothic Imagination* (Cambridge, MA: Harvard University Press, 1998).

Harlan, David: *The Degradation of American History* (Chicago: University of Chicago Press, 1997).

Hemingway, Andrew: *Artists on the Left: American Artists and the Communist Movement, 1926–1956* (New Haven, CT: Yale University Press, 2002).

Higham, John & Conkin, Paul K., eds.: *New Directions in American Intellectual History* (Baltimore, MD: Johns Hopkins University Press, 1979).

Hofstadter, Richard: *Anti-Intellectualism in American Life* (New York: Alfred A. Knopf, 1963).

Hollinger, David A.: *In the American Province: Studies in the History and Historiography of Ideas* (Bloomington: Indiana University Press, 1985).

Hughes, H. Stuart: *Consciousness and Society: The Reorientation of European Social Thought, 1890–1930* (New York: Alfred A. Knopf, 1958).

Kelley, Mary: *Private Woman, Public Stage: Literary Domesticity in Nineteenth-Century America* (New York: Oxford University Press, 1984).

Kloppenberg, James T.: *Uncertain Victory: Social Democracy and Progressivism in European and American Thought, 1870–1920* (New York: Oxford University Press, 1986).

Kloppenberg, James T.: "Deconstruction and Hermeneutic Strategies for Intellectual History: The Recent Work of Dominick LaCapra and David Hollinger," *Intellectual History Newsletter* 9 (1987), 3–22.

LaCapra, Dominick: "Of Lumpers and Readers," *Intellectual History Newsletter* 10 (1988), 3–10.

Lasch, Christopher: *The New Radicalism in America, 1889–1963: The Intellectual as a Social Type* (New York: Alfred A. Knopf, 1965).

Lears, T. J. Jackson: *No Place of Grace: Antimodernism and the Transformation of American Culture, 1880–1920* (New York: Pantheon, 1981).

Leja, Michael: *Reframing Abstract Expressionism: Subjectivity and Painting in the 1940s* (New Haven, CT: Yale University Press, 1993).

Lewis, David Levering: *W. E. B. Du Bois – Biography of a Race, 1868–1919* (New York: Holt, 1963).

Livingston, James: *Pragmatism and the Political Economy of Cultural Revolution, 1850–1940* (Chapel Hill: University of North Carolina Press, 1994).

Livingston, James: *Pragmatism, Feminism, and Democracy: Rethinking the Politics of American History* (New York: Routledge, 2001).

May, Henry: *The End of American Innocence: A Study of the First Years of Our Own Time, 1912–1917* (New York: Alfred A. Knopf, 1959).

Meranze, Michael: *Laboratories of Virtue: Punishment, Revolution, and Authority in Philadelphia, 1760–1835* (Chapel Hill: University of North Carolina Press, 1996).

Miller, Angela L.: *The Empire of the Eye: Landscape Representation and American Cultural Politics, 1825–1875* (Ithaca, NY: Cornell University Press, 1993).

Rodgers, Daniel T.: *Atlantic Crossings: Social Politics in a Progressive Age* (Cambridge, MA: Harvard University Press, 1998).

Rosenberg, Rosalind: *Beyond Separate Spheres: The Intellectual Roots of Modern Feminism* (New Haven, CT: Yale University Press, 1982).

Ross, Andrew: *No Respect: Intellectuals and Popular Culture* (New York: Routledge, 1989).

Ross, Dorothy: *The Origins of American Social Science* (Cambridge and New York: Cambridge University Press, 1991).

Rubin, Joan Shelley: *The Making of Middlebrow Culture* (Chapel Hill: University of North Carolina Press, 1992).

Sklar, Kathryn Kish: *Florence Kelley and the Nation's Work: The Rise of Women's Political Culture, 1830–1900* (New Haven, CT: Yale University Press, 1995).

Trachtenberg, Alan: *The Incorporation of America: Culture and Society in the Gilded Age* (New York: Hill & Wang, 1982).

Waldstreicher, David: *In the Midst of Perpetual Fetes: The Making of American Nationalism, 1776–1820* (Chapel Hill: University of North Carolina Press, 1997).

Warner, Michael: *The Letters of the Republic: Publication and the Public Sphere in Eighteenth-Century America* (Cambridge, MA: Harvard University Press, 1990).

Westbrook, Robert B.: *John Dewey and American Democracy* (Ithaca, NY: Cornell University Press, 1991).

Westbrook, Robert B.: *Why We Fought: Forging American Obligations in World War II* (Washington, DC: Smithsonian Institution Press, 2004).

White, Morton: *Social Thought in America: The Revolt against Formalism* (New York: Viking, 1949).

Williams, Raymond: *Culture and Society, 1780–1950* (New York: Columbia University Press, 1958).

Chapter Twenty-Seven

THE IMPACT OF THE CULTURE CONCEPT ON SOCIAL HISTORY

Lawrence B. Glickman

When practitioners of the "new cultural history" proclaimed the birth of the field in the late 1980s, they were quick to distinguish their methods, sources, and goals from those of the "new social history," which had been the major scholarly trend in history writing and the biggest growth area of the profession for the previous two decades. These new cultural historians were not just challenging, and occasionally rejecting, the techniques of their predecessors. They were also marking a turn in their own scholarship; for in many cases the new social history was the approach in which they had trained and written their first scholarship. As is often the case when a new frame-work is being developed, the new cultural historians emphasized the contrasts rather than similarities between their approaches and those of social history, promising that a radically different methodological and interpretive metric would govern their schol-arship. Where the new social history drew on Marxism, sociology, and the Annales school, the new cultural historians found their inspiration in literary theory, anthro-pology, and postmodern social theory. Where social historians described themselves as "listening" to the previously unheard inarticulate people in their quest to write history "from the bottom up," new cultural historians preferred the metaphor of "reading" cultures as texts. Where new social historians used extensive quantitative evidence to ascertain reality, cultural historians, influenced by the literary methods of deconstruction, highlighted the instability of texts and their multiplicity of meanings, and promoted a more freewheeling, boldly interpretative style. Where social historians aimed to recover unknown and ordinary lives, cultural historians sought to expose not just the ordinary but the unusual, the "other" against which the mainstream defined itself. Rather than responding to the explanatory question of "why," new cultural historians claimed to be more interested in the process of "how," and often embraced narrative history, a mode which had been famously rejected by many social historians. Where new social historians stressed deeds and actions, new cultural history preferred to focus on the linguistically inflected topics of memory, discourse, and representation. Where the paradigmatic genre of social history was the commu-nity study, cultural historians preferred what came to be called micro-history, the close analysis of an unknown life story, a symbolic incident, or an event. Finally, where new social historians emphasized the material world as the driving force of history, new cultural historians stressed the ways in which culture both informed the experience of peoples, groups, and nations and also played a constitutive role in creating that experience in the first place.

Self-proclaimed new cultural historians also aimed to distinguish themselves from an older style of cultural history, one that, unlike social history, was widely seen as old-fashioned. Understanding culture as, in Matthew Arnold's famous definition, "the best that has been thought or said," the older form of cultural history focused almost exclusively on high culture: painting, music, literature, and the theater. The new cultural historians, inspired by anthropology and the burgeoning field of cultural studies, preferred to understand culture as more democratic, popular, and all-encompassing. Furthermore, these culturally oriented historians understood culture not only as a noun, a thing that one took in occasionally, like an opera or a movie, but also as a verb, an activity that shaped groups of people even as it gave them resources to participate in the broader society.

Whereas the new cultural history has held firm in its rejection of older forms of cultural history, the distinction between cultural and social history, as they are currently practiced, is murkier. Despite the initial declarations of independence and difference, over the last decade social and cultural history have to a large degree converged. Over time, social historians have adopted many of the approaches recommended by cultural historians. Similarly, cultural historians have increasingly come to recognize something that was apparent from the outset: many of the roots of the cultural approach lay in the methods of the new social history.

From the beginning, even the most ardent proponents of the need for social historians to turn to cultural history recognized that "culture" was not absent from the new social history, which, after all, posited that understanding anonymous people meant understanding their daily lives, values, and beliefs. In *The Making of the English Working Class* (1963), perhaps the most influential English-language work of the new social history, E. P. Thompson famously proclaimed that the class experience had to be understood in "cultural terms," which he defined rather broadly as "value-systems, ideas, and institutional forms" (Thompson 1963: 10). Indeed, the centerpiece of the new social history was explorations of, variously, "working-class culture," "black culture," "slave culture," or "middle-class culture," often defined in a Thompsonian vein. Even though Thompson insisted that culture emerged from the experience of class relations, some Marxist critics denounced what they saw as the dangerous trend of "culturalism" in the new social history of Thompson and his many followers, a too-ready willingness to take culture seriously on its own terms. Critics of social history often singled out what they took to be its overemphasis on culture, which they complained was treated as if it operated independently of economics and power relations.

Thus, the new cultural history did not mark the kind of irrevocable break with new social history that, a generation earlier, new social historians had made with traditional political history or with the older forms of cultural history. Rather than the divorce, which many scholars foresaw, social history and cultural history have developed a productive, if occasionally acrimonious, marriage. Many articles in a forum on the state of the field in the Spring 2003 *Journal of Social History*, for example, treated social and cultural history as allies rather than adversaries. Institutionally, social history may appear to have the upper hand in this marriage. While periodicals such as the *Journal of Social History*, *Social History*, and the *International Review of*

Social History remain prominent, no *Journal of Cultural History* has emerged. Yet the dearth of journals specifically devoted to the subject should not be taken as proof of subordination. Nor have the ongoing criticisms of cultural history as overly speculative stopped its growth, or slowed the adoption of its methods. Indeed, one reason why social history is difficult to distinguish from cultural history is that many social historians have adopted the techniques and approaches of cultural history. The new cultural history may not have displaced social history, but it has nonetheless fundamentally altered the ways in which all history, especially social history, is written. Success, not failure, is the chief reason why cultural history has not developed the institutions of social history; it does not need them. New social historians needed their own journals because editors of the mainstream journals refused to publish their scholarship. New cultural history, notwithstanding continued resistance to its methods and claims, has rapidly made its mark in a wide variety of scholarly venues, many of them mainstream.

One way to track how the culture concept has transformed social history is to examine the recent output of scholars whose early work was in the tradition of the new social history, but who have subsequently modified their approaches. For example, in *A Shopkeeper's Millennium: Society and Revivals in Rochester, New York, 1815–1837* (2004 [1978]), a self-conscious and highly successful example of the new social history, Paul E. Johnson examined his topic largely through a variety of ingenious quantitative analyses. Johnson's unit of analysis, like much of the new social history, was the community study. His first chapter was on "Economy," suggesting that the economic base shaped the battles over culture traced in his book, which highlighted individuals only to the extent that they were representative of a group (the new middle-class elite drawn to evangelism, or the proletarianizing working class). By contrast, Johnson's more recent *Sam Patch, the Famous Jumper* (2003) is a micro-history. It focuses on one person rather than a community. Johnson employs many of the same techniques he used in his previous work to uncover the life of Patch, who was an obscure textile worker for most of his life: census, court, and church records. And Johnson suggests that Patch's precarious economic life as a member of one of America's first proletarianized families shaped his later development. But Johnson's *Sam Patch* is less the product of the author's "listening" – Sam Patch did not leave much information about his life, and the only statement attributed to him is drawn from a newspaperman's paraphrase – than the product of his vigorous "reading" of the meaning of Patch's life, by showing how it fitted into contemporary debates about popular amusements, aesthetics, and celebrity. Similarly, Shane White's first book, *Somewhat More Independent: The End of Slavery in New York City, 1770–1810* (1991), uses classic social history methods to explore the largely neglected topic of slavery and emancipation in the North. By contrast, his later work, including *Stylin': African American Expressive Culture from its Beginnings to the Zoot Suit* (White & White 1999) and *Stories of Freedom in Black New York* (2002), focuses on a fleeting African American theater company, African American clothing, and African American song and speech patterns, using material, aural, and visual culture to flesh out the meaning of slavery and emancipation in the North. Many other examples of social historians turned cultural historians could be adduced.

As the evolution of the work of Johnson and White suggests, while cultural history has developed a distinctive agenda, its approaches are not unrelated to the abiding concerns of social history. However, these approaches are not easily summarized and cultural historians, notwithstanding their bold agenda-setting announcements in the 1980s, have been far less successful at writing the kind of programmatic statements of what their approach means than were the new social historians. Peter Burke's admirable catalog of the various methods and emphases does not succinctly answer the question posed in his title, *What is Cultural History?* (2004). Burke is certainly correct in suggesting that no single moniker could symbolize a concept as multivalent as culture and a field as diverse as cultural history. Yet we can note some important, and generally shared, characteristics of social history after the cultural turn. One perhaps surprising emphasis of this style of history has been politics. This is surprising because new social historians were as a rule far more explicit about characterizing their field as a political endeavor than have been most cultural historians. Many advocates of social history described it as an historical offshoot of New Left politics; history "from the bottom up" was to many a corollary of participatory democracy. Yet, in part because of their reaction against the then-dominant style of political history, most social historians de-emphasized politics in favor of a focus on communities, families, and the triumvirate of concerns made famous by social history: race, class, and gender. Although social historians never accepted the view of their critics that social history amounted to "history with the politics left out," it is fair to observe that they understood themselves to be highlighting dimensions of the historical experience that lay beyond politics. To use the language of the pioneering French social historian Fernand Braudel, they sought to unearth the deep structures (of demography, geography, and culture) that underlay the "noise of mere events" that he, and many other social historians, understood politics to be.

Indeed, some steadfast social historians criticized the cultural turn in the scholarship of the eminent French historian Joan Scott – another former social historian, whose first book was a community study of French artisans – claiming that her emphasis on language and her postmodern theoretical apparatus led to a denial or undervaluation of the real experience of class oppression. These social historians feared what Bryan Palmer labeled an apolitical "descent into discourse" (Palmer 1990). For Palmer, discourse was subordinate to power, especially class oppression, and to the real engine of history, namely, historical materialism. (It is indicative of the confusion of labels that Palmer addressed his target as "social history" rather than cultural history; but clearly the main culprit, in his view, was the turn, among Scott and other self-described new cultural historians, toward understanding language and culture as driving forces of history.) Some social historians also feared that the small canvas of the micro-historical approach favored by cultural historians would leave little room for political interpretation; others worried that in the narrative approach storytelling would replace analysis.

The study of culture, especially the emphasis on language, has opened new understandings of politics. Culturally minded social historians have included politics itself in their definition of culture. Indeed, some of the pioneering works of the new cultural history, including Lynn Hunt's influential *Politics, Class and Culture in the French Revolution* (1984), were written by new social historians interested in what they called "political culture." In Hunt's work, for example, rather than addressing the question of *why* the French Revolution happened, she explored *how* it happened, by examining the revolutionaries' cultural attempts to remake the nation. In the political-culture approach, scholars like Hunt have examined canonical topics, often extensively treated in the political history literature, from cultural perspectives and with new questions, and in so doing helped revive the history of politics. This interest manifested itself in two related ways: some historians have emphasized culture as politics, while others, turning this formulation upside down, have stressed politics as culture – how economics, diplomacy, and foreign affairs operate culturally. Lauren Sklaroff, using the culture-as-politics approach, has suggested that the World War II-era struggle for representational civil rights, an effort to promote more positive, and less stereotypical, images of African Americans in popular culture at a time when political civil rights gains were stalemated by southern Democrats, was a politically significant effort (Sklaroff 2002). Noting that empire "requires stories as well as guns," Mary Renda's examination of US imperialism in Haiti, using the politics-as-culture approach, seeks to show not only that American control of Haiti was a cultural process (in which images of Haiti were recorded and imagined in theater, film, song, and soldiers' letters) and a military process involving violence and control, but that the cultural and military aspects could not be understood separately (Renda 2001). Lizabeth Cohen has argued that the development of postwar American consumer society (characterized by single-family suburban homes, shopping malls, and mass consumption) was an integral and intended outcome of a political project promoted by a set of elites who consciously sought to make America a "consumers' republic" (Cohen 2003). Perhaps the most ambitious attempt to reframe a canonical political event through the lens of social–cultural history is T. H. Breen's reinterpretation of the causes of the American Revolution. Breen's careful analysis of consumption patterns in colonial America, his use of business records, probate inventories, and material culture, bear the mark of the new social history. His discussion of the meaning of those patterns, and how they gave rise to political protest, especially the new political tool of the boycott, demonstrates the influence of the new cultural history (Breen 2004).

Cultural historians have made the study of category creation a key aspect of their political analysis. As Robert Allen has written, "power is expressed through ordination: that is, by attempting to regulate through the arrangement of things in ranks and orders – what is high, what is low; what is us, what is them" (1992: 34). In this conception, discourse, far from being distinct from politics (as Bryan Palmer and others saw it), actively shapes power relations. The keywords invoked by cultural historians imply that understanding how people, events, and even nations are represented, or represent themselves, is a political enterprise. Cultural historians employ words such as *construction, making, invention*, terms that suggest that a crucial political strategy of cultural history is *denaturalization* – taking what is thought to be natural, biological, and permanent and showing it be socially and culturally constructed. Although this emphasis on language and representation may seem to be far afield from the concerns of social history, the best of these works demonstrate the social historian's insight that discourse cannot be understood apart from experience. Lawrence W. Levine, for example, has argued that nineteenth-century theater audiences were as heterogeneous as the performances they witnessed. He has argued that "highbrow" culture – a sacralized form of entertainment that was to be appreciated passively and largely by audiences segregated by class – as well as its other, "lowbrow" culture, was not an age-old category but a social construction of the late nineteenth century (Levine 1988). George Chauncey's 1994 study of the development of a "gay male world" in New York City demonstrates, among other things, that homosexuality as a category of personhood is a relatively recent development, contingent on the invention of heterosexuality. Scott Sandage (2005) has shown that business success was partly created in the negative by the invention of a new sort of person, the failure, a concept that previously applied to businesses and not people.

New cultural historians not only study what ordinary people did but take seriously what and how they thought, felt, and even imagined. Social historians had been less interested in the thought of their protagonists than in their actions, for the recorded thoughts of individuals expressed in literary sources, such as diaries, letters, and fiction, were dismissed for being unrepresentative (a pejorative term for social scientists seeking replicability and precision). Robin Kelley's study of what he calls the "black radical imagination" (2002) focuses on a variety of utopian visions, on the theory that understanding how people dreamed tells us something significant about their worldview and culture. Helen Lefkowitz Horowitz (2002) has examined the competing ways in which Americans learned about sexuality, imagined how it operated, and circulated their ideas in genres ranging from tawdry exposés in the newly developed "sporting press" to scientific essays to pornography. For working-class women, according to Nan Enstad (1999), the search for pleasure in popular culture – through developing distinct fashions, reading dime novels, and attending movies – did not detract from their politics. Rather, these forms of consumer culture enabled them to "imagine recognition and value as workers" and as women, and made possible solidarity and resistance. By taking seriously not just the deeds but the thoughts of ordinary people, cultural historians have provided a framework beyond the material world in which to contextualize their activities.

In the hands of culturally minded social historians, narrative history has proven to be a powerful way of conveying complex meanings. When the narrative form was revived in the early 1980s, many social historians condemned the narrative approach as mere storytelling, the opposite of the analytical exposure of power relations that they claimed their method produced. As with many other aspects of the new cultural history, the roots of this analytically rich narrative approach can be found in many classic works of the new social history. For example, Leon Litwack's *Been in the Storm So Long: The Aftermath of Slavery* (1979) used the stories of ex-slaves and ex-masters to examine the experience of emancipation from many points of view. In the best works of the new narrative history, as in James Goodman's *Stories of Scottsboro* (1994), analysis and storytelling are interwoven into a seamless whole; through the careful choice of stories, they show rather than tell. Moreover, cultural historians have argued that there is nothing innocent or natural about narrative history; like all forms of history, it is constructed. As Goodman wrote, "I decided whose stories to tell and how to tell them. I chose central themes and some of the contexts in which I would like them to be understood. I decided who should have the first word, and who should have the last. I imposed order . . . out of the always seamless, often chaotic, flow of consciousness and experience" (Goodman 1994: xiii). Narrative, then, is both a mode of writing history and a means of interpreting it. By treating language as a cultural production, historians pay more attention not only to the stories they tell but to those they choose not to tell and to those that their subjects themselves tell, and the narratives in which they are enmeshed. They do not merely listen to and record these stories, although this is part of their task. They also contextualize and deconstruct such stories. Goodman, for example, shows how his protagonists' actions as well as their explanations of those actions can only be understood in the context of the narrative worldview they inhabited.

Drawing on the pioneering ethnography of Clifford Geertz, cultural historians have similarly interpreted events as texts that, properly interpreted, help to explain American culture. These events range from the famous (Paul Revere's ride) to the obscure (now-forgotten crazes, such as for the burlesque troupe, the "British Blondes"), and include performances (like Sam Patch's waterfall leaps), sensations (for example, the new sounds and sights of cities), and activities (including sexual acts like those discussed by Chauncey). As the French cultural historian Robert Darnton has written, "one can read a ritual or a city, just as one can read a folktale or a philosophic text" (Darnton 1984: 5). Reading events as texts requires what Geertz called "thick description," that is, a careful and theoretically informed examination of the meaning of an event or performance. Robert Allen's analysis of the rise and fall of burlesque (1992), a close reading of an influential 1868 burlesque show and its aftermath, proceeds on the assumption that this reading can only be persuasive in the context of shifts in gender relations, the behavior of theater audiences, and popular modes of amusement, giving the reader the literacy, as it were, to understand why this event set off so much outcry and disagreement about its meaning. Another example of this approach can be found in James Cook's interpretation of what he calls "the arts of deception" in nineteenth-century America (Cook 2001). In his study Cook interprets the meanings of events such as P. T. Barnum's traveling display of a woman purported to be the 161-year-old former slave of George Washington's father, the phenomenon of an "automaton chess-player," and other displays designed not so much to trick the viewer but to leave the viewer confused as to whether he or she had been tricked – and enjoying that confusion. Unlike Geertz's unitary interpretation of what the cockfight meant to the Balinese, Cook and other cultural historians have stressed the diversity of meanings and the divergent readings of such performances.

The political capaciousness of the culture concept in social–cultural history can also be seen in the emphasis on consumption in recent scholarship. The initial turn among social historians toward the study of leisure, especially working-class recreation, was met with some skepticism. In a critique of trends in the social history of leisure in the late 1970s, the prominent British historian Gareth Stedman Jones, himself an early advocate of linguistic explanations of history, declared, "The primary point of a holiday is not political; it is to enjoy yourself for tomorrow you must work" (1983: 89). Social historians continued to discuss leisure, but, paying close heed to the critiques of Stedman Jones and others, they often framed these discussions around questions of whether the popularity of American mass culture hindered the development of American socialism. With the cultural turn, however, historians, no longer bound by a Marxist framework that privileged production, began to explore consumption and leisure, not necessarily as subordinate to productive relations, but as areas with their own culture and politics worth exploring. Lizabeth Cohen's pioneering study of industrial workers in Chicago, *Making a New Deal* (1990), demonstrated that the new working-class solidarity of the New Deal era was as much a product of connections that workers and their families made as shoppers and consumers of mass culture as it was of workplace organizing. Workers' experiences with mass culture, in Cohen's telling, helped to make the pre-eminent political bloc of the twentieth century, the New Deal.

Although the history of consumer culture began with studies of what workers did away from the factory, new histories have felt less need to subordinate consumption to production or even to tether one to the other. As with other areas, cultural historians of consumption have sought to find politics where it had been presumed to be absent. Drawing on the burgeoning field of "cultural studies," some historians examined the ways in which individuals have used mass culture as a mode of expression and sometimes even subversion. Treating people as producers and not just consumers of culture, including mass culture, has enabled scholars to apply agency, one of the favored concepts of the new social history, to leisure time. Kathy Peiss's *Cheap Amusements* (1986) argued that single, working-class women in New York City were not merely, or even primarily, victims of the new heterosocial culture of the dance hall, amusement park, and movie theater but were actively creating new identities through an immersion in this culture. The trend, well anticipated by the works of Peiss and Cohen, has been toward an understanding of consumption that rejects a model of manipulation. Like the cultural turn of which it is a part, consumption has become a perspective through which almost any historical topic – from protest, to artistic expression, to aesthetics, to business – can profitably be examined.

Social historians have generally applauded the cultural transformation of their approach. At the same time, they, and even many self-described cultural historians, continue to point to pitfalls associated with the cultural turn. Peter Burke has warned of the dangers of what he calls "impressionism," a mode of history that can become anecdotal, in which a flashy reading of a small number of perhaps atypical sources replaces the hard work of actually collecting a persuasive database (Burke 2004). Other critics have charged that cultural historians' quest for the history of the "other" has led them to undervalue interrogating the "normal." Despite taking the cultural turn himself, Paul E. Johnson has expressed discomfort with new modes of history that analyze "nothing but middle-class psyches, feelings, imaginations, and interior decoration. Too much recent scholarly literature has chosen that alternative" (2004: xvii).

Despite these misgivings, there is wide acknowledgment that the culture concept has given new life to social history. If the new cultural history has proven to be less than a complete break from social history, it has provided a new way of looking at old questions and a framework for asking new questions and finding new topics, a transformation described by Peter Burke as "from the social history of culture to the cultural history of society" (2004: 75). At the dawn of the new social history in the early 1960s, the British historian E. H. Carr wrote that "the more sociological history becomes, and the more historical sociology becomes, the better for both" (Carr 1961: 84). At the dawn of the new cultural history in the late 1980s, Lynn Hunt revised Carr for the new era: "the more cultural historical studies become and the more historical cultural studies become, the better for both" (1989: 1, 24). Today, perhaps the best prospect for both social and cultural history is a continued convergence. Or, to put it in Carr's and Hunt's terms, the more social history becomes cultural and the more cultural history becomes social the better for both.

REFERENCES

Allen, Robert: *Horrible Prettiness: Burlesque and American Culture* (Chapel Hill: University of North Carolina Press, 1992).

Breen, T. H.: *The Marketplace of Revolution: How Consumer Politics Shaped American Independence* (New York: Oxford University Press, 2004).

Burke, Peter: *What is Cultural History?* (Cambridge: Polity, 2004).

Carr, E. H.: *What is History?* (New York: Random House, 1961).

Chauncey, George: *Gay New York: Gender, Urban Culture and the Making of a Gay Male World, 1890–1940* (New York: Basic Books, 1994).

Cohen, Lizabeth: *Making a New Deal: Industrial Workers in Chicago* (New York: Cambridge University Press, 1990).

Cohen, Lizabeth: *A Consumers' Republic: The Politics of Mass Consumption in Postwar America* (New York: Alfred A. Knopf, 2003).

Cook, James W.: *The Arts of Deception: Playing with Fraud in the Age of Barnum* (Cambridge, MA: Harvard University Press, 2001).

Cronon, William: "A Place for Stories: Nature, History, and Narrative," *Journal of American History* 78 (March 1992), 1347–76.

Darnton, Robert: *The Great Cat Massacre: And Other Episodes in French Cultural History* (New York: Basic Books, 1984).

Enstad, Nan: *Ladies of Labor, Girls of Adventure: Working Women, Popular Culture, and Labor Politics at the Turn of the Century* (New York: Columbia University Press, 1999).

Goodman, James: *Stories of Scottsboro* (New York: Vintage, 1994).

Higginbotham, Evelyn Brooks: *Righteous Discontent: The Women's Movement in the Black Baptist Church, 1880–1920* (Cambridge, MA: Harvard University Press, 1993).

Horowitz, Helen Lefkowitz: *Rereading Sex: Battles over Sexual Knowledge and Suppression in Nineteenth-Century America* (New York: Alfred A. Knopf, 2002).

Hunt, Lynn: *Politics, Class and Culture in the French Revolution* (Berkeley: University of California Press, 1984).

Hunt, Lynn, ed.: *The New Cultural History* (Berkeley: University of California Press, 1989).

Johnson, Paul E.: *Sam Patch, the Famous Jumper* (New York: Hill & Wang, 2003).

Johnson, Paul E.: *A Shopkeeper's Millennium: Society and Revivals in Rochester, New York, 1815–1837*, 25th anniversary edition (New York: Hill & Wang, 2004 [1978]).

Kelley, Robin D. G.: "We Are Not What We Seem: Rethinking Black Working-Class Opposition in the Jim Crow South," *Journal of American History* 80 (June 1993), 75–112.

Kelley, Robin D. G.: *Freedom Dreams: The Black Radical Imagination* (Boston, MA: Beacon Press, 2002).

Levine, Lawrence W.: *Highbrow/Lowbrow: The Emergence of Cultural Hierarchy in America* (Cambridge, MA: Harvard University Press, 1988).

Litwack, Leon F.: *Been in the Storm So Long: The Aftermath of Slavery* (New York: Alfred A. Knopf, 1979).

Palmer, Bryan D.: *Descent into Discourse: The Reification of Language and the Writing of Social History* (Philadelphia, PA: Temple University Press, 1990).

Peiss, Kathy: *Cheap Amusements: Working Women and Leisure in Turn-of-the-Century New York* (Philadelphia, PA: Temple University Press, 1986).

Renda, Mary: *Taking Haiti: Military Occupation and the Culture of US Imperialism, 1915–1940* (Chapel Hill: University of North Carolina Press, 2001).

Sandage, Scott A.: *Born Losers: A History of Failure in America* (Cambridge, MA: Harvard University Press, 2005).

Sklaroff, Lauren Rebecca: "Constructing G.I. Joe Louis: Cultural Solutions to the 'Negro Problem' during World War II," *Journal of American History* 89 (December 2002), 958–83.

Stedman Jones, Gareth: *Languages of Class: Studies in English Working Class History, 1832–1982* (Cambridge: Cambridge University Press, 1983).

Thompson, E. P.: *The Making of the English Working Class* (New York: Alfred A. Knopf, 1963).

White, Shane: *Somewhat More Independent: The End of Slavery in New York City, 1770–1810* (Athens: University of Georgia Press, 1991).

White, Shane & White, Graham: *Stylin': African American Expressive Culture from Its Beginnings to the Zoot Suit* (Ithaca, NY: Cornell University Press, 1999).

White, Shane: *Stories of Freedom in Black New York* (Cambridge, MA: Harvard University Press, 2002).

Zakim, Michael: *Ready-Made Democracy: A History of Men's Dress in the American Republic, 1760–1860* (Chicago: University of Chicago Press, 2003).

Chapter Twenty-Eight

RELIGIOUS HISTORY AND THE CULTURAL TURN

Leigh E. Schmidt

The cultural historian Inga Clendinnen turns a tiny theft of a tinier *Lantana* blossom into a transgression of Augustinian proportions in her memoir *Tiger's Eye* (2001). It was not the shrub's owner that concerned her, but instead, "it was God I was worried about." "The first time I tried, with my heart thumping and my stomach shaking and His great mad eye glaring full at me," she related in a chapter of fugitive child-hood memories,

> I couldn't do it. But the next time I did it almost without thinking – my hand just floated out, nipped off a flower, it was in my pocket, I was out the gate and home free . . . And nothing happened. My hand didn't wither, nobody found out, nothing bad happened at all. That's when I found out what I'd always suspected, that God was a fraud. So that was the end of Him, and of sin. (Clendinnen 2001: 50–1)

If Clendinnen got a feel for "ethnographic history" anywhere in her childhood, it was from "tickling trout" in the Wye River, not from holding religion close (ibid. 75).

Cultural historians have long had a fondness for the vignette, for the evocation of complex social and mental worlds out of the meticulously observed episode, gesture, rite, or breach. It would not be hard to interpret the ease with which the young Clendinnen slipped away from God and sin as a parable about the new cultural history's relationship to religious history. Rhys Isaac, a colleague of Inga Clendinnen's in that esteemed circle of cultural historians known as the Melbourne Group, had opened his heralded and crucially formative work on *The Transformation of Virginia, 1740–1790* (1982) with a disavowal. Even though "themes of religion" were the "main thread of continuity" in his book, make no mistake about this: "The intention has been neither to write religious history nor to present the story of a church" (Isaac 1982: 6). Even when they were ostensibly studying religion, the new cultural historians apparently had far more important tasks at hand than doing religious history. After all, when Raymond Williams, one of the primary signalers of the cultural turn, was setting out his generative list of *Keywords* in 1976, "culture" and "history" were definitely among them, as were "class," "art," "sex," and "democracy." Even though worship (the Latin *cultus*) was one piece of Williams's genealogy of the culture concept, "religion" itself did not make an appearance as an entry (Williams 1985 [1976]: 87). Was not the study of "culture" already vulnerable enough to the charge of being off base, given to poetic flights too far removed from socioeconomic structures and power relations? Why take the added intellectual risk of embracing the always-suspected fraud, religion?

As tempting as it may be to turn Clendinnen's tale of thievery into another fable of secular drift (religion gets nipped in the bud yet again), it is a temptation best resisted – not least because of the considerable attention that Clendinnen, Isaac, and the *éminence grise* of the Melbourne Group, Greg Dening, a former Jesuit, ended up paying religion in their historical work. The much-vaunted marriage of history and anthropology, a disciplinary coupling largely responsible for the emergence of the new cultural history, often had another consort in Religious Studies. True, from the perspective of the central courtship – say, of anthropologist Clifford Geertz and historian Robert Darnton – Religious Studies may have seemed more voyeur than partner, more observer than participant. Still, it hardly takes any deep archaeological digging to unearth the ways in which the study of religion was a fundamental part of this convergence of history and anthropology and the larger formation of the new cultural history.

When Lynn Hunt took the pulse of the field in her edited collection *The New Cultural History* (1989), the book was dedicated to Natalie Zemon Davis, a celebrated historian of early modern France, as font of inspiration for the movement from social to cultural history. Davis's work is also an appropriate starting point for exploring the initial intertwining of religious and cultural history, since she helped lead the way in making religion a central preoccupation in the cross-disciplinary exchange between history and anthropology. Her critical reorientation of inquiry was especially apparent in two regards: (1) the turn from religious institutions to religious cultures, from a high-culture view of religion to one far more attuned to the semiotics of popular culture; (2) the shift from clerical theology to cultural performance, from the written word to the ritual gesture. Accenting "religion as practised and experienced and not merely as defined and prescribed," Davis construed "popular religion" as a "religious culture" – a relational domain in which pastors and laity, clerics and crowds, interacted, collaborated, jostled, and contended (Davis 1982: 322). In those emphases Davis had many fellow travelers in early modern European cultural history, but her work was especially influential in moving religious history in the direction of cultural anthropology's deciphering of symbolic processes. Public ritual and popular religion – whether found in the carnival, the charivari, the confraternity, or the feast of Corpus Christi – had become central nodes of scholarly investigation by the early 1980s.

The cultural turn in the field of European history was soon felt in the domain of American religious history. One of the key markers of that trend was Jon Butler's prognostication of the field's future in 1985. Butler's essay expressly pointed American historians to the scholarship on early modern Europe for new models and methods for interpreting American religion and culture. Butler shared much of the wider enthusiasm for the study of popular religion and lay piety, but he did so more as a matter of "religious sociology" than cultural history (Butler 1985: 169). With at least one foot still firmly planted in the new social history of the 1960s and 1970s, Butler looked more toward a demographic rather than an ethnographic history of religious practice. Whereas most cultural historians, including Rhys Isaac, were placing a new emphasis on interpreting the dense meanings of ritual actions, Butler accentuated French statistical measures of participation in religious practices, especially the sacraments, as an important guide to questions of Christianization and de-Christianization. That kind of problematic, especially explaining the shift from thinly churched British colonies to a more heavily churched nineteenth-century nation, proved crucial to Butler's agenda. The relative failure of ecclesiastical establishments in the colonies also served as an opening for Butler to stress the importance of turning scholarly attention to the realms of popular religion, notably magic, astrology, healing, and life-cycle rituals. That research program came to fruition in Butler's *Awash in a Sea of Faith: Christianizing the American People* (1990).

If Butler himself still fell as much into line with the new social history as the emergent cultural history, other scholars would soon complete the transition. The bellwether in this regard was the scholarship of David D. Hall, the primary intermediary between American religious history and the early modern European cultural history of Natalie Davis, Peter Burke, Roger Chartier, Carlo Ginzburg, John Bossy, and Robert Scribner, among others. Hall's *Worlds of Wonder, Days of Judgment* (1989) became the benchmark of that dynamic exchange. With "no quantitative way of measuring commitment," Hall pursued the more elusive quarry of popular religious mentalities and everyday habits of devotion (Hall 1989: 17). Moving beyond "the spare meetinghouses of New England," beyond "sermons and the sacraments," Hall probed the social experience of religion in all its quotidian perceptions, subtle gestures, and familial desires (ibid. 17). Religion, as Hall defined it, "comprehends a range of actions and beliefs far greater than those described in a catechism or occurring within sacred space: it was a loosely bounded set of symbols and motifs that gave significance to rites of passage and life crises, that infused everyday events with the presence of the supernatural" (ibid. 18). With that formulation in mind, Hall blurred the distinction between religion and magic as well as the social and the religious; he emphasized the fluid negotiations between pastors and people of the import of performing – or refusing to perform – prescribed religious practices. Seventeenth-century New Englanders inhabited a compound world of wonders in which Christian apocalypticism, ghost lore, ancient meteorology, demonology, natural history, and tales of tormenting apostasy all commingled.

The marriage of religious and cultural history in the 1980s, which Hall's work especially exemplified, begat various lines of inquiry. Certainly, the attention to "popular religion" has remained strong, though that categorization has often mutated into the notion of "lived religion" since the mid-1990s. An artificial distinction between high and low, elite and vernacular, had always dogged the construct of "popular religion," even when those employing it were zealous to emphasize the negotiated terrain between pastors and people, the back-and-forth appropriations and adjustments within religious cultures. Hence Hall, among others, began using "lived religion" as "a shorthand phrase" for a historical anthropology of religion that attempted expressly to bypass the standard cultural oppositions that seemed inevitably present, however much denied, in studies of "popular religion" (Hall 1997: vii). That shift of nomenclature, though widely accepted now, does not represent a fundamental reorientation of the cultural history of American religion. The attention to lived religion is another way of emphasizing the everyday practices, popular mentalities, and multivalent symbols that constitute the cultural materials of American religious history. In many ways, it represents variations on the themes that Hall had made central to the historiography in *Worlds of Wonder, Days of Judgment*.

Notwithstanding the smooth transition from studies of popular religion to those of lived religion, there are certainly wrinkles and seams in the motley garment that cultural and ethnographic approaches to religious history have produced. The scholarship of Robert Anthony Orsi embodies this historiography's subtler textures. Orsi's first book, *The Madonna of 115th Street: Faith and Community in Italian Harlem, 1880–1950*, appeared in 1985 (with a new edition issued in 2002). Like Butler's work, Orsi's early research was poised between the new social history and the emergent cultural history. On the one hand, he was writing a social history of the immigrant experience: the settlement patterns of urban neighborhoods, the ongoing relationship to the homeland, the socioeconomic conditions of labor, the structures of the family, and the pressures around endogamy. On the other hand, he was constructing a fine-grained ethnographic history of Italian Harlem through close attention to popular ritual and celebration, the July festival dedicated to Our Lady of Mount Carmel. As an exploration of popular Marian devotion, Orsi's work moved well beyond the walls of the church, ranging through the varied activities of the streets and moving into the intimacies of the home. Riveting his attention on gender – especially the relationship between power and powerlessness for women within the family dramas of Italian Harlem – Orsi produced a work of disturbing insight into the entrapping, masochistic, penitential worlds of Christian practice. An absolutely formative work in the cultural history of American religion, *The Madonna of 115th Street* stands as a classic in this domain of scholarship.

Orsi struck similar chords in his next book, *Thank You, St. Jude: Women's Devotion to the Patron Saint of Hopeless Causes* (1996). Offering a densely contextualized history of prayer among twentieth-century American Catholic women, Orsi again explored the overlapping issues of power, agency, and gender in Christian devotionalism. In his approach Orsi blended close attention to popular religious literature (such as the *Voice of St. Jude* and *Ave Maria*) with ethnographic interviews, explicitly positioning his work at the intersection of history and cultural anthropology. Locating the rise of the cult of St. Jude in the matrices of economic change, the enduring effects of war, the travails of family life, and the nationalizing of Catholic devotional culture, Orsi imagined "the social history of praying" as inescapably connected to "the social history of hopelessness" (Orsi 1996: 49). "Women's prayers to Jude," he observes,

> were situated precisely at the point where personal, intimate experience intersected with the greater impersonal forces of history under way outside the door. Jude was called on at those moments when the effects and implications of changing historical circumstances . . . were directly and unavoidably experienced within the self and family, in women's relationships and responsibilities, and in their bodies.   (Orsi 1996: 49)

To the extent that women gain agency through the devotion, they do so, in Orsi's terms, through a charged, vulnerable, loving relationship to St. Jude, participating in "a discipline of disclosure" that opens up alternatives to the official disciplines of clerics, doctors, husbands, and bosses (ibid. 137). But, there is no romance of resistance here, since it is a mark of Orsi's subtlety (not to say perversity) that whatever reimagining of social and religious power the devout achieve is always cycled back through Christian discourses of sacrifice, resignation, submission, and dependency.

In his most recent book, *Between Heaven and Earth: The Religious Worlds People Make and the Scholars Who Study Them* (2005), Orsi has continued to recast the study of religious history in terms of relational dynamics – in the intricacies of family romances and tragedies, in the loving and yet sometimes cruel bonds that join the saints in heaven to their earthbound devotees. Here, as in his previous books, Orsi unbottles the anger, sorrow, sacrifice, and fortitude of twentieth-century American Catholic life: Jesus, Mary, the saints, and guardian angels remain the familiar, still unpredictable, companions in everyday struggles with illness, betrayal, resentment, submission, loss, and hope. These figures, in Orsi's understanding, do not provide the faithful so much with meaning or order (a swipe at long-standing symbolic and functionalist interpretations of religion). Instead, these invisible beings interact with the devout with all the psychological ambiguities of caprice and compassion, punishment and protection, that their immense power affords. Also, in this latest contribution, Orsi explicitly moves beyond the intersubjectivities of Catholic devotionalism to comment on the study of religion as an academic enterprise across the board. He effectively identifies two sets of relationships as his animating concerns: first, theorizing the divine–human relationship between religious practitioners and special beings; and, second, assessing the research relationship between the scholar and the religious subjects he or she studies. Given such emphases, *Between Heaven and Earth* now moves Orsi beyond the cultural history of American religion into the cultural history of the study of religion *tout court*. That added element in Orsi's most recent work is indicative of how histories of the critical terms by which religion has been categorized in academic and more popular discourses are now emerging alongside histories of the culture concept and other keywords.

Orsi's scholarship epitomizes much of the field's development over the last quarter-century as religious history has interacted with cultural history and moved from the study of popular religion to lived religion. But these generative cross-disciplinary exchanges have yielded other kinds of fruit as well, particularly in the realm of material culture studies. A standard in that area is Colleen McDannell's *Material Christianity: Religion and Popular Culture in America* (1995). Having worked previously on the Christian materialization of Victorian domesticity, McDannell set out to map the broader world of sacred stuff, the artifacts of American religious life from the monuments of the nineteenth-century rural cemetery to the T-shirt fashions of twentieth-century Christian retailing. More concerned with unpacking case studies than creating a historical narrative, McDannell convincingly critiqued the long-term marginalization of material religion through the combined apparatus of Protestant theology, anthropological categorizations of the sacred and the profane, and modernist aesthetics that dismissed the kitsch of mass culture. Her work served to foreground the material practices of religion – the landscape, architecture, souvenirs, statuary, garments, and healing objects of faith. In that endeavor McDannell has shared in the wider imagining of the material history of American religion with such scholars as Gretchen Buggeln, Paul Gutjahr, Jenna Weisman Joselit, David Morgan, Thomas Tweed, Judith Weisenfeld, Peter Williams, and Diane Winston, among others. Materializing religion, giving it flesh and sensuous complexity, remains very much a central ambition of those writing the cultural history of American religion. R. Marie Griffith's recent recovery of the evangelical and New Thought body in *Born Again Bodies: Flesh and Spirit in American Christianity* (2004) is an excellent example of these ongoing trends.

If material culture studies represent one of the now crucial intersections between religious history and cultural history, another close ally is visual culture studies. McDannell's own most recent work, *Picturing Faith: Photography and the Great Depression* (2004), pushes in that direction, but it is an area of inquiry that has especially benefited from the addition of art history as a disciplinary conversation partner. Two scholars, David Morgan and Sally M. Promey, have been especially instrumental in facilitating this exchange. Their jointly edited collection, *The Visual Culture of American Religions* (2001), is the premier source for surveying the terrain of that growing cross-disciplinary enterprise, and each of them has also made significant monographic contributions in this area. Promey's *Painting Religion in Public: John Singer Sargent's Triumph of Religion at the Boston Public Library* (1999) is a model of art history doubling (or tripling) as cultural and religious history. Seeing Sargent's grand work at the Boston Public Library as a visual commentary on the politics and imagined privacy of religion at the turn of the twentieth century, Promey explores through the conflicts over Sargent's artistic designs the paradoxes of the public display of a spiritualized and interiorized faith. While Morgan has been particularly interested in theorizing the creation and reception of popular religious art, he has also produced sustained historical accounts of the visual dimensions of American religion. Particularly notable in that regard is his *Protestants and Pictures: Religion, Visual Culture, and the Age of American Mass Production* (1999).

Scholars of material and visual religion do not like to moralize – or, when they do, they prefer to moralize against all the moralizing (Protestant and highbrow) that made popular religious art, sacred souvenirs, treasured relics, and shrine replicas seem banal at best and idolatrous at worst. Another strand of recent religious and cultural history has been less squeamish about – though sometimes equally suspicious of – the Protestant and civic republican discourses that make the ethical dimensions of a consumer culture an inescapable concern. The conundrums of simplicity and luxury, self-sacrifice and self-realization, modesty and display are deep-seated cultural dilemmas, and it has been well-nigh impossible to study the commercial revolution and the rise of a consumer culture without considering such moral and religious puzzles.

Richard Wightman Fox and T. J. Jackson Lears led the way with their edited collection of essays on *The Culture of Consumption* in 1983. Lears's own piece in that volume, "From Salvation to Self-Realization: Advertising and the Therapeutic Roots of the Consumer Culture, 1880–1930," made especially clear how important religion was within the struggles over the revised ethics of abundance. Lears had already explored the cultural yearnings for premodern simplicity and enchantment in *No Place of Grace: Antimodernism and the Transformation of American Culture, 1880–1920* (1981), but in this follow-up essay he especially stressed the religious quandaries that the ascendant culture of consumption produced. Focusing on the advertising leader Bruce Barton, a minister's son, who promoted both heady consumption and therapeutic faith, Lears dissected Barton's unease: "Sometimes clinging to older bourgeois values, sometimes doubting the worth of his own vocation, Barton yearned for transcendent meaning even as his profession corroded it" (Fox & Lears 1983: 30). And yet, for all Barton's inner turmoil, there remained little doubt that he was part of a much larger retailoring of Protestant Christianity "to fit the sleek new corporate system" (ibid. 31).

That sort of critical account of consumer capitalism's cooptation of Christianity carried considerable sway among cultural historians of American religion. It was mirrored, for example, in Susan Curtis's *A Consuming Faith: The Social Gospel and Modern American Culture* (1991); it had a parallel in Richard L. Bushman's account of how dreams of genteel consumption corrupted evangelical simplicity in *The Refinement of America: Persons, Houses, Cities* (1992); and it echoed in William Leach's lament of the full-scale secularization of the good life in *Land of Desire: Merchants, Power, and the Rise of a New American Culture* (1993). In turn, the narrative of secularization through commerce and consumption was, to some degree at least, disrupted by R. Laurence Moore's *Selling God: American Religion in the Marketplace of Culture* (1994), Leigh E. Schmidt's *Consumer Rites: The Buying and Selling of American Holidays* (1995), and Diane Winston's *Red-Hot and Righteous: The Urban Religion of the Salvation Army* (1999).

As important as the ethical quandaries posed by the consumer culture have been to American religious and cultural history, they pale before the moral predicaments of race. Albert J. Raboteau's *Slave Religion: The "Invisible Institution" in the Antebellum South* (1978), recently rereleased in a 25th anniversary edition, was of decisive importance in spurring greater attention to African American religion under slavery. Since then, the intersection of race, religion, and culture has become one of the most active and vibrant in American religious history. That vitality is evident across a vast spectrum: from Jon F. Sensbach's surprisingly rich accounts of Afro-Moravian Christianity in colonial North Carolina and the larger Atlantic world to scintillating studies of the twentieth-century exchange among religion, social reform, and civil rights. The latter include John T. McGreevy's *Parish Boundaries: The Catholic Encounter with Race in the Twentieth-Century Urban North* (1996), Charles Marsh's *God's Long Summer: Stories of Faith and Civil Rights* (1997), Patricia A. Schechter's *Ida B. Wells-Barnett and American Reform, 1880–1930* (2001), and David L. Chappell's *A Stone of Hope: Prophetic Religion and the Death of Jim Crow* (2004). Critical as well to this ferment has been the focal attention paid to the role of women in African American church life. Leading examples include Evelyn Brooks Higginbotham's *Righteous Discontent: The Women's Movement in the Black Baptist Church, 1880–1920* (1993) and Judith Weisenfeld's *African American Women and Christian Activism: New York's Black YWCA, 1905–1945* (1997).

In the last decade studies of religion and race have increasingly pushed in directions beyond African American Christianity, especially taking up topics in the borderlands of the Southwest. An exemplar of that variegated historiography is Linda Gordon's *The Great Arizona Orphan Abduction* (1999). Displaying the consummate gifts of a cultural historian in unpacking a densely charged vignette, Gordon takes up an episode of racial and religious conflict in the copper-mining towns of Clifton and Morenci, Arizona, in 1904. Caught in a tangle of Mexican–Anglo and Protestant–Catholic antagonism were 40 Irish Catholic orphans sent from the New York Foundling Hospital by the Sisters of Charity for adoption by Mexican Catholic families. The prospect of these "white" orphans being taken into Mexican homes scandalized a group of local Anglo-Protestants, who orchestrated the forcible removal of the orphans from the arms of the adopting families and successfully fought for control of the children in the courts. In many ways, "race trumps religion" in this local episode of white vigilantism; as Gordon writes, "The western pioneering project was racial. And nothing was more racial than the cause of protecting and saving children" (Gordon 1999: 71, 198). Yet, as she also observes, it is nearly impossible "to sever 'race' from religion in America," and the construction of whiteness and brownness in this case also built on underlying Protestant assumptions about Catholics as racially other (ibid. 198). Beyond Gordon's wonderfully revealing microhistory, the possible directions to pursue in these contact zones cover a very wide terrain indeed. Take just two highly disparate examples: Ramón A. Gutiérrez's *When Jesus Came, the Corn Mothers Went Away: Marriage, Sexuality, and Power in New Mexico, 1500–1846* (1991) and Thomas S. Bremer's *Blessed with Tourists: The Borderlands of Religion and Tourism in San Antonio* (2004).

A few years before the appearance of Inga Clendinnen's memoir, Greg Dening, a longtime colleague of hers in the Melbourne Group, had stepped back to offer his own autobiographical meditations in *Performances* (1996). Trained to the priesthood, Dening spent 22 years with the Jesuits before leaving the order, never quite content with "the replacement of the love of family and friends with 'charity'" (Dening 1996: 11). Unlike Clendinnen, who easily slipped away from religion as a child only to revisit it as a cultural historian of sixteenth-century Mexico, Dening finds himself enwrapped in Ignatian spiritual practices from the age of 16 forward. It is in Loyola's *Exercises* that Dening discerns some clue to his own academic ambitions as historian and anthropologist. The effort to focus the mind through the contemplative technique of the Composition of Place – the full engagement of the imagination in the work of remembering, the application of all the senses, and the re-presentation of a dramatic narrative in the mind's eye – was an appropriate intellectual preparation. "To make a Composition of Place," Dening remarks, "required some sort of ethnography. . . . I felt and would feel ever more strongly that to write the history of men and women one has to compose them in place and in their present-participled experience" (ibid. 16–17). Dening's personal observation about the training of his own mind, body, and spirit suggests the possibility of a religious history of cultural history itself. Is it mere coincidence – or meaningful providence – that two other founding figures in this mode of cultural inquiry were also Jesuits, Walter Ong and Michel de Certeau?

In "Soliloquy in San Giacamo," the last piece in *Performances*, Dening discusses his own experiences at a mass in Bellagio long after he has left the priesthood. Distracted by "my twisted anthropology" – "all the cultures in my head confuse me" – Dening nonetheless concludes:

The thousands of these communions in my life, for all their scruples and their arithmetic, have been sweet. Not mystic, I think, but sometimes moments of discernment, of cleared vision, occasionally even of a little breathless love. Why should I laugh at that? Why should I turn it upside down and say it is the effect of something else? Of deluded ambitions? Of subliminal class and sex? I have said to myself and anybody who would ask, that I would like to describe religious experience as it is, not in terms of something else. (Dening 1996: 272)

In that insistence, as in so much of his work, Dening, an unrivaled historical ethnographer of the eighteenth- and nineteenth-century Pacific, makes religion itself a keyword for cultural history. His colleague Rhys Isaac, to whom Dening actually dedicates *Performances*, may have contorted himself to avoid religious history's embrace at the outset of *The Transformation of Virginia*, and certainly in that denial Isaac has always had plenty of company in cultural history and cultural studies – all those who imagine religion's disappearance into race or sexuality, gender or class, art or politics, science or medicine. But, there is no need for any chips on any shoulders: Religious history has been integral to the cultural turn from the get-go and is still shaping many of the bends and curves now being navigated in American cultural history.

REFERENCES

Bremer, Thomas S.: *Blessed with Tourists: The Borderlands of Religion and Tourism in San Antonio* (Chapel Hill: University of North Carolina Press, 2004).

Bushman, Richard L.: *The Refinement of America: Persons, Houses, Cities* (New York: Alfred A. Knopf, 1992).

Butler, Jon: "The Future of American Religious History: Prospectus, Agenda, Transatlantic 'Problematique,'" *William and Mary Quarterly* 42 (1985), 167–83.

Butler, Jon: *Awash in a Sea of Faith: Christianizing the American People* (Cambridge, MA: Harvard University Press, 1990).

Chappell, David L.: *A Stone of Hope: Prophetic Religion and the Death of Jim Crow* (Chapel Hill: University of North Carolina Press, 2004).

Clendinnen, Inga: "Ways to the Sacred: Reconstructing 'Religion' in Sixteenth Century Mexico," *History and Anthropology* 5 (1990), 105–41.

Clendinnen, Inga: *Tiger's Eye: A Memoir* (New York: Charles Scribner's, 2001).

Curtis, Susan: *A Consuming Faith: The Social Gospel and Modern American Culture* (Baltimore, MD: Johns Hopkins University Press, 1991).

Davis, Natalie Zemon: "Some Tasks and Themes in the Study of Popular Religion," in Charles Trinkaus & Heiko A. Oberman, eds., *The Pursuit of Holiness in Late Medieval and Renaissance Religion* (Leiden: Brill, 1974), pp. 307–36.

Davis, Natalie Zemon: "From 'Popular Religion' to Religious Cultures," in Steven Ozment, ed., *Reformation Europe: A Research Guide* (St. Louis: Center for Reformation Research, 1982), pp. 321–41.

Dening, Greg: *Performances* (Chicago: University of Chicago Press, 1996).

Fox, Richard Wightman & Lears, T. J. Jackson, eds.: *The Culture of Consumption: Critical Essays in American History, 1880–1980* (New York: Pantheon, 1983).

Goff, Philip & Harvey, Paul, eds.: *Themes in Religion and American Culture* (Chapel Hill: University of North Carolina Press, 2004).

Gordon, Linda: *The Great Arizona Orphan Abduction* (Cambridge, MA: Harvard University Press, 1999).

Griffith, R. Marie: *Born Again Bodies: Flesh and Spirit in American Christianity* (Berkeley: University of California Press, 2004).

Gutiérrez, Ramón A.: *When Jesus Came, The Corn Mothers Went Away: Marriage, Sexuality, and Power in New Mexico, 1500–1846* (Stanford, CA: Stanford University Press, 1991).

Hall, David D.: *Worlds of Wonder, Days of Judgment: Popular Religious Belief in Early New England* (New York: Alfred A. Knopf, 1989).

Hall, David D., ed.: *Lived Religion in America: Toward a History of Practice* (Princeton, NJ: Princeton University Press, 1997).

Higginbotham, Evelyn Brooks: *Righteous Discontent: The Women's Movement in the Black Baptist Church, 1880–1920* (Cambridge, MA: Harvard University Press, 1993).

Hunt, Lynn, ed.: *The New Cultural History* (Berkeley: University of California Press, 1989).

Isaac, Rhys: *The Transformation of Virginia, 1740–1790* (Chapel Hill: University of North Carolina Press, 1982).

Leach, William R.: *Land of Desire: Merchants, Power, and the Rise of a New American Culture* (New York: Pantheon, 1993).

Lears, T. J. Jackson: *No Place of Grace: Antimodernism and the Transformation of American Culture, 1880–1920* (New York: Pantheon, 1981).

Marsh, Charles: *God's Long Summer: Stories of Faith and Civil Rights* (Princeton, NJ: Princeton University Press, 1997).

McDannell, Colleen: *Material Christianity: Religion and Popular Culture in America* (New Haven, CT: Yale University Press, 1995).

McDannell, Colleen: *Picturing Faith: Photography and the Great Depression* (New Haven, CT: Yale University Press, 2004).

McGreevy, John T.: *Parish Boundaries: The Catholic Encounter with Race in the Twentieth-Century Urban North* (Chicago: University of Chicago Press, 1996).

Moore, R. Laurence: *Selling God: American Religion in the Marketplace of Culture* (New York: Oxford University Press, 1994).

Morgan, David: *Protestants and Pictures: Religion, Visual Culture, and the Age of American Mass Production* (New York: Oxford University Press, 1999).

Morgan, David & Promey, Sally M., eds.: *The Visual Culture of American Religions* (Berkeley: University of California Press, 2001).

Orsi, Robert A.: *Thank You, St. Jude: Women's Devotion to the Patron Saint of Hopeless Causes* (New Haven, CT: Yale University Press, 1996).

Orsi, Robert Anthony: *The Madonna of 115th Street: Faith and Community in Italian Harlem, 1880–1950* (1985; New Haven, CT: Yale University Press, 2002).

Orsi, Robert A.: *Between Heaven and Earth: The Religious Worlds People Make and the Scholars Who Study Them* (Princeton, NJ: Princeton University Press, 2005).

Promey, Sally M.: *Painting Religion in Public: John Singer Sargent's Triumph of Religion at the Boston Public Library* (Princeton, NJ: Princeton University Press, 1999).

Raboteau, Albert J.: *Slave Religion: The "Invisible Institution" in the Antebellum South* (New York: Oxford University Press, 1978).

Schechter, Patricia A.: *Ida B. Wells-Barnett and American Reform, 1880–1930* (Chapel Hill: University of North Carolina Press, 2001).

Schmidt, Leigh E.: *Consumer Rites: The Buying and Selling of American Holidays* (Princeton, NJ: Princeton University Press, 1995).

Stout, Harry S. & Hart, D. G., eds.: *New Directions in American Religious History* (New York: Oxford University Press, 1997).

Tweed, Thomas, ed.: *Retelling US Religious History* (Berkeley: University of California Press, 1997).

Weisenfeld, Judith: *African American Women and Christian Activism* (Cambridge, MA: Harvard University Press, 1997).

Williams, Raymond: *Keywords: A Vocabulary of Culture and Society* (New York: Oxford University Press, 1985 [1976]).

Winston, Diane: *Red-Hot and Righteous: The Urban Religion of the Salvation Army* (Cambridge, MA: Harvard University Press, 1999).

Chapter Twenty-Nine

POLITICAL HISTORY AND THE TOOL OF CULTURE

Joanne B. Freeman

In the last few decades of the twentieth century, political history suffered something of an identity crisis. Politics, as traditionally defined, seemed out of place in a largely social-history-defined world. During the 1960s and 1970s, social historians transformed the historical landscape, restoring or adding long-ignored populations to the historical narrative and revealing the ground-level realities of their everyday lives. To be sure, the "new political history" played a role in this historical enterprise, using quantifiable data to trace patterns in voting and party membership. But such topics as political policy, the Constitution, and state building were peripheral concerns, when considered at all. As a result, the 1980s and 1990s gave rise to a series of grave pronouncements about the decline and impending death of political history. As Eric Foner wrote, in an edited volume on recent trends in historical scholarship, "The old 'presidential synthesis' – which understood the evolution of American society chiefly via presidential elections and administrations – is dead (and not lamented)" (Foner 1990: ix).

But, as Foner himself acknowledged in that same essay, the demise of the "old 'presidential synthesis' " did not mean the end of political history. Rather, it signaled the rise of a new, more broadly defined understanding of politics that reenergized the field. In essence, over the course of the 1980s and 1990s, political historians redefined "politics" guided by the tool of culture. Influenced by social history's interest in the culture of the masses, political historians gradually shifted their focus to what came to be called "political culture." Social history gave voice and influence to non-elite populations: ethnic groups, women, slaves, and the working class. The study of culture, applied to politics, showed these groups operating within a larger political framework; it emphasized the social *meaning* of political interaction as well as its patterns. This cultural turn focused on the human dimension of the quantifiable world of the "new political history," exploring the values, motives, and understandings that guided and shaped political interaction.

Of course, the study of political culture was not born in the 1980s, nor did it originate with historians. Despite the many ways in which historians have embraced it, the modern concept of political culture dates back to Cold War-era political scientists and their efforts to understand political systems (and thereby combat the threat of communism). Seminal works such as *The Civic Culture: Political Attitudes and*

Democracy in Five Nations (1963) by Gabriel A. Almond and Sidney Verba studied "the political culture of democracy" in the hope of spreading the "democratic model of the participatory state" to emerging nations (Almond & Verba 1963: 1, 3). According to Verba's definition, political culture was "the system of empirical beliefs, expressive symbols, and values which defines the situation in which political action takes place" (Pye & Verba 1965). But by researching matters as abstract and change-able as political attitudes using quantifiable data taken from polls, such works ulti-mately raised grave doubts about the possibility of quantifying culture. Doubting its usefulness, political scientists moved away from the concept of political culture, but political historians readily adopted it, defining it more broadly to encompass a complex web of ideas, beliefs, values, assumptions, and rituals related to public life. The work of anthropologist Clifford Geertz played a vital role in this methodological transition. Suggesting that "man is an animal suspended in webs of significance he himself has spun" (Geertz 1973: 5), Geertz argued that the study of humankind should be impressionistic and interpretative rather than grounded on scientific mea-surement. Many political historians followed this lead, just as they did Geertz's pre-scriptions about the value of "thick description": examining a single ritual or event in great detail to get at larger cultural patterns or understandings.

Geertzian logic is apparent in two seminal studies of political culture: Jean H. Baker's *Affairs of Party: The Political Culture of Northern Democrats in the Mid-Nineteenth Century* (1983) and Lynn Hunt's *Politics, Culture, and Class in the French Revolution* (1984); Baker also adopted Verba's definition of political culture as her working premise (Baker 1983: 12). In a sense, both works were a direct reaction against the new political history's quantitative, statistical bent. As Baker put it, "Given the data base available, I am convinced that the limits of such interpretation have been reached" (ibid. 11). Instead of focusing on what Baker called "social analysis," these works centered on questions of political language, behavior, and "style" (a term used by Baker). To describe an idea as potentially ambiguous as political style, both authors began their works by declaring what they were *not* attempting to do, thereby sketching the bounds of "conventional" political history as well. Baker declared that she was writing neither an "event-filled party narrative nor an investigation of the ethnic, religious, and economic background of mid-century Democrats" (ibid. 11). Hunt made an even bolder pronouncement, explaining that "although the subject of this book is politics, there is little in it about specific policies, politicians, partisan conflicts, formal institutions, or organizations" (Hunt 1984: 14).

Rather than studying formal political institutions and policies, these historians were interested in the *lived experience* of different populations in the realm of politics, as revealed by the study of culture. How did people experience politics? How did they learn their public roles? What customs, rituals, symbols, and rhetoric surrounded political behavior? How did education, urban living, or popular imagery shape politi-cal assumptions and habits? And how did these assumptions and behaviors shape the structure of politics itself? Baker explores these questions by examining the impact of such things as schooling and public ceremony on Democratic ideas and ideals. "Behind every set of Northern Democratic messages rested an accumulation of symbols and traditions," she writes, "a kind of switchboard on which languages, themes, and modes of expression connected belief and believer, past and present, perception and reality. Geertz calls this 'ideology as a culture system,' meaning a layer

of culture that fuses sentiments into significant belief systems" (Baker 1983: 147).
Along similar lines, Hunt studies such expressive forms as language, imagery, and
symbolism to get at "underlying patterns of political culture" that made possible the
appearance of new kinds of politicians and policies in revolutionary France (Hunt
1984: 14). These same few years saw several other major studies of political culture,
such as Daniel Walker Howe's *The Political Culture of the American Whigs* (1984)
and Ronald Formisano's *The Transformation of Political Culture: Massachusetts
Parties, 1790s–1840s* (1983), though each work defined the concept in subtly different ways. The fundamental assertion underlying these studies is that different populations experience political interaction in different ways, due to differences in their
values, assumptions, and beliefs, and that these beliefs in turn shape the nature of
formal politics. Get to the root of the culture of politics for a given population, and
it casts their "conventional" political interaction in an entirely new light. The result
was an outpouring of studies of political culture that continues to the present day.

In addition to its powerful influence on the study of politics generally, this focus
on language, habits, and *mentalités* reenergized the study of political ideology by
grounding it in a cultural context. One of the most noteworthy early scholars in this
field is Richard Hofstadter, whose interest in uncovering some sort of shared national
political culture led him to examine the link between politics and ideas in American
society, perhaps most notably in *The Paranoid Style in American Politics, and Other
Essays* (1965). By his own account, Hofstadter was interested in what he called
"the style of our political culture as a whole." The "paranoid style" was "a way of
seeing the world and of expressing oneself" – a good working definition of culture
as deployed by political historians in subsequent decades (Hofstadter 1965: 4).

Although Hofstadter's book was published too early to incorporate it, Bernard
Bailyn's *The Ideological Origins of the American Revolution* (1967) shared its logic.
By tracing the outlines of what would come to be known as political culture, Bailyn's
work had a seminal influence on early American history for generations to come.
Bailyn argued that the political rhetoric in Revolutionary-era pamphlets expressed an
underlying set of beliefs and assumptions that explained the origins of the American
Revolution. It was not unfair taxes but rather a conspiratorial mindset grounded in
a long-standing British intellectual tradition that ultimately escalated into an ideology
of revolution. Bailyn's next book, *The Origins of American Politics* (1968), focused
on this idea even more explicitly, beginning with a chapter entitled "Sources of Political Culture." Though Bailyn did not explicitly define "political culture" – nor indeed
did he even focus on the word "culture" – his exposure of this underlying network
of ideas and beliefs opened new realm of study for early American historians. Jack
P. Greene and Gordon S. Wood were early – and continuing – contributors to this
transformation in the understanding of early American politics. By his own account,
Greene made his first "serious foray into cultural history" in the 1960s, examining
colonial "identity formation" and its impact on the logic of revolution (Greene 1992:
xi). Wood, a Bailyn student, infused all of his work with his recognition of the shaping
influence of ideological attitudes and beliefs, perhaps most obviously in his essay,
"Conspiracy and the Paranoid Style: Causality and Deceit in the Eighteenth Century"
(1982). Cultural historian Michael Kammen, another Bailyn student, focused much
of his early scholarship on such topics as the meaning of colonization in American
Revolutionary thought; his later work addressed what one might call American

"constitutional culture" and the cultural significance of political language, images, and writings. Revolutionary America provided fertile ground for such studies for good reason. The American Revolution represented a period when political ideologies and nationalistic sentiments were evolving at a rapid rate in a distinctly self-conscious manner. Revolutions often bring accelerated political, social, and cultural changes in their wake, fostering a heightened self-consciousness about the structure of society and governance. In essence, creating a nation entails grappling with ideologies, making this period particularly inviting for the study of political culture.

Clearly, Bailyn was influenced by Geertz's 1964 essay, "Ideology as a Cultural System" (see Geertz 1973: 193–233). Particularly for historians of the American Revolution, Geertz's cultural grounding of ideologies was invaluable in their efforts to ground political events and ideas in a more encompassing social world; by giving shape and form to ideological constructs, Geertz sparked a methodological revolution in early American scholarship. As Daniel Rodgers observed in his 1992 article "Republicanism: the Career of a Concept," beginning in the 1960s, eighteenth-century political history was "suffused with references to Geertzian winks and twitches, cognitive road maps, and culturally constructed realities" for at least a decade. For political historians struggling to inform their work with the findings of social history, Geertz provided the right intellectual framework at the right time, enabling them to ground ideologies, ideas, and beliefs – concepts hovering on the edge of what one might define as "culture" – in social reality.

As suggested by the title of Rodgers's article, the concept of republicanism provides a good case study of the influence of culture on political history. As an explanatory concept, it accomplished a lot. Initially deployed in the study of early American politics, over time it raced its way across the entire American political narrative. Depending on who was writing, republicanism represented a shared tradition of political beliefs; a cultural construct shaping consumerism; an ideology that bound together the working class; or a political sensibility that defined roles for women in the new republic. Path-breaking studies explored labor republicanism, agrarian republicanism, radical republicanism, proto-Populist republicanism, and republican motherhood. A decade of scholarship seemed to prove that republicanism was everywhere – and herein lay a problem. What started out as a network of ideas advancing a revolution ultimately became something inherently "American." By seemingly explaining everything, the concept of republicanism ran the risk of explaining nothing. As Rodgers notes, "It was the investment of language and culture with coherence and social power that had made republicanism a historiographical concept to contend with. By 1990 the field was full of players of the republicanism game, tearing off in every conceivable direction. But the ball had all but disappeared" (Rodgers 1992: 37).

The rampant popularity of the concept of republicanism suggests the many ways in which the tool of culture has contributed to political history. It has expanded the political stage beyond polling places and legislatures, encompassing acts like attending a parade or wearing a cockade. Even for people who cannot vote, watching a parade march down the street on the Fourth of July can instill feelings of nationalism or inspire political activism. Such a realization is a reminder of an important insight that emerged from this scholarship (however obvious it may appear to us today): non-elite members of society have a vital political presence, political interests, and political sensibilities. They are political actors with their own language and logic, and not simply passive recipients of political ideas and ideals bestowed from on high. The 1990s saw an outburst of political studies centered on this concept of "the politics of the street," such as Simon Newman's aptly named *Parades and the Politics of the Street: Festive Culture in the Early American Republic* (1997), Len Travers's *Celebrating the Fourth: Independence Day and the Rites of Nationalism in the Early Republic* (1997), and David Waldstreicher's *In the Midst of Perpetual Fetes: The Making of American Nationalism, 1776–1820* (1997). By revealing the political influence of another non-elite population – newspaper printers – Jeffrey Pasley's *The Tyranny of Printers: Newspaper Politics in the Early American Republic* (2001) fits into this same rubric.

Along similar lines, the tool of culture has expanded the political population to include more than voters and politicians. Particularly in the area of gender studies, the study of political culture has had a powerful influence. The 1990s saw a series of major studies of women's political culture in the nineteenth- and twentieth-century United States, revealing distinct political subcultures characterized by forms of political participation that reach beyond voting. As historian Paula Baker explains in her 1990 article, "The Domestication of Politics: Women and American Political Society, 1780–1920," a broader understanding of politics as "any action, formal or informal, taken to affect the course or behavior of government or the community" brings together "the histories of women and politics" (P. Baker 1990: 56). Historians like Baker, Stephanie McCurry, and Kathryn Sklar revealed women expressing their political views and desires in voluntary associations and social reform, as well as in electoral rallies. In an early study of the political role of women, *Women of the Republic: Intellect and Ideology in Revolutionary America* (1980), Linda Kerber revealed the political dimensions of female domestic life in the early republic, creating the widely adopted concept of "Republican Motherhood," a particularly handy idea that bridged the gap between public and domestic life. The Republican Mother "integrated political values into her domestic life" by nurturing "public-spirited male citizens"; in essence, "the mother, and not the masses, came to be seen as the custodian of civic morality," contributing to the well-being of the republic through habits of childrearing (Kerber 1980: 11). To Kerber, this development reveals the inherent conservatism of the American Revolution. As with other seeming political outsiders, the extension of politics beyond the voting booth reveals the political dimensions of women's lives beyond the franchise.

Clearly, a culture-infused political history expands the definition of "politics." When understood to include ideas and habits from the lived experiences of people of all kinds, politics moves beyond elections and policy making, sometimes even beyond explicitly public acts. Reading a newspaper is not necessarily a public act; it can take place in the privacy of one's parlor, yet it links readers to a larger political public with shared political sensibilities, giving them a broader understanding of their partisan inclinations, their state, or their nation. Jürgen Habermas's *The Structure and Transformation of the Public Sphere: An Inquiry into a Category of Bourgeois Society* (1989) contributed much to this insight with its concept of a "public sphere" where people – women as well as men – join together to form a public, helped by the vehicle of the press; for Habermas, the public sphere links private concerns with public life. By envisioning a public, political space that existed apart from formal political institutions or the state, Habermas offered political historians a setting for expressions of political culture.

Even as it has broadened the scope of political history, the concept of political culture has not bypassed seemingly "conventional" political topics such as state building, political institutions, or the political elite. Richard John's *Spreading the News: The American Postal System from Franklin to Morse* (1995) details the rise of the state through the creation of the US postal system but, in doing so, it reveals assumptions about the role of the central government and the boundaries of American public life. Joanne B. Freeman's *Affairs of Honor: National Politics in the New Republic* (2001) explores the culture of political combat among the political elite on the national stage, revealing how the culture of honor shaped political interaction. Catherine Allgor's *Parlor Politics: In Which the Ladies of Washington Help Build a City and a Government* (2000) looks at the political influence of elite women on that same stage. By looking at seemingly familiar political populations and institutions through a cultural lens, such works reveal a deeper logic and a more complex dynamic underlying the conventional political narrative.

Yet, even as it has accomplished so much, or perhaps, *because* it has accomplished so much, the tool of culture should be deployed by political historians with care. As with the concept of republicanism, historians run the risk of finding it everywhere, thereby detracting from its analytical usefulness. Few political historians actually attempt to define what they mean by "political culture," though they make glancing references to "beliefs," "assumptions," "attitudes," "orientations," "values," "rituals," "traditions," "customs," "habits," "mindsets," "roles," "symbols," and other such concepts. Like the concept of republicanism, the concept of political culture is slippery and amorphous, sometimes deliberately so. As an ambiguous way of referring to underlying ideas of one kind or another, its fuzziness has made it a popular methodological shorthand. As Glen Gendzel notes in his historiographic survey of political culture,

> Sometimes it seems to denote not political symbols in context but minute procedural dissections of nominations, campaigns, patronage, and officeholding. Other times, it seems to encompass "common assumptions" about everything from "the legitimacy of the political process in general" to "the role of government in particular." Eager proponents have used the concept to investigate diverse matters, ranging from antebellum literary metaphors and the origins of New Deal liberalism to abolitionist fairs and George Washington's personality cult. Like political scientists before them, incautious historians are somewhat in danger of turning political culture into an indiscriminate uncaused cause once again. (Gendzel 1997: 245)

This is not to say that the study of political culture should be cast aside. As Jean Baker noted in a 1987 review of two self-described works of political culture, in one case, political culture created a brilliant study of "how a new approach can draw novel insights from familiar materials." But in the other case, it "serves as gloss" (Baker 1987: 60). Political culture may be running rampant through current political scholarship, but not all historians know how to deploy it with purpose.

Baker – herself a leading figure in the study of American political culture – also notes a second potential problem with the historical study of culture: it often "has a certain timeless quality foreign to historical concern with chronology" (Baker 1987: 65). History largely studies change over time, but the study of culture invites broad generalizations that tend to float above historical narratives. In their eagerness to employ the tool of culture in reenvisioning the world of politics, historians should not abandon their historical anchors. Nor should they forget the importance of comparison – between populations, organizations, or nation states. As Formisano explains in a recent historiographical essay on political culture, "The logic of political culture is always comparative, whether its unit of measure is a city, state, region, class, group, or nation. Historians vary widely in the extent to which they have made comparison explicit, and when they do compare, they usually do so by time rather than place" (Formisano 2001: 424). Perhaps future studies of political culture will become more geographically comparative, moving beyond national boundaries, as does much current historical scholarship; in the realm of recent early national American history, Andrew Robertson's *The Language of Democracy: Political Rhetoric in the United States and Britain, 1790–1900* (1995) and Seth Cotlar's work on the transatlantic dimensions of American popular political thought already move in that direction, one to which Robert Kelley's 1969 study, *The Transatlantic Persuasion: The Liberal-Democratic Mind in the Age of Gladstone,* pointed the way. Also yet to be seen are studies that focus on the interaction between the elite and non-elite, examining the political culture of a functioning political system operating on multiple levels. Among some historians, there is a lingering suspicion of the study of elite people or institutions as an invasive attempt to dominate the historical narrative. Such fears work against a full understanding of the conversation of politics in all its complexity.

Thus, in some ways, political history is still in the throes of an identity crisis. Certainly, it has escaped from the limits of the presidential synthesis; it is no longer restricted to a small population of political elites; and it encompasses more than elections and legislation. Revitalized as a field of study by the tool of culture, political history no longer hovers on the brink of death. But the precise contours of the political narrative are still under debate. If "all the past is political culture," as Jean Baker asserts, the challenge for future historians will be to define terms and boundaries so that the concept of political culture does not ultimately obscure more than it reveals.

REFERENCES

Allgor, Catherine: *Parlor Politics: In Which the Ladies of Washington Help Build a City and a Government* (Charlottesville: University Press of Virginia, 2000).
Almond, Gabriel A. & Verba, Sidney: *The Civic Culture: Political Attitudes and Democracy in Five Nations* (Princeton, NJ: Princeton University Press, 1963).
Almond, Gabriel A. & Verba, Sidney: *The Civic Culture Revisited* (Newbury Park, CA: Sage Publications, 1989).
Bailyn, Bernard: *The Ideological Origins of the American Revolution* (Cambridge, MA: Harvard University Press, 1967).
Bailyn, Bernard: *The Origins of American Politics* (New York: Alfred A. Knopf, 1968).
Baker, Jean H.: *Affairs of Party: The Political Culture of Northern Democrats in the Mid-Nineteenth Century* (Ithaca, NY: Cornell University Press, 1983).

Baker, Jean H.: "And All the Past is Political Culture," *Reviews in American History* 15 (1987), 59–65.

Baker, Keith: *Inventing the French Revolution: Essays on French Political Culture in the Eighteenth Century* (Cambridge: Cambridge University Press, 1990).

Baker, Keith, Lucas, Colin, Furet, François, & Ozouf, Mona, eds.: *The French Revolution and the Creation of Modern Political Culture*, 4 vols. (Oxford: Pergamon Press, 1987–94).

Baker, Paula: "The Domestication of Politics: Women and American Political Society, 1780–1920," in Linda Gordon, ed., *Women, the State, and Welfare* (Madison: University of Wisconsin Press, 1990).

Baker, Paula: *The Moral Frameworks of Public Life: Gender, Politics, and the State in Rural New York, 1870–1930* (New Haven, CT: Yale University Press, 1995).

Brooke, John L.: *The Heart of the Commonwealth: Society and Political Culture in Worcester County, Massachusetts, 1713–1861* (Cambridge: Cambridge University Press, 1990).

Foner, Eric, ed.: *The New American History* (Philadelphia, PA: Temple University Press, 1990).

Formisano, Ronald P.: *The Transformation of Political Culture: Massachusetts Parties, 1790s–1840s* (New York: Oxford University Press, 1983).

Formisano, Ronald P.: "The Concept of Political Culture," *Journal of Interdisciplinary History* 31 (2001), 393–426.

Freeman, Joanne B.: *Affairs of Honor: National Politics in the New Republic* (New Haven, CT: Yale University Press, 2001).

Freeman, Joanne B.: "The Culture of Politics, the Politics of Culture," *Journal of Policy History* 16 (2004), 137–43.

Geertz, Clifford: *The Interpretation of Cultures: Selected Essays* (New York: Basic Books, 1973).

Gendzel, Glen: "Political Culture: Genealogy of a Concept," *Journal of Interdisciplinary History* 28 (1997), 225–50.

Goodman, Paul: "Putting Some Class Back into Political History: 'The Transformation of Political Culture' and the Crisis in American Political History," *Reviews in American History* 12 (1984), 80–8.

Greene, Jack P.: *Imperatives, Behaviors, and Identities: Essays in Early American Cultural History* (Charlottesville: University Press of Virginia, 1992).

Greene, Jack P.: *Interpreting Early America: Historiographical Essays* (Charlottesville: University Press of Virginia, 1996).

Habermas, Jürgen: *The Structure and Transformation of the Public Sphere: An Inquiry into a Category of Bourgeois Society* (Cambridge, MA: MIT Press, 1989).

Hofstadter, Richard: *The Paranoid Style in American Politics, and Other Essays* (New York: Alfred A. Knopf, 1965).

Holt, Michael: "Political Culture and Political Legitimacy," *Reviews in American History* 11 (1983), 526–30.

Howe, Daniel Walker: *The Political Culture of the American Whigs* (Chicago: University of Chicago Press, 1984).

Hunt, Lynn: *Politics, Culture, and Class in the French Revolution* (Berkeley: University of California Press, 1984).

Jacobs, Meg, Novak, William J. & Zelizer, Julian E., eds.: *The Democratic Experiment: New Directions in American Political History* (Princeton, NJ: Princeton University Press, 2003).

John, Richard R.: *Spreading the News: The American Postal System from Franklin to Morse* (Cambridge, MA: Harvard University Press, 1995).

Kammen, Michael G.: "The Meaning of Colonization in American Revolutionary Thought," *Journal of the History of Ideas* 31 (1970), 337–58.

Kammen, Michael G.: *A Season of Youth: The American Revolution and the Historical Imagination* (New York: Alfred A. Knopf, 1978).

Kammen, Michael G.: *A Machine That Would Go of Itself: The Constitution in American Culture* (New York: Alfred A. Knopf, 1986a).

Kammen, Michael G.: *Spheres of Liberty: Changing Perceptions of Liberty in American Culture* (Madison: University of Wisconsin Press, 1986b).

Kelley, Robert: *The Transatlantic Persuasion: The Liberal-Democratic Mind in the Age of Gladstone* (New York: Alfred A. Knopf, 1969).

Kelley, Robert: "Ideology and Political Culture from Jefferson to Nixon," *American Historical Review* 82 (1977), 531–62.

Kerber, Linda K.: *Women of the Republic: Intellect and Ideology in Revolutionary America* (Chapel Hill: University of North Carolina Press, 1980).

McCurry, Stephanie: *Masters of Small Worlds: Yeoman Households, Gender Relations, and the Political Culture of the Antebellum South Carolina Low Country* (New York: Oxford University Press, 1995).

McGerr, Michael E.: *The Decline of Popular Politics: The American North, 1865–1928* (New York: Oxford University Press, 1988).

Newman, Simon: *Parades and the Politics of the Street: Festive Culture in the Early American Republic* (Philadelphia, PA: University of Pennsylvania Press, 1997).

Pasley, Jeffrey L.: *The Tyranny of Printers: Newspaper Politics in the Early American Republic* (Charlottesville: University Press of Virginia, 2001).

Pye, Lucian & Verba, Sydney: *Political Culture and Political Development* (Princeton, NJ: Princeton University Press, 1965).

Robertson, Andrew W.: *The Language of Democracy: Political Rhetoric in the United States and Britain, 1790–1900* (Ithaca, NJ: Cornell University Press, 1995).

Rodgers, Daniel: "Republicanism: The Career of a Concept," *Journal of American History* 79 (1992), 11–38.

Sklar, Kathryn Kish: *Florence Kelley and the Nation's Work: The Rise of Women's Political Culture, 1830–1900* (New Haven, CT: Yale University Press, 1995).

Travers, Len: *Celebrating the Fourth: Independence Day and the Rites of Nationalism in the Early Republic* (Amherst: University of Massachusetts Press, 1997).

Verba, Sidney & Pye, Lucian: *Political Culture and Political Development* (Princeton, NJ: Princeton University Press, 1966).

Waldstreicher, David: *In the Midst of Perpetual Fetes: The Making of American Nationalism, 1776–1820* (Chapel Hill: University of North Carolina Press, 1997).

Wood, Gordon S.: "Conspiracy and the Paranoid Style: Causality and Deceit in the Eighteenth Century," *William and Mary Quarterly* 39 (1982), 401–41.

Wood, Gordon S.: *The Radicalism of the American Revolution* (New York: Alfred A. Knopf, 1991).

Chapter Thirty

THE CULTURAL HISTORY OF FOREIGN RELATIONS

Andrew J. Rotter

Recently, US diplomatic historians have found the culture concept, in its variety of forms, helpful in understanding relations between Americans and others, and more broadly between all nations and peoples. To their older categories of analysis, including geopolitics, national security, and economics, foreign relations historians (a nomenclature now preferred over "diplomatic historians") have increasingly added culture. This movement is easy enough to spot. Since its publication in 1991, the methodological foundation text for the history of foreign relations has been *Explaining the History of American Foreign Relations*, edited by Michael J. Hogan and Thomas G. Paterson. It included a then-daring essay by Emily Rosenberg that suggested using gender as a "framework" for interpreting "national development"; a piece titled "Ideology" by Michael H. Hunt; and another, by Akira Iriye, called "Culture and International History." These chapters were sprinkled among a greater number of theoretically mainstream essays with titles such as "Balance of Power," "National Security," "Bureaucratic Politics," and "Public Opinion."

Now skip ahead to the second edition of *Explaining*, published in 2004. Many original essays remain, but additions include "Cultural Transfer" (by Jessica Gienow-Hecht), "Theory, Language, and Metaphor" (Frank Costigliola), "Gender History as Foreign Relations History" (Kristin Hoganson), and "The United States and the World, White Supremacy and Foreign Affairs" (Gerald Horne). The new introduction notes that foreign relations historians, in response "to criticism that portrays their field as parochial, ethnocentric, and hidebound," have turned more and more to cultural history to initiate "perhaps the most significant transformation in the field since the first edition" of *Explaining* was published. Derided for years as practitioners of the dull and the obvious, foreign relations historians had invigorated their work with cultural analysis.

This essay will trace the cultural turn in US foreign relations history. Briefly reviewing the origins of the field through its Cold War heyday and its subsequent fall from favor as elitist and staid, it will focus on the development of the cultural approach, investigating several ways in which diplomatic historians have applied culture to their subject. The essay concludes with some reflections on the problems and prospects for foreign policy "culturalism" (as the trend has come awkwardly to be called): what has worked and what has not in this encounter between, metaphorically speaking, men with buttoned-down collars and frisky teenagers with multiple body piercings. While alert to the difficulties of describing so tangled a concept as culture, the essay will nevertheless take as its definition the view of anthropologist Clifford Geertz: that culture is formed of "webs of significance" spun by human beings.

The celebration of American nationalism in the years following the Great War provided the context for the emergence of US diplomatic history. Having witnessed their nation come to the aid of "civilized" Western Europe in its battle with Central European autocracy, historians Samuel Flagg Bemis, Dexter Perkins, and Thomas Bailey extolled the exceptionalism of the United States and the wisdom and benefi-cence of its foreign policies, in narratives that reflected their convictions concerning America's ascent, Europe's decline, and the inconsequentiality of nearly everywhere else. A later generation would snidely rename the author of *The Diplomacy of the American Revolution* Samuel "Wave the" Flagg Bemis, and castigate him and others for their North American triumphalism and their cultural and racial insensitivity; Bailey's famous textbook *A Diplomatic History of the American People*, for instance, labeled the nineteenth-century Mexican general Santa Anna "cowering" and "slippery" (Bailey 1980: 239–40). Still, the insistence of the founders on conducting archival research both in the USA and abroad signaled their understanding that foreign relations had more than one point of origin, and that the United States was not the sole source of information about the international system in which it operated.

Disillusion set in during the 1930s and 1940s. As Bemis and others became, if anything, more convinced of American rectitude, they also came to believe that US foreign policy had been compromised by the very democracy it was supposed to represent, protect, and promulgate. Bailey's *The Man in the Street* (1948) cautioned against allowing an uninformed public to shape foreign policy. The new "realists," among them historian/diplomat George Kennan and political scientist Hans J. Mor-genthau, criticized what they saw as the excessive idealism of US policy and deni-grated efforts to impose on the world a single moral doctrine, no matter how ardently the American people professed to believe in it. The only sound basis for foreign policy was national interest; and the language of international relations was power. Realist analysis provided no room for the role of domestic institutions, politics, economics, or culture in either formulating or understanding foreign policy.

Both the inter-war exceptionalists and Cold War realists were challenged by a group of historians who were politically more radical and analytically more attuned to the United States itself. In the 1920s and 1930s, the progressive historians, led by Charles Beard, argued that US foreign relations were best understood from the inside out, through an examination of the assumptions and material bases of those elite groups responsible for US policy making. Beard, author of *The Idea of National Interest* (1934), did not dispute that national interest was the driving force behind US foreign policy, but he insisted that the national interest of the United States concerned the securing of "territory and commerce, including their connections with domestic affairs" (1934: 50). The United States was thus neither exceptional (all nations were interested in territory and commerce) nor necessarily harmonious (the nation's true national interest was often in dispute). Beard's views became popular among Americans suspicious that conniving bankers and munitions makers had beguiled the nation into war in 1917. But when Beard, staunchly isolationist into the 1940s, accused President Roosevelt of "lying" rather than "leading" the nation to war with Nazi Germany, his influence diminished. Such criticism of the consensual state and its leaders had no safe place in an America determined to defeat totalitarianism, first in its fascist, then in its communist form.

The Cold War proved a fertile period for exceptionalist or "consensus" historians, who proclaimed and celebrated the US determination to contain the communist menace, and only slightly less fertile for their realist critics, who differed from exceptionalists less over the goal of containment than the means by which the United States should pursue it. But by the late 1950s a neo-Beardian strain had emerged within the diplomatic field: "revisionism," whose leading exponent was William Appleman Williams. The revisionists argued that American ideology or "Weltanschauung" had projected the United States into the world as an expansionist newcomer in the first half of the nineteenth century, a rising power by that century's end, and the world's dominant nation after 1945. Like Beard, Williams argued that the pursuit of territory and commerce had always characterized US foreign policy. Americans had long believed their economic interests would best be served by an "Open Door" policy giving US farmers and manufacturers unfettered access to foreign markets. (The "Open Door" also implied approval of representative government, as long as it wasn't strong enough to deny American commercial demands.) Because of its newfound strength and its continued ideological resolve after World War II, the United States bore much of the responsibility for the Cold War; the Soviets had merely reacted to US initiatives.

The revisionist interpretation inspired the New Left during the 1960s and 1970s, especially as the US war in Vietnam intensified. But it won no friends among either exceptionalists or realists. And it spawned a backlash known as post-revisionism, which acknowledged that American interests played a role in US policy, but insisted that the United States had only reluctantly asserted its power after 1945; that American ideology was never as fixed as the revisionists claimed; and that communism was expansionistic and in need of containment. Led by John Lewis Gaddis, the post-revisionists attempted to restore the international system to a position of prominence in the study of foreign relations; the USA, though a superpower, was nevertheless constrained by the actions of other nations and the opinions of its own people. Foreign relations historians, they argued, should return to other nations' archives, following Bemis, and listen to the man in the American street, as had Bailey.

Seemingly lost in the politically charged debate over Cold War policy was the matter of national culture. Realists had no use for culture; they attended only to the apparently rational structures of the international system. If the exceptionalists had occasionally acknowledged the importance of national character, their post-revisionist heirs, embarrassed by or indifferent to the implication that white Americans were genetically exalted and Mexicans "slippery," left culture pretty much alone. The revisionists' version of American ideology made no room for cultural factors, which they knew only in the exceptionalists' racist form. For all these historians, the Cold War elevated the power struggle between the United States and the Soviet Union to the explanation of first and last resort. Whatever cultural differences might divide nations hardly registered on the vast global struggle between competing political and economic systems.

When the Cold War ended in 1991, it was as if a great tide ebbed, exposing previously hidden features of the world's landscape that included national cultures. Ethnic and cultural conflicts appeared prominently in areas of the world previously dominated by the Soviet Union, including Central Asia and the Balkans. The West's sense of triumph at the end of the Cold War was quickly deflated by bloody, ethnic fighting in Yugoslavia, Chechnya, and Azerbaijan. Policy pundits, political scientists, and even foreign relations historians noted the sobering vitality of culture as a force in international affairs, and it began to creep into their explanations of how nations and peoples behaved toward each other.

As the world was changing dramatically, so was the universe of ideas. Beginning in the 1980s, the historical discipline faced a challenge from poststructural (or postmodern) theory. Poststructuralists, among them the French philosophers Michel Foucault and Jacques Derrida, insisted that "reality," or "truth," were illusions, human constructs capable only of "representation." Language, the most confounding of human constructs, distanced people from reality. While most historians refused to abandon the quest for truth, many grew more self-aware of their own use of language and the lenses through which they viewed their subjects. Poststructuralism inspired greater interest in culture as both object of study and method of investigation. Unlike economics or politics, culture made no pretense to so-called Western logic, against which the postmodern challenge had proved most corrosive. Culture was the realm of language, emotion, unpredictability, all of which the postmodernists explored. Clifford Geertz's definition of culture treated as insoluble the relationship between cause and effect, denoting instead "a context . . . within which" various behaviors, social occurrences, and processes could be "thickly described." The study of culture might thus provide historians with a way to avoid a messy confrontation with "reality," befogged by language and resistant to full understanding.

While many historians had by 1990 made the cultural turn, or at least hand-signaled an interest in turning, the first edition of *Explaining the History of American Foreign Relations* demonstrated that diplomatic historians – with such notable exceptions as Emily Rosenberg, Michael Hunt, Reginald Horsman, John Dower, and Akira Iriye – were hardly first off the mark. Many foreign relations historians took note of the new approaches but continued working in their own idioms. Some attacked the new thinking as peripheral to the field, or analytically soft; others ignored it entirely. But the convergence of world events, intellectual trends, and bold thinkers unbounded by analytical straitjackets from the past resulted in the steady growth of culturalist methodology as a means of understanding relations between nations.

One important trend in the culturalist movement has involved shifting the analytical focus from the state to non-state actors and institutions. Inspired by Iriye in particular, a number of historians have pointed out that "foreign relations" need not concern only what one diplomat said to another. People get to know one another through any number of means: information exchanged via books, television, and the internet; tourism in each others' countries; contact with one another's bankers, missionaries, aid workers, soldiers, or (yes) diplomats; and the experience of others' art, architecture, literature, and music. It has become popular among political scientists to describe power as either "hard" – including military, political, or economic modes of domination – or "soft" – including the more subtle kinds of influence associated with propaganda, moral suasion, or cultural allure. But hard and soft power are never entirely distinct; and soft power, for all its subtlety, is power nonetheless. Still, acknowledging that power, *pace* Mao Zedong, may come not only from the barrel of a gun but also through the lens of a camera opens vast new areas of study to historians of foreign relations.

Historians of "cultural transfer" are interested in "cultural imperialism," a term they use to describe the hegemonic influence of one cultural system, usually that of the United States, over another. Analysts of cultural transfer treat imperialism as an encounter between goods, ideas, and identities – a two-way exchange between people, not always equal but nevertheless mutual. What do we think of them, their way of thinking, their fashions and food, their body language and smell? What do they think of us? A number of studies concern the relationship between American and French cultures (Wall 1992; Kuisel 1993; Ross 1995). The German–Central European–American encounter has also been a subject of considerable interest, given the vital role played by Americans and their cultural institutions in shaping the Federal Republic of Germany after World War II (Wagnleitner 1994; Gienow-Hecht 1999; Goedde 2003). Some ambitious works examine cultural transfer between the United States and Europe more generally (Costigliola 1984; Kroes 1996; Pells 1997).

Other works focus on particular modes of cultural transmission, sometimes taking the form of case studies, which can be particularly useful for illuminating chronologically or conceptually complicated relationships. Foreign relations historians have looked carefully at the economic, social, and intellectual impact of American tourists in Cuba, Puerto Rico, and France (Schwartz 1997; Merrill 2001; Endy 2004); and the cultural agency of American military families in Germany and Japan after 1945 (Alvah, 2007). Some scholars have focused on how US soldiers transmit a version of American values to those whom they encounter in occupied countries or near military bases, and carry home their impressions of others (Enloe 1990; Moon 1997; Renda 2001; Hohn 2002; Goedde 2003). A single study – Warren Cohen's *East Asian Art and American Culture* (1992) – explores international cultural transmission through the medium of art. Penny M. Von Eschen's *Satchmo Blows up the World* (2004) shows that touring jazz musicians, black and white, were simultaneously ambassadors for US foreign policy, transmitters of their own worldviews (especially on civil rights in the United States), and willing receptors of others' musical forms. During the 1940s and 1950s, musical theater profoundly influenced American ideas about Asians: Rodgers and Hammerstein's *South Pacific*, *The King and I*, and *Flower Drum Song* rendered Asians childlike and stubborn, yet ultimately receptive to Western plans for their modernization and democratization (Klein 2003).

Studies on cultural transmission have opened diplomatic history to new subjects and new interpretations, and constructively complicated its assumptions about what constitutes foreign relations. Some culturalists believe, however, that studies of fashion, tourism, and musical theater fail to address real power relations between nations. Fashion and tourism and musicals, they say, may reveal something about one people's attitudes toward another; but to understand why nations behave as they do, it is essential to bring the state back into the analysis. How, for example, do such cultural analysands as race, gender, and language help us parse hard power, including the mechanics of empire and the conduct of war? Can the Geertzian approach explain not just the context but the content, and even the cause/effect, of US foreign relations?

To be sure, many of the previously cited books do concern power; and the distinction between "cultural transmission" and "culture as power" may be artificial. Let us consider several specific ways in which historians have tried directly to connect attitudes, images, values, and prejudices to the practice of foreign policy, and the exercise of state power. Begin with race. For some years, scholars have noted that white racism has influenced US policy toward non-white others. For Michael Hunt, racism is one of three main elements of American ideology (1987). Reginald Horsman (1981) and Richard Slotkin (1985) have shown that white acceptance of racist social science during the nineteenth century enabled brutal treatment of Native Americans, Mexicans, and Filipinos, among others. John Dower's *War Without Mercy* (1986), a harrowing account of the Pacific War, demonstrates that white Americans and Japanese killed and maimed each other remorselessly because of their mutual racism. During the Cold War, US policy toward Africa was guided in part by the assumption that black Africans were unready for, and perhaps incapable of, self-government. In South Africa (Borstelmann 1993), Zimbabwe (Horne 2001), and all across the African continent (Noer 1985), white Americans sheltered too long and lovingly racist white minority governments that frustrated black aspirations to democracy.

Domestic race relations also played a role in US foreign policy. The rising civil rights movement after 1945 exposed American racism and embarrassed a succession of presidents trying to win the Cold War with the claim that communists represented tyranny, the Americans and their allies freedom. African Americans often identified with black freedom fighters in Africa, and vice versa, as both groups struggled against white power structures that denigrated and oppressed them. African Americans spoke out against racism at home and racist colonialism abroad, prompting State Department official (and later secretary of state) Dean Rusk to admit that race discrimination in the United States was "the biggest single burden that we carry" into the arena of diplomacy. A good deal of scholarly attention has been paid recently to the impact of domestic race relations on US policy making (Horne 1986; Plummer 1996; Von Eschen 1997; Krenn 1999; Dudziak 2000; Gallicchio 2000; Borstelmann 2001; Anderson 2003).

Along with race, gender has increasingly become an important analysand for historians of foreign relations. Joan Scott's influential essay "Gender: A Useful Category of Historical Analysis," first published in 1986, questioned why historians seemed to think that gender was "irrelevant to . . . issues of politics and power"; in her view, "high politics itself is a gendered concept" (Scott 1996: 48). Emily Rosenberg responded to this challenge (1990) and gradually thereafter, foreign relations historians began to apply gender analysis to their studies of diplomacy, imperialism, and war. Some saw gender as a way to consider the role of women in international encounters, as occasional makers of policy (Jeffreys-Jones 1995), as agents of foreign relations through non-governmental organizations (Tyrrell 1991), or as those on the receiving end of imperial power (Enloe 1990; Moon 1997; Findlay 1999; Goedde 2003; Shibusawa 2006). Some studies of gender included consideration of sexuality and/or race.

Other scholarship involving gender has concerned the role played by cultural constructions of the masculine and the feminine in shaping images of selves and others in US foreign policy. The United States has typically seen itself as a masculine nation, honor-bound to protect allegedly feminine others, or to discipline those whose flighty and effeminate misbehavior threatens international stability. The quest for manliness has been associated with certain American presidents; as Kristin Hoganson has written, "historians have turned Theodore Roosevelt into a virtual poster boy for the utility of gender in foreign relations history" (Hoganson 1998; Bederman 1995; Dalton 2002). Frank Costigliola has discovered significance in the gendered language of Cold Warrior George Kennan, who repeatedly warned against the "penetration" of the "West" by Soviet expansionism (Costigliola 1997). The fear of appearing soft on communism drove John F. Kennedy to insist on masculine toughness in his policy toward the Soviet Union and Vietnam (Dean 2001). Other historians have claimed that the United States is periodically seized by a "crisis of masculinity" that finds an outlet in an aggressive foreign policy, regardless of who is president. Rendering international others as feminine has enabled the United States, and other imperial nations, to naturalize or justify interference in others' affairs. Paternalism guided US policy toward Latin America and the Caribbean; the North Americans sought to control allegedly flighty and emotional Haitians, Cubans, and Puerto Ricans (Renda 2001; Perez 1998; Findlay 1999). The annals of US foreign relations are populated by tremulous Chinese, cowering Hindus, tough Muslims and weeping Muslims, manly Israelis, effete Frenchmen, and so forth. The "tough" and "manly" won praise and support from the United States. The "weak" and "soft" required firm, masculine guidance.

If foreign relations historians have confirmed that gender is "a useful category of historical analysis" even within realms of power, they have nevertheless found that gender alone, like race alone, has explanatory limits. The challenge for historians, as Hoganson puts it, "is shifting from demonstrating the relevance of gender to situating gender alongside strategic, economic, political, and other factors" (1998: 316). Some historians have opened their cultural analysis to a greater number of variables, by looking carefully at the language of foreign policy makers or those groups that influence them. Language, particularly in its metaphors, can convey a host of meanings inflected by the culture that produces it. Kennan's language in his famous "Long Telegram" (1946) was gendered – it feminized the Russian people, for whom Kennan had an almost sexual affection, and cast as rapacious the current Soviet leadership – but it also indulged in references to illness, as in the "Kremlin's neurotic view of world affairs" and Soviet leaders being "afflicted" with insecurity (Costigliola 1997). Geoffrey Smith has associated gender, pathology, and perceptions of national security in his explanation of the Red (fear of communism) and Lavender (fear of gay people) Scares that swept the United States in the late 1940s and early 1950s (Smith 1992). Homosexuality was purportedly a sexual perversion, a disease, and a risk to national security because gays were readily blackmailed by their communist handlers.

Increasingly, historians of foreign relations are trying to do justice to the complexity of culture and the disparate ways it affects perception and decision making. It is never neat work. Who is to say, for example, whether race or religion more insistently conditioned US policy toward Muslim Pakistan and Hindu India during the 1950s? How did interwoven ideas concerning gender, race, and class shape North American initiatives in Puerto Rico or Cuba at the beginning of the twentieth century? A number of scholars have skillfully blended the discrete elements of culture to offer satisfying explanations of American encounters with others (Stephanson 1995; Dower 1999; Bradley 2000; Connelly 2002; Klein 2003).

The most direct result of the poststructural challenge to the history of US foreign relations has been the emergence of postcolonial or subaltern studies, a movement closely associated with the late Edward Said, whose *Orientalism* (1978) was its foundation text. Postcolonial scholars admired Marx and especially the Italian Marxist Antonio Gramsci, but revealed their poststructural affiliations through their interest in literature, subjectivity, prisons, schools, and discourse, and through their footnotes, which cited more Foucault than Marx. The postcolonialists were emphatically interested in empire and power. While they were clear in their condemnation of colonialism, they looked imaginatively at the relationships empire created between the dominant nation, its agents, and colonized "subalterns" (*Subaltern Studies*, 1988–2000). Perhaps the most important contribution of the subaltern scholars was their ascription of agency to the weaker parties in the colonial relationship – men and women who, in spite of having limited power, shaped their own identities and forged resistance despite their subordinate status. Gender and often race figured prominently in these works.

Said and the *Subaltern Studies* quickly found their way into the arguments (and the footnotes)' of foreign relations culturalists. Essays in *Cultures of United States Imperialism* (Kaplan & Pease 1993) used poststructural theory to expand the horizons of historians more comfortable sorting through diplomatic correspondence than contemplating the prosthetics of empire, stuffed gorillas at New York's Museum of Natural History, and Tokyo Disneyland – all subjects of essays in the Kaplan–Pease anthology. As Rosenberg has noted, much of the foreign relations history inspired by poststructuralism has focused on the formal American empire: on the Philippines, and especially on Latin America (Joseph et al. 1998; Rosenberg 1999; Rafael 2000; Renda 2001). Adopting postmodern theory, regarding empire as an engagement of cultures, and exploring mutual images and attitudes as displayed in the media, in fiction, and in travel literature, these scholars have nevertheless combed the archives in search of affiliations between the official language of diplomacy and the broader discourse of encounter.

It would be satisfying to report that culturalism has swept the field, and achieved the stature of realist, revisionist, or even post-revisionist accounts of US foreign relations. There is no question that culturalism has gained a measure of respect, certainly among younger entrants to the field, and with some older scholars as well. Yet resistance remains. Some seems churlish: that cultural influence is harder to measure than, say, trade flows during the 1930s is self-evident, and hardly disqualifies culture as a meaningful category of analysis. But there is thoughtful criticism as well. Culture is an elastic concept; if it includes and explains everything, it threatens to explain nothing in particular. Culture, moreover, can occlude the operations of cause and effect. Exploring how selves see themselves and others does not necessarily illuminate *why* selves or others *act* as they do. And cultural perceptions are likely to depend on interests: Americans during the Pacific War hated and dehumanized the Japanese, but cherished the Chinese as honest, virtuous, and quaint. Above all, critics have charged, culture in the end has not much to do with power. Oppression is not, they say, about ridicule, stereotype, or ideas based on gender, race, or religion. Language does not kill people; war is not a discourse. In its affection for Geertzian context, its emphasis on image, culturalism neglects what is most important about US foreign relations.

If not always explicitly, the culturalists have responded to these criticisms in their work. Straightforward explanations of things – in terms of strategy or economics, for instance – have a certain elegance, but don't always suit the complexity of history. Cause and effect are surely important, but it is by no means clear that so-called "traditional" explanations of US foreign relations, including strategy, economics, or national interest, do any better at figuring them out. Did the Great Depression cause World War II? Most diplomatic historians reject such monocausal explanations as this, and some would admit to their lists of causes the mutual perceptions of the future combatants – that Americans were cowardly and would back down if delivered a powerful blow, that the Japanese were subhuman, could not be reasoned with, and therefore ought to be exterminated.

Most of all, many culturalists quietly insist that culture *is* about power, not an entity separate from it. How people see other people, how they construct and imagine them, affects how they treat them. If one people regards another as its racial inferior, it will behave toward the other with arrogance and cruelty. Feminine or effeminate others must allegedly be disciplined by those more decisive, reasonable, and therefore manly. If Christians see Israeli Jews as tough, they will admire and support them; if they see Muslims as fanatical, they will try to curb their perceived excesses; if they see Hindus as craven, they will try to put some spine into them, or, failing that, dismiss them scornfully as weak. When President Harry S. Truman used the language of poker to describe diplomacy with the Soviet Union, he soothed himself by comparing something threatening with something familiar; he masculinized the competition (poker was a man's game), and suggested that he would try to bluff the Russians while keeping a poker face. This seemingly loose connection between a game (culture) and high-level diplomacy (foreign relations) reduced the complex and dangerous to a crisp and simplistic reality that Truman could readily grasp.

It is unlikely that foreign relations historians will ever abandon the use of strategy, economics, or ideology as ways of analyzing their subjects. There is considerable merit in understanding, for example, the strategic triangulation that led to Richard M. Nixon's decision to seek a rapprochement with the People's Republic of China in 1971; the economic circumstances that presaged the creation of a new system of international finance at Bretton Woods in 1944; the ideological formulations that inspired a belief in Manifest Destiny; a faith in the Open Door; and the determination to resist communism in Korea and Vietnam. Culturalists must be modest in their explanatory claims. Culture doesn't explain everything, and arguments for its presence and significance in the diplomatic process require careful construction. But if culture itself is about human imagination, surely attempts to discern its presence in relations between nations demand imagination too. Diplomacy is a human activity. It is time for its historians to acknowledge that.

REFERENCES

Alvah, Donna: *Unofficial Ambassadors: American Military Families Overseas and the Cold War, 1946–1965* (New York: New York University Press, 2007).
Anderson, Carol: *Eyes Off the Prize: The United Nations and the African–American Struggle for Human Rights, 1944–1955* (New York: Cambridge University Press, 2003).
Bailey, Thomas A.: *The Man in the Street* (New York: Macmillan, 1948).

Bailey, Thomas A.: *A Diplomatic History of the American People*, 10th edn. (Englewood Cliffs: Prentice-Hall, 1980).

Beard, Charles A.: *The Idea of National Interest: An Analytical Study in American Foreign Policy* (New York: Macmillan, 1934).

Bederman, Gail: *Manliness and Civilization: A Cultural History of Gender and Race in the United States, 1880–1917* (Chicago: University of Chicago Press, 1995).

Bemis, Samuel Flagg: *The Diplomacy of the American Revolution* (Bloomington: Indiana University Press, 1935).

Borstelmann, Thomas: *Apartheid's Reluctant Uncle: The United States and South Africa in the Early Cold War* (New York: Oxford University Press, 1993).

Borstelmann, Thomas: *The Cold War and the Color Line: American Race Relations in the Global Arena* (Cambridge, MA: Harvard University Press, 2001).

Bradley, Mark: *Imagining Vietnam in America: The Making of Postcolonial Vietnam, 1919–1950* (Chapel Hill: University of North Carolina Press, 2000).

Cohen, Warren: *East Asian Art and American Culture: A Study in International Relations* (New York: Columbia University Press, 1992).

Connelly, Matthew: *A Diplomatic Revolution: Algeria's Fight for Independence and the Origins of the Post-Cold War Era* (New York: Oxford University Press, 2002).

Costigliola, Frank: *Awkward Dominion: American Political, Economic, and Cultural Relations with Europe, 1919–1933* (Ithaca, NY: Cornell University Press, 1984).

Costigliola, Frank: "'Unceasing Pressure for Penetration': Gender, Pathology, and Emotion in George Kennan's Formation of the Cold War," *Journal of American History* 83 (March 1997), 1309–39.

Dalton, Kathleen: *Theodore Roosevelt: A Strenuous Life* (New York: Alfred A. Knopf, 2002).

Dean, Robert D.: *Imperial Brotherhood: Gender and the Making of Cold War Foreign Policy* (Amherst: University of Massachusetts Press, 2001).

Dower, John W.: *War without Mercy: Race and Power in the Pacific War* (New York: Pantheon, 1986).

Dower, John W.: *Embracing Defeat: Japan in the Wake of World War II* (New York: W. W. Norton, 1999).

Dudziak, Mary L.: *Cold War Civil Rights: Race and the Image of American Democracy* (Princeton: Princeton University Press, 2000).

Endy, Christopher: *Cold War Holidays: American Tourism in France* (Chapel Hill: University of North Carolina Press, 2004).

Enloe, Cynthia: *Bananas, Beaches, and Bases: Making Feminist Sense of International Politics* (Berkeley: University of California Press, 1990).

Findlay, Eileen J. Suarez: *Imposing Decency: The Politics of Sexuality and Race in Puerto Rico, 1870–1920* (Durham, NC: Duke University Press, 1999).

Gaddis, John Lewis: *The United States and the Origins of the Cold War, 1941–1947* (New York: Columbia University Press, 1972).

Gallicchio, Marc S.: *The African–American Encounter in Japan and China: Black Internationalism in Asia, 1895–1945* (Chapel Hill: University of North Carolina Press, 2000).

Geertz, Clifford: *The Interpretation of Cultures: Selected Essays* (New York: Basic Books, 1973).

Gienow-Hecht, Jessica C. E.: *Transmission Impossible: American Journalism as Cultural Diplomacy in Postwar Germany, 1945–1955* (Baton Rouge: Louisiana State University Press, 1999).

Goedde, Petra: *GIs and Germans: Culture, Gender, and Foreign Relations, 1945–1949* (New Haven, CT: Yale University Press, 2003).

Hogan, Michael J. & Paterson, Thomas G., eds.: *Explaining the History of American Foreign Relations*, 2nd edn. (New York: Cambridge University Press, 2004 [1991]).

Hoganson, Kristin L.: *Fighting for American Manhood: How Gender Politics Provoked the Spanish–American and Philippine–American Wars* (New Haven, CT: Yale University Press, 1998).

Hohn, Maria: *GIs and Frauleins: The German-American Encounter in 1950s West Germany* (Chapel Hill: University of North Carolina Press, 2002).

Horne, Gerald: *Black and Red: W. E. B. Du Bois and the Afro-American Response to the Cold War, 1944–1963* (Albany, NY: SUNY Press, 1986).

Horne, Gerald: *From the Barrel of a Gun: The United States and the War Against Zimbabwe, 1965–1980* (Chapel Hill: University of North Carolina Press, 2001).

Horsman, Reginald: *Race and Manifest Destiny: The Origins of American Racial Anglo-Saxonism* (Cambridge, MA: Harvard University Press, 1981).

Hunt, Michael H.: *Ideology and US Foreign Policy* (New Haven, CT: Yale University Press, 1987).

Jeffreys-Jones, Rhodri: *Changing Differences: Women and the Shaping of American Foreign Policy, 1917–1994* (New Brunswick: Rutgers University Press, 1995).

Joseph, Gilbert, LeGrand, Catherine, & Salvatore, Ricardo, eds.: *Close Encounters of Empire: Writing the Cultural History of US–Latin American Relations* (Durham, NC: Duke University Press, 1998).

Kaplan, Amy: *The Anarchy of Empire in the Making of US Culture* (Cambridge, MA: Harvard University Press, 2002).

Kaplan, Amy & Pease, Donald, eds.: *Cultures of United States Imperialism* (Durham, NC: Duke University Press, 1993).

Kennan, George: *American Diplomacy, 1900–1950* (Chicago: University of Chicago Press, 1984).

Kennan, George: "Attaché George F. Kennan Critiques Soviet Foreign Policy in His 'Long Telegram,'" in Dennis Merrill & Thomas G. Paterson, eds., *Major Problems in American Foreign Relations*, vol. 2: *Since 1914*, 6th edn. (Boston, MA: Houghton Mifflin, 2005 [1946]), pp. 192–5.

Klein, Christina: *Cold War Orientalism: Asia in the Middlebrow Imagination, 1945–1961* (Berkeley: University of California Press, 2003).

Krenn, Michael: *Black Diplomacy: African Americans in the State Department, 1945–1969* (Armonk, NY: M. E. Sharpe, 1999).

Kroes, Rob: *If You've Seen One, You've Seen the Mall: Europeans and American Mass Culture* (Urbana: University of Illinois Press, 1996).

Kuisel, Richard F.: *Seducing the French: The Dilemma of Americanization* (Berkeley and Los Angeles: University of California Press, 1993).

Merrill, Dennis: "Negotiating Cold War Paradise: US Tourism, Economic Planning, and Cultural Modernity in Twentieth-Century Puerto Rico," *Diplomatic History* 25, 2 (2001), 179–214.

Moon, Katharine H. S.: *Sex Among Allies: Prostitution in US–Korea Relations* (New York: Columbia University Press, 1997).

Morgenthau, Hans J.: *In Defense of the National Interest: A Critical Examination of American Foreign Policy* (New York: Alfred A. Knopf, 1951).

Ninkovich, Frank: *Modernity and Power: A History of the Domino Theory in the Twentieth Century* (Chicago: University of Chicago Press, 1994).

Noer, Thomas: *Cold War and Black Liberation: The United States and White Africa, 1948–1968* (Columbia, MO: University of Missouri Press, 1985).

Pells, Richard: *Not Like Us: How Europeans Loved, Hated, and Transformed American Culture since World War II* (New York: Basic Books, 1997).

Perez, Louis: *The War of 1898: The United States and Cuba in History and Historiography* (Chapel Hill: University of North Carolina Press, 1998).

Plummer, Brenda Gayle: *Rising Wind: Black Americans and US Foreign Affairs, 1935–1960* (Chapel Hill: University of North Carolina Press, 1996).

Rafael, Vicente: *White Love and Other Events in Filipino History* (Durham, NC: Duke University Press, 2000).

Renda, Mary A.: *Taking Haiti: Military Occupation and the Culture of US Imperialism, 1915–1940* (Chapel Hill: University of North Carolina Press, 2001).

Rosenberg, Emily: "Gender, A Round Table: Explaining the History of American Foreign Relations," *Journal of American History* 77 (June 1990), 116–24.

Rosenberg, Emily: *Financial Missionaries to the World: The Politics and Culture of Dollar Diplomacy, 1900–1930* (Cambridge, MA: Harvard University Press, 1999).

Ross, Kristin: *Fast Cars, Clean Bodies: Decolonization and the Reordering of French Culture* (Cambridge, MA: MIT Press, 1995).

Said, Edward: *Orientalism* (New York: Pantheon, 1978).

Schwartz, Rosalie: *Pleasure Island: Tourism and Temptation in Cuba* (Lincoln: University of Nebraska Press, 1997).

Scott, Joan: "Gender: A Useful Category of Historical Analysis," reprinted in Joan Scott, *Gender and the Politics of History* (New York: Columbia University Press, 1996 [1986]), pp. 28–50.

Shibusawa, Naoko: *America's Geisha Ally: Reimagining the Japanese Enemy* (Cambridge, MA: Harvard University Press, 2006).

Slotkin, Richard: *The Fatal Environment: The Myth of the Frontier in the Age of Industrialization, 1800–1890* (Middletown, CT: Wesleyan University Press, 1985).

Smith, Geoffrey: "National Security and Personal Isolation: Sex, Gender, and Disease in the Cold War United States," *International History Review* 14 (May 1992), 221–37.

Stephanson, Anders: *Manifest Destiny: American Expansionism and the Empire of Right* (New York: Hill & Wang, 1995).

Tyrrell, Ian: *Woman's Work, Woman's Empire: The Women's Christian Temperance Union in International Perspective, 1880–1930* (Chapel Hill: University of North Carolina Press, 1991).

Von Eschen, Penny M.: *Race Against Empire: Black Americans and Anticolonialism, 1937–1957* (Ithaca, NY: Cornell University Press, 1997).

Von Eschen, Penny M.: *Satchmo Blows Up the World: Jazz Ambassadors Play the Cold War* (Cambridge, MA: Harvard University Press, 2004).

Wagnleitner, Reinhold: *Coca-Colonization and the Cold War: The Cultural Mission of the United States in Austria after the Second World War* (Chapel Hill: University of North Carolina Press, 1994).

Wall, Irwin M.: *The United States and the Making of Postwar France, 1945–1954* (New York: Cambridge University Press, 1992).

Williams, William Appleman: *The Tragedy of American Diplomacy* (Cleveland: World Publishing, 1959).

Index